Genres of the Credit Economy

Genres of the Credit Economy

Mediating Value in Eighteenth- and Nineteenth-Century Britain

MARY POOVEY

The University of Chicago Press
Chicago and London

Mary Poovey is the Samuel Rudin Professor in the Humanities and professor of English at New York University. She is the editor of *The Financial System in Nineteenth-Century Britain* and the author of *A History of the Modern Fact: Problems of Knowledge in the Sciences of Wealth and Society*, the latter published by the University of Chicago Press.

The University of Chicago Press, Chicago 60637
The University of Chicago Press, Ltd., London
© 2008 by The University of Chicago
All rights reserved. Published 2008
Printed in the United States of America

17 16 15 14 13 12 11 10 09 08   1 2 3 4 5

ISBN-13: 978-0-226-67532-9 (cloth)
ISBN-13: 978-0-226-67533-6 (paper)
ISBN-10: 0-226-67532-7 (cloth)
ISBN-10: 0-226-67533-5 (paper)

Publication of this book has been aided by a grant from the Abraham and Rebecca Stein Faculty Publication Fund of New York University, Department of English.

Library of Congress Cataloging-in-Publication Data

Poovey, Mary.
    Genres of the credit economy : mediating value in eighteenth- and nineteenth-century Britain / Mary Poovey.
        p.   cm.
    Includes bibliographical references and index.
    ISBN-13: 978-0-226-67532-9 (hardcover : alk. paper)
    ISBN-13: 978-0-226-67533-6 (pbk. : alk. paper)
    ISBN-10: 0-226-67532-7 (hardcover : alk. paper)
    ISBN-10: 0-226-67533-5 (pbk. : alk. paper)   1. Finance–Great Britain–History.   2. Consumer credit–Great Britain–History.   3. Money in literature.   4. Money–Social aspects–Great Britain.   5. Economics and literature–Great Britain–History.   6. Literary form–History.   7. English literature–History and criticism.   I. Title.
    HG186.G7P58   2008
    332.0941'09033–dc22

                                                          2007025921

In memory of my mother,
Mary Virginia Major Poovey,
and for my father,
William Edgar Poovey.

CONTENTS

ACKNOWLEDGMENTS

These days, it's a cliché to say that services that cannot be bought are "priceless," but, in the case of the support I've received for this project, the metaphor seems apt. My debts for this book are enormous, my gratitude even greater. My colleagues and students at New York University have helped me in various ways, raising questions that had not occurred to me, reading drafts, and generally providing an ideal intellectual environment in which to work. I would especially like to thank Jonathan Farina, Elaine Freedgood, John Guillory, Melissa Hillier, Leigh Claire La Berge, Karen Newman, Clifford Siskin, Gabrielle Starr, and all the students in "Genres of Enlightenment," the graduate course that Cliff and I taught together in the fall of 2005. I am grateful to New York University for funding the research leave during which I completed this project. Thanks also to Kevin Brine for many conversations about the financial world, past and present, and to Betty Flythe for reading an earlier draft of the introduction. Faculty and graduate students at King's College, Cambridge, Scripps, UCLA, the University of Chicago, the University of South Carolina, UNLV, and Vanderbilt invited me to conduct seminars at their institutions, and my project benefited enormously from these exchanges. In the fall of 2006, I taught two intensive, two-month seminars at Duke University, both of which influenced this project in unexpected ways. I want to thank Ian Baucom for inviting me to Duke and Michael Malone and Maureen Quilligan for treating me and my dogs to true Southern hospitality at Burnside. I hope that the extraordinary graduate students in my seminar at Duke will be pleased to find many of their suggestions incorporated into this book. Special thanks to Holly Bryan, Max Brzezinski, Nathan Hensley, Bill Knight, Joyoung Min, Jenny Rhee, and Philip Steer. Thanks also to members of the Barrow Street Book Club for reminding me why people love to read: Judith Altreuter, Eva Halpern, Toby

Knobel, Marie McGregor, Cindy Sirko, and Dorothy Tyler. Alice Geller deserves special thanks for her tireless efforts to purge this manuscript of errors, and Sarah Nash, Sherie Randolph, and Scott Spencer also helped track down loose ends for the bibliography. Eileen Bowman provided her usual expert help with problems technological and logistic, and I thank her, as always, for taking care of details large and small. *Genres of the Credit Economy* also received invaluable help from the three Press readers. James Thompson and Tim Alborn helped me strengthen my overall argument and fill a few remaining blanks, and Catherine Gallagher challenged me to clarify what the stakes of the project are. As with all my previous books, Alan Thomas provided the generous wisdom only an experienced editor could give. Finally, in the last stages of revision, both *Genres of the Credit Economy* and I enjoyed the altogether articulate support of Carla Mazzio, whose encouragement provided a much-needed incentive to put the book to bed.

Teddy and Jordan, who still have not learned to read, thoroughly appreciated all the days that writing kept me at home.

New York City
February 2007

INTRODUCTION

This book grows out of two questions I could not answer after writing *A History of the Modern Fact*: If the kind of knowledge that contemporary society values is really the modern fact, then why does the discipline of Literary studies matter? What can Literary scholars *do*?[1]

I don't know whether I've really answered the first of these questions, for, as the last sections of this book reveal, I continue to worry about the implications of many developments within Literary studies, especially as the discipline is now practiced in U.S. graduate programs. My suggestion about what Literary scholars can *do* is spelled out most explicitly in the last interchapter and demonstrated in chapter 6, but the entirety of *Genres of the Credit Economy* is intended to address the issues behind this question. For it has proved impossible for me to see what we might do until I have a better understanding of how this discipline became what it now is. I have tried to write the history of my discipline by understanding it as a particular genre. As a genre, Literary studies was developed to describe and explain another set of genres (Literary writing) as part of a more general process of generic differentiation, the gradual elaboration of sets of conventions and claims about method that were intended to differentiate between kinds of writing. This process of generic differentiation, in turn, belongs to the general history of specialization that we call *modernization*.[2]

Seeing Literary studies in this way is to ask about the *function* of the discipline, and, by extension, it has required me to think about the functions that Literary writing played during the last two centuries, as the process of specialization has accelerated. I have come to understand this function in terms of *value*: at the end of the seventeenth century, one of the functions performed by imaginative writing in general was to mediate value—that is, to help people understand the new credit economy and the market model of value that it promoted. As a subset of imaginative writing, Literary writing was delimited at the end of the eighteenth century, in an attempt to identify a special function that could be performed by some kinds of imaginative writing and not others.[3] By associating it with a special kind of value—one not defined by the market—writers like Wordsworth and Coleridge tried to free Literary writing from the function that imaginative writing had performed for most of the eighteenth century and, thus, to deny that other kind of value that Literary writing continued to have, as a commodity priced by market forces.

The changing function of imaginative writing, which was both reflected in and facilitated by the delimitation of Literature, can best be understood alongside two other sets of genres that also mediated value at the end of the seventeenth century. These two other sets are, on the one hand, monetary genres—gold and silver coins, paper money, and forms of credit paper—and, on the other, various types of writing about the market, credit, and price—shipping lists, prices current, economic theory, and so on. In the beginning of the period I examine here—the late seventeenth century and the first three-quarters of the eighteenth—these three genres were not consistently differentiated from each other. Not only did they perform variants of a single function, but they sometimes shared formal features as well. A shipping list was identical in format to the lists that appeared in poetic blazons or satiric catalogs, for example, and the promissory note used to acknowledge a debt contained phrases that also appeared in some imaginative texts. Because these genres—or the continuum of writing from which they would eventually be differentiated *as* genres—mediated the credit economy, all this writing helped make the system of credit and debt usable and the market model of value familiar as well. While the process of generic differentiation that this book describes was already under way in the eighteenth century, it was not until Literature was declared to be a different *kind* of imaginative writing that a secular model of value completely at odds with the market model was articulated. When this occurred, Literary writing gave up its claim to be valuable in the old sense, precisely by insisting that it was more valuable in another, more novel sense.

Even if champions of Literary writing repeatedly proclaimed the superiority of the value it was said to produce, by the middle decades of the nineteenth century this claim was widely disputed—or simply ignored—as other kinds of writing, including economic writing, acquired greater prestige. This prestige was partly a function of the kind of knowledge these non-Literary genres were said to produce—facts and information instead of fictions and imaginative truths—but, partly, it was a function of the social conditions that supported these claims about knowledge. As we will see in chapters 4 and 5, economic writers as a group were able to achieve a greater degree of what a modern sociologist would call *professional organization* than imaginative writers were. As we will also see, they were able to do so partly because the individuals who wrote economic and financial commentary distributed their efforts across the kinds of economic writing, without the rancorous feuds and fierce competition that so divided the ranks of imaginative writers.

In order to raise the prestige of fact-based genres like economic writing *relative to* the genres that circulated only fictions, of course, writers had to establish and maintain a strict distinction between fact and fiction.[4] In the first two chapters of *Genres of the Credit Economy*, I show how this distinction was introduced, as part of the breakup of the continuum of writing that mediated value at the turn into the eighteenth century. While the distinction between fact and fiction was crucial to generic differentiation and to the social status that various genres eventually attained, however, it proved virtually impossible both to distinguish absolutely between the two and to align fact and fiction perfectly with genres that were consistently distinguishable from each other. By the middle decades of the nineteenth century, as we will see in chapter 4, efforts to purge the fact-based genres of every element of fiction were visibly strained; and, as we will see in chapter 5, in the 1860s, some Literary writers tried to ban facts from novels in a desperate attempt to raise the status of this form. The impossibility of distinguishing absolutely between fact and fiction and the proliferation of publications that were neither completely factual nor totally fictitious continued to frustrate writers' efforts to use generic differentiation as a reliable instrument for enhancing social prestige.

Even a reader willing both to entertain the notion that generic differentiation is a social process, with implications for status, and to see economic and Literary writing as two outcomes of the distinction between fact and fiction might wonder what money is doing in this history. On the face of things, money does not seem to have anything to do with genre, and the distinction between fact and fiction simply seems irrelevant to the function or use of money. In my account of generic differentiation, however, money plays a crucial role, for reasons that are both theoretical and historical. For the very fact that we no longer notice that money consists of various kinds or that its function depends on writing means that money has been *naturalized*: through the social process that I describe in this book, money has become so familiar that its writing has seemed to disappear and it has seemed to lose its history as (various forms of) writing.[5] In being taken for granted, the writing that makes money serve its primary social function has passed beneath the horizon of cultural visibility. As a result of naturalization, money has come to seem simply like an instrument instead of something that was made to be used, in some ways and not others, as part of institutional practices that naturalization also tends to mask.

To the extent that we no longer see money as writing, then, and to the extent that we no longer realize that its various kinds function slightly differently (a banknote transfers value immediately; a credit card defers this transfer), we are experiencing the outcome of naturalization. As we will see in the preamble and chapter 1, various monetary genres were more or less susceptible to naturalization, but, in the course of the eighteenth and nineteenth centuries, money, as a general kind, was so effectively naturalized that the various genres it took came to seem incidental. We will also see, in chapter 6, that, in moments of fiscal crisis, the differences between monetary genres could become visible again, both as a sign that something had gone wrong in the credit economy and, when suitably interpreted, as a means of assuring worried Britons that the very instability of one kind of money could mean that other kinds were sound. Thus, the distinctions among kinds of money, which the process of naturalization tended to efface, could always be restored to visibility, always be *made* to matter, as a means of reinforcing the naturalization of the kind.

Economic and Literary genres did not undergo naturalization in exactly this way, for neither set of genres has completely lost its visibility as writing. The former, as explanations or accounts of the credit economy, came to seem most credible when its writing appeared to be *transparent*—that is, when texts seemed simply to describe or refer to economic and financial matters rather than calling attention to themselves as writing or books. The latter, by contrast, increasingly succeeded precisely to the degree to which its writing was *not* transparent and, sometimes, primarily because of its material embodiment in a beautiful or rare book.[6] Instead of making their status *as writing* disappear, as in the case of monetary genres, naturalization has erased the *historical relationship* between these two sets of genres; it has effaced the common function that once linked them and the historical process by which they were differentiated and ranked. In the process of becoming *disciplines*, of course, and partly because of the naturalization of money, economic and Literary genres have also lost their original affinity with monetary genres, which also mediated value in an earlier time.

Money plays another critical role in this history. For money—whether paper or coin—constitutes one of the earliest, and most important, forms of representation in relation to which it seemed crucial to make and reinforce a distinction between fact and fiction.[7] The version of this distinction that was articulated in relation to money was the distinction between *valid* and *invalid* monetary instruments. As we will see, the difficulties of making and defending this distinction were matters of concern even when coins constituted England's primary form of money; but the introduction of paper credit—first in the form of goldsmiths' receipts and bills of exchange, then in the bewildering varieties of credit paper that proliferated in the late seventeenth century and the eighteenth—considerably complicated efforts to distinguish between valid and invalid monetary forms. The challenges associated with maintaining this distinction in relation to monetary instruments foreshadowed similar problems that appeared in efforts to distinguish clearly and absolutely between fact and fiction and between the other generic kinds that also mediated value in this period, writing *about* financial and monetary matters and imaginative writing.

Economic, imaginative, and monetary genres were not the only kinds of writing that mediated value at the turn into the eighteenth century, of course, nor were these the only genres in which the distinction between fact and fiction came to matter. I also realize that economic writing and Literary writing acquired their modern, disciplinary forms through a process of differentiation that involved genres I do not discus in this book. What is arguably the most important seventeenth-century generic innovation, natural philosophy, also bore a complex relationship to value and the credit economy; and history, philology, and the classics, on the one hand, and physics, mechanics, and mathematics, on the other, undeniably influenced the delimitation of Literary studies and economics, respectively. While a more complete account of generic differentiation would include these (and other) disciplines, I have chosen not to do so. Partly, this expresses the limitations of my own knowledge, but, partly, it articulates a conviction that many contemporary scholars share—that economics and Literary studies have some special relationship to each other.

Before I describe the terms in which scholars have tried to understand this relationship, let me explain explicitly why I think these two disciplines should be studied together. What economic writing and Literary writing share, both historically and theoretically, is an engagement with the problematic of representation. This phrase—*the problematic of representation*—will be familiar to Literary critics, for it has become one way scholars describe the gap that separates the sign from its referent or ground (of value or meaning), whether the gap takes the form of deferral, substitution, approximation, or obscurity. Unlike most Literary critics, however, I do not present the problematic of representation as a property of *all* systems of representation.

Instead, I argue that representation *becomes* problematic—it presents problems that are both social and epistemological—only at certain times and under conditions that are historically and socially specific. A system of representation is experienced *as* problematic only when it ceases to work—that is, when something in the social context calls attention to the deferral or obfuscation of its authenticating ground. Thus, for example, when in 1720 the South Sea Bubble suddenly swelled up, then just as dramatically collapsed, the ground of its shares' value first seemed magical, then non-existent, and English men and women were left wringing their collective hands over the fictions inherent in the modern credit economy. By the same token, when in 1797 the Bank of England suspended its promise to redeem its paper notes with gold, the authenticating ground of paper credit seemed suddenly to disappear, and the nation's welfare seemed to be imperiled by a fiction whose effects had been contained for most of the eighteenth century.

When the problematic of representation becomes visible—as it did in the episodes just described—this can have grave implications for a society's economic and political stability, for it can jeopardize the prevailing model of value, the conventions that facilitate trust, and the signs that convey creditworthiness—monetary, social, legal, and political. The kinds of writing that eventually became economic and financial writing, on the one hand, and imaginative—then Literary—writing, on the other, were intimately involved in managing these troubling effects. This is why examining these genres together, and in relation to one another, is so revealing, for the different strategies by which each set of genres managed the problematic of representation helped give the modern disciplines their distinctive forms.

In the genres associated with economic writing, writers elaborated the category of fact by analogy to a distinction that natural philosophical writers had been making for decades, as a way to make market transactions seem as regular and harmonious as nature. Economic writers also helped neutralize the suspicion, often voiced by seventeenth-century writers, that financial matters were cloaked in secrecy by insisting that the very opacity of market transactions required someone to explain the secrets that made the market so difficult to understand; this figure, the economic expert, is the ancestor of the nineteenth-century economic theorist and of the modern economist as well. Imaginative writers, meanwhile, elaborated the category of fiction as a particular kind of relation between representation and the real world. Fiction helped manage the problematic of representation by creating a non-factual form of representation that was nevertheless *not a lie*. All the genres of fiction, in other words, became safe forms in which writers could explore the troubling and exciting possibility that representation could always float free of its ground.

Like economic and imaginative genres, money also constituted a form of writing in relation to which the problematic of representation became visible—especially in periods in which the nation's money supply was imperiled or speculative manias gripped the nation. Like economic and imaginative writing again, monetary genres could also be used to manage this problematic, as when the 1844 Bank Act fixed the relation between gold and the Bank of England's paper or when, in 1866, businesses' refusal to accept checks was interpreted as a sign that the Bank's paper was sound. In the beginning of the period I examine here, however, the most revealing relationship between monetary genres and the problematic of representation involved the difficulty that government officials faced in policing the distinction between valid and invalid money. As a prototype for the distinction between fact and fiction, the distinction between valid and invalid money was critical to all the strategies for managing this problematic; but, as a distinction that was nearly impossible to maintain, it was a constant reminder of the impermanence and inadequacy of every attempt to fix such distinctions.

By restoring monetary instruments, writing about economics and finance, and imaginative writing to the generic continuum that once linked them, I initially want to highlight the mediating function that these kinds of writing shared, the ways the problematic of representation appeared within them, and the ways various modes of writing managed this problematic. The majority of this book, however, is devoted to the story of the separation of these generic kinds. During the course of the eighteenth century, practitioners of both writing about financial matters and imaginative writing began to renounce their shared function—to deny that they shared the *same* function or practiced it in the same *way*. (They even more emphatically rejected their affiliation to the kind of writing that functioned *as* money.) By the 1740s, this denial began to take the form of generic distinctions (novels *as opposed to* financial commentary, political economic systems *as opposed to* romances), which were increasingly equated with—or used to define—the distinction between fact and fiction. Left suspended by these disavowals were specific words—like *credit* and *value*—that retained a place in the lexicons of both sets of genres and that remained as switchpoints or sites of overlap between them, even as these concepts became central to the function of various kinds of money.

Participants on both sides of what increasingly became a naturalized generic divide contributed to this separation. On the one side, eighteenth-century economic writers sought to emulate natural philosophical conventions for generating facts by producing political economic *systems* that first marginalized, then specifically repudiated any features associated with fiction. By the nineteenth century, the large field of economic writing had itself been informally subdivided into ranked kinds, a subdivision that included, at its higher rungs, tomes of increasingly mathematical economic theory and, at its lower, newspaper articles and periodical essays that helped familiarize readers with the operations of financial institutions. On the other side, eighteenth-century imaginative writers increasingly denied that their work had any meaningful connection to matters economic or financial—even (or especially) the connection that all forms of print so obviously continued to have to the market. As the volume of printed materials increased after 1770, and increased again in the wake of the mid-nineteenth-century repeal of the taxes on knowledge, imaginative writers struggled to enforce their own version of an internal hierarchy. As we will see in chapters 4 and 5, this hierarchy differed from its counterpart in economic writing in being characterized not by an informally agreed-on division of labor but by acrimonious accusations and internal policing, intended to distinguish between "refined" or "polite" variants of Literature and the lesser realm of "trash" or "print commerce."[8] As we will see in the first interchapter and in chapters 3 and 5, efforts to discriminate between the two kinds of writing (economic and Literary) intensified in the decades surrounding the turn into the nineteenth century, as the increase in the overall output of the publishing industry threatened to politicize all kinds of print—including paper money. I discuss the outcomes of these intensified efforts in chapters 4 and 5: a mode of economic writing that derived its descriptive and narrative conventions, and, increasingly, its method, from the physical sciences and mathematics and a mode of Literary writing that accommodated a variety of generic conventions but discriminated between itself and mere pretenders in terms of a set of values supposedly unique to Literature (originality, an elevated style, a form of textual autonomy that emulated an organism, and a distinctly *critical* relation to the credit economy).

During the middle decades of the nineteenth century, for reasons I explain in chapter 4, the monetary genres acquired the taken-for-grantedness that I have associated with naturalization. As the writing that enabled money to work became less visible, the monetary genres played an increasingly marginal role in the relationship between the two other genres with which I am concerned. After chapter 4, then—and apart from a critical reappearance in chapter 6—money virtually disappears from my narrative, which focuses increasingly on the version of naturalization that produced the modern disciplines of economics and Literary studies. During most of the century, economic and Literary writers both continued to stress the generic differences between them by differentiating between the modes of knowledge they claimed to produce. Even as political economists and Literary writers elaborated and reinforced this distinction, however, the two genres continued to have a complex relationship to each other. Most obviously, as we will see in chapter 4, writers on the economic side of the divide borrowed tropes and narrative conventions from imaginative writers when they encountered economic phenomena that defied the discipline's ordinary explanatory paradigms. On the other side, nineteenth-century Literary writers repeatedly—and, after 1845, increasingly—appropriated economic and financial themes and real-life situations for fictional treatment. As we will see in chapter 6, most of these Literary appropriations were only incidentally concerned with the explanatory function that was central to writing about money and finance; imaginative writers' tendency to mine contemporary financial events for characters and plots paradoxically cultivated in readers a tolerance for ignorance about the very financial mechanisms political economists sought to explain, and this strange symbiosis both underscored the differences between the two kinds of writing and bound them together in an increasingly complicated, increasingly misrecognized relationship of mutual indebtedness, masked by mutual disavowal and misunderstanding.

In the three penultimate sections of this book—the second interchapter and chapters 5 and 6—I turn to Literature and Literary criticism. While I devote two chapters to economic writing and two to its Literary counterpart, however, the latter contain a perspective that I have not been able to include in the former. In my discussions of Literary writing, I have been able to show how the disciplinary categories we now use—as a result of the refinement of Literary studies in university classrooms—grew out of and now influence the way we see these nineteenth-century Literary texts. In the best of all possible worlds, I would have been able to provide a similar discussion of the relationship between the modern discipline of economics and the way we see nineteenth-century political economic texts. I have not been able to provide this perspective partly because I am not trained in modern economics and partly because so many modern economists repudiate the theories and methods practiced by their disciplinary predecessors. If they do not explicitly deny that the discipline of economics has a history, they deny that its history matters. As a consequence, there seems to be a greater divide—or at least one that is difficult for an outsider to cross—between the protocols of the modern discipline and the protocols developed in the nineteenth century. I can only hope that some day an economic historian will write a version of this history from the other side so that Literary scholars like myself can see how this discipline's present informs the way we understand its past.

————

Many scholarly works populate the fields that overlap with or lie adjacent to the territory I cover here, and I want both to acknowledge these and to distinguish my work from them. In their introduction to the volume entitled *The New Economic Criticism*, Martha Woodmansee and Mark Osteen offer a useful overview of what, by the late 1990s, had already become a flourishing scholarly field. Surveying both Literary appropriations of economic themes and economists' use of Literary concerns, Woodmansee and Osteen identify four general areas of exciting work. These include studies of Literary production, often the economic conditions in which a given writer worked;[9] formalist studies of the internal "economies" of a text or of money or language as an "economy," which Woodmansee and Osteen call studies of "internal circulation"; studies that focus on the market forces that affect canonization and "economies of reading"; and a group of "metatheoretical" works that focus on the "practices, presumptions and protocols of economic criticism itself."[10] While this typology constitutes an interesting attempt to capture an emergent subfield of scholarly work, in the years since its publication the schema has been swamped by a veritable flood of new scholarship. While I cannot provide the kind of comprehensive typological system that Woodmansee and Osteen devised, I do want to offer a provisional grouping for some of these works in order to make my debts clear and to highlight the nature of my own contribution.

The territory is easier to map on the economics side of the disciplinary divide, for, as I have just stated, most modern economists are indifferent to the history of their discipline and relatively uninterested in the foundational metaphors that govern economic writing. The most telling contributions to this field have been made by Deirdre McCloskey, but, in addition to McCloskey, Philip Mirowski, Arjo Klamer, Thomas C. Leonard, and Robert M. Solow have also called attention to the relationship between language, generic features, and the production of economic knowledge.[11] In writing *Genres of the Credit Economy*, however, I have been less influenced by this work than by a group of economic histories, many of them quite old, that chronicle the development of specific financial institutions, practices, and instruments. Most important are histories by A. E. Feavearyear, L. S. Pressnell, David Kynaston, Ranald C. Michie, and George Robb.[12] Histories of the development of economics as a discipline or school of "thought" have also been extremely helpful, although, as I argue in a moment, *thought* is a category to which I want to add generic and disciplinary ballast. The histories of this kind I have regularly consulted include Joseph A. Schumpeter's influential *A History of Economic Analysis*, William Letwin's *The Origins of Scientific Economics*, Richard Olson's *Science Deified and Science Defied*, Deborah A. Redman's *The Rise of Political Economy as a Science*, and Margaret Schabas's *The Natural Origins of Economics*.

The scholarship on the Literary side of my subject is more extensive, and, although much of it could still be assigned to the categories that Woodmansee and Olson identified in 1999, I use a different set of groupings to highlight the theoretical and methodological differences among these works. The three large categories that I identify in this scholarship—all of which I have drawn on for this work—include one that treats economic matters as ideas (or "thought"), logics, metaphors, or structural paradigms; one that focuses on the economic conditions of Literary production; and one that deals with the formal, generic, and commodity features that have allowed Literary writing to attain a degree of relative autonomy since the late eighteenth century. In what is admittedly an inadequate survey, let me consider each of these categories individually.

The first category is the largest and most complex. In it I include, for example, histories of economic theory like those by David Kauffman, Regenia Gagnier, and Catherine Gallagher (to name only a few recent and important studies); considerations of an underlying "logic" of capital or capitalism, like the work of James Cruise and Deirdre Lynch; treatments of economic images or the metaphor of the "economy" itself, like the important works by Marc Shell and Jean-Joseph Goux; and various studies of representations of commerce, economic issues, and financial figures or attitudes toward business, capital, and finance, like the work of Edward Copeland, James Thompson, Liz Bellamy, Patrick Brantlinger, and Colin Nicholson (again, to cite only some of the most prominent).[13] Even though these studies are different in significant ways, I group them together because, in some important sense, they all focus on the *ideas* or *concepts* implicit in some system of representation, whether that system is eighteenth-century political economy, modern economism, capitalism, language, or one or more Literary texts. Even the work closest in subject matter to *Genres of the Credit Economy*, Catherine Gallagher's *The Body Economic*, is primarily engaged with the content of various texts and only incidentally attentive to genre or discipline.

While I agree that systems of representation, including economic representational systems (like money, political economy, and capitalism), can be said to contain and to convey ideas (like functional equivalence, free market individualism, and the effacement of labor by abstractions), and while I agree that these concepts have been important, in this book I argue that such ideas become operative only in and through the writing in which they are formulated and received. By emphasizing the genres by which such writings have been organized and the conventions and hierarchies of forms by which various kinds of writing were distinguished from each other, I want to stress how various ideas were rendered socially usable. Thus, I am less interested in the explicit content of economic treatises or the ideas that we can infer from the representational systems associated with them than in the way that various forms of writing participated in the social process of classification and ranking, by which economic writing and imaginative writing were first distinguished from each other as they were refined for different social roles, then ranked, both internally and in relation to each other. In this regard, *Genres of the Credit Economy* resembles Michael McKeon's *Secret History of Domesticity*, which also focuses on the early modern "division of knowledge." I discuss McKeon's work in more detail in chapter 2. Here, suffice it to say that, as his emphasis on "knowledge" rather than "genre" suggests, McKeon engages this subject at a greater level of abstraction than I do.

My second category contains samples of recent scholarship on the economics of Literary production. This work has been invaluable to me, and I could not have written this book without the painstaking research of scholars like Paula McDowell, James Raven, Peter Garside, Rainer Schöwerling, and William St. Clair.[14] They have uncovered new archives, found innovative (often digital) ways of sorting through known archives whose sheer size had previously stymied researchers, and organized their findings in usable systems of narratives, lists, statistics, and databases. Because of their labor, the printed materials of what is now called the *long eighteenth century* are searchable to a degree and visible in ways never previously possible. These scholars have added to an existing body of archival work on Literary publication, mostly involving the nineteenth century, that includes pioneering books by Richard Altick, John Sutherland, Guinevere Griest, Lee Erickson, and David Finkelstein.[15] While these scholarly works overlap with the category that Woodmansee and Olson call *production*, they tend not to focus on individual writers so much as the place that Literary publishing occupied in British economic and social relations. The shift away from individual writers to the *institution* of publishing helps replace the author-centric preoccupations of much traditional scholarship with a more sociological consideration of the ways that individual efforts are facilitated and constrained by the existing conditions of production. While these scholars—and I—give some attention to the technological innovations (in printing and papermaking) that helped accelerate Literary production during these two centuries, none of us insists that technology determined this speedup. Instead, many of the scholars I have cited assign more importance to legal, political, and industry-specific factors—like the passage, then repeal, of taxes on certain kinds of publications; various pieces of copyright legislation; and the cartel-like power exercised by printers and booksellers in the middle decades of the eighteenth century and by the circulating libraries between 1842 and 1894. I follow the lead of these scholars on this important matter, but I do expand their focus on the Literary publishing industry to include the factors that made the volume of economic and financial publications expand during these same decades. This expansion—in both volume and kind of financial genres—overlapped with and underwrote the expansion of the Literary publishing industry in interesting ways, and one of the themes I explore in the first interchapter in particular is how looking at these two expansions together changes our understanding of both.

The third important category of Literary scholarship contains fewer members than my first two groupings, but these works have influenced this book in profound ways. These works—the pathbreaking essays on genre by Ralph Cohen, studies of eighteenth-century print by Clifford Siskin and William Warner, and John Guillory's important treatment of the canon as a social form—differ from each other in their immediate focus: Cohen's essays tend to be theoretical metacommentaries on genre, both Siskin and Warner work on eighteenth-century texts, and Guillory moves from antiquity to twentieth-century Literary scholarship.[16] Nevertheless, all these scholars assign genres (and other classificatory systems) a central role in the configuration and reconfiguration of social situations. In allowing us to see some of the ways that the procedures of classification and ranking inherent in the process of generic differentiation participated in social processes, all these scholars present the history of our discipline in a new and exciting way.

This is the point at which my work parts company from the important contributions of these scholars. Even Siskin's inclusive term *writing*, after all—in failing systematically to discriminate among kinds of writing—understates the extent to which *disciplinary differentiation* was a critical counterpart to the classification and ranking that occurred within a single set of genres. More specifically, while attentive to generic differentiation, Cohen, Warner, and Guillory are all primarily concerned with Literary writing;

thus, they miss the opportunity to discuss the social processes by which disciplines were differentiated from each other alongside, and as part of, generic reworking and innovation. While one could certainly expand the number of disciplines beyond the two I isolate here, by focusing on the differentiation of economic writing from Literary writing, I can offer a methodological model that future scholars might adapt. By proposing that the relationships among genres and disciplines are the outcomes of a historical process of delimitation, ranking, and differentiation, I suggest a way of thinking about the relationship between the modern disciplines that might help explain why some now seem self-evidently more valuable than others.

Let me conclude this introduction with a few comments about the arrangement of this book, a description of the narrative that follows, and some observations on method. Since *Genres of the Credit Economy* focuses on generic differentiation, it has not seemed amiss to engage in a bit of generic innovation myself. Some of the materials that I have included in the following pages do not fit easily into the historical narrative that dominates the chapters, either because they contain information that is useful for understanding the entire book (the preamble), or because they contain historical or methodological treatments of issues that specifically comment on the chapters that follow them (the two interchapters). I have elected to place each of these discussions in a separate section as a way of signaling the departure they make from the chronological narrative the chapters unfold. This will also make it easier for readers to find the parts of this book most relevant to their interests. Readers already familiar with eighteenth- and nineteenth-century genres might want to skip the preamble, those familiar with the late-eighteenth-century takeoff of print and the Bank Restriction Act are excused from the first interchapter, and those not especially interested in debates among contemporary Literary critics can simply skim the second interchapter. These asides have allowed me to provide information or develop arguments that I consider essential to this book, but my feelings will not suffer if others don't agree.

After the preamble, which provides an overview of the genres I deal with in this book, I begin my chronological narrative. The first two chapters deal with the seventeenth and eighteenth centuries and illuminate the existence, then breakup of the continuum of writing that generated, then broke up the fact/fiction continuum. Chapter 1 highlights some of the intricacies that characterized the relationship between writing *about* money and the forms of writing that functioned *as* money in seventeenth- and eighteenth-century Britain. This relationship was intricate because, contrary to what we might expect (and unlike the correlation we find after 1797), the volume of writing about money did not simply increase as (or because) the forms of circulating money increased. Instead, before the Restriction period, commentaries about money proliferated in the years in which the value of the monetary instruments themselves seemed dubious—either because, as in the case of coins, these instruments had visibly lost some of the precious metal that theoretically guaranteed their worth, or because, as with paper money, the institutions that issued them seemed to have overreached themselves. Thus, the discussions of money that I explore in this chapter constituted attempts to use some kinds of writing to stabilize (or interrogate) the value of another by masking (or exposing) the problematic of representation that separates the tokens that represent value from its deferred ground in any money economy.

In chapter 2, I address the process by which the fact/fiction continuum was broken up during the eighteenth century, especially in imaginative writing. I begin with Daniel Defoe's early writings on credit, for these works reveal both the existence of the continuum in the first decades of the eighteenth century and the way that writing that was not generically marked, as subsequent writing was, could mediate value without distinguishing between facts and fictions. I also give considerable attention to the imaginative text that modern publishers title *Roxana*, first to explore the ways that Defoe helped readers understand, and, thus, learn to trust, unfamiliar features of the credit system, then to reveal how subsequent publishers revised Defoe's text (and changed his title) in order to make this volume conform to what was repeatedly identified after 1740 as the norms of a distinct—and distinctly fictional—form, the novel.

Chapter 2 also examines two other facets of the breakup of the fact/fiction continuum. These include, on the one hand, the emergence of an incipient *disciplinary* division and, on the other, the persistence of a *generic* reminder of the vitality the continuum had once had. Thus, we see in the appearance of Steuart's *Principles of Political Economy* and the launch of a series of periodicals dedicated to reviewing new imaginative works the rudiments of what would eventually become the distinct disciplines of economics and Literary studies. This disciplinary distinction, however, was not completely aligned with distinct genres, as one might expect. Instead, what we find are numerous texts that look, in retrospect, like generic *hybrids* because they contain features that were beginning to be separated and allocated to different generic kinds. The hybrids that I examine in this chapter, which include Thomas Bridges's *Adventures of a Bank-Note* and Steuart's *Principles*, reveal that vestiges of the fact/fiction continuum persisted even as genres were being distinguished from each other. The number and variety of these hybrids also suggest that they continued to make sense to readers, even though the process of generic differentiation was already under way. As we will see in chapter 5, subsequent attempts to reinforce the distinction between economic and Literary writing often targeted such hybrids, even though they continued to be written and published. Chapter 2 also inaugurates the discussion to which I return in chapters 3 and 4, showing how monetary instruments gradually passed beneath the horizon of cultural visibility as they lost their status as writing and came simply to seem to embody value.

The first of two interchapters provides a transition from the eighteenth-century materials to their nineteenth-century counterparts. In it, I discuss the dramatic increases in the volume of bank paper and book paper that occurred in turn-of-the-century Britain. While these increases occurred almost at the same time, they were different in significant ways: they were not caused by the same factors, and they did not take homologous forms. The writing that functioned *as* money proliferated as a direct consequence of the 1797 Restriction Act, for, by curtailing the obligation of the Bank of England to redeem its notes with gold, this legislation indirectly encouraged the formation of country banks and the issue of provincial paper. Writing *about* money was provoked by this legislation as well, both because the Restriction rendered the fictitious nature of all paper money visible and because, as the value of paper money rose and fell, contemporaries were driven to speculate about its merits. Thus, the 1797 act, as well as the 1810 Bullion Report (which advocated revoking the Restriction), immediately incited more writing of a theoretical kind, as a consequence of the written legislation that inaugurated the Restriction in the first place.

New legislation also led to a late-century increase in the volume of imaginative writing. The critical law in this regard was the 1774 act curtailing perpetual copyright, which had prevailed for most of the eighteenth century. As publishers rushed to take advantage of the opportunities introduced by the Booksellers' Act, imaginative writers also developed innovative genres that capitalized on Britain's growing market for all kinds of leisure goods, including print. Among these genres were Gothic novels, which drew their inspiration from sensational events in France, and cheap political tracts, which expressed the political yearnings of the British poor. As we will see in chapters 5 and 6, the increase in kinds of imaginative writing and the attendant commodification of print almost immediately provoked attempts by some writers to establish a boundary between what they considered Literature and every other form of imaginative writing.

Even though the proliferations of paper in the monetary realm and in economic and imaginative writing stemmed from different causes and took different forms, they need to be considered together, for they all had implications for the problematic of representation. This is clearest in regard to the monetary genres, for the explosion in the volume of paper money made the fiction inherent in this monetary form visible again. As economic writers scrambled to explain this fiction away, they invoked the more general distinction between fact and fiction to enhance the authority of their writing. For their part, writers like Wordsworth and Coleridge tried to deny that their work was related in any way either to developments in the market or to fact-based genres like economic theory. To do so, they tried to distinguish among kinds of imaginative writing—not by appealing to the distinction between fact and fiction, but by discriminating among various functions, which they claimed were natural to different kinds of writing.

Chapters 3 and 4 focus on the discipline of political economy, the antecedent of modern economics. Unlike most historians of economics, who focus exclusively on the discipline's march toward a fully mathematical science, I highlight three *sociological* features of nineteenth-century political economy. They include the ability of what I call *establishment* economists to elaborate and adapt the theories bequeathed to them by eighteenth-century theorists while denigrating rival formulations or attempts to make other issues seem more salient; the creation of a hierarchy internal to the genres by which theory was separated from the popular versions in which others extended the reach of theorists' ideas; and practitioners' ability, when they reached the limits of their scientific method, to revert to or borrow from imaginative writing to render aesthetically pleasing events that troubled the explanatory paradigms of economic writing.

In chapter 3, I show how establishment economists created a theoretical consensus. They did so partly by settling differences among themselves, as we can see in a debate that erupted immediately after the Restriction Act. This debate, which concerned the role that paper money should play in Britain's credit economy, involved a number of writers who differed on local issues but agreed about economic essentials. Even though Walter Boyd, William Harrison, and Lord Peter King challenged the Restriction Act and Henry Thornton and Francis Baring defended it, all these men simply assumed that competition meant progress, paper money extended credit, and no nation lacking either would prosper in the modern age. In the next section of this chapter, I show how establishment economists marginalized writers who disagreed with their theoretical commonplaces. Here my focus is William Cobbett, who insisted that the truisms of classical political

economy supported not the nation as a whole but only people who benefited from Britain's "funding system": the directors of the Bank of England,
stockholders, and the members of Parliament who protected them. Cobbett
was also engaged in a debate, then, but, because most establishment writers
wrote primarily to and for each other, he staged this debate in the pages
of his writing. By incorporating the words of his opponents into his own
texts, he tried to reverse the process by which the economic establishment
tried to marginalize him. By highlighting the position of marginality that
Cobbett simultaneously embraced and was assigned, I explain both the
ambition and the limits of his campaign: he wanted to expose the fiction
inherent in paper money to bring the government down, but members of
the economic establishment simply insisted that paper was not fiction and
that, even if it was, it was a fiction necessary to Britain's prosperity. The
third debate I consider in this chapter, the protracted discussions that led
up to the passage of the 1844 Bank Act, reveals how economic writers developed an increasingly technical vocabulary to account for phenomena
that contemporaries found deeply troubling. I conclude this chapter with
a discussion of another currency radical, the printer John Francis Bray.
Bray's *Labour's Wrongs and Labour's Remedies* (1838–39) shares with Cobbett's *Paper against Gold* (1810–11) the recognition that the Restriction Act
had politicized paper money, but the remedies suggested in it were so at
odds with the conventions of political economic writing that his impact
was as marginal as was the position to which Cobbett was relegated by the
third decade of the century.

Chapter 4 focuses on the division of labor informally adopted by
nineteenth-century economic writers. In this discussion, I not only highlight the way the discipline attained the status of a science but also test the
limits of political economists' claims to adapt scientific principles to describe
economic events. Specifically, I focus on various economic writers' treatments of the speculative manias and panics that periodically disrupted
Britain's mature credit economy. These treatments—and their failures—are
important both because manias and panics disturbed the optimistic picture
of capitalism that establishment economists tried to present and because
economists' inability to explain them marked the limits of their method. In
the first section of this chapter, I describe the process by which writers generally considered the century's leading theorists defined the characteristic
method and genres of political economy. These men include David Ricardo,
J. R. McCulloch, Thomas Chalmers (and, through him, Thomas Robert
Malthus), John Stuart Mill, and Stanley Jevons. After Ricardo (who died before the century's first speculative mania), each of these writers also tried to

accommodate manias and panics into their accounts of commercial society, and the limitations of their success tell us much about the similarities that continued to link economic and imaginative writing to each other. In the second section, I turn to a less prestigious kind of economic writing, financial journalism. Here, I show how Walter Bagehot, D. Morier Evans, and Laurence Oliphant tackled the problem of manias and panics in genres designed to appeal to readers not trained in political economic theory. Even though these popularizers also failed to explain why manias and panics occurred—in terms that modern economists would consider satisfactory, at any rate—their ability to demystify the operations of the City and to make even the arcane language of finance familiar to ordinary Britons helped make economic theory seem relevant to everyday life and, not incidentally, made investing in shares an acceptable thing to do with money.

In the final section of chapter 4, I engage one of the architects of what has been called the *Marginalist Revolution* in economic theory, W. Stanley Jevons. Jevons's work is important both because it signaled another stage in the professionalization of economics and because his attempts to model commercial crises reveal how attractive—and elusive—the dream of a fully scientific economics proved to be. As a professor, first in Manchester, then at University College, London, Jevons helped bring economic theory into the university, where it was further refined in subsequent decades. By insisting that commercial manias and panics could be correlated to a natural phenomenon whose occurrence seemed mathematically regular, he tried to dispel suspicions that some economic events were irrational by subjecting them to a fully rational, because mathematical, account. He held on to the idea that commercial crises were caused by sunspots, even when evidence failed to support this theory, because, by the late 1870s, he could assume that his formalist method, if not the figures he plugged into it, was essentially sound. As one expert writing to others, Jevons knew that, even if he could not make the numbers work, one of his colleagues eventually would.

In chapters 5 and 6, I turn to imaginative writing to show how a handful of poets, essayists, and reviewers progressively delimited the category of Literature by creating a hierarchy that resembled economic writers' division of labor. Whereas the groupings within economic writing divided and distributed the work of formulating and disseminating a relatively uniform interpretation of economic issues, the Literary hierarchy ruthlessly policed its own ranks in order to enforce the theoretical consensus that market forces discouraged. The public's appetite for new forms of print, in other words, and for cheap, political, and sensational genres in particular, did not necessarily accord with the values promoted by poets like Wordsworth and Coleridge, and, as a consequence, the stage was set at the beginning of the nineteenth century for a confrontation between writers already critical of the market model of value and readers who wanted their expectations met.

Chapter 5 begins with a discussion of the campaign, spearheaded by Wordsworth and Coleridge, to differentiate Literary writing from other modes of imaginative writing and from the political publications inspired by events in France. In this section, I discuss the relative status accorded different genres, Wordsworth's and Coleridge's equation of originality and longevity with Literary value, and the complex role played in the delimitation of Literature by minor Literary writers like De Quincey and reviewers like Jeffrey. I then describe the organization of the mid-nineteenth-century book market, giving particular attention to the circulating library system and its effects on writers, publishers, and readers. My argument here is that the confrontations among various sectors of the Literary establishment— elite writers, would-be popular writers, reviewers and critics, publishers and booksellers, library proprietors, and readers—produced, alongside a hierarchy of kinds of Literary writing, a hierarchical understanding of the modes of reading by which readers consumed imaginative writing. By examining efforts to discriminate among kinds of reading, I show how, by the third quarter of the century, (some) critics had managed to elevate the novel in the hierarchy of Literary kinds, in large part by endorsing the aesthetic criteria that, by that point, completely defined *Literary value* even in what had been (and continued to be) a popular genre.

In the second interchapter, I continue this discussion of reading, focusing now on the ways that contemporary Literary critics' treatments of texts differ so radically from the way readers not disciplined by graduate training read. This section contains my most explicit discussion of some of the methodologies used by modern Literary critics—the kind of textual interpretation often called *New Historicism* and a method that does not privilege interpretation, which Ian Hunter calls *historical description*. Using treatments of Harriet Martineau's *Illustrations of Political Economy* as examples, I show how contemporary Literary studies carries over the model of organic unity that Wordsworth and James associated with Literary value, and I explain why this kind of textual interpretation cannot provide evidence to support a historical argument, even one focused on something as amorphous as *discourse*. Historical description, which focuses on the classificatory schemes that group texts into various categories and the social function they played, constitutes an alternative to the presentist bias of most textual interpretation by recovering the historical conditions that made some uses of texts possible while rendering others nonsensical or obsolete.

In chapter 6 I demonstrate what the practice of Literary studies might look like if we were to provide historical descriptions of individual texts instead of trying to derive interpretations from them. In this chapter, I examine four canonical Literary texts through a series of interrelated questions: What occasioned this text? How do the conventions that the author deployed work as a narrative system? How does the system of narrative seek to manage both the way the text is read and its relation to the situation that occasioned it? My argument here is that the formalism that persists in most contemporary Literary methodologies is partly a response to Literary conventions developed to curtail reference. The particular novels I examine in this chapter—*Pride and Prejudice, Little Dorrit, Silas Marner,* and *The Last Chronicle of Barset*—all incorporate topics that economic writers also addressed, but they subject them to an aesthetic rationale. These novels have become canonical, in fact, partly because they lend themselves to the formalist methods now taught in most departments of English in the United States and the United Kingdom. Paradoxically, however, these novels were also popular in their own day, and generally remain so, because, to readers who have not been so disciplined, they seem to refer to the actual world, not simply to create the effect of reality within their pages. That such double modes of readings are possible suggests the transitional nature of these novels—they are simultaneously formalist, in approaching the Literary norm of the organic whole, and realistic, in the nontechnical sense of containing lifelike characters and situations. That such doubled reading is necessary reveals the fracture that runs through contemporary engagements with Literary texts, along the fault line of graduate training.

I return to the topic of the hierarchy of the modern disciplines in a brief coda, where I also offer a few thoughts about the new genres that are proliferating in cyberspace, apparently beyond the reach of all academic programs. Before closing this introduction, however, I want to make a few additional points about my own methodology.

The first concerns the kind of historical narrative I offer here. *Genres of the Credit Economy* provides neither a Foucauldian genealogy nor a traditional cultural history. Instead, by juxtaposing the way our modern disciplines—especially the discipline of Literary studies—encourage us to read to the way past readers engaged these texts, I try to enable my readers to see the process by which the classificatory schemes that undergird genres and disciplines changed. This shuttling back and forth and the repeated attention I give to the categories through which I read may be distracting to some readers, but I want to make it difficult to ignore the twin facts that every history is constructed through such categories and that these categories—as much as the details a writer chooses to emphasize—dictate *what* we can understand about the past by shaping the *way* we understand it.

The second concerns the scope of *Genres of the Credit Economy*. My focus on these decades—from the late seventeenth century through the 1870s—ignores the period distinctions most scholars recognize. The more expansive scope of this book enables us to see an array of changes in the way these genres mediated the credit economy that are obscured by traditional periodization, but, particularly in the case of Literary writing, it also allows us to see why scholars have tended to treat the years between 1798 and 1832 as a distinct Romantic period. As we will see in chapter 5, during these years some Literary writers announced the value of originality, declared that their writing broke completely with its predecessors, and equated Literary value with this self-proclaimed originality. Insofar as Literary scholars have isolated a Romantic period, cutting it free from both eighteenth-century imaginative writing and the Victorian writing that followed, they have tacitly accepted these claims; but, in so doing, they have failed to notice the continuities that link these imaginative productions or to comment on the role such claims have played in the creation of the modern disciplines. By contextualizing turn-of-the-century arguments about originality, both in relation to earlier and later Literature and in relation to writing of other kinds, I have tried to show the function that the Romantic model of value has played in Literary history, in debates about the nature of value, and in the modern separation of disciplines.

A third consideration has to do with organization and style. Because the modern disciplines are separate, in the ways this book chronicles, Literary and economic histories are typically written by different scholars, and versions of each tend to have their own narrative coherence as well as distinct stylistic conventions. Putting these subjects together in chapters that contain focused arguments has required me to respect the division in subject matter to a certain extent: as I have already noted, chapters 3 and 4 deal with the economic side of the history, and chapters 5 and 6 deal with the Literary side. While this division has allowed me to present coherent narratives, however, it also means that the overall chronology of the events I describe is sometimes out of order. Readers will encounter Jevons's sunspot theory, which he developed in the early 1870s, before they read about Wordsworth's early-nineteenth-century reflections on his poetic practice, for example, and they will be asked to engage with Jane Austen's late-eighteenth-century novel, *Pride and Prejudice*, after they have learned about Henry James's late-nineteenth-century theories about the nature of novelistic art. I have tried to provide enough thematic commentary and chronological narrative to overcome whatever difficulties this might pose, but I do acknowledge that the order of my narrative may require patience. In terms of stylistic conventions, I have decided to use present-tense verbs to describe the events that a text narrates, as Literary critics typically do, and past-tense verbs to describe historical actions, as some—but not all—historians do. In some sentences, this has led to what may seem like stylistic inconsistency, but I have wanted to call attention at the level of my style to the difference between textual events and actual ones—a difference that, as we will see in chapters 5 and 6, nineteenth-century Literary conventions helped efface by so expanding textuality that it seems to engulf everything outside the text.

Finally, in order to develop the argument of this book with enough detail to do justice to its complexities, I have found it necessary to limit my focus to Britain and British writing and to English money and the English financial system. By using variants of *Britain*, of course, instead of *Great Britain*, I artificially lop off huge sectors of what, by the late eighteenth century, had become an empire; and, by focusing only on English monetary arrangements, I exclude the two complex subjects of Scots and Irish money and the Scottish banking system, both of which were extremely important in these centuries. I am all too aware of the sacrifices that these limitations have exacted. Every credit economy is also an economy of debt, and, during these centuries in particular, English investors' extraordinary rate of return on their capital was largely obtained through overseas investment. As a consequence, to omit all discussion of India and the West Indies, in particular, is to present an admittedly one-sided picture of the global system of credit and debt whose legacy still casts such a long shadow across the world.[17] By the same token, because the monetary systems of Ireland and Scotland presented challenges that were different from those that English money posed, and because many of the solutions to banking problems were initially worked out in Scotland, failing to discuss these subjects deprives me of important comparative cases. Similarly, not even to mention the market for exported British Literary writing in Englished countries like India risks attributing too much credit for the delimitation of Literature to a few men and women in England.[18] While I fully acknowledge the importance of both comparative studies and placing the British story in a larger context, I have elected a narrower canvas in order to offer greater detail about the subjects I do address. The history of disciplinary specialization that I describe in the following pages helps explain why the grasp of any modern scholar is more limited than her ability to understand the bigger picture. Even if this history does not excuse the limitations of my effort, it should remind us of how much still remains to be incorporated in any attempt to understand the genres in which the credit economy in which we still live came to be naturalized and understood.

Mediating Genres

Before embarking on my account of generic differentiation, I provide an overview of the genres that emerged from this process. The organization of this preamble reflects the outcome of the history this book narrates: I separate the three forms of writing into three distinct groups because our modern disciplines do so; I describe the kinds of writing that appear in each group in terms of each other, instead of in relation to all the other kinds, because this is the way that modern disciplines generally understand generic affiliation—as variations on an identifiable, if historically changing, norm. While I use this organization for purposes of clarity, I want to emphasize at the outset what I make clear elsewhere in the book. All these genres initially performed a single function—they helped Britons understand and learn how to negotiate the market model of value. Preserving this dual perspective—looking back from where we are now *and* looking at situations that once existed but no longer do so—is a challenge I will repeatedly ask readers to meet in the chapters that follow, but, for now, I will simply look back, from where we are now, and with the help of terms that should be familiar to most readers.

One further theoretical point is in order. Even though it has become conventional (i.e., it accords with the conventions of the modern disciplines) to treat these genres as different from each other, some modern critics have identified structural homologies between some of these kinds of writing. I have already mentioned some prominent examples of this theoretical position—Jean-Joseph Goux's discovery of a "structural parallel" between money and language, for example, or Marc Shell's claim (following A. R. J. Turgot) that speech and money are both languages.[1] These claims undeniably help us understand genres that now seem so different, precisely because of the process of disciplinary differentiation that this book chronicles. Nonetheless, in this preamble, and in the remainder of *Genres of the Credit Economy*, I want to insist that the genres I describe are not simply homologous. Even if we can identify formal similarities—especially structural similarities—between some of them, such insights are possible only because we have attained a certain kind of distance on these genres. This distance reflects our use of *theoretical* paradigms; it is a product of the articulation of the level of abstraction that discipline-specific theoretical paradigms produce and in relation to which some features of the genres, but not others, become prominent. To this theoretical perspective, I want to juxtapose a *historical* perspective, which brings other features of these genres into relief and tends to highlight not their structural similarities but their manifold differences from each other. From this perspective, the genres I describe here can be said to have served a single function, but the different ways they did so are what matters. From this perspective, these genres appear to be *incommensurate*, not *homologous*. There are at least two important senses in which this is true.

First, even though all the genres I describe in this preamble mediated value and the credit economy, they did not do so in the same way. On the one hand, the three sets of genres represented different relations to value (and, in the case of Literary writing, claimed to represent a different *kind* of value). Monetary instruments were understood to approach a literal relation to value, for one of their functions—to serve as a common denominator in exchange—required that monetary tokens be taken *as* valuable instruments in and of themselves. At the same time, of course, most of the tokens used as money before the general acceptance of paper *did* literally incarnate value, for they were at least partially composed of the gold or silver that Britons considered the most precious metals. As I will argue in a moment, it was with the introduction of paper that monetary instruments can also be conceptualized as genres, and this makes them resemble in some ways (although not others) other kinds of texts. Writing about economic matters, by contrast, like imaginative writing, engaged value more indirectly: these modes of writing were thought to be *about* value rather than to approach or embody literal value (at least not until a particular volume achieved the degree of scarcity and desirability that rendered it a valuable commodity in the rare book market). These kinds of volumes can be said to have been valuable as well because they constituted *symbolic capital*—that is, they represented visible achievements that could help a particular individual establish the kind of reputation that could secure national prominence and a lucrative professional appointment. This, as we will see in chapters 3 and 4, was increasingly possible for (male) economic writers during the second half of the nineteenth century. As we will see in chapter 5, even though there were some notable exceptions (like Walter Scott and Charles Dickens), it was generally possible to become a professional Literary writer—a writer who made a living by publishing imaginative writing of various kinds—only at the end of the nineteenth century.

On the other hand, the three forms with which I am concerned in this book were incommensurate because their relationships to the fact/fiction continuum differed. As I will argue in chapter 1, the monetary counterpart to what became the *distinction between* fact and fiction was the distinction between valid and invalid monetary instruments; and, even though this distinction has never been established in such a way as to permit effective enforcement, as a conceptual and practical necessity it preceded and helped model the dichotomy that was gradually created in the other two types of writing, that between fact and fiction. As writers of various kinds gradually devised strategies and genres intended to distinguish fact from fiction (for reasons both social and professional), however, they began to give more priority to this distinction than to the monetary distinction between valid and invalid that had helped inspire differentiating gestures in the first place. In other words, as the bulk of this book chronicles, economic and Literary writers began to distinguish their work increasingly from *each other's* writing, rather than to belabor the founding distinction between valid and invalid, which remained crucial for monetary instruments. In the course of the late eighteenth century and the nineteenth, economic and Literary writers developed what we might call a *primary relationship* to each other, through which each group of writers increasingly defined the uniqueness of its own products *by differentiating these from the products produced by the other set of writers.* In the course of this disciplinary disaggregation and specification, the relationship that both kinds of writing had once obviously had with monetary writing simply disappeared—even though traces of this relationship persisted, both in the common function all three shared, that of mediating value, and in the fact that every book written to be sold was a commodity. As economic writers increasingly differentiated their work from that of Literary writers, and vice versa—both as the difference between fact and fiction and as mediations of two different *kinds* of value—both also elaborated the different types of investment in the status of writing per se to which I referred in the introduction: economic writers minimized the crafted nature of their prose (even as they continued to borrow features from imaginative writing); and imaginative writers drew attention to, and increasingly fetishized, this quality (even as they told stories taken from or meant to illuminate "real" life). Meanwhile, the creators of monetary instruments, which continued to derive their value from the fictions their apologists ignored, tried to make these tokens approach the level of transparency or abstraction that would enable them to attract no more notice than what would allow a user to distinguish between a "good" (valid) and a "bad" (invalid) note or coin.

In the descriptions that follow, I emphasize the incommensurability of these genres, which a historical perspective enables us to see, rather than the homologies that a theoretical perspective might highlight, because variations that were once social or functional have now come to seem essential or definitive. These apparently essential differences have become familiar, whether or not we extrapolate from them to structural homologies that provide a theoretical bridge over the chasm opened by history. It is the (historical) opening of this chasm, rather than the construction of the (theoretical) bridge, that I chronicle in this book. In this preamble, I want simply to provide an overview of the generic products of this history so that readers can embark on the history of their separation with a clear sense of the outcome of the story.

Imaginative Genres

As we will see in chapters 2, 5, and 6 in particular, imaginative genres took many forms in the period with which I am concerned, and, because many of these are familiar to modern readers, I give the least attention to them in this preamble. Nevertheless, a brief summary of some of the imaginative genres that preceded the late-eighteenth-century appearance of distinctively Literary writing seems to be important, if for no other reason than to remind us that imaginative genres were not identical to fiction and that—even in the late seventeenth century and the eighteenth—fiction was not limited to prose, or to what we call *the novel*. This last point in particular has sometimes been difficult to see, for, even though all kinds of imaginative writing in the early part of this period bore a complex relation to the fact/fiction continuum, modern Literary historians have tended to treat the genre of the novel as the normative—or even the exclusive—form that fiction took in eighteenth-century Britain. Indeed, three of the most helpful discussions of the fact/ fiction continuum—those by J. Paul Hunter, Lennard Davis, and Michael McKeon—appear in book-length studies of the novel, and this has tended to reinforce the novel-centrism of the modern discipline.[2] In this book, I do not fully disentangle my account of the breakup of the fact/fiction continuum from a discussion of eighteenth-century novels, and I acknowledge my dependence on these important scholars' work. Even if I do not fully explore the interrelation of eighteenth-century imaginative forms, however, and even though my most extensive discussion of poetic writing appears in my chapter on the nineteenth century, I want to restore the fact/fiction continuum to visibility partly in order to urge other scholars to trace out the intricacies I do not examine.

What Hunter, McKeon, and Davis have enabled us to see is that the writing that came to be recognized as distinctively *Literary* had a number of seventeenth-century antecedents that did not systematically distinguish between (what we call) fact and fiction.[3] Among these, Hunter highlights the news ballads and broadsides that I discuss in chapter 1; the genres of occasional meditations, metaleptics, and Providence books, which enabled Puritan writers, natural observers, and Anglicans, respectively, to record and reflect on everyday events, both momentous and ordinary, physical and spiritual; conduct materials of various kinds (including guides, commentaries, casuistic writings, and devotional manuals); private histories and diaries; the quasi-autobiographical, quasi-didactic genre of the apology; and the sometimes overlapping genres of travel writing, history, and biography. To this already extensive catalog, Michael McKeon has added the romance, the antiromance, natural history, apparition narratives, spiritual biographies, allegories, and secret histories. Once we expand our consideration beyond the novel to include poetry, we need to enlarge the genealogy yet further so that it incorporates Greek and Roman genres like the epic, various modes of satire, the georgic, the elegy, and the ode and other kinds of lyric. To this list, we might also want to add oral ballads, hymns, the Bible, and the medieval and early modern poems and play texts that Britons considered their national literary heritage.

As this no doubt incomplete list suggests, the antecedents of what eventually came to be considered distinctively *Literary* writing are numerous, and sorting out their relationship to each other has constituted an important facet of the scholarly activity that we call *canon formation* since at least the 1770s, when the first editions of standard British poets were published. In later chapters, I contribute to this scholarly effort, but my primary interest is not in either establishing a lineage for Literature or in identifying the principles of canon formation. Instead, in the chapters that follow, I explore the social process by which imaginative writers delimited the general field of Literature, by distinguishing between Literary and other kinds of writing (including economic writing) and by establishing a hierarchy within Literary writing that ranks and evaluates genres. This process of delimitation is not identical to canon formation because it does not rank individual works; my discussions of it emphasize the range of writers who contributed to the delimitation of Literary writing (reviewers and critics as well as poets and novelists) as well as the relationship between changes in the conditions governing publishing and efforts to establish the social prestige of Literary writing. The features shared by the various kinds of writing included in the category of *Literature* have changed as the definition of *Literature* has changed, of course, but, from the perspective of this book, what matters is that they all constitute mediations of value—efforts to provide readers an imaginative relationship to the economic, social, and (increasingly) ethical and aesthetic issues raised by Britain's maturing credit economy.

As I have already stated, the kinds of writing gradually grouped into the general category of *Literature* (with a capital *L*) typically performed the related functions of entertaining and improving their readers. They also, increasingly, tended to call attention to their own artistry as one means of distinguishing between the kind of value they mediated and its antithetical counterpart, the monetary value associated with commodification and the market. Poems announce this artistry in virtually every formal feature, from the spatial arrangement of the lines on a page to the meter, rhyme, and diction, and, as we will see in chapter 5, poets and their advocates took the initiative in defining the kind of value that was uniquely associated with Literature. In chapters 2 and 6, by contrast, I focus on prose fiction, for, in these chapters, I am interested in the ways in which a genre that shared formal features with nonfiction prose (including economic writing) both differentiated itself from and drew on the features it shared with its informational counterpart. One of my objects in chapter 5 is to show that, because poets and reviewers successfully yoked a distinctively Literary form of value to *poetry*, nineteenth-century novelists had to struggle to make their work fit into the hierarchy of Literary genres that poetry had long headed. In this chapter, I show how novelists gradually elevated the status of their genre—all the while negotiating the relationship between novels and the other, nonfiction kinds of prose that also mediated value.

Financial Writing

The various genres that I have been calling *economic writing* actually constitute a subset of a more capacious set of genres, which, for want of a better term, we might call *financial writing*. This more expansive term enables me to highlight the link between economic commentary, which could be written only after geographically and temporally discrete market transactions were conceptualized as belonging to a single conceptual entity, and financial information, which was being made available even before writers began discussing *the market* or *the economy*. Indeed, the regular availability of information about shipping, exchange rates, and current market prices was a precondition for conceptualizing various transactions as belonging to the same kind; thus, the relationship between these genres was as overdetermined as was the theoretical formulation of *the market* or *the economy* itself. Without trying to sort out this relationship, I want simply to summarize the major developments within the broad set of genres I'll now call *financial writing*. This set of genres contained both financial information and—in increasing volume after the 1760s—works of economic theory.

News sheets that listed the market prices of commodities originated in Antwerp and Venice in the sixteenth century; by 1608, they were being printed in London, and, by 1716, a London merchant would have been able to subscribe to as many as seven weekly or semiweekly news sheets, at a cost of about £6 a year. From these news sheets, the merchant would have been able to obtain information about ships, cargoes, prices, and exchange rates across the trading world.[4] These news sheets were published under license from the English Crown until the 1670s, and they were not free of government control until the Licensing Act was allowed to lapse in 1695. At that point, enterprising publishers began to circulate financial news in papers that often originated in, and were sometimes named for, London coffeehouses. Thus Lloyd's coffeehouse was associated with *Lloyd's News* from 1696 (soon renamed *Lloyd's List*), and *The Course of the Exchange*, which I discuss in chapter 1, was associated with Jonathan's. Both these news sheets were single pages, printed in columns on either one side or both.

Financial information briefly became financial *news* in the boom and bust year of 1720, but, with the collapse of the South Sea Bubble, much writing about the event moved into the adjacent genres associated with imaginative writing.[5] By the 1740s, public interest in this topic was great enough to warrant the inclusion of some financial information (beyond advertisements for company shares) in London and provincial newspapers, and, by the end of the century, a column entitled "remarks on trade" was a staple of nearly every British newspaper. London papers also carried shipping news, lists of bankrupts, and the prices of commodities, staples, and securities. As important was the introduction into British papers of what one historian has called "business opinion." Beginning in earnest in the 1780s, writers began to use newspapers as a forum to discuss commercial subjects, such as whether Britain should export wool. By the end of the century, the reading public was accustomed to reading about financial and commercial topics in its local papers—a fact, it has been suggested, that contributed to the emergence of political economy (or economic theory) in the second half of the eighteenth century.[6]

The development of the financial press, like the delivery of commercial information more generally, must be considered alongside the history of British taxation, for the British government used various taxes to control the circulation of all kinds of information and opinion during the entire eighteenth century and the first half of the nineteenth. The first stamp taxes were imposed on newspapers in 1712; in 1776 and 1789, the stamp tax was increased, until it reached 2d. per page. Advertisements, meanwhile, which were essential to the economic viability of newspapers, were taxed at 3s. apiece. Taken together, these prices (which were included in the cover price of the paper) made newspapers too expensive for most working-class and poor Britons.[7] They also increased the likelihood that a newspaper would be read aloud to numerous listeners, rather than being purchased and read silently by individuals; this both increased contemporary fears that newspapers fomented revolutionary sentiments and now makes determining how many readers a given newspaper reached all but impossible. When the stamp taxes were eventually repealed, beginning in the 1850s, this was a tacit admission that high prices had not had the desired deterrent effect.[8]

As we will see in chapter 2, stand-alone volumes of political economic theory began to be published in 1767, and these volumes joined theoretical pamphlets and essays like the ones McCulloch included in his collections of scarce and valuable tracts (I return to these tracts in chapter 1). Beginning in 1802, the concepts and arguments formulated in such works began to be made more widely available in the pages of the *Edinburgh Review*, a quarterly largely devoted to publishing lengthy and often quite theoretical discussions of economic subjects. Although, like the other quarterlies soon launched as rivals, the *Edinburgh Review* was relatively expensive, it is reported to have attained a large readership—as many as about fifty thousand readers within a month of each issue's publication, by some estimates.[9]

In the 1820s, another new financial genre appeared, this time in the pages of newspapers. Sparked by a dramatic increase in the number of publicly traded stocks in the early years of the nineteenth century, newspaper editors began to make writing about finance a regular part of their papers. Unlike the numerical tables and lists of market information that appeared in eighteenth-century newspapers, however, the new City columns treated the financial world as a distinct culture, which writers strove to make interesting even to readers who did not need to know about international exchange rates or economic theory. The first such column appeared in 1818 in the Sunday papers, but such articles became commonplace only in 1821, when W. I. Clement took over the *Morning Post* and decided to make City coverage a daily item. In 1825, the *London Times* followed this lead, introducing a

column entitled "Money, Market, and City Intelligence," which was typically written by the paper's City editor, Thomas Massa Alsanger. The *Times*'s
reports on the City were entertaining, generally provided reliable information, and were sometimes sharply critical—even of the advertisers whose
fees helped support the paper. In the 1840s, for example, Alsanger repeatedly warned readers that the speculative railway bubble would soon burst,
even though, like other papers, the *Times* carried numerous advertisements
for new railway ventures.[10]

In addition to the political economic theory published in stand-alone
volumes, essay collections, and the pages of the quarterlies, and the newspapers' chatty, informative City reports, British readers also had access, from
1843, to a weekly periodical designed to show the relationship between
economic theory and business. This was the *Economist*, which was founded
by James Wilson. Initially a mouthpiece for the Anti-Corn Law League, the
Economist published articles that supported free trade, political reform, and
the theories of classical political economists like Adam Smith and David
Ricardo. Even though it was founded as a partisan organ, the weekly consistently tried to detach the financial information it provided from articles
expressing its political agenda, and, by the late 1840s, it presented itself as a
politically neutral forum. The weekly was quite widely distributed: the 1845
circulation of 2,894 rose to 4,483 in 1847, then leveled off, after the repeal
of the Corn Laws, to about 3,500.[11] By that point, the goal of the *Economist*
was to combine economic reasoning, practical business matters, and political
observations. According to Walter Bagehot, who began to write for the weekly
in 1857, the periodical launched "the economic age," for it was a great
"belief-producer" that made members of the middle class feel like members
of a single, if complex, economic community.[12] Bagehot himself, to whom
I return in chapter 4, was one of the period's most respected writers on economic, commercial, and financial issues. During the eighteen years for which
he wrote for the *Economist*—from 1857 through 1875—he came to be considered the greatest interpreter of commercial sentiment and economic ideas
of the day.[13]

Bagehot's contributions to the *Economist* should be seen in the context of
another generic innovation in financial writing: the emergence of financial
journalism. I discuss some of Britain's most prominent financial journalists
in chapter 4, where I also explore the relationship between the appearance
of this genre in the late 1840s and the recurrence of speculative manias and
panics. The causes of these periodic economic events were widely debated
in the second half of the nineteenth century; and, as I demonstrate, financial journalists like D. Morier Evans and Laurence Oliphant developed

an investigative mode that simultaneously exposed details of some of the more flagrant crimes associated with the boom phase of each episode and rendered these puzzling events imaginatively engaging—even to reader-investors who lost money as share prices fell. Financial journalism, then, constitutes a mid-nineteenth-century example of an economic genre that borrowed liberally from imaginative writing, which had become a recognizable set of genres by 1850. While they were not the only writers who tried to explain manias and panics, financial journalists help us see how the disciplinary divide whose development I trace in this book could be crossed by writers who knew that their readers consumed numerous kinds of writing that offered different views of a single event.

The last decades of the nineteenth century also witnessed the emergence of additional new genres of economic writing. While I do not deal with them in this book, it is worth mentioning two of these. The first, which tended to narrow what counted as economic news to *investment advice*, appealed to the audience of British investors, which had been considerably broadened by midcentury legal provisions that encouraged the formation of joint-stock companies. In 1878, Sir Robert Giffen and Thomas Lloyd founded the *Statist*, which devoted increasing attention to detailed and technical accounts of the stock exchange and money markets. The *Statist*'s emphasis on the factors that underwrote investment opportunities explicitly became advice in the pages of the daily financial newspapers that began to appear in the 1880s. The two most significant financial dailies were the *Financial News*, which was launched by Harry Marks in 1884, and the *Financial Times*, which was founded in 1888. These two papers, along with their numerous imitators, analyzed individual company share offerings, carried numerous advertisements, printed letters from readers, and generally presented themselves, as the subheading of Marks's paper proclaimed, as "Devoted to the Interests of Investors."[14]

A second important generic innovation of the last part of the nineteenth century presented economic theory in a highly technical, often mathematical format that was specifically intended for expert—usually professional—political economists. I explore the beginnings of the professionalization of political economy in chapter 3, but during the period I examine there—the middle decades of the nineteenth century—professionalization was a goal to which individuals like J. R. McCulloch might aspire, rather than a widely attainable possibility. The founding of the *Quarterly Journal of Economics* in 1886 and the *Economics Journal* in 1890, along with the establishment, also in 1890, of the Royal Economics Society, signaled the fully professional status that the discipline had attained by the end of the century. The technical nature of the articles published in the two professional journals, moreover—articles written by and for economic specialists—revealed the extent to which, by the century's end, at least one economic genre had completely renounced its early affiliation with imaginative writing.

Monetary Genres

In order to treat monetary instruments as genres, it seems important to make a provisional distinction between coins and paper (credit) documents.[15] The concept of genre that I am using in this book—as a set of formal features whose interrelation with each other and with the features of other genres dictates their function—seems to privilege *written* or *printed* texts or documents over material objects like coins, primarily because the stylistic features that accompany inscription are not incidental to the nature or function of a given text, as they arguably are to their counterparts in objects like coins: a written text ceases to be the same text if its words are altered, and it ceases to perform its signifying function if the words with which it is inscribed are effaced, but a coin can pass current regardless of whether its value is inscribed in numerals, words, or some other signifying system, and, in many instances, it will still be accepted even after use has rendered its inscription illegible. In chapter 1, I will argue that eighteenth-century coins and paper money posed the same theoretical problems for contemporary users; nevertheless, and even though I highlight financial *instruments* throughout the bulk of this book, in this section I distinguish between coins and paper instruments and I emphasize the *genre*, rather than the instrumentality, of the latter because I want to show that the stylistic features of various monetary instruments determined the way each mediated value. Equally important, I also want to compare the challenges that each monetary instrument's stylistic features posed to the user, for these challenges helped determine the kind of discrimination various monetary instruments required for use. This, in turn, helped dictate which monetary forms could become so familiar to so many people that they passed beneath the cultural horizon of visibility or so abstract that they disappeared from sight. Once in the cultural realm of the taken-for-granted (or fully abstract), a monetary form could become invisible or go unremarked—that is, either it could seem simply to *be* valuable, not to represent or mediate deferred value, or it could *record* value, not seem to carry value in itself at all. To highlight the stylistic differences among monetary texts or credit documents, then, I omit from my present discussion both first-order monetary instruments, which actually embody valuable material (coins), and third-order monetary instruments (insurance documents, e.g.), which become valuable only when a first- or second-order mediating instrument is lost or fails.[16] I divide the second-order, paper credit instruments (which mediate value by representing it) into three groups: bills of exchange; various kinds of bank money; and checks.[17]

Bills of Exchange

A bill of exchange was initially a handwritten order that facilitated long-distance commerce by allowing a seller of goods to receive payment as soon as he shipped his product. Such bills were devised by early modern merchants who wanted to conduct business in different countries without having to carry large sums of money or to negotiate the wide variety of local currencies they were likely to encounter. Beginning in 1697, foreign bills of exchange began to be supplemented with bills drawn up and intended for use within the British Isles. These bills, called *domestic* or *inland bills*, gradually came to dominate the London bill market that developed during the eighteenth century, as bankers and bill brokers invested in the bills of merchants to augment their own profits and to provide merchants the short-term finance they needed. In the wake of the commercial crisis of 1825, banks began to put their own reserve cash into inland bills, and, as the number of bills proliferated, bill brokers gradually became bill dealers, and an extensive bill-discounting industry sprang up in and around London's Lombard Street. With the extension of the telegraph to more parts of the globe in the 1870s, inland bills began to decline in importance, and, by the 1880s, foreign bills once more dominated the London bill market. By 1880, the number and variety of foreign bills that passed through London enabled the City to finance ever-greater volumes of international trade and to solidify its position as the hub of the international financial market. In 1887, Bertram Currie stated what was by then a commonplace when he told a Royal Commission that London was the "center of the business of the world." "Wherever there is an exchange of any sort there is an exchange upon London," Currie told his interlocutor. "Bills upon London are always in the market; everybody has debts to pay in London, therefore everybody wants bills on London."[18]

In form, foreign bills differed from inland bills in two primary ways. First, the former were issued in sets, while the latter were issued individually. Sets of foreign bills—each set usually comprising three copies of the bill—were used to protect against some unforeseen accident like the loss of a ship at sea. By sending each copy of the bill on a different ship, a merchant was able to guarantee that his order would arrive promptly and safely; and, by clearly designating each bill as a specific member of the set, he was able to guarantee that the order was not paid multiple times. Thus, the first bill typically contained the words, "Pay this my *first* of exchange (the second and third not being paid)." Once any copy was paid, the others lost all value. Second, foreign bills were often drawn at "usance" after date, whereas inland bills were drawn for specified times and typically allowed three days' grace. The usance, or customary time before a bill was due, varied from country to country. Thus, usance from Amsterdam, Rotterdam, or any place in Germany was one month, from France thirty days, from Spain and Portugal two months, from Sweden seventy-five days, and from Italy three months. Bills from Russia posed special problems because they were dated according to the old style. This meant that the merchant had to add twelve days to the written date in order to determine when the bill was due.[19]

Whether foreign or inland, all bills of exchange had to be inscribed with specific information, which was generally arranged in a designated form.[20] This information was grouped into three parts, which typically appeared in three distinct sections of the note (fig. 1). The top of the bill generally contained the amount of the bill (rendered numerically and placed in the upper-left-hand corner) and the date at which the bill was drawn (in the upper-right-hand corner). The center of the bill was generally occupied by an imperative sentence ("pay to the order of"), which dictated the date at which the bill was due, the person to whom the bill was to be paid, the amount of the bill again (rendered in words), and an allusion to the security that backed the bill. Immediately following this sentence was the signature or printed inscription of the person or firm that drew the bill (on the right-hand side of the bill); beneath that, the addressee of the imperative sentence appeared in the bottom-left-hand corner, and the space for the acceptor's signature or imprint appeared in the lower-right-hand corner of the bill. The bill's acceptor did not have to sign the bill in the blank space at the lower-right-hand corner, but he did have to sign its front, for any signatures that appeared on the back of the bill represented by law the bill's endorsers.

Special terms were used to signify each party to the bill's transactions. Thus, as the respected Victorian banker J. W. Gilbart explained: "The person who draws a bill is called the drawer; the person on whom it is drawn is called the drawee: after the bill is accepted the drawee is called the accepter. The person who indorses a bill is called an indorser; the person to whom it is indorsed is the indorsee. The person who pays a bill is the payer; and the person to whom it is paid is the payee." To anchor these terms in his reader's mind—and to leaven his relatively technical description—Gilbart illustrated

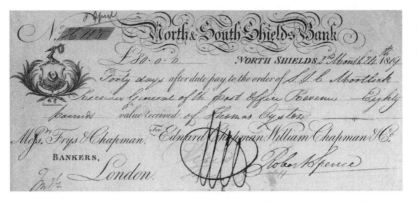

Figure 1. Bill of Exchange. In this inland bill of exchange, we can see how information was arranged on the bill. In the upper-left-hand corner, we find the number of the bill (113) and the amount (£80). In the upper-right-hand corner, we see the location at and the date on which the bill was drawn (North Shields, 2nd month 24, 1819"—i.e., 24 February 1819). On this bill, the imperative "pay to the order of" is preceded by its due date, which is forty days after the bill's date of issue. The £80 is to be paid to S. J. C. Montlock (?), receiver general of the Post Office Revenue (middle line) against a security obtained from Thomas Oyston ("value received"). The next line contains, on the left, the name of the bank's London agents ("Frys & Chapman") and, on the right, the name of the firm on which the bill was drawn ("Edward Chapman, William Chapman & Co."). Robert Spence, the "drawer," has signed the bill on the lower-right-hand side. Someone, presumably at Frys & Chapman, has written in hand on the upper-left-hand side of the bill the actual date at which it is due ("8 April"). *Source*: Booker, Travellers' Money, fig. 10 (on interleaves between 86 and 87).

his explanation with a little anecdote about the cross-examination of a witness in a mortgage trial: "*Counsellor.* 'Now, sir, you are a witness in this case; pray do you know the difference between the mortgager and the mortgagee?' *Witness.* 'To be sure I do. Now, suppose I nod at you, I am the nod-er, and you are the nod-ee'" (*HPP*, 1:261).

Gilbart's humorous courtroom example, as do the details I have already given, begins to suggest the complexities involved in the drawing and use of bills. In the first place, once drawn, a bill could be absolutely accepted, accepted conditionally, or partially accepted. As these last two terms suggest, this means that the acceptor could impose restrictions on the obligations the bill placed on him; to do so, he had simply to notify the other party to the bill of his conditions. By the same token, the endorsements that transformed the bill into a negotiable instrument also varied in kind and implication. Once a bill had been accepted by the drawee, that is, it could circulate as cash until the date it fell due, passing from hand to hand as each recipient signified his (or her) willingness to take responsibility for the bill by signing its back.[21] A simple signature, which constituted a general endorsement, allowed the bill to be paid to anyone; a special endorsement, by contrast, was made to a particular party and consisted of the signature plus the name of the party ("Pay to Messrs. John Doe & Co., or order"). Once a bill had been signed with a general endorsement, it was not supposed to be signed with a special one; but, as Gilbart explained, a bank was often unwilling to accept a bill not endorsed specifically to it, so this rule was generally honored in the breach. From the mid-nineteenth century, the Bank of England applied a stricter rule to bills sent through the post; it refused to acknowledge any special endorsement that followed a general endorsement on a bill so received (*HPP*, 1:260). Finally, endorsements could take the form of a "case of need" endorsement. When this form was used ("In case of need, apply to Messrs. A. B. & Co."), a bill not paid on the day after it fell due was passed to the named party to be honored. According to Gilbart: "The advantage of placing a case of need upon a bill is, that the party endorsing it receives it back sooner in case of non-payment. It also makes the bill more respectable, and secures its circulation" (263). This is the kind of endorsement that Caleb Garth allows Fred Vincy to affix to his bill in George Eliot's *Middlemarch*, to the near ruin of the Garth family.

Another matter that complicated the use of bills of exchange was the fact that various bills were payable (due) at different times. That is, they could be payable either at a specified time, after the date of the bill, on demand, or "on sight." The last phrase refers to the date at which the drawee saw the bill; he signified this date by writing it after his signature (generally, although not always, on the lower-right-hand corner of the bill). If an inland bill was payable on demand or on sight, it was not allowed the usual three-day grace period; if it was payable at a specified date, this grace period obtained, unless the due date was a Sunday or a public holiday ("Good Friday and Christmas-day, and every day of fast or thanksgiving appointed by his Majesty" [7 & 8 Geo. 4, c. 15 (1827)]), in which case the bill was due on the day before. An act of 1871 (34 Vict., c. 17) expanded the number of bank holidays to include Easter Monday, the Monday in Whitsun week, the first Monday in August, and 26 December; in addition, when Good Friday and Christmas day fell on a Sunday, the following Monday became a bank holiday. To determine whether a bill was good and when it fell due, then, one had to read the front and the back of the bill carefully and know one's calendar of bank holidays.

Numerous considerations also affected the value of a given bill. In the first place, since all bills fell due several weeks after their date of issue, and since, if a bill was not payable on sight, its date of payment could be several days after the due date named, bills were generally bought for a lower sum than the face value named. To describe this feature, which allowed someone to hold a bill until maturity without financial loss, we might say that a bill was an interest-bearing instrument; contemporaries more commonly said that a bill was bought "at discount."[22] When a bank or a bill broker purchased a bill before its due date, the bill was said to be "discounted" again (or rediscounted) because the purchase price was once again less than the face value of the bill. As we are about to see, in the valuation of foreign bills, the practice of discounting bills—which had become an everyday part of the circulation of credit by the third decade of the nineteenth century—raised all sorts of complications. Even with inland bills, discount rates varied. Primarily, the variation was a function of the state of the bill market at any given time (the number of bills for sale and the demand for particular kinds of bills) and the quality of the signatures a given bill contained. The quality of these signatures, in turn, was a measure of the probability that the individuals whose names appeared on the front and back of a bill were real, could be located, and would be willing to pay the bill's face value. It was because endorsers were sometimes fictitious and sometimes difficult to locate that Gilbart recommended requiring endorsers to write their addresses on the backs of the bills they signed (*HPP*, 1:263). In order to determine the quality of a bill, one also had to be able to evaluate the relationship linking the drawer of the bill to its drawee (acceptor). In theory, the relationship between the two individuals these signatures represented involved some kind of business, and the transaction was (also theoretically) secured by the transfer of property or deeds from the drawer to the drawee. In practice, however, the drawee was sometimes willing simply to *accommodate* a friend or a relative by promising to accept the bill without requiring the drawer to deposit security. So common were such dubious bills that contemporaries devised a host of terms to describe them, calling them, among other things, a "pig upon bacon bill," an "accommodation bill," or (in Scotland) a "kite." These are also, presumably, the "queer bills" that Dickens mentions in *Our Mutual Friend*. Bills drawn in this way generated money when the drawer took the bill to a bank or some other lender for rediscounting (i.e., to exchange for cash).

The complications in form, due date, and value help explain why every bill purchased by a bank (discounted) was immediately submitted to the bank's accountant for verification and evaluation (Gilbart, *HPP*, 1:258). These complications also explain why the use of bills was restricted to merchants for most of the nineteenth century (with the exception of Lancashire, whose residents, before 1826, preferred bills to both local and Bank of England notes [ibid., 283–84]) and why a flourishing bill-broking industry developed in London after 1825. The complexities of bills were such that even large banks needed to outsource the all-important task of evaluation to experts, for doing so was necessary to diminish the risk that trading in bills involved.[23] Even though the London bill-broking houses, led by the famous Overend, Gurney, and Company, rapidly assumed the task of discrimination for large institutions and banks, individual bank officials, especially in provincial banks, were still regularly faced with the task of evaluating bills. This is why nearly every nineteenth-century handbook on banking includes one or more chapters devoted to helping the banker distinguish good bills from bad—a practice of interpretation that writers referred to as learning to "read" the bills.[24]

Before leaving the topic of bills of exchange, it is important simply to note—without rehearsing all the attendant complexities—the additional challenge to valuation (and evaluation) posed by foreign bills. We have already seen that the value of an inland bill varied according to its quality and the number and kind of bills in the market at any given time. In addition to these variables, foreign bills were also subject to additional conditions. These included fluctuations in the two currencies the bill was intended to bridge, changes in the rate of exchange between the two currencies, and estimations of the likelihood that either of these factors—or some other material circumstance (like an outbreak of war)—would change during the time that separated a bill's issue from its due date. This means that a merchant who wanted to pay a debt or make a purchase in a foreign country had to calculate the probability of a host of factors before he could decide what a given bill was worth or even whether using a bill was more advantageous than using cash. To give just a sense of the complexities involved, I cite two examples given by J. R. McCulloch in his *Dictionary of Commerce and Commercial Navigation*, a volume that was intended (among other things) to help merchants master the intricacies of credit and foreign trade:

The cost of conveying bullion from one country to another forms the limit within which the rise and fall of the *real* exchange between them must be confined. If 1 per cent. sufficed to cover the expense and risk attending the transmission of money from London to Paris, it would be indifferent to a London merchant whether he paid 1 per cent. premium for a bill of exchange on Paris, or remitted money direct to that city. If the premium were less than 1 per cent., it would clearly be his interest to make his payments by bills in preference to remittances: and that it could not exceed 1 per cent. is obvious; for every one would prefer remitting money to buying a bill at a greater premium than sufficed to cover the expense of a money remittance. If, owing to the breaking out of hostilities between the two countries, or to any other cause, the cost of remitting money from London to Paris were increased, the fluctuations of the *real* exchange between them *might* also be increased; for the limits within such fluctuations *may* range correspond in all cases with the cost of making remittances in cash.

In conducting the business of exchange, a direct remittance is not always preferred. When a merchant in London, for example, means to discharge a debt due by him in Paris, it is his business to ascertain not only the state of the direct exchange between London and Paris, and, consequently, the sum which he must pay in London for a bill on Paris equivalent to his debt, but also the state of the exchange between London and Hamburg, Hamburg and Paris, &c.; for it frequently happens that it may be more advantageous for him to buy a bill on Hamburg, Amsterdam, or Lisbon, and to direct his agent to invest the proceeds in a bill on Paris, rather than remit directly to the latter.[25]

As these two examples make clear, determining the value of a foreign bill was extremely complicated—even though the complications simply took the complexities entailed in evaluating an inland bill to their logical (because transnational) extreme. These complications, which always attended the use and evaluation of bills, helped render bills of exchange the most opaque of all the credit documents commonly used between the seventeenth and the nineteenth centuries. By this I mean that bills of exchange could never be taken for granted because of familiarity or abstraction, for determining the value of a given bill always required diligent inspection (preferably by a financial expert), and every bill had to remain in its original material form, complete with original signatures, dates, and figures. Any alteration of the amount, date, term, or place at which a bill was payable, as Gilbart reminded his readers, was a "*material* alteration . . . , and would affect the validity of the bill" (*HPP*, 1:258).

Bank Paper

The history of private banking in England is obscure, both because of the tendency of early guilds to guard trade secrets and because of the uneven nature of the records that survive. Nevertheless, modern historians generally agree that there were two sets of antecedents to modern private bankers: the scriveners and the goldsmiths, both of whom sometimes issued receipts for the goods deposited with them.[26] Scriveners, who were usually located in London, acquired prominence during Queen Elizabeth's reign, when graziers began to entrust them with the proceeds of late summer slaughters in exchange for handwritten receipts. This simple banking function was augmented in 1617 when a second Company of Scriveners was formed.[27] Scriveners (also called *brokers* or *notaries*) concentrated on one of the few areas in which handwritten documents continued to be important after the advent of print: conveyancing, which involved both drawing up and registering the title deeds to land and money bonds. Conveyancing documents were not negotiable, but the trust that their execution inspired in landowners encouraged some depositors to allow scriveners to put their money out for interest and, thus, to perform another of the operations associated with modern banking.

The second group of early financiers, the goldsmiths, also accepted deposits—of plate and other valuables as well as gold and silver coins—and they also issued receipts for the goods they held. According to F. G. Hilton, in the 1650s some goldsmiths also initiated two of the most characteristic banking functions: they lent these deposits to borrowers and allowed clients to draw drafts on demand.[28] Some of these goldsmiths probably modeled their practices on the activities of well-to-do merchants, like Thomas Gresham and the Vyners, who had lent money to the Crown before the Restoration.[29] This function was later taken over by the Treasury, then the Bank of England.[30]

The two ancestors of private banking—the scriveners and the goldsmiths—were, thus, associated with a number of written documents, some of which were or became monetary instruments: conveyancing records; receipts for deposit; international and inland bills of exchange; and checks (or "cheques"), which both groups issued to borrowers for limited use against deposits. Receipts, bills, and checks were all negotiable to various degrees, but their relationship to value was no more fixed than was that of a bill of exchange. In the case of the early banker's receipt, the variable relationship between the written document and the value it represented was partly a function of invisible fees, which the goldsmith or scrivener charged for holding his client's money or goods, and partly a function of the use to which the money represented by the receipt could be put while in the goldsmith's keeping. Early bankers were often called on to find loans for their clients, in other words, and they often used deposited money to answer this demand. Such loans were legal, but they were valued at different rates. When a banker loaned money from his personal funds, he was operating as a simple lender and was entitled to collect the maximum legal rate of interest; when the goldsmith loaned deposited money, he technically became a loan broker and was allowed only a brokerage fee. Because the source of a loan was not visible to borrowers, however, and because the lines dividing cashiering, personal lending, and brokering were not always clear, an early banker could generate a tidy sum by taking advantage of the ambiguity surrounding loans.[31]

Truly negotiable bank paper was first introduced in the late seventeenth century by a new company, one founded in 1694.[32] This company, the Bank of England, was, from the beginning, a private banking company (it remained a private company until 1946), but it enjoyed a special relationship with the British government, and the Whig Party in particular, because it was founded by advisers to the king to manage the national debt, which had been created in 1692 to finance the War of the Grand Alliance against France. As we will see in chapter 1, the Exchequer initially used tally sticks to record incoming loans, and it supplemented this recording system with paper notes in the 1690s. While these notes were legally negotiable, the acceptance of this paper seems to have been initially impeded by the belief that the notes were simply receipts for debt. Once the Bank of England began to exercise its chartered prerogative to issue notes, however, Britons began to accept both its running cash notes and government paper as legitimate money.[33] In 1697, a revision of the Bank's charter authorized it to replace running cash notes with negotiable notes payable on demand, and these notes constituted the prototypes of modern banknotes.[34] Like their prototypes, the receipts issued by goldsmiths and scriveners and the Bank's running cash notes, these notes were initially handwritten receipts issued on ordinary paper and made out for odd sums.

Even more than bills of exchange, which were always drawn to order, the Bank's early notes were intended to be general or all-purpose notes—that is, to circulate without a named acceptor or endorser. After 1752, the general function of the notes was made explicit when they began to be made out to the chief cashier ("Daniel Race," e.g.) or "to bearer"; it was the last phrase that made them fully negotiable. The general nature of the Bank's notes also made them vulnerable to forgery and fraud. To reduce the possibility of counterfeit, the Bank began to introduce the material and stylistic innovations that (ideally) made Bank notes both interchangeable with other notes of the same denomination and distinct from rival (counterfeit) notes. As we will see in a moment, Bank notes did not acquire the first characteristic until after 1855; the second is still a challenge for the Bank's Printing Department. The first innovation intended to foil counterfeiting and make the Bank's notes pass as cash was material: within two weeks of the first issue of its new notes, Bank officials began to require that notes be issued on marbled, indented paper rather than easily obtainable plain paper. This innovation was soon followed by a second material change: the adoption of paper watermarked with a looped border and inscribed with a scroll on the left side and a panel containing the words *Bank of England* at the bottom. This paper was produced and supplied by Rice Watkins. Soon, a third innovation was mandated: the use of partially printed, instead of handwritten, notes graced with a medallion of the seated Britannia holding a spear and an olive branch. In 1707, the Britannia medallion was altered by the addition of a foliate border surround, and, in 1725, the Bank began using special paper produced by Henry Portal, printing its notes by copperplate, and issuing the notes in fourteen set denominations (beginning with £20 and going up to £1,000). Earlier notes had been issued for odd sums, usually no smaller than £20.[35] Lest these stylistic features not be a sufficient deterrent on their own, the singular legitimacy of the Bank's notes was backed by the full force of the government: from 1697 through 1832, forging a Bank of England note was a capital crime, punishable by death.

Despite the Bank's efforts to authenticate and legitimize its notes, and despite the unofficial monopoly over note issue granted the Bank in 1708, Bank paper continued to have only limited circulation until the middle of the nineteenth century.[36] Initially, Londoners entertained doubts about the Bank's notes simply because they were new, but, even after the novelty wore off, the large denominations of early notes made them difficult to use. Suspicion of the Bank's notes was also provoked by the link between the Bank and the Whig Party, with which it continued to be associated. As promissory notes—promises to exchange, on demand, the note for the amount of gold or silver represented on its face—all Bank notes issued after the cessation of the running cash notes required the recipient to trust the institution issuing them; if an individual did not trust the Whig government, he would not be likely to trust notes issued by what seemed to be (but was not) a government organ. We get a sense of the suspicion that circulated alongside the Bank's notes from Jonathan Swift's satirical poem "The Bank's Thrown Down":

> The Bank is to make us a New Paper Mill,
> This Paper they say, by the Help of a Quill
> The Whole Nation's Pockets with Money will fill.[37]

Because the Bank's paper depended on both the company's prosperity (and its directors' willingness to limit their own dividends) and the government's willingness to keep routing tax revenue into the Bank's coffers, even Britons less skeptical than Swift might well have thought twice before accepting the Bank's notes. Because the Bank's reserve was always rumored to be what it in fact was—dramatically smaller than the amount represented by the notes in circulation—its notes retained their value *only* so long as the individuals who held them did not all seek to exchange them for gold at the same time. For all these reasons, Bank of England notes did not pass as currency beyond about a twenty-mile radius of London for the entire eighteenth century. This meant that a majority of eighteenth-century Britons, especially those who lived outside London, did not see a single Bank of England note during their lifetimes.

As we will see in a moment, the campaign to naturalize Bank of England notes—to render them identical to each other, so familiar and trustworthy that recipients would not hesitate to accept them, and both sufficiently numerous and user-friendly that they could be taken for granted—was still under way in the middle of the nineteenth century. Indeed, this campaign did not begin in earnest until the first decade of that century, for, during the eighteenth century, the Bank was content to circulate its notes alongside other kinds of paper money, issued by a variety of individuals and companies for local use. Much of this paper was informal, taking the form of paper tokens issued by shopkeepers or employers. Some was more regular, even if it did not have much greater currency than informal chits. Among the variants of more formal paper that circulated in eighteenth-century Britain were the notes issued by private banks, which had begun to be established early in the century. For reasons I explain in a moment, the number of private banks rapidly increased after 1797. Although precise figures do not exist, one modern historian estimates that there were 119 English banks in 1784, with 129 offices; that by 1798 the number of banks had grown to 312 and the number of offices to 335; and that by 1813 there were 761 banks, with at least 922 offices.[38] Not all these banks issued paper notes, but those that did—and this number also increased after 1797—often found people more willing to accept their notes than paper issued by the Bank of England. Local notes were often more desirable for several reasons: they were more familiar to provincial Britons than Bank of England notes; because they did not circulate much beyond fifteen miles of the bank of issue and were readily identifiable by local bankers, they were less susceptible to fraud than the Bank's notes; and, because they were issued in small denominations (after 1797), they were more useful for everyday transactions. Locals could also become attached to the images printed on country banknotes, as signs of civic pride. Thus, people who lived near Settle in the 1820s often requested the note "wi' the cow on," as an expression of confidence in the Craven bank, which issued notes showing the famous Craven heifer.[39]

As this reference to the Craven cow suggests, country banks' notes were anything but standard in their size, imagery, or denomination. Unlike Bank of England notes, they were issued not only in small denominations but also for odd figures, such as the £2 11s. 8d. note issued in 1779 by the Exchange Bank of Bristol.[40] They were made of various kinds of paper and came in different sizes, with one of the largest, issued by the Miners' Bank in Truro, measuring 5 × 8 inches. Most country banks' notes also tended to avoid the image of Britannia, which appeared on all of the Bank's notes, sporting instead one of a variety of pictures, including town scenes, coats of arms, and animals. For those who could not read or whose literacy was limited, these images often constituted the most legible feature of the country banks' notes, and they could even help an individual identify a note's value. The Welsh Aberystwith and Tregaron Bank, for example, used figures of sheep to help customers recognize the value of its notes; one sheep signified one pound, two sheep signified two pounds, and a lamb signified ten shillings (figs. 2, 3). Arguably, such images—especially the vines, animals, and country scenes—constituted a rudimentary, because literal, attempt to naturalize country banks' notes. By depicting scenes from nature and animals that could be counted, country bank officials wanted to persuade customers that their notes did not impose artificial or arbitrary barriers between the client and the gold for which they stood but simply depicted "natural" money or even stood in for the "living money" that had once circulated in Britain.[41]

The event that caused the number of country banks to explode and the volume of their note issue to swell was the passage in 1797 of the Bank Restriction Act. This act, which relieved the Bank of England of the obligation to redeem its notes with gold, was adopted when rumors of a French invasion threatened to provoke a run against the Bank. Although the Restriction was supposed to last for six weeks, it continued for nearly a quarter of a century—provoking, as we will see in the first interchapter and chapter 3, an avalanche of controversy.[42] During the Restriction, Bank of England notes became fiat money instead of promissory notes—that is, they had value *only* because the government said they did, not because they could be exchanged for gold.

The Restriction Act also granted private banks permission to issue notes in small denominations (as low as one pound), and this lucrative privilege, along with the limited circulation of the Bank of England's notes, encouraged the proliferation of country banks and local notes. While the exponential increase in the volume and variety of paper money facilitated local trade, it also constituted a problem for Britain's economy as a whole.

Figures 2 and 3. Aberystwith & Tregaron Banknotes. These notes, issued by the Aberystwith & Tregaron Bank in Cardiganshire, Wales, show the use of a figure to illustrate the denomination of the note. One sheep stands for £1; two sheep stand for £2. By permission of Llyfrgell Genedlaethol / The National Library of Wales.

Because no one knew whether any of these notes—even Bank of England notes—were backed by sufficient treasure, and because there were no restrictions on the volume of notes a bank could issue, people suddenly confronted the problematic of representation inherent in all paper money: because it simply represents, instead of embodying, value, paper always defers its ground and, thus, is always subject to deflation, that is, a decrease in its value against the gold it represents. That the value of paper could fluctuate became painfully obvious after 1800 and acute in 1810, when the purchasing power of all paper notes fell dramatically. To address this problem—and to stem the competition posed to Bank notes by private bank paper—Parliament passed a law making it illegal to receive or pay Bank of England notes at less than their face value. This legislation unofficially made the still inconvertible Bank of England notes legal tender.[43]

The government's decision to back one bank's money with a law (instead of gold reserves) while continuing to allow other banks to issue unrestricted (and inadequately secured) notes provoked another monetary crisis at the end of the Napoleonic Wars. When the price of corn began to fall in 1815, the value of all paper money plummeted again; unemployment soared; and country banks, unable to attract depositors or secure loans from the Bank of England, failed in droves. As they did, people were forced to confront another harsh reality of the credit economy: paper money was only as good as the bank that issued it, and, when a bank failed, its paper became worthless. Meanwhile, protected by the law that sutured the value of its notes in *English* markets to the numbers printed on their faces, the Bank of England continued to increase its issue of paper, even though the international exchange continued to value gold at a higher rate than paper. As we will see in chapter 3, the ensuing chaos made currency and value, banking and banknotes, volatile political issues. The increase in the volume of its note issue can also be linked to what I am calling a *campaign* on the part of the Bank to naturalize its notes—to make them so familiar and so reliable that users would simply take it for granted that they were worth the sums printed on their faces.

The controversy over how Bank notes could secure the value they claimed to represent did not begin to subside until 1844, when Parliament passed Peel's Bank Charter Act. By strictly limiting country banks' issue of notes, this act reinforced the priority of Bank of England notes, and, by establishing a ratio between the Bank's gold reserve and the notes it issued, it helped curtail the Bank's tendency to increase note issue in periods of high demand. Even after the passage of the 1844 Bank Act, however, the campaign to naturalize the Bank's notes still had to be waged, for the Bank Act did not lay to rest all the questions about the currency. Nor was it yet technically possible to make Bank notes *identical*—that is, to make one ten-pound note indistinguishable from every other ten-pound note. Even though the Bank's Printing Department had been working on a new note design since 1842, the wear that continued use inflicted on the Bank's plate transfer press meant that two notes of the same denomination could still look quite different. It was not until the 1855 issue, which deployed a new printing technology, that identical notes could be produced.[44]

Before technological innovations could ensure uniformity in the Bank's paper notes, the campaign to naturalize these notes was waged in print of another kind—in periodical articles intended to inspire the confidence that Bank notes could not yet generate on their own. One such article appeared in Dickens's popular weekly, *Household Words*, in 1850. Written (and published anonymously) by Dickens's subeditor, W. H. Wills, this review of a "popular publication," a Bank of England note, insisted that the note's stylistic features—its "pithy terseness" and its graphic "flourishes"—instantaneously and automatically inspired confidence in its user. The note "strikes conviction at once," Wills asserted:

> It dispels all doubts, and relieves all objections. There is a pithy terseness in the construction of the sentences; a downright, direct, straight-forward, coming to the point, which would be wisely imitated in much of the contemporaneous literature that constantly obtains currency (though not as much). Here we have no circumlocution, no discursive pedantry, no smell of the lamp; the figures, though wholly derived from the East (being Arabic numerals), are distinct and full of purpose; and if the writing abounds in flourishes, which it does, these are not rhetorical, but boldly graphic: struck with a nervous decision of style, which, instead of obscuring the text and meaning, convinces the reader that he who traced them when promising to pay the sum of five, ten, twenty, forty, fifty, one hundred, or a thousand pounds, means honestly and instantly to keep his word: that he *will* pay it to bearer on demand, without one moment's hesitation.[45]

As we will see in chapters 5 and 6, the implicit criticism against which Wills set his explicit praise of the Bank note—criticism of that other kind of "contemporaneous literature" that we associate with Literature—was one facet of the distinction, which was also being naturalized in 1850, between Literary writing and writing of every financial kind, both writing about financial matters and writing that functioned as money. In 1850, Wills's humorous article suggests, monetary writing hovered on the tipping point between seeming *note-worthy* (because Bank notes had so recently been singled out from all competitors) and being *self-evident* or *beneath comment*. Once new technology helped bring to pass the taken-for-grantedness that Wills sought to will into being, Bank notes began to shed even the affiliation they had long maintained with writing about money. By the 1880s, even though questions remained about the nature of money, how it should be subdivided and defined, and the role it played in the nation's overall economy, the Bank of England note itself had ceased to look like the text it always was, for it ceased to require the kind of scrutiny that rival credit instruments required, much less the arduous interpretation that Literary writing increasingly solicited.

Checks

The third kind of credit instrument that deserves our attention aspired to achieve a kind of invisibility that differed substantially from the taken-for-grantedness that proponents of Bank of England notes coveted. The invisibility structurally associated with checks had less to do with the familiarity of this credit form, the uniformity of each document, or the prominence of any individual bank than with the role that checks came to play in the institutional *system* of English banking. This role, in turn, involved banks' willingness to treat all checks as being of the same kind, no matter what bank issued them, and despite the variations that distinguished one bank's checks from another's. More specifically, it involved bankers' willingness to treat checks as equivalent to the numbers by which accountants recorded their receipt in an accounting book; once returned to any bank in the system and recorded in the bank's book, the material check lost the importance that it initially enjoyed as a mediator of value, for it was simply absorbed into—that is, replaced by—the figures a clerk wrote down. Offsetting monetary transactions by means of book accounting thus helped realize one of the fundamental advantages that proponents of the credit economy had long promised: it decreased the number of physical monetary tokens needed to make the economy work by substituting writing for material objects.[46] This substitution constitutes a prime example of the *abstraction* to which all credit systems theoretically aspire and that, arguably, the late-twentieth-century investment instrument called *derivatives* takes to a logical extreme.[47]

As we have already seen, some form of the check was used in the seventeenth century as one of the monetary innovations developed by goldsmiths and other moneylenders to stand in for the goods and cash deposited with them.[48] The form of these handwritten "drawn notes" was initially simple: a check was a piece of paper that was drawn against deposited goods, typically made payable to an individual or "to bearer." Like a banknote, a check was not an interest-bearing instrument, and there was, as a consequence, no reason for the individual who received it to hold it for any specific time. A check could circulate from hand to hand by endorsement, as a bill of exchange did, and, also like bills of exchange, checks could be made out for odd sums. With the development of banking in the eighteenth century, checks began to be addressed to and drawn on a bank and required the banker to pay the sum named on the check to its bearer on demand. The form of the instrument then remained relatively constant through the next century and a half, but, sometime in the middle of the nineteenth century, banks began to print uniform books of blank checks for their depositors to use as payment.[49] Probably in the early 1870s, it became more common to make checks payable to a particular individual than "to bearer," but, as late as 1885, it was still possible to make out a check "in blank"—that is, to a number or the initials of the payee instead of to a named individual.[50] Sometime in the middle of the nineteenth century it also became common for a payer to draw two lines across the check when making it out; a check that was "specifically crossed" in this manner had to be presented at a particular bank for credit to a specific individual's account. This means that a crossed check was not a fully negotiable instrument, as generally endorsed bills of exchange, banknotes, and uncrossed checks were.

The material form of the printed checks entailed both potential problems and clear advantages, both for the individual who used them and for the banking industry as a whole. The problems associated with bank-issued books of blank checks were openly acknowledged in nineteenth-century commentaries on credit. Because different banks used different formats for their checks, W. Stanly Jevons noted, the "perpetration of fraud" was always a possibility, especially to a public not "in the habit of daily receiving and paying cheques without minutely inquiring into their validity" (Money, 241). Then, too, thieves might be tempted by these printed documents, for all an enterprising thief had to do to cheat both the bank and the checkbook holder was to steal a checkbook and fill up all the checks for an amount that exhausted or exceeded the deposited funds. Finally, the bank that held a check user's deposits could fail, leaving the creditor without his or her money even if a valid check was in hand.

By and large, however, the advantages of checks were held to outweigh these liabilities. In particular, the last possibility—the ramifications of bank failure—were thought to be offset by the principle of "reasonable time," which dictated that every check had to be presented at a bank for collection soon after receipt. While everyone agreed that it was impossible to determine exactly what constituted reasonable time, most commentators maintained that a check should be presented for collection or deposit before the close of business hours on the day after it was received (Jevons, Money, 241). Since the principle of reasonable time originated in the anxieties caused by numerous bank failures in the nineteenth century's successive commercial crises, it seems paradoxical that this principle soon served to bolster the collective power of the banking industry as a whole. It did so because, as bankers began to rely on each other—and on written accounts that could be shared—to shore up the position of individual private and joint-stock banks, they were able to make do with less cash by substituting written entries in bank ledgers for monetary instruments. Foremost among the instruments that could be offset by book entries were the various checks that increasingly dominated the nation's circulating currency.

Bankers all over Britain were able to convert checks into a single set of ledger entries because, by the middle of the nineteenth century, nearly all the banks in England belonged to a single system, which contemporaries called the *check and clearinghouse* system. Its center was a private organization, the London Clearing House, which was set up in 1775 by a group of London bankers. In the late eighteenth century, the operations of this organization were both simple and secret. At the end of each business day, clerks from the participating banks met in a designated room to settle the day's accounts. They did so not by exchanging notes or gold but through the old practice of book credit—that is, by entering numbers in an accounting ledger, which kept a running total of each bank's debts and credits with other banks; cash payments were made only when a balance became inconveniently large. According to McCulloch, on an average daily transaction of several millions, only about £200,000–£500,000 had to change hands in cash.[51] By the middle of the nineteenth century, the London Clearing House had renounced both its secrecy and its exclusivity, thus drawing banks of different kinds and in different parts of England into its system. In 1854, the London Clearing House admitted the London joint-stock bankers to the association, and, in 1858, the system was extended to country bankers (Jevons, *Money*, chap. 20).

It was possible to forge this institutional banking system because, by the middle of the nineteenth century, local English banks had begun to adopt the branch-and-agency format that had characterized Scottish banking for more than a century. By midcentury, almost all the English country banks that survived the financial crises of 1825, 1837–39, and 1847 (or that were founded after these waves of bank failures) were either part of trunk-and-branch systems (legalized for the Bank of England in 1826) or allied with one or more of the twenty-six agency banks located in London. Individual banks kept running accounts with their branch's head office and/or their agency bank by which they offset the credits and debts that returned and outstanding checks and bills of exchange represented. These agency banks, in turn, participated in the London Clearing House, and, as ledger totals and bundles of checks and bills were passed along from bank to bank, all the transactions that occurred throughout the country were eventually cleared with only minimal exchanges of Bank notes or gold. When inconveniently large balances did exist among the clearinghouse banks, a final transfer was made in the books of the Bank of England, which, as the ultimate bankers' bank, kept the accounts of all the banks that belonged to the Clearing House. For Jevons, one of the leading economic theorists of the last quarter of the nineteenth century, this system approached the ideal to which economic theorists and bankers had long aspired: a fully abstract monetary system in which all representative money had been transcended: "The settlement of the reciprocal claims of the twenty-six principal banks is therefore a business of the utmost magnitude and importance, representing as it does the completion of the business of no small part of the world. In a room of moderate dimensions . . . debts to the average amount of nearly twenty millions sterling per day are liquidated without the use of a single coin or bank-note. In the classic financial neighborhood of Lombard Street, and even in this very chamber, the system of paper commerce has been brought nearly to perfection" (*Money*, 263).

According to Jevons, then, the combination of checks and the clearinghouse system brought paper commerce "nearly to perfection" by abstracting value from the credit documents in which it circulated, reducing the amount of gold and Bank notes the nation needed to operate, and fixing the disparate operations of the nation's (domestic) economy in a centrally located, carefully guarded, generically uniform set of books. The pair of Clearing House books that reconciled the heterogeneous credit transactions that occurred all over England—the out-clearing book and the in-clearing book—reduced all the circulating monetary genres to numbers, the placement and treatment of which conformed to the rules of double-entry bookkeeping (*Money*, 266–67). Thus, the operative generic conventions, which ultimately governed the form into which all monetary genres were distilled, were the stylistic conventions developed in the sixteenth century to make the merchant's honesty visible to his trading partners and to God.[52]

Before leaving the subject of monetary genres, it is important to note one final thing. No matter how close to "perfection" the clearinghouse system brought the British monetary system by abstracting value from the physical documents that represented it, vestiges of the monetary instruments and the clerks who inscribed the figures in the Clearing House books always haunted the system of writing that sought to supersede materiality. At the end of the nineteenth century, F. A. Walker ruefully acknowledged this when he sought to limit the definition of *money* to Bank notes: "After all that credit can do in the mutual cancellation of indebtedness, there still remains, in the community most highly advanced, even where banking has been carried to its utmost limits, a vast volume of transactions which must be effected by the use of money. The sufficient proof that these must be effected by the use of money is found in the fact that they are so effected, for money would not be used, since its use involves expense, unless this were economically necessary."[53] Perhaps more poignantly, this principle was also acknowledged in 1875 by Jevons, the economist who so longed to see the monetary system perfected. For Jevons, the system's materiality lingered in the room where the clerks were crowded together in the London Clearing House. Calling this room "unwholesome," Jevons worried that "the intense head work performed against time, in an atmosphere far from pure, and in the midst of bustle and noise arising from the corrections shouted from one clerk to another across the room, must be exceedingly trying. Brain disease is occasionally the consequence" (*Money*, 268). As we will see in the rest of this book, even as Britain's monetary genres became so familiar that the stylistic conventions and individual variations of their various incarnations faded through habit and use, such traces of their materiality lingered, as reminders of the kinds of writing every monetary instrument once so obviously was.

CHAPTER ONE

Mediating Value

In the late seventeenth century and the early eighteenth, money was a necessary but uncertain feature of British life. This was true for reasons that were simultaneously historical and theoretical. Historically, money was necessary because of the nation's dramatic increase in trade, both domestic and international. It was uncertain because official coins were in such short supply. The shortage of coins had been chronic since 1540, but the situation began to be acute during the seventeenth century because of increased demand, the government's refusal to mint additional tokens, and the clipping, export, or hoarding of many of the coins that surfaced.[1] The uncertain quality of the coins exacerbated—and was further exacerbated by—theoretical issues that accompanied representative money. In seventeenth- and eighteenth-century Britain, money was thought to serve three functions: it was a unit of account; it served as a common denominator in exchange, both immediate and deferred; and it was a commodity whose value fluctuated according to market factors. While the first function could be stabilized (because a unit of account is abstract and not necessarily linked to any intrinsically valuable ground) and the second seemed neutral (because it rendered equivalence universal), the third could not be stabilized or construed as neutral (because the value of any commodity is dictated by supply and demand). In the early part of the period with which I am concerned, it was the interdependence of the last two functions that most frequently led to complications and confusions about money, for the fact that the value of gold or silver could fluctuate, according to international market conditions, seemed to undermine the function of these metals as a common medium of exchange.

One plausible solution to this last problem would have been for the government to dictate the value of some intrinsically valueless material that functioned as money; this solution—the government issue of fiat money—was the course pursued by France in the second half of the eighteenth century and, as we will see, by Britain between 1797 and 1819 (and by the United States today). By and large, however, most early modern governments—including England's—did not choose this route because they believed that the value of monetary tokens should be anchored in and refer to something that was itself intrinsically valuable. They chose gold and silver because these were scarce and easily divisible and because the volume of these metals was relatively stable and their price fluctuations therefore minimal.[2]

The English government's attachment to what contemporaries called the principle of "intrinsick value" compounded the uncertainty of coins because it discouraged monarchs from using base metals to mint additional money. The Tudor monarchs routinely rejected making coins from copper and lead. James I issued farthing tokens in 1613, but he did not command the Royal Mint to produce these coins, nor did Parliament make it compulsory to accept them; in 1644, the Puritans curtailed the production of these coins.[3] As Deborah Valenze has argued, the resulting monetary situation was confusing, for a few "real" coins, made of silver or gold (but often defaced or clipped), circulated alongside countless "imaginary" coins, which were created by tradesmen for use in local markets: "Town councils authorized their own token production and business establishments boasted their own coin presses.... Makers sold packs of tokens at a profit to tradespeople and shopkeepers, who then offered them as change in transactions. Town councils also contracted with tokeners, selling halfpence and farthings to those who needed them, sometimes for the best price offered. Their value rested simply on the assumption of continuing neighborhood custom and popular trust."[4]

Valenze has also demonstrated that the mixture of kinds of coin encouraged traditional superstitions about money to linger, even as the foundations of the modern economy were being laid. "As a metonym for avarice," she explains, "money in the shape of coins circulated as moralistic religious and literary messages writ small, functioning as potent signs with multiple meanings."[5] As pimps to indulgence, talismans of luck, or vehicles assumed to carry mysterious power, coins conveyed a range of connotations, from the ability to ward off damnation to a sign that the devil had already triumphed.[6] In Valenze's account, this unstable monetary situation not only allowed multiple meanings to accumulate around coins but also elicited considerable creativity on the part of English tradesmen and -women. Forced to adapt to the presence of multiple kinds of coin of uncertain worth, early modern Britons developed great "technical virtuosity in exchange relations" that enabled them to evaluate a coin by weight, "chink," color, thickness, or design, to decide when and how to deploy better and less good coins, and to determine which coins should be hoarded and which ones paid away.[7]

The social process by which various kinds of money were gradually naturalized is one of the chief concerns of *Genres of the Credit Economy*. Whereas historians like Valenze have been interested primarily in the material conditions that helped neutralize what now seem like the extraneous connotations of early money, I focus on the role played in this naturalization process by other kinds of writing—other genres—that circulated alongside money in the period. For, whatever role material conditions like geographic mobility played in making people treat coins as money, every kind of monetary token also relied on some kind of writing to enable it to serve the three functions that money had to perform. This writing might be as simple as an inscription on the face of a coin, where the writing typically shared space with images; or it might be complex and not confined to the monetary instrument at all. From a very early date—1667—Parliament signaled the superiority of monetary instruments that were inscribed with writing when it officially declared that paper orders should take the place of the tally sticks that had previously acknowledged loans to the Crown. These orders were registered in a Treasury book for future redemption in order of issue; during the period between issue and redemption, the orders were negotiable by endorsement. The point of this example, of course, is that the writing on the orders themselves could represent value only because other kinds of writing—the official decree and the entry in the Treasury book—declared that it did so. As various forms of paper were increasingly used to address the scarcity of coins, the theoretical problem presented by all forms of representative money became increasingly clear, as did the inextricable relationship between all monetary forms and writing. As we will see, in addition to the material and technological developments that historians typically emphasize, volumes of writing about money were essential to its gradual naturalization—its increasing invisibility *as* writing.

It is partly because of the necessary, but supplementary, relationship between the writing that functioned as money and writing about money that the volume of monetary publications in any period can be correlated to the relative confidence people feel toward the institutions entrusted with overseeing the money supply. Immediately preceding the recoinage of 1696, for example, over four hundred publications spewed from Britain's young press about the nature of monetary value.[8] For most of the eighteenth century, by contrast, there was relatively little writing on the subjects of paper currency and banking. In 1857, John Ramsay McCulloch, one of the most vocal apologists for the financial institutions that resolved the seventeenth-century monetary crisis, attributed this dearth of publications to the "equable system" by which the Bank of England had earned the nation's "unlimited confidence" by circulating its notes on a par with gold.[9]

In this chapter, I begin to discuss the naturalization of money by examining two, apparently incidental features of late-seventeenth- and eighteenth-century *monetary writing*—a term I use to describe both the writing that functioned as money and writing about money, whatever its generic form. The first feature is an effect of the historiography through which this writing was made available to a later reading public. In the first main section below, I show how many of the late-seventeenth- and the eighteenth-century pamphlets that did address monetary issues were packaged a century later into two volumes that implicitly celebrated Great Britain's rise to the international dominance it had attained by 1850. The double perspective that these collections afford enables us to see two things at once. On the one hand, because the seventeenth- and eighteenth-century pamphleteers exposed many of the theoretical problems that all representative money introduces, they help us understand these issues *and* why they were considered to be relatively *un*problematic during the eighteenth century. On the other hand, the form in which these pamphlets were collected, edited, and published in the mid-nineteenth century begins to reveal how the solution devised to address these issues could be mobilized in a different cultural context to serve another social purpose. The mid-nineteenth-century function that these volumes served was disciplinary as much as theoretical: as two of the many publications printed for the Political Economy Club, the volumes of "scarce and valuable tracts" on monetary issues helped canonize a set of texts that articulated the theoretical position associated with Adam Smith's *Wealth of Nations*. In so doing, they helped present the central terms of the emergent discipline of classical political economy as part of a century-long consensus—even though, as we will see in chapter 3, this theoretical position had long faced considerable opposition from rival economic theories.

A second feature of monetary writing in the late seventeenth century and the eighteenth is even more consequential for the narrative I develop in this book. The campaign to distinguish between valid monetary forms and their invalid counterparts, a campaign conducted partly through the pamphlets I examine in the first section, intersected in complex ways with another eighteenth-century development, one that had immeasurable consequences for all modern forms of writing. This development was the gradual breakup of a continuum that once linked (what we call) fact to (what we call) fiction. In the second section, I argue that the breakup of the fact/fiction continuum was modeled on the distinction between valid and invalid monetary tokens; this distinction, in turn, was the necessary precondition for making representative money seem to *be* rather than simply to *represent* value. Thus, the breakup of the fact/fiction continuum, through the related, but not parallel, processes I call *factualization* and *fictionalization*, simultaneously drew on and helped stabilize the distinction between valid and invalid monetary tokens, a distinction that was essential to the naturalization of money. Factualization was also the precondition for the social category of *expertise* in the realm of economic writing and was, thus, a crucial component of the authority retrospectively conferred on the pamphleteers I examine in the first section. Fictionalization, in turn, was the precondition for imaginative writers' claim that their writing was different in kind from the informational and theoretical writing published in these pamphlets. Fictionalization, as we will see in chapter 2, was, thus, the generic precondition for the argument that a different kind of value circulated alongside, but in competition with, the kind of value monetary writing incarnated, represented, and explained.

Writing about Money in the New Credit Economy

In order to appreciate the social function played by all three kinds of writing discussed in this book, it is important to remember that the growth of Britain's credit economy created not only new economic opportunities but also, to use Jonathan Lamb's phrase, "a new sort of ignorance, productive of a keen anxiety about the tendency of events and the constitution of the self." "Instead of relying on Providence for a sense of history," Lamb continues, "people confronted an engine for social development that they had constructed themselves, but that they could neither govern nor understand."[10] In this novel situation, "a sense of history" was not the only truism imperiled by the new and mysterious "engine"; once assumptions about Providence were challenged by rival accounts of change, the very nature of value seemed to be at stake, especially when it was so unmistakably clear that *value* had become a market, as well as a moral, category.[11] The three kinds of writing I discuss in this book all mediated the general category of value in the sense that they constituted the media in which contemporaries formulated definitions of *value*, measured or defined *market worth*, and forged ways of understanding the relative status, usefulness, or importance of persons and things in relation to the changes introduced by market society.

Because money was most obviously an index to one kind of value, its uncertain status repeatedly aroused alarm. As we have just seen, the uncertain status of money in relation to value was partly a function of the multiple roles it played; in the seventeenth and eighteenth centuries, this theoretical uncertainty was compounded by the scarcity of legitimate coins. But, partly, money was uncertain because its very nature dictates that its value depends on a gap between its material form and the ground of the value it supposedly represented. Thus, even though paper money was supposed to solve the practical problems associated with scarce coins, it simply made the theoretical problem inherent in all money visible: even a legitimate coin, whose face was not worn and whose edges had not been clipped, always contained only a fraction of the precious metal its face value proclaimed. Paper money simultaneously exacerbated this discrepancy and introduced new dilemmas, which emanated from the even more indeterminate relationship paper tokens bore to the ground of their value. Since paper did not literally embody any gold or silver, it was possible for private banks, employers, or other credit agencies simply to issue paper in whatever volume was necessary to meet demand; and, when demand dictated the volume of paper in circulation at home, it was even more likely that the value of paper would fall against the price of gold, as the latter was established by the international market. Even though paper money was useful, then, in extending credit to a nation strapped for quality coins, the very properties that made paper attractive threatened to exacerbate the theoretical problem that always haunted coins, for the ease with which paper could be printed meant that there was *no* necessary relationship between a monetary token and what it claimed to represent.

This slippage in the relationship between representative money and the value of the metal that grounds its various forms is an example of what I am calling the *problematic of representation*. As I stated in my introduction, the representational nature of money—which allows for this slippage—becomes problematic only when the mechanisms intended to manage the gap between the representative of value and its ground fail to work efficiently. During the seventeenth century, there were three such periods, all correlating to the upsurge in the volume of writing about monetary issues. The first was the 1620s, when a shortage of currency and an outflow of bullion provoked the debates about the balance of trade that we associate with mercantilism; the second was the 1640s, when religious and political conflicts inspired an increase in all kinds of print; and the third was the late 1680s and early 1690s, when the new financial arrangements imported by William of Orange to finance international conflicts sparked debates about how best to deal with the country's debased coins. After the late-seventeenth-century recoinage, as we have seen, and before the late-eighteenth-century war with France, the volume of writing about monetary issues decreased, although important pamphlets did sporadically appear. Modern historians, for the most part, have treated these debates separately, as episodes in the complex process by which Britons began to conceptualize a "market system" at work alongside Providence.[12] Before microfilm collections and electronic databases made such intensive analyses possible, however, these pamphlets were not generally available, even to scholars of the subject, and it is, thus, hardly surprising that the form in which they were remediated—published in a different form—influenced the way their significance was understood.

In 1856 and 1857, J. R. McCulloch, whom we will meet again in chapters 3 and 4, published two fat volumes of seventeenth-, eighteenth-, and early-nineteenth-century monetary pamphlets. Entitled *A Select Collection of Scarce and Valuable Tracts on Money* (1856) and *A Select Collection of Scarce and Valuable Tracts on Paper Currency and Banking* (1857), these volumes were privately financed (the second by Samuel Jones-Loyd, first Baron Overstone), printed in small numbers (150 copies), and intended "for distribution among his [Overstone's] friends" (*SCPCB*, vii). For McCulloch, these volumes constituted the fruits of a lifetime of labor—the collection of ten thousand pamphlets and volumes dealing with economic and financial matters. They were also fitting pendants to two volumes that he had published earlier in the century: a new edition of Smith's *The Wealth of Nations* (1828) and an edition of the works of Smith's most prominent nineteenth-century disciple, David Ricardo (1845).

As we will see in chapters 3 and 4, McCulloch published many more volumes of economic writing during his long and productive life, most of which can be seen as supplements to these midcentury canonizing projects. For now, however, it is important simply to remark the audience for whom these volumes of scarce and valuable monetary tracts were intended. The London-based Political Economy Club, which James Mill founded in 1821, boasted many of the century's most influential economic writers. Before midcentury, these included—in addition to Mill, Lord Overstone, and McCulloch—Ricardo, Thomas Robert Malthus, John Stuart Mill, Thomas Tooke, Nassau Senior, William Newmarch, and Jane Marcet. When McCulloch presented his volumes to this august company, he could have been reasonably certain that the ideas explored in the collected pamphlets would be discussed, debated, and circulated far beyond the pamphlets themselves. In deciding which pamphlets to include, then, and—equally important—which ones to exclude, McCulloch was setting the tone for much of what counted as economic orthodoxy in mid-nineteenth-century Britain.

Before discussing the consensus that McCulloch retrospectively imposed on seventeenth- and eighteenth-century writing about monetary issues, it is important just to note the most significant perspective that his selection omitted. This other point of view, which, for the sake of convenience, can be associated with Tories like Lord Bolingbroke and Edmund Burke, insisted that all credit money was pernicious because it undermined the hegemony of property, which was the true, because natural, ground of value. For writers who held this position, the salient opposition was not between grounded and ungrounded money, as it was for the writers McCulloch anthologized, but between any representative money and literal ground (property), which was also the anchor for Britain's virtue and the nation's deserved superiority over France.[13] While this position was extremely important in the eighteenth century, I do not discuss it at length here because, with the general acceptance of paper money, it became a distinctly minority position, one that seemed increasingly outmoded as the years passed and more paper circulated.[14] The authors McCulloch chose to anthologize, by contrast, articulated what eventually emerged not simply as the majority position but as the commonsensical way to understand money. The Whig position acquired this centrality, as we will see in chapter 3, in part, at least, because nineteenth-century political economists like McCulloch chose to resurrect the pamphlets of these writers rather than to present eighteenth-century writing on this subject as a *debate*. What looked like a consensus was given additional weight by Thomas Babington Macaulay's *History of England*, which, along with McCulloch's numerous publications, helped rewrite the history of English money so that the monetary tokens that were so controversial in their own time retrospectively seemed like the groundwork for Britain's international power and the economic stability the nation claimed uniquely to embody.

Two sets of questions echo through the pamphlets McCulloch anthologized. The first, and most persistent, squarely raised the problematic of representation, for it concerned the source of money's value. Among the questions contemporaries raised about value we find the following: Is the value of a coin anchored in the stamp by which its face is imprinted? Is the source of value the quantity and quality of the gold or silver a coin contains? Does value reflect the scarcity or plenty of the coins themselves? The second set

of questions, which is related to the first, focused more narrowly on prices—
of commodities in general as well as of gold and silver more particularly.
What, contemporaries demanded, determines price? Is price a function of
the quantity of gold and silver in the international market at any given
time? Is it a function of a monarch's reputation or of a nation's willingness
to back its own currency? Does paper money cause prices to rise? And,
if it does so, does this offset the benefits that paper confers on a nation
by amplifying the available credit? As they tried to find solutions to these
questions, the authors McCulloch selected gradually produced something
that, when viewed from the perspective of McCulloch's volumes, looks like
a consensus. McCulloch articulates this consensus explicitly—as statements
of fact—in the introductions to the volumes: the value of coins comes from
a nation's willingness to adopt and legally enforce a monetary standard;
prices are a function of the relationship between the quantity of precious
metals in the international market and a nation's support for its own domestic currency; paper money does not adversely affect prices when it is
backed by a reserve of precious metals or securities. In the anthologies
themselves, the bulk of this consensus is articulated most explicitly in the
longest of the selections, the two-part treatise by Joseph Harris entitled
"An Essay upon Money and Coins," which was initially published in 1757
and 1758. When McCulloch called this work "one of the best and most
valuable treatises on the subject of money that has ever seen the light," he
implicitly endorsed its conclusions—especially Harris's warnings about the
"disgraceful" practice of degrading the value of a nation's coin.[15]

Harris's treatise helps McCulloch dispel some of the "errors" that previous writers had made in their attempts to understand money. The most
egregious of these is what McCulloch scornfully dismissed as the "old and
deeply-rooted heresy" that the source of a coin's value is the stamp imprinted on its face. This theory of value prevailed in the seventeenth century
and highlighted "Extrinsical" value; its proponents attributed the value of
a coin to its stamped inscription because they equated the value of the coin
with the monarch whose face was emblazoned there (SCM, 12–13).[16] A
rival theory of value is the one we have already seen; this theory—which
was endorsed by McCulloch and Rice Vaughan, the author of the earliest
treatise in McCulloch's volumes—attributed a coin's value to its "Intrinsical" worth, which Vaughan associated with the international market as
indexed by the balance of trade and exchange rates. The problem with the
"Extrinsical" formulation, according to Vaughan, was that, if a monarch
could dictate the value of coin, then monarchs could "give what value they

list to Gold and Silver, by enhancing and letting fall their Coins"; if the "Intrinsical" formulation was true, by contrast, the value of a coin would depend on "the consent of other Nations" (ibid., 12).

The "Intrinsical" theory, however, also raised questions, for the "consent of other Nations" might be complicated, in practice, by the plenty or scarcity of the coins in circulation at any moment—or even by the quantity of gold or silver available to mint coins as the discovery of new mines or hoarding raised or lowered the always unknowable international totals of gold and silver. A third possibility for anchoring the value of a coin, therefore, was by the quantity of metal a coin actually contained. This apparently common-sensical possibility, which Harris (and McCulloch) vehemently repudiated, would have meant that any coin that circulated needed to be weighed and assayed in order to be assigned a true value. The alternative to this unwieldy value-by-weight solution, and the solution that Harris (and McCulloch) endorsed, was to value the coins by tale—that is, by measure or count. In practice, however, value-by-tale is actually not as straightforward as the allusion to counting implies, for one can measure or count coins only after one has determined which coins to measure or count, and one can do this only by assuming that a particular coin of a certain denomination can be said to *stand for*, even when it does not *embody*, the precious metal it *would have* contained *if* it had actually embodied the gold or silver represented by the stamp on its face.

Thus, the solution of value-by-tale placed a kind a fiction at the heart of a coinage's value—a fiction that, not incidentally, invokes the other meaning the word *tale* carried in this period: "a mere story, as opposed to a narrative of fact; a fiction, an idle tale; a falsehood."[17] Even if the word *tale* carried this connotation, however, to most economic writers, applying value-by-tale to coins was preferable to value-by-weight; and, by the middle of the eighteenth century, it was universally considered preferable to the "Ex-trinsical" theory of value-by-stamp. Indeed, as two of McCulloch's other seventeenth-century pamphleteers proclaimed, it was the fact that England had not followed the example of other rulers in allowing monarchs to change the value of coins that had upheld "the Honour of England."[18] Actually, Joseph Harris admitted, England had *almost* never been dishonored by a monarch's debasement of the coin, for, in fact, Henry VIII *had* notoriously done just that. And, although Queen Elizabeth had restored the luster to the nation's reputation by taming the "monster" of debasement, even she had ultimately resorted to this measure at the end of her reign.[19] Nevertheless, by the middle of the eighteenth century, the adage that Sir Robert Cotton articulated in the 1620s was accepted as gospel: "Princes must not suffer their Faces to warrant Falshood" (*SCM*, 127). Or, if they did so, they profited from debasement at the cost of their nation's honor.

As McCulloch had to admit, however, the temptation to debase money was difficult to resist, especially when the coins were in the deplorable condition to which they had deteriorated by the 1690s. McCulloch acknowledged that even reasonable individuals could back debasement by including a pamphlet by William Lowndes, secretary to the Treasury under James II. This pamphlet, "A Report, Containing an Essay for the Amendment of the Silver Coins," was published by order of the Treasury Commission in 1695. In it, Lowndes cited the confusions that underweight coins caused: "Persons before they conclude in any Bargains, are necessitated first to settle the Price or Value of the very Money they are to Receive for their Goods accordingly" (*SCM*, 233). Instead of recommending value-by-tale (or any other alternative valuation), Lowndes suggested adding 25 percent to the nominal value of coins in the general recoinage that Parliament had already agreed to undertake. As an interim measure, he also recommended issuing paper receipts for the clipped coins submitted for exchange; during the period before they were redeemed, these receipts would circulate as money, as goldsmiths' receipts already did. It was Lowndes's pamphlet that provoked the famous response by John Locke ("Further Considerations concerning Raising the Value of Money" [1695]). McCulloch did not reprint Locke's pamphlet because, he said, editions of it were relatively easy to find, but he did pass judgment on Locke's response, commenting that the pamphlet, "though involving sundry errors," refuted Lowndes's suggestions "with an amplitude, or rather a redundancy, of illustration, that leaves nothing to be desired" (ibid., x).

But Locke's pamphlet did leave something to be desired—at least according to Joseph Harris, who was the king's assay master at the Royal Mint in the 1750s, when repeated calls for debasement once more echoed in the British press. "Considered as a system of the theory of money," Harris explained, Locke's writings were "very deficient and imperfect," for they did not address the all-important question of the *standard* and how a standard could—and should—be used to refute the tempting alternative of debasement (*SCM*, 437). In Harris's endorsement of *theory*, over and above the kind of practical solutions that could address immediate problems (like a nation's worn coins), we see the emergence of the kind of abstract, systematizing approach that Sir James Steuart would soon take to the issue of money in his *Principles of Political Economy* (1767). In chapter 2, I discuss the way such systematic, theoretical treatises helped transform the scattered and miscellaneous pamphlets of which economic writing had previously consisted into a body of generically recognizable writings capable of founding a *discipline*. For now, it is important to see why Harris thought that establishing a standard could stabilize the value of British money—even though the coins were once more worn, illegible, and in short supply, sixty years after the great recoinage.

According to Harris, money is like any other measurable good—wheat or land, for example. It can—and should—be valued by its quantity, not by the quality of the materials that individual coins contain. Harris admitted that money posed a challenge to the idea of a standard measure, but, instead of saying that money's function as a commodity is in tension with its function as a unit of measure, he pointed out: "Money is not only a measure, but also an equivalent, and as such passes from one to another; whilst other measures, may rest indifferently in the buyer's or the seller's, or a third person's hands, it matters not whose they be" (*SCM*, 372).[20] Harris did acknowledge the more common objection (that the value of gold and silver coins fluctuates), but, in dismissing this objection and emphasizing instead the circulation of money, he opened a new possibility for stabilizing money's relation to value. By denominating a standard that could be rendered exact by measurement and then kept out of circulation so that its mass would never be diminished by use, a country could, Harris thought, protect the value of its money.

Establishing and encrypting such a standard would restore to English coins the quality that they had (theoretically) once enjoyed: an exact equivalence between their weights and their names. It was the loss of this equivalence, Harris asserted, that explained the current confusions that surrounded money; and, if the equivalence could be restored, his contemporaries would stop demanding (again) that the coinage be debased. Harris's argument about this subject is worth examining in some detail:

> In former times, the coins agreed exactly in quantities with the common weights of the country, and had the same names with them; as pounds, shillings, and pence, were the names of the common weights, as well as those of specific coins and sums of money: At those times, the bare names of coins and of given sums of money, did manifestly specify or define the precise quantity of silver which they ought to contain; and then every one could readily judge for himself, without the assistance of a law-book, and prevent any fraud or imposition. (*SCM*, 456)

When a nation enjoys a perfect alignment between the common weights of the country (standard weights and measures) and the coins that represent those units, *and when both can be signified by a single name*, the problematic of representation disappears because there can be no slippage between the name that signifies value, the embodiment of that value, and the standards by which value is quantified. In Harris's account, this alignment had once obtained, but it had been disrupted "by the strange pranks that were afterwards played in the dark succeeding ages with money"; as a consequence of these "pranks" (debasement), "this business [had] become somewhat more obscure" (*SCM*, 456), and people were confused about money because discrepancies had opened between the signs or representations and the ground of value to which these signs seemed to refer.

Thus, Harris's analysis—weight should (and once did) equal value, and both should be (as they once were) signified by a single name—identified a solution: make the weight of the coin determine its value, and let its name signify both its weight and its value. If the nation had preserved this original equation, Harris explained, the situation that Britain faced in 1757 would not have come about: "Every one would have readily known, how much silver each piece of money ought to contain; and [this] would naturally have led people to compare coins with weights, which probably would have produced long ago, some of the regulations now so much wanted in regard to money, and which would have saved this nation from great loss and perplexity. It were to be wished also, that our silver and gold coins were of the same fineness one with another, for then their respective values might have been the easier compared" (*SCM*, 449).

The most obvious reason that names could not simply be realigned with the weight of the circulating coins, as Harris's last sentence admits, was that the wear sustained by the coins had diminished their weight. A related, and more pressing, problem in the mid-eighteenth century was that the debased coins had driven almost all the full-weight coins out of the country; this meant that there were too few coins of any kind to conduct the nation's business. Harris largely ignored this second problem, concentrating instead on the first. If names could no longer correspond to the weight of the coins that actually circulated, he maintained, they could be realigned with an *ideal* coin, which could be established by law as a monetary standard. The existence of this standard would anchor the circulating currency by making individual coins—no matter how light—pass current *as if* they were actually equivalent to the weight their names once signified. The standard, along with valuation by tale, would thus provide indisputable value for the coinage, even if it did so by means of a necessary fiction: "In the currency of coins by tale, no regard at all is had to their lightness, or deficiencies arising from mere wear; but all pass, as if they were of their due standard or full weight, as they first came out of the mint" (*SCM*, 483). Given the notorious tendency of mint masters to slight the weight even of newly minted coins, Harris had to acknowledge that, even in their pristine state, coins might not actually embody "their due standard or full weight." The value of a coin, in the end, was dictated by law, not by weight: "It is not the mint, but the laws, and the universal concurrence of mankind, that makes money" (489).

Even assigning laws responsibility for anchoring the value of coins did not stop the slippage that the problematic of representation occasioned at midcentury, however, for, as Harris also admitted, laws were not fixed but could be altered by legislatures or monarchs. This, in fact, was why debasement was such an attractive solution to a nation's deteriorated coinage, as the example of France revealed: a simple change in the law could apparently both realign a coin's stamp with its value and net the royal coffers revenue. To foreclose this possibility, Harris was forced to find another support for value; he did so, not in the stamp that represented the king, or in coins' reference to a standard weight, or in the nation's laws, but in the nation's workers and their *belief* in a law that is immune to change because it is "old" and "established":

> Labourers, handy-craftsmen, and manufacturers of all sorts, are paid their daywages in silver: What they receive is palpably, and manifestly their standard; and as labour is the main foundation of all riches, what goes to pay the price of it, will be the real standard of the nation, even though laws were enacted to the contrary. Laws, though they may, and perhaps too often do, perplex, yet they cannot eradicate settled ideas. Workmen of all sorts here, have fixed ideas annexed to shillings; they do not know, perhaps, the precise quantity of silver which they ought to contain; yet they know that there is an old established law, that hath settled this matter: Whilst this law is not abrogated or tampered with, they think themselves safe; they are content with their usual wages, without scrutinizing into the precise quantity of silver in the respective coins; whilst the same laws subsist, they expect these coins will fetch them as much necessaries as usual, and they look no farther. (*SCM*, 492)

Harris hints here at the kind of labor unrest that British landowners always feared and that high prices provoked in the 1790s ("whilst this law is not abrogated . . . they are content"). That he does so suggests how desperate he was to identify something that could halt the slippage that haunted the concept of value. Because this slippage was a function of the gap inherent in any system of representative money, of course, his antidote to the threat that money might be politicized (as it manifestly was after 1797) could not really work. The solution that he ultimately adopted, in other words—a material standard that did not circulate—could not counteract the slippage between sign and referent, for it too performed its social function only through representations that could at best approximate the gold to which they claimed to refer:

> The standard should be one clean piece of metal, kept under the locks of some of the principal officers of state; and, I think, it should not be accessible to any one, without their personal presence, if not of a certain number of other privy-counsellors. All the use that there need be made of this standard, would be for the adjusting of duplicates or representatives of it, which might be kept in the several offices, as those things called standards are at present. These, being adjusted with due care and exactness, together with their artificial parts and multiples, the law might declare to be sufficiently exact, or near to the true standard, for common use. And to these all persons might have recourse at such proper seasons as the law should direct, upon paying of very moderate fees. (*SCM*, 511n)

Harris's solution to the problematic of representation tried to halt the slippage implicit in substitution and approximation by identifying a single, physical incarnation of value that would serve as an ultimate ground. This physical referent could not completely solve the problem—because its place always had to be taken, in practice, by "duplicates or representatives"—but this did not detract from the appeal of this idea in the mid-eighteenth century. Indeed, in the 1750s, the appeal of a physical standard emanated not only from the commonsense notion that a "clean piece of metal" could actually embody (not just represent) a precise measure of gold or silver, whose value (for all intents and purposes) did not change, but also from the proximity of Harris's method to that of natural philosophers, whose prestige had been steadily rising for the entire eighteenth century. If one set aside for a moment the props that Harris found necessary in the heat of his argument, in other words—the props of laws and the workers' belief in an older, more absolute "established law"—then Harris's argument seemed to rest on the indisputable procedures of measuring and weighing, by means of which natural philosophers like Newton had made such persuasive claims about the physical world.[21] Joseph Harris's affiliation with natural philosophy, and with the Royal Society in particular, was critical to his own professional advancement, in fact, for, as the son of a carpenter, he had been able to rise to the prestigious position he enjoyed in the 1750s only because of the patronage of Edmond Halley, the astronomer and mathematician.

Harris wrote pamphlets about navigation and technical measuring instruments that were published by the Royal Society, and, largely as a consequence of Halley's support, he obtained a position at the Royal Mint in 1736. From there, he rose rapidly, with salary increases commensurate to his growing responsibilities, until he attained the position of king's assay master. Harris had been working with the Royal Society to establish a system of standard weights and measures since 1749; for the Mint, he oversaw the creation of the reference weights that he mentions, which were adjusted (presumably under his supervision) to mint standards. In 1824, long after Harris's death, one of his mint standards was adopted by Parliament under the new imperial system.[22]

If the adoption of a physical standard sought to address the problems of substitution and approximation, it did not even approach the root of the problematic of representation: the gap between the monetary token and its ground of value. As we have seen, Harris evaded this issue partly by discounting the changing market value of gold and silver (which would have imperiled the value of the guarantor). Partly, he evaded it by insisting that all monetary tokens had to incarnate, as well as represent, value. This was his reason for opposing paper money, which was being issued in several forms by the 1750s, but which was still controversial. If a nation's monetary tokens did not have some intrinsic value, Harris insisted, "private property will be precarious"—presumably because, like bills of exchange, paper money consisted of "mere promises or obligations of payment" (*SCM*, 374). To clarify this point, Harris alluded in the second part of his treatise to a distinction between "real and fictitious" money (409). By the last phrase, he meant paper credit, which he countenanced *only* if its volume was "restrained within due bounds": "Should they (paper bills) increase much beyond the real stock of bullion that ought to be in their stead, they would prove mischievous two ways; by increasing in effect the quantity of circulating cash beyond its natural level; and by endangering, in a cloudy day, their own credit" (412).

The distinction that Harris made here—between real and fictitious money—was echoed by McCulloch a century later, but McCulloch amended the distinction in such a way as to legitimate (some kinds of) paper money, which was ubiquitous by 1857. McCulloch's distinction separated "paper money, properly so-called," from "bank-notes payable upon demand" (*SCPCB*, v, x) in order to distinguish between what we would call *fiat money*—inconvertible paper backed only by the dictate of a government[23]—and the convertible notes issued by the Bank of England before 1797 and after 1819. His acceptance of convertible banknotes accorded with the opinion expressed by several of the sources he anthologized, including the pamphlet by Dr. Robert Wallace; in so doing, it also departed from the opinion of another of his pamphleteers, David Hume. In fact, McCulloch applauded the prescience of Wallace (and another, unnamed contributor) specifically in order to chastise Hume for his shortsightedness: "Hume, who survived the publication of the *Political Essays* for about five and twenty years must have seen, in the extension of banking, and in the rapid progress of all sorts of improvements in Scotland after the peace of Paris in 1763, a practical refutation of his statements in regard to the mischievous influence of bank-notes" (ix–x).

Wallace, David Ricardo (whose 1810 tract McCulloch called one of the "ablest in this volume" [*SCPCB*, xiv]), and McCulloch may have applauded paper money, but they could not deny that it introduced an even more obvious version of the gap implicitly associated with coins. Even if a writer like Harris, in other words, could try to stabilize the relationship between representation and value by insisting that a coin embody (some of) the precious metal for which it stood, no such expedient was possible with paper, whose inherent value—while not negligible in the eighteenth century—could never rival that of gold or silver. With paper, the problem of the deferred ground of value was, therefore, unavoidable: paper did not simply approximate or substitute for value; it seemed either to defer indefinitely or completely to float free of whatever theoretically secured its value. This facet of the problematic of representation surfaced most frequently in the question of what would *limit* the issue of paper—since, without any immediate or necessary connection to its ground, there seemed to be nothing to keep a bank from issuing as much paper as it could afford to print.

Writers addressed this question in a variety of ways. Wallace argued that there was a "natural" limit to the issue of paper, even for private banks, but, when he tried to specify the nature of this limit, he, like Harris, had to invoke belief. In this case, the belief belonged to the bankers who issued paper money, not to laborers, and its object was not Harris's "old established law[s]" but the creditworthiness of those who demanded paper: "Credit can never be given without end. None will give credit but to men either of substance, or of integrity, prudence, and activity. Here then are *natural* checks and limits, beyond which credit will not be extended" (*SCPCB*, 84). The unknown author of *Reflections on Coin in General* (1762) addressed the issue of limiting paper obliquely when he argued that the problem of its ground was no different from the situation that obtained with gold and silver: "Paper in the general Chain of Credit and Commerce, is as valuable as they [coin or bullion] are; since the Issuers or Coiners of that Paper have some *Equivalent* to answer for what the Paper is valued at: *nor more* can any *Metal or Coin* do, than find its *Value*" (*SCM*, 523). Ricardo addressed the problem by advocating a mixture of coin and paper notes that could be converted into coin on demand; these measures, he thought, would ensure that the value of a nation's currency would "neither rise above nor fall below the value of the metallic currencies of other countries, by a greater sum than will suffice to defray the expense of importing foreign coin or bullion if the currency be deficient, or of exporting a portion of the existing supply if it be redundant" (*SCPCB*, xv).

This last quotation constitutes McCulloch's summary of Ricardo's actual words. As we will see in chapter 3, Ricardo's own phrasing was often even more difficult to understand than this summary, and McCulloch's attempts to clarify Ricardo's opaque style—so as to popularize his ideas—proved essential to the success of political economy as a discipline. For now, I want simply to emphasize the way that McCulloch dealt with the challenges paper money presented, especially in the aftermath of what was, by any account, a signal departure from the principle so emphatically endorsed by Ricardo (and McCulloch): to retain its value, paper money must somehow be secured, preferably by being convertible on demand. This departure, to which I return repeatedly in this book, occurred during the Restriction period (1797–1819/21), when the Bank of England suspended its promise to redeem its paper for gold. In the first interchapter, and in chapter 3, I discuss some of the effects of this suspension—on the issue of paper by other banks, the value of Britain's currency, and Britons' confidence in the Bank and the Whig government with which the Bank was so intimately connected. So dramatic was this departure from accepted theories about the relationship between money and value and so inescapable its practical fallout that it provoked more writing about economic matters than any previous fiscal event. The 1797 Restriction Act, McCulloch admitted, "awakened the attention of the public" to the subject of money; and the 1810 Bullion Report (whose conclusions were influenced by Ricardo's pamphlet) occasioned more comment. "Few if any parliamentary papers ever occasioned so much controversy as the latter," McCulloch admitted. "It gave birth to myriads of pamphlets" (*SCPCB*, vii).

Given how disruptive the Restriction was to the principle that all money—especially paper money—had to be secured by precious metal, and given the volume of writing it generated, it would seem logical that McCulloch would address this issue, either by defending or criticizing the Restriction Act or by retheorizing the relationship between monetary tokens and the ground of their value. As we will see in chapter 3, he did address this issue at somewhat greater length in other writings, but his lifelong strategy was to deemphasize the significance of the Restriction by reducing it to a minor chapter in a history that celebrated both Britain's rise to international financial supremacy and the nation's embodiment of a moral superiority that rested on its financial institutions. In practical terms, this entailed assigning preeminence to the late-seventeenth-century events that modern historians call the *Financial Revolution*, especially the founding of the Bank of England and the establishment of a permanently funded debt, and presenting the Restriction period as an "exception" to the "unlimited confidence" these arrangements inspired. Thus, in the preface to his second monetary anthology, McCulloch dealt with the Restriction in passing ("with the exception of the period from 1797 down to 1819 . . . " [*SCPCB*, vi]), and he immediately undertook his triumphal history of the Bank of England and the "unlimited confidence" that anchored its notes (vii). In the preface to his first monetary anthology, he chose a more circuitous route to the same end. Here, in a one-paragraph editorial on the "disgraceful" practice of monetary debasement, he alludes to the effects that many of his contemporaries attributed to the Restriction, but he does not name the legislation that inaugurated that period or associate it directly with the Bank of England:

> What was formerly done by degrading the standard of coins, is now done with greater facility, and to an inconceivably greater extent, by making that paper legal tender which has ceased to be exchangeable for the coins it professes to represent. This though a less direct, is a more dangerous and disgraceful species of fraud. A degradation of the standard is an open and avowed act of injustice, of which the extent and limits are defined and known to every one; but none can tell how far the depreciation of paper may be carried. It has frequently, indeed, arrived at such an excess, as to appear almost incredible. In France, for example, after the explosion of the Mississippi Scheme, and again, after the country had been deluged with assignats, a man might have died of want, with notes of the nominal value of 100,000 frs. or 1,000,000 frs. in his pocket! Even in this country, we have had, and at no distant period, ample experience of the baleful influence of the over-issue, and consequent depreciation, of paper. (*SCM*, xiii)

Identifying France as the most egregious abuser of monetary principles was a staple of British economic writing during the entire period covered by this book; and, while McCulloch's last admission ("even in this country") might seem to invoke the Bank of England's apparent overissue during the Restriction, it almost certainly applies not to the Bank but to the provincial banks, which McCulloch repeatedly charged with overissuing notes, not just during the Restriction, but until legislation severely curtailed their note issue.[24] In McCulloch's account, then, banks' overissue of notes was tantamount to a monarch's debasing the coinage, but this was a transgression limited, in Britain, to institutions not associated with the state, for, McCulloch insisted, the bank most closely tied to the well-being and honor of the nation, the Bank of England, had never overissued notes.

McCulloch's decision to emphasize the financially beneficial aspects of the Glorious Revolution and to gloss over the government's departures from its own stated policy of convertible notes is typical of the Whig version of British history most famously set out by Thomas Babington Macaulay in his influential *History of England* (1848–61). Like McCulloch, Macaulay highlighted the role that stabilizing the nation's monetary system played in stabilizing the nation itself, and he equated the government's fiscal decisions—to create a permanently funded debt, charter the Bank of England, and adopt the old standard in the recoinage—with providing an enduring basis for the nation's honor.[25] Because his history never reached the controversial Bank Restriction, of course, Macaulay did not have to account for the country's departure from the policy of convertibility. Nevertheless, by emphasizing the way that fiscal policies grounded national virtue, he effectively displaced the question of what could ground the value of paper notes (and the volume of their issue).

Or, more precisely, Macaulay left all such questions to political economists, the experts who had firmly established their prerogative over such issues by the 1840s. As Macaulay pointed out, in the late seventeenth century, when the idea of establishing a national debt was first introduced, it provoked a "cry of anguish and despair" from all kinds of people—statesmen, politicians, and ordinary traders and merchants. Such amateurs, however, could not be expected to understand the intricacies of complex financial matters; and, while Macaulay allowed himself to speculate about why the debt had proved so successful, he also insisted that the legitimate explanation for such matters must come from experts, not amateurs—"to point out that fallacy is the office rather of the political economist than of the historian."[26]

Macaulay's bow to economic expertise, like his substitution of one kind of ground (the ground of the nation's honor) for another (the ground of money's value), epitomizes the strategy by which mid-eighteenth- and nineteenth-century writers best managed the problematic introduced by all forms of representative money. By insisting that economic experts had a monopoly over economic issues, writers like Macaulay reinforced the authority claimed by eighteenth-century writers, like Sir James Steuart, David Hume, and Adam Smith (to name only the most influential). As we will see in the next chapter, establishing this authority was partly a matter of establishing a way of writing—a genre—that seemed capable of addressing complicated economic issues at a relatively abstract level and in a systematic form that seemed to mirror the system they claimed to find in market relations. Writing in the nineteenth century, J. R. McCulloch simultaneously reinforced the authority of his predecessors by reprinting, editing, and promoting their writings and anchored his own authority (as a popularizer of these writings) in the authority he helped establish for them. Before taking up the story of how political economy was created as a discipline associated with a distinctive form of writing, however, let me turn to an adjacent issue, one that considerably complicated eighteenth-century efforts to establish economic writing as a reliable, because factual, source of information and expertise.

The Fact/Fiction Continuum

One of the preconditions for establishing the authority of economic expertise, which most of us now unquestionably accept, was the creation of a stable, self-evident distinction between the categories we call *fact* and *fiction*.[27] From one perspective, this seems too obvious even to mention: why would anyone accord the kind of economic pamphlets McCulloch collected authority if she did not believe that the theories they expound are based on fact? From another perspective, it seems impossible to prove that the distinction between fact and fiction was ever in doubt since we can argue that a continuum linked fact to fiction only retrospectively, from a vantage point that postdates such a distinction, and in terms that early modern Britons would, presumably, not have recognized. Despite these undeniable challenges, scholars have identified such a continuum in sufficient kinds of writing to give such retrospective analysis considerable weight. In this section, I discuss some of the late-seventeenth- and early-eighteenth-century manifestations of the fact/fiction continuum and the historical conditions that imperiled or helped preserve it as the new modes of knowledge production, which we associate with the Enlightenment, the Scientific Revolution, and natural philosophy, were being codified in innovative ways of writing. Throughout this discussion, I also keep an eye on the eventual breakup of this continuum, for, as I have just noted, it is impossible to recover the generic and ontological continuums that have disappeared except through the discrete forms and categories that have taken their place.

In recent years, a number of scholars have identified a range of early modern genres that did not distinguish clearly between fact and fiction. These include seventeenth-century "news" ballads and broadsides, histories, almanacs, travel writings, secret histories, and satirical writings.[28] A few examples will suffice to illustrate some of the manifestations of this continuum. In 1666, for example, Robert Boyle described *"factitious* bodies" as physical entities produced through experiments; such entities resembled "natural" bodies in being material, yet they were not identical to natural bodies because they had been created by human initiatives.[29] Whereas Boyle's "factitious bodies" was a term that referred to actual entities, most instances of the fact/fiction continuum were strictly linguistic and were produced within certain kinds of writing or genres. News ballads, for example, which Lennard Davis describes as "the dominant type of publication" between 1560 and 1650, capitalized on the ability of print to report rapidly on recent events, yet they often did so in entertaining ways that ignored any distinction between events that had actually occurred and their imagined counterparts. Even the terms used to describe these ballads and the news books to which they were related invoke an ambiguity similar to Boyle's category of "factitious bodies": the seventeenth-century news books were called *corantos, nouvelles, novels,* and *newes,* all of which (with the exception of *corantos*) were also used in the period for books of imaginative tales.[30] Secret histories embodied the same ambiguity, for they supposedly reported on the intrigues of actual people but did so through characters whose names or initials pretended to mask their referents. Similarly, almanacs, which William St. Clair places "at the heart" of the alliance between the government and the book trade in the late seventeenth century, did not distinguish between astronomical data and astrological pronouncements. "Almanacs contained . . . both the official state and ecclesiastic calendar and the astrological forecasts, prognostications, and advice on auspicious days whose efficacy depended upon knowing the date," St. Clair explains. "In almanacs, the legitimate and the illegitimate supernaturals depended so intimately on one another that they often coexisted within the covers of a single book."[31]

According to St. Clair, the coexistence of astronomical findings and the astrological predictions to which they were textually adjacent in almanacs was protected by the complex compromise by which the printing industry protected its monopoly over the proceeds of these profitable volumes. That is, even though formal censorship was applied to almanacs soon after the Restoration in 1660, the English government tacitly tolerated almanacs' continued dissemination of magic and superstition because printers paid hefty taxes for the right to preserve their monopoly over the production and distribution of these texts. Even in the eighteenth century, when many of the astrological predictions had been superseded by astronomical facts, almanac publishers continued to include supernatural material: "Provided they contained nothing politically dangerous, such as forecasts of social unrest, riots, dearth, or of a second fire in London, they were allowed to be printed under the royal arms and much Latin, traditional guarantees of authority and truth."[32] In the case of other genres, especially the periodicals that flourished from the late seventeenth century, the continuum between fact and fiction was explicitly part of the medium's appeal. Quasi-autobiographical characters like Isaac Bickerstaff or Mr. Spectator explicitly toyed with the ambiguity that came to inhabit the fact/fiction continuum as its two poles began to pull apart: such characters were as self-consistent and recognizable as any real individual (probably more so), yet their fabricated nature enabled their authors to move them around in society at will and to play up their superhuman canniness. Such personae epitomized the playfulness by which early-eighteenth-century periodicals in particular solicited the participation of their readers, for the fictive characters who superintended such periodicals as the *Tatler*, the *Spectator*, and the *Examiner* had their counterparts in the sometimes actual, sometimes fictive correspondents whose letters supplemented contributions written by the editors. So cleverly did Joseph Addison, Richard Steele, and the members of the Scriblerus Club exploit the epistolary model originated in 1691 by John Dunton that they were soon able to surpass the achievement of Dunton's *Athenium Mercury* by turning all their readers into would-be writers and a good part of their publications into material voluntarily contributed by readers.[33]

In the late seventeenth and early eighteenth centuries, then, various kinds of imaginative writing preserved the fact/fiction continuum in order to *exploit* the problematic of representation. Such writing, in other words, populated the gap opened by the deferral of reference with possibilities: the possibility that a named character might refer to a real person or the equally plausible possibility that an apparent reference to an actual person might simply function as a character.[34] Unlike money itself and, equally, writing about money, both of which sought to *manage* the problematic of representation, imaginative writing—whether or not it invoked financial issues— flaunted deferral, obscurity, substitution, and approximation to generate ambiguity, uncertainty, and opportunities for intrigue and play. Like the masquerade, one of the many nontextual forms in which the fact/fiction continuum flourished in the eighteenth century, imaginative writing made the most of print's ability to conjure something out of nothing—or simply to obscure the ontological status of the figures it created.

In the next chapter, we will see how some writers we now associate with Literary genres tried to preserve the fact/fiction continuum, even as it came under pressure from other writers and from social events. We will also see that fictionalization—the creation of explicitly imaginative characters and situations that had no real-life referent—was used by other imaginative writers to break up the fact/fiction continuum, as part of a more general campaign to specify the properties and functions that were unique to imaginative writing.[35] Before I pursue that argument, however, I want to emphasize its counterpart: just as fictionalization was a strategy devised to disrupt the fact/fiction continuum, producing new genres and rationales for fiction in the process, so too was factualization articulated in new genres, genres devised to authenticate another kind of knowledge, in this case, informational and/or theoretical knowledge. Elsewhere, I have described one of these genres—double-entry bookkeeping—as an amalgamation of theological claims, rhetorical strategies, and numerical language designed to express the honesty and moral rectitude of merchants by equating these virtues with the exactness of numerical facts.[36] Here, I continue that argument by suggesting that, in the genres elaborated by economic writers, the distinction between fact and fiction, which occupies such an important place in our modern understanding of knowledge, was modeled on a similar distinction forged in relation to monetary instruments: that between valid and invalid monetary tokens. The difficulty inherent in making and enforcing this discrimination, however—a difficulty compounded both by the problematic that discrimination was intended to manage and by opportunistic financial innovations themselves—necessitated additional social measures. Among these was the creation of the epistemological and social categories that we have already seen in writing about money, those of expert knowledge and the knowledge expert or specialist. The transformation of the previously suspect (because self-interested) merchant into the (disinterested) economic expert was, in part at least, a function of the creation of new, authoritative genres by which financial information could be conveyed. Paradoxically, these new genres, including political economy itself, were both modeled on and intended to reinforce the ever-elusive distinction between valid and invalid monetary forms.

Any monetary system needs to be able to distinguish between valid and invalid tokens, and the ability of any particular instrument to seem self-evidently valid is one quality that makes it preferred over others. Tally sticks, which preceded paper notes, embodied validity as a literal mark, for only when the notches cut into the two halves that had once formed a single whole could be realigned would a debt or credit be acknowledged. When in the 1660s tally sticks were replaced by orders written on paper, validity could no longer simply be embodied, for paper, like the metal of coins, was always subject to duplication and other forms of abuse. Counterfeiting and forgery have been as ubiquitous in the history of English money as were sweating and clipping in the seventeenth and eighteenth centuries, and the introduction of every new monetary instrument has been both characterized by official measures designed to discourage counterfeiting and accompanied by criminal efforts to make a passable substitute for the new money.

The chronic difficulty involved in stabilizing and enforcing the distinction between valid and invalid monetary instruments was compounded in the last two decades of the seventeenth century by financial innovations that accompanied and facilitated the proliferation of English joint-stock companies. Joint-stock companies had existed in England since the mid-sixteenth century, but it was only in the 1680s that an active London market developed for buying and selling shares in these companies. This market became active, in large part, because of new publications designed to advertise the availability and prices of company shares. John Houghton's *A Collection of Letters for the Improvement of Husbandry and Trade*, which made its initial appearance in 1681, was one of the first serials dedicated to regularly publishing share prices. This followed the brief appearance, in 1680, of James Whiston's *The Merchant's Remembrancer* and was soon joined, in 1709, by John Castaing's *The Course of the Exchange*. The latter became the definitive guide to stock prices. The number of companies listed by these publications grew rapidly: in 1689, there were fewer than 20 joint-stock companies whose shares were announced for sale; by 1695, this number had grown to about 150.[37]

The reason that the availability of shares in joint-stock companies compounded the difficulty of distinguishing between valid and invalid monetary instruments is that the value of the shares was *intended* to fluctuate in the market, as a function of supply and demand. That is, the price of a share in the East India Company rose or fell not simply as the company's overseas ventures prospered or failed but also as fewer or greater shares were available for purchase than were in demand. Shares in joint-stock companies constituted *speculative* investments, and the risk involved in speculation simultaneously increased the potential return on one's investment—beyond the value of the money actually pledged—and exaggerated the capacity of every monetary instrument to gain or lose value as the market altered the relationship between supply and demand. Shares both made the problematic of representation inherent in every monetary instrument visible and capitalized on that problematic. As a result, by the 1690s, this form of financial transaction was regularly characterized as a "trick," which took advantage of sellers' and advertisers' "art":

> 'Tis by this means, that our noble *Trade* had degenerated into *Trick*, and instead of employing a Stock in honest and generous Adventures abroad, according to the laudable Practice of Merchants; There is lately set up a new Society of *Artificers*, who blow the Price of Stock up and down, as best suits their Design of enriching themselves by the ruin of others; and this *Legerdemain* is manag'd by a strange sort of *Insects* call'd *Stock-Jobbers*, who devour men on our *Exchange*, as the *Locusts* of old did the Herbage of *Egypt*.[38]

Outrage about this form of financial instrument reached a crescendo at the end of 1720, when the collapse of the South Sea Bubble provoked countless complaints about trickery, artifice, and the kind of fictions that lay at the heart of stockjobbing. Often represented as a collective madness or delusion,[39] the South Sea mania might also be described as a period during which the continuum that linked fact to fiction became invisible or ceased to matter—*even though* the distinction between valid and invalid monetary instruments that underwrote it had yet to be stabilized. As we have just seen, in fact, one reason that the distinction between valid and invalid monetary instruments did not matter in the case of publicly traded shares was that *every* share attained its value not (just) from some underlying gain by the company it represented but (also) from the desire of other buyers to purchase the company's stocks.

If the mania that fueled the South Sea Bubble ignored or even exploited the fact/fiction continuum in monetary instruments, then the Bubble's collapse produced a kind of backlash—a widespread intolerance toward permitting financial instruments to harbor, much less turn on, fictions of any kind. This intolerance was expressed in a number of ways. Some critics equated stockjobbers' promises of immediate wealth with overt lies and challenged the practice of using fallacious names to cover the truth.[40] Others targeted the mystery and secrecy with which stockjobbers had long been associated. The parliamentary history that recorded the mania, for example, emphasized "the mysterious springs" that "wound up" investors' fantasies; since the "foundation" of this machine was "fraud, illusion, credibility, and infatuation," it "fell to the ground as soon as the artful management of its directors was discovered." To capture the extent to which secrecy was bound up with the perceptions that fed the mania, we might note that one of the most preposterous—but symptomatic—of all the speculative ventures was a "company for carrying on an undertaking of great advantage, but nobody to know what it is." To convey how closely secrecy was associated with deceit, we have only to note that the aptly named House Committee of Secrecy found in February 1721 not only that some of the books kept by the South Sea Company recorded false and fictitious entries but also that others "had been taken away or secreted."[41]

I stress the prominence of secrecy in accounts of the fictions that were said to feed the South Sea Bubble because it was, in part, the secrecy that merchants embraced as a necessary facet of competitive trade that created the social opening for experts who claimed to be able to dispel such mysteries for ordinary Britons. As early as the mid-seventeenth century, titles of publications about financial matters promised to expose the secrets associated with money and finance. Such titles—*Mysteries and Secrets of Trade and Mint-Affairs* (1653) and *The Mystery of the New Fashioned Goldsmiths or Bankers* (1676), to name just two—simultaneously granted monetary matters a version of the opacity also associated with sorcery and alchemy and claimed to subject those practices to the kind of rational analysis that was beginning to be applied to the natural world. One legacy of this paradox was a split, in monetary matters, between those who engaged in such practices and those who wrote about economic issues. The former tended to guard the secrets of their business (which were often unique to particular companies or guilds), and the latter sought to describe these activities—increasingly, at a relatively general, systematic, and abstract level.

This division—between secretive practitioners and the experts capable of writing up and exposing practitioners' secrets—eventually put pressure on the fact/fiction continuum in the realm of economic writing, for, as we have just seen, in the aftermath of the South Sea debacle, writing associated with secrecy was also associated with pernicious—indeed, ruinous—fictions. Such fictions, which were intended to deceive, were said to resemble counterfeit money: both passed off worthless tokens as valuable; both netted rewards for hidden artificers. Thus, events like the collapse of the South Sea Bubble not only exposed the existence of the fact/fiction continuum in a monetary instrument; they also fueled public intolerance for this continuum *in monetary matters* even though the continuum continued to attract readers to periodicals, secret histories, and satires.

Actually, intolerance toward the fact/fiction continuum, which provoked the most controversy in relation to monetary tokens, was already being expressed in relation to imaginative writing as well. Even before the Bubble, in 1719, Charles Gildon challenged Daniel Defoe to clarify the status of *Robinson Crusoe*: Was this a true adventure, as Defoe maintained, or an imaginative tale? The anxieties provoked the next year by the collapse of the Bubble—the fear that God was punishing speculators' greed or that the Stuart monarchy would be restored—exacerbated the intolerance Gildon expressed for the fact/fiction continuum, for, as E. J. Clery has argued, the backlash focused on quasi-fictional, quasi-factual figures.[42] Critics castigated the genre of secret histories in particular because these were said to encourage the general licentiousness they associated with the nation's manic phase, and, after the late 1720s, partly in response to such criticism, the popularity of secret histories began to wane. Even Eliza Haywood, who had published many secret histories (including, as late as 1727, *The Secret History of the Present Intrigues of the Court of Caramania*), turned away from this subgenre to pure fictions, which were intended to inculcate morality in impressionable young readers; this was the case, for example, with *The History of Miss Betsy Thoughtless*, which Haywood published in 1751.

As authors of imaginative genres gradually began to renounce the fact/fiction continuum and to create characters that had no real-life referents, they might seem to have been adopting the explanatory function embraced by the self-proclaimed experts who wrote about economic matters. Some significant differences distinguished the two kinds of explanation, however. Unlike economic writers, who tended to distinguish their explanatory function from the secrecy kept by goldsmiths and money lenders, imaginative writers typically included explanations of their fictions in the very texts in which they created the fictions themselves—in the form of prefaces, addresses to the reader, appendices, and other paratextual materials. Placing the division between practice and commentary within a single volume also helped break up the fact/fiction continuum, for doing so graphically distinguished between the parts of the text that were fiction (the action, the characters) and the parts of the book that were fact (the author's addresses to the reader). This difference *within* imaginative texts also meant that the inadequacy of the commentary to the fiction was always visible to the reader—unlike in economic writing, where any inadequacies of explanation in relation to practice were both masked and rendered irrelevant by the physical separation between the two.

The tendency to place commentary within imaginative works generated several additional effects, especially in prose fiction, the century's most consistently innovative genre: secrecy persisted, but it changed its form, moving, as we will see in chapter 2, from the areas of authorship and reference to the kind of character that began to dominate novels after 1740; ambiguity, suspense, and difficulty increasingly became characteristic features of imaginative writing; and these features encouraged the kind of consumption associated with earlier forms of romance, not the periodic consultation associated with financial ledgers, the totalizing overview promoted by theorists' systems, or the inattentiveness encouraged by naturalized monetary tokens, but a sequential mode of consumption that privileged imaginative engagement, interpretation, and evaluation. As we will also see, this kind of consumption could not exhaust the ambiguity that increasingly became the characteristic feature of novelistic character; and the evaluation of character—the skill ideally inculcated by this kind of reading—constituted an integral aspect of this genre's claim to be able to mediate the credit economy. Evaluating character, in other words, was what everyone who accepted a token of credit was required to do; and the skills necessary to evaluate character were what forms of imaginative writing like the novel claimed uniquely to teach.

Eighteenth-century imaginative writers thus gradually assailed the fact/fiction continuum through various strategies of fictionalization, which were the counterparts to the strategies of factualization by which economic (and natural philosophical) writers also repudiated this continuum. If the former eventually relinquished the link between fact and fiction, however, they did so without giving up their claim to be able to mediate value. In fact, as we will see in chapters 5 and 6, nineteenth-century imaginative writers presented their work as an alternative kind of value as well as an effective vehicle for understanding the sorts of value associated with credit, commerce, and money.

CHAPTER TWO

Generic Differentiation and the Naturalization of Money

In the last chapter, I argued that the challenge to the continuum that once linked (what we call) fact and fiction was modeled on a distinction that was always important in the realm of monetary instruments, for the ability of the latter to represent value depended on creating and maintaining a distinction between valid and invalid monetary tokens. I also argued that, even as the Bank of England instituted measures that tried to police this distinction, the currency of its money (like that of all credit instruments) also relied on certain constitutive fictions: the fiction that coins contained all or nearly all the precious metal whose sum was stamped on their faces; the fiction that the paper money issued by the Bank represented and could always be redeemed for an equivalent amount of gold; the fiction that the numerical figures written on the faces of bills of exchange and credit notes of all kinds represented their current value, both what was paid for them and what they were worth in exchange.[1]

For the most part, and under normal circumstances, the monetary instruments that originated in the seventeenth century did pass current during the next century, even when coins were clipped or worn, and even though paper instruments were always subject to controversy. Sometimes this currency was limited geographically; sometimes the instruments were privately produced and had no official or nationwide status. Whatever the limits imposed on individual kinds of money, however, the monetary demands of Britain's rapidly growing economy were simply too great for tradesmen and government officials to object too strenuously to these limitations. Indeed, as we will see at the end of this chapter, much of the writing published during the eighteenth century—both economic and imaginative—reveals a general *indifference* to the fact that many, often competing kinds of money circulated in Britain. For virtually all Britons, an imperfect monetary system was preferable to none, and, given the near impossibility of creating perfect monetary instruments, it was more important to treat the available money as good than to question the nature of the tokens that circulated.[2]

There were, of course, relatively brief periods during the century in which this generalization did not hold true—months in which the fictions inherent in all credit instruments threatened to undermine public confidence, as at the end of 1720, or years in which the scarcity and debasement of the available monetary instruments provoked demands for some remedy, as in the 1750s, 1770s, and 1790s. But, given the state of British currency—both coin and paper—during the eighteenth century, these periods were remarkably few in number, short in duration, and easily brought to an end. The overall level of public confidence in the British monetary system seems even more remarkable in the context of the nation's almost constant military engagements, for these wars—with Spain, France, and the Dutch Republic, to name only Britain's most prominent opponents—led to an unprecedented expansion of the national debt, which, in turn, meant higher taxes for the vast majority of Britons, alongside the increased investment opportunities for the few that I began to discuss in the preamble. J. G. A. Pocock has famously argued that the growth of the debt, and the extent to which its very existence anchored the nation's political and economic stability in fantasies and speculations about the future rather than tangible land or material productivity, created a psychologically volatile situation, in which hopes and fears fed a combustible mixture that some politicians were eager to exploit.[3] While I concede that, to modern readers, the combination of this innovative model of state financing and a heterogeneous and inadequate domestic currency might seem potentially explosive, I also want to point out that none of the eighteenth-century politicians who tried to fan the flames of monetary alarmism—not even Edmund Burke—succeeded in galvanizing much public outrage. Throughout the century, religious and political leaders were able to arouse more passion among their followers when they addressed nearly any subject other than the national debt, the state of British coins, or the varieties and nature of paper money.

In part, of course, the relative indifference of eighteenth-century Britons to monetary and economic issues, compared with the interest many of our contemporaries (periodically) express in these matters, is a function of the different kinds and amounts of information available to each audience. As late as 1843, a British writer who wanted to stir up concern about the escalating national debt deployed a graphic (and imprecise) verbal picture of carts of gold lined up between Land's End and John O'Groat's House in Scotland rather than citing numbers.[4] This reminds us that, even with the eighteenth-century expansion of financial publications that I outlined in the preamble, economic and especially monetary information was often indigestible and primarily attracted the attention of readers already concerned about commerce or the probity of government. The vast majority of Britons were content to use whatever monetary instruments came to hand, to let the administration finance the nation's wars with the permanently funded (and growing) debt, and to worry primarily about making ends meet, keeping personal credit intact, and paying down debts with whatever small sums could be set aside after purchasing the necessities of everyday life.

In this chapter, I argue that this general acceptance of Britain's credit economy—from its most grandiose incarnation in the national debt to its most minute manifestation in everyday credit instruments—was furthered by the two other kinds of writing with which this book is concerned. More specifically, I argue that one of the effects of the differentiation between economic and imaginative writing—along with the concomitant differentiation between fact and fiction—was to naturalize the peculiarities of the credit economy and the monetary instruments on which it depended so that ordinary people would take all this for granted. By so doing, naturalization helped manage the problematic of representation that periodically emerged into visibility. The gradual process of naturalization was made possible by two interrelated, but not parallel, adaptations of the dichotomy that governed monetary instruments (valid/invalid): in the realm of fiction, the negative connotations associated with invalid money were neutralized by the claim that imaginative writing did not have to refer to anything in the actual world; in the realm of (economic) theory, the fictive elements intrinsic to credit instruments were neutralized by the introduction of abstractions, which could claim simultaneously to be true and not to be referential. Each of these adaptations helped manage the problematic of representation inherent in the credit economy in a different way. Fiction, which was not held to a standard of referential accuracy, did so by helping readers practice trust, tolerate deferral, evaluate character, and, in a general sense, believe in things that were immaterial; theory, which also bore an indirect relation to reality, did so by making abstractions seem like credible accounts of a market economy whose manifestations were inescapable but that, as a whole, was impossible to see.

In discussing the naturalizing function of this generic differentiation, I do not want to imply that economic and imaginative writers deliberately or intentionally divided up their topics or generic features so as to address concerns about monetary and economic issues. The generic differentiation I describe here, as I have already said, was part of the more general social process of specialization by which Britain acquired prominence in the new hierarchy of Western nation-states that emerged at the end of the eighteenth century. From one perspective, in fact, the function I highlight here—naturalization or normalization—seems incidental to the more general process of specialization by which Britain seized the initiative in international finance. From another perspective, by contrast, the naturalization of the credit economy seems essential (even if we cannot assign agency for it), for, if ordinary Britons had not been willing to use whatever money was available, to accept the growing national debt, and to take the financial arrangements that funded Britain's economic expansion for granted, British brokers and bankers would not have been poised to step in when the international money markets in Amsterdam and Paris collapsed at the end of the century, British merchants would not have been able to expand their domestic and international markets so dramatically, and British investors would not have been willing to risk their savings on the joint-stock ventures that proliferated in countries where the physical and economic infrastructures, administrative arrangements, and political conditions were less elaborate or less stable than their counterparts in Britain.[5]

The naturalization of the credit economy was intimately tied to the mediation of value, of course, for writing that embodied, interpreted, or made (what counted as) value comprehensible helped individuals accept deferral, slippage, substitution, and obscurity, which are constitutive components of any credit economy, and abstraction, which is a feature of the capitalist system in particular. During the first two decades of the century, these twin offices—naturalization and mediation—generally occurred within what I have been calling the *fact/fiction continuum*—that is, in kinds of writing that, like their seventeenth-century counterparts, did not explicitly or consistently differentiate between objective data, which seemed simply to reflect the natural world, and imaginative or rhetorical representations, which clearly elaborated or transformed the observable world. Even though it is possible to find earlier attempts to develop genres and formal features that could institute this differentiation (seventeenth-century bookkeeping and reports of natural philosophical experiments, e.g.), by and large, the distinction between our modern senses of fact and fiction—and between the formal and the generic features by which an educated reader could immediately recognize this difference—was a product of the middle decades of the eighteenth century.[6] Along with this generic differentiation, as we are about to see, the always complex concept of value also came to be more decisively differentiated—to be divided more precisely into one kind of value that could always be adjudicated by the market and another that was, by definition, considered immune from market considerations.

To trace these changes, I divide this chapter into three sections. Generally speaking, the first two focus on the gradual breakup of the fact/fiction continuum through the interrelated processes that I call *fictionalization* and *factualization*, and the third focuses on the way that imaginative writing contributed to the general cultural drift that eventually made the writing on monetary instruments invisible *as writing*—that is, as mere artifice or representation. More specifically, in the first section, I use some of Daniel Defoe's writings to illustrate in greater detail than I was able to do in the last chapter the nature and some of the tensions that developed within the fact/fiction continuum. I argue that Defoe is an exemplary figure for understanding this continuum, partly because his early writings so clearly reveal some of the generic features that characterized it, and partly because, as some contemporaries began systematically to distinguish between fact and fiction, Defoe resisted making this distinction in a simple or straightforward way. I argue that Defoe's resistance to breaking up the fact/fiction continuum was part and parcel of his fascination with the extent to which the relatively new technology of print could generate belief. The capacity of print to make readers believe was not an abstract matter in the early eighteenth century, for belief—like its corollaries, trust and creditworthiness—was essential both to fueling the market for all kinds of imaginative writing and to the efficient operation of liberal governmentality, which Defoe championed throughout his life. Experimenting with print's ability to generate and sustain belief, Defoe helped cultivate in readers the mental habits they needed to negotiate the credit economy. At the same time, and without fully articulating the modern category of fiction, he also explored the possibility that print could generate belief in events and characters that had never existed but that were, nonetheless, valid. I conclude the section on Defoe's writings with a brief survey of the way that eighteenth-century booksellers altered the title and ending of one of his late works, the text we call *Roxana*, in order to make the editions of this work published after Defoe's death conform to the criteria that had been developed to evaluate this nonreferential but nonetheless valid realm, which, after the 1740s, had clearly become *fiction*, in our distinctive, modern sense.

In the second section, I further explore the generic differentiations that began to distinguish economic from imaginative writing in the middle decades of the eighteenth century. The introduction of these features did not occur all at once, nor can we say that their use always expressed a deliberate or conscious attempt to create two separate kinds of writing. Indeed, as we will see, the agendas that gradually came to organize the features of (what we call) economic writing—the delivery of factual information and the production of theoretical models—was often pursued through features that also appeared in (what we call) imaginative writing, and the agendas that had long governed imaginative writing—the conveying of instruction and entertainment—were sometimes pursued through features that incidentally conveyed information or modeled theory. Only gradually, and only through the elaboration of the theoretical principles and institutional supports that we associate with *professionalization*, did economic and Literary writers articulate self-consciously the differences between their modes of writing and the kinds of value each produced.

In order to illuminate some of the continuities and differences that characterized this early phase of generic differentiation, I focus in this section on three midcentury texts. The centerpiece of my analysis is Sir James Steuart's *Principles of Political Economy*, a long treatise that was researched and written while Steuart was an exile from his native Scotland and published, on his return to Britain, in 1767. When scholars place this text within the history of economic writing, they generally present it as the first theoretical system of political economy, but it also conveys the factual information, both historical and contemporary, that Steuart collected during his decades on the Continent. By placing Steuart's *Principles* alongside Henry Fielding's *Tom Jones* (1749), I show that it shared a surprising number of features with the variant of fiction that Fielding called the *novel*. Even if these two texts did share features, however, by considering the texts together we can also see that *Tom Jones* and Steuart's *Principles* organized these features according to the different agendas that were beginning to be associated with two distinct kinds of writing. When I add Adam Smith's *Wealth of Nations* (1776) to this constellation, I can more clearly demonstrate that Steuart's *Principles* did not fully subordinate its fictional features to its informational or theoretical agendas and highlight the kind of formal adjustments that Smith made in order to do just that. Smith's *Wealth of Nations*—not Steuart's *Principles*—became the model emulated by subsequent economic writers, and, as those writers imitated Smith's work, they helped codify not just Smith's ideas but also the generic conventions by which generations of readers would recognize economic facts and identify economic value as strictly a function of market relations.

In the brief final section of this chapter, I consider one of the side effects of the breakup of the fact/fiction continuum. While the splitting apart of the rationales associated with economic writing, on the one hand, and imaginative writing, on the other, may seem inevitable or natural to modern readers, in the middle decades of the eighteenth century many texts pursued both agendas simultaneously. As fewer of them tried to provide both information and theory, on the one hand, and the kind of aesthetic pleasure increasingly associated with imaginative writing, on the other, and as they began to judge the two kinds of writing by two separate sets of criteria, writers sought to narrow the expectations of readers in a corresponding way: by the end of the century, writing that was recognizably fiction was being treated in a different way—by critics and reviewers at least—than was writing that explicitly provided information or theoretical models. This split in expectations and kinds of writing corresponds to the emergence of a recognizably segmented market for print, of course; but it also helps explain the phenomenon I describe in the opening paragraphs of this chapter: even though a bewildering variety of monetary instruments circulated in eighteenth-century Britain, contemporaries who were not involved in trade seem not to have sought or provided guidance for understanding or evaluating these instruments. In this section, I begin to link the generic division I have just described to what seems to me like tolerance for a certain kind of ignorance. More precisely, I begin to argue that the generic division I describe in this book encouraged the majority of readers to believe that not understanding the details of Britain's increasingly complex economy *in any terms other than those offered by imaginative writing* had no consequences. Such ignorance might seem to have no consequences precisely because, as one effect of the proliferation of imaginative genres, another kind of value was seen to circulate alongside monetary value, just as another kind of probability circulated alongside referential accuracy. While the text I examine in this section—Thomas Bridges's *Adventures of a Bank-Note*—is a slender reed on which to hang such a momentous argument, I return to this point repeatedly in the course of this book, with evidence intended to bolster a claim I can only initiate here.

Inciting Belief through Print

The writings of Daniel Defoe (1660–1731) provide a particularly interesting perspective on the fact/fiction continuum, both because his early texts in particular seem so oblivious to the generic and ontological distinctions that seem self-evident to us and because the critical treatment that this writing received after Defoe's death reveals that defining these categories has been central to the differentiation of the disciplines with which this book is concerned. I will take up the mid-eighteenth-century treatment of Defoe's writing in a moment, but, by way of beginning, it is useful simply to note how challenging the mixture of factual and fictional elements has made Defoe's work for modern scholars, who are, for the most part, fully schooled by their (our) disciplinary training. Thus, even though Defoe wrote many treatises that deal with economic issues, economic historians rarely consider Defoe's writing at any length;[7] and, when Literary historians write about Defoe, they tend both to isolate the six works we call *novels* and to marginalize any features that depart from the norms that began to be stabilized for this genre in the 1740s.[8] In this section, I want initially to approach some of Defoe's writings by showing how they depart from our generic norms and how they might have looked to contemporaries. Doing so allows us to see both why these works now look strange and why they were perfectly recognizable to contemporary readers.

All the publications I examine in this section—Defoe's pamphlets and essays on credit, his pseudodocumentary on Mrs. Veal, and the prose work we call *Roxana*—can be considered, in general terms, parts of a single project, if we use the term *project* as Defoe did. "The true definition of a project," he explained in 1702, "is . . . a vast undertaking, too big to be managed."[9] The "vast undertaking" to which these works belonged was an apparatus that could incite in members of the public a voluntary willingness to engage in behaviors that simultaneously enhanced commerce and virtue. When I discussed this project in *A History of the Modern Fact*, I connected it to the challenge posed by liberal governmentality, the mode of government that emerged after the demise of absolute sovereignty and as part of the emergent market society; liberal governmentality requires that most individuals "freely" conform to social norms without requiring coercion from a central authority.[10] The project of encouraging such voluntary compliance was "too big to be managed" both because so many people were involved and because the mechanisms of the apparatus were so diverse and unmanageable. As I argue in this section, these mechanisms included the routinization of certain habits of mind (belief, trust) and the technology of print (which helped cultivate belief and trust). Here, I also want to make it clear that, as I consider these texts as part of this project, I am approaching them as guides or handbooks. That is, I argue that Defoe treated print as a technology that could incite belief and cultivate trust, but I cannot say that enough readers read these texts—or read them in this way—actually to bring about the changes in attitude and behavior that Defoe's guides sought to naturalize.

One of the subjects that preoccupied Defoe in his early writings was credit.[11] This topic was important to the journalist, tradesman, sometime spy, and chronic debtor for reasons that were simultaneously personal and patriotic, practical and political. As a manufacturer and tradesman (of brick and tile), the young Defoe depended on credit for his often-precarious private business (as did almost all his contemporaries); and, as an early defender of William III and the financial arrangements William brought with him from Holland, Defoe had a professional and political stake in promoting the system of public credit anchored by the national debt. While most of Defoe's publications on credit clearly engaged this topic as an economic matter, however, their generic features do not always conform to the features we associate with economic writing. Repeatedly, for example, Defoe used elaborate systems of metaphors and personifications to describe economic activities and an explanatory method that depends on association and amplification rather than analysis or abstract models. One of his first allusions to credit provides a rudimentary example. This appears in the 1701 pamphlet entitled "The Villainy of Stock-Jobbers Detected and the Causes of the Late Run upon the Bank and Bankers Discovered and Considered." In this pamphlet, one of many turn-of-the-century attacks on stockbrokers, Defoe introduced credit with two figures to which he frequently returned, credit as both the "moon" and the "soul of trade":

> Trade in general is Built upon, and supported by two essential and principal Foundations, *Viz.* Money and Credit, as the Sun and Moon in their *Diurnal Motion* alternately *Enlighten* and *Envigorate* the World, so these two Essentials maintain and preserve our Trade; they are the Life and Soul of Trade, and they are the support of one another too. Money raises Credit, and Credit in its turn is an Equivalent to Money.[12]

As the title of the pamphlet implies, Defoe was led to address credit by a specific event, the run on the Bank of England sparked (in Defoe's account) by competition between the old East India Company and its newer offshoot, the new East India Company. According to Defoe, the old company's directors had incited the run either by employing stockjobbers to manipulate the price of shares or by manipulating these prices themselves.[13] Given the chronic shortage of capital available for investment at the turn of the century, if the old company directors had been able to generate enough demand for their shares, they could, presumably, have drained London of its ready money and, thus, undermined their upstart competitors, who were also trying to attract capital. The description I have just offered does not accurately capture the way Defoe narrated these events, however, for his account is couched in language that, by modern standards, seems to obscure both the actual events and what caused them. Instead of a straightforward narrative of what happened and an analysis of underlying causes, which we might find in a modern economic history, the pamphlet offers a combination of details that only seem precise and rhetorical figures that offer primarily elaboration:

> The Old *East India* Stock by the arts of these unaccountable People, has within 10 Years or thereabouts, without any material difference in the Intrinsick value, been Sold from 300 l. *per Cent.* to 37 l. *per Cent.* from thence with fluxes and refluxes, as frequent as the Tides, it has been up at 150 l. *per Cent.* again; during all which differences, It [*sic*] would puzzle a very good Artist to prove, That their real Stock (*if they have any*), set loss and gain together, can have varied above 10 *per Cent.* upon the whole; nor can any Reasons for the rise and fall of it be shown, but the Politick management of the Stock-Jobbing Brokers; whereby, according to the Number of Buyers and Sellers, which 'tis also in their Power to make and manage at will, the Price shall dance attendance on their designs, and rise and fall as they please, without any regard to the Intrinsick worth of the Stock. ("Villainy," 75)

The numbers given in this passage suggest precision, but this quasi precision coexists with—indeed, is subordinate to—the tropes Defoe was beginning to develop: the figure of the sea with its moon-driven tides and the metaphor of the stockjobbers as puppet masters. In a subsequent passage, Defoe elaborated the latter by segueing from a metaphor that compares stockjobbing to the artistry of the puppeteer to one that associates stockjobbing with a military campaign:

> These People can ruin Men silently, undermine and impoverish by a sort of impenetrable Artifice, like Poison that works at a distance, can wheedle Men to ruin themselves, and *Fiddle them out of their Money*, by the strange and unheard of Engines of *Interests, Discounts, Transfers, Tallies, Debentures, Shares, Projects*, and the *Devil and all* of Figures and hard Names. They can draw up their Armies and levy Troops, set *Stock* against *Stock*, *Company* against *Company*, *Alderman* against *Alderman*; and the poor Passive Trades men, like the Peasant in *Flanders*, are Plundered by both sides, and hardly knows who hurts them. ("Villainy," 92)

Compare this to a modern explanation of stockbrokers and fluctuations in share prices: "*Brokers* handle buy and sell orders placed by individual and institutional clients in return for a commission. . . . The price of the stock moves up or down depending on how much you and other investors are willing to pay for it at the time."[14] In the modern account, the authors link their description to no specific occasion or setting, they use no rhetorical figures or personifications, and they attribute the fluctuating prices to buyers, not brokers. In Defoe's description, by contrast, the explanation that is provoked by a particular historical event proceeds by an elaborate cluster of figures, which includes artistry, poisoning, and warfare. These figures are related to and build on each other—they all describe work conducted invisibly, and all these activities somehow enlist the victim in his own ruin—but they do not precisely describe the activities of the stockjobber. Apart from the list of "Engines" the jobber uses, which, like the numbers in the previous passage, merely simulates precision (without providing definitions), Defoe does not offer any details about what the jobber actually did. He pursued his case that jobbers caused the fluctuations in share prices largely by creating an aura of mystery and by choosing rhetorical figures that provoke ominous connotations: invisible poisoners and unseen generals command "strange and unheard of Engines" and "wheedle Men to ruin themselves."

Even though these passages do not look like the explanations that appear in a modern work of economic explanation, they *functioned* as explanation for Defoe and his readers. The rhetorical figures that modern readers might consider merely ornamental or extraneous were not decorative or incidental to Defoe, in other words: they were essential to explanation because, according to the conventions that prevailed at the beginning of the eighteenth century, explanation required the writer to engage the reader imaginatively, not to break down and convey information in simple, discrete parts, as modern explanation requires. A modern reader might also say that the conclusion Defoe reached—that stockbrokers, not buyers, control prices—is incorrect; but this conclusion (or, more accurately, assumption) is of a piece with Defoe's rhetoric: Defoe held the jobbers responsible because he viewed market transactions in terms of puppetry, poisoning, and military campaigns; he viewed market transactions in these terms because, in the absence of abstract concepts, which might have enabled him to transcend the particular situation he witnessed, and precise information, which might have enabled him to specify share prices and to name market instruments, he supplemented what he could actually see with his belief that villainy was afoot. Thus, it is not particularly helpful to say that his explanation is wrong, nor would it be accurate to say that it is a fiction. Instead of being errors or fictions, his conclusions and assumptions belong to a mode of understanding the world that did not distinguish clearly between fact and fiction, and, in this instance at least, they did not do so because the generic conventions he used asked readers to imagine invisible actions and believe the author's account.

The kind of explanation that governed Defoe's narrative looks strange to us because its logic derives from classical rhetoric, which is a mode of analysis with which most modern readers are unfamiliar. To Defoe and his contemporaries, it would have seemed normal to conduct an argument in this way, for such argument by amplification drew on one of rhetoric's fundamental devices, elaboration or *copia*.[15] In classical rhetoric, which was an oral art, the purpose of such elaboration was to persuade listeners to believe by drawing them imaginatively into the speaker's flight of eloquence, then to prolong and direct their engagement by means of numerous interpretive variations. In such disquisitions, in other words, explanation was a subset of elaboration, not the other way around, and elaboration was enlisted in the general aim of persuasion, which was the overall goal of the communicative act. When argument was transferred to the *printed* page in the sixteenth and seventeenth centuries, elaboration was often retained because the intensity it provided could help compensate for the absence of the speaker's body and voice. Thus, even as explanation began to rival persuasion as the goal of printed pamphlets like Defoe's, elaboration continued to play a critical role, for its emotional and imaginative potential helped the writer engage the reader despite the absence of the embodied voice. Defoe's elaborate metaphors—and, equally important, his elaboration *by* metaphor—thus performed the function once carried out by the speaker's presence and voice: they drew the reader into an imaginary situation that built on, but then departed from, what the reader might personally have known and then enticed the reader to make another imaginative leap into a quasi-imaginary realm where the writer's own beliefs held sway. Unlike modern explanation, then, which appeals to the reader's judgment by subdividing, simplifying, and clarifying a phenomenon at a relatively abstract level, Defoe's rhetorical mode appealed to the imagination and to belief through amplification, association, and metaphor.

We can see how this mode of explanation works more clearly in another of Defoe's engagements with credit. In this essay, which appeared in the Tory *Review* in 1706, Defoe gestured toward Renaissance figures like *fortuna* and *occasione*, but he used these to launch an even more complex family of explanatory tropes.[16] By quoting this passage at length, I can show how Defoe elaborated familiar figures until his tropes seem to inhabit a world of their own, then used the autonomy of this imaginary world to draw his readers into situations that were wholly imagined:

> Money has a younger Sister, a very useful and officious Servant in Trade, which in the absence of her senior Relation, but with her Consent, and on

the Supposition of her Confederacy, is very assistant to her; frequently supplies her place for a Time, answers all the Ends of Trade perfectly, and to all Intents and Purposes, as well as Money herself; only with one Proviso, That her Sister constantly and punctually relieves her, keeps Time with her, and preserves her good Humour: but if she be never so little disappointed, she grows sullen, sick, and ill-natur'd, and will be gone for a great while together: Her Name in our Language is call'd CREDIT, in some Countries Honour, and in others, I know not what.

This is a coy Lass, and wonderful chary of her self; yet a most necessary, useful, industrious Creature: she has some Qualification so peculiar, and is so very nice in her Conduct, that a World of good People lose her Favour, before they well know her Name; others are courting her all their days to no purpose, and can never come into her Books.

If once she be disoblig'd, she's the most difficult to be Friends again with us, of anything in the World; and yet she will court those most, that have no occasion for her; and will stand at their Doors neglected and ill-us'd, scorn'd, and rejected, like a Beggar, and never leave them: But let such as have a Care of themselves, and be sure they never come to want her; for, if they do, they may depend upon it, she will pay them home, and never be reconcil'd to them, but upon a World of Entreaties, and the severe Penance of some years Prosperity.

Tis a strange thing to think, how absolute this Lady is; how despotickly she governs all her Actions: If you court her, you lose her, or must buy her at unreasonable Rates; and if you do, she is always jealous of you, and Suspicious; and if you don't discharge her to a Title of your Agreement, she is gone, and perhaps may never come again as long as you live; and if she does, 'tis with long Entreaty and abundance of Difficulty.[17]

Once more, this passage is not exactly fiction, in our modern sense, for, even though it describes events that did not actually occur, the characters are not like the characters that populate later novels, and the situation is not wholly imaginary. Nor is the passage an account of facts, in our sense. In some senses, Defoe's elaborate family drama resembles allegory,[18] but he was asking his readers not simply to invoke allegory's stock figures but also to remember what they knew about real sisters (and women in general), then to think about what a "coy Lass" *might* do, and then to accept an account that "explains" why credit is so fickle without using either concrete examples or abstract models. The culminating account is abstract in one sense, of course—it describes a personified abstraction. But it is not abstract in the sense that modern economic writing is—it does not analyze or generalize in order to construct a formal model. What an early-eighteenth-century reader would have gained from reading this passage was not a more particularized understanding of credit, or a formal model of this abstract mechanism, but an imaginative experience of the passivity and wonder Defoe says the tradesman felt. As with my last example, this experience is a function of the *way* that Defoe develops his account; that is, it is a function of the passage's tropes and syntax, which cast credit as the charming, enigmatic dominatrix. Whereas the feminized (and typographically marked) Credit regularly occupies the subject position of Defoe's sentences and takes active verbs ("court," "pay," "govern"), only two human beings are referred to in his discussion—and they are invoked without proper names or capital letters. Designated simply as "those... themselves" and "you," these (implicitly masculine) figures twice occupy the object position ("she will court those most," "let such as have a Care of themselves"), and, when the latter commands a verb, as it does three times, its agency is revoked by the syntactic reversal entailed by "if... then" ("if you court her, you lose her," etc.).

Even though contemporaries would, presumably, have recognized such accounts as explanations, they would not have considered them to be either factual or fictional accounts. Such categories simply do not apply to these descriptions, just as one could not say that they either provided or failed to deliver *information* or to construct a theoretical *model*. Such accounts were intended to entertain and instruct in order to incite virtuous behaviors that would enhance commercial success, but what they could tell a reader about how to maintain creditworthiness was ethical or psychological rather than informational or theoretical. By the same token, even though these two pieces helped mediate the reader's relationship to the credit economy, they did so not by promoting a rational understanding of particularized or abstracted data but by eliciting imaginative engagement with individualized and interpretive personifications and tropes. Because Defoe's explanations begin with specific historical situations, then move from them—via elaborate metaphors and personifications—to imaginative pictures that depict complex interrelations among imaginative personifications, his accounts tend both to target the individuals he could actually have seen and to project on them (via the tropes they inspired) motives and relationships he could only have imagined. Defoe's emphasis encouraged contemporaries to revile the individuals who performed this service (the stockjobbers), not to blame—or even see—an abstract market system that we might say was replacing state-directed trade, of which (a modern economist would say) competition, price fluctuations, and stockbrokers were merely outward signs. By the same token, presenting credit as a mysterious, dominating female, as he did in the *Review* essay, encouraged tradesmen to both accept and—to a certain degree—enjoy their inability to control their financial fates, not to engage actively in analysis that could produce rational responses to market conditions. This explanation-by-amplification, moreover, helped interpret the obscurity that Defoe found in the practices of stockjobbers and that appeared in all early attempts to explain the credit economy, including Defoe's own. What we might interpret as Defoe's *failure* or *inability* to explain why share prices rose or how credit worked, in other words, might well have looked to readers who did not have our expectations about explanation like a credible account precisely because it captured the obscurity they too experienced. In both conforming to the rules of classical rhetoric and repeating their own experience of the inexplicable tides of credit, Defoe's account might well have been effective because readers did not see *the market* as an abstraction that they could hope to understand by analyzing its underlying laws.

In a somewhat later pamphlet, the *Essay on Public Credit* (1710), we can see at least one of the reasons why Defoe might have preferred this mode of explanation to its modern counterpart. I stress that Defoe's reliance on copious rhetoric did constitute a choice because, by the early eighteenth century, classical rhetoric coexisted with modern explanation-by-analysis-and-synthesis, the mode that had been refined by late-seventeenth-century natural philosophers. By the first decade of the eighteenth century, this mode of analysis was regularly being used by members of the Royal Society, and, as they used the features that characterized this kind of writing to authorize their own credibility, Society members gradually helped distinguish the fact as a particular kind of knowledge and rendered facts credible by separating them from conjectures, assumptions, and a priori assertions (*not* by distinguishing facts from *fictions*).[19] The *Essay on Public Credit* suggests that, even though explanation-by-analysis-and-synthesis was available to Defoe, and even though he was not specifically creating fictions, in our modern sense, the old rhetorical mode of explanation remained attractive because it offered a *political* advantage: it enabled him to avoid the partisan disputes in which his peers were so bitterly embroiled.

Like "The Villainy of Stock-Jobbers," the *Essay on Public Credit* was a response to a particular situation, the fallout from the Whigs' defeat in the general election of 1710.[20] The Whigs, whom Defoe had previously supported, were thrown out of office in part because of popular hysteria aroused by the conviction, in March, of the High Church Reverend Henry Sacheverell, who supported the restoration of the Stuart monarchy. In June of that year, Queen Anne further alarmed the Whigs when she replaced the secretary of state, the Earl of Sunderland, with Lord Dartmouth and appointed Robert Harley, who was also rumored to support the Stuart cause, chancellor of the Exchequer. In response, some Whigs began to withdraw money from the funds (the national debt), and this both exacerbated the financial depression already under way in England and made it clear that wealthy Whigs posed as great a threat to the nation's well-being as did the Stuart supporters, who wanted to challenge Britain's commitment to the Protestant religion. Even though self-interest was pulling him toward the victorious Tories, Defoe still wanted to protect Britain from the Stuart (Catholic) Pretender. To do so, he argued that the system of public credit that the debt represented was a *national* resource that was—or ought to be—immune from party interests.

To encourage his readers to think of credit as a national property that was public in being good for everyone, Defoe argued that particular individuals should always subordinate themselves to—and be considered subordinate to—general principles. In his account, this held true even when the individuals involved were the most powerful people in the nation—in this case, the queen and members of Parliament. In the events that had recently saved the nation's credit, Defoe explained, the particular individuals who held the positions of monarch and lawmakers mattered less than did their willingness to adhere to general principles of honesty and good faith:

> Neither does our credit depend upon the person of the queen, as queen, or the individual House of Commons, identically.... But it will remain a truth, that every queen or every king, and every parliament succeeding the present, that shall discover the same justice in government, the same care in giving sufficient funds, the same honesty in supplying the deficiencies, if they happen, the same concern for the burthen of the subject, and the same care to put the treasure into the hands of faithful and experienced officers; shall keep up the same character, have the same credit, and restore all these declinings to the same vigour and magnitude as ever.[21]

Defoe obviously formulated this argument specifically to reassure Whigs who were skeptical about the new ministers; but, in doing so, he also presented credit not simply as an enigmatic trope but also as the predictable product of a bureaucratic process overseen by rules and principles. Theoretically, if his readers could have seen public credit in these terms—not as a personification but as the predictable outcome of principles faithfully followed—they would have renounced their party interests in favor of the principles that supported the rules.

Thus, Defoe briefly turned away from the figurative language that was more common in his engagements with private credit (and that also opens the *Essay on Public Credit*) and moved toward a mode that approaches modern explanation. His account in this pamphlet is more analytically detailed, and it moves toward more general principles (if not an abstract model): the queen, he tells us, "threw in" a hundred thousand pounds to prop up the securities market, and members of Parliament agreed to put the national interest before party interests (*Essay*, 6).[22] Such a particularized narrative that breaks down events and emphasizes general principles rather than relying on elaborate tropes represents a significant departure from his characteristic mode of explanation, and, if he had pursued it, it might have generated an account of credit that resembles a modern sociological (if not quite economic) explanation. It is clear from the way he introduced this account, however, that Defoe did not intend to replace explanation-by-amplification with such analytic, generalizable accounts. Instead, when he apologized for his "descend[ing] to particulars," he revealed that he associated descriptive particularity with divisive, party interests. "This nice case requires me a little to descend to particulars, and touch matter of fact nearer than was intended," he wrote. "I shall do this as modestly as I can; for it is not the present work to open sores, but to heal them, to prevent more from breaking out" (ibid.).

Thus, Defoe seems to have thought that "touch[ing] matter of fact"—that is, citing observable particulars—threatened to exacerbate political divisiveness and that this constituted an adequate reason for continuing to use explanation-by-amplification, even though a rival mode of explanation was available to him. Using the older generic conventions, of course, also preserved the continuum that linked fact to fiction. Positioning accounts of economic issues on this continuum, rather than modeling them, as later writers would do, on natural philosophical conventions—and doing so *for political reasons*—also helped Defoe keep economic issues and politics aligned, rather than separating them, as later economic writers did. Defoe's writings on the subject of credit, then, resisted what we might call *factualization*—the attempt, pursued by natural philosophers in particular, to devise conventions of writing that would clearly signal that certain kinds of statements expressed apolitical or disinterested *facts*, instead of articulating opinions or a priori assumptions.

If Defoe's writings on credit did not support factualization, many of his other writings—including the ones we now call *novels*—can be seen to

have approached, without wholeheartedly participating in, another specification, one that was just beginning to be made in the first decades of the
eighteenth century. Even though contemporaries did not use this term, we
might call the process that produced this new category *fictionalization*, for
its ultimate product was the realm of fiction, in which characters and events
can be plausible (or probable) without either referring to real people
(truthfully or libelously) or simply reworking familiar tales. Although it did
not develop, strictly speaking, in chronological stages, fictionalization can
be broken down into two parts: in one, writers (and readers) distinguished
facts from other kinds of statements; in another, and on the basis of
this distinction, they began to invent and appreciate wholly imaginative
characters and situations without referring them to real referents or familiar
fables. When in 1719 Charles Gildon demanded that Defoe reveal whether
Robinson Crusoe was a "fable" or "a just history of fact" (as Defoe called this
story), he was taking the first of these steps, for, by insisting that a "fable"
was different in kind from a "history of fact," he was imagining a distinction
not possible while the fact/fiction continuum prevailed.[23] It does not seem
that Gildon was finding a third term to complicate the resulting opposition,
however, for his use of the word *fable* does not allow for the new *fictional*
realm that scholars have identified in writing from the 1740s.[24] Gildon,
that is, was imagining an alternative to the fact/fiction continuum, but not
one that necessarily accommodated the kind of nontruth/nonlie we call
fiction.

Defoe's place in this development is particularly complex, for, while he
resisted the distinction Gildon wanted to make—between a "fable" and "a
just history of fact"—he did repeatedly experiment with writing's capacity
to inspire belief in events that were, strictly speaking, neither true nor false.
This capacity—and the writer's ability to cultivate it—was essential to the
kind of writing we call *fiction*, of course, just as it was essential to the working of liberal governmentality and the credit economy in particular. Defoe's
various forays into the ambiguous domain that would eventually be opened
alongside fact, then, can be seen as extensions of his writings on credit, for,
in all these texts, he sought to explore the dynamics by which credit can be
produced as well as managed. In the text I take up now, which forms one
of his many treatments of the supernatural, Defoe explicitly explored the
possibility that credit might be a function of print—that is, that printed texts
might be able to generate belief *even when* a reader could not determine
whether the events they narrated were true. Even though one cannot say
that, in this text, Defoe was self-consciously delimiting an arena of *fiction*,
as Richardson and Fielding were later to do, one can identify in it strategies

that suggest that he was exploring *how* print worked as a medium. After such explorations, it would prove relatively easy to cut the ties between the medium or technology of print and its referents, whether these were actual events and people or previous versions of familiar tales.

The title of this early pamphlet, "A True Relation of the Apparition of One Mrs. Veal the Next Day after Her Death to One Mrs. Bargrave at Canterbury, the 8th of September 1705," immediately foregrounds the issue of credibility and, hence, belief: the account is a "true relation" of the appearance of a ghost. Just as the title uses precise details—specific names, places, and dates—to authenticate the relation's veracity, however, its insistence that the "relation" is true allows doubt to linger. After all, the *relation* may be true—in the sense that someone told this story—even if the *events* the story describes did not actually occur. That a "relation" might simultaneously be "true," in the sense of authentic, *and* generate content that is undecidable, or impossible to verify, is precisely the possibility that seems to have fascinated Defoe.

As a modern editor notes, Defoe was not the only writer to chronicle the events narrated in "The Apparition." At least one early-eighteenth-century letter also told Mrs. Bargrave's story, and other documents suggest that the account circulated as a popular tale, not unlike countless other testimonials to a life hereafter.[25] Defoe's version of this tale, however, differs from its other incarnations in at least one significant regard: Defoe's "Apparition" immediately and repeatedly calls attention to its status as a *printed* text. Print plays a central role in the contents of the pamphlet, for, in Defoe's version of Mrs. Bargrave's story, the conversation that took place between the two women named in the title—Mrs. Bargrave and the "apparition" of the friend from whom she has been estranged, the "pious" spinster Mrs. Veal—repeatedly returned to the books they had read.[26] Even more striking is the fact that Defoe's version of Mrs. Bargrave's account is framed by an introduction, supplied by an unnamed editor, that specifically describes how the tale made its way into print. While this introduction might seem to authenticate the "relation"—in the sense that it documented the fact that someone told the story—it also raised questions that complicate the veracity of the narrated events, even as the editor seemed to authenticate them.

The events narrated in "The Apparition" can be easily summarized. A respectable resident of Canterbury named Mrs. Bargrave opens her door one day to find her old friend Mrs. Veal on her doorstep. Mrs. Veal, who had moved away from Canterbury some years before, tells Mrs. Bargrave that she wants to rekindle their friendship before embarking on a long voyage. The two women discuss several books about death and friendship, Mrs.

Veal asks Mrs. Bargrave to write a letter to Mrs. Veal's brother naming some bequests she desires to make, and Mrs. Veal reveals that she has left a purse of gold in her locked cabinet. Mrs. Bargrave admires her friend's dress, then, when Mrs. Bargrave offers to kiss Mrs. Veal, the latter turns her face away. At Mrs. Veal's request, Mrs. Bargrave steps out to call her daughter, but, when she returns, she finds Mrs. Veal already outside the door, preparing to leave. After Mrs. Veal's departure, Mrs. Bargrave searches for her friend at the home of the relative with whom Mrs. Bargrave thought Mrs. Veal was staying. At this point, she is told that Mrs. Veal had died the day before the visit, and the remainder of the narrative details various efforts to persuade Mrs. Bargrave to tell her story, the principal claim of which never varies. "She appeared to be as much a substance as I did, who talked with her," Mrs. Bargrave explains (265).

The narrated events of "The Apparition" thus turn on the ontological ambiguity of the apparition: she seems to be "substance," but, being already dead, she must not be. This ambiguity is repeated and amplified by the epistemological ambiguity introduced by the "relation" itself. For, as the preface informs us, this "relation" made its way into print by a complicated route, which involved many hands. "As it is here worded," according to the preface, the relation proper was written by "a gentleman, a justice of peace at Maidstone, in Kent," who first heard the story from his "kinswoman," who was a neighbor of Mrs. Bargrave. But the composer of the relation, the gentleman "justice of peace," was not the author of the preface, which is the textual sign that the relation passed from manuscript to *print*; an editor, who presumably both wrote the preface and arranged for the tale to be printed, is never named, and he reveals his own point of view primarily in his concluding comments about the pious "use which we ought to make of" this story (251). Just as the "relation" passed through the editorial hands of the preface's author, so it passed through two other sets of hands on its journey from Mrs. Bargrave's mouth to print: the justice of the peace in Maidstone sent the (presumably handwritten) "relation" to a friend, who lived in London; this unnamed friend then presumably gave it to the editor, who presumably gave it to a wholly invisible, because unmentioned, printer. Thus, in Defoe's version of Mrs. Bargrave's story, numerous male hands wrote up, conveyed, and then set in print the chronicle of a conversation that originally occurred between two women. By framing the event itself—the conversation—with this elaborate tale of gendered mediation, Defoe made print simultaneously the medium that authenticated the relation of the story and the barrier that now makes it impossible for a reader to know whether the events it describes actually happened.

The way Defoe frames Mrs. Bargrave's story thus directs the reader's attention not primarily to its content but to its transmission—that is, to mediation. From its apparently unambiguous first sentence, the editor's preface insists that the story should inspire belief: "This relation is matter of fact, and attended with such circumstances as may induce any reasonable man to believe it" ("The Apparition," 251). Yet the way the editor frames the story makes it clear that it is not the story itself that inspires belief but the circumstances that attend its "relation." Initially, it seems that the reputation of those who have passed the tale along will suffice to authenticate the events, but, as he names these people, the editor increases the doubt that he seems intent upon banishing. In the quotation that follows, I supply in brackets the probable antecedents of various pronouns, but note that, without my editorial amendments, these antecedents are not always clear. The editor tells the reader that the "relation"

> was sent by a gentleman, a justice of peace at Maidstone, in Kent, and a very intelligent person, to his friend in London, as it is here worded; which discourse is attested by a very sober and understanding gentlewoman and kinsman of the said gentleman's [the justice], who [the kinswoman] lives in Canterbury, within a few doors of the house in which the within-named Mrs. Bargrave lives; who [the justice] believes his kinswoman to be of so discerning a spirit as not to be put upon by any fallacy, and who [the kinswoman] positively assured him [the justice] that the whole matter as it is here related and laid down is what is really true, and what she herself had in the same words, as near as may be, from Mrs. Bargrave's own mouth, who, she [the kinswoman] knows, had no reason to invent and publish such a story, nor any design to forge and tell a lie, being a woman of much honesty and virtue, and her whole life a course, as it were, of piety. (ibid.)

In this account, both the authenticity of the "relation" and the credibility of Mrs. Bargrave rest on the belief of the justice's unnamed kinswoman; her credibility, in turn, rests on the justice's belief in her; and his credibility rests on the editor's belief that the justice is "a very intelligent person." The ambiguity of the pronouns allows for an even more unstable system of verification, however. If the second *who* refers not to the justice but to Mrs. Bargrave (the most proximate noun), then the basis for the justice's kinswoman's belief in Mrs. Bargrave is Mrs. Bargrave's belief in her.

Whether the logic of authentication in the preface is circular or simply torturously distended, it is further compounded by the "relation" itself. The author of the "relation," who is presumably the justice of the peace, seconds his kinswoman's belief that Mrs. Bargrave is reliable by the authority of his own experience: the narrator tells us that Mrs. Bargrave is "my intimate friend, and I can avouch for her reputation for these last fifteen or sixteen years" ("The Apparition," 253). This narrative frame, which asks the reader to believe in Mrs. Bargrave because the narrator does, almost immediately recedes, and, by the fourth paragraph of the "relation," Mrs. Bargrave becomes the focalizer of the narrative. For about half the tale, her story of the events proceeds without comment from the narrator, with the result that it is impossible for the reader to determine whether any given detail originated with Mrs. Bargrave or with the justice of the peace. This matters because it is precisely these details that now seem to authenticate the tale. In other words, the authority initially ascribed to the reputation of the various characters—the justice, his kinswoman, and Mrs. Bargrave—is now being propped on another kind of authority—that of the formal features associated with (what we call) fact. These features include the use of specific dates and place-names, the almost complete absence of rhetorical elaboration or amplification by metaphor, the use of a chronological narrative that enables the reader to be a virtual witness to the events related, and an absence of editorial commentary. A brief passage will give a sense of this: "In this house, on the 8th of September last, viz., 1705, she was sitting alone, in the forenoon, thinking over her unfortunate life. . . . [She] took up her sewing-work, which she had no sooner done but she hears a knocking at the door. She went to see who it was there, and this proved to be Mrs. Veal, her old friend, who was in a riding-habit: at that moment of time the clock struck twelve at noon" (255).

The narrator announces his mediating presence (which is implied by the use of the third-person pronouns) only when the narrative reaches Mrs. Veal's departure, at "three-quarters after one in the afternoon" ("The Apparition," 260). At this point, the narrator informs the reader that Mrs. Veal had died on "the 7th of September, at twelve o'clock at noon" (ibid.), and describes the initial transmission of the story (Mrs. Bargrave told Captain Watson's family, Mrs. Watson "blazed all about the town, and avouched the demonstration of the truth of Mrs. Bargrave's seeing Mrs. Veal's apparition; and Captain Watson carried two gentlemen immediately to Mrs. Bargrave's house to hear the relation from her own mouth. And then it spread so fast that gentlemen and persons of quality, the judicious and sceptical part of the world, flocked in upon her" [261]). Then the narrator bolsters his earlier positive assertion of belief in Mrs. Bargrave's credibility with a rebuke to those who doubt: "To suppose that Mrs. Bargrave could hatch such an invention as this from Friday noon till Saturday noon (supposing that she knew of Mrs. Veal's death the very first moment), without jumbling circumstances, and without any interest too, she must be more witty, fortunate, and wicked too, than any indifferent person, I dare say, will allow" (264). The narrative concludes with the narrator's definitive verdict, which rests on the two bases of feeling and faith: "This thing has very much affected me, and I am as well satisfied as I am of the best grounded matter of fact. And why should we dispute matter of fact because we cannot solve things of which we have no certain or demonstrative notions, seems strange to me. Mrs. Bargrave's authority and sincerity alone would have been undoubted in any other case" (265).

This compact tale, which, including the preface, is only fourteen pages long, claimed to be an efficient mechanism for generating belief, but it was also a medium for exploring what made a narrative credible in the first place. Because of the editor's preface, the belief that the tale aimed to inspire—the conviction that Mrs. Bargrave was telling the truth—is placed in the service of another belief, the conviction, as the editor phrases it, "that there is a life to come after this" ("The Apparition," 251). But the elaborate framing, with its repeated emphasis on the credibility (or lack thereof) of the tale's *handlers* suggests that this narrative was not simply an endorsement of apparitions or an afterlife. Even if it was commonplace in the early eighteenth century to link religious piety to belief in spirits, this combination still provided a rich vein for a more radical project: an experiment that tested the medium itself to see whether print could inspire belief for its own sake, not belief in anything in particular.

I place my emphasis on print because, in Defoe's presentation of this material, print is what finally confers credibility on the relation (and, less certainly, on the events described therein). Only when a series of men had shepherded the "relation" from the domestic sphere and the ephemeral realm of orality into the autonomous and semipermanent world of print could it be authenticated, and only as printed material could the tale circulate beyond Mrs. Bargrave's immediate audience. As we have seen, printed texts also play a central role in the events, for books constitute the focus of much of the two women's conversation. And each member of the story's chain of custody (the justice of the peace, his London friend, the author of the preface) can attest only to the "matter of fact" nature of the printed "relation," not to the accuracy of Mrs. Bargrave's report. In fact, once the focalization shifts away from Mrs. Bargrave and back to the justice-narrator, the latter informs us that the conversation Mrs. Bargrave reported was *not* accurate, at least with regard to the actual words Mrs. Veal used: "The apparition put [this discourse] in words much finer than Mrs. Bargrave said she could pretend to, and was much more than she can remember (for it cannot be thought that an hour and three-quarter's conversation could all be retained, though the main of it she thinks she does)" ("The Apparition," 258). Thus, print has fixed Mrs. Veal's words more reliably than Mrs. Bargrave was able to do, for, even though Mrs. Bargrave actually heard Mrs. Veal's words, she could not retain them in the same way or to the same extent that print was able to capture hers.

Because they were delivered orally, Mrs. Veal's actual words are now lost. What we have instead—what was preserved and fixed by Defoe—is a printed substitute for those words (and the events they describe) that authenticated itself precisely *because* it was printed, because it had been printed by men willing to vouch for each other and then to disappear into the production of this text. As a medium, that is, print seems not to require authenticating by its most immediate agent (the printer) because, as mediation, it seems to disappear, to require no hands. Print becomes invisible as it becomes familiar, of course, but, as it does so, it has the ability to neutralize the problem of authentification altogether.

"The Apparition of One Mrs. Veal," then, constitutes a complex and self-reflexive test of the ability of print to generate belief. In the process, it also hints at—though it does not explicitly create—a new generic possibility: a form of writing that might make events that were neither verifiable nor refutable plausible and that might enable a writer and a reader to imagine that events that were neither truths nor lies were, nevertheless, persuasive. The product of this kind of writing, which we now call *fiction*, required and cultivated a version of the same belief that enabled worn coins and worthless paper to function as currency in the early eighteenth century, of course, for both fiction and representative monetary instruments directed their users' attention away from the medium itself and toward that for which each token might be exchanged: pleasure, instruction, or commodities. In learning how to use the medium of print to generate such belief, then, Daniel Defoe was also revealing what his contemporaries demanded of both media: the instruments themselves should disappear so that what they seemed to represent could circulate (as) value.

The process I have been describing, which I have called *fictionalization*, has recently been linked to the distinctively modern differentiation between the public and the private. In making this compelling argument, Michael McKeon has helpfully named and described the special textual effect that helped facilitate this split. Calling it "concrete virtuality," McKeon identifies

Fielding as the author who initially theorized this effect as part of his attempt to distinguish satire from libel:

> In confining itself to the realm of the general, satire does not necessarily lose touch with the particularity of private individuals. Rather, it engages that particularity by offering readers a concrete individual, a fictional character, from whom they can learn through an equalizing process of identification—holding the glass to thousands of private readers in their closets—which depends on and is enabled by generalizing from the realm of the actual to a realm that is virtual but also concrete. . . . The effect of Fielding's rationale is to separate out two aspects of particularity, actual and concrete particularity, whose difference had lain dormant in traditional ways of thinking about that category in the absence of the unprecedentedly normative force of empirical actuality in early modern experience. . . . The emergence of these doctrines amounts to the emergence, not of fiction, but of our kind of fiction, which openly proclaims its fictionality against the backdrop of its apparent factuality. Only through the modern valorization of the actual—of the factual, the empirical, the historical—does the ancient and equivocal whole of "fiction" become resolvable into separate and unequivocal parts: falsehood and fiction, deceit and the aesthetic mode of truth, what is made up and what is made.[27]

McKeon's argument operates at a more abstract—and, thus, inclusive—level of analysis than I can pretend to attain, but our projects are compatible: we both aspire to illuminate what he calls the modern "division of knowledge," which contains (but also exceeds) the generic and disciplinary differentiations with which I am concerned. McKeon's notion of "concrete virtuality," moreover, helpfully clarifies the peculiar (though now familiar) status of the fictional character, which is both *concrete*, in being fully detailed by circumstantial particulars, and *virtual*, in not referring to an actual person. As McKeon suggests in the passage I have quoted (and as he explains at length in *The Secret History of Domesticity*), the authority granted to circumstantial particulars follows from "the modern valorization of the actual," which, as others have amply demonstrated, was cultivated through the generic features and social conventions associated with natural philosophy.[28] The emergence of fiction as a distinct product of imaginative writing required the elaboration of a distinct variant of circumstantial particularity—a variant that was concrete but not referential and that, therefore, was to be judged not by its accuracy but by altogether different criteria. One of these criteria was the density of particulars that characterized a text. Indeed, as Catherine Gallagher has argued, once fiction was fully separated from the continuum that had previously contained it, the dense weave of concrete but virtual particulars became a generic marker *for* fiction itself: "Thinness of detail almost always indicated specific extra-textual reference. But the more characters were loaded with circumstantial and seemingly insignificant properties, the more readers were assured that the text was at once assuming and making up for its reference to nobody at all."[29]

My interest in Defoe centers on his relation to the emergence of this identifiable realm of the fictional, which Fielding, Richardson, and other writers were soon to practice and theorize. Thus far, I have argued that Defoe resisted the breakup of the fact/fiction continuum even as he experimented with print's ability to elicit belief in events and characters that were neither decisively factual nor wholly imaginary. I now turn to another text in which Defoe engaged more thoroughly with the formal conventions that came to be associated with fiction before I show how booksellers (the forerunners of modern publishers) helped package this text in such a way as to push it into what had, by the 1740s, become the recognizable market category of fiction.

The watershed event that separated Defoe's early writings from his late productions was the rise, then fall, of the infamous South Sea Bubble in 1720. Numerous historians, literary scholars, and imaginative writers have chronicled the vertiginous events of this momentous year and contemporaries' reactions to them,[30] and a quick summary will be sufficient for my purposes. The South Sea Company was chartered in 1719 by a group of (largely Tory) Britons who were worried about the influence that the Bank of England was exercising on the government through its monopoly over the permanently funded national debt. It was a publicly traded corporation that invited public creditors to exchange their investments in government securities for South Sea stock; had it been successful, it would have created a strong rival to the Bank and, thus, a Tory financial interest capable of offsetting the influence of the Whigs. Parliament granted the company's charter, but, because legislators failed to set a rate for the exchange, South Sea stock was immediately subject to puffing by its directors, who hoped to sell their stock for an inflated price at the same time that they were investing heavily in the Bank of England. Investors thought (incorrectly) that the stock was backed by the authority of the government, and, with the example of the Mississippi Company and John Law's French land bank before them, they began to run up the price of South Sea shares. Very few investors really understood the scheme, which relied on secret books, insider manipulation of the market, and bribed politicians, but they poured their money into the venture nonetheless. South Sea stock opened above par in 1720, with £100 worth of stock bringing in £128 on the Exchange; by June, the shares were trading at £745; and, in July, the price peaked at over £1,000. As we saw in the preamble, multitudes of companies were launched in the wake of the South Sea Company's apparent success, and London was suddenly gripped by what nineteenth-century economists called a *speculative mania*. When the price of the company's shares began to fall precipitously in the late summer and early fall, investors began to panic, and sellers outnumbered buyers in a frenzy of escalating distress. By early December, the price had fallen to £191, having lost nearly six hundred points since early September. Realizing that Parliament was complicit in the fiasco, the public expressed its outrage in pamphlets, broadsides, and some of the most virulent satire of the century. Suddenly, credit seemed poisonous by its very nature, any government that derived its security from credit seemed suspect, and trusting any venture one could not personally control seemed potentially ruinous. In the terms that I have been using in this book, this constituted a full-blown crisis of the problematic of representation, for the collapse of the Bubble cruelly exposed all the fictions inherent in the credit economy, and, for a time at least, the government teetered on the brink as the public's outrage and despair threatened to render the country ungovernable.[31]

E. J. Clery has argued that the collapse of the Bubble and the personal losses experienced by writers like Alexander Pope and Jonathan Swift provoked not only a general decline in public confidence but also a tide of misogynistic writing, which proliferated as writers personally injured by the crash sought scapegoats to blame for their losses. Clery also argues that the stylistic and thematic innovations that Richardson introduced into the genre of the novel in the 1740s were designed to counteract this misogyny by associating women with virtue and by severing the long-standing connection between femininity and *fortuna*.[32] While I find Clery's argument persuasive, I want to emphasize a point that she engages only in passing: one of the strategies by which writers like Richardson counteracted the debilitating effects of the Bubble was to cultivate a distinctive realm of fiction, in which writers and readers might explore uncomfortable cultural anxieties without suffering their consequences. Through the medium of fiction, a writer might teach a reader to believe once more in possibilities that could not be proved; in so doing, a writer could encourage readers to accept the deferral that was essential to credit, both private and public, without feeling imperiled by risk. Even in the decades before Richardson began to feminize virtue, writers like Defoe were experimenting again with the relationship between print and belief as they gradually began to identify the special, healing virtues that might be associated with the distinctive form of representation we call *fiction*.

The text that we now call *Roxana* (1724) is not a *modern* fiction, for reasons that will become clear. Instead, like "The Apparition of One Mrs. Veal," this text opens with a preface that places the work within the fact/fiction continuum by both claiming that the events the text relates are facts and rendering that claim suspect. As with "The Apparition" again, this preface self-consciously constitutes one segment of an elaborate chain of transmission, in the course of which, once more, the tale is transferred from a woman's speech to the domain of print, which is overseen by men. The unnamed author of the preface, who has, presumably, arranged for the text to be printed, introduces an unnamed "Relator" (who either is also called the "Writer" or dictates the story to the Writer); the Relator heard the story from the "Beautiful Lady" who will subsequently be called Roxana. It is the Relator who vouches for the veracity of the tale: *"He* [the Relator] *takes the Liberty to say, That this Story differs from most of the Modern Performances of this Kind, tho' some of them have met with a very good Reception in the World:* I say, *It differs from them in this Great and Essential Article,* Namely, *That the Foundation of This is laid in Truth of* Fact; *and so the Work is not a Story, but a History."*[33] The Relator proceeds to undermine this claim about facts when he offers as *"a Pledge for the Credit"* of the story his personal acquaintance with *"this Lady's First Husband,* the Brewer" (35). This familiarity introduces doubt, both because the Brewer's initial role in this story is too limited for knowledge of his *"Bad Circumstances"* to count for much (he soon abandons Roxana) and because, when the Brewer briefly reappears (after more than a third of the narrative), he is revealed to be a chronic liar.

The Relator further sustains—and calls attention to—the fact/fiction continuum when he offers as verification for the bulk of the tale the fact that Roxana—another inveterate liar—has told the tale herself: *"As she has told it herself, we have the less Reason to question the Truth of that Part also"* (*Roxana*, 36). If the details of the story come from Roxana, however, the actual words come from the Relator, who apologizes for *"dressing up the Story in worse Cloaths than the* Lady, *whose words he speaks, prepared it for the World"* (35). By insisting that a gap separates the original telling of the events from the (printed) version in which they are now accessible, Defoe directs the reader's attention to mediation, as he had done in "The Apparition." Unlike "The Apparition," however, this narrative does not return the story to the narrator who opened it; in failing to do so, the text drops its formal emphasis on mediation. This abandonment of the frame, along with the length of the narrative and its focalization through a single character, also makes the theme of mediation disappear: in the course of the text's three hundred or so pages (in a modern edition), most readers forget that Roxana's story is being translated into the words of a Relator.

The erasure of the framing (and authenticating) Relator is important because it pushes the text toward what McKeon calls "concrete virtuality": once the authenticating apparatus of the Relator disappears, the only feature that authenticates the narrated events is "Roxana" herself, and she authenticates them not by referencing a real or quasi-autobiographical person (as the Relator might be said to do) but simply by speaking in the manner that the fully realized characters we associate with fictions do. Unlike Lady Credit, in other words, and unlike Mrs. Veal, Roxana is neither a rhetorical figure, nor a character taken from another story (real or imaginary), but a concretely virtual character that elicits that "equalizing process of identification" that McKeon describes. This is the kind of character with which we are now thoroughly familiar as one of the signature features of realist fiction—and of the novel in particular. In many instances, this feature distinguishes a text *as* fiction because it does not refer to a real individual but is, nevertheless, *realistic*—that is, a plausible because recognizable, concretely detailed, lifelike, and self-consistent individual.

Even though it approaches this kind of fiction, however, the text we call *Roxana* does not conform to all the norms that came to be associated with fiction during the middle decades of the eighteenth century. The text does fulfill the criterion I have already mentioned—it has plenty of dense particularization—but, in at least two other respects, *Roxana* falls short of a recognizably modern fiction. Both these constitute violations of a criterion that was at least as important as density of particularization for identifying and judging a fiction. The criterion I have in mind was unity, which was a property that seventeenth- and eighteenth-century writers derived from Aristotle's discussion of the categories. Aristotle had described six categories—the moral, the fable, character, sentiment, language, and spectacle—but assigned them all a single normative feature: each category should be self-consistent so as to render the entire imaginative construction self-consistent and, therefore, "probable."

By the beginning of the eighteenth century, as Douglas Patey has shown, British writers had begun to adopt the criterion of unity that Aristotle applied to the drama, and, during the next decades, other writers adapted this standard to fit imaginative writing of all kinds.[34] As writers like Joseph Addison, Henry Fielding, George Campbell, and Samuel Johnson began to do so, they also introduced what Patey calls a "split" into the concept of probability. This split can be mapped onto the division between imaginative and informational writing, for the two kinds of probability were increasingly viewed as two different kinds of mediation; they also established two different but related standards for judging a printed work. "Beginning in mid-century," Patey explains, "ordinary probability is usually thought to take its objects particularly from the mundane details of everyday social life; 'poetical probability' is fidelity to deeper psychological truths, permanent truths of the heart and its emotions."[35] As part of this generic and philosophical split, the concept of *nature*, when used by imaginative writers and theorists, came to mean almost exclusively human nature, and, as imaginative writers restricted the meaning of *nature* in this way, they also elevated character in the hierarchy of formal features by which one could identify a text as fiction. By the 1760s, character had become the most important feature of any imaginative text; but, even before the hierarchy of "poetical probability" was fully reorganized, some writers insisted that unity of character was capable of organizing the unity of all the other categories and, thus, the unity of the text as a whole. In the words of James Harris, writing in 1744, a character could render imaginative action credible if the narrated actions are "*various, and yet consistent . . . ; a* Succession, *enabling us to conjecture,* what the Person of the Drama will do in the *future,* from what already he has done in the *past.*"[36]

Probability, which was the philosophical and formal effect generated by a writer's adherence to the unities, was held to be important for yet another reason. In Patey's words: "The probable mediate[d] the falsehood of the fictional work and the truth of the reality it imitate[d]."[37] In other words, for writers and theorists who were attempting to neutralize the negative connotations that some eighteenth-century Britons associated with fiction because it was *a lie,* the concept of probability, and the availability of clear criteria by which to judge it, rendered imaginative writing immune from the truth test to which informational writing had to submit. Having recognizable and socially agreed-on criteria by which to judge fictional probability, in turn, helped manage what I am calling the *problematic of representation* because such criteria provided a reliable system that allowed one to evaluate the features internal to a text *but not* the relationship between the text and the ground of its referential system. Adherence to the unities, especially the unity of character, was held to reinforce fiction's immunity from this kind of evaluation, for even eighteenth-century divines associated unity with the harmony God installed in the universe. If an imaginative work could be shown to contain self-consistent characters that organized a formally unified plot to advance a single moral in sentiments that followed naturally from each other and that produced a unified spectacle in language that was consistent too, then that work was held to be demonstrably virtuous. Even if it was not referential, it constituted a model, in miniature, of God's masterwork.

We will see in chapter 5 how the split within the concept of probability, and the relative autonomy this enabled theorists to grant the imaginative work (in the guise of organic unity), opened the door for later writers, like Wordsworth and Coleridge, to elaborate a model of value that was not simply an alternative to the value accorded informational writing but an alternative to the *form* of value economic writers associated with the credit economy. Lest we get ahead of ourselves, however, let me return to Defoe's *Roxana*, which was published hard on the heels of the South Sea Bubble but before the criteria of unity and probability had been articulated in this modern way. In 1724, it seemed critical to neutralize the problematic of representation, but the modern, aesthetic model by which this would be done had yet to be refined: probability had yet to be split into its constitutive parts, and the criterion of unity had yet to be successfully transferred from drama to other kinds of imaginative writing. It should not surprise us, then, that Defoe's text does not conform to all our modern criteria for fiction. Nor should it surprise us that, as these critical concepts were elaborated and refined, subsequent publishers tried to alter Defoe's text so that it would do so. Before showing how midcentury publishers altered Defoe's text, I will describe its two most noticeable violations of the criteria that midcentury writers used to evaluate fiction.

The first appears in the realm of character. Character in *Roxana* fails the test of unity or consistency in two senses. First, the text contains two different modes of characterization: while the characterization of Roxana and her maidservant Amy features the dense particularization and virtuality that McKeon associates with realist fiction, another character is characterized in an altogether different way. This character, Sir Robert Claypole, is neither particularly concrete—that is, circumstantially detailed—nor virtual—that is, fictional rather than referential. Instead, Claypole, who advises Roxana about certain investments, is barely described at all; and, more important, this character refers to a real historical individual who, in actual life, performed exactly the services for real people that this character provides Roxana in Defoe's text. Thus, Claypole helps Roxana "raise [her] Fortune to a prodigious Height" by convincing her to save, invest, and take advantage of the ability of capital to accrue interest (*Roxana*, 207). That Defoe chose not to develop the text's only historically referential character by giving a wealth of concrete particulars is in keeping with the theoretical conviction we have already seen: in cases involving actual people, he associated using too many particulars with divisiveness and injury. As he explained of another, nonfictive narration: "If this unhappy Story were a Romance, a Fiction, contrived to illustrate the Subject, I should give it you with all its abhorred Particulars, as far as decency of Language would permit.... But when Facts, however flagrant, are too near home, and the miserable Sufferers already too much oppressed with the Injury, we must not add to their Afflictions by too publick a use of the Calamity to embellish our Story."[38]

In mixing two kinds of characterization in a single text, Defoe preserved the fact/fiction continuum, which the concrete virtuality of the rest of the characters might otherwise render obsolete. But including the referential character Claypole in the concrete virtuality of *Roxana* also introduced questions that the text could not address or resolve. The real Sir Robert Clayton prospered during the reign of Charles II and died in 1707; but, in the opening pages of her story, Roxana tells the reader that she was ten years old in 1683, when her father brought her to London (37). A birth date of 1673 would make Roxana thirty-four in the year of Clayton's death; even though this is a plausible age at which an eighteenth-century individual might have conducted complicated financial transactions, it is obviously not the age that the character Roxana has attained by 1707. It is clear from other references in the text that Roxana amassed the bulk of her English wealth *after* the real Clayton's death—that is, after 1715—for much of this action is explicitly set during the period of George I's court.[39] In 1724, this mixed mode of characterization would not have seemed particularly troubling, for its first readers would presumably not have required the text *either* to refer consistently to actual facts, as a referential text would later be asked to do, *or* to be internally consistent, as an imaginative work would eventually be asked to do. It was only with the split between kinds of probability and kinds of genres that these criteria became applicable and mutually exclusive, as we will see.

Roxana's second violation of the norm of consistency concerns the title character herself. This character is inconsistent in two senses. Thematically, she is consistently inconsistent: inconsistency as *deceit* is Roxana's modus operandi. Thus, she is almost never who she says she is—she is not a lady of quality, as she pretends to be, nor is she French, which she sometimes claims; she does not consistently tell the truth; and Roxana is not even her real name. But this character is inconsistent in another sense as well: she is also inconsistent in her self-representations to the narrator and in the narrative.[40] As the Relator notes in the preface, the character sometimes professes remorse but more frequently seems hardened to her crimes; sometimes she attributes her misfortunes to fate, and sometimes she takes responsibility for them. Even more significantly, at a critical moment in the narration, she suddenly reveals an entire story that she now claims has been unfolding all along as an unnarrated preoccupation she supposedly felt but did not relate.

This story, which erupts into the narrative about two-thirds of the way through, concerns one of Roxana's children, the daughter who (she now tells us) is named for her—Susan. As with nearly all the references to her children, Roxana introduces this story in a manner that explicitly calls attention to its disruptive relation to her main story, the story of herself: "I must now go back to another Scene, and join it to this End of my Story, which will compleat all my Concern with *England, at least,* all that I shall bring into this Account. I have hinted at large, what I had done for my two Sons, one at *Messina,* and the other in the *Indies.* But I have not gone thorow the Story of my two Daughters" (*Roxana,* 311). The remainder of the narrative focuses on Susan's attempts to corroborate her suspicion that her former mistress Roxana is actually her mother, the maidservant Amy's determination to eliminate Susan, the likely (but not narrated) murder of Susan, and Roxana's final—if characteristic—alternation between enjoyment of her wealth and remorse for having let Amy kill Susan. The last two paragraphs of the first edition bring the narrative to an end, but they neither resolve the inconsistency that marks the character's attitudes nor explain why what (presumably) happened to Susan was narrated out of the order in which it occurred:

> I can say no more now, but that, *as above,* being arriv'd in *Holland,* with my Spouse and his Son, *formerly mention'd,* I appear'd there with all the Splendor and Equipage suitable to our new Prospect, *as I have already observ'd.*
>
> Here, after some few Years of flourishing, and outwardly happy Circumstances, I fell into a dreadful Course of Calamities, and *Amy* also; the very Reverse of our former Good Days; the Blast of Heaven seem'd to follow the Injury done the poor Girl, by us both; and I was brought so low again, that my Repentance seem'd to be only the Consequence of my Misery, as my Misery was of my Crime. (378–79)

Both the inconsistencies that we can identify in the overall system of characterization in *Roxana* and the ones manifested by the character Roxana challenge the Aristotelian criterion for probability—unity. By so doing, they reveal that this text was not quite fiction in our modern sense. The very inconsistencies that keep *Roxana* from conforming precisely to our modern definition of *fiction,* however, did perform a social function in the early eighteenth century: they prolonged the process by which the reader tried to form an opinion about Roxana. Because the text makes it so difficult to know what to make of Roxana, the reader had to keep making conjectures about her. Unlike a referentially accurate narrative, in other words, in which a reader would have known to convict Roxana of lying, or a realist fiction, in which lying might seem like a recognizable behavior in a flawed character, this text asked readers to test and retest the status of the narrative, the veracity of its chief character, and the relationship between this character's words and her creditworthiness. In so doing, *Roxana* encouraged readers to examine their own process of evaluation so as to determine whether—and what—to believe.

My point is that, in one sense at least, *Roxana* constituted a primer in the kind of evaluation that everyday credit transactions required in the eighteenth century and whose importance was magnified by the speculative possibilities—and fiasco—of the Bubble year. Before extending credit to a stranger or investing money in a speculative venture, an individual had to decide, by a complex process of evaluation and prediction, whether what the debtor or company promoter said about himself or the company was true, whether the assets he described were real, whether he was likely to be able (or willing) to repay the debt when it fell due, and whether the predicted profits were likely to materialize. If the tradesman (or tradeswoman) or investor knew at the beginning of the transaction that the stranger was a liar, then the decisionmaking process was unnecessary; if the tradesman or investor knew that the assets, willingness to repay, and productive potential were real, then the decision was easily made. It was only in a situation of undecidability, like that created by *Roxana*, that evaluation had to take the form of *deliberation*—a self-conscious consideration of evidence, probability, and generalization. Because he was not restricted to the narrative features from which later imaginative writers would forge fully virtual worlds, Defoe was not asking readers to suspend their disbelief. Instead, he rendered *Roxana* an exercise in the social process of evaluation that made the credit economy work. Engaging with this text, an early-eighteenth-century reader would have been encouraged to make precisely the kind of judgment later, explicitly fictional texts did not require: that about whether to believe or doubt, whether to extend one's credit or withhold it.

Even if the text we call *Roxana* initially exercised this social function, it soon lost its ability to do so. Once the features we associate with fiction were assembled and associated with the form we call *the novel*, in texts like

Richardson's *Pamela*, and theorized, in works like Fielding's *Joseph Andrews*, the fact/fiction continuum could not remain intact. Its breakup did not have the catastrophic effects that accompanied the emergence into visibility of the problematic of representation, however. On the contrary: by creating a distinct category of fiction that neutralized the gap between sign and referent, this breakup helped push the problematic back out of sight. But this breakup did have deleterious effects for works like *Roxana*. In the context of the separate *aesthetic* and *informational or theoretical* agendas that took the place of the fact/fiction continuum, attempts to serve the kind of *social* agenda I have associated with *Roxana* began to seem increasingly incoherent. Fiction became a recognizable realm that assumed the reader's ability to suspend disbelief; and information, and its attendant theory, became the customary products of other kinds of writing, kinds that used facts and models to generate conviction. As character was gradually moved higher in the hierarchy of features that made a fiction probable, moreover, subsequent readers also grew intolerant of characters that displayed the kind of inconsistencies we see in Defoe's last heroine.[41] During the middle decades of the century, as prose fiction became the site of some of the most imaginative stylistic and marketing innovations of the century, publishers tried to make Defoe's final imaginative work fit the criterion applied to all aesthetic properties so as to capitalize on the popularity of his first fiction-like production, *Robinson Crusoe*. In altering the text to make it conform to the market model, they also left clues about how *Roxana*'s social agenda was transformed in order to serve the aesthetic agenda associated with modern fiction.

I discuss the market relations that linked authors, publishers, and texts in more detail in the first interchapter. Here, it is important just to note that, once an author sold the copyright to a work, he or she did not typically control the way in which the text was packaged or marketed. Publishers and printers enjoyed considerable latitude in determining how a book looked, and they were understandably eager to imitate any format that had proved its market appeal. Among the successful mid-eighteenth-century texts, none was more noteworthy than *Pamela*, which Richardson issued from his own printer's shop in 1740. Just two years later, Defoe's text was reprinted, but not under the elaborate title it had originally borne: *The Fortunate Mistress; or, A History of the Life and Vast Variety of Fortunes of Mademoiselle de Beleau, Afterwards call'd The Countess de Wintselsheim, in Germany. Being the Person known by the Name of the Lady Roxana, in the Time of Charles II.*[42] Instead of this copious, descriptive title, the text was reprinted as *Roxana*, and this name featured prominently in all subsequent eighteenth-century editions.[43] While we cannot say for certain that Defoe's publisher was imitating Richardson's work, a text advertised under a woman's single proper name had at least one feature in common with Richardson's novel. Treating *Pamela* as "the hitherto much-wanted Standard or Pattern for this kind of Writing," as one of Richardson's admirers advised,[44] in other words, had implications for publishers as well as authors. For both, making an imaginative work allude to or resemble *Pamela* was a way of making it visible in a market beginning to be crowded with competitors.

Beyond making *Roxana* resemble *Pamela* superficially, the change in the title of Defoe's text might also have affected readers' expectations about—or even their experience of—this book. Using a single proper name in the wake of *Pamela* might have encouraged readers to expect that Roxana would be as consistent as Richardson's heroine claimed to be and, thus, to overlook the inconsistencies that I have identified in Defoe's text.[45] Publishers of editions in 1740, 1750, and 1755 reinforced such expectations when they introduced changes designed to make the text conform to the Aristotelian norms the first edition violated. Some of these changes clarified the relationship between the author of the preface (the Relator) and the principal character, thereby giving the transmission of the story a coherent history.[46] Others provided the closure that the original story lacked by underscoring and elaborating the moral transformation that Roxana just hints at in the 1724 edition. Thus, in the 1740 edition, Roxana "freely resigned her Soul to the Mercy of him who gave it"; in the 1750 edition, she "repented of every bad Action, especially the little Value she had for her Children"; and, in the 1775 edition, her husband assures the Relator that his wife, "being sensibly touched with the remembrance of her former follies[,] . . . had for several months past been truly a penitent."[47]

John Mullan points out that most versions of *Roxana* published in the mid-eighteenth century and the nineteenth also "erased the possibility that the daughter might have been murdered, and made the protagonist discover some of the maternal feeling that she had scandalously failed to display (and noticed herself failing to display) in the course of her history."[48] Such changes were consistent not only with eighteenth-century publishers' efforts to make their products sell but also with the aesthetic agenda of elevating the status of the novel in particular in the hierarchy of kinds of imaginative writing, an elevation that began in the wake of the South Sea Bubble. To elevate this form, publishers and writers alike tried to disavow any connection between new novels and the secret histories or criminal tales that had proliferated in the preceding decades.[49] Making new novels conform to the Aristotelian categories also helped encourage readers and reviewers to evaluate these texts as *fictions*, not as references to real people, and this, in turn, helped consolidate the category of fiction as a distinctive kind of representation that demanded evaluative criterion of its own. In a recursive dynamic that would operate effectively until the 1790s, publishers and fiction writers rapidly formulated and promoted increasingly self-evident standards for evaluating the increasingly recognizable products we call *novels*. Because of the conditions of the publishing industry that I describe in the first interchapter, these standards simultaneously fulfilled aesthetic, ethical, and economic rationales. That is, during the middle decades of the eighteenth century, a novel—that is, a new, generically particular kind of fiction—could simultaneously conform to the Aristotelian categories, thus satisfying aesthetic criteria, convey moral lessons by eliciting identification with a virtual character, thus satisfying ethical criteria, and appeal to readers, thus prospering as a commodity. As we will see in the first interchapter and in chapters 3 and 5, at the turn into the nineteenth century, the temporary coincidence of aesthetic and economic rationales collapsed under the twin pressures of a dramatic expansion in the number and kinds of new imaginative texts and a critical backlash, by poets in particular, against what they viewed as the degradation of Literary writing by popular fiction. To writers like Wordsworth and Coleridge, the aesthetic and economic rationales briefly sutured together by mid-eighteenth-century writers and publishers were fundamentally incompatible, and this incompatibility led Wordsworth to theorize the nonmarket criterion of value that was implicit in the emergent aesthetic agenda. This kind of value was theoretically indifferent to, and protected from, the vicissitudes and dynamics of the market.

In many of the 1740s texts that provided the norms for the new kind of fiction we call *the novel*, we can see harbingers of the breakup that was to come. One sign of the rupture that was eventually to separate the aesthetic and the informational rationales is mid-eighteenth-century novelists' tendency to marginalize financial themes and to subordinate references to money to an ethical agenda that serves the categories of characterization or plot. In the next section, I show how this marginalization works in Fielding's *Tom Jones*. Here, I want simply to note that the kind of passages one finds in *Roxana* that precisely (and accurately) detail the way money could be transferred from country to country in the early eighteenth century, the way compound interest worked, or the way that mortgages could function as modes of investment are absent from novels like *Clarissa* (1747–49). In the latter novel, Richardson's references to Clarissa's inheritance feature prominently only at the beginning of the text, and they function here and throughout primarily as indices to this and other characters' moral worth or as incidents in the novel's complex plots. The ability to use money, in other words, or to transcend the desire to do so, becomes one among many markers of a character's "deepest" nature, and references to financial matters are often used to initiate or turn the plot.[50] Indeed, as indices of a character's interior "depths," novelists' references to money helped naturalize plot turns that could otherwise have been attributed to coincidences; they did so, paradoxically, by fictively rendering a character's relationship to money a psychological, rather than a material, matter. Thus, the marginalization of monetary matters *in* fictions helped naturalize the psychologization of economic behavior at the same time that it helped attenuate the relationship between the medium that conveyed this lesson—the book itself—and the market in which it was produced, distributed, purchased, and consumed.

As the final section of this chapter reveals, by the 1770s, the relationship between representations *of* monetary matters in fictional works and the operation of the credit economy had already begun to submit to the effacements and mystifications that accompanied the disciplinary disaggregation that this study chronicles. This effacement, of course, was not simply an effect of transformations within the kind of writing we call *Literary*; it was also one among many of the outcomes of the systematization of the writing we call *economic*.

Sir James Steuart's Principles of Political Economy: Between Fiction and Theory

If Defoe's essays on credit seem to belong to a guidebook on effective commercial behavior, the tale of Mrs. Veal and the text we call *Roxana* resemble experiments in the ways in which print could generate belief. While Defoe did not call these texts *experiments*, and even though they did not use either the procedures of late-seventeenth-century natural philosophy or the method that Francis Hutcheson began to associate with experimental moral philosophy in the 1720s, these forays into the capabilities of print were thematically (if not formally) affiliated with the eighteenth-century philosophical experiments that theorized the relationship between individual behavior, national progress, and the dynamics of commercial society.[51] Like some of Defoe's earliest writings, which oscillated between encouraging self-government and invoking some kind of central authority to ensure discipline, moreover, all the writings I have thus far examined reveal that, like the Scottish moral philosophers, Defoe was trying to figure out how to cultivate the subjective motivations that would promote self-government in an increasingly commercial society. If, as he explained in *The Complete*

English Tradesman, creditworthy behavior inspired the kind of belief that encouraged lenders to extend more credit to the tradesman, then figuring out how to use writing to produce creditworthy behavior was a socially constructive goal.[52] And, if the creditworthy behavior of the tradesman could be generalized to the members of polite society as a whole, then writing about credit could actively contribute to the progress of a commercializing nation like Britain.

We can see this tendency fairly easily in Defoe's writings because so many of them focus explicitly on belief and its relationship to print, credibility, and credit. Defoe's imaginative writings did not consistently *theorize* the subject of credibility, as *The Complete English Tradesman* did mercantile credit, but they made it possible for readers to engage in the process of extending credit—or refusing to do so—because they solicited the kind of evaluative process I have associated with *Roxana*. Many of Defoe's imaginative writings, moreover, incidentally provided financial *information*. As the publication history I have described reveals, however, in the decades after Defoe's death, the social and informational agendas that texts like *Roxana* initially performed were subordinated to the aesthetic agenda according to which recognizable fictions were increasingly evaluated, as writers and publishers increasingly began to insist on the differences that distinguished various kinds of writing instead of the continuum that had once linked them.

As I pointed out in my introduction, the process by which writers and publishers differentiated imaginative and economic writing during the middle decades of the eighteenth century was gradual and uneven. I can describe the various facets of this process only in relatively general terms, and I will use the metaphor of levels, rather than that of chronological stages, in order to convey its unevenness. At one level, particular works were increasingly shaped to differentiated agendas or rationales—in this case, imaginative writing was adapted to fit the aesthetic rationale derived from Aristotelian poetics, and economic writing was adapted to an informational or explanatory rationale. At another level, and to serve these rationales, writers selected formal features and gave each one more or less emphasis in order to make a particular work conform to what were emerging as generic norms. At still another level, writers introduced distinctions *within* each of the broad kinds of writing precipitated out of the fact/fiction continuum. Sometimes, as in the case of economic writing, these distinctions made different subsets of the general kind serve different, but related, purposes. Thus as we saw in chapter 1, from the mid-seventeenth century, the subset of economic writing called *money* functioned to *mediate value* and *facilitate exchange*; by the end of that century, another subset of economic writing was providing *information* in the form of specialized lists of prices and shipping news; and, during the eighteenth century, another variant of economic writing began to circulate economic *theory* in the form of political economic treatises, which I discuss in just a moment. In the broad category of imaginative writing, authors introduced their own innovations. Some of these elaborated existing generic distinctions, which sometimes crossed over into differences in format as well (satire sometimes took the form of prose, sometimes that of poetry, e.g.). Others tried to alter the relative prestige accorded various genres and formats (all kinds of poetry continued to be valued more than prose fiction, but some kinds of poems—like lyric—gradually rose in the hierarchy of poetic forms). Still others rearranged the order of features within the hierarchy that defined a given subgenre (character rapidly rose in importance as a feature of prose fiction, e.g.; the rhymed couplet gradually fell as a valued feature of poetic forms). One of the innovations imaginative writers (and publishers) experimented with installed a variant of difference *within* individual texts; thus, as I mentioned in the preamble, prefaces, letters to the reader, and the kind of appendices Richardson attached to *Clarissa* provided venues for metacommentary within the pages of a single book. These instructed readers about how to understand various features of the fiction themselves and sought to preempt—or influence—critical responses to these works.

This process of generic distinction accelerated during the eighteenth century. Even as it did so, however, numerous publications continued to appear that contained features associated with or borrowed from the kinds of writing that were rapidly being differentiated from each other. It is useful to examine a few of these texts, for they reveal some of the ways that the sorting out and differentiation occurred. In this section, I place three texts in relation to each other in order to highlight their similarities and differences against the backdrop of this differentiating process; in chapters 3, 4, and 5, and in the second interchapter, I examine additional texts in some detail to show how what were rapidly becoming genre-specific features, when housed in a single text, might enable a particular text to serve both the aesthetic rationale associated with imaginative writing and the informational and explanatory rationales associated with economic writing *or* render a text generically anomalous because it did not conform to either rationale. Here, and in later sections of this book, I call such texts *hybrids*, but I need to make it clear that these texts were not all hybrids in the same sense. The earlier texts I discuss, including the ones I examine in this chapter, look to us like hybrids because we can recognize in them competing rationales and the features that supported these agendas; but, to contemporaries, they might not have looked like hybrids at all because, as was the case with Defoe's writings on credit, they were published before the aesthetic and informational agendas had been so clearly separated. We can make sense of some of the other texts I examine later, especially the novels of Charles Reade, by calling them *hybrids*; but, again, to contemporaries, this term might not have seemed appropriate because, by the late 1860s, the aesthetic and informational agendas had come to seem *so* different that readers could not imagine consulting a novel for reliable information. My use of the concept of hybrid, then, is heuristic; in each case, I am describing not a compound made up of two identifiable, historically distinct parts but a phenomenon that looks like a compound to us because it was precipitated out during a process of generic and disciplinary change.

I need to make one more prefatory point. Even though I argue that all the texts I examine here performed the general function of mediating the credit economy, I want to remind readers that they did not do so in the same way. Thus, I am not arguing, as many scholars have done, that there was a single "economic discourse," "plot," or "narrative" that all these texts articulated or to which they contributed.[53] Instead, I am arguing that *one* of the functions performed by each of these texts was to naturalize the credit economy; but, in each case, this function coexisted with other agendas, which, as genres became increasingly differentiated, increasingly seemed incomparable too. These differences seem to me as important as the texts' similarities, and I do my best to respect them in the pages that follow.

In this section, I examine Sir James Steuart's *Inquiry into the Principles of Political Economy* (1767) in relation, first, to Henry Fielding's *Tom Jones* (1749) and, second, to Adam Smith's *The Wealth of Nations* (1776). The first pairing will no doubt be more surprising than the second, but, as we will see, Steuart's work shares almost as many features with *Tom Jones* as it does with *The Wealth of Nations*, and placing the economic treatise alongside the novel enables us to see the overlap that persisted between the two kinds of writing, even after the fact/fiction continuum had been broken up. Placing these two texts side by side also enables us to see how this overlap was managed—or disciplined—as part of the process by which the features that we associate with political economy or economic theory were grouped together and used to define a new, relatively stable genre. The norms of this genre were established by Smith's text, even though later political economists continued to experiment with variations on the features Smith used, in terms of both their relative importance and the way they could be mixed—for example, how mathematical language might be mixed with historical narratives or how such narratives might be mixed with abstract, theoretical models. By comparing Steuart's *Principles* with *The Wealth of Nations*, we can see how Smith omitted some features that Steuart borrowed from imaginative writing because, by 1776, these features had come to seem too fictive for the informational and explanatory agendas that economic writing was increasingly expected to advance.

————

Sir James Steuart (1713–80) was an aristocratic Scotsman whose outspoken support for restoring the Stuart monarchy led him to flee his homeland in the wake of the failed uprising of 1745. During his eighteen-year exile, Steuart lived primarily in France, but he also traveled extensively in Europe, in part at least to collect materials for the elaborate treatise on political economy that he finally published in 1767, soon after his return to Britain.[54] Given the relatively small numbers in which such books were printed and their typically high price, we can assume that Steuart's audience was quite limited during his lifetime. As was the case with many of the economic pamphlets McCulloch anthologized, Steuart's *Principles* was deemed to be important only retrospectively, from the perspective of the *discipline* of political economy, and as part of what eventually became a canon. From the vantage point of modern historians of the discipline, Steuart's work has seemed important because it is the first example of *systematic* political economy.[55] Beyond this, modern scholars have highlighted Steuart's arguments about money and monetary policy, his theory that inadequate demand might slow the development of modern economies—the argument that led him to emphasize monetary theory—and his belief that legislators should be ready to intervene in monetary policy. For the nineteenth-century economic writers who were trying to create a canon, by contrast (writers like McCulloch), these positions disqualified Steuart as a candidate for canonization. His position on failing demand, as we will see, directly contradicted the orthodoxy of Say's law; and his support for government intervention ran afoul of the doctrine of laissez-faire, which reigned virtually unchallenged from Adam Smith through the 1870s.[56]

In this discussion, I primarily emphasize not the content of Steuart's *Principles* but its formal features—that is, the formal contributions his treatise made to the genre we now call *political economy* or *political economic theory*. I emphasize form because doing so enables me to show how Steuart's work shared some of the features that appeared in midcentury imaginative writing but adapted those features to serve the informational and explanatory rationales increasingly associated with theoretical writing. Even though Steuart altered these features, however, simply including them made his examples seem inadequate beside the fully abstract model that Adam Smith was soon to produce. Steuart did want to present a general account of market society. As he explained in his preface, his purpose in writing the *Principles* was to "reduc[e] . . . to principles, and to form . . . into a regular science, the complicated interests of domestic policy."[57] As we are about to see, however, Steuart was suspicious of purely theoretical accounts, abstraction as a mode of knowledge, and formal models in general. He identified as his primary addressee a figure that, ontologically, hovered between the pure abstractions that populated theoretical treatises and the kind of concretely virtual character we find in novels of the period. He called this figure "the statesman." In order to influence the actual lawmakers this figure represented—as well as the people the statesman governed—Steuart deemed novelistic features appropriate, for, if he could encourage readers to project themselves into the historical and geographically distant situations he had discovered in his research, he might persuade them to sympathize with the statesman, to adopt the policies the statesman endorsed, and to submit to the government he superintended.

Steuart was not the first writer to attempt to persuade readers to take one or another position on economic subjects, of course. As we have already seen, some versions of what we might call *economic theory* appeared in the seventeenth century, alongside and as part of texts designed to provide both market information and political advice. The primary innovation of Steuart's *Principles* was to separate economic theory from politically interested advice by providing a comprehensive picture of a market system that was simultaneously national and international in nature. To provide this systematic picture, and to reduce his observations to "principles," Steuart created a mode of presentation that helped order his vast archive of materials by subdividing the subject into seven general categories: population and agriculture, trade and industry, money and coin, credit and debts, interest and circulation, banks, exchange, and public credit, and taxes. In his multivolume work, these subsections are linked by a chronological narrative that provides a developmental account of modern society; the theme of development recurs within each of these topics and in their relation to each other as well.[58] This developmental narrative is repeatedly interrupted, however, by addresses to the reader, which sometimes explicitly solicit imaginative engagement with the situation Steuart is describing and sometimes comment reflexively on the work's organizational plan, its strengths, and its weaknesses. The result is neither the kind of protofictional imaginative conceit we saw in Defoe's writings on credit nor the fully schematic analysis that economists like David Ricardo would compose half a century later. Instead, Steuart's *Principles* can be said to occupy the generic territory *between* prose fiction (the novel) and theory, as one example of how two genres that were already being separated out from each other could still overlap in the 1760s.

We can measure the distance between Steuart's work and the kind of theoretical treatise that Ricardo wrote by noting Steuart's repeated desire to "avoid abstraction as much as possible." As part of his aversion to abstraction, Steuart also insisted that he was not creating a "system" but only providing the materials from which someone else might create such a model. "By tracing out a succession of principles, consistent with the nature of man and with one another," he wrote, he was trying to "endeavour to furnish some materials towards the forming of a good one" (*Principles*, 1:24). His repudiation of the system was largely a renunciation of French theorists' work, as he made clear when he rejected "*Systemes.*" Such treatises, he explained,

> are no more than a chain of contingent consequences, drawn from a few fundamental maxims, adopted, perhaps, rashly. Such systems are mere conceits: they mislead the understanding, and efface the path to truth. An induction is formed, from whence a conclusion, called a principle, is drawn and defined; but this is no sooner done, than the author extends its influence far beyond the limits of the ideas present to his understanding, when he made his "definition." The best method, therefore, to detect a pretended system, is always to substitute the definition in place of the term. (9)

Elsewhere, Steuart referred to "the modern vice of forming systems, by wiredrawing many relations in order to make them answer" (3:165). Wiredrawing was a metal-shaping process in which a wire rod was drawn through a single, narrowing die or adjacent dies in order to reduce the diameter of the rod. Because the volume of the wire remained the same, its length changed in proportion to its new diameter. By associating this method with French writers, and by metaphorically invoking the kind of industrial process chronicled in Diderot's *Encyclopédie*, Steuart distinguished between (British) "principles," which remained closely related to observable data, and (French) "principles," which followed the logic of (or inspired the production of additional parts for) the "system" to which they belonged.

Instead of organizing his argument according to the "conceit" of first principles, Steuart wanted to mix deduction with induction by using illustrations derived from actual observations to generate conclusions that were general without being abstract. Noboru Kobayashi calls the result "*descrip-*

tive history"; whereas Adam Smith tended to separate theoretical observations from historical description, as we will see in a moment, Steuart tried to keep them "intertwined."[59] It was in an effort to keep theory or "principles" intertwined with historical and eyewitness accounts that Steuart mixed the features I have described: particularized, often detailed accounts of historical and contemporary illustrations, descriptions of principles that he presented as universal or ahistorical, and first-person narrative intrusions that commented self-reflexively on his own method. The resulting mix of features constituted the first comprehensive model of market society, even if this model was neither abstract nor, formally, a system. It also preserved a formal link between two genres that were in the process of being separated from each other: fiction and theory.

In setting Steuart's *Principles* alongside *Tom Jones*, I do not mean to imply that any readers—whether Fielding's contemporaries or ours—would read the two texts in the same way. By 1767, the protocols for the two different kinds of writing were sufficiently differentiated to prevent what had already begun to seem like a category mistake; even by 1749, when Fielding published *Tom Jones*, the formal features that characterized fiction had begun to be codified—in part through the metacommentary about the novel that Fielding had included in *Joseph Andrews*. Thus, the concrete and virtual characters that appear in *Tom Jones* differ markedly from their counterparts in the *Principles*; the events chronicled in the former are explicitly made up, not derived from historical examples, as most of the events narrated in the latter are; the overall plot and characters of *Tom Jones* famously conform to the Aristotelian unities, whereas the developmental plot that organizes Steuart's text is interrupted by digressions and asides; and the explicit aim of the novel's narrator—to place this "historic kind of writing" within a typology of *fictional* types—differs from the implicit aim of the narrator in the *Principles*, which is to help the reader follow the argument Steuart was developing.[60] Despite these obvious differences and the fact that the protocols for fiction had already diverged from their counterparts for other kinds of writing, however, the two texts also share numerous features. The author of each presented his work as a "new" kind or "province" of writing, claimed to have discovered the "laws" of human nature and to have followed the rules that govern a particular kind of writing, and punctuated the body of his narrative with digressions intended to "refresh" the reader's mind. Each work also contains a narrator who directly addresses the reader and comments on the events and the nature of the narrative; alternates between generalizations, which the narrator supplies, and historical chronicles, which unfold as if without artistic direction; contains identifiable characters in addition to the narrator; and self-consciously chronicles a "revolution," whether in kinds of writing (*Tom Jones*) or in types of economic societies (*Principles*). Both authors, finally, explicitly claimed to present, as well as to embody, a comprehensive picture of historically particularized actions and to have derived from this comprehensive picture general principles that were (and are) universally true.

A few examples will give some sense of these formal similarities. First, both the novel and the treatise elevate character to a prominence it did not have in the early eighteenth century. Indeed, Fielding used the principle that "dramatic critics call conservation of character" to justify much of the plot of *Tom Jones* (337), and he explained this principle by explicitly invoking the midcentury elaboration of probability: "I will venture to say, that for a man to act in direct contradiction to the dictates of his nature, is, if not impossible, as improbable and as miraculous as anything which can well be conceived" (337–38). The consistency of Tom Jones's character thus formally organizes and renders his various exploits probable, for, from the beginning of the novel, Tom is represented as honorable but imprudent, generous but impulsive. These mixed qualities organize and explain the scrapes Tom gets into as well as the way he repeatedly survives and surmounts them. Other characters also consistently enact their characters: Mr. Allworthy is consistently generous; Blifil is consistently self-interested; Sophia is consistently virtuous; and so on. While Steuart's *Principles* contains no single character as concrete or developed as Fielding's characters, its action is also organized by a self-consistent figure that intermittently functions as a character; this is the statesman, who makes his first appearance in the opening pages of book 1, and who is also Steuart's primary addressee: "The *statesman* . . . is neither master to establish what oeconomy he pleases, or, in the exercise of his sublime authority, to overturn at will the established laws of it, let him be the most despotic monarch upon earth." The ellipsis in my sentence contains the following parenthetical explanation, which seems to contradict my claim that Steuart's statesman can be construed as an individualized character: "this is a general term to signify the legislature and supreme power, according to the form of government" (1:20). Despite this initial claim that "the statesman" refers to a collectivity, in the remainder of the *Principles* the figure gains increasing individuality as Steuart enumerates his powers and responsibilities. Thus, Steuart says that the role of the statesman is to "create reciprocal wants and dependences among [his] subjects" (135) and that the statesman must "combine" all the "principles" of a nation (work, demand, foreign trade) "and adapt them to his plan" (249). Unlike all the subjects he oversees, the statesman is not motivated by self-interest; and he is, by nature, reliable because consistent: "I suppose him to be constantly awake, attentive to his employment, able and uncorrupted, tender in his love for the society he governs, impartially just in his indulgence for every class of inhabitants, and disregardful of the interest of individuals, when that regard is inconsistent with the general welfare" (168).

As even these brief quotations should suggest, the notion that a states-man should oversee and invisibly "model the minds of his subjects so as to induce them, from the allurement of private interest, to concur in the execu-tion of his plan" (*Principles*, 1:21) helped turn nineteenth-century economic writers against Steuart's work, for ceding a nation's economic management to an individual (or group of individuals) ran counter to Smith's principle of laissez-faire. As we will see in a moment, moreover, it was the decision to replace Steuart's statesman with an impersonal abstraction—the invisible hand—that helped Smith reorder the hierarchy of features that character-ized Steuart's treatise; by so doing, Smith transformed a quasi-novelistic account into a fully theorized description of the apparently self-governing system of commercial society. In Steuart's *Principles*, by contrast, the consis-tent use of a personalizing noun gives the statesman considerable promi-nence in the hierarchy of stylistic features, thus making this treatise more closely resemble a fiction than Smith's account does. The resemblance be-tween Steuart's quasi-virtual statesman and a fictional character is most obvious in a "rhapsody" intended to "refresh" the reader's mind. In this passage, Steuart depicts the statesman riding a metaphoric horse, then over-coming unnamed opponents in his struggle to create a system of public credit. The entire scenario resembles an episode in a medieval morality play, when a "type" enacts some universal situation. If Steuart's character is more generalized than a character like Tom Jones, however, the states-man is still more imaginatively realized than a mere type, for the details Steuart includes encourage his reader to engage imaginatively in a dilemma that was certainly not universal or typical. As the statesman "looks upon" a "wide field," he "sees" wealthy individuals beginning to rival his power:

> The statesman looks about with amazement; he, who was wont to consider himself as the first man in society in every respect, perceives himself eclipsed by the lustre of private wealth, which avoids his grasp when he attempts to seize it. This makes his government more complex and more difficult to be carried on; he must now avail himself of art and address as well as of power and authority. By the help of cajoling and intrigues, he gets a little into debt; this lays a foundation for public credit, which, growing by degrees, and in its progress assuming many new forms, becomes, from the most tender begin-

nings, a most formidable monster, striking terror into those who cherished it in its infancy. Upon this, as upon a triumphant war-horse, the statesman gets astride.... He gets the better of all opposition, he establishes taxes, multiplies them, mortages [sic] his fund of subsistence, either becomes a bankrupt, and rises again from his ashes; or if he be less audacious, he stands trembling and tottering for a while on the brink of the political precipice. From one or the other of these perilous situations, he begins to discover an endless path which, after a multitude of windings, still returns into itself, and continues on an equal course though this vast labyrinth: but of this last part, more in the fourth book.

It is now full time to leave off rhapsody, and return to reasoning and cool inquiry. (226–27)

The features Steuart used in this description resemble those in fictions like *Tom Jones* and in moral philosophical treatises like Hutcheson's works on beauty: on the one hand, Steuart attributed specific emotions to the statesman (amazement), and he placed him in a localized setting that could be said to provoke concrete, virtual responses ("he stands trembling and tottering"); on the other hand, he gave this character no name, located him in no specific geographic or historical place, and described his actions in metaphoric or generalized (but not universal) terms (the "brink" he stands on is simply "the political precipice," and the "path" he discovers is not described). This passage, moreover, is self-consciously marked off from the surrounding narrative ("it is now full time to leave off rhapsody"), with the result that, even if it does contain fictional devices, it is at most an interlude, which disrupts as much as it advances the "reasoning and cool inquiry" that Steuart presented as his narrative norm.

While all this is true, it is also the case that Steuart's *Principles* is filled with such interludes, many of which contain characters that do have specific names, geographic settings, and historical referents. Some of these interludes, like the long digression on the republic of Lycurgus ("a perfect plan of political economy; because it was a system, uniform and consistent in all its parts" [1:275]), are explicitly referential in nature but composed from a combination of facts and fictions; that is, the Spartan republic Steuart describes did exist, but, because the available records about it were impressionistic and filled with gaps, his representation was based on conjecture as well as written materials. Other interludes are frankly and explicitly imaginative or virtual, as is the elaborate narrative by which he illustrated how agricultural improvement might have increased national populations; without reliable records, Steuart must have imagined that such was the case. Such imaginative narratives—of which there are many—clearly borrowed from the genre of conjectural history or the conjectural mode of the philosophical thought experiment, but the way Steuart's narratives typically open as well as the detail they rapidly accumulate and the virtual concreteness they acquire *as stories* make them seem as much like a novel's embedded narratives as the philosopher's abstract conjectures. Thus, the narrative about agriculture and population begins with the formula by which many philosophical conjectures begin: "*Let me suppose* a country fertile in spontaneous productions, capable of improvements of every kind, inhabited by a people living under a free government, and in the most refined simplicity, without trade, without the luxurious arts, and without ambition" (45; emphasis added). Almost immediately, Steuart abandons features common to conjectural histories and turns instead to features a reader would also have found in fiction: the conjectural mode (*let me suppose*) gives way to indefinite past-tense verbs and to terms, like *therefore* and *actually* that indicate causation within a concrete but virtual universe (46). Some of these embedded stories also prominently rely on individuated characters and dialogue, features they share with the embedded narratives that punctuate novels like *Tom Jones* (cf. the "island of small extent" [147–54] and *Tom Jones*'s Man of the Hill episode).

Steuart's *Principles* and Fielding's novel also share a common attitude toward Britain's developing credit economy. Both acknowledged the importance of credit and commerce but also tended to look backward to the agricultural economy Britain was leaving behind rather than forward to the commercial society that was already well developed by midcentury. In Kobayashi's terms, Steuart captured the "modern commodity economy... at the stage immediately preceding the capitalistic form of production"; in the *Principles*, Steuart never recognized the importance of industrial capital, nor did he gesture toward capitalist speculation.[61] James Thompson, in his careful analysis of the credit instruments in *Tom Jones*, attributes a similar attitude to Fielding's novel. Noting that "Fielding's novels are situated in between, calling up a nostalgic vision of a stable agricultural economy yet situating his protagonists on the road in a cash economy," Thompson argues convincingly that Fielding associated the former with virtue, generosity, and safety and the latter with temptation, corruption, and risk.[62] In particular, the embedded stories that punctuate Steuart's narrative, which almost all deal with past events (historical or conjectural), seem to belong, affectively as well as substantively, to the period in which an agricultural economy reigned, even if the genre Steuart was developing looked forward to the new mode of abstract analysis soon to be developed by Adam Smith. By the same token, Fielding's entire imaginative output (at least before *Amelia*) looked backward in content, even as he proclaimed the generic novelty of his formal innovations.

All these similarities, of course, do not make Steuart's *Principles* and Fielding's novel generically identical, and, by way of transition to my discussion of *The Wealth of Nations*, let me elaborate what I see as the most important formal difference between the *Principles* and *Tom Jones*. Once more, this distinction should be placed within the function they shared: both texts mediated the reader's relationship to the credit economy, even if Steuart and Fielding expressed more ambivalence about it than Defoe did. The mediating function of the *Principles* is obvious, especially in the discussions of paper money and banks, for Steuart was explicitly instructing his readers about how to understand the role of these credit instruments in the domestic and international markets. While *Tom Jones* is not usually read as a handbook about how to use (or avoid) credit, it contains so many examples of virtuous and criminal, productive and foolish behaviors with money and credit that we might be tempted to read it as such. Thus, for example, we learn from the Man of the Hill that one should not live on credit, nor should one scorn or renounce riches altogether; we learn from the example of Squire Western that the "just value and only use of money" is not, as he imagines, "to lay it up" (222) or hoard it; we learn from numerous characters, including the Man of the Hill and Black George, that one should not steal or keep money that one has not earned or inherited; we learn from the mishaps of Tom and Sophia that one should keep an eye on one's purse, especially when it contains credit instruments like banknotes; and, most important, we learn from Mr. Allworthy, Tom, and the narrator that the best thing to do with money of every kind is to give it away, in acts of generosity that are unremarked, unmotivated (except by the recipient's merit), and unremarkable (apart from their inherit virtue). In one of many passages stressing this last point, the narrator reminds the reader "that beneficence is a positive duty, and that whenever the rich fall greatly short of their ability in relieving the distress of the poor, their pitiful largesses are so far from being meritorious, that they have only performed their duty by halves" (632).

Even if Steuart's *Principles* and Fielding's novel can both be said to have helped instruct the reader about how to use and understand the credit economy, they did so in quite different ways. For Steuart, instruction was one of the primary functions of his treatise; along with the supply of information and explanations, the formulation of instruction organized the relationships among the various parts of the treatise. Thus, after his preliminary discussions of population and the historical backgrounds of trade and industry, Steuart devoted the remainder—the vast bulk—of the four-volume *Principles* to explaining how the modern institutions of credit (public and private), debt, banking, and taxes worked. *Tom Jones*, by contrast, consistently subordinates its narratives about economic behaviors and credit instruments to its aesthetic and ethical rationales, which do not depend on understanding how credit worked or obtaining information about various levels of national productivity. While it is possible for a reader to determine the precise nature of the "bank-bills" that Mr. Allworthy gives Tom when he sends him away early in the novel, in other words, it is not necessary to do so.[63] In fact, figuring this out does not enhance one's understanding of or appreciation for the novel because the fiction's *primary* function is not to help readers obtain information about or understand the money economy but to encourage them to cultivate moral virtues like prudence, moderation, and generosity.

To show how Fielding used references to money without mobilizing the informational or explanatory function these references could have had (and do have in *Roxana*), let me offer a few of many possible examples. From the opening pages of *Tom Jones*, the narrator emphasizes the "fortune" Mr. Allworthy has inherited, yet nowhere does Fielding reveal the monetary value of Allworthy's estate. Indeed, when the narrator introduces Allworthy, the word *fortune* does not even refer to riches or land but to one of the two personified deities that bestow "favours" on Allworthy (the other is Nature): "Fortune had only one gift in her power; but in pouring forth this, she was so very profuse, that others perhaps may think this single endowment to have been more than equivalent to all the various blessings which he enjoyed from Nature" (3). The only episode in which Fielding gives any hints about the monetary value of Allworthy's "fortune" occurs in book 5, chapter 7, when, under the mistaken impression that his death is imminent, Allworthy makes a will. The will does specify several monetary bequests, but what matters in the scene is not how much individual legatees will receive but the attitude they express toward the possibility that Allworthy will die. Thus, Tom proves himself to *deserve* the bequest because he loves Allworthy so much that he would rather have his benefactor live than receive the money he will inherit. In both these scenes, economic transactions serve agendas that are either aesthetic or ethical or both; but they do not explain or theorize the market system. Allworthy's wealth sets up the plot of *Tom Jones*, but it does not matter to this plot exactly how much Allworthy's estate is worth; Tom's ability to love distinguishes him from his half brother Blifil in moral terms, regardless of how much money the two characters have at any point in the novel.

This principle operates consistently in *Tom Jones*. The reader is told that Sophia Western has a "vast fortune" (225–26), and we are even given some specifics: "She was entitled to her mother's fortune at the death of her father, and to the sum of £3000 left her by an uncle when she came of age" (292). Nevertheless, what matter about Sophia—as a character in the fictional plot and as a moral exemplar for the reader—are her moral values or virtues: her constancy, her generosity, her love for Tom. By the same token, money does play a significant role in the plot: it is Tom's loss of the five £100 notes that propels him into many of the scrapes he suffers in his exile from Mr. Allworthy and Sophia, but these notes, though found, are never treated as money (they are never spent or exchanged for gold); and, when Allworthy recognizes them at the end of the novel (826), they function primarily as an index to the "black ingratitude" of George Seagrim (872), not as additional riches for Allworthy or Tom. When Sophia loses her pocketbook and the £100 it contains, this episode similarly has aesthetic and moral significance, not economic repercussions: the lame fellow who finds the purse does not even look inside (and would not have recognized the value of the note if he had, for, as the narrator tells us, he "could not read" [549]). And, when Tom finds and recognizes the purse, the discovery primarily serves as an excuse for him to regain admission to Sophia, not as an opportunity to get the money he so desperately needs. Indeed, Sophia sends the purse and its contents back to Tom with a note whose reference to the money is so euphemistically entwined with an invocation of a more metaphoric "fortune" that Fielding is prompted to provide an explanatory note. The note Sophia appends to her letter to Tom reads, in part: "Accept this, which is now of no service to me, which I know you must want, and think you owe the trifle only to that fortune by which you found it." Fielding's note reminds the reader that Tom's "fortune" now consists not only of Sophia's notice but of money too: "meaning, perhaps, the bank-bill for £100" (756). At the end of the novel, when Tom refers to Sophia as his "treasure" (864), the translation of monetary into ethical value is complete, and the reader can enjoy the superiority to mere earthly riches that the narrative as a whole celebrates. After all, throughout *Tom Jones*, Fielding depicts only the "low" characters—ladies' maids, manservants, and stablemen—thinking about money obsessively and in specific amounts.

If *Tom Jones* subordinated the informational and explanatory agendas embraced by Steuart's work to aesthetic and ethical rationales, then *The Wealth of Nations* made two different adjustments to the generic mixture that the *Principles* contains. On the one hand, Smith marginalized or formally contained the features borrowed from fictions, like concretely virtual characters, the intrusive narrator, and embedded stories. On the other hand, he transformed Steuart's quasi-descriptive, quasi-theoretical "principles" into reified abstractions whose relation to particularized historical situations was increasingly attenuated. The result is a text that not only achieves the internal coherence of a system in its organization but also produces the image of a system as one of its effects.[64] Despite the obvious similarities between Steuart's *Principles* and Smith's *Wealth*, that is, in the former, and despite Steuart's repudiation of the term *system*, it is primarily the writing itself—the plan, with its subdivisions and orderly chronological progression—that displays systematicity; *The Wealth of Nations*, by contrast, represents the market itself as systematic in its coherence, autonomy, and ability to regulate itself. That the British economy had not achieved this coherence, autonomy, or level of self-regulation by 1776 was, in a very real sense, incidental to Smith's project, for he insisted that, if he could describe the market as it ought to be, he would be able to help make that ideal real. That the fictional component of Smith's model has tended to disappear with the passage of time (and the fulfillment of many of Smith's wishes) is one measure of the success that political economy has enjoyed in arrogating to itself the exclusive prerogative of explaining the modern credit economy.

In *A History of the Modern Fact*, I have described the process by which Scottish conjectural historians elaborated the ambition expressed by experimental moral philosophers to make the study of society as systematic as their disciplinary predecessor, natural philosophy, had made the study of nature.[65] To realize this ambition, conjectural historians like William Robertson and Adam Ferguson substituted for the universals that appeared in the writings of moral philosophers like Francis Hutcheson ("human nature") abstractions of a different kind. These abstractions, such as Robertson's "the human mind," were able to function as personified agents in the writings of the conjectural historians and, thus, to provide links among historical events that might otherwise have appeared unconnected—or whose connection was solely a function of the historian's retrospective perspective. At the same time, as concepts created by the method of conjectural history itself, these abstractions brought into imaginative existence phenomena that existed only in the writing of the conjectural historians. It was this last function that Adam Smith so brilliantly adapted to political economic writing. The first-order abstraction Smith claimed to describe—the market—as well as the second-order, quantifiable abstractions that followed from this—labor, happiness, and so on—were products of his method and of the writing through which he realized it. The market system, in a very important sense, was the product of *The Wealth of Nations* and of the theory or belief that guided Adam Smith.[66]

I will return in a moment to the all-important subject of belief, but first let me demonstrate how Smith marginalized—or disciplined—those features that Steuart's *Principles* shared with novels like *Tom Jones*. One section in which we can see this appears in book 3 of *The Wealth of Nations*, for the discussion this book contains represents one part of the content we find in book 1 of Steuart's *Principles*. Smith's book is entitled "Of the Different Progress of Opulence in Different Nations." As this title suggests, the book chronicles the historical events that prepared the way for the emergence of commercial society; like Steuart's first book, Smith's third book is essentially historical and draws on both written records and the kind of conjectures with which eighteenth-century British philosophers typically filled in the gaps that characterized all their available printed sources.

Even though the two books cover more or less the same ground, however, there are also some important differences. First, the placement of the two historical accounts signals the heart of the methodological difference that divides these two works. Smith's historical account appears *after* he has laid out certain basic principles (the division of labor, the nature and accumulation of stock [including, importantly, capital]), and Steuart's appears *as part of* the naming of principles. Smith's placement suggests both the logical priority he assigned to abstractions (they came first) and his conviction that such abstractions were *separable* from the historical events from which he had presumably derived them (they not only came first but could also stand alone). Steuart's embedding of general principles within a historical account exemplifies what Kobayashi calls the "intertwining" of theory and historical description.[67] This tendency is also what led Karl Marx, who found much to like in Steuart's work, to complain, in 1859, that Steuart never managed to abstract the principles of political economy from his examples. "All the abstract categories of political economy still seem to be with him in the process of differentiation from the material elements they represent and therefore appear quite vague and unsettled," Marx wrote.[68]

The "vague and unsettled" nature of the "abstract categories of political economy" in Steuart's *Principles* is partly an effect of the role played by the narrator: as this narrator guides the reader through his examples, he repeatedly calls attention to the gap between specific examples and the general principles Steuart supposedly wanted to stress, the inadequacy of his terminology, or the fictional nature of the episodes he introduces. In *The Wealth of Nations*, there is no equivalently delineated narrator, and those few narrative intrusions Smith interjected gesture toward the narrator's modesty, not toward the nature or features of the narrative itself. Thus, book 3, like the rest of *The Wealth of Nations*, contains numerous instances of the following phrases: *I believe, so far as I know, I reckon it not improbable,* and *however this may have been.* These phrases tend to substantiate the reliability of what is being narrated rather than suggest that the chronicles are conjectural or fictions, as Steuart's narrative intrusions often do. Smith also avoids the "vague and unsettled" "abstract categories" to which Marx objected in Steuart's work by depicting abstractions as natural and inevitable products of historical change. Thus, phrases like *must always* make historical outcomes seem inevitable, and the unremarked introduction of analogies enables the narrative (*not* a personified narrator) to abstract general principles and a historical logic from particular examples: "That order of people, with all the liberty and security which law can give, must always improve under great disadvantages. The farmer compared with the proprietor, is as a merchant who trades with borrowed money compared with one who trades with his own. The stock of both may improve, but that of the one, with only equal good conduct, must always improve more slowly than that of the other, on account of the large share of the profits which is consumed by the interest of the loan" (371 [bk. 3, chap. 2]). Because the narrator does not call attention to himself or to the metaphor that lifts a claim about history ("that order . . . must always improve") to a general principle ("the farmer . . . is as a merchant"), the presence of the trope tends to pass unnoticed, and abstract "laws" emerge as if they are simply phenomena that have been observed.

Thus, Smith literally contained the features associated with virtuality or fiction in Steuart's narrative by relegating the historical account (which has to have been derived partly from conjecture) to a section separate from the sections in which he laid out theoretical principles. But he also, more subtly, contained the features associated with fiction by simultaneously demoting individualized characters and introducing abstractions that could function as agents in his narrative. While some of Smith's historical narratives do specify names (or, more typically, subject positions, like "farmer"), there is no character equivalent to Steuart's statesman. The two roles this figure plays in Steuart's work—the statesman is the addressee and the chief actor in almost all the historical tales as well as the figure Steuart looked to for reform—are subsumed in Smith's work into a single figure whose realization solicited a different kind of imaginative participation on the part of the reader. As addressee, that is, Steuart's statesman provided a fictional counterpart with whom an actual statesman reading the work could identify;

by identifying with this figure, the reader of the *Principles* could imagine himself acting as Steuart said he should—disinterestedly and with his subjects' well-being consistently before his eyes (and with his political economic advisor at his side). Thus, the figure of the statesman functioned like the exemplary figure in a novel—Clarissa Harlowe, for example, or Tom Jones. As McKeon explains, this figure holds an imaginative mirror up to readers so that, through identification, the reader could imagine herself or himself into more principled, more ethical behavior.

In *The Wealth of Nations*, by contrast, where there is no named addressee and no single character with whom to identify, the reader needs to engage the text at a more abstract level—as a philosophical exercise, not (primarily) as an opportunity for imaginative projection. Even more important, because the agents who do have efficacy in Smith's narrative tend to be abstractions, the reader must be willing to extend to these abstractions a variant of the belief that she would extend to a fictional character. In some senses, however, it seems more difficult to make a reader believe in the reality of an abstraction like "the invisible hand" than in a named character like Tom Jones. In the passage in which Smith introduces this abstraction, we can begin to see one of the stylistic features by which he courted his reader's belief. The passage opens with what looks like a straightforward statement of fact (but is actually a theoretical assertion), then introduces a generalized figure, to which the culminating abstraction seems simply to belong:

> But the annual revenue of every society is always precisely equal to the exchangeable value of the whole annual produce of its industry, or rather is precisely the same thing with that exchangeable value. As every individual, therefore, endeavours as much as he can both to employ his capital in the support of domestic industry, and so to direct that industry that its produce may be of the greatest value; every individual necessarily labours to render the annual revenue of the society as great as he can. He generally, indeed, neither intends to promote the public interest, nor knows how much he is promoting it. By preferring the support of domestic to that of foreign industry, he intends only his own security; and by directing that industry in such a manner as its produce may be of the greatest value, he intends only his own gain, and he is in this, as in many other cases, led by an invisible hand to promote an end which was no part of his intention. (423 [bk. 4, chap. 2])

What makes this passage credible is a complex syntactic system: first, we are given a collective noun (*every individual*) that secretes, as if in a logical progression, a singular noun that becomes a specific—although nonreferential—pronoun (*he*); this noun is syntactically parallel to, and, thus, links, two agents, only one of which (*the invisible hand*) carries any connotations of the abstraction they actually have in common. In other words, as the subject of an elaborate trope ("*as* every individual"), the *he* who "intends only his own security; and . . . only his own gain" is as abstract as *the invisible hand*, but, because the pronoun *he* could—and generally does—refer to an individual (virtual or real), the abstraction of this figure is diminished; and, by extension, it diminishes the abstract nature of that other, parallel agent, the invisible hand. Such abstractions (both *he* and *the invisible hand*) take the place of the concrete, virtual characters of fiction *and* the quasi-concrete, nonreferential statesman of Steuart's text, and, by so doing, they organize a different kind of imaginary universe differently. In *The Wealth of Nations*, character is not the dominant feature in the hierarchy of stylistic devices, imaginative projection is not the appropriate mode of engagement, and historical reference is not an essential vehicle for generating evidence. Instead, the features of *The Wealth of Nations* are organized in relation to a series of abstractions, the function of which is to generate an abstract model that is universally applicable for readers who have learned to understand that the educational value of abstractions rests precisely in this general—not fictive and not specific—applicability.

Smith did include a few of the features that are so prominent in Steuart's work. His metaphoric account of banking as "a sort of wagon-way through the air" is one example (*Wealth*, 305 [bk. 2, chap. 2]). By and large, however, he tended either to downplay his use of tropes, as in the example I just described from book 3, or to mark the presence of a figure of speech so emphatically that its artifice is clear. Thus, Smith introduces his metaphor about banking with a pseudoapology. "If I may be allowed so violent a metaphor," he writes. His most expansive discussion of money, in which this metaphor appears (bk. 2, chap. 2), contains numerous tropes, but, even though he is forced to use them, Smith generally dismisses such figures as, at the very least, distracting. Having referred to money as "the great wheel of circulation," for example, he then disdains the trope: "It is the ambiguity of language only which can make this proposition either doubtful or para-doxical. When properly understood, it is almost self-evident" (274 [bk. 2, chap. 2]). Smith's overall treatment of money implies that its use is similarly "self-evident" and that it is, as a consequence, immune from the taint of language's ambiguity. Thus, when he describes the introduction of money, he identifies its adoption as a natural episode in the historical process of specialization. "It is more natural and obvious" to measure value by money, he explains, than to define *value* in any other terms (32 [bk. 1, chap. 5]).

Smith's professed disdain for metaphoric language and his ability to populate his text with abstract agents (including various incarnations of "he" as well as "the invisible hand" and "the market system") may constitute the stylistic keys to the credibility of *The Wealth of Nations*, but formal features cannot fully explain the influence this text exercised, especially after the beginning of the nineteenth century. In other words, developments beyond the formal and stylistic innovations I have just described were necessary to make large numbers of readers believe in abstractions like the invisible hand. As we will see in chapter 3, these developments were institutional, social, political, and religious: they included the codification of political economy by Dugald Stewart and Thomas Robert Malthus; the popularization of the science of wealth by writers like J. R. McCulloch, Jane Marcet, and Harriet Martineau; the political triumph of the Whigs in 1832; and the rise of evangelical Christianity, which developed its own variant of political economy. Finally, these developments were disciplinary: it was as much the embrace by practitioners of prose fiction of rationales that were exclusively aesthetic and ethical as the repudiation by political economists of the fictional elements their works still contained that finally made these two kinds of writing seem to require different kinds of belief and to concern two different kinds of value. Or, more precisely, it was imaginative writers' increasing indifference to informing readers about the credit economy or instructing them in the use of its instruments that made their writing bear an increasingly opaque—or even misrecognized—relation to commercial society. This relation and its misrecognition are the subjects of chapters 5 and 6.

Money Talks: Thomas Bridges's *Adventures of a Bank-Note*

In this section, I examine a text that is even more generically anomalous than Steuart's hybrid *Principles*. This text, Thomas Bridges's *Adventures of a Bank-Note*, is also admittedly more marginal to our modern disciplines than Steuart's treatise, for, despite the efforts of a handful of modern Literary critics and at least one historian to incorporate this and other works like it into the genealogy of the novel or an account of the humanization of the economy, Bridges's text seems to have had almost no lasting influence on Literary form or the historiography of this period. Despite its oddity and current obscurity, *Adventures of a Bank-Note* interests me for two reasons. First, its status as a generic hybrid enables me to provide another perspective on the distance that opened between the aesthetic rationale associated with fiction and the informational and explanatory rationales associated with various kinds of economic writing during the last quarter of the eighteenth century. Second, the fact that this distance did open—and that it did so within an accelerating market in kinds and volume of print production—enables me to shift the focus of this study away from the formal features of texts and toward the social and economic conditions that informed such formal matters. Indeed, the gap that has opened in our modern disciplinary practice between a consideration of formal matters and the study of social conditions reflects—and encourages us to reflect on—the distance opened in the last decades of the eighteenth century between the two rationales I have associated with the genres of imaginative and economic writing.

When modern scholars discuss *Adventures of a Bank-Note*, they typically group it with other works that share its most distinctive feature: narration by a character that is fictional, in being concrete and virtual, but unrealistic, in being nonhuman. Denominating such texts "money-centered narratives," "it narratives," "object narratives," "spy narratives," "novels of circulation," "novels about non-human characters," or "traveling coins,"[69] scholars usually treat them as a subgenre of the novel;[70] they tend to trace British variants of this subgenre to a French prototype, Alain René Le Sage's *Le double boîteaux* (which was translated in 1708 as *The Devil upon Two Sticks*);[71] and they identify as the period of these texts' greatest popularity the last quarter of the eighteenth century (1770–1800), the decades that coincided with the "takeoff" of British print.[72] During this period, an astonishing range of household commodities (and pets) spoke for themselves in printed fictions. The animated speakers include (among many others) a corkscrew, a kite, a pin, a quire of paper, a watch, a black coat, a whipping-top, and a lapdog. Among the monetary narrators, contemporary readers could encounter the testimony of a half guinea, a halfpenny, a shilling, a silver penny, a silver three-penny piece, a sovereign, a Birmingham counterfeit coin, a twenty-pound banknote, and a rupee.[73] The most popular of all the narratives of this kind, Charles Johnstone's *Chrysal; or, The Adventures of a Guinea* (the first two volumes appeared in 1760, the last two in 1765), was so well received that, by 1800, it had appeared in twenty editions; it was still familiar enough in the middle of the next century for George Eliot to mention it, as Fred Vincy's morning reading material, in *Middlemarch*.[74]

Instead of considering *Adventures of a Bank-Note* as a member of this group or treating these works as an episode in Literary history or the humanization of exchange, I want to use this work to advance the history *of* the Literary that I offer in this book. To do so, I want first to highlight the features this text shared with (or borrowed from) the two genres with which I am concerned: economic writing and imaginative writing. The first two volumes of *Adventures of a Bank-Note* are particularly interesting in the context of the generic differentiation I am describing, for these two volumes, which were published in 1770, intermittently pursued *both* the informational agenda that was already associated with economic writing and the aesthetic agenda increasingly arrogated to imaginative writing. In the next two volumes, which were published in 1771, Bridges seems to have abandoned the first agenda and opted instead to model his text solely on the imaginative fictions that were being published in ever-greater numbers. *Adventures of a Bank-Note* thus presents in miniature an example of the splitting apart of the two agendas, and it also provides another, more extreme version of the way in which imaginative writers increasingly subordinated their treatment of financial themes to an aesthetic agenda.

It is clear from the opening pages of *Adventures of a Bank-Note* that this text both borrowed features from and pursued the aesthetic agenda increasingly associated with eighteenth-century imaginative writing. The characters are all concrete and virtual, as are the narrated events, and it is filled with references to other, contemporary fictions, especially Sterne's *Tristram Shandy* (1759, 1761, 1762, 1765, 1767) and, in volume 3, sentimental fiction like Goldsmith's *Vicar of Wakefield* (1766) and Sterne's *Sentimental Journey* (1768). Bridges's plot is picaresque in form, like the plots of these fictions, and, like Sterne's incidents in particular, many of Bridges's episodes are euphemistically risqué or bawdy. Even if the work is recognizably an imaginative fiction, however, in the course of the first two volumes, *Adventures of a Bank-Note* also supplies a surprising amount of information about Bank of England paper. Early in volume 1, for example, the narrator, having revealed that he is a twenty-pound Bank note, tells the reader how such a note might be procured: a man whom the Note calls his "father" deposits coin in the Bank that he received for writing a poem, and, in exchange, he receives this piece of paper.[75] The Note also reveals, in passing, that such notes were made out, by hand, to their initial bearer by the Bank cashier. To justify including this information, the Note states that the poet's motive for obtaining the note was vanity, not prudence: wanting a title, and being unable to afford its purchase price, the poet has asked the Bank's cashier to issue the note to "Timothy Taggrhime, Esq" (1:14). An honor thus conferred, the Note jokingly tells the reader, will persist even after the note is passed to other hands. "After the Bank has dubb'd you an esquire," Timothy's Muse assures him, "no man will dare to say a word against it; you may then boldly add the title esquire to your name the very next work you publish. Your title to the title will then be as indisputably a title, as your own title to your title-page" (1:14–15).

In subsequent episodes, the Note offers additional information: he explains that the numbers printed on a Bank note's face constituted its identifying serial number, that they signified the note's date of issue, and that the Bank of England was required by law to record this number in a ledger when it issued the note.[76] The Note also explains how this number could be useful when he describes what happened when an individual lost a Bank note: if the holder had recorded the serial number of the note, he could advertise for its return, and, if the note did not appear, he could notify the Bank that the note was lost and receive reimbursement for its value; the Bank, in turn, would stop the note—that is, refuse to redeem the note if someone else tried to cash it. Bridges's Note describes this provision in an anecdote about a dishonest landlord who has substituted a grocer's bill for an illiterate tinker's twenty-pound note. Realizing that the tinker might recognize his fraud, the landlord has to wait to see if the note is "advertised and stopped at the Bank." "On the sixth day, when he saw an advertisemen[t], Lost on the road between * * * and * * * a twenty pound bank-note, number forgot," the landlord knows that the tinker did not record the number and therefore will not be able to claim ownership of the note. At this point, the landlord "conscientiously mark'd me down for his own" and passes the note to another customer (*Adventures*, 2:149).

In addition to information about what happened when a Bank note was lost, Bridges's text also reveals how long a Bank of England note typically circulated (less than two years) and describes what happened to a note when it was cashed at the Bank. Imagining his own demise, the Note reveals that, when a note was returned, a clerk clipped its serial number off, crossed the corresponding number out of the Bank ledger, and destroyed the note—or, as the Note relates these events, "a fellow with a hangman-looking face" deprives the note of its "spinal marrow" (*Adventures*, 1:166–67). The text also points out the social inequalities that jeopardized the validity of Bank notes when the Note complains about the scandalous provision that allowed members of Parliament to default on their debts without penalty (148–49).

To see why I call these offhand, incidental, and humorous comments *information*, it is helpful to recall two facts about the monetary situation that prevailed in Britain in 1770. We saw the first peculiarity in the preamble: in the middle decades of the eighteenth century, a bewildering variety of kinds of paper money circulated, some of which was issued by the Bank of England, some by private banks, some by shopkeepers or merchants, and some by counterfeiters.[77] The second peculiarity follows from the relatively limited scope of circulation for these various notes: because each kind of (legitimate) note typically circulated only in a small geographic area, the vast majority of Britons would not have known how to evaluate the quality of various notes, might never have seen a Bank of England note, and would not have known how to realize the value of the notes that passed through their hands. In this confusing monetary environment, we might expect precise and useful data of any kind to have found a receptive audience—as was the case with the handbooks for merchants that had enjoyed great popularity in Britain since the sixteenth century and the numerous guides to currency published during a similar monetary situation in the United States (in the 1860s).[78] As far as I have been able to determine, however, the middle decades of the eighteenth century saw the publication of no such monetary handbooks for laymen. Even the *Encyclopaedia Britannica*, which was published in Scotland between 1768 and 1771, included in its long entry on money no practical advice about how to recognize a valid banknote, when it was advisable to exchange country notes for coin, or how to transfer money between one bank's currency and another's.[79] Sir James Steuart did offer general *principles* for evaluating the quality of notes in his economic treatise, but he also acknowledged that, because no bank (not even the Bank of England) was required to disclose the amount of its securities, it was impossible for anyone actually to know the relative merits of paper notes—including those issued by the Bank (*Principles*, 3:173, 230).[80]

As a onetime banker himself, Thomas Bridges (1710?–75) would have known something about currency. As a partner in the Hull firm of Sell, Bridges, and Blunt, moreover, he would have known about both local currencies and transactions between a country bank and the Bank of England; and, because no more than about a dozen "bankers' shops" operated outside London in the 1750s, he would have known that what he knew about paper notes was still a specialists' knowledge in 1770. Finally, as someone who turned to writing after the failure of his banking company (in 1759), Bridges would have realized that he could turn what he had learned about money from banking into income from another source—the writing of a book about how money circulated and what it saw along the way.[81] That he decided to make the narrator of his tale a *paper* note instead of a coin, as all the other eighteenth-century money-narrators are, suggests that he wanted to capitalize on the special features of this particular kind of money and on his specialist's knowledge about it.

Even if capitalizing on his knowledge about paper currency constituted one motivation for Bridges's first two volumes, however, by 1771, when he published the next two, he seems to have completely abandoned this plan. After the end of volume 2, nothing that happens to the narrator requires the speaker to be a paper note, and nothing the note tells us conveys any information about Bank of England or any other monetary paper. The small size and masculine gender of the Note do enable him to engage in numerous sexually titillating encounters (as when he twice finds himself secreted in a woman's bosom), but a coin could also have found itself lost between a matron's ample breasts. The fact that the Note is small and light does encourage his holders to stow him in portable containers, like a snuff case and an apothecary's clyster-pipe holder, but, when he simply narrates scenes he sees on the street (like the slapstick episode that ends volume 1, in which the leash of a blind man's dog entangles his owner with a bandy-legged pastry cook), his presumed identity as a Bank of England note does not have any material implications for the narration. As the narrative unfolds in volumes 3 and 4, in fact, Bridges seems to have cared less and less that his narrator was supposed to be a paper note; he even seems to have forgotten that, in volume 1, the Note told the reader both that he is the only Bank note that can speak (*Adventures*, 1:166) and that his words are being recorded for print by a human being ("a secretary, or, more properly speaking[,] . . . a machine, whose utmost qualification before was . . . just to be able to write his name, and read it when he had done" [3]). In volume 3, the Note meets another Bank note who talks, and he begins to imply that he is writing the tale himself instead of using a human recorder: first, he tells the reader that the "bookseller pays me by the sheet" (3:157); then, in volume 4, he refers to his "pen" (4:71), as if he has dismissed (or forgotten about) his amanuensis.

By volume 4, the Note has come to resemble a human character in numerous respects: he tells us that he reads the *Morning Chronicle* every day (*Adventures*, 4:70); that he once possessed twenty books (which he has pawned [87]); and that he drinks liquor (71). Having purchased a dram with one of the pennies he got for pawning the books, he finds his "bowels" upset (75). The Note twice states that, "at present, I am a great man" (201, 204), he has long discussions with an imaginary critic, whom he denominates "a presbyterian parson" (96–100), and he repeatedly addresses the reader as an equal (120, 133–34, 138–40, 200–204). While the Note does continue to circulate in these volumes, Bridges's representation of circulation is so cursory and so rapid that the Note's movement seems like a parody of the more stately circulation he narrated in the first two volumes. Thus, late in volume 4, we find passages like the following: "I was paid to a wool-stapler; he paid me to a long-legg'd hosier; the hosier paid me to a Nottingham weaver; the weaver changed me with the landlord, at the Bull in Bishopsgate-street; the landlord paid me to the one-eyed Norwich warehouse-keeper; from him I went to a gingerbread-baker, for gingerbread sent by the wagon into the country. By Timothy Treaclebread the gingerbread-baker, I was paid to Mrs. Coppernose, a rich brazier's widow, for rent: all this was performed in less than three hours" (142–43).

In volumes 1 and 2, then, it matters to the action of Bridges's narrative that the narrator is a Bank of England note, the note function is explicitly separated from the writer function, and the informational and aesthetic agendas overlap. In volumes 3 and 4, by contrast, the narrator ceases to be recognizably a monetary token of any kind, the Note merges with the writer, and the informational agenda simply disappears. While the text as a whole never attains the unity of character or action that critics were increasingly identifying with aesthetic merit, Bridges seems to have decided to model his last two volumes exclusively on imaginative writing. In one sense, he was simply returning to the pattern he first adopted when he initially took up writing in 1762; his first two productions (both poems) were parodies of well-known imaginative works.[82] In another sense, however, he seems no longer to have considered information about money essential to the production or marketing of imaginative writing. Accelerating the generic split I describe in this book to an almost comic pace, Bridges so dramatically subordinated the informational rationale to its aesthetic counterpart that the former simply vanishes, leaving no trace in the last two volumes of the work.

It is impossible to say how contemporaries responded to Bridges's text, for the only critical notice I have found of these narratives does not mention it by name. What this review does stress is that works like Bridges's had become "fashionable" by 1781: "This mode [of writings narrated by inanimate things] . . . is grown so fashionable, that few months pass which do not bring one of them under our inspection."[83] This comment confirms that Bridges struck a rich vein of interest when he launched his chatty Note into the world of print in 1770, but both his abandonment of monetary information in the last two volumes and the fact that his seems to be the only narrative that features an informative paper note suggest that providing even incidental information—at least about money—was not essential to the popularity of this kind of work. By 1771, Bridges seems to have become convinced that alluding to other imaginative fictions, borrowing sentimental scenes from some, and taking the loose plot structure from others, would enable his volumes to ride the rising tide of demand for imaginative writing.

It is important not to make too much of Bridges's change of direction. *Adventures of a Bank-Note* belongs to what was, by all accounts, one of many passing fashions in the increasingly heated book trade of the 1770s and 1780s, and it remains something of a curiosity, one that few modern scholars have noticed.[84] But, as one small barometer of the late-eighteenth-century book trade, *Adventures of a Bank-Note* does illuminate a phenomenon that became much more pronounced in the nineteenth century: as books became market commodities, in ways and to an extent that had not previously obtained, authors of imaginative fiction increasingly turned away from the informational and theoretical agendas pursued by other kinds of writing, embraced the aesthetic agenda that seemed best suited to distinguish their works from those of their competitors, and tried to deny that the value of their writing had anything to do with the market in which they circulated. As we will see in chapter 5, the kind of value imaginative writing was increasingly said to create was soon to be theorized, celebrated, and canonized by poets who proclaimed themselves practitioners and prophets of Literature. For these writers—Wordsworth, Coleridge, and their minions—money, the book trade, and market value were subjects too degrading for Literature to touch. As these writers provided a theoretical account of what Literature should be and do, they tried to portray the century-long breakup of the fact/fiction continuum as a historical inevitability that had as its natural product a new form of value, one that imaginative writers were uniquely fitted to grasp and render accessible to future readers.

There is one more sense in which *Adventures of a Bank-Note* might be considered a barometer. As we saw in the preamble, Bank of England notes did not attain the level of uniformity that enabled them to become truly identical—that is, culturally invisible—until after technical innovations were introduced in the Bank's Printing Office in 1855. We have also seen that, even before the campaign to achieve uniformity succeeded, the Bank implemented numerous stylistic and material changes intended to make its notes uniquely valid; these ranged from new kinds of paper, to new forms of embossing and watermarking, to new denominations. These alterations, however, were not sufficient to render Bank of England notes so familiar that Britons would take them for granted and accept them at face value, for the Bank's notes had only limited circulation for the entire eighteenth century and, thus, remained a rarity compared to the notes of local banks. In the context of the country's circulating paper, then, we can see that one, probably unintended, effect of Bridges's fictional text was to help make the Bank of England note familiar to readers who might never have seen one. In volumes 1 and 2, the chatty Note travels far beyond the twenty-mile radius of London that would have marked the boundary of a real note's circulation, its validity as legitimate currency is never questioned, and no one in the fiction balks at its relatively large denomination. In the world of the fiction, in other words, the Note's circulation is geographically un-limited, ontologically certain, and monetarily unproblematic. In the world of the fiction, in short, the Note achieves precisely the kind of currency to which Bank officials could only aspire; and, insofar as Bridges's fiction could circulate beyond the boundary that circumscribed the currency of the Bank's actual notes, it might be said to have helped prepare Britons to accept notes about which they had only read. As a fictional device that indirectly assisted the Bank's campaign to naturalize its notes, *Adventures of a Bank-Note* reminds us of one kind of connection that continued to link monetary writing with its imaginative counterpart, even as practitioners of fiction and Bank officials alike stepped up their efforts to deny any substantial link between these two kinds of writing.

"The Paper Age"

The last decades of the eighteenth century and the first half of the nineteenth witnessed a dramatic increase in the volume and kinds of paper circulating in Britain. This proliferation had at least three fronts and several staggered points of acceleration. In the book trade, the volume of all kinds of publications increased after the passage of the Booksellers' Act in 1774, then again when the price of paper fell at the end of the war with France (1815); publications increased once more when the introduction of machine-made paper lowered the cost of production (1820s) and yet again in the late 1850s and 1860s after the repeal of the window tax and the stamp duties known collectively as the *taxes on knowledge*. In the banking industry, the acceleration of note issue followed the passage in 1797 of the Restriction Act. Among country banks, note issue then increased every time a new group of banks was founded and fell when some of these, along with other banks, were forced to close.[1] The Bank of England, in turn, increased its note issue significantly in 1799, 1809, and then periodically, usually in response to demand, until the passage of the Bank Act in 1844.[2] Finally, and bridging the gulf that seems to separate these two kinds of paper, commentary about financial matters, the currency, and the economy also proliferated during these decades. Some of these publications, as we will see in chapters 3 and 4, were direct responses to the monetary situation produced by the wartime economy (1793–1815); some capitalized on the new market for economic commentary created by the investment opportunities generated by the war; and some sought to replace such opportunistic publications with volumes intended to outlive their immediate provocation. Many of the latter took the form of political economic treatises that, by offering models of the economy as a whole, tried to attain a place in the emergent canon of political economic analysis.

Contemporaries were intrigued by this avalanche of paper. In 1837, for example, Thomas Carlyle looked back on the French counterpart to Britain's threefold print takeoff with a mixture of fascination and foreboding. Calling the decade between 1774 and 1784 the beginning of "the Paper Age," he linked "Bank-paper" to "Book-paper." Both, he wrote in his inimitable style, captured the spirit of the "Age of Hope," when delusive dreams of endless riches as well as "Theories, Philosophies, Sensibilities . . . mount[ed] heavenward, so beautifully, so unguidably . . . specifically-light" on the "wind-bags" made of paper.[3] In the French case, one set of windbags—the paper currency known as *assignats*—soon became the "dishonoured Bills" that financed an abortive revolution, while another—the "beautiful art" that hid "the want of Thought" in the visionary publications—was soon banned or burned or used to justify the waves of executions known as the Terror. For Carlyle, the French example constituted a sobering example of the dangers an unrestrained flow of paper might herald. "Paper is made from *rags* of things that once did exist," he remarked ruefully. "There are endless excellences in Paper.—What wisest Philosophe, in this halcyon uneventful period, could prophesy that there was approaching, big with darkness and confusion, the event of events? Hope ushers in a Revolution,—as earthquakes are preceded by bright weather."[4]

By and large, modern historians, both Literary and economic, have forgotten the Paper Age or, in the few instances in which they have examined bank paper and book paper together, have found in these two kinds of publications a *structural* similarity that has led to fascinating, but not specifically historical, speculation.[5] In this brief interchapter, I place these various accelerations in paper production side by side as a way of introducing my discussion of the disciplinary disaggregation whose story occupies the remainder of this book. I will not argue that the accelerations in these forms of paper were connected in any simple, causal manner. While technological improvements in paper manufacture and printing did eventually affect the production of both bank and book paper, these innovations were not adopted in the two industries at the same time or to the same extent.[6] By the same token, the increase in the volume of imaginative, political, and financial publications did not cause banks to print more paper money, nor did the increased volume of circulating currency by itself make it easier for contemporaries to purchase books or subscribe to circulating libraries. It is undeniably the case, by contrast, that the overlap of the first two increases facilitated the third—that is, the increase in possibilities for publication and the proliferation of paper money made it both easier and seem more urgent to air one's opinion about the credit economy in print.[7] It must also be said, however, that the overlapping takeoffs in the production of bank paper and that of book paper were not strictly coincidental. Both of these were, in the simplest sense, symptoms of Britain's growing commercial economy, which thrived on the credit represented by the expansion of paper notes and prospered, in part, because of the commodification of a wide range of fashionable and leisure products, including books and pamphlets.[8] To say that these increases were symptoms of something else, however, casts scant light on the relationship between bank paper and book paper, nor does it enable us to understand the different dynamics that characterized nineteenth-century developments in these kinds of writing. To show how bank paper gradually moved beneath the horizon of cultural visibility, becoming taken for granted in the ways I have discussed, and how both financial and imaginative writing acquired the relative degrees of visibility that characterize their modern forms, I need to examine the way all three kinds of writing took off together, then followed trajectories so different in outcome.

As we will see in just a moment, the speedup of production in the book trade preceded its counterpart in the banking industry, a chronology to which I adhere in this brief discussion. In the chapters that follow, however, I reverse this chronology. There are three reasons for examining developments in banking and financial writing before their counterparts in Literary writing. The first is my desire to achieve narrative clarity. Because the speedup in the issue of paper money spiked more dramatically (after 1797) than did its counterparts in financial or imaginative publishing, because this matter was settled more decisively (by the Bank Act of 1844), and because the history of monetary events is generally less well-known to today's readers, it seems important to begin with the narrative I provide in chapter 3. Second, as we will see in chapter 4, financial and economic writers rapidly adopted measures that gave their productions sufficient social authority to force imaginative writers to respond to them (whether directly, in critiques, or indirectly, via appropriation, reworking, or marginalization). As a consequence, the body of financial and economic writing I examine in chapters 3 and 4 constituted one of the *cultural contexts* in which imaginative writers developed their generic innovations. Restoring this context can help us understand the treatment Literary writers gave to financial and economic issues in their work. And, finally, imaginative writers' most *characteristic*—or generically definitive—response to the consolidation of the credit economy and the upsurge in economic commentary about it was to repudiate all but the most attenuated connection between the market economy and imaginative productions. For this reason, the monetary genres that underwrote the expansion of credit and the economic genres that tried to explain it can be said to have been the negative or misrecognized conditions of possibility for the writing we call *Literature*. I discuss this dynamic *among* genres in chapter 5, and I devote chapter 6 to some of the consequences that this denial had for Literary writing per se.

The Takeoff in the Book Trade

Our understanding of the eighteenth- and early-nineteenth-century book trade has been immeasurably enriched in recent decades by the pioneering work of James Raven, Peter Garside, Rainer Schöwerling, and William St. Clair, and much of the summary I provide in this section draws extensively from their published work.[9] In St. Clair's narrative of developments within the book trade, the first point that merits attention is the intimate connection between the expansion of publishing in Britain and innovations in credit like the ones I examined in the preamble. Because printing required both outlays of fixed capital (for presses and type) and a constant supply of working capital (for book production, warehousing, advertising, and distribution), the expansion of the print trade depended on establishing both innovative modes of financing and distinctive relationships among various parts of the industry. Among the innovative credit arrangements, the most prominent were the use of postdated promissory notes, which enabled English book producers to establish two-way relationships with geographically distant markets where credit was well established (like colonial America), and the subdivision of shares in copyrighted titles, which allowed publishers to spread the cost of production yet funnel most of the profits to families whose members were in the trade.[10] Within the industry, both a strict hierarchy and a division of labor helped maximize profits: writers and editors were initially subcontractors to printers, and printers soon joined them as subcontractors to booksellers (the forerunners of modern publishers). A highly centralized, collectively protected cartel of book producers grew up as these modes of financing, ownership, and labor were established. By the third decade of the eighteenth century, St. Clair explains, after the lapse of the Licensing Act (1695), and despite the passage of Queen Anne's Act (1710),[11] booksellers in England were able to create and protect monopolistic pricing structures because their concentrated and internally organized corporate institutions linked writers, printers, booksellers, and potential buyers throughout Britain and across Europe and North America in an elaborate network of production, distribution, profit, and credit. In what St. Clair calls the "high monopoly period" (1710–74), English booksellers enjoyed the ability to set prices, control the volume of print production, and dominate the production and distribution of virtually all the printed materials produced in London and the English provinces.

Several characteristics distinguish the high monopoly period of publishing, in St. Clair's account: the printing of anthologies and abridgments was strictly curtailed; high book prices became the norm; and the pressruns of most books were deliberately kept small. Even though the publishing monopoly was not absolute—Scots and Irish publishers managed to defy it, and a few titles, like *Robinson Crusoe*, escaped the net—the virtual monopoly over new titles meant that the writers who prospered from the high price of books had little incentive to challenge the publishing system. It also meant that the vast number of English readers had very limited access to books written by their contemporaries and virtually no access to anthologies or abridgments, which would have made excerpts of longer works available to more readers lower down the social scale.

For the purposes of my argument, the significance of St. Clair's thesis is that the ability of the publishing cartel to limit access to new titles condemned the vast majority of English readers to a steady diet of works published before the Act of Anne (along with the books that St. Clair includes in the "official supernatural," like the Bible). These works included old folktales, like *Jack and the Giants*, and pseudoscientific/medical handbooks, like *Aristotle's Compleat Masterpiece* and *Dreams and Moles, with Their Interpretation and Significance*. Such writing, by and large, did not make a distinction between fact and fiction, as much of the eighteenth-century writing that we now value was beginning to do. Nor did these seventeenth-century titles demand of readers the sophisticated intellectual skills or leisure to read necessary to enjoy a work like Hume's *Enquiry*, Gibbon's *Decline and Fall*, or even Sterne's *Tristram Shandy*. Instead of cultivating a single nation of readers whose members developed commensurate skills because they read the same things in the same way, as St. Clair's title (*The Reading Nation*) implies, the eighteenth-century publishing industry helped create two nations of readers with two, very different sets of skills and expectations about reading: one, a tiny minority, practiced discriminating fact from fiction by reading expensive, time-consuming books that commented self-consciously on their own epistemological and stylistic status; and the other, the vast majority, sought escape and self-improvement by reading cheap works that were rapidly consumed and that preserved the superstitions, mysteries, and ignorance that prevailed at the dawn of print.

Virtually all the imaginative and financial writing I examined in chapter 2 was published during this high monopoly regime, and much of it belonged to the expensive material consumed by the elite. Then, in 1774, the conditions that governed publishing in England suddenly began to change. As with the late-seventeenth-century lapse of the Licensing Act, this change was inaugurated by a legal development. While the story behind the passage of the Booksellers' Act is too complex for me to rehearse here, suffice it to say that the success of the lawsuit that challenged the English courts' failure to enforce the Act of Anne had momentous implications. As St. Clair describes this contest, it was really a struggle between an old, monopolistic way of doing business and the commercial model described by political economists like Adam Smith:

> The scene was now set for the most decisive event in the history of reading in England since the arrival of printing 300 years before. It was a struggle between the ancient guild approach to economic management and the emerging world of free trade and economic competition, between entrenched interests and challenging innovatory forces, between elegant old money and vulgar business, between the clear words of modern statute law and the fuzzy talk of common-law rights, between a static *ancien régime* view of society based on hierarchy, heredity, property, and allocation of roles, and the new Enlightenment science of political economy that aimed to use the power of reason to bring about social and economic improvement. According to the Lockian view of property, the booksellers' portfolio was the intellectual property equivalent of a rich real estate originally tamed from a wilderness by the ancestors of the present owners, and subsequently improved and added to over the centuries by careful stewardship. Seen in terms of political economy, the portfolio was a fortune amassed by monopolistic businessmen derived from centuries of monarchical usurpation, restrictive trade practices, and price exploitation.[12]

As St. Clair's description makes clear, the Booksellers' bill ironically pitted the *ideas* promoted by eighteenth-century political economists against the *mode* in which their works had initially been published, for, if the monopolistic conditions St. Clair describes had not obtained, it is not at all clear that such small-market, high-cost volumes as Steuart's *Principles* or Smith's *Wealth of Nations* would ever have made their way into print. Whatever the ironies involved, in the end, political economic theory triumphed: the House of Lords decided against the English publishers, reinstated the terms of copyright established by the Act of Anne, and (however briefly) allowed Smith's dream of open competition to flourish in the book-producing industry.

In the wake of the 1774 decision, the English publishing trade threw off the shackles of monopoly, and the proliferation of paper that I have described began. The first increase in the output of imaginative writing seems to have occurred in what the *Critical Review* called the "prolific scribblerian year" of 1771–72, but this speedup became steady and sustained only in the early 1780s, when the effects of the 1774 act began to be felt. Whereas the average annual rate of growth for both new titles and reprints was 1.58 percent between 1740 and 1780, from 1780 to the end of the century this rate more than doubled, rising to 3.37 percent.[13] As Raven points out, this takeoff in imaginative publications consisted of an increase in the number of titles and editions rather than in edition sizes; it reflected both the expansion of the provincial distribution network, which, by 1800, included at least 112 circulating libraries in London and 268 in the rest of England, and new productivity and marketing sophistication on the part of printers and booksellers.[14] In the 1790s, a period during which new novel titles appeared at about three times the rate at which they had been published in the 1750s, the ranks of imaginative writing were joined by a flood of cheap printed material, much of which was political in nature. Despite successive attempts on the part of the government to suppress such materials (in 1794, 1796, and again in 1819), publications like *Salamagundi for Swine* and *Hogs' Wash* formed a staple of the reading materials of the masses.

Even during the brief window of publishing competition that the Booksellers' Act opened, according to St. Clair, Britain remained a nation divided into two reading audiences. This was true not only because publishers responded to the pent-up demand of the majority with new works that appealed to the lowest common denominator of ability and taste but also because the old materials they repackaged in cheap new editions tended to represent a distinctively conservative point of view that did not accommodate the substantive and formal innovations elite readers had learned to appreciate. Much of this "old canon"—stories like *Guy of Warwick, Robin Hood,* and *Bevis of Southampton*—was very old indeed, and its continued availability helped preserve the fact/fiction continuum for the lower classes long after elite readers had become used to seeing a difference between the two.[15] The newer volumes of the "old canon" included various series of "standard novelists" and "English poets," but most of these were, generally speaking, conduct literature: "The publishers of old-canon lists, whether mainstream or newly joining outsiders, not only ignored the discoveries of the Enlightenment, but offered a Counter-Enlightenment to readers who knew nothing of the Enlightenment."[16] The pricing structure of new publications also reinforced the bifurcation of British readers and ensured that this situation would survive the Booksellers' Act. While the prices of works included in the "old canon" fell sharply, the prices for works not so included rose steeply. Copyright legislation passed in 1808, 1814, 1836, and 1842 reinforced the publishers' control over both pricing and the volume of print runs by gradually extending the length of copyright from fourteen years to the length of an author's lifetime plus seven years (or forty-two years from date of publication, whichever was longer). This legislation effectively closed the window briefly opened to competition and made the works of most early-nineteenth-century elite writers—even those who populate the modern Literary canon—available to only a relatively small number of readers because no affordable English editions of these works existed.

As we will see in chapter 5, creating, then preserving, two nations of readers had momentous consequences for the social dynamics that characterized the nineteenth-century Literary world. For the gap that separated the expectations of the two groups of readers, compounded by the discrepancy in the sizes of the two audiences and the profits to be made by catering to the majority, meant that, every time a legal or price barrier fell, opportunistic publishers rushed to respond to (or create) demand with works that were cheap and easy to read. This, in turn, led the minority of elite readers and writers increasingly to fear that the very nature of English Literature was in peril, for, every time the volume of cheap publications increased, the overall quality of the nation's writing seemed to fall. In response, elite writers, aided by reviewers and critics, repeatedly sought to discriminate among kinds of imaginative writing and ways of reading. Not surprisingly, such discriminations were difficult to define and police, and they did little to close the gap between reading audiences that the publishing industry had perpetuated.

There were two substantial exceptions to publishers' ability to control the pricing of new books after 1800, both of which further complicated relations between the two nations of readers. The first exception consisted of works considered too controversial (usually too "obscene") for publishers to risk protecting their rights by prosecuting piracy. The most notorious examples of such works, Southey's *Wat Tyler*, Shelley's *Queen Mab*, and the first two cantos of Byron's *Don Juan*, were issued in pirated editions whose prices fell in direct relation to the quality of the paper on which they were printed and the number of words squeezed onto each page. As a consequence, these works became available to the large audience of "general readers," whose taste elite writers had already come to fear.[17] Instances of the second exception, new novels, were indirectly priced by the circulating libraries. After 1842, these libraries exerted so much pressure on the publishing industry by their willingness to purchase in bulk that their influence over new fiction resembled the eighteenth-century monopoly that the booksellers had exercised over publishing in general. While the circulating libraries' fees (and the high prices assigned to new novels purchased by individuals) did restrict the size of the audience for these works, the libraries could not stop alternative modes of publication—like cheap weekly magazines—from printing increased numbers of formulaic fictions; nor could they guarantee that the novels they did stock would approach the particular taste increasingly refined by the increasingly ambitious (and anxious) minority elite. As we will see in chapter 5, the result was a competition among models of value offered by members of the Literary world, each of which intersected in complex ways with the market model of value theorized by economic writers. The force field created by these complicated factors shifted as each condition was curtailed or altered. Thus, the ability of British pirates to cut into legitimate publishers' profits by underselling them was curtailed in 1839 by the repeal of the law that required printing presses to register with the state. The power exercised over the price of new fiction by Mudie's and other circulating libraries ended in 1894 when the circulating libraries voluntarily agreed to stop purchasing primarily novels published in the triple-decker format. And the gap between the two nations of readers did not even begin to close until the 1870s, when the adoption of compulsory schooling began to have an effect; arguably, the gap did not begin to close until the twentieth century. In my coda, I suggest that, even though schooling has undeniably narrowed the nineteenth-century version of the gap between elite and general readers, another gap has now replaced it: this one separates specialist readers, who have been trained in graduate programs, from the vast majority of readers, who are not disciplined by such training.

The Proliferation of Bank Paper

Before 1833, it was impossible for anyone—even a Bank of England director—to say how much credit paper circulated in Britain at any given time. It was clear to everyone that the volume and kinds of monetary paper had increased since the passage of the Restriction Act in 1797, but, with no regulation requiring that banks publish any part of their accounts, and with conventions of secrecy shrouding the denominations and volume of the outstanding bills of exchange, accurate information was simply unavailable. As we will see in chapter 3, the Bank Charter Act of 1833 began to require banks, including the Bank of England, to make some of this information public, but, as late as 1851, when William Newmarch tried to determine the exact volume of currency circulating in Britain, he was forced to rely on estimates for at least part of his conclusions.

The impenetrability of Britain's paper currency, at least in terms of volume, constitutes an important feature of the turn-of-the-century monetary situation for two reasons. The first has to do with the political issues that surrounded the currency. Given the relationship that was presumed to exist between the elevated commodity prices of the war years and a large volume of credit paper, the impenetrability of the currency meant that contemporaries on all sides of the political divide were free to speculate about which banks were issuing too much paper. Opponents of the Bank of England charged the Old Lady of Threadneedle Street with overissue during the Restriction period; supporters of the Bank, in turn, accused the country banks of issuing paper irresponsibly. Since the legislation that enacted the Restriction allowed banks to issue notes in small denominations, and because alleviating the requirement that note issue be redeemable for gold made the currency extremely elastic, all banks were tempted to issue paper to meet demand, and, as far as anyone could tell, most banks were succumbing to this temptation. Everyone agreed that prices were rising, in other words, but no one was sure why; and, when the end of the war with France brought no price stability and banks continued periodically to fail, everyone accused everyone else of monetary irresponsibility. Because no one could know exactly how much paper individual banks issued, then, speculation and accusation flourished, and the volume of writing *about* the currency issue increased, as writers tried out theories and floated volumes of imprecise information.

The second reason that the impenetrability of the volume of currency matters is that, as long as competing kinds of paper credit circulated, and as long as no one—not even the Bank of England—took responsibility for controlling the nation's currency, paper money remained controversial. No credit money could be taken for granted, in other words, because every banknote was as subject to evaluation in relation to the notes of competing banks as every bill of exchange always was. Until some institution took control over note issue in general, and until it was possible to rank and keep track of various kinds of paper credit, all notes would compete with each other, and, as a consequence, they would remain objects of cultural scrutiny. The Bank Act of 1844 finally began to exercise some control over this chaotic situation, thereby creating the conditions by which Bank of England notes could begin to attain the level of taken-for-grantedness that W. H.

Wills celebrated (prematurely) in his 1850 essay in *Household Words*. By strictly limiting the right of country banks to issue notes, and by establishing a specific ratio between securities and note issue for the Bank of England, the 1844 legislation began to rationalize the English banking system, to make Bank of England notes the most stable (and, therefore, desirable) form of paper currency, and to make information about the currency regularly available to anyone who wanted it. This legislation was controversial from the moment it was adopted, and it continued to be controversial for the rest of the century. Nevertheless, along with the technical improvements in printing that I described in the preamble, the 1844 Bank Act did help push the Bank of England note beneath the horizon of cultural visibility, and, even though rival forms of paper continued to circulate, Bank of England notes ceased to provoke the questions other kinds of paper repeatedly raised.

In this section, I briefly chronicle the related histories of attempts to find out about the volume of currency and attempts to control the effects of too much, or too little, credit paper. I return to these histories in chapters 3 and 4, but an overall picture should help frame those more detailed accounts. The Bank of England plays a central role in both stories, of course, for its ability to issue paper against securities, the monopoly it had been granted over note issue in London, and the special relationship it enjoyed with the government and the national debt placed this private institution at the center of the nation's money supply—even if it was not assigned an official role in controlling the volume of currency. During the eighteenth century, there were sporadic attempts to discover (and disclose) the volume of notes issued by the Bank and the amount of the securities that backed these notes, but the results were, at best, estimates and, more often, simply educated guesses. Meanwhile, beginning in the middle of the century, the number of country banks slowly began to increase. One estimate puts the number of provincial banks at 119 in 1784; by 1851, when Newmarch published the results of his investigation, he counted 900 non-London bank offices in England and Wales.[18] Most of these country banks issued notes, but, because no one knew the volume of this paper or the value of securities that stood behind it, no one could evaluate with confidence the relative validity of any country bank's notes.

In the last decades of the eighteenth century, two pieces of legislation gave investigators some insight into part of the circulating currency. First, in 1775, bills of exchange for amounts less than 20s (£1) were made illegal; two years later, this restriction was increased to £5 bills. This meant that, from 1775 until the Restriction Act, the small, easily counterfeited bills that circulated in such great numbers in the middle decades of the century largely disappeared.[19] Second, in 1782, the government required that all inland bills of exchange and promissory notes carry a stamp; the duties set in that year were repeatedly increased until 1815. This meant that the Stamp Office in London theoretically held records of all bills issued in England and Wales and, thus, that it was possible to find out how many bills of what value were outstanding. In practice, as Newmarch discovered, these records could sometimes be misleading because (among other reasons) they were not inclusive, they did not record the exact amount of each bill, and they did not include foreign bills at all.[20]

The Restriction Act, as we will see in chapter 3, provoked a flood of new writing on the currency, much of it intended to figure out which banks were issuing excessive currency. In addition to the pamphlets I discuss in chapter 3, the decades of the Restriction period (1797–1819/21) saw the publication of two additional contributions to the currency debates. The first was Henry Thornton's *Nature and Effects of the Paper Credit of Great Britain* (1802), which not only attempted to exonerate the Bank of England from the charge of overissue but also, in the process, tried to ascertain the volume and value of the bills of exchange currently in circulation. Determining this figure was important to any attempt to understand the currency, for most contemporaries thought (in 1810 at least) that bills of exchange constituted part of the nation's circulating medium, even if one held, as Thornton's critic Walter Boyd did, that bills were not, strictly speaking, money.[21] The second important contribution to the currency debates reported the findings of the 1810 House committee appointed to consider the price of bullion. Testimony before this committee, which issued the important (if controversial) Bullion Report of 1810, included significant statements by Thomas Richardson, one of the founders of the famous bill-broking house that became Overend, Gurney, and Company. As familiar as he was with the state of the bill market, however, Richardson was unable to determine the exact volume of the circulating medium.

In 1832, after the resumption of gold payments by the Bank, Henry Burgess, the secretary of the Association of Country Bankers and one of the chief contributors to the *Bankers' Circular*, confidently assured the Bank Charter Committee that a reduction in the volume of Bank of England notes invariably led to a contraction in the number of bills of exchange. This opinion was echoed in 1840 by Lord Overstone, one of the government's leading experts on financial matters, in testimony before the Committee on Banks of Issue. When Newmarch published his findings in 1851, he was forced to contradict this principle and to agree instead with the observations published in three short papers by Mr. Leatham, head of the Wakefield banking firm of Leatham, Tew, and Company. Even though Leatham's figures were based on estimates and averages at crucial points, Newmarch essentially confirmed what the banker had observed: when the Bank of England contracted its issue, the volume of bills of exchange did not decrease but actually increased substantially.[22] Despite his best efforts, however—he personally examined 4,367 bills of exchange held by five London bankers and bill brokers—even Newmarch could not determine with precision the volume of the circulating medium. In the course of his long and careful article, he had to acknowledge that his conclusions were only "approximate estimates."[23]

Even though the Bank Charter Act of 1833 required all banks to publicize the volume of their paper notes, then, the overall volume of the circulating medium, as well as the principles that governed the internal relations of its parts, remained elusive.[24] Since country banks continued to issue notes—albeit in ever-decreasing volume—through the entire nineteenth century, and because foreign bills of exchange remained untaxed (and, thus, unregistered), the volume of the currency continued to provoke controversy. Since rising prices (or the devaluation of the pound) constituted only one of the controversial symptoms of a currency that had exceeded the securities it presumably represented, moreover, contemporaries repeatedly returned to the matter of money to try to determine why Britain's credit system did not simply generate more profits, as the classical political economists said it should. As we will see in chapter 4, the most worrisome signs that something was wrong with the system were the periodic manias and panics that punctuated the nineteenth century. The panics that erupted with alarming regularity after 1825–26 brought down scores of banking firms, along with other businesses that had previously prospered. These panics seemed to herald some problem even more pervasive and less comprehensible than the impenetrable volume of the nation's money supply; but one thing was clear to everyone who wrote about these subjects: without both reliable information and theories about how the credit system worked, no one would be able to anticipate, much less forestall, the crises that continued to shake Britain's economy.

Differential Forms

In the remainder of this book, I trace the measures taken by producers of monetary, financial, and Literary genres to differentiate their works from each other during the course of the nineteenth century. In the process of naturalizing this differentiation, I argue, the producers of financial (and economic) writing and Literary authors implicitly supported two different models of value. The most dominant model, as we have already begun to see, defined *value* in market terms—as a function of exchange, price, labor, utility, or some other measurable index. The other, less prominent model defined *value* in terms of subjective qualities that defied quantification, were immune to exchange, and were sometimes difficult to grasp or convey. Writers used words like *imagination, genius,* and *originality* to characterize the qualities by which this value could be recognized, but, because every individual experienced it differently, the exact nature of the value these objects conveyed often seemed impossible to describe. Indeed, instead of focusing on the differentiation of value, which was implicit in their projects, the imaginative writers whose works I examine in the following pages often concentrated on differentiating the *formal* characteristics of their writings and linked these formal features to the contribution their works supposedly uniquely made to the mediation of value in general. As we will see, in other words, most writers who aspired to offer an alternative model of value tended not to do so explicitly but rather, by a combination of tactics, simply to distance themselves from the dominant, market model of value. Among these tactics was the elaboration of the idea that only posterity was fit to judge the merits of a Literary production, the celebration of imaginative artworks as constituting formally self-contained worlds that were immune from market price, and the development of an internally differentiated cadre of workers, all devoted, in different ways, to the perpetuation of Literary genius.

In arguing that nineteenth-century Literary writers tried increasingly to differentiate their work both from the writing produced by political economists and from the market model of value, I am, of course, flying in the face of much recent scholarship. As I noted in the introduction to this book, many Literary scholars have described the structural, metaphoric, and linguistic continuities that can be found in writings by nineteenth-century political economists and novelists in particular. I do not dispute the claims that Victorian political economists and novelists, for example, both showed an interest in organicism (as Catherine Gallagher argues) or that we can identify a "logic of capital" in novels by Dickens and the economic writing of Ricardo (as Claudia Klaver argues). My point is that these continuities now have to be *discovered* precisely because nineteenth-century writers devoted so much energy to denying them and because their efforts were, to a certain extent, successful. Nineteenth-century writers denied the continuities we now see in their works for several reasons. In the first place, these writers saw themselves as competitors, not only with other members of their own profession, but also, disciplinarily, with writers of other kinds of works; they saw themselves as competitors because they knew that they were all seeking to mediate some kind of value, even if they were not always able to define the kind of value their writings conveyed. In the second place, precisely because the model of value promoted by classical political economists was so antithetical to the kind of value Literary writers sensed but could not define, the latter often tried simply to extract themselves from market relations altogether—to deny, in one way or another, that the political economists' understanding of the world had anything to do with Literature. This led to what I have been calling the *misrecognition* of Literature's relation to the market.[25] And, in the third place, because it was impossible for Literary writers to repudiate the market in practice, they developed elaborate defenses of their own work meant to mask or obscure the ineluctable fact that books circulated in the market too. Our contemporaries find metaphoric resemblance at the levels of form and structure, then, because nineteenth-century writers tried so hard to deny that any other kind of relationship existed, even when this meant obscuring the common project that united Literary writers and economic theorists.

The momentum behind this denial (or misrecognition) came from economic and imaginative writers alike and took the form of both differentiation from their professional or political coworkers and differentiation from work produced in other genres. On the one side, because critics of the government repeatedly denigrated paper notes as "fictive" substitutes for "real money" (by which they meant first gold or silver, then convertible Bank of England notes), writers who sought to defend the credit economy increasingly felt it necessary to deny *any* association between imaginative writing and paper money—not to mention imaginative writing and their own, supposedly superior theories about value. By the same token, as we have seen, because no bank publicized the volume of its notes (before 1833), and because the Bank and Pitt's ministry did not make public the rationale behind the Bank's unprecedented loans to the government in the 1790s, speculation flourished about both these matters—especially as economic conditions became more volatile in the first decades of the nineteenth century. To counter these speculations—and to brand them as unfounded, incendiary fictions—economic writers offered alternative accounts that either took the long view, by emphasizing Great Britain's historical march to commercial supremacy, or struck a greater level of abstraction, by emphasizing political economic theory. In their responses to critics' cries for information and disclosure, in other words, financial writers offered historical narratives that sought to submerge recent events in a longer context, and economic writers composed theoretical treatises that tried to transcend the call for information by offering abstract, supposedly universal principles.

On the other side, authors who wanted to elevate the social prestige of imaginative writing increasingly struggled to identify some axis of discrimination that could distinguish their work not only from the writings of political economists but also from the floods of formulaic, sensational, and political writing that proliferated in the decades immediately before and after the turn of the century. To do the latter—to enhance the status of (some kinds of) imaginative writing and to distance this from other kinds that only superficially resembled serious Literature—many authors sought to deny the extent to which their writing depended on commercial transactions. By treating financial matters as content—as themes, plot elements, and, most important, indices to a character's moral worth—Literary writers followed the example already set by Richardson; they sought to subsume their unavoidable participation in the market into imaginative (and voluntary) choices that primarily served an aesthetic, not a commercial, rationale. Even more pointedly, beginning in the last decades of the eighteenth century, writers at nearly every rung of the hierarchy of imaginative kinds began to fill their works with stereotypical, generally negative depictions of business characters. That these negative portrayals coincided with the growth of the book trade suggests that many writers were attempting to manage, at the level of content, what James Raven calls the "embarrassing dilemma" created by the book trade's structural implication in the commercialized fashion industry its more elite participants criticized.[26]

With financial and economic writers offering history and theory as correctives to charges about the fictive nature of paper money or demands for more information, and with imaginative writers increasingly desperate to deny their works' status as commodities, the early-eighteenth-century continuum that linked fact to fiction was finally, completely severed. As a result, by the second half of the nineteenth century, economic writers who invoked imaginative images to explain phenomena that otherwise seemed inexplicable, as W. Stanley Jevons did when faced with the conundrum of speculative manias, embarrassed even their staunchest admirers; and imaginative writers who wanted to bring information back into fiction, as Charles Reade did in the 1850s and 1860s, found themselves increasingly pushed to the margin of serious Literary writing. In the chapters that follow, I respect this separation by treating the two kinds of writing separately. In doing so, I may risk reifying a distinction whose origins and successive stages require historical explanation, but I can provide this explanation only by examining contemporary efforts to make the separation seem natural.

CHAPTER THREE

Politicizing Paper Money

By the 1790s, fiction was an acknowledged product of particular kinds of writing, related to but distinguishable from its counterpart, facts. I do not want to overstate the separation between fiction and fact in relation to individual texts, for less prestigious kinds of writing in particular, like publications addressed to the lower classes or to a mass readership, continued to produce the two side by side; and, beginning in 1829, one of the nineteenth century's most respected authors, Walter Scott, enhanced the popularity of his already critically acclaimed fictions by including informational notes and appendices. Indeed, as we will see in the next two chapters, the inclusion of both fact and fiction within individual works sometimes helped critics rank these texts within the hierarchies that ordered financial writing, both informational and theoretical, and imaginative writing. This complication notwithstanding, it is fair to say, I think, that, by the end of the 1790s, most British readers would have recognized the first differentiation with which this book is concerned: contemporaries might disagree about whether fiction was good for some people—especially young women—and whether facts could be comprehended by others—especially lower-class readers—but all but the most disadvantaged readers could recognize fiction and fact when they encountered them, even when the two appeared in the same text.[1]

In this chapter, I address one genre in which fiction continued to pose cultural problems even after it had become recognizable. This genre is paper money, whose cultural efficacy, as we have repeatedly seen, depended both on maintaining and on neutralizing the fictions that enabled it to pass current. Unlike the fiction associated with imaginative writing, in other words, the fictional quality of paper money always had the potential to reanimate the problematic of representation. This was true partly because none of the evaluative criteria that helped contemporaries rank works of imaginative writing relative to each other and that assigned all these works to a socially acceptable but marginal place was applicable to paper money, whose aesthetic merits were inconsequential, and whose social importance continued to grow along with Britain's burgeoning economy. In simplest terms, paper money could always activate the problematic of representation because the single evaluative criterion that did apply to notes (their relative validity) was impossible to enforce as long as rival variants of paper circulated and as long as the notes that eventually became the standard—Bank of England notes—had yet to achieve the currency or uniformity that would enable users to take them for granted.

Given the crucial role that, in retrospect, all kinds of credit instruments can be seen to have played in the spectacular expansion of Britain's economy during the first three-quarters of the nineteenth century, it may be difficult to remember that paper money was once so controversial or—more precisely—so closely aligned with the problematic of representation. But it is precisely the proximity of paper money to this problematic that its centrality to capital growth has helped efface. Recovering this problematic now can help us make sense of various early-nineteenth-century campaigns to politicize paper money and to grant Bank of England notes priority in the country's sea of paper. It can also help us see the process by which at least one of the cultural instruments that mediates value in the modern economy began to pass beneath the horizon of visibility, taking with it the questions that its constitutive relationship to fiction has always had the capacity to raise.

As we will see in this chapter and the next, the campaign to render Bank of England notes the unassailable standard of paper money and the official representative of English monetary value was conducted by several sets of individuals and against the backdrop of several interrelated debates. Some of the contributors to this campaign were what might be called *money amateurs*, in the sense that they either attained their understanding of currency from practical experience (often in banking) or came on the subject accidentally, in the course of other, typically legislative, work (as Robert Peel did). Others belonged to the categories of economic experts, monetary professionals, or financial popularizers, which were all roles associated with the institutional developments examined in the next chapter. All the advocates for regularizing the paper money system and effacing the problematic of representation, however, belonged to what I will call the *economic establishment*; that is, they shared the assumptions that paper credit was essential to the expansion of Britain's economy, both domestic and international;

that the expansion of the British economy was an undeniable goal, both national and personal; and that certain social and economic inequalities were inevitable by-products of or preconditions for this expansion, however regrettable they might be. Most of the critics of the English monetary system, by contrast, did not share these assumptions. Some of the individuals I call *currency radicals* were socially and professionally marginalized in ways we are about to see; others, like David Ricardo, played central roles in the political establishment and in the monetary solution that eventually prevailed. What united these otherwise disparate men was that all the currency radicals questioned the Bank's right to control the money supply because they considered the Bank "the locus of Old Corruption."[2] To promote this claim, they tried to politicize the subject of paper money—to keep the problematic of representation visible. One of the ways they did so was by arguing that the concept of value was expansive and should be kept so: value, they insisted, should not simply be a function of competitive market conditions, subject to measurement by volume, demand, or price. In significant ways, this position overlapped with that taken by a far more (politically) conservative faction, a heterogeneous group known as the Bullionists, some of whom insisted that the value of money was inherent and absolute, not dictated by the market.[3] I return in a moment to the Bullionist debate. For now, it is sufficient to note that the currency radicals who proposed new *kinds* of money did not always propose a genuine alternative to the market model of value, as the Bullionists did. Nevertheless, in the face of the economic establishment's increasingly organized and vehement support for the market model, all alternative senses of value were increasingly marginalized as the century wore on. Even if it now seems quaint or naive, the articulation of this possibility in the first decades of the nineteenth century is worth recovering, for the questions that its proponents raised about money and value remind us of what we have lost in acquiescing to this facet of modern specialization.

I divide this chapter into two sections that correspond roughly to the two major monetary controversies of the first half of the nineteenth century. In the first section, I address some of the debates that broke out during the Restriction period (1797–1819/21). Participants in these debates, both members of the establishment and various currency radicals, repeatedly flirted with the possibility that the paper money that proliferated in Britain's wartime economy could expose the problematic of representation. They did not use this term, of course, but, when they worried about (or celebrated) the "fictitious" nature of paper money, the indeterminate relationship between the representative of value and its ground was implicit in their concerns (and hopes). The currency radical whose writing dominated this period was William Cobbett, and the enormous popularity of his *Paper against Gold* signals just how close the radicals came to making the problematic of representation visible during these decades. In the second section, I turn to a series of writings produced in the wake of the Bank's restoration of payments and the passage, in 1826, 1833, and 1844, of three important pieces of legislation intended to strengthen the position of the Bank of England. While all these events supported the Bank, they did not specifically make the Bank directors assume responsibility for the nation's money supply. As a result, questions about the ground of paper money's value continued to surface, even as establishment writers gradually succeeded in narrowing *the concept* of value to the more restrictive terms that dominated the discussions of the political economists I consider in chapter 4. The two currency radicals I discuss in this section are Robert Owen and John Francis Bray. While both advocated the more expansive definition of *value* associated with early counterestablishment campaigns, neither was finally able to reverse the establishment's increasing monopoly over the definition of *value*— at least partly because both proposed monetary innovations instead of challenging the principle of deferral naturalized by paper money.

The First Currency Radical: William Cobbett Pits Paper against Gold

As we have seen, the Bank of England was effectively granted a monopoly over note issue in London in 1708 by a provision that denied issue to banking corporations with more than six partners. The ban against corporations was extended to the rest of England and Wales by the Bubble Act, which was enacted in 1720 in the wake of the South Sea Bubble.[4] But, as we have also seen, the restriction on corporate banking in the nation's capital and on joint-stock corporations throughout England and Wales did not give the Bank of England a national monopoly over the issue of paper money. On the contrary, from at least the beginning of the eighteenth century, privately funded banking operations existed in England, even though these were not devoted exclusively to banking or note issue. At the same time, as we have seen, other credit instruments circulated alongside banknotes.[5] As we have also seen, the proliferation of kinds of paper, almost all of which circulated locally, was partly a response to the poor quality and inadequate supply of Britain's coinage; partly, of course, it was an articulation of—as well as a spur to—the growth of the British economy, which, fueled by overseas trade, war expenditures, and a dramatic rise in domestic demand for luxuries, rapidly and dramatically exceeded the coin available to transact domestic business.

I pointed out in chapter 1 that paper currency was intermittently a source of concern for prominent eighteenth-century Britons, and sometimes—although not always—this concern was expressed in political (party) terms. Especially after the collapse of the South Sea Bubble, for example, writers like Alexander Pope, Jonathan Swift, and Lord Bolingbroke tied speculation, the escalating national debt, and paper currency into a stick with which to spank the governing Whigs. But paper money also provoked worries that were not (or not explicitly) political, as it did, for example, for Lord Elibank and David Hume, two Scots who publicly opposed the use of paper money in the middle decades of the century. Both writers based their opposition on the claim that paper money was, in Elibank's words, "a fiction" and, in Hume's, "a counterfeit." According to Elibank, the increased reliance on this "imaginary money of paper" was a sign but also a cause of a dangerous lethargy among his contemporaries: "the evil consequences of this implicit faith, this unlimited trust, this lethargic carelessness of my countrymen, with regard to paper-credit," had led, in his view, to the "public calamity" of increased prices and devalued notes.[6] According to Hume, paper money distorted the "natural proportion" between the circulating medium, labor, and commodities. He favored limiting private banking to banks of deposit, which would simply hold the money they received and not issue part of their holdings as paper.[7]

In 1767, Sir James Steuart tried to counter the charge that paper money was "a fiction" by drawing a distinction between "money of the world," gold and silver, and "money of the society," paper. Steuart argued that, especially in periods in which the international balance of trade was unfavorable to a country, "good citizens" should accept paper money as an expression of faith in their nation's honesty.[8] Similarly, in 1776, Adam Smith supported without much comment the judicious issue of paper money, stating simply that the amount of paper money should never exceed the value of the gold and silver it represents.[9] Thus, paper money was debated in the eighteenth century—especially when increased prices or commercial crises, like those of 1763, 1772, 1783, and 1793, brought the subject to writers' attention—but this sporadic debate was minor by contrast with the controversy that followed the Restriction Act of 1797. In order to explain why this act so rapidly led to the politicization of paper money and the proliferation of writing about it, I need briefly to summarize its causes and effects.

At the end of 1796, Britain was at war with France, the national debt had reached an unprecedented size, and the reserves in the Bank of England had fallen to a dangerously low level. The Bank's deplorable condition was partly a result of Pitt's attempts to use the Bank to finance the conflict with France: since the war's beginning in 1793, the government had repeatedly pressed the Bank for further advances, largely in the form of short-term bills, which the Bank was expected to discount. Partly, the state of the Bank's reserve was an effect of the concern expressed by country bankers, who sought to anticipate a possible run on their own reserves by drawing on the Bank. The Bank tried to stop the outflow of gold by restricting the discounts it allowed, but this policy could not withstand the effect of rumors, which began to circulate just before Christmas 1796, that the French were poised to invade England. Early in February 1797, a large number of farmers in Newcastle simultaneously demanded their money from local banks, and, because of insufficient reserves, these banks were forced to close. By 25 February, with rumors about an invasion intensifying, the price of consols (government securities) having fallen to a frighteningly low level, and a credit crisis gripping the City, Pitt, the king, and the Bank of England's governor and deputy governor decided that the Bank of England should stop redeeming paper notes with gold. An Order in Council dated 26 February made the stoppage of payment official, and, in May, the king inaugurated the period known as the Restriction by signing the Restriction Act.[10]

The Restriction Act almost immediately produced two dramatic effects. On the one hand, as we will see, the suspension of cash payments meant that contemporaries critical of the government rushed into print to charge the Bank—and the moneyed interests who benefited from the national debt—with violating the promise printed on the face of every note. On the other hand, the Restriction also encouraged the proliferation of provincial banks' notes and banks of issue. It encouraged this increase by inviting country banks to issue notes in any denomination in order to compensate for the shortage of coin; it also encouraged more entrepreneurs to form banks by suspending the requirement that country banks back their notes with gold. Initially, the Restriction period was expected to last only a few months, but, as it dragged on for more than twenty years, it led to an increase in paper notes that variously encouraged, bewildered, and alarmed contemporaries.

The Restriction Act sought to curtail a new kind of commercial crisis—one that differed substantially from the nation's previous commercial crises. Whereas each of the crises of the late eighteenth century had followed a speculative boom and was alleviated by the Bank's willingness to extend credit, the events leading up to the Restriction provoked a crisis of confidence in the overall monetary and banking systems: Britons were terrified that no policy of the Bank of England could protect country banks, which depended on the Bank for gold. The mere declaration of war in 1793 had already brought many provincial banks to their knees, for, without a large base of backers, and with poor credit facilities themselves, these small concerns could not meet depositors' panicked demands for cash. Since its reserve had dwindled to the alarming sum of £2 million by 1791, the Bank could not have stopped provincial banks' failures had it wanted to. The Restriction Act did manage to quell the immediate crisis—historians argue that signs of returning confidence began to appear in the banking system by August 1797—but the dramatic legislative interference could not stop the domino-like cascade of bank failures. Pressnell reports: "Between 1750 and 1830 at least 343 firms, the members of which described themselves as 'bankers,' failed in the country; 334 of them failed between 1790 and 1826, sixty-seven in the three years 1814–16; and sixty in the period July 1825 to June 1826."[11] Because country banks constituted the public face of banking for most Britons, and because these banks were not insured (as most modern banks are), their failure could have done permanent damage to Britons' confidence—not just in local banks, but in the entire British financial system, which, as we have seen, was fully based on credit by the end of the eighteenth century. For the first three decades of the nineteenth century, this possibility, along with the price volatility that occurred during the Restriction, provoked a miscellaneous group of writers to identify paper money as the most visible weakness of the credit economy. These writers represented a variety of political positions, and they occupied various positions in the business, legislative, religious, and journalistic communities, but their common focus on the fictive quality of paper money shows just how close to the surface the problematic of representation was in the first decades of the century.

When they are discussed at all, the members of the first group of writers I consider here are generally seen as participants in the "Bullionist controversy," the debate about whether and when note holders should be able to redeem their paper for gold.[12] This controversy was partly a response to the dramatic fall in the value of the pound in relation to gold, which seemed, to some contemporaries but not others, like an obvious consequence of an increased volume of paper money. The pound's value fell in four successive waves, waves separated by brief, but not sustained, rebounds: 1799–1802, 1809, 1811, and 1817. Every time the pound lost value, contemporaries gestured toward the increase in the numbers of country banks of issue (from about eighty in 1793, to seven hundred in 1810, to nine hundred in 1815), and some mentioned the corresponding increases in the Bank of England's note issue (in 1799 and 1809).[13] I say that contemporaries *gestured* toward these factors because, as we have seen, no official data were available about the number of banks in operation, the volume of their note issue, or the role the Bank was playing in the unfolding situation. The two things no one could fail to notice were that prices began to rise dramatically after passage of the act and that they seemed to rise in some relation to the volume of notes in circulation.

Partly, the controversy about whether paper money should be returned to the "discipline" of the gold standard reflected more general worries about the nature of Britain's chaotic wartime growth. With credit readily available, the national debt on the rise, and overcrowded cities engulfing the surrounding countryside, some conservatives, like Edward Copleston, worried that the "shadowy and ideal" riches of the new speculative age were displacing the "real" wealth generated by the land.[14] This position obviously mapped onto the early-eighteenth-century Tory opposition to the moneyed interests and Burke's Harringtonian preference for traditional values, but it also dovetailed with a newly pertinent concern that the Bank of England directors might be withholding information out of self-interest, instead of acting patriotically, in the nation's best interests.[15]

To dispel the obscurity that masked the volume and the composition of the nation's money supply—which, as we have seen, constitutes one facet of the problematic of representation—some writers began to demand that the Bank of England disclose the size of its note issue. In 1801, for example, four years after the Restriction Act, Walter Boyd, a Scots financier and merchant banker (a partner in Boyd, Benfield and Co.) made this demand in print; if the Bank refused to make its note issue public, he implied, the public would know that the Bank was using the act as an excuse to inflate (and hide) its note issue and profits. His professed aim was to challenge the fiction that enabled paper to pass as money, but Boyd also offered a more general monetary lesson: he wanted to teach readers that, because of its crucial role in the nation's banking system, the Bank of England had an interest in keeping the quantity of paper high.[16] He assigned responsibility to the Bank of England, not country bankers, because he insisted that the former encouraged the latter to issue more paper by (deceptively) guaranteeing its own notes (which implicitly backed country banks' notes);[17] if the Bank did not somehow raise the value of its notes, he warned, the deceit would be revealed, Britons would stop taking any paper money, and the nation's credit system would collapse.[18] The only way to increase the value of its notes, he continued, was for the Bank to decrease the volume of its issue; and the best way to ensure this was to return to the time when "the great primary wheel, which set it [the currency issue] in motion, turned upon an axis of Gold and Silver."[19] Boyd was arguing, in other words, that country banks' notes could be inconvertible (for gold) as long as they could be exchanged for Bank paper and as long as the Bank's notes were really what they claimed to be—that is, redeemable for gold.

While Boyd's pamphlet is interesting for its content (as an international financier, Boyd had a personal interest in restoring the gold backing of notes), it is most revealing as an instance of the kind of publication the act provoked: it is relatively short, probably privately financed, and aimed at a middle-class, largely commercial audience. This pamphlet, moreover, not only typified one response; it also prompted responses of its own. Thus, Francis Baring, one of the Bank's directors, retaliated with his own brief response, and Henry Thornton, one of the authors of the 1810 Bullion Report and the brother of Samuel Thornton, another Bank director, published his much longer pamphlet *On Credit* to refute publications like Boyd's.[20] One of Boyd's implicit charges was that, without a basis in gold, Bank paper was patently fictitious, and this roused Thornton to answer "the common charge" levied against Bank paper—that it is "merely a fictitious thing." Thornton's response to this charge was succinct but, he no doubt hoped, decisive: "To reproach it with being merely a fictitious thing, because it possesses not the intrinsic value of gold, is to quarrel with it on account of that quality which is the very ground of its merit. Its merit consists in the circumstance of its costing almost nothing."[21]

The complexities of this debate are impossible to overstate, for, while Boyd opposed the note-issue monopoly of the Bank, he was not an anti-Bullionist. That is, he did not argue that English money should float free of a ground of gold or that the profits that the wartime credit had generated were the signs that a new financial age had dawned. By the same token, the men who answered him were not opposed to all the positions he endorsed. Henry Thornton, an evangelical banker and one of the three primary theorists of the Bullionist position, shared Boyd's desire to return to the gold standard. The other two architects of Bullionist theory agreed with this basic position but offered variants of their own: David Ricardo, a Jewish currency radical, thought that the Bank should be stripped of its note-issue power; and Francis Horner, a financial journalist, largely endorsed Adam Smith's stance on the Bank.[22] Thus, while the differences among the positions taken by these men seemed momentous to them, what matters now is that they all exposed a "common charge"—that paper money was based on a fiction.

We can see this common charge in at least two other pamphlets published soon after the Restriction Act. In 1803, William Howison, a Scots financial writer, invoked the "fictitious state of paper money" and charged that, when a government relied exclusively on its authority to back paper, people inevitably began to suspect that the currency had no value at all.[23] Like Boyd, Howison was generally concerned about the obscurity that shrouded the Bank of England's actions.[24] Like Boyd as well, Howison recommended ending the Restriction as soon as possible so that Bank paper would once more rest on gold, public confidence would revive, and gold would (presumably) flow into the Bank's coffers. In 1804, Lord King, the prominent landowner and member of Parliament, repeated the worry that paper money was fictitious and called again for ending the Restriction. Calling "the substitution of paper money for metal" the "most curious and important fact in the commercial history of modern times," Lord King (who, as we will see, provoked Parliament to reinforce the status of the Bank's notes after the Bullion Report was rejected in 1811) charged that the "natural standard" for value had to be set by a nation's gold and silver.[25] In the absence of this standard—which should also back the Bank's convertible paper notes—the volume of paper would inevitably fluctuate according to demand and the (dubious) wisdom of the Bank directors. While Lord King was willing to allow the Bank to keep the volume of its note issue secret, he insisted that the Restriction Act was "a law to suspend the performance of contracts" and that the issue of inconvertible Bank notes was tantamount to "a breach of parliamentary faith."[26]

These three writers, like the men who answered them (Thornton and Baring, among others), belonged to what I am calling the *economic establishment*, even when, like Boyd, they challenged the decisions of the Bank or, like Boyd and Howison, they hailed from Scotland (where banking rested on a more stable foundation).[27] By saying that these men were part of the economic establishment, I mean not simply that they belonged to the classes that benefited from trade, banking, and the national debt but also that they wrote from the shared set of social assumptions I have already described. Most important, even though they differed from Pitt's administration and the Bank's directors about the necessity of an inconvertible paper currency, they all endorsed the position that Lord King explicitly articulated: paper money formed a crucial part of an advanced nation's circulating medium, and whatever taint of "fiction" it carried could be neutralized by making at least some of the nation's paper convertible. Gold, in short, provided a "real" ground for value, and, when paper was convertible, in the last instance (of the Bank), it traveled back from an "imaginary" realm to the land of the "real." During subsequent decades, other establishment writers voiced opinions similar to Boyd's, Howison's, and Lord King's—especially in the years immediately preceding the Bank's resumption of gold payments (initially, as a sort of trial, in 1819; then officially in 1821). Both before and after the Bank resumed payment, this position was also endorsed by evangelical political economists, who played a prominent role in these discussions for the first half of the century, as we will see in the next chapter. Meanwhile, some establishment writers voiced opinions I otherwise associate with the currency radicals. These included not only Ricardo, who wanted to curtail the Bank's note issue, but also Joseph Hume, G. Poulett Scrope, and J. W. Gilbart, who supported a free trade in money.[28] In addition to these anti-Bank (but not anti-Bullionist) voices from within the political establishment, some of the most outspoken critics of the Bank, Bank money, and the Restriction linked their criticisms to a larger claim: the entire system of social, as well as monetary, inequity should be overthrown.

————

The most prominent and prolific currency radical of the first third of the nineteenth century was William Cobbett (1763–1835), the farmer, soldier, journalist, and eventual member of Parliament. Cobbett spent much of his life chronicling and protesting the narrowing of the more expansive understanding of value that he associated with Britain's eighteenth-century agrarian society. His most comprehensive assault on the paper money system appeared in a series of letters initially addressed to the "gentlemen of Salisbury" and published in his journal, the *Weekly Political Register*, between September 1810 and August 1811. Issues of the *Political Register* sold for 1s. each, thus putting the paper beyond the means of most working-class readers and making it clear that the "gentlemen" Cobbett initially addressed were small farmers, tradesmen, artisans, and local merchants, not laborers or the unemployed. The twenty-nine original letters, along with three new ones, were reissued, as both a 5s. book entitled *Paper against Gold* and 2d. or 3d. parts, in 1815. In these formats, the letters are estimated to have sold over 150,000 copies in the two years before they were again reissued in the cheaper, unstamped version of the *Weekly Political Register* that Cobbett launched in 1816. In 1828, Cobbett claimed that over 30,000 copies of the twopenny version of *Paper against Gold* were purchased in 1817 alone, and, later that year, he said that over 100,000 copies of the book had been bought. In book form, *Paper against Gold* remained in print for at least the next dozen years. Such figures, which, even if somewhat inflated, are remarkable for the period, have led one of Cobbett's modern biographers to call *Paper against Gold* "the most widely read book ever published purely on monetary questions."[29]

Cobbett was provoked to write *Paper against Gold* by a series of bank failures and the government's inadequate response to the monetary problems they disclosed. The first failure to attract Cobbett's notice was that of a London bank that crashed in July 1810. Within three weeks, an Exeter bank failed, as did banks in Salisbury and Shaftesbury; in August, another London bank failed, bringing additional country banks down with it. In response, tradesmen in Salisbury refused to accept local banknotes, and this caused even the provident poor to lose everything: in Cobbett's words, they "saw their little all vanish in a moment, and themselves reduced to the same state with the improvident, the careless, the lazy, the spendthrift, the drunkard, and the glutton."[30] By the end of the summer, the *Monthly and Commercial Report* announced that the "stoppages and compositions [bankruptcies] are equal in number to one-half the traders in the Kingdom.... In Manchester and other places, houses stop not only every day but every hour."[31] To many contemporaries, such failures seemed like the symptoms of a more general economic crisis: wages were low, prices and unemployment were high, and the drawn-out war with France, with its accompanying embargo, had made even necessities difficult to obtain. The government's response, as we have already seen, was to try to raise more money from an already overextended Bank by issuing new short-term, unfunded debt in the form of Exchequer and navy bills.[32]

At the time he began the letters about the currency (which I will refer to by their volume title, *Paper against Gold*), Cobbett was serving a two-year sentence in Newgate Prison for seditious libel, a charge resulting from his defense of a group of Ely militiamen who had been flogged for demanding back pay. This situation is important for three reasons. First, and most simply, imprisonment gave Cobbett time to develop the argument that he had been intermittently pursuing since 1803, when he read Thomas Paine's 1796 pamphlet attacking Britain's funding system. Second, his initial campaign—in favor of the militiamen's rights and against flogging—positioned Cobbett against the campaign that William Pitt's government was trying to promote, the campaign to encourage Britons to join local militias to prevent a French invasion. To support fair treatment of the local men who composed the militia, in other words, was to oppose the government's attempts to present patriotism as the counterpart to—and support of—belief in what the government represented as the other bulwark of national security, the system of public credit.[33] This position also, significantly, marked Cobbett's retreat from the conservative, pro-Pitt stance he had voiced during the 1790s, when he wrote under the name of Peter Porcupine from his self-imposed exile in

America. And, third, the actual charge for which Cobbett was imprisoned—seditious libel—placed him in the company of the radicals who had been prosecuted in England during the 1790s. This makes it clear that his transgression was a crime of print, that freedom of the press was one of the causes he defended, and that writing could still serve as a political weapon.[34] If the government had momentarily succeeded in confining Cobbett, he seemed determined to use print to defy his imprisonment and to make his accusers answer for their crimes against the people.

Before considering Cobbett's attack on the paper money system, I need briefly to specify the nature of the position he occupied in relation to other writers, both financial and imaginative. This position, especially in relation to financial and economic writers, was one of *marginalization*. In Cobbett's case, this marginal position was overdetermined, for it was simultaneously imposed and consciously adopted. On the one hand, because of the very mode of his publications, Cobbett occupied an institutionally marginal position: in the same decade that saw the founding of the first university position in political economy (at the East India College at Haileybury, Hertford, in 1807) and the launch of the first quarterly largely devoted to economic topics (the *Edinburgh Review*, in 1802), Cobbett published his *Weekly Political Register* independently, from a position located outside the university, the paid lecture circuit, and the circle of influence that enabled contemporaries like Francis Horner to attract the notice of patrons and legislators. On the other hand, his elective marginalization was stylistic. Self-consciously adopting a mode of writing that alluded to the radical writings of the 1790s yet departed from the style typical of those cheap, incendiary publications, Cobbett developed a mode of writing that was clearly outside the establishment yet difficult to ignore.[35] Described by William Hazlitt as "plain, broad, downright English," this style relied on concrete nouns and everyday examples yet harnessed this unadorned writing to antiestablishment messages.[36]

As numerous scholars have pointed out, this style was designed to address two audiences simultaneously: the politically disenfranchised, largely self-educated readership that self-mockingly referred to its members as the "swine" and the politically and sometimes economically advantaged readership whose members nonetheless also suffered from the hardships of the war years.[37] The commercial success of both the 1s. and the 2d. versions of the *Register* suggests that Cobbett's stylistic gambit worked. Indeed, as Jon Klancher argues, Cobbett's stylistic innovation not only enabled working-class audiences to understand his message; it also "forced" middle-class readers to respond. Because middle-class and aristocratic readers could relate to the way Cobbett wrote yet could not help but think that he spoke for the silent masses, they feared that Cobbett was "the very emblem of an English radical public." Thus, at least two conservative papers were launched to denounce him, and a writer for *Blackwood's Magazine* parodied his style.[38] Whether mocking or reviling him, Cobbett's politically more conservative contemporaries could neither make him one of their own nor simply dismiss him as a "mob writer."[39] Even the Literary elite, who, as we will see, had already begun to intensify efforts to distinguish serious Literature from less respectable kinds of imaginative writing, could not ignore him, even when they expressly disapproved of him. In 1805, for example, Samuel Coleridge, who was devoting much of his energy to defining a "clerisy" qualified to protect British Literary culture (and who was a monetary relativist), called Cobbett a "Political Harlequin," charged him with being dull, and, as Leonora Nattrass points out, immediately undercut this charge by devoting an entire series of articles to him.[40] Percy Shelley was equally ambivalent. "What a pity that so powerful a genius should be combined with the most odious moral qualities," he wrote.[41]

The horrified fascination expressed by Coleridge and Shelley was reflected in the attention that other, more minor Romantic writers devoted to this self-educated turnip farmer–turned–writer. William Hazlitt wrote a "Character of Cobbett," for example, and Leigh Hunt credited him with virtually inventing the popular press: "The invention of printing itself scarcely did more for the diffusion of knowledge and the enlightening of the mind than has been effected by the Cheap Press of this country. Thanks to Cobbett!"[42] As we will see in chapter 5, the position of "minor" *Literary* writer, which both Hazlitt and Hunt occupied, was also a social position created during the early decades of the nineteenth century. While the position of minority has certain features in common with Cobbett's position of marginalization, Literary minority also differed from marginalization by— or within—financial writing in significant ways. In large part, the relatively early consolidation of economic or financial writing—through its incorporation into the education system, its theoretical codification in the writings and teachings of Dugald Stewart (then David Ricardo and others), and its wide dissemination via lectures and writings by J. R. McCulloch, Harriet Martineau, and evangelical political economists like Thomas Chalmers— provided a more unified, socially identifiable position from which practitioners could accrue social prestige for their work. Writers whose politics or style departed from the norm this position represented could be relegated to the margins either institutionally, by being denied official venues, or informally, through negative reviews that dismissed their ideas as "vulgar" or merely political. Unlike imaginative writers, that is, in the early nineteenth century, financial and economic writers inevitably worked in relation to (even when they did not write from within) identifiable stylistic and substantive norms, and such norms enabled participants actively or passively to marginalize writers whose work did not conform (and to support those whose efforts did). For would-be Literary writers, as we will see, the absence of an institutional base (even after the first vernacular Literature classes were taught in universities) and a single, identifiable stylistic norm meant that those who aspired to raise the status of their work had to normalize distinctions of two kinds (both of which were extrainstitutional): on the one hand, they disparaged other imaginative writers whose content, format, or features did not reach the lowest horizon of serious Literature; and, on the other hand, they informally agreed among themselves that some serious writers would devote themselves to promoting other, more deserving peers, as a means of enhancing the status of their collective enterprise (thus creating the positions of the minor writer and the critic).[43] That some minor members of the Literary establishment expressed interest in William Cobbett does not simply imply the unspecified "possible relationship between Cobbett and figures like Keats and Leigh Hunt" that Nattrass suggests, then.[44] More precisely, this interest reveals that, at the outer edges of the increasingly differentiated kinds of Literary and financial writing, there was still enough overlap to provoke self-appointed gatekeepers of the Literary, like Hunt and Hazlitt, to step up their efforts against writers like Cobbett, whose stylistic innovations both resembled and challenged the specifically Literary nature of the more properly Literary style.

As a marginalized author (in relation to financial and economic writing) who was also of interest to Literary writers, Cobbett is particularly important to my argument. Significantly, the overlap he represented (between financial and Literary kinds of writing) is most visible in his writing style. As we will see in the next section of this chapter and in my discussion of Harriet Martineau's *Berkeley the Banker* in the second interchapter, the gap between financial and Literary writing was widened and naturalized in the late 1830s and 1840s. Only for a brief period in the nineteenth century, in other words, did the *formal* possibility exist that writing could be both informative about financial matters and appealing from an aesthetic (Literary) perspective. The short duration of this possibility, as we have already begun to see, was an effect of *social*, or, more properly, *institutional*, factors. Once financial and economic writing was established in one set of institutions (university courses, paid lectures, the pages of the *Edinburgh Review* and government Blue Books) and Literary writing had begun to find a toehold in another set of (albeit less formalized) institutions (critical reviews, manifestos like Wordsworth's "Preface" to the *Lyrical Ballads* or De Quincey's periodical article about the "literature of power"), whatever borrowing of features one kind of writer did from the other kind of writing looked like just that: an importation of features whose provenance lay elsewhere. The separation of the two writing genres then provoked (or became the precondition for) various writers' attempts to forge artificial or second-order connections that would bring these kinds of writing back into some other, nonsocial kind of relationship, as, for example, when a writer like John Bray established a metaphoric connection between the alphabet and money. Before turning to the aftermath of this separation, however, it is important to see what the style associated with the final phase of the continuum of writing kinds (although *not* the fact/fiction continuum) looked like. For that, I turn to Cobbett's *Paper against Gold*.

In content, Cobbett's argument, which occupies 332 closely printed pages in the 1828 edition, is both historical and theoretical. In offering historical information and a theoretical model as the twin wings of his argument, Cobbett animated both facets of eighteenth-century financial writing; paradoxically, in doing so, he also anticipated the kind of response that other, more conservative economic writers would use to dismiss radical complaints like his. In Cobbett's account, the creation of a permanently funded national debt had enmeshed the British government—and, thus, the British people—in an ever-growing morass of obligation and paper. While everyone agreed that William III had established the debt to finance the war against France, Cobbett stressed that the debt had not primarily supported Britain's financial and military power (as Thomas Macaulay was to argue) but simply inaugurated the proliferation of paper in which the nation was now drowning. In other words, in Cobbett's version of these events, the lack of gold that had led to the creation of the debt in the first place meant that some *alternative* to gold was necessary to pay the interest on the debt; the need to finance the debt had then led the government to create an institution—the Bank of England—that was empowered to print paper. In this account, the Bank was originally simply a kind of financial printing press, and the existence of paper money was tantamount to acknowledging that England had no real money at all. Paper notes were, in Cobbett's words, the "*representatives of Debt*, and not of *wealth*" (*Paper*, 74). This charge, of course, made the problematic of representation visible by revealing that, because the relationship between the paper and its supposed ground of gold was attenuated, arbitrary, and obscure, the "value" that paper claimed to represent could consist of anything—or nothing—at all.

For most of the eighteenth century, Cobbett reminded his readers, the Bank's notes had represented something more than just the nation's debt; they had represented the government's promise to redeem its paper with gold. But, as his readers knew too well, this situation changed in 1797. When the Bank stopped redeeming its paper, it essentially defaulted on its promise, and, since the Bank had been issuing paper money in denominations as small as five pounds since 1793, it had already managed to attract to its coffers many of the coins previously in circulation. With almost no viable coin remaining and too few available Bank notes, the same legislators who had authorized the Bank to stop payment had then encouraged private individuals to form country banks. Thus, in Cobbett's account (which obscures the chronology here), country banks had been established as even less responsible paper mills: they had been created solely to print and circulate increasingly devalued money for local use (*Paper*, 74–75, 104). With the situation out of hand by 1810—with the country awash in various kinds of paper money, the national debt at an all-time high, and paper devalued in relation to gold—Cobbett insisted that the government could not make good on its promise to resume cash payments in two years, as critics of the Restriction, including members of the Bullion Commission, urged it to do.[45] The only solution Cobbett could devise was for the government to repudiate the debt immediately and return to a full metallic currency. If this did not occur, he insisted, the paper money system would collapse under its own weight, and the government based on false promises would fall.[46]

Some modern historians have charged that Cobbett's critique of the British funding system constitutes a "demonology" rather than a coherent analysis.[47] Yet behind his litany of accusations lies an agenda more coherent than most critics have allowed. It centers on the formal structure of the market model of value: formally, as we have seen, value in a credit economy is not a matter of the precious metal that monetary instruments contain but a function of deferral, both temporal and material. This structural property, which abstracts value from material things so that it can be expanded through judicious uses of time and distance, was also (although not so explicitly) the target of the establishment critics who complained about the "fictitious" nature of paper money. Unlike these critics, however, who supported competition in commercial society, Cobbett rejected both competition and the deferral that paper supposedly introduced. In *Paper against Gold*, Cobbett did not elaborate his criticism of competition, nor did he explore the relationship between the competitive system and the abstraction (and quantification) of value. What he did elaborate was what I am calling the *problematic of representation*—the idea that the deferral inherent in paper money constituted a *problem* that could not be resolved simply by limiting the volume of circulating paper. The problem of deferral could not be so resolved, according to Cobbett, because all paper money both rested on and represented *belief*, not gold. To expose the problematic of representation, Cobbett insisted that Britons had to pursue three goals: they should make demands instead of accepting the government's assurances; they should claim immediate redemption instead of accepting promises about future returns; and, most important, they should analyze the contemporary situation instead of simply believing what they were told.[48]

We will see in a moment that Cobbett did not consistently or explicitly elaborate the model of value that theoretically obtained in eighteenth-century Britain—a nonmarket model of value based on customary privileges and responsibilities.[49] As far as I have been able to tell, in fact, Cobbett did not even directly engage the distinction that Adam Smith had introduced between use value and exchange value, nor did he participate directly in the debates about value that classical political economists launched in the wake of Ricardo's *Principles of Political Economy and Taxation* (1817). Instead of a consistent or theoretical engagement with the question of value, Cobbett's contribution was to stage confrontations between one kind of value and another so that readers could see for themselves the limitations of the market model of value. From these imaginative confrontations, an attentive reader might infer that some things and places and experiences could be treasured for what they *are*, not because they could be exchanged for something else; what one treasured in this way, Cobbett implied, could not be measured or given a price. Because these treasured things were already passing away in the years in which Cobbett composed *Paper against Gold*, however, he primarily invoked them allusively and in general terms; even in the papers that composed his later collection, *Rural Rides*, he was forced to use conventions associated with fiction to evoke scenes and experiences that were, by 1821, more often memories than current realities.

Even after most writers and readers could distinguish between fictions and facts, of course, the stylistic conventions used to produce the two remained available for appropriation and adaptation. But Cobbett did more than simply appropriate formal features associated with fiction to develop an argument about what he considered fact. He also raised the entire issue of fictionalization to the level of visibility, with the result that, in his writing, appropriation became critique. We can see how Cobbett simultaneously used and commented on language's capacity to create fictions in an early section of *Paper against Gold*. In his second letter from Newgate Prison, Cobbett constructed an imaginary dialogue to show how words—in this case, the phrase *having money in the Funds*—could produce an illusory materiality that masked the reality that a metaphor—and a dead one at that—was producing the *effect* of fact, not referring to an actual situation:

> Being here in the elementary, the mere horn-book part of our subject, we cannot make the matter too clear to our comprehension; and, we ought, by no means, to go a step further till we have inquired into the sense of this saying about people's "*having money in the Funds;*" from which any one, who did not understand the thing, would naturally conclude, that the person who made use of this saying, looked upon *the Funds*, as a *place*, where a great quantity of gold and silver was kept locked up in safety.... A place, indeed, of a sort of mysterious existence; a sort of financial Ark; a place not, perhaps, to be touched, or even seen; but, still the notion is, that of a place, and a place, too, of more than mortal security.
>
> Alas! *the Funds* are no place at all! and, indeed, how should they, seeing that they are, in fact, one and the same thing with the *National Debt?* But, to remove, from the mind of every creature, all doubt upon this point; to dissipate the mists in which we have so long been wandering, to the infinite amusement of those who invented these terms, let us take a plain common-sense view of one of these *loaning* transactions. Let us suppose, then, that the Government wants a *loan* ... and ... [that] the money is lent, by Mssrs. Muckworm and Company.... Well: what does Muckworm get in return? Why, *his name is written in a book; against his name is written, that he is entitled to receive interest for a million of money;* which book is kept at the Bank Company's house, or shop, in Threadneedle Street, London.... "Well," you will say, "but *what becomes of the money?*" Why, the Government *expends it*, to be sure.... "What? Then the money all *vanishes;* and *nothing remains in lieu of it but the lender's name written in a book?*" Even so: and this, my good neighbours, is the way, that "*money is put into the Funds.*" (*Paper*, 16–17)

In this passage, Cobbett did not abandon the informational agenda of factual writing: his primary goal was to give his readers clear and explicit information, in this case, about how the funding system operated. The way he conveyed this information, however, was to use not only direct explanations—"the Government *expends it*"—but also a mimetic strategy that sought to place his readers imaginatively in the situation he described. Since terms like *the Funds* had gradually hidden the process to which they actually referred through the kind of repetition that causes metaphors to die, and because this linguistic ossification had substituted a new, *fictive* reality for the social process it obscured, Cobbett's readers had to simultaneously experience the mystification and, somehow, dispel it. What they saw as Cobbett pulled back the veil was that the fictional universe created by dead metaphors was a self-enclosed system. In it, words led only to other words, both metaphorically (as when *the Funds* was another way of saying *the national debt*) and metonymically (as when the phrase *money in the Funds* led to a name being written in a book). To step outside this system, which is cloaked by the mystifying veil, readers had to imaginatively take up the position Cobbett offered them in the dialogues that make up the bulk of *Paper against Gold.*

For Cobbett, the dialogue form offered an alternative to a linguistic system that was merely tautological because it could simultaneously expose and evade the self-enclosed and interlocking systems he saw everywhere around him.[50] To expose these systems, Cobbett used conventions taken from informational writing: he repeatedly *named* the systems and explained how they worked. To evade the pernicious systems, especially the linguistic system, he also used a feature associated with epistolary fiction of the eighteenth century. Unlike most eighteenth-century uses of dialogue, however, his deployment of this convention did not seek to naturalize it, for he thought that the naturalization of any formal convention brought with it the very blindness that he was trying to cure. Instead of naturalizing dialogue by effacing its artifice, he repeatedly called attention to its presence as a formal device. Even though he had to use language to create the position he wanted his readers to occupy—a vantage point outside language—Cobbett tried to use the dialogue form self-consciously to encourage readers to see how and why they were being so positioned.[51]

Variants of the dialogue form constitute the single most important rhetorical strategy in *Paper against Gold.* When Cobbett wanted the reader to recognize the absurdity of the government's position, for example, he typically quoted an opponent's words, altering only the typography for emphasis. Seeing Cobbett's emphasis (added to the citations with capital letters and italics) enabled the reader imaginatively to hear Cobbett's sarcasm while reading someone else's words.[52] Ideally, seeing the original writer's words while imaginatively hearing Cobbett's interpretation would encourage the reader to agree with Cobbett and to see the foolishness of the government's apologists. Thus, in his letter of 14 September 1810, Cobbett quoted a government supporter who had attacked him in the *Morning Post.* According to this writer, paper money "offers to Government a *most indestructible support,* because IT MAKES THE DAILY BREAD OF EVERY INDIVIDUAL DEPEND SUBSTANTIALLY ON THE SAFETY OF GOVERNMENT. . . . Money [i.e., gold], which may be hoarded, separates the individual from the public safety. In the present revolutionary state of the world, I think our paper currency a most *miraculous mean*[s] *of salvation,* and the man who would *propose the payment of bank-notes in specie at any period,* to separate individual property from public safety, might as well propose *the burning of the Navy to protect the commerce of the world"* (*Paper,* 44–45). Since Cobbett *had* advocated paying Bank notes in specie, these words obviously referred to him. By equating this position with proposing that Britain burn the navy's ships, the *Morning Post* writer had implicitly charged Cobbett with treason. By printing this quotation in this way, however, without quotation marks but with copious capital letters and italics for emphasis, Cobbett tried to point up the absurdity of the charge. He did so, moreover, in such a way as to indicate his willingness to engage with his critic—a courtesy not extended to Cobbett by the anonymous writer. Citations printed like this one thus constituted a double dialogue: they visually reflected Cobbett's engagement with another writer, and they repeated that encounter for the reader in a form altered— that is to say, interpreted—by Cobbett's typographic emphasis.

These typographic engagements with his critics sought to make Cobbett *virtually present* for the reader in the reading experience itself. Since these letters might well have been read aloud, moreover, by one bankrupt trades- man to another or by disgruntled workingmen over pints of beer, Cobbett's typographic alterations resemble stage directions intended to guide an actor's delivery of his lines. For the individual who read the words aloud, these directions dictated emphasis and tone; for the auditors who listened, the translation of typography into tone constituted cues about when to laugh, when to sneer, when to pat a comrade on the back. At the same time, of course, the typographic alterations by which Cobbett directed his readers' responses also sought to convey a specific argument. Because some of his allusions are now lost to us, we can grasp this argument only by turning to the two sources with which Cobbett was engaging in these passages. Uncov- ering this engagement reveals that his dialogue tried to operate on multiple levels: beyond engaging his readers and inviting them to see him engaging his critics, he also generated his own arguments by engaging other writers. His writing style, then, sought to animate a social chorus of like-minded Britons, all of whom readers could dimly sense as they read or listened to his words.

The first passage I cited, in which Cobbett refers to the "horn-book" part of his argument, alludes to Thomas Paine's 1796 pamphlet "Decline and Fall of the English System of Finance." Cobbett credited this influential pam- phlet with awakening his interest in the subject of paper money.[53] In the pamphlet (which is not organized as a dialogue), Paine explained that, during the eighteenth century, the British funding system created two groups of creditors. The first group, the initial "generation" of fund holders in the national debt, loaned money to the government in exchange for dividends. The "second generation of creditors, more numerous and far more formidable and withal more real than the first generation," consisted of "every holder of a bank note."[54] In the first dialogue I quoted from Cobbett's text, both "generations" appear: Messrs. Muckworm and Co. corresponds to the first set of creditors, the fund holders; the reader, along with his surrogate, the implied addressee, corresponds to the second. Thus, Cobbett both built on Paine's explanation and departed from it rhetorically by distinguishing between the two kinds of creditors not analytically but formally: he cast the fund holder as a character and the note holder as the letter's addressee (the reader).

Cobbett's argument followed Paine's thesis this far and then departed from it. In Cobbett's account, when the Bank suspended cash payments in 1797, the interests of the eighteenth-century fund holders and the note holders diverged. Instead of one group, described by Paine as two "generations" of a single metaphoric family, Cobbett represented his contemporaries as divided into two distinct groups with two distinct, competing interests: the fund holders profited from the nation's debt, and the note holders (and taxpayers) bore its costs. This is the division to which Cobbett alluded in the second passage I quoted, when he cited (and altered) the government supporter's words. That writer, Cobbett's typographic emphasis implied, sought to conjure a single "public," united by fear of the French and by belief in the British government's credibility. For Cobbett, this illusion should have been dispelled long ago, for it was exposed by Edmund Burke, who was one of Paine's implied interlocutors.[55] Cobbett reprinted a passage from Burke to make his point: "REAL MONEY can hardly ever multiply too much in any country; because it will always, as IT increases, be the *certain sign of the increase of* TRADE, of which it is the measure, and consequently of the soundness and vigour of the whole body. But this PAPER MONEY may, and does increase, without any increase of Trade; nay often when Trade greatly declines, FOR IT IS NOT THE MEASURE OF THE TRADE OF ITS NATION, BUT OF THE NECESSITY OF ITS GOVERNMENT; and it is absurd, *and must be ruinous,* that the same cause which naturally exhausts the *wealth* of a Nation should be the only *productive cause of money*" (*Paper*, 60).

By juxtaposing Burke's statement with the claim of the government apologist, Cobbett was implicitly arguing that his contemporaries' problems stemmed from the coexistence of two kinds of money—"REAL MONEY" and "PAPER MONEY." These two kinds of money embodied and signified two different things to Cobbett: the first signified the "vigour of the whole body" because it could actually measure the strength of a nation by the produce it created; the second incarnated lies because it substituted for measurable, tangible products the government's promises (which were no more than expressions of bad faith). Cobbett's response to Burke thus altered, even as it echoed, the original. It did so because, for Cobbett's contemporaries, the situation had changed. Whereas Burke could still invoke a single national body because the Bank's promise still obtained and because gold could still be said to measure tangible products, the only way one could conjure a single, productive Britain in 1810 was to do what the government spokesman did: use threats to coerce that homogeneity from a frightened population made up of different interest groups and pretend that riches deferred were identical to riches actually in hand. In Cobbett's account, the government's image of a nation that was homogeneous and inclusive, that transcended neighborhoods and parishes, that united all Britons in a common struggle against the French, and whose credit was a form of wealth was a lie—just as false as the promises printed on the Bank's money. Instead of this single nation, whose credit was backed by gold, Cobbett saw a country that was divided into an "us" and a "them": the ordinary workingmen and -women who were forced to accept paper and support the national debt and the investors who profited from the credulity of the majority. This is the vision he wanted his readers to see, and he wanted them to see themselves—by reading his words—occupying the position of the duped. In this vision, the only acceptable way to create a single national body would be to purge Britain of fallacious credit by reneging on the national debt. Once freed from the yoke of Bank money and deaf to the tautologies of the government, he argued, Britain would regain its vigor and the vitality it had momentarily lost: "The corn and the grass and the trees will grow without paper-money; the Banks may all break in a day, and the sun will rise the next day, and the lambs will gambol and the birds will sing, and the carters and country girls will grin at each other, and all will go on just as if nothing had happened" (*Paper*, 325).

All it would take to realize such a vision, Cobbett insisted, was for ordinary people to stop believing in the Bank's paper, the government's promises, and the claim that the interests of the fund holders both supported and represented the nation's interests. To curtail belief would end the government's lies and halt the reign of credit because credit, Cobbett reminded his readers, "is a thing wholly dependent upon *opinion*. The word itself, indeed, has the same meaning as the word *belief*. As long as men *believe* in the riches of any individual, or any company, so long he or they possess all the advantages of riches. But once *suspicion* is excited, no matter from what cause, the *credit* is shaken: and a very little matter oversets it" (*Paper*, 110).[56] In 1819, Cobbett took this argument to one of its logical conclusions when he recommended that some radical engraver flood London with counterfeit paper money in a "puff-out" intended to explode the monetary system. According to his modern biographer, Cobbett thought that "an engraver of ordinary ability ('any boy of common capacity can learn in six months') could produce good imitations of the existing banknotes. If a large quantity of the existing notes were put into circulation at one time—for example—by dropping parcels of them on the streets of London on some dark night—such a panic would occur that everyone would refuse to accept paper money. 'In 48 hours not a note would pass. The mails would carry the news to the land's end. A dread, such as never was before heard of, would spread over the country like lightning.'"[57]

I say that Cobbett's puff-out suggestion was *one* of the logical conclusions of his critique of the problematic of representation because, even though it radicalized the idea that all paper money is a fiction, it did not argue that all representation is fictive. Nor did Cobbett argue—or even imply—that all fiction is misleading or suspect. In fact, as I have already suggested, when he tried to invoke an alternative to the market model of value, he typically resorted to conventions associated with fiction. Or, more precisely, he resorted to a mode of description that alluded to or borrowed features from imaginative writing but that was vague and generic rather than detailed and precise, as descriptions in imaginative writing had come to be: "The corn and the grass and the trees will grow . . . the lambs will gambol and the birds will sing. . . . " This principle holds true even in *Rural Rides*, where his language is intermittently more detailed and referential; for every flourishing asparagus bed Cobbett actually saw and described in detail, we find a dozen general invocations of foxhunts long gone and farms swallowed up by tax collectors or debt.[58] His tendency to allude to or invoke fiction when he wanted to conjure up an alternative to the market model of value but *not* to use the stylistic conventions that his readers would have recognized *as* fiction suggests how important—and how difficult—it was simultaneously to criticize prevailing conditions and to remind readers of what they might one day have, *not* as a fiction, but as a (not-yet-attained or already-lost) fact. At the same time, his refusal to extend his critique of paper money to writing or representation of all kinds reveals how desperate he was to contain his critique—presumably so that the alternative model of value to which he alluded might one day seem realizable, even if he could not quite see how to bring it into being.

Cobbett's *Paper against Gold* was repeatedly reprinted, widely bought, and widely read, but it had little effect on British monetary policy, the use of paper money, or the fate of the banking system. Indeed, even when what Cobbett had so long predicted actually occurred—when numerous country banks failed in December 1825 and the Bank of England came within a hair's breadth of bankruptcy—the central targets of his campaign remained unshaken. If anything, in fact, subsequent developments suggest that Britons' willingness to believe in the Bank's money and the banking system as a whole grew stronger as the years passed, not weaker, as Cobbett would have liked.

While there are numerous ways to explain the ineffectiveness of Cobbett's critique, I want simply to raise one generic possibility here. Even as Cobbett was trying to develop a style that would encourage middle-class readers to take his work seriously, that could invoke an alternative to the market model of value *without* presenting this as a mere fiction, and that would also engage readers across a wide class spectrum, establishment writers were refining the definition of what counted as authoritative financial—or economic—writing in such a way as to make stylistic hybrids like Cobbett's seem merely nostalgic or recreational. During the first decades of the nineteenth century, a group of writers who not only embraced the assumptions I have associated with the establishment but also saw themselves as *specialists* in economic matters began to adopt a shared set of stylistic conventions. As these conventions and the ideas they were used to advance were imitated by evangelical political economists and popularized by writers like McCulloch and Martineau, what counted as financial writing was simultaneously narrowed—both stylistically and in terms of ideas—to *economic* writing—and enlarged—in terms of sheer volume—to the flood of paper I have already described. This simultaneous narrowing and expansion rendered some styles and kinds of writing "amateurish" in relation to self-defined "scientific" or "useful" writing and made arguments like Cobbett's seem entertaining, at best, and, at worst, simply nostalgic. At the same time, of course, the audience for such specialist writing began to grow, especially as the number of individuals seeking to profit from investment, both domestic and international, increased. Even before Parliament began to enact the legislation that helped rationalize the British monetary system by giving Bank of England notes the priority that Bank officials had just begun to covet, Britons with capital to invest were interested in learning about how to make the financial system more stable, not figuring out how to bring it down. Before turning to the writers who codified the style that came to signify authoritative economic writing, I briefly consider another currency debate that developed in the wake of the restoration of payments. When Peel's Act of 1819, which provisionally curtailed the Restriction period, failed to stabilize prices, a new series of debates broke out about Britain's paper money and, more generally, how to control credit. As part of these debates, two currency radicals—Robert Owen and the Leeds printer John Bray—attempted once more to raise questions about paper money, even though, as we will see, political economists had already so narrowed the terms of debate that credit paper had come to seem like a natural part of Britain's credit economy.

Labor Notes and a Coinage of Pottery: Robert Owen and John Bray

Between 1810, when Cobbett began writing *Paper against Gold*, and 1844, when Parliament passed the Bank Act that endorsed the Bank's notes, the subject of Britain's paper currency continued to provoke controversy. Contributions to this controversy came in successive waves: the defeat of the 1810 Bullion Report produced one outpouring of print; in 1819, the convening of a second Bullion Commission and the passage of the Resumption of Payments Act led to another; the official resumption set more pens to work in 1821; the anticipation of the expiration (or renewal) of the Bank's Charter in 1833 caused more public debate; and continuing fluctuations in prices, along with three serious commercial crises (1825–26, 1836–37, and 1839), ensured that the topic did not lose its urgency. Historians have generally focused their treatment of this writing on the decades between the resumption of payments in 1821 and the passage of the 1844 Bank Act. Typically, they limit their accounts to a set of debates about how (or whether) to regulate the volume of paper in circulation, and they identify in these debates either two positions (the Currency school and the Banking school) or three (a Free Banking position in addition to the other two).[59] While these debates were no doubt responsible for the most influential publications about the currency, it is also important to place them within the context of developments in the radical and popular press. This is important not only because radical writers occasionally addressed the issue of currency, but also because the increasing marginalization of radical contributions was one consequence of the narrowing of what counted as legitimate economic writing. Equally important, the narrowing of economic writing—which, as we will see in the next chapter, was directly related to the creation of a canon of political economic texts and the emergence of a general agreement about what analytic method was appropriate to a complex subject like money—occurred in relation to significant changes within the segment of the publishing industry devoted to "cheap," "popular," or "mass-produced" imaginative writing. When John Bray took the establishment's statements about money to another logical conclusion in 1839, his suggestions were virtually unreadable—both, paradoxically, because they looked so different, in content, if not in form, from the kind of economic writing most of his middle-class peers were devouring and because they did not conform to the paradigm of "entertaining" or "useful" knowledge that had begun to dominate the market for popular print. We will see an example of the latter in the second interchapter when I consider Harriet Martineau's *Illustrations of Political Economy*. First, I want to identify some of the factors that helped keep the controversy about Britain's paper currency alive and outline the issues that dominated the currency debates in the decades immediately preceding the 1844 act.

Presumably, the Restriction Act was intended not only to protect the Bank of England but, by extension, and especially as the provision was repeatedly renewed, to make the entire English banking industry more stable. If this was the legislators' intention, however, the act did not have this effect. In 1826, Thomas Joplin claimed that three hundred banks had failed in the nearly three decades since the turn of the century; this figure proved that banks were more likely to fail than any other kind of business, Joplin argued. That same year, J. R. McCulloch reported that "no fewer than ninety-two commissions of bankruptcy were issued against English country banks" between 1814 and 1816, and "*one* in every seven and a half of the total of these establishments existing in 1813 . . . was entirely destroyed." In 1837, J. W. Gilbart compiled an annual record of country bank failures for the period 1809–30, which showed that the average annual failure rate of English banks was more than four and a half times greater than the failure rate for Scottish banks.[60] Even after the Bank resumed payments of gold, then, banks continued to be exceptionally vulnerable to failure. In the commercial crisis of 1825–26, for example, banks failed in even greater numbers than before the resumption of payments. In a single month, seventy-three banks stopped payment, and Gilbart claimed that eighty commissions of bankruptcy were issued against country bankers that year. Writing in 1866, another historian of banking, H. D. Macleod, insisted that Gilbart's estimate was too low; Macleod argued that "from the different ways of making compositions, etc., the number of failures should probably be estimated at four times the number of commissions of bankruptcies."[61]

Bank failures were only one sign of the instability of Britain's credit economy in the first half of the nineteenth century, and, in and of themselves, they can even be seen as a comparatively minor problem. Bank failures, after all, were, in some senses, relatively simple to understand and prevent: they affected primarily the clients who held deposits in the fallen banks; they could be attributed to a single weakness of the English banking system, the ban against partnerships involving more than six people; and this inhibition might be (and was) addressed by legislation (the 1826 and 1833 Bank Acts). Unlike bank failures, however, the early nineteenth century's dramatic fluctuations in prices and in the value of money affected everyone, albeit differently; these fluctuations seemed to emanate from numerous, sometimes conflicting causes; and no one could agree what—if any—laws might help stabilize prices. Thus, for example, in the wake of the 1810 Bullion Report's defeat, the value of paper money fell dramatically. This meant that, if one were a leaseholder with a long-term commitment, rent increased in proportion to the price of staples; if one were a farmer, it meant that crops could face falling demand while the price of necessities soared. If one were a landowner, by contrast, or a fund holder in the national debt, the depreciated currency yielded higher returns. In 1811, Lord Peter King drove this lesson home when he announced his decision, first in the upper House, then in print, to refuse to honor Bank of England notes at face value. Instead of accepting the depreciated notes, he demanded rent payment in gold.[62] Lord King's audacious demand raised the specter of long-term creditors taking advantage of the fall in the value of the Bank's money at the expense of tenants and long-term borrowers. To foreclose the chaos this threatened, Parliament passed legislation that mandated that Bank of England notes pass at face value. A second bill, enacted in 1812, stated that, when a court ordered payment in "money," creditors were required to accept Bank of England notes. Together, these acts effectively—but unofficially—made Bank of England notes legal tender.[63]

The issue at stake in the contest between Lord King and Parliament was how to conceptualize the value of the British pound. This was important because, if the government were to resume payments in gold, it had to determine whether to redeem pound notes at their old value or at some new value, a value that fluctuated during the years of the Restriction. In theoretical terms, the question could be posed in either of two ways. First, did the pound note represent a definite piece of metal that incarnated the quantity of gold bullion fixed by the proclamation of 1717, as Lord King insisted, or could its value fluctuate according to other factors? Second, was the value of a pound note affected by the volume of paper notes in circulation? In 1811, when the Commons rejected the Bullion Commission Report, it was effectively asserting that the value of notes did not fluctuate, especially in relation to the volume of currency in circulation. Almost immediately, however, the wisdom of this formulation was called into question: at the end of 1813, the value of paper money began to rise in relation to gold; then, in the wake of the commercial pressure that accompanied the end of the war with France (1815), it fell again (1817). In 1819, Parliament convened a second Bullion Commission (chaired by Sir Robert Peel) that essentially reversed the Commons' earlier decision by accepting the analysis the original Bullion Commission Report had offered: relying on the testimony of economic theorists like David Ricardo instead of the practical bankers whose testimony had dominated the first committee's hearings, Parliament this time agreed that the value of paper money could—and did—fluctuate according, among other factors, to the volume of Bank notes in circulation. The committee thus recommended that the Bank of England phase in the resumption of gold payments at the old (i.e., now-appreciated) rate. Even this measure did not have the desired effect, however, in large part because the legislation did not require the Bank of England to take responsibility for the amount of paper in circulation. When full resumption finally took effect in 1821, the results were anything but reassuring: the Bank contracted its credit; commodity prices fell; many industries suffered; unemployment spread through numerous industries; and the value of gold soared. Returning from America in 1819, William Cobbett registered the misery that ensued; everywhere he traveled, he "not[ed] the depressed condition of agriculture, attend[ed] distress meetings of farmers, and arous[ed] them against the fund-holders who, under Peel's Act, were to receive full payment of interest and principal in an appreciated currency even though the producer might be bankrupt."[64] With gold flowing unchecked in and out of the nation according to the exchange and country banks issuing small notes without restraint, the country soon faced another commercial crisis. This crisis, in 1825–26, was inaugurated by what economic historians generally consider the first of the century's speculative manias. It ended as manias typically do: in widespread business failure and general panic. With the Bank of England's reserves nearly depleted by calls from the country banks, the Bank stood on the brink of failure, and the country was on the verge of barter. The Bank was saved by luck when the directors found a box of unissued, small-denomination notes. They began to issue these notes freely against nearly any security borrowers could offer, and by this means the Bank was able to curtail the panic.

The near catastrophe of 1825–26 made it clear that legislative action had to address the banking system as a whole more directly. Parliament's first response was the Bank Act of 1826, which eased restrictions on the system by allowing joint-stock banks to incorporate, outside a sixty-five-mile radius of London, and permitted the Bank of England to form branches. Because the act did not assign responsibility for overseeing the volume of currency to anyone, however, note issue remained unregulated; the government seems simply to have expected a combination of public demand and competition among banks to manage the currency. In 1833, Parliament tried to address the problems again, this time strengthening the Bank's ability to control credit, easing restrictions against the formation of joint-stock banks within the radius around London, and requiring the Bank to furnish the Treasury a weekly account of its reserves, securities, circulation, and deposits; this account was also published, as a monthly average, in the *London Gazette*.[65] This legislation still did not directly address the volume of note circulation, however, and, like the 1826 act, it failed to quiet controversy about money or stabilize the value of paper. In 1836–37, and again in 1839, pressures in the money market kept the issue of the circulating medium alive and made it clear that none of the current analyses were sufficient to explain—much less control—the fluctuating value and volume of paper money.

The various debates that crystallized around these events can be confusing to modern readers, in part because economists no longer use most of the categories introduced by Victorian writers. If concepts like the real bills doctrine, the law of the reflux, the needs-of-trade doctrine, and the law of proportion no longer figure in economic textbooks, however, they do signal the development in this period of a specialized economic terminology by which writers tried to capture the "laws" that governed Britain's economy.[66] Instead of explaining what each of these terms conveyed to Victorians, I want simply to identify three of the largest questions that repeatedly surfaced in these debates and to outline the methodological and generic issues they implied. In general terms, these questions would have been familiar to most nineteenth-century readers, but it is important to point out that the relatively technical way that writers typically formulated them shows how specialized the subjects of finance and currency were becoming by the late 1820s. The relatively commonsense formulations Cobbett had advanced in 1810—if prices are high, there is too much paper; to lower prices, return to gold—no longer seemed adequate; and the plain, straightforward language he preferred was beginning to look like a sign of amateurish naïveté. Stated simply (not as Victorians phrased them), the three questions are versions of those raised in the eighteenth century and again during the Restriction: What is the ground of paper money's value? What should determine how much paper circulates? What is money? The methodological and generic issues these questions raised all turned on whether it was possible for anyone to gather and present all the information relevant to formulating policy about money—whether, in short, something more than information might be necessary for writers who were trying to understand and describe the credit economy.

Here, I need only rehearse briefly the way that nineteenth-century writers addressed the questions I have named, but it is important to note at the outset that specific formulations depended not only on a writer's political and theoretical alliances but also on the precise circumstances particular phases of the debate addressed. What I am calling a *debate*, in other words, did not look to contemporaries like a single conversation but seemed instead to be a series of sometimes overlapping, sometimes contradictory, and sometimes redundant responses to conditions that seemed as different as they did alike. Retrospectively, by contrast, we can see that variants of the same issues surfaced repeatedly and were answered in a limited number of ways. Thus, for example, some writers thought that the ground of paper's value was labor (Malthus and Ricardo, following Adam Smith); others thought that it was metal or gold (members of the so-called Currency school and Sir Robert Peel, following David Hume); others thought it was simply the quantity of money in circulation (this was the consensus after the 1810 Bullion Report); and still others thought it was prices (members of the so-called Banking school). On the matter of what should dictate how much paper circulated, some writers (members of the Currency school, following Hume again) thought that this should be a function of the gold reserve; others (members of the Free Banking school, following Smith) argued that paper should be issued in response to demand; and others (James Mill, John Horsley Palmer, and some members of the Currency school) thought that abstract principles, implemented and overseen by legislation, ought to decide how much paper was issued.

The question of what counted as money provoked even more complicated responses. In the wake of the Restriction Act's passage, Charles Fox had argued that money consisted only of coin; because he wanted to downplay the effect of the Restriction, Pitt responded that the category should be more inclusive: "anything that answered the general purposes of trade and commerce, whether in specie, paper, or any other term that might be used," should be considered money, he said.[67] Also following (and seeking to justify) the Restriction, Henry Thornton argued, unsuccessfully, that the definition of *money* ought to include bankers' drafts and deposits. The Bullion Commission of 1819 rejected this suggestion and insisted that checks and bills of exchange should not be considered part of the nation's money supply. In the 1830s, when the debate between what historians call the

Currency school, the Banking school, and the Free Banking school raged, more definitions were advanced. Thus, members of the Currency school, led by Samuel Jones Loyd, J. R. McCulloch, George Warde Norman, and Robert Torrens, argued that *paper circulation* referred strictly to the notes issued by the Bank of England and the country banks and to the coin that circulated alongside paper; they considered bills of exchange, deposits, checks, and the accounts kept by the London Clearing House to be simply "the means of economizing the money." Members of the Banking school, led by Thomas Tooke, John Fullarton, and James Wilson, by contrast, re-garded notes and coin as only a small part of the circulating medium; checks and bills of exchange should also be included because they were undeni-ably—and in ever greater volume—used in everyday exchanges. Proponents of the less organized Free Banking school, finally, such as Sir Henry Parnell, Thomas Hodgskin, Samuel Bailey, G. Poulett Scrope, and J. W. Gilbart, in-sisted that it was less important to determine what counted as money than to make sure that all monetary instruments were treated as what they ac-tually were: commodities whose volume and price were (or ought to be) subject to the free play of competition. To these men, notes and deposits were simply alternative forms of bank liabilities; "circulating credit" (bank-notes) and "book credit" (checking deposits) should, thus, be treated in the same way. The function of all banks, by this account, was not (as both Cobbett and members of the Currency school claimed) to produce and sell money but to exchange unfamiliar forms of credit that did not easily circu-late (inland bills of exchange and some banks' notes) for forms of credit that were backed by the reputation of their issuer and, thus, circulated more easily (the notes issued by the Bank of England and reputable London and country banks). To Scrope, who formulated this principle, the substitution of banknotes for private bills of exchange was "a simple step in the division of labour."[68]

These questions, however they were phrased and answered, were always formulated in relation to another set of issues that were both methodolog-ical and generic in nature. These issues involved information and how best to gather and present it. At one level, the problem turned on the respect typically extended to the secrecy that businesses had long claimed was es-sential to competition. Thus, for example, legislators did not require the Bank of England directors to reveal the volume of circulating notes or the amount of gold held in reserve until 1833; private banks were also exempt from this requirement during the first three decades of the century. Such obscurity, as we have seen, was one facet of the problematic of representa-tion, and, when it began to seem like the source of social difficulties rather than simply the solution to a commercial challenge, it could be used to arouse public resentment. This is what John Wade, the radical editor of the *Gorgon*, tried to do in 1831 when he exposed the extent of the Bank's privileges in the *Extraordinary Black Book*. In the wake of Wade's exposé, legislators began to call for more information and more publicity—at the same time that the Bank found more defenders, at least one of whom sought to humanize the "Old Lady of Threadneedle Street" by allowing "her" to tell "her" own story.[69]

At another level, the problem involved more than simply obliterating the obscurity with which traditionally secretive companies had protected their competitive edge. For, as members of the Free Banking school insisted, no one was capable of gathering or effectively presenting the massive amounts of information that would be necessary to manage the banking and monetary systems. This supposed impossibility followed partly from the fact that, in an operation as variable as banking, local knowledge and personal expertise trumped efforts at centralized management. This was the point Samuel Bailey made in 1840 when he wrote: "In banking, as in any other trade, the most productive organization of resources depends crucially upon local facts known only to the agent on the spot. Such questions as the size of a firm's capital, its proportion to the volume of business transacted, its profits, and the number and location of the firm's office cannot efficiently be centrally dictated: Such points are to be determined by the vigilance of the parties—requiring minute knowledge of a thousand particulars which will be learned by nobody but him who has an interest in knowing them." To Bailey, the proper response to this situation was to gather less information, not more, for his desire was to let the market govern itself: "No wisdom, short of omnipotence, could so well proportion the number and extent of these establishments to the wants of the community, as those principles of human nature which spontaneously work out the result."[70] Partly, the challenge that banking posed to the collection and dissemination of useful information was said to stem from the complexity of the needs it was intended to serve. Thomas Hodgskin, who later adopted a more radical position, expressed this idea in the late 1820s: "To provide for *general* social welfare seems to me an object much more beyond the power of man than to estimate the bulk and density of the planets. However admirable the faculties of each individual are adapted to provide for his own wants, they are quite incompetent to grasp, much less to regulate the complicated relations of society; and these relations, growing more complicated as our race multiplies on the earth, make the puny ambition of the lawgivers appear every day more and more contemptible."[71]

The problem of gathering information and making it useful was further complicated by the complexity of the phenomenon that writers were trying to understand. As Walter Boyd had pointed out in 1801, in matters as complicated as money it was often difficult to decide which factors were primary causes and which were secondary.[72] When William Cobbett refrained from ranking the influence of the various systems he held responsible for the nation's woes—or even from identifying some as symptoms and others as causes—he implicitly echoed—without remarking on—this confusion. (At one point, Cobbett even implicitly equated "Pitt's false money"—i.e., Bank paper—with "Walter Scott's poems.")[73] This issue had far-reaching implications for action, for, if it was possible that the underlying problem was not the volume of circulating paper but something else, how could critics—or legislators—know whether their efforts to quantify and curtail issue were properly directed? As we will see in the next chapter, writers who wanted to enhance their own prestige as economic writers took advantage of what we can identify as the old tension between two facets of factual writing—information and theory—by supplementing—or replacing—the information that was available with theoretical models and abstractions. In the not very long run, this generic solution helped elevate political economy to the status of *expert* or *specialist* knowledge, which required the assistance of more popular genres to make its conclusions seem like common sense. Before turning to these generic and institutional developments, however, I want to place the debate I have been discussing, which, in my account, has thus far involved only middle-class writers, in the context of events that were occurring simultaneously in (and to) the radical press.

The year that Parliament convened the second Bullion Commission— 1819—also witnessed the mass meeting in Manchester that came to be known as Peterloo, which was called in response to the government's punitive effort to crack down on seditious print and public meetings (the passage of the Six Acts). In the wake of the extension of a tax buried in one of these acts, 1819 also marked the beginning of the virtual demise of the radical weekly press.[74] This marked a reversal of the brief upsurge in the number of radical weeklies that followed the expiration of the Seditious Meetings Bill in 1818. A list of the beginning and termination dates of the leading weeklies makes the effectiveness of the legislation clear: *Sherman's Political Register* (1817–19), the *Gorgon* (1818–19), the *Medusa* (1818), the *Cap of Liberty* (1818–19), and the *Black Dwarf* (1817–24). As Ian Haywood has argued, however, the government did not repress radical efforts in the long run: even though the Six Acts ran many of the radical weeklies out of print and drove up the price of the few that remained, this legislation eventually laid the groundwork for the "next 'heroic' phase of the radical press, the 'unstamped' wars of the 1830s."[75] The Six Acts required that all periodicals and pamphlets display their credentials prominently, and this prompted clever writers and publishers to use titles and other paratextual materials to proclaim their allegiances and promote their causes. Thus, an 1833 volume displayed the title *Poor Man's Advocate; or, A Full and Fearless Exposure of the Horrors and Abominations of the Factory System in England, in the Year 1832* and devoted a column (entitled "Midnight Robbers") to naming factories that operated throughout the night.[76]

During the decades in which middle-class writers were discussing the volume and value of paper money, establishment publishers who sought to cash in on the mass readership the radical press had helped create were beginning to do so with a new, more capacious kind of publication—the "library" of "useful" or "entertaining" knowledge. Such ventures took their inspiration from what Richard Altick calls the "cheap book crusade of 1828–32," which was intended to steal the fire the radical press had ignited by making "improving" but inexpensive reading materials available to the masses.[77] Charles Knight initially conceived the idea for a "cheap and wholesome Literature for the People" in December 1819, in the aftermath of Peterloo, but the project was not realized until 1827, when the newly formed Society for the Diffusion of Useful Knowledge launched its Library of Useful Knowledge, which cost 6d. per fortnight, and the Library of Entertaining Knowledge, which consisted of texts issued in weekly 6d. parts. If this crusade was intended, as Altick argues, to neutralize the effect of radical writers, the concept of the "library" was soon appropriated by other, more liberal (but no less opportunistic) publishers, such as John Doherty, the Manchester trade union leader. In 1832, Doherty used his periodical the *Poor Man's Advocate* to advertise another of his publishing enterprises, "The People's Library of Cheap and Entertaining Knowledge." The list of titles this library contained, as Haywood observes, "is a striking testament to the remarkable expansion of 'cheap' print culture in the adversarial atmosphere of the unstamped wars." This list also enables us to see how easily publishers crossed over from fact-based materials, with their informational agenda, to fictions, which sought to instruct by entertaining. For the mass readership publishers hoped to court, neither the hierarchy of kinds of imaginative writing that I examine in chapter 5 nor the distinction between fact and fiction was particularly relevant. The audience these publications sought to reach, after all, had only recently had access to anything other than the "old canon" of eighteenth-century works and the even older, seventeenth-century texts in which the fact/fiction continuum obtained.

Haywood groups these works into a category he calls "the new hybrid of 'entertaining knowledge'":

> A selection of unstamped journals comes first, including the satirical *Figaro in London* . . . , the "useful knowledge" *Penny Cyclopaedia* . . . , the *Doctor*, "a penny medical magazine," the *New Casket*, "a journal of fiction" . . . and John Limbird's *Mirror of Literature, Amusement, and Instruction*. . . . There is a breezy latitudinarianism in the "People's Library." Its proletarianisation of the production of knowledge involves more than the proliferation of plebeian periodicals—it also redistributes the "standard works" of the literary canon. An even longer list offers such texts ("all with engravings") "in numbers" for 2d. per issue. Hence, Doherty's readers could purchase most of the "standard" eighteenth-century authors in cheap installments (*Tom Jones*, for example, in twenty-five issues; Inchbald's *Simple Story* in eight issues). There is no question of this list of "standard" texts exerting a superior cultural authority. Indeed, the "standard" works are sandwiched between lists of cheap periodicals. High culture is only one of the cultural tools of improvement, not an end in itself.[78]

To discuss "standard works," the "literary canon," and "high culture" is to broach the topics I take up in chapter 5. For now, I want simply to note the emergence in the 1830s of the hybrid, capacious categories of "useful entertainment" and "entertaining knowledge," to point out, following Haywood, that the kinds of writing these categories included anticipated the "truly mass-circulation literature" of the 1840s,[79] and to observe, as Haywood does not, that they also harkened back to the publications of the late seventeenth century and the early eighteenth that predated the breakup of the fact/fiction continuum.

It was a combination of the popularity of this capacious kind of writing and the narrowing of what counted as authoritative economic writing that conspired to make publications like John Bray's *Labour's Wrongs and Labour's Remedy* seem generically anomalous when this volume appeared in 1839. Even if Bray's work never achieved the popularity Bray sought, however, for the purposes of my argument it is important to devote some attention to it, for Bray (along with Owen) was one of the few radical writers, after William Cobbett, to identify money as a potential target of political action. Whereas Cobbett tried to use his attack on paper money to criticize the funding system that classical political economists defended, Bray wanted to co-opt the monetary system and the conventions of political economy as well; he wanted both to substitute a new kind of money for the paper that currently circulated and to borrow the tactics—even the literal words—of political economists to make a case for a noncompetitive economic system. Like Cobbett, then, Bray tried to make paper money's reliance on the problematic of representation visible, but he did so in the very form that others were using to manage or neutralize the effects of that problematic.

John Francis Bray (1809–97), who was born in the United States and moved to England when he was thirteen, had his first exposure to the radical press in 1833–34, when he worked for the unstamped paper the *Voice of West Riding*. His first foray into print was a series of five essays published in the *Leeds Times* as "Letters for the People in Leeds" between December 1835 and February 1836. In November 1837, Bray delivered a lecture to the Leeds' Working Men's Association, a radical organization for which he served as treasurer. He published his most important work, *Labour's Wrongs and Labour's Remedy*, at his own expense, in weekly parts in 1838, then again in 1839, as a 2s. book.[80] Even though Marx considered Bray one of the few "Ricardian socialists" to understand that an attack on money was tantamount to an attack on "the capitalistic mode of production,"[81] *Labour's Wrongs* was indifferently reviewed, and, disappointed with both its reception and the radical movement's commitment to political (as opposed to financial or economic) reform, Bray returned to the United States in May 1842.

As Marx's phrase "Ricardian socialists" suggests, Bray pursued his argument in relation to and, stylistically, from *within* the generic conventions used by establishment political economists like Smith and Ricardo. Unlike Cobbett, then, who constructed dialogues to stage his fierce antipathy to apologists for the credit economy, Bray imagined that sympathetic employers and disgruntled employees had more in common than more militant radicals believed and that they would, as a consequence, respond to the same kind of writing. Like many Owenites and the group that has been called the Birmingham Radicals, Bray thought that skilled workers and sympathetic employers could make common cause against the aristocracy, the Bank of England, the national debt, and the system of Bank money.[82] Thus, the formal strategy with which he ended *Labour's Wrongs*—the citation of long, unattributed quotations from classical political economists to support the more radical arguments he had made—enacted his literal effort to position his radical argument within the conventions by which the credit economy's apologists advanced their more conservative agenda.

Given Bray's assumptions about the fundamental compatibility of radicals and (some) establishment writers, it is not surprising that, in method, conventions, and style, *Labour's Wrongs* resembles Steuart's *Principles of Political Economy* (and subsequent treatises published under that name) more than Cobbett's writings. Even more explicitly than Steuart, Bray wanted to construct a comprehensive *system*, a *theoretical model*, that could account for and order all the components in what contemporaries viewed as an incomprehensible array of symptoms and causes.[83] Whereas Steuart tried to organize and analyze the elements of the credit economy, however, Bray wanted to address the problem of priority that Walter Boyd had identified: Was the chief cause of laborers' suffering low wages? Were low wages more or less important than workers' lack of political representation? Were the division of labor, new machines, and the corporate form part of labor's problem, or were they part of the solution? To produce his theoretical model, Bray imitated the conventions that, as we will see in the next chapter, early-nineteenth-century economic theorists like David Ricardo helped normalize: he reasoned from "First Principles" rather than marshaling concrete examples, he organized his reflections according to a logic that flows from these principles, and, even though his language occasionally borrowed from the apocalyptic books of the Bible, his style is generally transparent—that is, he avoided personifications, embedded narratives, dialogues, and other devices common in imaginative writing as well as the kind of direct addresses to the reader that might disrupt his logical argument. The one noun that does approach a personification is *Labour*, which, as we will see, functions both rhetorically, to solicit his readers' identification, and performatively, to enact the unification of interests that Bray wished to bring about.

In Bray's analysis, the root of the multiple wrongs that afflicted labor in the 1830s was the institution of private property. From this followed another version of Adam Smith's distinction between "the productive classes," who labored, and the "unproductive classes," who profited from the labor of others (*LW*, 23). Bray reached this conclusion deductively, by reasoning from the three principles he took from "the great Book of Nature": (1) "all men are alike"; (2) labor is necessary to confer value on "the materials requisite for the preservation of life"; and (3) "as the nature and wants of all men are alike, the rights of all must be equal; and, as human existence depend[s] on the same contingencies, it follows that . . . the earth is the common property of all its inhabitants" (28). These three principles "force . . . upon us" the conclusion "that individual possession of the soil has been one cause of inequality of wealth—that inequality of wealth necessarily gives rise to inequality of labour—and that inequality of wealth, and labour, and enjoyments, constitute the wrong as a whole" (32).

His attack on private property and his promotion of a strict labor theory of value aligned Bray with other, better-known radicals of the early nineteenth century, like Robert Owen and William Thompson. The solution he ultimately proposed, moreover—a reorganization of British society according to the principles of cooperation—was frequently advanced in this period, most notably by Owen, whose writings and example had inspired the creation of as many as five hundred cooperative societies by 1832.[84] Whereas Bray was sympathetic to Owen's ideas, however (he led a breakaway Owenite contingent from the more militant, Chartist-sympathizing Leeds' Working Men's Association in 1839), the emphasis he placed on money as a revolutionary tool distinguishes his work from Owen's.[85] In *Labour's Wrongs*, Bray called money "the first great element of the power of the capitalist" (136), and he identified monetary reform as a critical weapon of the working-class revolution. To see what distinguishes Bray's ideas about money from Owen's, it is necessary to look briefly at the paper money Owenites introduced and used between 1832 and 1834.

As early as 1820, Robert Owen had proposed that an "equitable" stage of social intercourse would be achieved only when the medium that facilitated exchange ceased to obscure the "natural standard of value." To use the terms I applied to Cobbett, Owen was suggesting that "equitable" social intercourse required changing the structure of value: in order to curb the abuses that followed from the fact of mediation, one had to address the element of deferral built into the market model of value. Recognizing that it was impossible to eliminate deferral by making the medium incarnate its ground (making gold, not paper, the circulating medium), Owen opted for the opposite solution: he suggested using a circulating medium that had *no* intrinsic value at all. The British government had unintentionally done this when Parliament passed the Restriction Act in 1797, of course, but, when the Bullion Commission of 1819 argued for resuming payments, it restored what most people considered the normal or natural relationship between the paper medium and gold. To avoid the problems he associated with such a metal-based currency, Owen recommended that the working classes issue their own paper notes; these notes might defer value momentarily, but they would not do so substantively or for an extended period of time, for each note would represent a unit of the labor that Owen (like Bray) considered the true ground of value and would do so only until labor could be exchanged in kind. Owen suggested that the proper unit for these notes was the day; and, in 1823, he proposed that "notes representing any number of days' labour or part of a day's labour" be issued.[86]

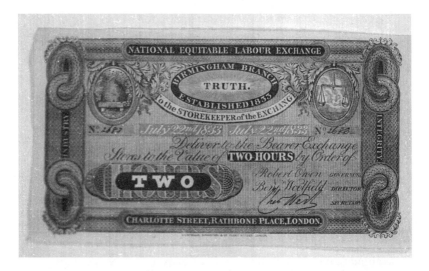

Figure 4. National Equitable Labour Exchange Note. This note, issued by the National Equitable Labour Exchange in Charlotte Street, Rathbone Place, London, in July 1833, represents two hours of labor and could be used only in the Exchange Shop. By permission of People's History Museum, Manchester, United Kingdom.

Owen's scheme did not materialize until 1832, when cooperative societies briefly formed a nationwide network. The first English cooperative venture had been organized in 1827; the London Co-Operative Society set up a cooperative store that used labor notes in its union exchange, but it used these notes only to pay store clerks. As soon as cooperative associations were set up in additional locations, members began to expand the use of labor notes. The British Association for Promoting Co-Operative Knowledge officially proclaimed the federal idea in January 1830, and, in April 1832, the *Crisis* advertised an exchange bazaar in New Road, Marlebone, that functioned "on an equitable time valuation." While Owen did not lead this initiative, when William Lovett said that "equitable time valuation" referred to the use of labor notes, Owen was provoked to provide a full account of his monetary scheme, complete with draft labor notes and rules for using them (fig. 4).[87] An office for collecting deposits—of labor *hours*, not the days that Owen had initially proposed as the unit of value—was established at Bromley's Bazaar, Gray's Inn Road, London, in September. After a month, a branch office, set up in Blackfriars, recorded 32,759 hours' deposits and 16,621 hours' exchanges.[88]

Owen's labor notes were issued on the basis of hours worked (which were registered or "deposited" with the exchange), and they entitled a worker to purchase goods from the issuing store in amounts equal to the value of the notes. For convenience, labor was valued at 6d. per hour, and goods were priced according to the number of hours of labor required to produce them. The scheme prospered for the first few months, but the very success of the cooperative exchanges soon led to the establishment of rival institutions, and these—along with the unscrupulous use of notes by non-cooperative tradesmen, who banked no hours to secure them—caused the public to lose confidence in the labor notes.[89] It soon became obvious, in other words, that, if one could not guarantee that some relationship—even an attenuated one—secured the representative medium, it was possible to print countless notes and impossible to sustain confidence in them. This wholly ungoverned relationship between paper notes and the reserves they only presumably represented precisely replicated the currency situation that had obtained during the Restriction, of course, but, when this elastic relationship appeared within the fragile cooperative community, which lacked assurances from institutions like Parliament and an established Bank, there was insufficient collective belief to support the notes. Then, too, the necessity to make the labor notes circulate beyond the community of workers—in order to increase the products for which they could be exchanged—meant that the general public, not just cooperative workers, would have had to believe in the notes. One contemporary's account of the London Exchange and its currency captures the excitement—and the disappointment—this experiment aroused: "Every avenue to the Exchange, during the whole week, was literally blocked up by the crowds of people that constantly assembled—some attracted by the novelty of the institution; some to watch its progress . . . ; some to make deposits and exchanges. . . . But, alas! It was soon discovered that the beautiful labour notes . . . could not by any means be forced into general circulation, on which account the supply of provisions failed and a complete failure was the result of one of the most extraordinary movements that was ever attempted in this or any other country."[90]

Writing at the end of the nineteenth century, the political economist J. Bonar argued that labor notes were not, strictly speaking, comparable to country banks' notes (much less Bank of England notes): "They were not issued for profit or on a calculation of probable demands for payment, but simply to effect the exchange of two supposed equivalents both actually existing at the time of exchange. Over-issue was impossible, for the goods might be said to go with the notes, as with bills of lading. In theory they were always convertible. If depreciation occurred, it was because of the spread of disbelief in the possibility of carrying out the conditions of the scheme, not from the nature of the case owing to an issue beyond the needs of the public."[91] Robert Owen did not see things in precisely these terms: he seems to have considered the labor notes the ideal to which Bank of England notes should have aspired; if the labor notes were not subject to overissue or intended to make a profit, these were advantages, not flaws. "A paper representative of the value of labour manufactured on the principle of the new notes of the Bank of England will serve for every purpose of their [the association's] domestic commerce or exchanges and will be issued only for intrinsic value received and in store," Owen explained.[92] Although Owen did not emphasize this, it was his last point that constituted the most significant difference between the labor notes and Bank of England paper, even notes redeemable for gold: labor notes were intended to represent the *intrinsic* value Owen attributed to labor and to circulate only where cooperation obtained, not merely to function as tokens of exchange in a general market where the terms of value fluctuated and redemption was always deferred. As the representatives of labor, which was not universally recognized as the ground of value, Owen's notes could be used only within the closed community whose members agreed on their terms. Once the enclosure literalized in the labor store was breached, members of the community lost faith in the notes, and, as they did so, labor notes lost the value they had momentarily incarnated.

Despite his endorsement of the labor note scheme, Robert Owen was not particularly interested in the theoretical nature of money or in the contemporary controversies about what led to fluctuations in the price or volume of bank paper. These are precisely the topics that interested John Bray, however, for he thought that the contemporary debates about money could be used as a springboard to more radical speculations. Bray's argument about money belongs to his attempt to alert his working-class readers to the numerous "secrets" that "political economists and capitalists" kept from them (*LW*, 59). Revealing these secrets was far more important to Bray than discovering the number of notes the Bank of England printed or the amount of gold it held in reserve, for he considered the operations of money to be "the secret of the almost omnipotent might of the capitalist" (136); banking, by extension, he held to be "the great armoury from which the capitalists derive all their weapons to fight with and conquer the working class" (146).[93] "Devise what he may, it is impossible for the ingenuity of man to create any instrument which will enable him to exercise such power over his fellow-man as he now obtains by means of the system of banking, or the creation and issue of money" (146). The combination of workers' ignorance about money ("the great body of the people have no precise idea of what is meant by the term 'money,' nor do they ever reason upon the cause or the nature of its power" [139]) and money's centrality to the establishment's strength placed this topic at the center of Bray's agenda. Like apologists for the paper money system, Bray wanted to explain what counted as "money," but, as he did so, he also wanted to reveal how the circulating medium could be used against the system that issued it.

Like the unscrupulous tradesmen who undermined Owen's labor notes, Bray realized that, if the medium of money could sometimes be detached from the ground that theoretically secured its value, as the Restriction Act had done, then it must be the case that money bears no fixed or necessary relation to what it claims to represent. In one sense, this is simply another way to say that (paper) money is a fiction, as critics of Britain's credit economy had done since the late seventeenth century; Bray took this position when he declared: "The note has been created as a substitute for gold; and common consent has stamped it with a fictitious, a merely representative value, altogether distinct from and independent of its own intrinsic value" (*LW*, 143). In another sense, his insight repeated the position that his contemporaries in the Free Banking school were advancing—any bank should be able to issue paper notes because money is a commodity; "the creation of a circulating medium is, under the present system, just as much a trade as the making of shoes or hats," Bray explained (148). In yet another sense, however, his claim went further than either of these observations, for, at several points in *Labour's Wrongs*, Bray argued that money constitutes a self-contained system of signs that obtains its value *only* because of social conventions—only "by the custom of society," as he phrased it (140). If this is so, according to Bray, then society *could* decide to change what counted as money—not, as the Currency and Banking school advocates were doing, by dickering over which monetary instruments should be considered money, but by creating an altogether new circulating medium that functioned on a different set of principles. Like Owen, Bray endorsed the principle of "EQUAL EXCHANGES" (62); but, whereas Owen wanted to restrict these exchanges to the closed system of the equitable labor shop, Bray wanted them to proliferate throughout the world. As the medium that would supersede paper money and link all the nations into a single, cooperative network, his new form of money was central to this ambition.

Like Owen, Bray considered value to be a function of labor, not market exchanges or some precious metal, like gold. Whereas Owen wanted to create labor notes that would represent labor in temporal units, however, Bray thought that money was a second-order form of mediation; money represented not labor itself but the things—houses or implements or food—that labor had created. Bray considered such objects "real capital" or "real wealth," and he thought that the media that represented this "real capital" should be issued in exact proportion to the "worth" of these objects (*LW*, 140). His account omitted the crucial question of how this "worth" could be evaluated or priced, but his conclusion followed logically from his premise. If money represented "real capital," and if labor had generated this "real wealth" by transforming nature into usable products, then there was not enough money in England to represent the products labor had created; therefore, more monetary tokens had to be issued:

> Money is to capital, or real wealth, what the alphabet is to written language; and as the latter consists merely of a number of arbitrary signs, signifying certain sounds, so in like manner do coin and bank-notes, in larger or smaller quantities, signify houses, or implements, or food, or anything else. The alphabets of all languages are sufficiently extensive to be made, by various combinations of the letters composing them, to express every variety of sound contained in these languages: the letters are neither too few nor too many. But in our monetary alphabet we have never yet followed this simple and natural plan of apportioning the means to the end.... There are in the United Kingdom upwards of three millions of buildings, we are possessed of above one hundred and fifty thousand vessels of various descriptions, and we have likewise an immense quantity of implements and machinery of different kinds. All these things are real capital—something to assist in further production. The whole of this wealth has been calculated to be worth above five thousand of millions of pounds sterling. But, under the present system, this enormous mass of capital cannot be said to have any representative whatever; for there is not in the nation a sum of money equivalent even to one hundred millions sterling; and yet the whole of this capital, if necessary, might be represented just as easily as a part. (141–42)

One might be tempted to say that, with this last point, Bray was obliquely commenting on the political situation of the British working classes, who also lacked representation in Parliament, but I think this would misconstrue his argument. Bray was adamant that the Chartist focus on extending the franchise was shortsighted, and he repeatedly insisted that merely gaining political representation would be ineffective. Only a change in the "principles" that governed British society would bring about genuine change: the "evils" currently suffered by "the productive classes" were "so interwoven into the present system—so ramified and entangled—so assimilated into every social and political institution—that the productive class can only free themselves by cutting through all at one blow" (*LW*, 64). What Bray wanted

was not to extend the franchise to workers but for the entire society to substitute the principle of equal exchange for the capitalist principles that
enshrined private property and inequitable exchange.

The question that remains is whether Bray's recommendation that the
productive classes produce a new form of money could have had this effect.
If he considered paper money the instrument by which one class currently
dominated another, why did he think that a new circulating medium would
bring about equality? It is difficult to answer this question from the argument of *Labour's Wrongs*. What is clear is that Bray thought that the form
of money he proposed—which consisted of pottery and paper tokens, each
inscribed with both a unit of labor hours and a sterling price (143, 172,
198)—would facilitate the necessary *transition* from the current state of class
oppression to a new condition of global equality:

> The past, the present, and the future transactions of Capital all depend upon
> Labour for their fulfillment. Such being the case, why should not Labour itself
> make a purchase? Why should not the bond of *Labour*, to pay at a future time
> what itself only can produce, be as valuable as the bond of *Capital*, to pay what
> this very same Labour is to produce? . . . If security be wanted by the capitalist,
> that the contract shall be abided by, is the security offered by a people of less
> worth than that offered by an individual? There are innumerable instances of
> individual breach of faith . . . but there cannot be found one solitary instance
> of the infringement of a contract by a people. (173)

What seems most striking about Bray's argument is not the radical nature of his ideas but how closely his operative assumptions resemble those
of establishment political economists like Smith and Ricardo. Even though
he wanted eventually to overthrow the reign of capitalists, in the transition to this state Bray wanted to preserve contracts, property, credit, and
a representative circulating medium, and it is difficult to imagine how a
transition that so closely resembled the status quo would ever be brought
to an end. Moreover, while the specific monetary instruments he recommended were new—both in their compositional materials and in the kind
of inscriptions embossed on their faces—it is difficult to see how pottery
tokens would have differed from the existing paper money. Bray's monetary tokens would have reminded users that two models of value existed
side by side during the transition; but, as long as these tokens were *credit*
instruments, they would have functioned exactly the way Bank of England
notes did. Bray never said whether he wanted such instruments eventually
to be phased out, nor did he say how this might happen or what might

take the place of representative money. Nor did he comment on the fact that his pottery notes could never attain the level of cultural invisibility that Bank of England notes were increasingly designed to achieve: as printed embodiments of a relationship *between* labor and sterling, those tokens, no matter what they were made of, would have reminded their users that, every time money changed hands, labor had already been abstracted into tokens with no intrinsic value.

Bray's attempt to use representative money to end prevailing inequalities, in other words, did not put an end to the deferral inherent in Britain's credit economy and its system of paper money. Thus, it did not offer a genuine alternative to the market model of value, even though Bray clearly thought that it did. His monetary tokens, with their twin inscriptions, would have kept the problematic of representation associated with paper money visible, but there is no reason to believe that simply keeping this problematic visible—instead of managing it, as the naturalization of Bank of England paper was to do—would have led to the changes he so obviously desired.

The primary lesson we learn from Bray's pamphlet is not that a new kind of money could have inaugurated social change but just how thoroughly the arguments of the classical economists had triumphed by 1839. The central role Bray assigned money in his proposed solution to labor's problems, in fact, suggests just how essential some form of representative money had come to seem by that time, even to a critic of the capitalist system like Bray. Bray could recognize that the existing forms of paper credit constituted part of labor's problem, in other words, but he seems not to have been able to imagine a society—even a society where equality reigned—without some form of representative money to function as a promise and a bond.

Bray's pamphlet seems to have had little impact on his contemporaries. Once he left the Leeds' Working Men's Association, Bray had no institutional base from which to promote his ideas; without the backing of one of the mass market publishing firms, he had none of the resources necessary to make his pamphlet circulate widely; and, in a market already saturated with popular renditions of classical political economy, like those of Martineau and McCulloch, his critique of capitalists and banks simply sank into obscurity. Indeed, as we will see in the next chapter, by 1839, the struggle over the definition of *value* had virtually come to an end, for, apart from the lingering influence of evangelical political economists, establishment writers had so thoroughly appropriated this concept and narrowed its definition that alternative concepts of value were beginning to seem reactionary or unrealistic. Although Ricardo used the word *value* in seven different ways in his *Principles of Political Economy and Taxation*, all but two of these ("value in use" and "natural value") constituted variants on what even by then had come to seem like its normative sense—value in exchange or exchangeable value. Some writers did question Ricardo's use of *value*, but most of those who did, like Thomas De Quincey and Samuel Bailey, focused on his failure to define the term precisely, not his association of value with exchange.[94] Like Bray, these writers did not offer an alternative definition of *value*—one that emphasized the pleasure an individual might experience, the process by which this pleasure might be obtained, or even the spiritual rewards that denying pleasure might confer. As we will see in chapter 5, imaginative writers had begun to formulate such an alternative by the turn of the nineteenth century, but, as De Quincey's early response to Ricardo reminds us, in the first decades of the century, even self-proclaimed champions of aesthetic value could easily be seduced into answering the supposed enemies on their own terms. By 1844, when De Quincey tried more concertedly to formulate an alternative model of value in *The Logic of Political Economy*, he was clearly waging a rearguard action against the successful narrowing of this concept.

If Bray's pamphlet failed to attract the attention he wanted for it, it does contain one interesting feature that deserves a final look. As I have already pointed out, Bray followed the lead of political economists in reasoning deductively, from first principles, rather than inductively, from historical or contemporary examples. As we are about to see, in normalizing deduction and insisting on principles, political economists like Ricardo had extracted one facet of the hybrid methodology Sir James Steuart introduced from the other modes of analysis that originally accompanied it. In *On the Principles of Political Economy and Taxation*, historical accounts and particular examples are so completely subordinated to theoretical abstractions that Ricardo could present his conclusions as universal, context-free laws. In *Labour's Wrongs*, principles also both follow from and reinforce what Bray presented as natural laws, but, while these laws might be universal *in theory*, they had yet to be realized in British society. Unlike Ricardo, then, and in order to help institute the laws that ought to (but did not) prevail, Bray allowed his preference for abstractions to manifest itself thematically and stylistically as well as in his method. For Bray, that is, in order to realize the laws that nature has supposedly given, individuals would have to subordinate themselves to a greater collective, which he repeatedly personified as *"Labour."* When he capitalized (and sometimes italicized) this noun, he intended it to be self-actualizing or performative: in his sentences, the word *Labour* seeks to unite readers by soliciting them to identify themselves with this collective abstraction. Like the imperative address that rendered the same directive more explicitly in the writings of later socialists—"workers of the world, unite"—Bray's single noun solicited identification not with an individual leader but with a social movement. As an activity that engaged both the imagination and reason, reading ideally functioned to generate a "mass" or collective from individuals.[95]

This vision of a mass—where most political economists emphasized the individuals who composed it—is precisely what champions of the kind of imaginative writing we call *Literature* despised, of course. According to writers like William Wordsworth and Samuel Coleridge, only the development of the individual imagination could yield meaningful improvement; reading was the preferred means of such development, not a vehicle for performing (or forming) collectives. To economic writers, meanwhile, the vision of the collective was also disturbing—even after the demise of Chartism in the 1840s. For, under certain circumstances, a collective could express itself in frightening ways—and not simply in the kind of crowd or mob action so feared in the eighteenth century. In the speculative manias and panics that punctuated the nineteenth century, collective action—not by radical workers, but by the hardworking citizens who risked, then lost everything when share prices rose, then fell—posed a new kind of threat. This threat challenged not just the security of the nation (although, arguably, it did that too); it also challenged the prestige of political economists, who increasingly viewed themselves as specialists—as professionals and scientists—not as participants in a political debate. Before turning to the Literary counterpart of the professionalization of economic writing, I take up the challenge that manias and panics posed to the economists' professional prestige, for this is one place where fictional strategies appeared alongside facts and information, even after economists succeeded in dismissing the radical claim that paper money was, by its very nature, fictitious.

CHAPTER FOUR

Professional Political Economy
and Its Popularizers

The 1844 Bank Act went a long way toward establishing the *legal* conditions in which Bank of England notes could fall beneath the horizon of cultural visibility—in which they could pass without scrutiny or question. It established these conditions gradually and incidentally, for this was not the primary aim of the legislation. It did not go so far as to make all Bank notes legal tender, for example; the final provision for this was not formally adopted until 1928.[1] Nor did it outlaw the issue of notes by country banks: banks that issued notes were allowed to continue doing so, but strict conditions intended to phase out issue were imposed; the last country bank notes were issued in 1923.[2] The two measures that granted Bank of England notes priority were specifically aimed at shoring up the stability of the banking system as a whole: by fixing the volume of the Bank's issue to a specified security of gold, the act bolstered public confidence in the nation's monetary supply, but it also supported belief in the Bank's notes and these notes alone; by dividing the Bank into two departments, it separated the Bank's variable note-issue function from its everyday business in order to insulate the former from the latter, but, by so doing, it also made the Bank's issue of notes as important as its other banking activities.[3]

As we saw in the preamble, the *technological* conditions necessary to render Bank notes culturally invisible had to await improvements in the Bank's plate transfer press, but, as we also saw, writers began to celebrate the reliability of Bank notes even before uniformity had technically been achieved. Partly because the government's legal provisions continued to nudge the Bank toward assuming responsibility for the nation's currency, and partly because momentum within the radical movement shifted away from financial reform, then dissipated with the defeat of Chartism in the late 1840s, the Bank's notes ceased to be controversial after midcentury. As the percentage

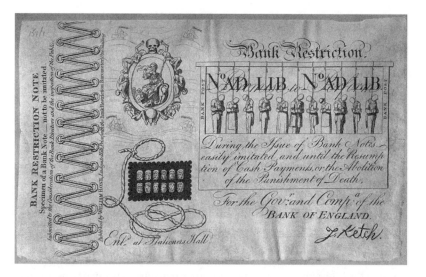

Figure 5. George Cruikshank, "Bank Restriction Note; Specimen of a Bank Note–Not to Be Imitated" (engraving on Bank-post paper, 13–21 cm, 1819). This skit note parodies the notes issued by the Bank of England during the Bank Restriction period (1797–1819/21). On the right, Cruikshank's note shows a line of forgers, hanged for imitating or receiving counterfeit notes. The emblem of Britannia has been replaced by a medallion of death's-heads, and the note is signed by "J. Ketch," the nickname for the state hangman. By permission of the William Hone Collection, Special Collections, Adelphi University Libraries.

of these notes in the nation's currency increased, and as their visual inter-changeability with each other did too, Bank of England notes ceased to merit characterization, as they had done for Thomas Bridges; they ceased to be symbols of tyranny, as they were for George Cruikshank; and they ceased to spark fantasies of radical reform, as they did for William Cobbett (fig. 5).

Bank of England notes constituted only one of the many financial instruments that facilitated the growth of the British economy, of course, and, as this economy continued to expand in the middle decades of the nineteenth century, credit instruments also increased in kind and complexity. It is not my intention to list or describe all these instruments; the account I provided in the preamble gives a good idea of the creativity with which lenders encouraged the public to use credit instruments in nineteenth-century Britain, and I return to this subject again in chapter 6. For my present purposes, it is time to shift attention away from the medium of banknotes toward the discipline, venues, and genres in which writing about the economy proliferated in the Victorian period. In this chapter, I argue that, during the middle decades of the nineteenth century, writing about economic and financial matters, which was increasingly distributed across specialized professions and circulated in a variety of publications, was as instrumental as monetary instruments in helping naturalize—and, thus, promote—the growth of Britain's credit economy. As we will see, writers who discussed the economy continued to perform the mediating function eighteenth-century writers initiated. As they did so, they also helped manage the problematic of representation, which repeatedly threatened to become visible whenever disturbing events roiled the British economy.

I want to make two preliminary points about the approach I take in this chapter. The first concerns organization. While my discussion is generally chronological, I also repeatedly highlight and sometimes follow the logic of a series of overlapping distinctions that characterized the entire field of nineteenth-century financial and economic writing. The first distinction, which we have already seen in Sir James Steuart's work, was articulated in various ways by nineteenth-century writers—as the difference between *information* and *theory*, between *facts* and *principles*, or between *practice* and *explanation*. In general terms, the members of these pairs were not considered incompatible with each other, and readers looked to economic writing to supply both—both information about existing conditions and theoretical models that could explain them, both practical suggestions based on facts and general principles derived from discrete experiences. Nevertheless, and with increasing vehemence as political economy acquired social prestige and several institutional homes, most economic writers insisted that accumulating facts and generalizing theoretical models constituted two separate activities, activities best conducted by two distinct sets of writers.[4]

Thus, we have a second distinction, one that we might characterize as a division within economic and financial labor. In the course of the century, as we will see, one group of writers, whose work was generally considered rudimentary or preliminary, collected factual information, and another group of writers, whose work was held to be more prestigious, used these data to generate models that, especially after the 1870s, aspired to the logical rigor and formal abstraction of mathematics. Finally, the division between collecting facts (which was often associated with, and eventually institutionalized as, the practice of *statistics*) and generating theory (which was associated first with political economy, then, after 1890, with *economics*) was superimposed on another set of distinctions. This set of distinctions can be said to have formed another, quite different division of labor. This division manifested itself in the genres in which the findings of statisticians and theorists were set out. While some writers formulated their findings, whether informational or theoretical, in pamphlets and books intended to reach an audience of specialists, others wrote in a style intended to communicate expert knowledge to as wide an audience as possible. As we will see, the nineteenth century saw a number of generic innovations designed to popularize statistical data and political economic theory, and the compatibility that characterized the relationships among kinds of financial and economic writing helps explain why what Carlyle called the "dismal science" acquired such popularity in the middle decades of the century. It also provides a salutary contrast to the competitive relationship that developed among—and continued to divide—the ranks of imaginative writers, which I discuss in chapter 5.

There are two reasons why I have tried to capture the layering of these three sets of distinctions. First, the fact that nineteenth-century political economy, then modern economics, matured in the context of a growing volume of more accessible, more practical writing about an everyday form of economic information meant that, even as the science of wealth was becoming narrower and more arcane, many of its basic principles were being disseminated to a growing number of readers, who sought to apply these principles in their everyday lives. Second, because the split within economic writing—between accessible writing on practical matters and specialized theory—generally compensated for (or even masked) the lack of fit between various contributions to the field, the fact that political economists' theories could not always explain the phenomena that practitioners reported did not always register with readers. Explanations and theories, in other words, were sometimes judged sensible in and of themselves, whether or not they made sense of economic events. Economic theorists offered a variety of ways to explain the disjunction between (unreliable because particular) "facts" and (reliable because general) "principles,"[5] but more important than the specific formulations used to dismiss this disjunction was one of the unintended effects this gap created: increasingly—and even though both theoretical and practical economic writers wanted to clarify and explain their subject—it became acceptable to most readers *not* to understand how financial institutions worked, much less the theories developed to explain economic factors. Such ignorance was partly a response to the subject's inherent complexity, but the cultural tolerance for ignorance was also a reflection of the fact that one could learn the jargon of finance, develop a working knowledge of economic principles, and conduct one's everyday financial affairs without really understanding the workings of individual financial institutions or the theoretical laws they presumably obeyed. As we will see in chapter 6, an entire range of writers, primarily Literary, helped cultivate this cultural tolerance for ignorance by referring to economic topics in fictions that did not require readers to understand the principles or the institutions that underwrote them.

My second general point concerns the focus of this chapter. Much has been written about the development of political economic "thought," disputes among schools of political economists, and the interplay between specific political or legislative events and political economic theory.[6] While I am indebted to this scholarship, I do not rehearse its findings here. Instead, I focus on two topics: the professionalization of political economic expertise, along with the proliferation of genres that helped popularize this expert knowledge, and the various ways that writers, both specialist and popular, tried to explain the speculative manias and panics that periodically disrupted the nineteenth-century economy. I will have more to say about the importance of manias and panics in a moment. Here, it is sufficient to note that both these topics enable us to see how nineteenth-century economic writing helped manage the problematic of representation that repeatedly became visible in nineteenth-century Britain. The relationship between these two topics, moreover, helps us see how writing about financial and economic matters assumed the function of cultural naturalization performed, in relation to Bank of England notes, by the 1844 Bank Act and the technological improvement of the Bank's new printing press. At first glance, the relationship between expertise and the anxiety that panics repeatedly expressed may seem obvious: in periods of economic uncertainty, it seems natural for people to look to experts for the reassurance that facts and models promise. On closer inspection, however, this relationship will prove more complex, for, before the impulse to consult experts could become natural, people had to assume that the manias and panics *could* be modeled and explained. In order for *this* to happen, in turn, people had to learn to believe in political economic theory as they believed in Bank of England notes, and they had to be taught to discount all the signs that the theories were not actually explaining the phenomena they claimed to make sense of.

Raising the Profile of Economic Theory: Ricardo, McCulloch, Chalmers, and John Stuart Mill

As Claudia Klaver has reminded us, David Ricardo played a critical role in the campaign to establish the prestige of economic "science." Ricardo made at least two crucial contributions to this effort. On the one hand, he was largely responsible for narrowing what had been, in the writings of Sir James Steuart and Adam Smith, the more capacious practice of jurisprudence into a more focused study of a reified, law-governed entity specifically conceptualized as an *economy* rather than *the market* or simply *trade*. On the other hand, Ricardo devised a form of writing that effectively excluded much of the British reading audience, thereby opening a space that could be filled by a more accessible form of economic writing devoted to explaining everyday economic events.[7] The most important component of the first contribution was Ricardo's revision of Smith's model of human nature. Whereas Smith thought that human beings were inherently social creatures motivated by multiple, often conflicting passions, Ricardo insisted that economic agents could be treated as if they were fully autonomous beings, motivated exclusively by the rational pursuit of self-interest. The most important effect of Ricardo's second contribution was the creation of a diverse group of writers who published in various genres and interpreted economic phenomena in various ways but who all essentially endorsed—and, thus, helped popularize—the liberal ideas Ricardo carried over from Smith (although not always the radical position Ricardo took on the currency).

As Klaver notes, Ricardo narrowed Smith's jurisprudence into what became the science of economics by a process of methodological and stylistic abstraction. This abstraction is evident everywhere in Ricardo's most important work, *Principles of Political Economy and Taxation* (1817), but nowhere is it more striking than in his use of hypothetical scenarios. As I pointed out in chapter 2, such scenarios were common in Steuart's work as well, but, whereas Steuart drew on fictional devices to enliven such scenarios, Ricardo rigorously excluded from his hypothetical scenarios any details that might seem extraneous to the abstract principles they illustrated. In Klaver's instructive summary, the effect of this method was to block any possibility that a reader might be imaginatively engaged with what Ricardo was describing:

> These scenarios allow Ricardo to recreate the abstraction of his theories in the prose through which he explains them. They enable him to strip his human representations of all features except those directly related to his economic point. There are no complicating circumstances unwittingly imported by an actual, or even realistic, anecdote. Collaterally, there are no grounds for the complicating emotions of sympathetic identification in the reader. In fact, because Ricardo reifies the actors in these scenarios into one-dimensional economic figures, he produces a narrative version of rational economic man without the capacity for mutual sympathy—or any other moral or affective capacities. The reader can relate to this figure only through his or her rational capacities, rather than through the nonrational and subjective sensibilities that stimulate sympathetic investment in other narrative forms and agents.[8]

The challenge posed by Ricardo's expository mode was (and is) undeniable. Even his most ardent supporter, J. R. McCulloch, acknowledged that his prose was difficult, noting, without quite apologizing for, "the brevity with which Mr. Ricardo has stated some of his most important propositions, the fewness of his illustrations, and the mathematical cast he has given to his reasoning."[9] When Thomas Robert Malthus, who famously sparred with Ricardo over both substantive and stylistic matters, challenged Ricardo to bring political economy back from the brink of mathematics toward "morals and politics," Ricardo reiterated the principle he thought key to making political economy a science. In a true science, one had to privilege abstraction because prejudices and preoccupations too easily made their presence felt in a practice with so many variables: "If I am too theoretical, which I really believe is the case—you I think are too practical. There are so many combinations—so many operating causes in Political Economy, that there is a great danger in appealing to experience in favour of a particular doctrine, unless we are sure that all the causes of variation are seen and their effects duly estimated."[10] While his ideas were undeniably influential in the nineteenth century—and while his place in the canon of political economic writers is secure—it is almost certainly the case that Ricardo influenced more theorists of political economy than nonspecialist readers. Indeed, while the abstractions he helped naturalize became a goal that nearly all economic theorists aspired to produce, his style was almost never imitated in the nineteenth century, even by theorists who achieved a greater level of mathematical rigor than he was able to.

––––––––

Ricardo's ideas attracted the attention of middle-class Britons almost exclusively through the lectures and writings of his followers, especially John Ramsay McCulloch (1789–1864). A Scot, McCulloch initially caught Ricardo's eye in 1815, when he sent Ricardo a copy of his first publication on political economy, *Essay on the Question of Reducing the Interest of the National Debt* (1815). McCulloch went on to review Ricardo's *Principles of Political Economy*, first for the liberal paper the *Scotsman* (in May 1817), which McCulloch edited from 1817 to 1821, then—more prominently—for the *Edinburgh Review* (in June 1818). This marked the beginning of McCulloch's nearly twenty-year association with the *Review*, for which he wrote most of the major economic articles, often (in the beginning) after consultation with Ricardo. When Ricardo was elected to Commons in 1819, McCulloch regularly consulted him about materials relevant to his journalism, and McCulloch also urged Ricardo to speak in Parliament on issues of particular interest to Scots. The two men finally met in 1823, and their mutually productive relationship ended only with Ricardo's death later that year.[11]

It is doubtless the case that McCulloch's renditions of Ricardo's ideas substantially altered both the form and the content of the master's works, as Klaver argues.[12] Nevertheless, the two men agreed on the principal tenets of political economy, and McCulloch also undeniably extended the reach of Ricardo's ideas beyond that which Ricardo's writing could have had on its own. It is McCulloch's career, in fact, and not Ricardo's, that reveals how proponents of political economy were able to establish the prestige of the new science. McCulloch has been called "the first professional economist"[13]—a position made possible not only by McCulloch's personal energy and determination but also by the confluence of print, extrainstitutional, and academic opportunities newly available in the first half of the nineteenth century. It is worth dwelling for a moment on this conjuncture, for the overlap between new opportunities, made possible by the expansion of print, and older forms of publicity, which depended on physical presence, powerfully shaped political economy's rise to prominence.

Unlike his most notable predecessors—Sir James Steuart, the Edinburgh professor Dugald Stewart, and Adam Smith—J. R. McCulloch was able to take advantage of the upsurge in print publications that I have already described. And take advantage he did. McCulloch published tirelessly and copiously—often increasing the sheer volume of his output by reproducing in new articles entire sections from essays that had already appeared. Admittedly, some of his pressruns, especially at the beginning of his career, were relatively small; in 1825, for example, he published his own *Principles of Political Economy* in a run of only fourteen hundred copies.[14] But McCulloch more than made up for this modest effort with ventures specifically designed for the flourishing market for entertaining knowledge. He was particularly adept in the popular genre of the encyclopedia. He published three such compilations of statistics and analyses (in addition to twenty articles in the *Encyclopaedia Britannica* and its supplements). The most popular of his compilations was the *Dictionary, Practical, Theoretical, and Historical of Commerce and Commercial Navigation*, the first edition of which appeared in 1832. Compiled and written almost single-handedly, this reference book contains accounts of an extraordinary range of places, products, and commercial activities as well as numerous foldout maps and elaborate charts. The *Dictionary* was popular not only in Britain but in other countries as well; so great was demand for it that McCulloch revised and reissued the book nine times during his lifetime. Each edition grew in girth and comprehensiveness, until the 1869 edition, which was published immediately after McCulloch's death, reached an astonishing fifteen hundred double-column pages filled with type almost too tiny for the eye to decipher. According to Hugh Reid, the editor of this edition, "if printed like ordinary books, [the *Dictionary*] would make at least thirty volumes octavo."[15]

In addition to his theoretical treatise addressed to specialists and popular reference books designed to engage those who wanted entertaining knowledge, McCulloch also packaged his ideas for an intermediate readership largely composed of middle-class men and women who wanted to know about—or be able to display their familiarity with—Britain's most current, most fashionable ideas.[16] These readers were likely to consume periodical articles, especially those published in the popular, but intellectually demanding, *Edinburgh Review*, which averaged a circulation of over eleven thousand and no doubt reached more people through circulating libraries and reading rooms. McCulloch, of course, was the leading economic writer for this publication for much of his publishing career. Nor was his periodical output limited to its pages: by the end of 1818, he had already published over fifty articles on economic themes in a range of periodicals, and his efforts in this venue never slowed. He also reached a more specialized market with his editions of the texts he helped turn into political economy's canon. As we saw in chapter 1, he published an edition of Smith's *Wealth of Nations* (1828) that made the entire text available for the first time in the nineteenth century,[17] an edition of Ricardo's works (1845), and the series of "scarce and valuable" economic tracts that he published for the Political Economy Club.[18]

The varied and market-savvy publications by which McCulloch exploited the power of the press capitalized on his expertise in an older mode of disseminating knowledge (and earning money): the public lecture. McCulloch began his teaching career in 1820, in a course of private—that is, extrauniversity—courses for Edinburgh students; by 1823, his students numbered sixty, and this led Ricardo to suggest that McCulloch develop a similar course for "some of the grown gentlemen in the House of Commons."[19] While he never offered such a course, McCulloch did lecture in London in April 1824 to an audience that included government ministers and members of Commons. This was his inaugural address as the first recipient of the newly endowed Ricardo Memorial Lectureship, and it proved successful enough for him to repeat it in Liverpool the following autumn. In 1825 and 1826, McCulloch's reputation grew: his London lectures were so popular that he gave them both at City and West End locations; and he supplemented these twenty-six twice-weekly lectures with private classes for especially eager students. One of his lectures, delivered at the opening of the City of London Literary and Scientific Institution—is said to have attracted nearly eight hundred people; his audiences sometimes included such luminaries as the chancellor of the Exchequer, the president of the Board of Trade, and the lord mayor of London.

McCulloch's ability to supplement the old medium of the lecture with the new medium of mass print did not ensure his success in another venue, which was simultaneously old and new. This was the university classroom. As I have already noted, the first university professorship in political economy was created at the East India College at Haileybury in 1807; from 1807 through 1834, this post was by occupied by Thomas Robert Malthus, who was indisputably one of the leading English political economists at the beginning of the nineteenth century. Meanwhile, in Scotland, Dugald Stewart had successfully lectured on political economy from his post as professor of moral philosophy at Edinburgh from 1799 to 1809; but neither that venerable university nor Oxford or Cambridge established chairs in political economy per se. In fact, an effort to create such a chair at Edinburgh was defeated when McCulloch's friends recommended him for the position. In 1828, McCulloch did receive a university post when a chair of political economy was established at the newly founded University of London; but, as Phyllis Deane points out, the university setting did not prove conducive to McCulloch's talents. He quarreled repeatedly with the university council, and the ranks of his students dwindled. He finally resigned his university post in 1837. In 1838, McCulloch left the academic world altogether, accepting a government position in the Stationery Office at a salary of £600 per annum (this rose to £1,200 by 1854).[20]

That McCulloch achieved such success outside the university setting—where modern professions most often achieve prestige and where the disciplines are typically defined—should not surprise us, for, even though universities were traditionally associated with the old professions—law, the clergy, and (some kinds of) medicine—in the first half of the nineteenth century there was no necessary connection between the university and the prestige of an individual or the social authority of a subject. This was true for several reasons. In the first place, the Latin- and Greek-based curriculum taught in the old universities was largely irrelevant to the kind of knowledge an individual needed to understand economic matters; even the most respected theorists of the subject—like John Stuart Mill—were largely informally schooled in political economy. New universities, where political economy courses or even chairs were initially created, lacked the prestige of the old universities, and, because some of them (like the East India College) were directly linked to specific (nonprofessional) kinds of work or companies, these courses did not command the respect accorded a classical education. In the second place, the dynamics of patronage almost always overrode the appeal of whatever intellectual content one might learn in a university. This meant that, if a member of Parliament wanted to consult someone about a topic associated with the economy—or to staff a government post—he was more likely to turn to a friend than to recruit a stranger from a university. And, in the third place, as McCulloch's career so aptly demonstrates, as audiences grew, and as the reasons for wanting to learn about economic matters proliferated, media that could reach out—through the printed page or the mass lecture—and that could create the kind of interest that we call *buzz* generated more prestige than the closed shop of the university could. The university did not take over the role of training and credentialing political economists until the 1870s, by which time demand for specialists in political economy had grown—both on the part of young men who wanted formal instruction in the subject and on the part of employers—and the practitioners of political economy had adopted a methodology that resembled those of other subjects taught in universities, especially the physical sciences and mathematics.

I want briefly to examine one of McCulloch's many treatments of economic topics, the long (47-page, 104-column) encyclopedia entry on banks and banking that was published in the 1859 edition of his *Dictionary*.[21] This entry will enable us to see one of the strategies by which a popular rendition of political economic orthodoxy addressed the aspect of the problematic of representation exposed by the century's recurring financial crises. As we are about to see, events called *crises* occurred roughly every ten years (in 1825–26, 1836–37, 1847–48, 1857, 1866, and 1890), various people explained them in various ways, and the losses associated with them varied in magnitude and extent. What these events had in common was a two-stage dynamic: a period of widespread and accelerating demand, often for new investment opportunities or speculative ventures, followed by a period of rapid sell-off and profit taking accompanied by failing businesses and bankruptcies. As manifestations of the problematic of representation, the manic phase of this dynamic opened a vertiginous gulf between the apparent manifestation or sign of value and its ground; and the panic phase both articulated the anxiety the problematic of representation could always provoke and demonstrated that this anxiety could become an active economic agent itself: panicked selling begat panicked selling, just as frenzied investment provoked emulative speculation in the manic phase. Taken together, the two phases of the dynamic raised the disturbing possibility Britons had encountered in the South Sea Bubble: rather than being a self-regulating, stable mechanism, the economy might be subject to fits of irrationality driven by nothing more than a collective, self-perpetuating madness. Clearly, if the practitioners of political economy were to establish the credibility of the liberal ideas Smith had introduced, they had to find some way to account for these crises, which seemed to strike at the heart of the orthodoxy Smith and Ricardo had established.

McCulloch never addressed commercial crises at length, but he did repeatedly allude to them, in what turns out to be a characteristic strategy of containment. The entry on banking provides a good example. While early editions of the *Dictionary* contained a relatively brief article on this subject, McCulloch significantly revised and enlarged the entry for the 1859 edition, following the Bank directors' decision to give him access to the Bank's archives. They were no doubt prompted to let him see these papers by the same events that made him want to expand the entry: by 1858 (when he composed the article), the Bank Act of 1844 had been suspended twice, each time in response to demands for additional credit provoked by a commercial crisis. In 1847, the Bank had been allowed to increase its note issue to stanch the hemorrhaging of the collapsed market for railway shares, and, in 1857, it acted to contain the fallout from a series of bank failures, sparked by failures in the United States. McCulloch's article was ostensibly a history of British banking, but (in its 1859 version) it was really a defense of the 1844 act, which the 1847 and 1857 panics had tested and, critics said, found wanting.

The heart of McCulloch's defense reiterated the compromise that Adam Smith had offered for the all-important questions of whether and when a government should intervene in commercial matters. The question about government "interference" was repeatedly raised in economic publications both by establishment writers, who generally supported only limited intervention in areas like public security, and by radicals, most of whom rejected the liberal ideal of unfettered competition. Even though the 1844 Bank Act, by which the government granted special powers to the Bank of England at the expense of country banks, could be (and was) interpreted as a violation of the liberal ideal of free trade, McCulloch argued that it did not actually violate laissez-faire. Every nation recognized that regulating note issue was an essential responsibility of any government, he argued, as essential as protecting public safety:

> Though a free and liberal course of policy be in general most for the public advantage, there are very many cases in which it is necessary to impose restric-

tions. It is admitted on all hands that governments are bound to suppress or regulate every business or pursuit which is likely otherwise to become publicly injurious. And does anyone doubt that the issue of notes payable upon demand is in the foremost class of these businesses? The experience of all ages and nations is conclusive as to this point. It has been everywhere regulated, in the most democratical as well as in the most despotical states, in England and Russia, Holland and France, the United States and Austria. The reasonableness of the practice accords with its uniformity. ("Banks," 88)

McCulloch elaborated this defense with two additional arguments. First, he claimed that, in the absence of national legislation, members of the "public" would be powerless to refuse the issue of local banks, for, since everyone had to use money, they would inevitably use whatever money was available ("Banks," 88). Second, he argued that, even though the Bank Act had strengthened the Bank of England's priority in note issue, this did not actually violate the principle of laissez-faire, for it simply moved the site of free trade to a higher level: instead of multiple bankers establishing the value of paper money by self-interested competition within Britain, the Bank of England now acted self-interestedly—but on behalf of the nation— to set the value of paper in relation to the international exchange, where gold was freely traded. Thus, the Bank—representing the nation—competed freely with other nations in the international market for gold, and the "public" benefited both because it was protected from unstable local banks and because public demand governed the volume of notes in circulation within Britain.[22]

To make the argument that the Bank Act actually supported the principle of free trade without expanding his history beyond Britain's banking system, McCulloch used an interesting rhetorical strategy: he offered two, conflicting (and gendered) definitions of *the public*. On the one hand, when he wanted to argue that Britain's country bankers took advantage of powerless individuals, he defined *the British public* as a feminized—or effeminate—group: "persons living on fixed income, women, labourers, minors" ("Banks," 88). On the other hand, when he wanted to argue that neither the Bank nor the government interfered with the volume of paper credit, he defined it as a masculine group, which consisted of "merchants, bankers, and money-dealers" ("Banks," 103). In his account, these are the individuals who "carr[y] bullion to the Mint or the Bank, that they might obtain coins, or notes, or both, with which to increase the currency." "It is one of the chief merits of the Act of 1844," McCulloch explained, that, under its agency, the supply of money is not to any extent or in any degree regulated or influenced by the proceedings of the Bank or the Government. They have nothing to do in the matter, unless it be to coin the bullion which individuals of firms carry to the Mint for that purpose, and to exchange, when called upon, notes for coins, and coins for notes. The supply of money, like that of all non-monopolised articles, is wholly dependent upon, and is determined by, the free action of the public. It would, indeed, be quite as true to say, that the Act of 1844 limits the amount of corn, of cloth, or of iron produced in the country, as that it limits the amount of money. It maintains the value of the notes issued by the Bank on a level with the coins for which they are substitutes; but beyond that its effect is *nil*. It has nothing whatever to do with the greater or less amount of the currency. That depends entirely on the estimate formed by the public of its excess or deficiency, an estimate which, when wrong, is sure to be corrected by the exchange. (103)

Using two definitions of *the public* enabled McCulloch to distinguish between a passive function (being forced to accept country bank notes) and an active function (taking bullion to the Mint). This double definition has its counterpart in the two characterizations he offered of banks. Once again, moreover, he gendered the distinction between these two kinds of banks. On the one hand, like the "merchants, bankers, and money-dealers" who acted aggressively when an opportunity arose, country bankers are masculine characters in his account. Unlike the trio of bullion holders, however, country bankers displayed a form of self-interest that violated the public good. By so doing, they revealed that masculine aggression could be either constructive or destructive, depending on whether it conformed to or violated laws. "The issue of notes is of all businesses that which seems to hold out the greatest prospect of success to the schemes of those who attempt to get rich by preying on the public," McCulloch warned ("Banks," 88); "the history of the joint-stock banks . . . discloses some of the most flagrant instances to be met with of recklessness, imposture and fraud" (90); "villainy is fertile in resources; and no severity of punishment has ever been found to be effectual for the suppression of crime" (92). On the other hand, McCulloch consistently gendered the Bank of England feminine. Representing the Bank as a woman, of course, did not imply that the institution was weak; instead, like Queen Victoria, the Bank of England could be a martial mother, like Britannia, the female figure whose image each note bore. Gendering the Bank feminine was conventional in the nineteenth century; ever since William Gillray had used the phrase in a(n antigovernment) cartoon, the Bank had been referred to colloquially as "the

Figure 6. "Political-Ravishment; or, The Old Lady of Threadneedle-Street in Danger!" (22 May 1797). This political cartoon, by James Gillray, shows William Pitt, the prime minister, picking the pockets of the Bank of England, who is covered with the inconvertible £1 paper notes the Bank issued during the Restriction period. The loan receipt in the lower-right-hand corner refers to the debt the government was incurring to finance its war with France. Courtesy of The Lewis Walpole Library, Yale University.

Old Lady of Threadneedle Street" (fig. 6). McCulloch took conventional wisdom one step further when he implied that the rumored run on the Bank of 1797 threatened an assault, or even a metaphoric rape, not by the prime minister (as in Gillray's cartoon), but by country bankers: "Demands for cash poured in upon the Bank from all quarters; and on Saturday, Feb. 25, 1797, she had only 1,272,000*l.* of cash and bullion in her coffers, with every prospect of a violent run taking place on the following Monday" (99).[23]

Defending the 1844 act by linking it to the international free trade in gold was one thing; but, as we have just seen, it was equally pressing in 1858 to defend the *suspension* of the act. Even if he could demonstrate that controlling the note issue was a matter of national security that did not violate the international free trade in gold, McCulloch still had to explain why, since the act had repeatedly had to be suspended, it was even necessary. To do so, he provided an account of the Bank's history that simply subsumed the crises of 1847 and 1857 into a triumphal narrative in which these crises (and, thus, the suspensions of the act) barely register. In his account, in fact, each of the century's commercial crises received successively less attention, and, when he came to the two most recent events, he barely paused over them. Thus, he provided a fair amount of detail about the events that led up to the 1826 panic, but he dismissed the next downturn (the 1836–37 crisis), saying only that "it is needless now to enter upon any investigation of the circumstances which led to the overtrading" that sparked it ("Banks," 102). The 1847 panic received even less attention, for McCulloch was intent on characterizing the suspension of the act as "doubtful policy." "In whatever way the crisis may have originated," he explained, "there can be no question that the suspension of 1847 was a measure of doubtful policy." After blaming events in the United States for the 1857 crisis ("a fire originating in a pig-sty may destroy a palace"), he also turned away from this event, again dismissing the suspension of the Bank Act with almost no comment: "This, though a brief, is, we believe, a sufficiently accurate account of the circumstances that led to the suspension of the Act in 1857" (105). As his treatments of these events suggest, McCulloch could minimize the importance of suspending the Bank Act by training his eye on the overall well-being of the Bank: when the Bank was in danger, whether from overtrading (as in the century's first two panics) or from miscellaneous precipitating causes (as in 1847 and 1857), any measure that could protect it would serve the interests of the nation. Thus, McCulloch placed all four crises in a single narrative *about the Bank* in order to argue that, if accorded sufficient integrity, this institution would always survive the brief—and, ultimately, trivial—expressions of doubt that contemporaries called *crises*. Because the 1844 act protected the Bank, he argued, it should not have to be suspended, for whatever led to such a lapse of faith was, ultimately, less important than the survival of the Bank.

Taken together, the two narrative devices I have described—McCulloch's creation and gendering of two "publics" (and two kinds of banks) and his subordination of the century's commercial crises to an account of the Bank of England—presented the entire history of British banking as the story of the Bank's rise to a position that enabled "her" to protect "the public." Individuals whose businesses collapsed in various panics, bankers whose note issue had been limited, and even the political economists who had tried to explain commercial events as "crises" barely figure in this narrative. By the same token, individual events—apart from the Bank's two definitive moments (the 1797 Restriction Act and the Bank Act of 1844)—simply became illustrations of the "sacred master principles" that governed economics and human nature alike, according to McCulloch.[24] It did not matter to him that the crises of 1825, 1836–37, 1847, and 1857 could be said to have differed from each other in significant ways. What mattered was that "the solemn engagement into which the public had entered with the national creditor" had finally been realized ("Banks," 100): by the Bank Act of 1844, the effeminate, sometimes obstreperous little groom—the public—and his great warrior-mother bride—the Bank of England—had been decisively and fruitfully wed.

————

The offhand, even dismissive way that McCulloch dealt with commercial crises was not atypical for nineteenth-century economic theorists. This may seem surprising at first, for such events might seem to demand a response from writers seeking to justify Smith's optimistic account of a self-regulating economy. Then, too, even before the century's first major crisis, two Continental theorists had already offered accounts of periodic variations in the trade cycle, accounts that might have been used to explain the much more severe ups and downs that followed. In 1803, the Frenchman J. B. Say had tried to affirm Smith's assertion that capitalism always strives for equilibrium by arguing that supply always produces an equal demand; in the account he offered in *Traité d'économique politique*, Say implied that unusual increases or decreases in trade were merely episodes in a larger dynamic striving for balance. J. C. L. Simonde di Sismondi, writing after the end of the Napoleonic Wars, countered the optimism voiced by both Smith and Say by arguing, in his *Principes d'économie politique* (1819), that trade cycles reflect the intrinsically disorganized nature of a system that distributes capital unevenly.

Even with these theoretical models before them, and despite the provocation of the century's repeated waves of speculative manias and panics, the leading British economic theorists addressed these events only in passing. When they did not subsume them into an apology for a specific financial institution or law (as McCulloch did), they tended to take one of two approaches to manias and panics. On the one hand, they treated crises as part of another topic. For much of his career, for example, the question of "gluts" preoccupied Malthus, and, while a general glut—the superabundance of all a society's commodities, which would make prices fall below the cost of production—was not thought to be identical to the sudden economic downturn some theorists called a *crisis*, it seemed, in some ways, related. Other, somewhat later theorists focused on oversaving rather than manias and panics per se; thus, John Lalor argued that oversaving created pressure to invest and that this could, but did not always, lead to speculative manias. F. W. Lloyd and William Sargant also promoted variants of this idea.[25] On the other hand, theorists tended to focus on abstract principles and to treat all individual events—no matter how dramatic—as relatively unimportant instances whose departures from the norm would even out over time.

One group of writers that did focus on crises deserves mention—in part because its influence was considerable during the first three decades of the century and in part because its members' interest in this subject proves my general point that crises were not a topic addressed by economic *theorists*. This group has been denominated *evangelical* political economists by Boyd Hilton, who has also identified as its most prominent spokesperson Thomas Chalmers (1780–1847), the Scots divine who mesmerized both local parishioners and London audiences with the fiery sermons he delivered between 1815 and 1844.[26] Even in the loose sense in which I have been using the term, Chalmers was not a *professional* political economist, nor was he an economic *theorist*. He initially became interested in political economy when he assumed the chair of moral philosophy at St. Andrews University in 1823, and, while he did publish three volumes devoted to economic ideas, he remained primarily a social reformer and a preacher who used Malthus's theories to advance his social and spiritual programs.[27]

Joseph Schumpeter has called Chalmers the "McCulloch of the Malthusian school" to indicate the popularizing role played by both men.[28] As we have seen, McCulloch relied on a combination of lectures, articles, books, dictionaries, and collected editions and series to disseminate the ideas of Ricardo and Smith; Chalmers's efforts on behalf of Malthus's theories were less diverse but no less ardent, for, after reading Malthus's *Principles of Political Economy*, he became convinced that the economic growth Britain experienced during the war years was fated to end. Unlike Ricardo and Smith, who believed (with Say) that supply would always create a corresponding demand, Malthus feared the development of a "general glut" that would flood the market with unwanted goods and bring economic progress to a halt. This theory (which was finally endorsed by Keynes in the twentieth century) dovetailed with Chalmers's conviction that spiritual demand was also limited and that, as a consequence, it needed constant cultivation: "It is just as necessary to create a spiritual hunger, as it is to afford a spiritual refreshment," he wrote.[29]

For Chalmers, the idea that demand for material goods might be as limited as its spiritual counterpart did not mean that the former needed to be cultivated, as the latter indisputably did. Instead, Chalmers adopted another of Malthus's principles, this one from his earlier work on population. Just as the increase in population, which tended naturally to outstrip the supply of food, had to be limited by self-restraint, lest famine and disease take their course, as Malthus had argued in 1798, so, according to Chalmers, the economic growth of the war period had to be constrained by economic discipline; if it was not, commercial crises like the one that erupted in 1826 would inevitably occur. In the third volume of *Christian and Civic Economy*, which he wrote during the months this crisis exploded, Chalmers proposed the analogy that was to prove so influential to so many of his peers: "What disease does with the redundant population, bankruptcy does with the redundant capital of our land; relieving the overdone trade of its excess, and so reducing capital within those limits beyond which it cannot find any safe or profitable occupancy."[30] According to this view, economies did not naturally expand, nor were financial crises insignificant interruptions of a system striving for equilibrium. Instead, Chalmers viewed Britain's economy as a static entity whose dynamics were cyclic and inevitably disrupted by undue growth. Bankruptcies were the safety valves of overproduction, overambition, or both; as such, they "reliev[ed]" the "overdone trade" of the nation, even though they injured the individuals who suffered them.

As Hilton has argued, some of Chalmers's contemporaries took his Malthusian model of countervailing forces even further, arguing that crises like the 1826 panic were special providences—divine interventions directed at what the *Christian Observer* called "our commercial sins, and the retributive distresses which have accompanied them."[31] By 1846, when three such crises had occurred, providential intervention might have seemed less special—that is, directed at a single event—than regular—that is, part of God's system for imposing order on the financial world. Such interpretations encouraged some devout Britons to treat individual bankruptcy as sign of a personal spiritual failure and waves of bankruptcy as a cleansing agent, "exterminating noxious weeds and destroying the seeds of spreading mischief."[32] They also added to the nearly constant attempts to distinguish between legitimate profit and judicious *investment*, on the one hand, and excessive profit and destructive *speculation*, on the other. As a contributor to the *Ecclesiastic and Theologian* wrote in 1860, only "a very strong religious spirit" was thought sufficient to identify this all-important difference:

> In this speculating world, amid all these risks and ventures which perhaps must be entered into to make business prosperous and to keep pace with the age, it is only a very strong religious spirit, a practical exercise of religion, that can make anyone judge accurately between legitimate and reckless commercial speculation. . . . From the danger we are all in of taking our moral standard from the tone of the common morality of society, we are apt to forget the higher standard of the law of CHRIST. We are every now and then recalled to a

sense of the difference of these two standards by some tremendous commercial failure; in which we see that speculation has been carried so far into the region of uncertainty and risk, that trust and confidence has been abused, and the ruin of one man has involved in it that of hundreds, who trusted him.[33]

Chalmers's Malthusian ideas were undeniably influential. Samuel Jones Loyd (Lord Overstone) held many of these positions, and his impact on Peel's 1844 Bank Act was informed by them. As a leading member of the Currency school, Overstone believed that money should incarnate value; if the Bank's circulating currency was backed by gold, as the 1844 Bank Act dictated, it could theoretically offset the dangerous potential for speculation unleashed by excessive credit. Even though Chalmers's ideas had a long afterlife in this slightly watered-down form, however, his own influence effectively ended in the late 1830s. Chalmers's brief, meteoric prominence was curtailed by a combination of the failure of his voluntarist approach to the problem of poverty, his controversial endorsement of church extension, and Peel's decision to appoint a commission of inquiry into the Scottish Poor Laws in 1843. As we will see, some financial journalists (as well as novelists like Mary Ann Evans [George Eliot]) continued to associate financial overreaching with spiritual weakness (think of Bulstrode in *Middlemarch*), but, by and large, as political economy was taken over by expert theorists, who emphasized aggregates and abstractions, such associations tended to fall by the wayside. Finally, the passage of limited liability legislation in the 1850s put a juridical end to the possibility that an individual could be held personally responsible for the failure of his (or her) unwise speculations.[34]

––––––––

John Stuart Mill (1806–73), the most influential theorist to develop Ricardo's Smithian position, was openly skeptical of Chalmers's ideas. How, Mill wondered, could a clergyman "inculcate on capitalists the practice of a moral restraint in reference to the pursuit of gain"?[35] Mill's disdain for Chalmers's individualistic approach to commercial activities was part and parcel of his tendency to view the economy as a law-governed system best understood in the abstract, as an aggregate of nonpsychological participants. Even though Mill did not devote sustained attention to commercial crises, it is important briefly to consider the passages in which he did so because this approach proved so important for the discipline in which this work (and not Chalmers's) became canonical.

Mill's most important economic treatise, *Principles of Political Economy*, was published within a year of the century's third (or fourth, depending on one's view of the 1839 downturn) commercial crisis; after the first, 1848 edition of the *Principles*, subsequent editions appeared (during Mill's lifetime) in 1849, 1852, 1857, 1862, 1865, and 1871. While Mill explicitly considered his treatise to be "popular," and even though a students' edition was published (in 1862), the popularity to which Mill could reasonably aspire was very different from that Cobbett attained in 1810, not to mention Chalmers's popularity or even what Charles Knight and McCulloch achieved with their volumes of useful knowledge in the 1820s and 1830s. As we will see in the next chapter, two years after Mill's first edition Wilkie Collins discovered (to his horror) that an altogether different scale of popularity lay beyond the wildest ambitions of middle-class writers like Mill and McCulloch, in the 3.5 million readers who indiscriminately devoured cheap weekly periodicals. In 1848, the appeal of even a "popular" economic treatise (as long as it was not a collection of sermons) was really limited to the educated middle classes, and a "students'" edition was likely to have been consumed by aspiring specialists or pupils. Mill himself had been just such an aspiring pupil, one who learned from books and talk rather than university training. His expertise was acquired through private reading (directed by his father), conversation (with Ricardo, among others), and participation in debating societies (populated largely by Bentham's followers). The popularity of his published writing, then, should be measured in terms of serious, self-directed, and well-educated readers like himself, not the thousands who attended Chalmers's sermons or the millions of readers who remained largely invisible to middle-class writers until the 1850s. While this popularity was sufficient to solidify Mill's reputation as the leading economic theorist of his day, and while we can attribute it to the market, the market in question was the growing middle-class demand for serious printed materials and the growing desire (among the same readership) for political economy in particular, not the mass market that was just beginning to make its presence felt. Just as he was a self-taught and (in this limited sense) market-made expert, so Mill was, from our perspective, an amateur political economist. Never employed as an economic specialist, he spent much of his adult life, from 1823 until 1858, working as a bureaucrat—first as a clerk, then as an examiner at the East India House.

In his *Principles of Political Economy*, Mill did not address commercial crises in a sustained way, and his adherence to Say's law gave him *theoretical* reasons for doubting that crises were inherent in the credit economy. Nevertheless, he considered commercial crises in four passages, which, taken as a whole, suggest that, for *practical reasons*, he was beginning to see the century's recurring economic downturns as versions of the same kind of phenomenon. Of the four passages in which he discussed these crises, three followed up on the pre–Bank Act currency debates and presented commercial crises as causes or manifestations of some problem in the money supply.[36] The other, which is the first to appear in the book, belongs to Mill's discussion of credit "as a substitute for money" (511). In this passage, Mill offered a definition of "the ideal extreme case of what is called a commercial crisis" (527):

> There is said to be a commercial crisis, when a great number of merchants and traders at once, either have, or apprehend that they shall have, a difficulty in meeting their engagements. The most usual cause of this general embarrassment is the recoil of prices after they have been raised by a spirit of speculation, intense in degree, and extending to many commodities. Some accident which excites expectations of rising prices, such as the opening of a new foreign market, or simultaneous indications of a short supply of several great articles of commerce, sets speculation at work in several leading departments at once. The prices rise, and the holders realize, or appear to have the power of realizing, great gains. In certain states of the public mind, such examples of rapid increase of fortune call forth numerous imitators, and speculation not only goes much beyond what is justified by the original grounds for expecting rise of price, but extends itself to articles in which there never was any such ground: these, however, rise like the rest as soon as speculation sets in. At periods of this kind a great extension of credit takes place. Not only do all whom the contagion reaches employ their credit much more freely than usual; but they really have more credit, because they seem to be making unusual gains, and because a generally reckless and adventurous feeling prevails, which disposes people to give as well as take credit more largely than at other times, and give it to persons not entitled to it. . . . In this manner, in the celebrated speculative year 1825, . . . the prices of many of the principal articles of commerce rose greatly, without any fall in others, so that general prices might, without incorrectness, be said to have risen. When, after such a rise, the reaction comes, and prices begin to fall, . . . speculative purchases cease. . . . [And to the rational desire not to overextend one's credit] there is superadded, in extreme cases, a panic as unreasoning as the previous over-confidence; money is borrowed for short periods at almost any rate of interest, and sales of goods for immediate payment are made at almost any sacrifice. Thus, general prices, during a commercial revulsion, fall as much below the usual level as during the previous period of speculation they have risen above it: the fall, as well as the rise, originating not in anything affecting money, but in the state of credit; an unusually extended employment

of credit during the earlier period, followed by a great diminution, never
amounting, however, to an entire cessation of it, in the later. (527–28)

The fact that this description focuses on the last phase of the mania/
panic dynamic reveals how difficult it was for observers to spot a commercial crisis in the making. Only when prices began to fall could the theorist
see that one was under way. In other words, the first part of the dynamic,
which Mill only alluded to, did not immediately attract the political economist's attention because the activities that inaugurated a speculative mania
were ordinary commercial activities, like trade and investment. The beginning of what was retrospectively termed a *mania*, then a *panic*, then a *crisis*,
was simply the natural desire for profit; it was only when the ordinary
"expectation of profit" intersected with something else—"an extra demand,
a short crop, obstruction to importation, or any other cause" (*Principles*,
526)—that the snowball of trade and investment began to turn into the
avalanche of speculation and commercial crisis. In Mill's account, these
"accidents" lay outside the economic theorist's purview, for the Smithian
picture of an economy always in—or searching for—equilibrium did not accommodate such outriders. By the same token, the availability of credit,
which was also considered a natural part of a mature economy, did not provoke the political economist's notice until it began to be drawn into and accelerate speculation. Because both the desire for profit and the availability
of credit were considered normal parts of the economy, the political economist could see that something had begun to go awry only when falling
prices announced the presence of a crisis.

The difficulty of discriminating between ordinary commercial activity
and the extraordinary activities that could be called a *crisis* was compounded
by the fact that different crises were precipitated by different causes and ran
courses that were not always the same. As we will see in my discussion of
Walter Bagehot, some economic writers faced the challenge posed by variations in commercial crises by constructing a typology of types of downturns.
Such typologies enabled writers both to group such phenomena together
and to discriminate among them, and detailed descriptions enabled analysts to identify the historically specific conditions that provoked each crisis.
Mill gestured toward each of these approaches, but, instead of generating a
comprehensive typology or individualized accounts of the century's crises,
he tended to see them simply as (unfortunate) episodes in the natural
course of trade. In book 4 of the *Principles*, he suggested that commercial
crises not only took ordinary economic behaviors to an extreme but also
constituted an innate part of the modern economy's dynamic. Thus, he

wrote that "commercial revulsions" (a term that encompassed the fall in prices, the business failures, and the unemployment that followed contractions in trade) were "almost periodical" because they were "a consequence of the very tendency of profits [to decrease so far but no further] which we are considering" (734).

Mill's approach to commercial crises may not have been identical to the tack taken by other economic writers, but some of the features of his treatment did become normative for economic theorists. One of these is especially worthy of note—in part because it differs so markedly from the evangelicals' formulations. This is his preference for theoretical abstractions over concrete description. Mill presented the crisis through a group of disembodied abstractions, not in terms of the individuals who actually engaged in trade. Thus, phrases like *spirit of speculation, expectations of rising prices*, and *the public mind* are the primary agents in Mill's sentences. Such descriptions dwarfed the concrete particulars from which the abstractions were drawn, subsumed the ambiguities inherent in unfolding events into a defined (albeit abstract) phenomenon, rendered all individuals interchangeable, and made their emotional states seem merely the effects of objective (if invisible) causes. At only two points in the passage—the words *contagion* and *imitation*—did Mill even allude to the social process by which the desire to speculate spread—a topic that was of considerable interest to some of his contemporaries.[37]

Mill's reliance on abstractions, of course, was the sign that political economy was becoming—that is, still aspiring to become—a science.[38] In such a science, there was not room for the individualizing accounts that some of Chalmers's followers provided because the individual was not the focus; no amount of personal soul-searching or self-restraint could affect an economy conceptualized in the abstract as a mechanism governed by secular laws. By the same token, Mill's reluctance to pursue his observations about commercial crises was, in part at least, an expression of his desire to leave the theory he had inherited from Smith and Ricardo unchanged. Indeed, his transitional position can be seen in the important fifth article in his *Essays on Some Unsettled Questions in Political Economy*, which he composed in 1829 and 1830. In this essay, Mill explained that political economists knew that the assumptions that underwrote their method were artificial; they had to make such assumptions, Mill explained, because a science in its infancy often had to assume what it could not yet prove:

> Political Economy considers mankind as occupied solely in acquiring and consuming wealth, and aims at showing what is the course of action into

which mankind, living in a state of society, would be impelled if that motive [the desire for wealth] . . . were absolute ruler of all their actions. . . . All
these operations, though many of them are really the result of a plurality
of motives, are considered by political economy as flowing solely from the
desire of wealth. The science then proceeds to investigate the laws which
govern these several operations, under the supposition that man is a being
who is determined, by the necessity of his nature, to prefer a greater portion
of wealth to a small in all cases . . . ; not that any political economist was ever
so absurd as to suppose that mankind are really thus constituted, but because this is the mode in which the science must necessarily proceed. When
an effect depends on a concurrence of causes, these causes must be studied
one at a time, and their laws separately investigated, if we wish, through
the causes, to obtain the power of either predicting or controlling the effect;
since the law of the effect is compounded of the laws of all the causes which
determine it. . . . In order to judge how he will act under the variety of desires
and aversions which are concurrently operating upon him, we must know
how he would act under the exclusive influence of each one in particular.[39]

This statement implies that, as political economy matured, the science
would be able either to jettison its preference for abstracting a single motivation or join with other sciences to produce a more comprehensive account
of complex behaviors. Ironically, of course, the specialization that abstraction promoted militated against the former, for Mill was also acknowledging that the very artifice that political economy needed in order to become
a science narrowed the understanding of human nature and, with it, the
definition of *value* that the science could acknowledge. I will return at the
end of this chapter to this process of narrowing, which had both professional and substantive implications, but, for now, it is important to turn
to the ranks of auxiliary economic writers, whose contributions continued
the effort McCulloch had launched early in the century: the campaign to
popularize the findings of theorists like Smith, Ricardo, and Mill.

Financial Journalism: Economic Writing for Middle-Class Readers

The marginalized position to which radical writers like Cobbett were relegated, which I discussed in chapter 3, and the role of spiritual guide, which
Chalmers occupied, were not the only positions from which nineteenth-
century financial writers could play a role subsidiary to that of the theorists.
The most important auxiliary position, as measured by numbers of both

writers and readers, was that of the financial journalist. Most of the writers who published in nineteenth-century periodicals and newspapers were not theorists, like Ricardo and Mill, nor were they typically critical of the credit economy, as Cobbett and Bray were. Indeed, as explicators of and—to a large extent—apologists for the credit economy, financial journalists played a unique role in popularizing classical political economy and in natural- izing the economists' narrowed definition of *value*. This role, which had no precise equivalent among imaginative writers, involved mediating be- tween aspects of the economy that seemed opaque—either because financial institutions shrouded their operations in secrecy or simply because of the- orists' abstruse terminology—and middle-class readers, who increasingly wanted to learn something about economic matters, whether from general interest or to improve their own financial situations. Unlike reviewers and critics—the closest Literary equivalents to financial journalists—the peri- odical writers who explained how the economy worked did not typically try to enhance their own importance by calling attention to their person- alities or work. Partly as a result, the cooperation that characterized the division of labor among economic writers actively supported—and helped generate—the considerable prestige that economics enjoyed by the end of the century. Unlike Literary writing, which, as we will see, achieved its reputation through an elaborate system of internal discriminations and public backstabbing, economic writing achieved its authority through a process that produced a hierarchy of kinds of knowledge and information, packaged for various groups of readers with different interests and needs.

Journalists were quick both to spot the segmentation of British readers and to take advantage of this by providing accessible translations of expert knowledge. As early as 1813, Francis Jeffrey, the editor of the *Edinburgh Re- view*, noted the specialization that was subdividing the growing body of readers and writers. "The age of original genius, and of comprehensive and independent reasoning is over," Jeffrey wrote. "Instead of such works as those of Bacon, and Shakespeare, and Taylor, and Hooker, we have En- cyclopaedias, and geographical compilations, and country histories, and editions of black-letter authors. One man spends his life in improving a method of dyeing cotton red;—another in adding a few insects to a catalogue which nobody reads ... and five hundred others in occupations equally liberal and important: each of them being, for the most part, profoundly ignorant of everything out of his own department."[40] In 1855, Walter Bage- hot offered a keen (if somewhat wistful) appraisal of the opportunity that specialization, along with the gulf opened by expertise, offered journalists, whom he refers to here as *we*:

It is, indeed, a peculiarity of our times, that we must instruct so many people. On politics, on religion, on all less important topics still more, everyone thinks himself competent to think,—in some casual manner does think,—to the best of our means must be taught to think rightly. Even if we had a profound and far-seeing statesman, his deep ideas and long-reaching vision would be useless to us, unless we could import a confidence in them to the mass of influential persons, to the unelected Commons, the unchosen Council, who assist at the deliberations of the nation. . . . And this appeal to the many necessarily brings with it a consequence. We must speak to the many so that they will listen, that they will like to listen, that they will understand. It is of no use addressing them with the forms of science, or the rigour of accuracy, or the tedium of exhaustive discussion. The multitude are impatient of system, desirous of brevity, puzzled by formality.[41]

At the beginning of the nineteenth century, it was not clear that journalists would ever be influential enough to play the role Bagehot described. Until the last two decades of the century, journalism was a poorly defined and, typically, poorly paid activity. Granted, increasing numbers of newspapers and periodicals were launched during the century, in waves that generally followed the repeal of politically or fiscally repressive legislation, but writing for a magazine or a newspaper required no particular credentials, and simply getting an article published did not inevitably open a path to a career—or even promise a second assignment. Generally speaking, journalists worked within a hierarchy similar to those that characterized nearly every facet of nineteenth-century Britain: at the top of this particular ladder were editors, followed, in order of status, by leader writers, subeditors (who generally assembled and oversaw the production of each issue), reporters, and essay writers; this last group included freelancers, who typically wrote on nearly any subject for a wide variety of publications, and a smaller number of writers who enjoyed a more regular relationship with one or more periodicals. Nor was this activity well remunerated. Alan Lee estimates that, in the 1830s, the editor of a London daily might have made £600–£1,000 a year; by contrast, ordinary reporters earned much less, probably about 75 percent of a bricklayer's annual income.[42] It was not until the 1880s, according to Walter Besant, that numerous enough and sufficiently lucrative opportunities existed for individuals to be able to support themselves through periodical writing.[43]

Financial journalism, as a subset of this broad sector of periodical writing, was even less formally defined in the period, although one can argue that it acquired a recognizable form and sufficient variants to be identifiable from the mid-1840s.[44] It did so for a number of reasons internal to the economic world: by the middle of the 1840s, the institutions that composed the British money market—what Walter Bagehot called "Lombard Street"— had acquired sufficient regularity and habits of internal record keeping to produce detailed accounts like those already appearing in government Blue Books; with the invention of the electric telegraph in the late 1830s, journalists could transmit their stories more rapidly; and, by the mid-1840s, financial information was copious and public enough to support the kind of second-order commentary that characterized most financial journalism. Beyond these internal factors, financial journalism responded to two external factors: first, the mid-1840s witnessed the railway boom, the third of the century's episodes of speculative mania and panic, and the ensuing economic volatility was undeniably "news," in the sense of being both current and of almost irresistible appeal to readers and writers alike; second, in the early 1840s, books and pamphlets that were critical of the credit economy had increased in number and kind, thus inciting apologists for the system to respond.

It is impossible to identify all the financial journalists, for, unlike their closest Literary counterparts, the "Bohemians," these reporters founded no self-advertising magazine like *Punch*, nor did a recognized leader emerge from their ranks, as Dickens and Thackeray did from the Bohemians.[45] The convention of publishing anonymously also impedes our efforts to identity these writers, but we can certainly say that, between 1845 and the 1880s, the ranks of financial journalists included Walter Bagehot, Thomas Massa Alsanger, W. E. Aytoun, Bonamy Price, David Morier Evans, Ronald Laing Meason, Sidney Laman Blanchard, Laurence Oliphant, and even, on occasion, Charles Dickens himself. All these writers sought to capitalize on—and incite—the same interest in financial matters that led people to flock to McCulloch's lectures in the 1820s and to purchase (even if they did not fully understand) economic treatises like Mill's *Principles*. Financial journalists often alluded to the theories of the writers whose work I have already examined, just as they sometimes (and with increasing regularity in the last decades of the century) described daily fluctuations in share prices. By and large, however, the products of financial journalists differed from both theory and stock reports. Instead of formulating economic laws or offering investment advice, most financial journalists sought to present portraits of the City that could make its idiosyncratic culture interesting, if not fully comprehensible, to readers. The three journalists with whom I am particularly concerned—Walter Bagehot, David Morier Evans, and Laurence Oliphant— clearly saw themselves as intermediaries whose liminal positions—both inside and outside the City—enabled them to translate the arcane jargon of the financial world into a language that any middle-class reader could appreciate, even if the finer points of economic theory remained elusive.

My treatment of the way that financial journalists dealt with commercial crises moves from accounts that more closely resemble economic theory to narratives that include so many imaginative features that one might mistake them simply for fictions. This section thus provides a bridge to chapter 5, where I take up Literary writing as an increasingly distinct subset of nineteenth-century print, and it also anticipates what I describe in the next interchapter—that, despite efforts to discriminate among the genres of the credit economy, the boundary between economic and imaginative writing remained permeable. The growing overlap between kinds of writing that my order of presentation suggests does not reflect a historical trend, however. Indeed, as we will see in the remainder of this book, efforts to make this differentiation intensified with the passage of time, even though, in retrospect, they can be seen to have had various degrees of success and to have been established at considerable cost.

Walter Bagehot (1826–77) was educated at University College, London, in classics, Roman history, mathematics, and poetry, and, while he worked in some branch of his family's bank for much of his life, he seems always to have wanted to be a writer. In the early 1850s, Bagehot acted on this wish, founding the *National Review* (with the help of his friend the reviewer and critic Richard Holt Hutton). This periodical, for which Bagehot served as coeditor and contributing writer, was largely devoted to reviewing imaginative writing; his nine-year association with the *Review* enabled Bagehot to write on Shakespeare, Cowper, Dickens, Scott, and Gibbon, among others. During the entire period he edited the *Review*, Bagehot continued to work as a banker, first in Langport, then in Bristol. Then, in 1859, his career took a decisive turn away from practical banking when James Wilson, the founding editor of the weekly *Economist*, appointed Bagehot (who had recently married Wilson's daughter) director of the paper. While Bagehot continued his affiliation with the London branch of his family's bank, from 1859 until the end of his life he increasingly subordinated banking and reviewing to writing about economic and political matters.[46] He became the *Economist*'s editor in 1861, and, during the next sixteen years, he wrote at least one article a week for the periodical, published several greatly admired books, and became a regular consultant for legislators and cabinet members. So indispensable did William Gladstone consider his services that he called

Bagehot "a sort of supplementary Chancellor of the Exchequer"; in 1876, the actual chancellor of the Exchequer, Sir Stafford Northcote, asked Bagehot to devise a plan to raise short-term revenue, and, in response, Bagehot invented the Treasury bill.[47]

Bagehot's most enduring contribution to economic writing is undoubtedly the monograph *Lombard Street* (1873), an overview of the British financial system that, like McCulloch's encyclopedia entry, focused specifically on the Bank of England. Written both to explain how the system as a whole worked and to defend the 1844 Bank Act, *Lombard Street* also took a strong stand on the responsibilities entailed by the Bank's role as repository of England's gold reserve, and Bagehot formulated concrete suggestions, derived from his own experience, to help the Bank act as the national bank that, in everything but name, it had already become. In the mid-1870s, Bagehot began working on a treatise on political economy, which, like *Lombard Street*, emphasized practical rather than abstract formulations. He never completed this work, however, publishing only the first part—*Postulates of Political Economy*—in 1876; the remaining fragments were published posthumously, in 1880, as *Economic Studies*.

In *Lombard Street*, Bagehot offered several suggestions about how the Bank could help even out the course of commercial affairs, including that the Bank increase gold reserves in periods of prosperity so that it could advance more credit in economic downturns. For the purposes of my argument, however, the scattered suggestions about commercial dynamics in *Lombard Street* are less important than are two pieces of Bagehot's financial journalism, both of which appeared in the *Economist* in the midst of the turmoil surrounding the collapse of the nation's most important bill-broking house, Overend, Gurney, and Company, in May 1866. The first article appeared on 12 May, two days after the widely respected London bill-broking house failed. The second was published the following week, on 19 May, after the worst of the panic had subsided, but before the causes and effects of the failure were known. Like the country's other commercial crises, the closing of "the house on the corner," as Overend and Gurney was known, threatened to expose the problematic of representation, but the collapse of this house posed a particularly serious threat. This was true for three reasons: first, because Overend and Gurney, which had been founded in 1805, served as a buffer between the Bank of England and the banks that depended on it, its failure revealed the fragility of Britain's distended banking system; second, because the house failed only a year after it had incorporated as a joint-stock company, its collapse made it clear that even incorporation, which had been created to distribute risk, could not protect investors; and third, as a symbol of the stability and rectitude of Britain's overall credit system, Overend and Gurney had served a symbolic function that was destroyed by the house's failure. When the house closed on 10 May, then, a panic rippled throughout the financial system: there were runs on London and country banks, which caused ten important banking establishments to close; the Bank of England was forced to lend over £4 million in a single day; and the Bank's reserves fell to £3 million. It was to calm this panic and mitigate its long-term effects that Bagehot addressed his readers in these two articles. By coolly explaining how the "machinery of credit" operated in ordinary times, then arguing that, with a slight modification, the 1844 Bank Act could accommodate such periods of "discredit," Bagehot tried to present the events that Mill called a "crisis" as "a calculable, though unpleasant, piece of business"—that is, as simply one among many episodes in a dynamic that could be trusted, in the long run, to operate smoothly.[48] In so doing, Bagehot also revealed how the Bank notes' practical taken-for-grantedness could be used to manage the anxiety panics expressed.

As a weekly, the *Economist* was not primarily intended to report the news, and readers would not have turned to it for an up-to-the-minute narrative of recent events. Unlike dailies, weeklies were expected to convey the considered opinion of writers who had achieved a bit of distance on immediate events, even if the distance was, as in this case, only a matter of days. Bagehot himself best captured the special function performed by the *Economist*: perhaps more than any comparable publication, it was a "belief-producer" that created in its readers both the feeling that they belonged to a single (commercial) community and the conviction that the items the paper reported were critical to their everyday lives.[49] As belief-producer extraordinaire, Bagehot considered it his responsibility to assuage his readers' anxieties rather than capitalize on their fears. Unlike reporters for the dailies, then, he used the events in May as an opportunity to teach his readers how to understand what they were experiencing as part of a larger, ultimately comprehensible, economic process. His hope was clearly that some degree of understanding would help quiet the panic and, thus, restore to regular operation the ordinary machinery of the credit system.

We can appreciate the tone of Bagehot's accounts by glancing at a few other reports of the panic. Even the ordinarily staid *London Times* registered the gravity of Overend and Gurney's closing by highlighting the shock it provoked. On 11 May, the day before the first of Bagehot's articles appeared, the *Times* proclaimed the closing of the bill-broking house "a national calamity" and warned that "unless prompt steps are taken the close of the week will be marked by disasters such as have never been equaled in our commercial history." Three days later, it implied that even this strong language was inadequate when its columnist assured readers that he had thus far used "delicacy and discretion" to report events.[50] In between these two columns, on 12 May, with the first panic beginning to abate, the *Times* risked a brief description of the scene, the imagery of which would not have been out of place in the mob passages of Dickens's *Barnaby Rudge*: "About midday yesterday the tumult became a rout. The doors of the most reputable Banking-House were besieged, more perhaps by a mob actuated by the strange sympathy which makes and keeps a mob together than by creditors of the Bank, and throngs heaving and tumbling about Lombard Street made that narrow thoroughfare impassable."[51] On 10 May, the morning that Overend and Gurney actually failed, even Bagehot had to acknowledge that panic was sweeping the City—although he did so privately, in a note hastily penned to Gladstone. "A complete collapse of credit in Lombard Street and a greater amount of anxiety than I have ever seen," he wrote.[52]

In the two articles that appeared in the *Economist*, Bagehot masked whatever anxiety he personally felt by pitching his discussion at a relatively general level. Instead of describing the scenes of panic or predicting their dire consequences, he provided a general explanation of how the British credit system worked. His closest approach to a description, in fact, decisively downplayed the threat posed by the panic by comparing it to a country fair. "Last week," he reminded his readers on 19 May, "Lombard Street looked more like a country fair than its usual self."[53] In the opening pages of his first article, Bagehot did not even mention the collapse of Overend and Gurney by name, preferring instead a general reference to the "state of alarm and confusion" that occasionally prevailed in the financial world. He also pointed out that the word with which he was to title his second article—*panic*—was actually a "technical" term, one that did not mean that "a general destruction of all confidence, a universal distrust, a cessation of credit in general" had occurred. Used in its technical sense, Bagehot explained, a "panic" was simply "a state in which there is a confidence in the Bank of England, and in nothing but the Bank of England." To explain why the prevailing fear should not be taken as an index to a larger problem, Bagehot directed his readers to the "state of quiet and tranquility" that ordinarily obtained in the English monetary system. "There is," Bagehot explained, "in the ordinary working of banking in England, a refined mechanism of diffused credit" ("What," 88).

In an account that seems positively laconic by contrast with the descriptions that appeared in the *Times*, Bagehot patiently described how this mechanism worked. It did so by dispensing two kinds of credit: one, which took the form of checks, bills of exchange, and entries in bank ledgers, Bagehot referred to as "wholesale" or "supplementary" currency ("What," 89; a week later he called checks "auxiliary credit money" ["Panic," 95]); the other, which consisted only of Bank of England notes, he called "retail" currency ("What," 89; a week later he called Bank notes "the simpler credit money" ["Panic," 95]). In ordinary times, merchants and provincial bankers were willing to accept checks as payment, and bankers were able to cancel the debts they represented through the London Clearing House. "The marvelous result" was "that the most important bargains are settled without the use of any bank notes or coin whatever" ("What," 88). In periods of what Bagehot called "discredit," by contrast, the "auxiliary" currency ceased to be acceptable, for "its very foundation is taken away" (89). To use the terminology I have been using in this book, in periods of discredit, the problematic of representation became visible because it suddenly became obvious that "auxiliary" currency was not secured to any form of value. Because Bank notes had passed beneath the horizon of cultural visibility, however—because they were treated as if they incarnated the gold they actually only represented—people continued to believe in them even when the groundlessness of other credit instruments was exposed. It was the taken-for-grantedness of Bank of England notes that explained why, in periods of general "discredit," people continued to demand them and only them: "There is an increased demand during a panic for Bank of England notes; at such times an enlarged trust is reposed in the Bank, but there is a much diminished confidence in everyone else. Discredit is diffused, but the Bank of England does not feel it: the use of its credit is augmented" (88). Since the Bank gained strength as other lenders lost it, Bagehot argued, the public did not have to worry. The only measure necessary to reinforce public trust was to allow the Bank, at the request of the chancellor of the Exchequer and the first lord of the Treasury, to issue more notes (91). This proposal, which would have required an amendment to the 1844 Bank Act, would have made the kind of suspension that Parliament authorized in 1847 and 1857 seem less like a "sin" ("Panic," 95). In other words, it would have made the kind of "discredit" the commercial world was experiencing seem like a "calculable... piece of business" ("What," 92).

Two of the strategies by which Bagehot conveyed this lesson to his readers are particularly interesting. The first is his repeated use of the word *discredit* instead of any of the more alarming terms that other writers used to describe similar events: *national calamity* (the *Times*) or *commercial crisis* (John Stuart Mill). In general usage, *discredit* refers to a company's loss of funds and the dishonor that many associated with commercial failure.

Bagehot invoked these judgmental connotations when he used *sin* and *evil* in the second article, but he was careful not to imply that Overend and Gurney had sinned or was evil, even though it was this company's financial discredit—its inability to pay its debts—that provoked the panic in the first place. Instead of saying that the company (or its board of directors) had sinned, Bagehot applied *sin* and *evil* to the public's (mis)perception about the Bank Act: when the public believed that suspending the act was a "sin" (i.e., a mistake), this was "evil" (i.e., dangerous). "The present evil is that many persons think we have committed some sin, not a great one perhaps, but still a little one. . . . But in a time of discredit, such as we have described, the suspension of that Act is not contrary to economical theory, but is the precept of that theory" ("Panic," 95).

When Bagehot wrote these words, just nine days after the house failed, it would have been impossible for anyone to know precisely what caused Overend and Gurney to close its doors, even though Bagehot implied that he, along with others in the financial community, had long suspected that the company could not reverse the disastrous affairs it had inherited from the old, private firm. Three and a half years after the collapse, when Overend and Gurney's directors were brought to trial, the sordid details finally became public: the company had, in fact, been bankrupt *before* it incorporated in 1865; and the partners, "whether stimulated by zeal or enthusiasm, or whether actuated by the insane cupidity which was too largely a characteristic of the present day," began to speculate wildly in ventures as disparate as shipping, railways, iron, and grain.[54] Even if Bagehot could not have known the nature or extent of the directors' speculations, however, other reporters did not hesitate to accuse all "finance companies"—which, they charged, Overend and Gurney had become—with reckless overtrading. Calling finance companies "gaudy and volatile butterfl[ies]," for example, a columnist for the *Times* detailed the kinds of activities such companies promoted as early as 14 May 1866.[55] For Bagehot, by contrast, anxious not to inflame his readers or cast blame on any particular individuals or company form, it was important to represent bad management as the "evil" of discredit in general. Thus, he transformed what might have been poor management or even fraud on the part of the company's managers into a more general condition: "a time of discredit"; he replaced what some might have called the "sin" committed by particular individuals with the "sin" of suspending the 1844 act; and he shifted what others might have considered the "evil" of corporate greed onto the more general "present evil . . . that many persons think we have committed some sin" in suspending the Act ("Panic," 95).

These generalizing and, to a certain extent, mystifying phrases served a function similar to Mill's abstractions: both kinds of language directed attention away from individual instances (culprits or events), which Chalmers's followers might have highlighted, toward larger principles. Whereas abstractions implied the existence of universal laws, however, Bagehot's generalizing phrases asked contemporary readers to understand the situation in a new, more complex way: instead of seeing the suspension of the Bank Act as a sin or the panic as a sign of systemic breakdown, readers should view both as indications that Britain's financial system was working as it should. Both the theorists' abstractions and Bagehot's generalizations privileged what could not be seen over what participants actually experienced, but, whereas the theorists' abstractions assigned the theorist responsibility for knowing what others could not see, Bagehot's generalizations simply asked readers to remember what they already knew by redirecting their attention from what they currently felt to what, in ordinary times, they had come to know: the Bank of England and its notes incarnated the value they claimed. Certainly, the journalist played a critical role in redirecting readers' attention, but, unlike the economic theorist, Bagehot did not claim that his knowledge was superior because it was more abstract; he simply pointed out that he could remember what others had temporarily forgotten.

Bagehot reinforced his argument that readers should consider the current "discredit" a sign of the stability of the system rather than a "crisis" by presenting a historical taxonomy of similar events. The panic of 1866, he explained, was a credit panic; thus, it both resembled and differed from the panic of 1847 (which was a capital panic) and the near panic of 1864 (which was a bullion panic) ("Panic," 94). His taxonomy elaborated Mill's rudimentary attempt to discriminate among commercial crises, but, by focusing on "panics," not "crises," Bagehot shifted his emphasis to investors' emotional response to economic events and away from the events themselves. This shift enabled Bagehot to imply that the responses were disproportionate to the causes, just as substituting *discredit* for *crisis* implied that the problem might not herald a flaw in Britain's economy but express a temporary—and limited—failure of trust on the part of the British public.

A second strategy confirms this reemphasis, but, in doing so, it also converted individual responses into a collective force. Bagehot repeatedly used the word *malignant* in these two articles, but not to describe the individuals who directed finance companies. Instead, he characterized fear as "malignant," and, as he developed this point, he abstracted the emotion from the individuals who experienced it and metaphorically objectified the feeling:

The country world, which always trusts the London world largely, became frightened. It was disconcerted beyond example, and it did not know what to do. Even in London itself the effect, though mitigated in some degree by previous preparation, was very great. It was like a spark falling upon tinder. The diffused though slight discredit caused by the known bad finance speculations, and the uncertainty who might be mixed up in them, was at once aggravated into malignant fear.... Suspicion got abroad not because our whole reserve of bullion was too low to support the credit of the country; not because our annual expenditure had dangerously surpassed our annual saving; but because the lenders of money were *suspected* of misusing it; because the most celebrated of old houses evidently had misused it; because no one knew who else might not be to blame; because all persons under obligations to pay on demand felt they must strengthen themselves because the floating peril might come their way, and if they did not they might perish. ("Panic," 94)

It was this general, contagious emotion that actually imperiled the credit system, Bagehot implied, not the failure of a single bill-broking house or the mismanagement of its directors. Bagehot could have offered a general account of how such collective emotions worked, of course, as other nineteenth-century writers had already tried to do,[56] or he could have written at a level of abstraction that would have removed the reader from the scene of panic, as Mill had done. In mixing his metaphoric description of an emotion generalized and rendered collective, however, Bagehot simultaneously discredited the suspicions that fed it, suspended his judgment of any particular individuals who might have feared the worst, and mocked the fear itself. As a "spark falling upon tinder" that ignites a "*floating* peril" (emphasis added), the fear Bagehot depicted is ineffectual; the fire that floats on water is fated to be short-lived, for it can withstand the element that will drown it only momentarily. Writing as a journalist, not a theorist, Bagehot wanted to dispel such fears gently but effectively. For this, the kind of marginalization McCulloch used and the theoretical accounts Mill provided were less useful than the reassurance a practical banker could give. By making light of the fear but not of those who were afraid (or at fault), Bagehot intervened in such a way as to keep a general "discredit" from becoming the "crisis" that might have spread even to the Bank of England notes whose taken-for-grantedness could stop the current panic.

Historians have credited the *Economist* with creating a new kind of financial journalism,[57] but, in 1843, when James Wilson founded the weekly as a partisan organ for the Anti–Corn Law League—that is, a proponent of free trade—other journalists were already publishing versions of the informative, entertaining articles for which the *Economist* became famous. One of the most prolific was D. Morier Evans (1819–74), who began his career as the assistant City correspondent to the *Times*. After leaving the *Times*, Evans contributed financial articles to two other dailies, the *Morning Herald* and the *Standard*. He also wrote for the *Bankers' Magazine*, the *Bullionist*, the *Stock Exchange Gazette*, and the *Bankers' Almanac and Diary*, but his most enduring contributions are the six books he published, most under his own signature, between 1849 and 1864. Most relevant to my argument are the two volumes that chronicle the period's speculative manias and panics: *The Commercial Crisis, 1847–48* (1849) and *History of the Commercial Crisis, 1857–58, and the Stock Exchange Panic, 1859* (1859). Although these books are not journalism per se, many of the chapters included in them were originally published in periodicals, and most draw heavily on such articles, whether written by Evans or others. These capacious, eclectic accounts of the crises also reveal how the journalist's desire to chronicle recent events could generate both the kind of detailed information that economic theorists tended to disregard and a mode of reassurance that theorists were not always able to deliver. While some of Evans's remarks were specifically critical of theoretical writing, then, his works actively supported theorists' efforts to raise the prestige of economic writing and to present the credit economy as law-abiding and regular. For, although Evans approached commercial crises in a different way than theorists did, his writings were intended to make readers so familiar with financial institutions that they would neither fear nor distrust their operations. After I discuss Evans's two books on crises, I take up some of his journalistic essays to show how, even when he was not writing about such exceptional events, he helped neutralize the problematic of representation crises exposed by providing a human guide to steer readers through the unfamiliar terrain of finance.

Speculative manias and panics were obviously news, but Evans seems to have realized rather quickly that these events could also be presented in a genre more permanent than the dailies, with their up-to-the-minute reporting, and the weeklies, with their pulse-taking reflections. The genre Evans chose adapted the formula of useful knowledge that Charles Knight had bundled into libraries for the working classes so that it would appeal to readers "who may be engaged in banking and mercantile pursuits" or who might want simply to retrace "the career of the crisis."[58] For such commercial readers, a volume was useful if it privileged information over theory and data over news; such reporting also required the writer to subordinate individual personality to the presentation of these facts—so much so that Evans occasionally presented himself as merely the editor of the volumes and often referred to himself in the third person.[59] For example: "Studiously avoiding attempts at dissertation, and strictly eschewing theories, he has endeavoured to confine himself to a description of 'Facts and Figures,' which while they may prove serviceable to most parties connected with mercantile pursuits, can be looked upon as offensive by few" (*Commercial*, vi). In 1859, Evans reiterated what he considered the proper relationship between facts and the individual who gathered them; the former could "tell their own tale" so effectively that they effaced their human facilitator: "Investigation is . . . to be commended, since it lends assistance to the multiplication of facts and inferences, which otherwise would remain dormant and concealed; but these once eliminated [*sic*] and prominently displayed, will tell their own tale without the aid of embellishment, to give a particular colouring to events, or to raise a fanciful theory, the basis of which is frequently destroyed by the practical results of a few short weeks" (*History*, 29).

As these two quotations suggest, Evans's suspicion of political economic theory stemmed from two convictions, which derived largely from the particular market to which he sought to appeal: he believed that theoretical positions could be partisan, offensive, and, by implication, harmful to the needs of commercial readers, who might hold a variety of beliefs; and, because theories could not accommodate every circumstance or fact, he maintained that they could quickly become dated, thus impeding a book's long-term sales. To engage as many commercial readers as possible in a format that would continue to have appeal, Evans borrowed features from the encyclopedia and from dictionaries like McCulloch's: each book contains statistical tables, lists of bankrupt companies, and price lists along with Evans's narrative accounts. In addition, the principal narrative of each book is printed atop an impressive foundation of notes, much of whose material is taken from periodical articles and government reports and which, taken together, contain the raw data from which Evans constructed his narrative. Evans sometimes included entire documents, either in the body of the text itself or in a note, even though some of their contents contradicted the position he was taking. Thus, for example, in 1859, he included almost the entire report from the Select Committee on the Bank Acts, which had been appointed to investigate the 1844 Bank Act, even though the conclusions of this report specifically exonerated the Bank of England directors, whom Evans elsewhere blamed, and endorsed the 1844 Act, which he considered unnecessary. These inclusions suggest that, unlike John Stuart Mill and J. R. McCulloch, who used different publishing formats but insisted on theoretical consistency, Evans was not interested in advancing only one doctrine; he never presented evidence in such a way as to ensure that it supported the argument he developed in his narrative; and he included as much undigested data as he could fit on a page, even though it might draw the reader's eye away from his own writing.

One can piece together an argument about commercial crises from Evans's two books, but the presentation of this argument is disjointed, to say the least. Reduced to a few words, his point seems to have been that individuals matter: in his accounts, each crisis has its own character, and the individuals who caused and suffered them are memorialized. Thus, Evans explained how the conditions specific to each crisis allowed a speculative mania to arise, and he included a 48-page appendix in the 1849 volume that lists every bankrupt company and tallies their remaining assets, debts, and compositions. In 1859, the equivalent appendix grew to 241 pages. He did replace the names of individual transgressors with the conventional long-dash form of abbreviation ("Was Mr.——, Provisional Director of more than one railway?" [*History*, 48n]), but this seems to have been designed to avoid charges of libel rather than to express a theory-based preference for generalizations over specific references.

In Evans's narratives, *wickedness* and *evil* figure prominently, but these refer neither to the collective human feelings that some theorists tried to quantify nor to the mistaken views that Bagehot ascribed to the public in 1866. Instead, for Evans, "wickedness" manifested itself in actual behaviors, which proliferated when certain legislative and financial conditions obtained, and "evil" was the collective product of such behaviors, which "spread like a pestilence" when international events permitted (*History*, 11). In using such terms, Evans was clearly carrying on the tradition of the evangelical economists, but he was adapting their assertions to a secular context. Thus, "three kinds of evil" conspired in 1857 to precipitate the crisis: an unprecedented increase in British exports; an increase in gold from new mines in California and Australia, which caused an increase in the circulating medium; and an increased volume of credit. Even though he did not ascribe "wickedness" and "evil" to particular persons, Evans did identify groups who colluded in the crisis: a "throng of greedy speculators anxious to work the credit system to the utmost possible extent . . . lenders [who were] utter[ly] reckless in making advances . . . borrowers [possessed by] unparalleled avidity in profiting by the occasion" all leaped at the "apparently boundless amount of capital waiting to be borrowed" (33). When American banks failed, the "unwieldy edifice of borrowed capital" began to totter, and the ensuing panic exposed both the "utter rottenness" of the system and the victims it left behind: "Once and once again comes the story of reckless mismanagement on the part of directors, and of the sacrifice of helpless depositors.... But even the fate of depositors was mild compared with that of shareholders, who having already lost their paid-up capital were subject to heavy calls, not with the prospect of an ultimate profit, but simply to wind up the unfortunate speculations in which they had embarked" (36).

While Evans did not name names here, this account is more informative, because more detailed, than McCulloch's metaphoric allusion to the American failures ("a fire . . . in a pig-sty may destroy a palace"), and readers could have learned more about the kinds of losses the 1857 crisis entailed from Evans's book than from Bagehot's generalized descriptions of "malignant fear." While it is true that, more than any of the other secular writers I have examined, Evans was constructing a cautionary tale in language that sometimes carried biblical overtones, he did so in a manner that refused to cushion the catastrophe with abstractions and euphemisms. For every passage in which Evans's prose reaches Old Testament heights—"Never did wickedness and commerce seem so intimately allied as during the great panic of 1857 . . . ; it spread like a pestilence" (*History*, 11)—numerous lists tally the precise amount of money lost, the specific creditors who suffered, the meager payoffs bankrupts scraped together. All his notes and appendices helped Evans present commercial crises not as vague, "calculable . . . piece[s] of business" (Bagehot), and not as divine checks (Chalmers), but as particular businesses that had failed, specific sums squandered, and precisely named transgressions, whether foolish or criminal.

Repeatedly, Evans claimed that his only motivation for compiling these accounts was "to put into shape, for reference, 'a plain unvarnished tale' of circumstances which, either regarded as of present or of future interest, cannot fail to engross attention" (*Commercial*, v). While this motivation may have animated his two books on crises, however, in many of his other essays and articles Evans expressed another desire, one requiring him to take a more aggressive stance than the editorial role he played in these two books. This is important to my argument because the role of intermediator, which Evans assumed in these essays, provided a more imaginatively engaging, hence, arguably, more effective, antidote to the anxiety that panics expressed. Even though these articles do not expressly concern manias and panics, then, they presented a picture of financial institutions that helped neutralize the anxiety occasioned by extraordinary crises by making these institutions seem familiar and safe.

We can see that Evans was gravitating toward this mediating role in a collection of essays published anonymously in 1852. Unlike the two volumes on crises, *City Men and City Manners* focuses on figures and institutions that would have been familiar to anyone who frequented the City: the stag, the peripatetic speculator, 'Change (the Royal Exchange), the coffeehouses associated with finance, and the Bank of England. What made these topics interesting to the general reader, of course, was that most Britons were *not* familiar with the City; few people without financial business would have visited the City, and many, no doubt, considered it a mysterious, confusing, even menacing place. Free to play up the City's mystery so that he could expose its secrets, Evans used these essays to unveil the City's denizens, decode its arcane jargon, and open the doors of institutions closed to the general public. Thus, he took advantage of the position he actually occupied—as a journalist assigned to the City—to provide a perspective that was otherwise unavailable to readers. The perspective he offered promised novelty (tales of heretofore unimagined creatures: the bull, the bear, the stag), intrigue (revelations about crimes past, present, and in the works), and the thrill of detection—in short, many of the qualities that Charles Dickens was using to such effect to market serial fictions like *Dombey and Son*.

Evans's first efforts to teach readers about the City did not efface his own role as completely as the two books on crises did, but they still did not feature the journalist as intermediary. Instead, the essays in *City Men and City Manners* initially emphasized the information network that had grown up alongside the City's network of financial institutions. The point where the two networks intersected, according to Evans, was the North and South American Coffee-House, a Threadneedle Street establishment that served as the City's "complete centre for American intelligence." This coffeehouse, which was frequented primarily by merchants and newsmen, housed a collection of current newspapers from "every quarter of the globe."[60] In Evans's description, it is clear that much effort lay behind this collection, but it is not immediately clear whether the labor to which Evans was alluding belonged to the coffeehouse owners, who collected the newspapers, or to the reporters, who had gathered the information and composed the articles the papers contained:

> Much exertion and much expense must have been employed to bring together the mass of intelligence regularly received at this house, which, whether regarded in the light of immediate utility to the parties who are subscribers, or of subsequent reference for others who may succeed them,

exhibits method and arrangement not anywhere else excelled. When it is considered, that at least three or four hundred files of papers are here at the disposal of the reader, who may turn from America to the East or West Indies, thence to Australia, the Havannah, France, Germany, Holland, Russia, Spain, and Portugal, and consult the leading journals published in those countries, and watch in all these sources, if it suit his interest, the progress of business, no one can complain of the want of field of research opened to the merchant, or whoever may wish to make himself acquainted with the various political and commercial relations of the respective governments. (*City Men*, 119)

Immediately after this general description, Evans turned to the journalists, especially the "'City-correspondents' of the morning and evening press" (120), that select group of writers who, since 1824, had been publishing regular financial columns for the dailies. In Evans's account, these City correspondents are educated men who direct a swarm of news bees from their thrones at the center of the information hub: "They are generally men of sound education, possessing a knowledge of two or three modern languages. . . . Two or three of the 'City-article' writers have separate offices, paid for by the proprietors of the journals with which they are connected, and here their friends visit them, and communicate what news or information they may wish to impart" (*City Men*, 120–21).

Evans respected the writers of the City articles not simply because they oversaw the collection and arrangement of financial news but also because their commitment to accuracy and integrity enabled them to do what Parliament had proved unable—or unwilling—to do: police the activities of the financial world.[61] By collecting and printing information that was otherwise unavailable—even secret—financial journalists had become a power, one that was increasingly recognized by readers and legislators alike:

By continuing this description of contribution, and by sparing few of the failing houses from the merited odium of their proceedings, it was discovered that a new power had erected itself, through the medium of the press, over the commerce of the country, and such was its influence that many feared to come in contact with it. On 'Change and at the coffee-houses the greatest dismay was apparent; for through this channel the roguery and tricks of designing speculators were held up to public contempt, and a ready explanation given of the success or failure of bubble companies.

The fearless exposure of anything like fraud or foul dealing gave scope for the display of reason and judgment, which before long stamped the individuals who then preeminently occupied that position, as being persons

who were well qualified to fill the important post confided to their care. . . .
The service they have done the country, in connection with foreign loan
transactions and other subjects which legitimately come within the scope of
their pen, has been admitted both in and out of the legislature. (*City Men,*
125–26, 120)

Evans may seem to have been describing himself here, but, in 1852, he still
occupied only a subordinate position in the newspaper—he was merely the
assistant City editor at the *Times.* Even if he was still the onlooker here, as
he was in his books on crises, in elevating the City correspondents to this
preeminent position, he was discovering a vehicle through which he could
simultaneously neutralize the strangeness of the City and capitalize on the
occupational role he played within it. All that remained was for him to find
generic conventions that would give his sketches an imaginative appeal for
general readers as great as he thought the appeal of information was for
commercial readers.

In his last two books, Evans found these conventions in the kinds of
imaginative writing that were proving so popular for purveyors of fiction.
Two kinds of imaginative writing provided the most obvious models for
Evans: the genre of true crime writing, which had flourished since the
early eighteenth century and which was still used to sell cheap working-
class periodicals,[62] and sensation fiction, which was already appearing in
working-class magazines and would soon be packaged for middle-class
readers by Wilkie Collins, Mary Elizabeth Braddon, and Charles Dickens.
As we will see in a moment, Evans's borrowing from these genres was sometimes so extensive that his late essays, in particular, seem indistinguishable
from imaginative writing; but his original, explicit aim in turning to the
material by which imaginative writers achieved such sensational sales was
to provide the policing function he outlined in *City Men.* In his penultimate
volume, the gargantuan (727-page) *Facts, Failures, and Frauds: Revelations Financial, Mercantile, Criminal* (1859), Evans presented the financial journalist as a detective whose proximity to City institutions and insiders enabled
him to expose the crimes the public could not see. Because the documents
he "exposed" in this volume were in the public domain, however, and
because all his "revelations" appeared well after the miscreants had been
prosecuted, this volume was generically closer to his compilations on crises
than to the generic hybrid he was beginning to develop. It was only in his
last collection of essays, *Speculative Notes and Notes on Speculation* (1864),
that Evans explicitly began to use features drawn from imaginative writing
to place himself—in the form of a quasi-autobiographical character—in the

midst of a landscape animated, like fiction, by intrigue and mystery yet based on, and intended to illuminate, the facts of the financial world he knew so well.

Evans clearly viewed these late essays as both emerging from and transcending the limits of journalism, for the cavalier manner in which he alluded to yet brushed off their original place of publication simultaneously affiliated these articles to a specific newspaper or periodical and lifted them free of their original home. Thus, in a preface addressed "To the Public," Evans explained: "A few of these papers have, during the last twelve months, appeared in the 'London Review,' the 'Bankers' Magazine,' and other publications; the great majority, and the longest of the series, are now presented for the first time."[63] Presented in a longer format than a newspaper would have allowed, and published (for the first time) with his own signature attached, many of these sketches feature as first-person narrator a character expressly modeled on Evans who repeatedly reminds his readers that what he reveals is based on intimate knowledge of the City: "I am . . . the personal witness of this scene" (*Speculative Notes*, 1); "I have become so completely identified with the City . . . that I fancy I am somehow or other welded into a portion of that great heaving mass of machinery" (66).[64] Such autobiographical allusions enabled Evans explicitly to become the detective whose presence he previously masked under the guise of editor, and this stylistic insertion into the action enabled him to become his reader's active guide through the strange byways of the financial world.

In an essay entitled "Credit Assistance to Country Cousins," we can see how the detective persona could assuage readers' anxieties about otherwise impenetrable aspects of finance. In this essay, the journalist-narrator penetrates a "nest of bill forgers" located in a London suburb (*Speculative Notes*, 246). The sketch obviously drew on Evans's knowledge about how easily bills could be forged, but it used features associated with sensation fiction to cast his knowledge in an entertaining, suspenseful narrative. Thus, the account is organized by the narrator's journey; he confronts graphically described (though unnamed) characters at his destination; long descriptive passages give local color to the setting; and dialogue punctuates passages of narrative commentary. The narrator creates the kind of retrospective temporal organization typical of first-person detective fiction by alluding to the past events that led him on his chase; by anticipating events yet to come ("it will be seen hereafter the part he played" [254]), he attributes to himself the same kind of "burn[ing] desire" (259) to capture the bill forgers that we see in characters like George Talboys (from Braddon's *Lady Audley's Secret*); and he concludes the narrative, as Dickens does in *Oliver Twist*, with the suicide of the besieged chief criminal—here referred to only as "old fur collar." Evans conveys this event in a manner reminiscent of Dickens's narration of the death of Bill Sikes when he focalizes the criminal's death through this character:

> He had been concealed in an old out-house abutting on the canal, and there as he looked out upon the dark surrounding water, it required only a little nerve to accomplish that which he had often promised himself should be his fate, sooner than accept the responsibility of a trial. Since the time of his flight he was quite aware that he possessed one means only of escaping from the paths of his pursuers; viz., through the dread portals of death.
>
> He was worked into a state of strong excitement through the fear of speedy arrest and imprisonment. The resolution once formed was soon carried out. An old but vigorous man, he mounted the scantling that could scarcely bear his weight. The moon was up, and her clear, bright rays threw a cold, still light athwart the stream; he plunged head foremost with a dull leaden sound. There was a momentary struggle, then he sank, and as his form was lost to view, heavy black clouds floated onward, overshadowing the scene of that dark but long meditated crime. A low, short, hollow cough seemed to rise from the depths of the waters, reverberating in mocking tones for an instant on the dull night air, and then there reigned the silence of death! (262)

Needless to say, even if this narrative was based on firsthand knowledge, Evans could not have been privy to the bill forger's thoughts, and the phantasmatic nature of the last narrated sound ("seemed to rise") underscores the imaginative license that colors the entire description. In such essays, the aesthetic coherence typical of imaginative writing has taken the place of the theoretical coherence economic theorists sought to produce, and the focalizing narrator formally arranges details in a manner intended to keep the reader reading as the detection plot unfolds.

Metaphorically, at least, Evans assigned his autobiographical narrator several roles in these essays: in addition to describing him as a detective (*Speculative Notes*, 3, 237), he also says that he hunts stocks with the care of a "military man ... planning a campaign" (23), pursues inaccessible characters like an explorer in search of "*terra incognita*" (237), and tracks down leads like a spy engaged in the "great game of speculation" (161). Interestingly, some of Evans's personae do not exhibit the level of energy these metaphors imply, but their passivity does not undermine their ability to guide the reader—or to animate the narrative. In "The Great Enigma—Who Can Solve It?" for example, the narrator simply stations himself on the sidelines of

'Change, from which position he follows a mysterious speculator of foreign extraction referred to only as "Count D——." For over thirty years, this
Merdle-like figure (Merdle appears in Dickens's *Little Dorrit*) sweeps in and
out of the world's financial markets and the narrator's view like "a meteor"
(195). During this time, the narrator repeatedly thinks about the once-great
man and even dreams about him ("I occasionally, in a dreamy, loose sort
of manner, pictured to myself what he would resemble" [205]); but, every
time he finds himself face-to-face with Count D——, either he is overcome
by faintness ("I felt giddy and faint, and left the room" [207]), or he ducks
out of sight ("I stepped aside, if possible, to avoid recognition, and was fortunate enough to escape his glance" [209]). This narrator resembles a fla-
neur, the figure who wanders, unnoticed, through the byways of the urban
landscape, collecting observations for later, more aesthetically disengaged
meditations or witty bons mots. While clearly an updated version of Addison and Steele's urbane Mr. Spectator and Laurence Sterne's squeamish
Sentimental Traveler, the financial voyeur is also a vehicle through which
Evans was able to let his reader experience what it *felt* like to occupy the
inner sanctum of the City—to be one of its members but not a player on a
grand scale. In this essay, the narrator's emotions run the gamut from disinterested amusement to quasi-erotic obsession, but, since nothing explicit
happens to Count D—and the two men exchange no words, the reader's
emotional engagement remains suspended, like that of the narrator.

In one other essay, Evans took this experiment in vicarious affect further,
as he used the combination of his insider's position and the ability of
imaginative writing to engage readers to expose what it felt like not simply
to watch a great speculator but actually to engage in speculation oneself. In
"Review of Some Extraordinary Operations," the narrator allows the reader
access to a secret most Britons were never able to see and to overhear a
conversation held behind doors closed to most readers. Even though the
speculator who chronicles his passions is not the narrator, "Review" provides one of the very few examples in all the century's financial writing of
what the emotions felt like that sparked and sustained commercial crises.

As we have already begun to see, the majority of nineteenth-century
economic theorists did not elaborate the emotional states that drove a mania or a panic. Ricardo, McCulloch, and Mill focused their attention on
abstractions and universal laws rather than subjective emotions, Bagehot
wanted to generalize (and neutralize) the effects of panic, and even W.
Stanley Jevons, whose work I examine in a moment, highlighted only the
aggregate manifestations of emotions in a form that could be quantified
(prices). Even the writers who did offer what we might call *psychological*

accounts, like John Mills and William Purdy, did so in terms so vague and collective that the reader was buffered from the subjective affect of the speculator's emotions. While it is easy to understand why theorists and journalists like Bagehot did not explore in agitating detail the feelings that fed speculative manias and panics, it is, nonetheless, noteworthy that almost every nonfiction representation of these events completely neglected their affective component. For every financial crisis could also have been said to have begun in the desires of individuals—not in some abstract, generalized "propensity to truck, barter, and exchange," as Adam Smith phrased it, but in the desires of particular individuals to buy or sell shares in specific commodities or stocks. Among nonfiction writings, the perspective Evans offered in "Review of Some Extraordinary Operations" uniquely enabled readers to get an imaginative sense of these emotions while continuing to inform them why such feelings were dangerous.

In "Review," the narrator is once more the disengaged voyeur, who has accepted an invitation to an impromptu West End dinner party. From the beginning, he teases the reader with what he knows but will not reveal: even though one of his companions, "a *millionaire* in figures, . . . if more accurately described . . . would at once be recognized as a power in Lombard Street" (*Speculative Notes*, 16), the narrator refuses to specify his name. Generically, this refusal, especially because it is accompanied by the wealth of concrete particulars that had come to be the signature convention of fiction, suspends this essay halfway between a real account of actual people and an imaginative tale. As a generic hybrid, however, the essay could accomplish something neither an explicit fiction nor an abstract theoretical essay could hope to do: it could instruct readers about the dangers of speculation in a way that was as engaging as fiction but as informative as Bagehot's cool delivery of the facts about the financial system. Thus, the names Evans chose for his distinguished companions—"Optimist" and "Millionaire"—are both generic and provocative, and the scene in which he placed himself incited his reader's voyeuristic fascination with all things monetary without providing enough details to inspire actual emulation. In the story itself, the "men of money" indulge themselves in a vaguely described conversation about the preoccupations they share—"rates of discount, the state of money—that inscrutable mystery—the action of the foreign exchanges" (17)—until one of the men utters the word *speculation*. "As if by magic, the whole conversation at once takes a different direction," and the dinner guests begin to rehearse the "dreadful effects" of the speculations they have personally witnessed (18). Even the narrator becomes animated as he describes the railway mania, the gold speculations of 1851–

52, and his own brief foray into the share market when he purchased some worthless gold mine script. Even though the narrator confesses that he speculated, however, Evans reserves the essay's most extensive emotional confession for Optimist, who prefaces his monologue with the comment that his story "will perhaps afford its lesson in its way" (22):

> He lights a cigar, rolls the end carefully, and proceeds:—
>
> "You must know, friends, that it was in one of my periods of financial depression—and they have not been unfrequent—I was at home, moodily looking over that crowded sheet, called the railway share list, when my eyes lighted upon the Lombardo-Venetian Stock. . . . From the strain on my mind of other engagements, I fancied a little change would prove beneficial, and I meditated a trip to the metropolis, and at the same time a venture in Lombard-Venetian shares. . . .
>
> "When I reached town all my available cash was £1000. I went to a London banker, and consulted him, upon what I termed, my investment. He shook his head doubtfully; he was not favourable at such a moment, to placing money in such a security, but if I thought of doing it he could introduce me to a broker, who would transact any *bona fide* business I might require. Clever bank manager—link the first: I sought the broker—link the second: here was I on the high road to gambling, and my hobby riding with all the easy grace of a lady's park hack. . . . The contract is made out, the commission paid, and I return to my hotel, and still cogitate on those shares. I have a friend in the country who has plenty of cash, and the thought strikes me, that if I can borrow £2000 of him, it will increase my interest in this great line, and *when* the rise comes—as I feel sure it must—I can repay him with £5 per cent. interest." (22–24)

With the shares purchased—for himself and his friend, who turns out to be his wife's cousin—Optimist displays the speculator's obsessive ingenuity and, not incidentally, shows the reader how to raise money when credit is tight. He gives a promissory note to another banker in exchange for a loan, purchases more shares from the astonished, because "steady-going" (25), broker, then returns to the country to wait for the price to rise. Back at home, poring over the news from Italy, Optimist finds his emotions fluctuating along with the stock's price:

> The news from Italy was discouraging; prices fell. . . . My spirits drooped. I was out of sorts. I hardly mixed with my family, and for a night or two I could get no rest. . . . All this time the market was in a very unsatisfactory

state; the reaction which had set in was gradual, and it required but another half per cent. fall, to place me in that position from which there could scarcely have been a recovery. The anxiety I experienced threatened to terminate in madness. My brain seemed on fire, and the weight of suspense was most overwhelmingly oppressive. (25–26)

So distraught is Optimist that he confesses to his wife that he has borrowed money from her cousin, and he confides to the reader that, if he loses the borrowed £2,000, "it would break the family connection" (*Speculative Notes*, 26). Just as his health begins to fail, good news arrives from Italy, prices begin to rise, and, as they do, Optimist's spirits soar. He is elated, his wife is elated, his son is elated, and, before the shares have reached their highest point, he sells, thereby securing not only his original investment, the £2,000 he owes his wife's cousin, and the loan he took from the banker but also "a clear gain of upwards of £2700." Despite the advantageous outcome of his investment, Optimist draws from it a cautionary conclusion:

Fortunate as was the result, the torture I passed through, the harrowing influence exercised upon my home, when the great secret [of his having borrowed from his wife's cousin] was revealed, and the enormous risk involved, determined me, if I could possibly restrain myself, to avoid ever again entering the arena of the Stock Exchange. Since then, I have lost nearly £3000 in a contested election, and several other large sums in mercantile adventures, but never have I known the exhaustion, produced by the alternation from apprehension to joy, and the intermediate stages of languor, which I experienced during the comparatively short interval, absorbed in the conception, and completion, of those very doubtful share operations. (27)

The narrator winds up this anecdote with a moral as ambiguous as Optimist's worrisome allusion to his continuing need to "restrain" himself: "I add that I only hope the experiment once tried, will never be repeated, for usually if such engagements are successful, they are either followed till a fortune is assured, or, on the other hand, ruin entailed" (28).

This essay provides only a rudimentary narrative, for the narrator does not follow up on many of the plot details he introduces (the hint that failure would cause a break between the families, Optimist's failed run for Parliament, the nature and extent of his mercantile adventures). Nor does the essay prolong its brief foray into monomania, as some contemporary works of fiction did (Trollope's *He Knew He Was Right*, Dickens's *Dombey and Son*). Its rationale, in other words, was not the aesthetic, ethical, or psychological rationales that nineteenth-century novelists pursued, nor was it the explanatory, informative rationale that organized works of economic theory or analysis. Instead, its rationale mixed elements of these agendas: Evans wanted to provide readers an imaginative sense of what speculation and panic felt like, and he also wanted to remind them of particular speculative episodes that had actually occurred. In doing so, he began to offer something like a psychological account of real manias and panics, which writers like Margaret Oliphant and Anthony Trollope also tried to do for the fictional manias they depicted. I do not want to overstate the extent to which this or other essays in Evans's collection devised a vocabulary for exploring the psychological dimension of speculation, for, every time the narrator broaches the subject, he pulls himself up, as if Evans considered immersing readers in such passions unseemly—or impossible—for a journalist committed to giving his readers information and facts. The most intense emotions the narrator displays in these essays is the altogether legitimate "thirst for knowledge" about some financial subject (*Speculative Notes*, 5) and the anxiety aroused by the "weight of the responsibility" his position imposes on him (39).

As a journalist, whose slightest hint could heighten the emotions his readers already felt, Evans more typically sought to repress rather than agitate passionate feelings. At most, he permitted himself to use an occasional disturbing metaphor or to chronicle someone else's obsession with shares.[65] Even if he did not elaborate the emotions that fed speculative manias and panics, however, Evans did acknowledge the role feeling played in commercial crises; by doing so, he helped give the kind of economic theories Mill developed a recognizably human face. While matters of emphasis and substance clearly divided Evans from the theorists whose work I have examined, his books and sketches did help humanize the economic forces theorists tried to abstract, generalize, and quantify. To appreciate Evans's essays, it was not necessary for readers to understand the labor theory of value or to choose between various positions in the currency debate. By presenting another side of the century's economic activities, his essays enabled more readers to believe that financial topics were interesting, for he made them palatable and—in a manner intended to use but not inflame the emotions they aroused—even matters of intrigue.

In an essay entitled "The 'Reign of Terror' in the Share Market," Evans noted in passing that the violent emotions that erupted in manias and panics were not aberrant by-products of an ordinarily rational economic machine; instead, he commented: "The Stock Exchange literally lives, in a great measure, upon this kind of excitement" (*Speculative Notes*, 298). By acknowledging, albeit briefly, that Britain's credit economy required the excitement that occasionally threatened to destroy it, he inadvertently introduced a possibility most theorists did not address. It was possible that commercial crises were not simply exceptions to—or even regular parts of —Britain's ordinary credit mechanism, as Mill and Bagehot implied, but manifestations of an irrationality that was essential to the credit economy itself. Evans did not develop this idea, but, a decade after Evans's last book, another journalist took a slightly more jaundiced attitude toward this possibility. This journalist was Laurence Oliphant, a cousin of the novelist Margaret Oliphant. Before leaving the topic of financial journalism, I want briefly to show how Oliphant provided readers a view of the financial world that was just beginning to be visible in the final decades of the century.

By 1876, the year in which he composed "The Autobiography of a Joint-Stock Company (Limited)," Laurence Oliphant (1829–88) had already survived more than his share of exotic adventures. The son of an evangelical Scot stationed at the Cape of South Africa, Oliphant was raised primarily in Ceylon and England. While still a young man, he tried out several careers as he made his way across the world: he served as a secretary to Lord Elgin, a freelance writer for the *Daily News*, and a war correspondent for the *Times*; in these capacities, he visited Nepal, India, Katmandu, Russia, the Crimea, America, Canada, Japan, Egypt, Greece, and Poland. As a journalist, Oliphant published news stories and travel accounts about many of these places; in 1865, after he returned to England, he also published a satirical send-up of the English upper classes.[66] In 1865, Oliphant was also elected to Parliament, but, too restless for administrative work, he pursued the religious mystic Thomas Lake Harris to America. While trying to raise money for Harris's religious community, Oliphant became tangentially involved in Wall Street, where he met Jay Gould, the consummate nineteenth-century American financier. While it is not clear whether Gould was the real-life subject of the "daring and pungent piece of satire" that Oliphant published in *Blackwood's* in 1876, it is obvious that the information he received from an inside source (referred to only as "C.") provided "the stimulus of sudden wrath and indignation" that led him to dash off the satire in a single night of frenzied writing.[67] As far as I know, this is the only piece of financial journalism Oliphant ever published, and, if his cousin's assessment is true, its singularity suggests that physical risk—preferably in an exotic country—was more to Oliphant's taste than finding out about finance.[68]

Like Thomas Bridges's *Adventures of a Bank Note*, "The Autobiography of a Joint-Stock Company" is a spy narrative, told from the point of view of an object. In this case, the narrator is "an abstract being," the joint-stock corporation known only as "XYZ."[69] The narrative opens on the eve of the company's dissolution, and the retrospective this occasions leads the narrator to meditate philosophically both on the conditions that led to his creation and on the frauds that checkered his career. As a behind-the-scenes view of the "trouble it takes to prepare the gaudy fly by which you [investors] are ultimately to be hooked" (106), the "Autobiography" lets the reader see the institutional mechanisms and human cupidity that made speculative manias possible. Thus, even though an actual commercial crisis is mentioned only once (120), as a factor that prevents the company's directors from raising additional capital, the "Autobiography" belongs to the body of periodical writing about manias and panics, for it shows how the same legislation that enabled the credit economy to grow (the Companies' Acts of 1862 and 1867) actually encouraged the fraud perpetrated by unscrupulous company promoters.

The narrator begins his retrospective when he—that is, the company XYZ—is still an "embryo" ("Autobiography," 113), a mere prospectus for a concern whose unspecified "works" are to be conducted abroad. The "complicated and incomprehensible prospectus" that eventually becomes XYZ is drafted by a company promoter, whom the narrator denominates "Captain Hawk" ("in consideration of his natural predatory habits" [98]). In the narrator's account, Hawk first imagines the concern, then seeks to give it "real value" by "obtain[ing] certain concessions and permissions from foreign Governments and municipalities" (99). To pay for his travels, Hawk needs a capitalist, which he finds in a young heir named Sir Twig Robinson, whose newfound wealth and "weakness of intellect" fit him for partnership with Hawk (99). Backed by Twig's capital, Hawk flits through Europe for a year, then returns to England to begin promoting the company's shares. Knowing that "the confiding country investor" (101) will not buy solely on his recommendation, however, Hawk proposes to Twig that they open the first "vicious circle" of company formation: they need a "rich rogue" to recruit a board of directors and a contractor "upon the certain assurance that money can be found; and at the same time . . . [to] induce the public to subscribe the money upon the no less certain assurance that the directors and contractors have been found" (101). This "vicious circle" rests on another, equally vicious circle. In order to convince the public to buy, Hawk will first offer shares to a syndicate, a combination of influential capitalists with the right to purchase shares below par. After Hawk rigs the market to inflate the price of shares, the syndicate will sell its members' shares to the public, which will want to buy stocks because they seem to be rising in value.

In the end, things don't work out quite the way Hawk anticipates. He tries to work his shell game on various contractors and capitalists, but he soon meets sharpers more cunning than he is. A German Jew named Mire agrees to head the syndicate and hires the contractor Messrs. "Chisel Bros.," but Sarmist, a canny evangelical who has also joined the syndicate, highjacks its first meeting and, along with Mire, wrests control of XYZ away from Hawk and Twig. Secretly colluding against Hawk and the other syndicate members, Mire and Sarmist replace Chisel with "Gouge & Co.," a contractor whose profits they can skim, and, even as the company's works are launched, Mire and Sarmist begin to bull and bear the price of the company's shares: "They carried out their operations by spreading rumours sometimes detrimental, sometimes favourable to my interests. They never failed to take advantage of the turn of the market which had thus been influenced by them" ("Autobiography," 115). The company's success soon inspires another promoter to form a rival company, but Mire and Sarmist also commandeer it by convincing one of its unscrupulous directors, Sir Verrikute Trimmer, to divulge confidential information. With this triumverate manipulating the price of both companies' shares, XYZ finds its stock "the instrument of gambling on the Exchange" (117). Next, Mire, Sarmist, and Trimmer launch a trust company to fend off irate shareholders, who demand more control of XYZ. Not realizing that the same men control all three companies, the public pours more money into the trust company, and, soon, XYZ is propped up by a half million sterling, and Mire, Sarmist, and Trimmer are swindling everyone, directors and shareholders alike. Then, when the ousted contractor, Chisel, opens another rival company, the triumvirate strikes back with all the weapons at its disposal:

> They invoked the aid of their influential shareholders, of the Peers and Commoners who had assisted at my banquet, and, above all, of the Press. Many baser members of the journalistic world wrote up those gentlemen and their enterprises on every possible occasion, and opened upon my rival with a chorus of slander like a pack of hounds upon a hot scent. Every disgraceful transaction of which they had themselves been guilty, Messrs. Mire and Sarmist darkly insinuated was practised by the Directors of the A. B. C. Co.... The consequence was that the poor A. B. C. Co. had a very rough time of it, and was generally regarded as one of the most dishonest, gambling, stock-jobbing concerns in the city—an impression which certain

of the less reputable members of my own Board found it easy to produce, by getting up "rings" to bull and bear its shares, heaping discredit upon it thereby, while they at the same time filled their own pockets. . . . I knew the A. B. C. Co. intimately; and I used to tell it that I felt like a skunk who squirted its own vile odour all over it, and then cried aloud to all the passers-by to shun it on account of its noxious effluvium. (119)

As the campaign against the A. B. C. Company accelerates, the narrator admits that he has begun to be "painfully conscious of the seeds of incipient disease" in his own foreign works ("Autobiography," 118–19). With all the company's capital going to its unscrupulous directors, these works fall into disrepair, and, even though Mire and Sarmist soon realize that they must raise additional capital, it is too late. Just as Mire and Sarmist ready a prospectus for first mortgage debenture bonds, "a serious financial crisis shak[es] the confidence, not only of the money circles in the city, but of the investing public at large" (120); in the midst of this crisis, the public fails to purchase the bonds. Mire and Sarmist then assemble the company's shareholders in a last desperate effort to raise cash, but the shareholders, irate and now gaining control, demand an inquiry into the company's transactions. The inquiry reveals that the company is penniless, that it has routinely been plundered by its directors, and that "the elderly and highly respectable manager" has fled to Bologna (121). XYZ, now utterly sapped of its "vitality" (120), is relegated to the Court of Chancery ("that borne from which no company returns" [121]); and, in a final twist, Captain Hawk successfully sues Mire and Sarmist for violating a relatively obscure provision of the 1867 Companies Act (clause 38): failing to disclose the company's agreement with a new contractor in the original company prospectus. This lawsuit "reveal[s] the whole of the fraudulent transaction" to the public (121); the judge demands that Mire and Sarmist repay shareholders £100,000; Sarmist wallows in an orgy of evangelical guilt; Mire dies; and the narrator last glimpses Captain Hawk "dash[ing] past the office in which I am now lying, behind his high-stepping bays, bent on the promotion of a new Company" (121).

This brief summary cannot do justice to the twists and turns of this rapidly unfolding tale, but it should convey some sense of what a nineteenth-century Briton could have learned from reading it. In addition to informing his readers what technical terms and financial slang like *debenture bonds*, *bulling*, and *bearing* meant, Oliphant was also ushering the reader behind the scenes of company formation to expose the fraud made possible by

Britain's permissive companies law.[70] By using a narrator who is initially naive, moreover, Oliphant provided a fictional surrogate for the reader; the gradual enlightenment of this narrator offered an equally gradual education for the reader.[71] As the narrator becomes aware of what is going on, his commentary directs the reader's attention to the lessons he is learning: "For the first time I became aware that the *concessionaires* were practically powerless, and that those who had most capital at their backs really divided the spoil" ("Autobiography," 111). This narrative device enabled Oliphant to suggest, albeit indirectly, that the operations by which the public is bilked in his tale are criminal only because they take permissible financial behavior to its logical extreme. Taken to this extreme, the ordinary business of finance turns out to be a series of scams: a corporation that seems productive is actually a scheme to make its directors rich; share prices that seem to reflect market forces are actually manipulated by the company directors; a prospectus that promises a company is actually a ploy to plunder the public; and even the company's schedule of costs and profits is simply an elaborate ruse intended to deceive.

Early in his narrative, speaking with the sad wisdom of hindsight, XYZ insists that every one who reads this essay should be "interested, deeply interested, in the story [he] has to tell" ("Autobiography," 96) because every reader was, directly or indirectly, implicated in the explosion of companies the new company legislation allowed. While Oliphant did not explain precisely why this would have been so, the ominous tone with which XYZ reconciles himself to death suggests that this legislation was permitting a morass of guilt, suffering, and deceit to spread throughout Britain:

> In a few brief days my brief and stormy career will finally close. I can calmly, and even thankfully, contemplate this premature extinction of an existence which has ruined reputations, shattered fortunes, and carried want and misery into hundreds of humble homes; for I am wearied and worn out with the effort it has caused me to achieve these deplorable results, and utterly disgusted with the advanced state of civilisation which has made me the victim of its immoral tendencies. . . . What philosopher can explain to me the nature of the causes of which I am the vile effect? It was not my own fault that, like those who first hatched me, I was conceived in sin and shapen in iniquity, and became almost immediately the means of demoralising every one who came into contact with me, of deceiving those who trusted in me, and of crushing those who opposed me, until my own turn came, and I fizzled out in a gutter of fraud like a bad squib. (96)

What such passages omit is as telling as what they include. For example, Oliphant does not cite the dramatic increase in the number of corporations that filed with the new Registry Office (created in 1844); historians tell us that registrations increased from 966 in the dozen years between 1844 and 1856, to nearly 2,500 in the next four years, to nearly 4,000 between 1862 and 1868.[72] Nor does Oliphant cite the corresponding increase in stock market participation: we now know that investments rose from about £200 million (invested in 900 companies) in 1843 to £1,300,000,000 (invested in 24,000 companies) in 1897.[73] As these numbers suggest, shareholders also multiplied as investment opportunities increased. One historian, for example, estimates that the number of serious shareholders quadrupled between 1870 and 1914.[74]

Even in 1876 (by which time some of these data were available), Oliphant did not cite such numbers—partly because most of his readers would have been at least vaguely aware that dramatic changes were under way in Britain's financial landscape—if not because they were personally investing, then because they could not miss the waves of criminal proceedings that had been exposing ever-greater numbers of white-collar criminals since the mid-1840s.[75] Partly, he did not include numerical information about shares and investors because, like Evans's late essays, the "Autobiography" had a mixed rationale: the essay did provide specific information, but the form Oliphant chose borrowed features from imaginative writing in order to give readers what no numbers could provide, an inside look at the way such crimes were actually launched. That such criminal activities festered alongside of—or were even encouraged by—the company legislation that helped Britain's credit economy grow in the second half of the nineteenth century was a lesson political economists were not quick to convey. Like Evans's brief investigations of the passions that fed speculative manias and panics, Oliphant's cautionary tale reminded readers that the theorists' abstractions captured only one facet of the mature credit economy. Behind the numbers and general laws might stand a Hawk, a Sarmist, or a Mire, ready to swoop in and feed off unwary investors.

Despite the fact that Oliphant's "Autobiography" offered an implicit critique of Britain's permissive company legislation and an explicit critique of one unscrupulous group of company promoters, it can, nonetheless, be seen to have contributed to the general campaign to naturalize financial activities and to have neutralized anxieties associated with the problematic of representation. It must be noted, however, that these contributions were complicated. In the first place, the very fact that William Blackwell was willing to publish the article—without an explanatory appendix or notes—

means that new corporations and shares were topics of interest in 1876 and familiar enough to have needed no explanation beyond what the article itself provided. This, in turn, means that, just as stories like Oliphant's could be used to expose financial crimes, so they could be used to sell the magazines that printed them. Then too, as Oliphant's allusion to the "baser members of the journalistic world" puffing new companies suggests, the press did not simply circulate commercial information in a neutral way;[76] simply informing readers that XYZ's directors were cheats did not, by itself, compensate for the fact that many periodicals ran advertisements for new companies, some of which were, no doubt, as fraudulent as this one. Despite the undeniable complexities that characterized the relationship between the press and commercial institutions by the 1870s, however, articles like Evans's and Oliphant's did help naturalize the workings of financial institutions by providing a norm against which aberrant behaviors could be judged. By drawing distinctions between such practices as (legitimate) investing and (illegitimate) speculation or (legitimate) saving and (illegitimate) theft, for example, and by showing that the financial sector could police itself, financial journalists like these helped make the extreme upheavals epitomized by commercial crises and the flamboyant crime caricatured in Hawk's actions seem like departures from the normal, everyday business that ordinarily prevailed. Even if these articles revealed that such businesses needed the kinds of excesses journalists exposed, moreover, they offered their revelations in entertaining forms more likely to provoke laughter than to prompt a parliamentary investigation.

W. Stanley Jevons and the Narrowing of Economic Science

In this chapter, we have seen that a twofold dynamic characterized the development of nineteenth-century economic writing. On the one hand, among practitioners and promoters of political economy, a division of labor developed in which theorists elaborated increasingly abstract accounts of economic events, while, on the other hand, another group of writers, which I have referred to as *popularizers* and *financial journalists*, offered a variety of imaginatively engaging, easily understandable versions of economic matters and financial institutions. Both sets of writers helped naturalize the operations of Britain's increasingly complex credit economy—even the bouts of mania and panic that exposed the problematic of representation always implicit in this economy. On the other hand, and as part of the professionalization of the theoretical branch of economic writing, the definition of *value* was rapidly narrowed as political economy, which had once been the capacious study of human nature and jurisprudence, was increasingly restricted to the more focused science of a form of value that could be measured.

Before turning to the imaginative counterpart to economic writing, it is important to consider one final episode in this history. As numerous scholars have pointed out, in the 1870s political economic theory was decisively narrowed once more. In what has been called the Marginalist Revolution, W. Stanley Jevons and Alfred Marshall in Britain, Leon Walras in Switzerland, and Carl Menger in Austria rejected the labor theory of value in favor of a model of value that focused on taste, demand, and price. According to this theory, the modern economy was no longer organized by the problem of scarcity, with its auxiliary dynamics of production, distribution, and needs; instead, in an economy of abundance, the dynamics that mattered were consumption and desire, for, when individuals were able to choose among an almost infinite variety of consumable goods, the way that they developed and articulated their tastes was more important than labor and the accumulation of capital. As Donald Winch explains, the theorists of marginal utility

> focused attention on the subjective determinants which underlie the demand for goods, rather than the objective factors which determine the cost and supply of goods. The proper foundation for a new economics, they argued, lay in the quasi-psychological law of diminishing marginal utility—a law which posited a definite (if subjective) relationship between the quantities of goods possessed and the extra satisfaction to be derived from additional amounts of them. With such a law in his possession the economist was able to explain the market behaviour of buyers faced with an array of prices, their responses to changes in price, the gains to be made from exchange, and the optimal allocation of a given stock of resources among alternative uses. The classical approach to economics was dominated by the problems of capital accumulation, population growth, and diminishing returns in agriculture. The interest of the classical theorists in the economics of allocation and value in exchange, though it was profound and led them to make permanent contributions to our understanding of these questions, was largely subservient to their interest in economic growth and macrodistribution. After the marginal revolution attention shifted away from such grand speculations towards a narrower and more precise inquiry into the determination of relative prices. Economics became a quasi mathematical discipline in which the important questions were posed as scarcity or choice problems.[77]

For my purposes, the Marginalist Revolution is important for two reasons. First, the success that Jevons and Marshall enjoyed—a success associated with their socially recognized *expertise*—was directly related to their affiliation with various universities; and, second, economics' embrace of mathematical modeling, which was inextricably linked to the theory of marginal utility, helped widen the gap between a mode of explanation that was obviously (if not always perfectly) related to the phenomena it sought to describe and another mode whose referential capacity was arguably less important than its formal coherence. The link between economics and universities is important, in turn, because this marked the beginning of a final stage of the professionalization of economic writing. The increasing formalism of a mathematical variant of economics is important because it suggests that, by the last third of the nineteenth century, the mere fact of expertise was beginning to serve the cultural function of naturalization that the 1844 Bank Act had helped provide for Bank of England notes at midcentury.

The link between economic writing and the university system is clear from the careers of Jevons and Marshall. Whereas John Stuart Mill and J. R. McCulloch obtained their knowledge about political economy outside the university system, Jevons was trained in a university (in chemistry and botany), and he subsequently held several university posts (at Owens College, Manchester, from 1866 through 1875, and at University College, London, from 1875 through 1880). Alfred Marshall was even more deeply enmeshed in the university system: he studied mathematics at St. John's, Cambridge, where he became a lecturer (in moral science) in 1868; he served as professor of political economy (and principal) at the new University College, Bristol, from 1877 through 1881; and he returned to Cambridge in 1885, where he served as professor of political economy until his retirement in 1908. Marshall was mentor to the group of economists known as the Cambridge school; he circulated his theoretical ideas through his lectures for several decades before publishing them; and he worked tirelessly to introduce political economy into the Cambridge curriculum. The School of Economics at Cambridge, which Marshall promoted, was founded in 1903. At the time of Marshall's death, his former pupils held almost half the economics chairs in Britain. That political economy (as economics) was becoming a science for university-trained scholars can also be seen in the creation of specialist journals and professional organizations in the last two decades of the century; the *Quarterly Journal of Economics* was launched in 1886, and in 1890 the *Economics Journal* began publication and the Royal Economic Society was founded. In 1895, the London School of Economics opened, the first university devoted specifically to advanced study in the science.

The complex role that the formalism of economics played in the social function of economic writing is less easy to summarize, but I can give a symptomatic—if somewhat idiosyncratic—example by citing one of the formal models offered by the first British marginalist to explain the century's economic crises. This model was not intended to quiet the anxiety manifested in a panic, as Bagehot's articles were; nor was it written to downplay the importance of such events, as was McCulloch's dictionary entry, or to render them useful, as Evans's two books on the crises attempted to do. Instead, W. Stanley Jevons's papers on commercial crises were written for fellow specialists, and, in them, he developed an explanatory model as part of a more general attempt to create a reliable—because mathematical—model of the dynamics of the economy.[78] Only by "detect[ing] and ex-hibit[ing] ... every kind of periodic fluctuation," Jevons insisted, could the economist measure and explain the overall regularity of the economic system.[79] Manias and panics posed the greatest challenge to creating such a model, of course, because these "fluctuations" threatened to defy even the power of mathematics to introduce order where chaos seemed to rule.

In order to anchor the apparent irregularity of commercial crises in events that could be observed and modeled mathematically, Jevons decided that manias and panics were caused by sunspots. His belief in the sunspot theory was serious and lasting. In the final paper he devoted to this topic, he explicitly reiterated that he was "never more in earnest." "I am perfectly convinced that these decennial crises do depend upon meteorological variations of like period," he wrote. "It is no jest at all" ("Commercial Crises," 215, 221). While this conviction may initially seem strange—to us and to many of Jevons's contemporaries[80]—it is worth noting that other nineteenth-century writers also offered unusual explanations for commercial crises. In 1867, for example, John Mills, a Manchester banker, told the Manchester Statistical Society that manias and panics were "not, in essence, a matter of the *purse* but of the *mind*." In 1876, William Purdy offered an equally speculative explanation when he said that manias and panics were correlated to the composite life cycle of business: when younger men predominated in the commercial world, he thought, speculations, then panics, were likely to occur; when older men regained control, equilibrium was restored.[81] By the same token, Jevons was not the only economic writer who tried to correlate economic events to variations in a natural phenomenon. Harvests, in fact, which Jevons thought connected solar activities to economic events, were repeatedly singled out by James

Wilson and other contributors to the *Economist*.[82] Jevons's theory, then, is important not primarily because of its strangeness but because it reveals the aspiration that lay at the heart of the campaign to win prestige for political economy: by insisting that observable meteorological phenomena caused apparently inexplicable economic events, Jevons was arguing that the social world resembles the natural world in being completely legible, that is, perfectly aligned with the explanatory system of a fully scientific political economy.

Jevons initially turned his attention to the problem of "periodic commercial fluctuations" in 1862, nine years before he published his influential *Theory of Political Economy*. His initial thought was that these fluctuations were irregular and nonperiodic—and that this was what both made them interesting and made keeping track of other, more regular "fluctuations" worthwhile: "Every kind of periodic fluctuation, whether daily, weekly, monthly, quarterly, or yearly, must be detected and exhibited, not only as a subject or study in itself, but because we must ascertain and eliminate such periodic variations before we can correctly exhibit those which are irregular or non-periodic, and probably of more interest and importance" ("Commercial Crises," 4). By 1866, Jevons had begun to fear that, even though such phenomena were observable (and therefore measurable), they might be inexplicable; even in 1866, however, he did suggest that harvests might be one of many causes that could precipitate a panic: "It is the abnormal changes which are alone threatening or worthy of very much attention. These changes arise from deficient or excessive harvests, from sudden changes of supply or demand in any of our great staple commodities, from manias of excessive investment or speculation, from wars and political disturbances, or other fortuitous occurrences which we cannot calculate upon and allow for" ("Frequent Pressure," 166, 167, 170).

It was in 1875 that Jevons's ideas took two dramatic turns: he stopped treating commercial crises as "irregular" and incalculable and began presenting them as fixed in a precise, and, thus, foreseeable, eleven-year "cycle"; and he stopped viewing the causes of such events as "fortuitous," attributing them instead to specific meteorological events. The paper in which Jevons made these dramatic claims, which he delivered to Section F (the Statistics Section) of the British Association for the Advancement of Science, immediately announced the departure from his earlier formulations:

It is a well-known principle of mechanics that the effects of a periodically varying cause are themselves periodic, and usually go through their phases in periods of time equal to those of the cause. There is no doubt that the energy poured upon the earth's surface in the form of sunbeams is the principal agent in maintaining life here. It has lately been proved, too, beyond all reasonable doubt, that there is a periodic variation of the sun's condition, which was first discovered in the alternate increase and decrease of area of the sun-spots.... Little doubt is now entertained, moreover, that the rainfall and other atmospheric phenomena of any locality are more or less influenced by the same changes in the sun's condition.... The success of the harvest in any year certainly depends upon the weather.... Now, if this weather depends in any degree upon the solar period, it follows that the harvest and the price of grain will depend more or less upon the solar period, and will go through periodic fluctuations in periods of time equal to those of the sun-spots. ("Solar Period," 175–76)

Jevons confidently cited 11.11 years as the average length of the principal sunspot cycle, but he also admitted that the prices of grain during the last century, not to mention the commercial crises, did not map onto this periodic cycle. Rather than abandon his thesis, he dismissed the data collected during his own century and turned instead to a list of prices from the thirteenth and fourteenth centuries. During these centuries, he claims, before "credit cycles, crises, floods of paper money, and other causes" could have interfered, it was possible to detect "variations [in grain prices] due solely to meteorological conditions" ("Solar Period," 178, 176, 177). Unfortunately, however, the precision of the information about grain prices during these earlier centuries was not matched by reliable data about sunspots. Such data, in fact, did not exist, and Jevons was forced to acknowledge that all he could offer was a "surmise." "As the years of maximum or minimum sun-spots are quite unknown as regards such earlier centuries, and even their occurrence is only a matter of inference, the exact relation of prices to the sun-spots cannot be disclosed at present by this inquiry," he conceded (178). Despite its hypothetical nature, however, his surmise, Jevons insisted, deserved both further investigation and bold articulation:

It is now pretty generally allowed that the fluctuations of the money market, though often apparently due to exceptional and accidental events, such as wars, great commercial failures, unfounded panics, and so forth, yet do exhibit a remarkable tendency to recur at intervals approximating to ten or eleven years. Thus the principal commercial crises have happened in the years 1825, 1836–39, 1847, 1857, 1866, and I was almost adding 1879, so convinced do I feel that there will, within the next few years, be another great crisis. Now, if there should be, in or about the year 1879, a great collapse comparable with those of the years mentioned, there will have been five such occurrences in fifty-four years, giving almost exactly eleven years (10.8 years) as the average interval, which sufficiently approximates to 11.11, the supposed exact length of the sun-spot period, to warrant speculation as to their possible connection. (183–84)

As a concession to the skeptics, Jevons cited the work of John Mills, but he was not content with Mills's psychological explanation, even when emotions were attributed not to individuals but to a collective abstraction ("the commercial mind"): "But it seems to me very probable that these moods of the commercial mind, while constituting the principal part of the phenomena, may be controlled by outward events, especially the condition of the harvests." Having staked his claim on a "mechanical" model, Jevons completed his paper with a flourish, claiming to discover "remote causes" in ever more distant spheres: "Now, if the planets govern the sun, and the sun governs the vintages and harvests, and thus the prices of food and raw materials and the state of the money market, it follows that the configurations of the planets may prove to be the remote causes of the greatest commercial disasters" (184, 185).

In his last two papers on commercial crises, Jevons continued to refine his formulation of what had by 1878 become a conviction. He did so, moreover, despite the fact that each of his data sets proved inadequate. In the paper presented to the Dublin meeting of the British Association for the Advancement of Science in August, Jevons admitted that he could not find evidence to support his theory about periodic harvest failures in the English or European records; arguing that the climate conditions in these parts of the world were too "complicated," he turned to India, where, according to Dr. W. W. Hunter, famines occurred regularly ("Periodicity," 196). Since Lancashire mills depended on India for raw materials and markets, Jevons exulted, the periodic famines in India had to influence the commercial state of Britain. When he sought to document the connection, however, by graphing "the value of merchandise exported to India in each year from 1708–9 to 1809–10," he had to renounce his triumph. Still, he remained convinced, attributing the imperfection of the figures to the novelty of the subject, and dismissing altogether the graph's failure to produce the desired result: "The subject is altogether too new and complicated to take the absence of variation in certain figures as conclusive negative evidence" (198).

In November of that year, Jevons tried again. Rejecting his earlier efforts with "disgust," Jevons seized on a new account of sunspot periodicity—the theory advanced by J. A. Broun that sunspots peak every 10.45 years, not every 10.3, 10.46, 10.44, or 11.11 years, as Jevons had previously thought. Using Broun's figure, Jevons returned to the data about eighteenth-century commercial crises. Initially reporting a "beautiful coincidence" between these crises and the 10.45 year sunspot interval, he acknowledged disappointment again when historical reports failed to confirm the interval: "I have... spent much labour during the past summer in a most tedious and discouraging search among the pamphlets, magazines, and newspapers of the period, with a view to discover other decennial crises. I am free to confess that in this search I have been thoroughly biased in favour of a theory, and that the evidence which I have so far found would have no weight, if standing by itself" ("Commercial Crises," 205, 207, 208). Not only did he grasp at evidence that was slight; he also continued to dismiss any evidence that failed to corroborate his theory ("In spite... of the doubtful existence of some of the crises... I can entertain no doubt whatever" [210]). As he had done in the August paper, Jevons interposed Indian famines between the crop failures he needed to find and the commercial crises he was having difficulty documenting; then, when the figures about India failed to support his thesis, he added "tropical Africa, America, the West Indies, and even the Levant" to his list of the sunspot affected countries that might have influenced British commerce (212).

Having failed to find evidence of exact commercial crises, Jevons next acknowledged that the sunspots might not be as regular as he had once reported; and he was reduced to speculating that the commercial crises, which he still could not document, might actually have been *more* regular than the sunspots, even though he had thus far been using sunspot regularity to guide his interpretation of the historical evidence ("Commercial Crises," 214). Finally, refusing to admit defeat, he called for direct observation of the sun to document, once and for all, the periodic variations in which he so adamantly believed:

> Why do we beat about the bush when all that is needed is half-a-dozen of Pouillet's pyrheliometers with skilled observers, who will seize every clear day to determine directly the heating power of the sun? Why do we not go direct to the Great Luminary himself, and ask him plainly whether he varies or not? If he answers No! then some of us must reconsider our theories, and perhaps endure a little ridicule. But if, as is much more probable, he should answer Yes! then the time will come when the most important news in *The Times* will be the usual cablegram of the solar power.... An empire on which the sun never sets, and whose commerce pervades every port and creek of the sunny south, cannot wisely neglect to keep a watch on this great fountain of

energy. From that sun, which is truly "of this great world both eye and soul," we derive our strength and our weakness, our success and our failure, our elation in commercial mania, and our despondence and ruin in commercial collapse. ("Commercial Crises," 214)

The most constructive way to interpret Jevons's repeated assertions, his willingness to overlook or dismiss contradictory evidence, and his determination to prove what he already assumed is to treat these as signs of his unwavering commitment to the dream of a fully scientific political economy. The inquiry into the causes of phenomena as complex as commercial crises could not approach the rigor or mathematical purity of a science unless Jevons purged this subject of all traces of human emotion, unless he *assumed*—even if he could not prove—that some physical cause was acting on events others might describe as social. He was determined to link sunspot periodicity to the periodicity of commercial crises, in other words, because, without some observable natural phenomenon to serve as causal agent, commercial crises threatened to become *uninterpretable* and, thus, to mark the limit of political economy's ability to become a science.

It is also important, however, to note that the failure of Jevons's model to explain commercial crises did not really matter—not to him and certainly not to the ordinary Britons who suffered through these events. For, by the time Jevons published his essays, in periodicals intended primarily for specialists, the prestige of the economic expert had come to be so taken for granted that the gap between any given model and what it purported to explain was less important than the fact that an economic expert was working on the problem. Expertise had become an effective antidote to anxiety in and of itself, in other words, and, even if commercial crises continued to disrupt the British economy, ordinary Britons could rest assured that reliable explanations would be generated in time, as the science continued to mature, as all mathematical sciences could be counted on to do.

CHAPTER FIVE

Delimiting Literature, Defining
Literary Value

In this chapter, I describe some of the factors that informed nineteenth-century imaginative writers' efforts to define a distinctively Literary form of value.[1] As we will see, the complexity of these factors created problems for authors of imaginative writing that economic writers did not face. These problems took several forms. Some were conceptual: they followed from the challenges posed by the particular qualities turn-of-the-century writers chose to emphasize. Some were social: the rivalry that developed among workers in this field prevented them from achieving both the degree of professionalization and the level of cooperation that strengthened economic writers as a group. Finally, some were practical: the Romantic definition of *Literary value* made it difficult for authors of genres that were popular—whose value *as commodities* was unmistakable—to claim that their works were also valuable in aesthetic terms.[2] In the course of this chapter, I show how nineteenth-century Literary writers' solutions to these problems gave rise to the modern versions of Literary writing, Literary reading, and professional Literary criticism; but I also argue that the compromises and rivalries these solutions entailed laid the groundwork for the paradoxical status that has bifurcated contemporary versions of these practices. This paradox will be familiar to many readers of this book: on the one hand, Literary texts seem to be universally valued because they are required reading in almost all secondary and tertiary educational institutions in the United States and the United Kingdom; on the other hand, the way that some students are taught to read these texts, especially (but not exclusively) in graduate programs (British postgraduate programs), tends to make them (or these readings of them) *inaccessible* to readers who are not so schooled. One unintended product of the triumph of the Romantic model of Literary value, then, as it was elaborated in the practices taught in late-twentieth-century graduate schools, has been a mode of Literary interpretation that is so arcane that many consider it to have no value at all.

I divide this chapter into three sections. In the first, I take up a number of the factors that eventually led to the specialization of advanced (professional) Literary studies. First, I examine some of the qualities turn-of-the-century writers emphasized in their efforts to devise a model of value that could challenge the market evaluation registered by *popularity* or *demand*. Then I turn to the rivalries and competitions sparked by privileging these qualities. These contests developed among various groups of imaginative writers—major writers and their minor disciples, on the one hand, and Literary writers and reviewers, on the other. My argument is that the combination of the Romantic model of value and changes in the publishing market helped pit subsets of Literary workers against each other, even though it was arguably in their collective interest to work together. In this section, I also discuss the way that changes in the hierarchy of imaginative kinds of writing—the creation of a host of new periodicals, the fall in the market value of poetry after 1824, and the rise in the popularity of novels—put pressure on the Romantic model of value that Wordsworth and other poets advocated. Finally, I examine the effect that circulating libraries like Mudie's had on writers' efforts to retain control over the definition of *Literary value* and on the conditions in which novels in particular were produced and evaluated.

In the second section, I turn to one of the challenges created by the decision to equate Literary merit with stylistic originality, and I show how the way this challenge was eventually met transformed the problematic of representation into a source of value instead of a problem, as it continued to be for credit instruments and in the accounts of credit offered by economic writers. This section, "Hierarchies of Reading," focuses on late-nineteenth-century journalists' attempts to map the differences among kinds of imaginative writing on differences in reading practices. These differences were social and institutional as well as theoretical, for they reflected the gap between the way an elite minority read outside formal schools and the way the majority of readers were taught to use Literature in schools. Ian Hunter has called the reading practice of the elite minority an "aesthetics of self-cultivation"; in schools, by contrast, reading was used "like singing, drawing and nature-study . . . [to] focus and support the techniques of 'correction through self-expression.'"[3] In the periodical articles I examine in this section, I show how members of the minority elite emphasized the trope of organic unity, which enabled them to locate in the Literary object the source of the pleasure and fulfillment they experienced through reading; this trope also enabled them to specify the nature of Literary value, which Wordsworth and Coleridge had struggled to do. The combination of a model of reading that attributed value to the *effort* involved in *interpreting the connotations of language* and an image of an *organic whole* that explained how a work of art could exist in and of itself, apart from the social world to which it only incidentally referred, enabled Literary writers to revalue the deferral inherent in the problematic of representation. In these late-century accounts of (elite) reading, we can see that the gap that always separates a representational sign from the ground of its value (and from its referent) came to be cast as the site of the uniquely aesthetic *kind* of value produced by—or through interaction with—Literary texts.

In the final section of the chapter, I return to the challenge this model of value presented to novelists—and vice versa. By the last decades of the century, many novelists claimed that their works were Literature too, yet the formal similarities between prose fictions and informational writing, as well as the fact that most novels' language seemed denotative rather than connotative, made it difficult for novelists to satisfy the demands of a model that defined *value* in terms of organic unity, linguistic connotation, and textual autonomy. We can also see this challenge in terms of the fact/fiction continuum, for one way that novelists tried to approach the aesthetic ideal was to deemphasize the similarities between their works and the kinds of writing that conveyed factual information by drawing a sharp distinction between "facts" and "fiction" (or "facts" and "truth"). In this section, I focus on a series of debates about the novels of Charles Reade, for Reade's insistence that imaginative writing *should* refer to actual events provoked his peers—even fellow novelists like Margaret Oliphant—to repudiate his aesthetic and find ways to make the novel fit the model of value that early-nineteenth-century poets had promoted. By the end of the century, as we will see, novelists who aspired to elevate the status of prose fiction devised ways to describe the novel that made it seem to conform to this model. As I argue in chapter 6, this campaign to cast (some) novels as Literature elaborated a novelistic practice that already existed in the early nineteenth century and that continued to be refined by later novelists eager to distinguish the aesthetic value of their works from their market value—that is, from their status as commodities.

Literary Value and a Hierarchy of Imaginative Genres

In his compelling account of the late-eighteenth-century emergence of a "discourse of value"—or, more precisely, a "double discourse of value"—John Guillory has demonstrated that the very notion of *aesthetic value* depended on a development within economic writing: the invention of the concept of *use value*, in analogy to *exchange value*, as a theoretical means of squaring the problematic relationship between economic production and consumption.[4] Before the development of this concept, Guillory explains, there was no model for a distinctive "aesthetic" kind of value, or even for "value" in general, despite the fact that people had always evaluated works of art. Before the last quarter of the eighteenth century, according to Guillory, "the comparison of authors or works to one another need not . . . be expressed as the comparison of their relative 'aesthetic values,' because neither the concept of the aesthetic, nor the concept of value, [was] as yet defined in such a way that they [could] be yoked together." What provoked these definitions, in Guillory's account, were two forms of "uneasiness" whose intersection led to a reworking of the "discursive classification of objects," then the disaggregation of two distinct "discourses." One "uneasiness" was social, a widespread discomfort "with the lack of any systematic regulation of consumption," such as the Renaissance sumptuary laws had provided; the other was theoretical, the perception on the part of moral philosophers that the analogy they had previously used to link the harmony of God's handiwork to the social totality (the relationship between production and consumption) did not fit what they actually saw. To address this double discomfort, Guillory argues, Adam Smith tried two, quite different tacks: first (in the *Theory of Moral Sentiments*), he argued that the imaginative "pleasures" attendant on the possession of certain objects constituted the "deception" that stimulated human industry; then (in *The Wealth of Nations*) he substituted for this (implicitly aesthetic) theory of value *another* theory that located value "in the pole of production" rather than consumption. This substitution—the invention of the concept of *use value* to displace the problem of affect and to explain the relationship between production and consumption—was immediately covered over by the generic differentiation I have been describing, a differentiation that, in Guillory's powerful account, entailed two kinds of forgetting:

> The failure to construct a theory of the harmonious relation between a continuum of production and a continuum of consumption marks the point of the irrevocable disengagement of political economy from aesthetic questions, and thus its emergence as a separate discourse. Aesthetics, on the other hand, continues to name a set of questions or a subdiscourse within the larger discourse of philosophy, from which it had no reason to detach itself, and never did. Nevertheless it still betrays its consanguinity with political economy in several respects: Once aesthetics has ceded to political economy the

defense of the rationality of the social order . . . it need no longer assume that all man-made objects are by definition "works of art," and it can define the "work of art" as distinct from both "craft" objects and the commodity. It then proceeds to analyze this object as though it had always existed, but it can only make such an assumption by *forgetting* political economy, by forgetting the fact that the "fine arts" emerged as such in contradistinction to commodities of immediate utility, or commodities as such. This distinction must be continuously reimposed upon the domain of production, in response to the fact that works of art continue to be exchanged in the marketplace as commodities which are commensurable with other commodities. . . . The very concept of aesthetic *value* betrays the continued pressure of economic discourse on the language of aesthetics. Of course aesthetics immediately reasserted, against the universality of economic commensurability, a theory of the incommensurability of aesthetic and economic values, on the basis of the inutility of the aesthetic object. In that sense aesthetics learns to forget political economy just as political economy forgot aesthetics. This mutual forgetting constitutes aesthetics and political economy as antithetical discourses, which between them divide the world of cultural production into works of art and commodities.[5]

I cite Guillory's work at length because this is the best account of the way that the concept of aesthetic value was produced through a process of *discursive* differentiation, which had profound implications for our understanding of *disciplinary* history: the breakup of the eighteenth-century *discipline* of moral philosophy into the modern *discourses* of economics and aesthetics laid the groundwork for the creation of our two modern *disciplines*, economics, on the one hand, and, more complexly, Literary studies, on the other.[6] If one adds to Guillory's account the notions of *genre* and *print*, this history can be rendered even more precise, for his discussion of the two modes of "uneasiness" eighteenth-century Britons felt fails to specify the conditions that intensified this discomfort *differentially* with regard to particular *genres* of *print*. Even though the distinction between *use value* and *exchange value* was made in the genre of economic theory, in other words, as a way to displace the problem of subjective desire (or pleasure), the pressure to discriminate among instances of the same genre was *not* registered by the authors of these texts. By and large, these authors were not affected by the market model of value because their works continued to be printed, in small numbers, for an elite audience of specialist readers, and they, for the most part, did not depend on book sales for their livelihood. The writers who *were* pressured to invoke the aesthetic model of value, of course, were the authors of imaginative writing, for it was this large category of print whose volume increased so dramatically after the passage of the Booksellers' Act. It was this increase in the production of (some kinds of) printed materials, in other words, that made the concept of aesthetic value *socially attractive* to writers seeking a way to distinguish between their works and those of everyone else, on some basis *other than* mere popularity (demand). Guillory's reliance on the Foucauldian notion of *discourse* makes it easy to imagine that the distinctions between use value and exchange value and between aesthetic value and market value were simply matters of theoretical interest (or primarily of interest to theorists), whereas the rubrics of *genre* and *print* remind us that making such distinctions could seem like a matter of economic life or death to writers who feared having their works buried—and their livelihoods cut off—by the flood of publications pouring from a newly liberated press.

Thus, while the turn-of-the-century campaign to delimit the nature of Literary value was not the first effort to rank instances of imaginative writing, the version of this campaign launched by Wordsworth and Coleridge seemed to its participants more urgent than earlier skirmishes.[7] Armed with the newly available aesthetic model of value as a *differential* category (i.e., as incommensurate with market value), these poets tried to manage the torrent of print by proposing various categories designed to help readers discriminate between "good poetry" and other, inferior kinds of imaginative writing. "All good poetry is the spontaneous overflow of powerful feelings," Wordsworth wrote in the "Preface" to *Lyrical Ballads*; "but though this be true, Poems to which any value can be attached, were never produced on any variety of subjects but by a man who being possessed of more than usual organic sensibility had also thought long and deeply."[8] For my purposes, the telling word in this often-quoted sentence is *value*, for the value Wordsworth wanted readers to appreciate was the new, nonmarket model of value spun off by the disciplinary division Guillory describes.

Invoking this model of value enabled Wordsworth to draw the large distinction he introduces here, that between "good poetry" and nearly every popular variant of imaginative writing: "frantic novels, sickly and stupid German Tragedies, and deluges of idle and extravagant stories in verse" (*PW*, 1:128). Simply invoking the differential category of aesthetic value, however, could not identify the particular features that were essential to "good poetry." Wordsworth praised poems that inspire "enjoyments, of a purer, more lasting, and more exquisite nature," and he frequently used vague phrases like "genuine poetry," but his comments about "elevation and moral purity" were too imprecise to explain, in *positive* terms, what aesthetic value entailed (157–58).[9] The difficulty subsequent readers had in determining exactly what Wordsworth meant has been compounded, as we are about to see, by the role some of his contemporaries played in elaborating, extending, and, sometimes, slightly altering his ideas, but most modern Literary scholars agree that the qualities Wordsworth wanted to endorse were the originality of the poem and its ability to appeal not to contemporaries but to "posterity." In 1815, he stressed both these qualities in his famous rebuke to reviewers: "Every author, as far as he is great and at the same time *original*, has had the task of *creating* the taste by which he is to be enjoyed. . . . The predecessors of an original Genius of a high order will have smoothed the way for all that he has in common with them;—and much he will have in common; but, for what is peculiarly his own, he will be called upon to clear and often to shape his own road:—he will be in the condition of Hannibal among the Alps" (2:80).[10]

This definition of *aesthetic value*, which stressed originality and immunity from the judgment of an author's peers, enabled Literary writers to distinguish among kinds of imaginative writing and to exempt their efforts from the market definition of *value*, but it also presented certain problems. In the first place, by definition, very few writers could be said to be "original," even if one allowed that "predecessors" could "smooth" the way of the "Genius"; in the second place, if the judgment of "posterity" was necessary to identify a writer as an "original," a poet's relationship to other writers would necessarily be vexed. Then, too, there was the problem of money, which some writers might have professed to despise, but which very few—including Wordsworth—could afford completely to ignore. We will see in a moment how complicated the issue of money proved to be for Wordsworth, but first let me show some of the ways that privileging originality and the judgment of posterity created complex networks of dependence and rivalry among Wordsworth's contemporaries.

Even though Wordsworth insisted, against the evidence of flagging sales and poor reviews, that his poetry would eventually receive the recognition it deserved, he also realized that, if the poems were not to be forgotten, someone needed to teach readers how to read them. In the 1800 "Preface" to *Lyrical Ballads*, the poet suggested the magnitude of this task, and, even though he halfheartedly began it, he was clearly reluctant to devote himself to this work: "I was unwilling to undertake the task, knowing that on this occasion the Reader would look coldly upon my arguments. . . . I was still more unwilling to undertake the task, because, adequately to display the opinions, and fully to enforce the arguments, would require a space wholly disproportionate to a preface" (*PW*, 1:120).[11] Wordsworth need not have worried about helping readers remember him, however, for, virtually as soon as he began to publish, a host of minions clamored to help him out. This group of acolytes and imitators—which Coleridge called "a company of almost religious admirers"—has been deftly analyzed by Margaret Russett under the rubric of "Romantic minority."[12] Foremost among these self-designated minor writers was Thomas De Quincey, who first encountered Wordsworth's "We Are Seven" in 1799, when he was only fourteen. De Quincey finally met Wordsworth, briefly, in 1807; then, after leaving Oxford, he joined Wordsworth and Coleridge at Allan Bank in 1808. From this precious, physical proximity—a position sacrificed when De Quincey moved to London to help Wordsworth publish his work—the young man launched his lifelong project of promoting, interpreting, and disseminating Wordsworth's writing, all of which ultimately served to enhance the reputation of the increasingly reclusive older poet.

De Quincey was not the only self-proclaimed minor writer to assume the role of passionate publicist for the leading Romantic poets and their ideas. The "young men of ardent minds, liberal education and not with 'academic laurels unbestowed,'" as Coleridge described the "literocracy" that buzzed around Wordsworth and Coleridge, also included Leigh Hunt, Thomas Hazlitt, and Charles Lamb as well as more remote satellites like Henry Crabb Robinson. But De Quincey was "the very earliest . . . to honour and welcome" the new light, as he liked to remind his own readers, and the way he chose to do so is worth recalling.[13] As Russett explains, the way that De Quincey helped transmit Wordsworth's poetry and augment its reputation involved the lesser writer's offering himself up to the greater, identifying with and emulating Wordsworth so that he could, in a manner of speaking, *embody* him for others.[14]

The early nineteenth-century position of minority writer was dictated, in part at least, by the qualities Wordsworth associated with Literary value, for, if an original genius was fated to be misunderstood in his own time, then he had to surround himself with a blessed few who could keep his name before the public, explain the nature of his genius, and protect him from the hardships of ordinary life. If minor writers like De Quincey performed these offices for Wordsworth, however, they also introduced problems that the genius might not have anticipated. Thus, as Russett reminds us, assisting a great writer was not always a simple task: when De Quincey tried simply to facilitate the editing and publication of Wordsworth's *Convention of Centra*, for example, he inevitably altered the text as he struggled over questions of grammar, syntax, and compositor's errors. As Wordsworth watched his minion enhance his own reputation by dropping public hints about Wordsworth's unpublished poems and domestic secrets, the great poet lost control of the reception he so desperately wanted to manage.[15]

To grasp the advantages and liabilities conferred on Literary labor by the presence of minor writers, it is useful to contrast the position of minority with that of marginality, with which I associated William Cobbett in chapter 3. Unlike a marginalized writer, who typically was forced out of the mainstream or elected a contrarian position, the minor writer embraced subservience, for he (or she—think of Mary Shelley) found in the auxiliary position a way to be close to power without having to assume the responsibilities associated with it.[16] The minor writer also materially assisted in the transmission of the major writer's works so that the former's status could be enhanced by the rise of the reputation of the latter. A marginalized writer, by contrast, spun in an orbit ever further from the star, and, as the discipline to which he was a satellite gained a set of definitive norms, as political economy did in the first decades of the nineteenth century, he was likely to have no voice, no place, and no legacy apart from what scholarly curiosity might subsequently award. We should also note, however, that, even though a writer who was marginalized during his or her lifetime is typically effaced from accounts of the discipline's history, a discipline that gains definition and an institutional home by exiling the figures on its margins is more likely to present a unified front than is a practice that does not draw distinct boundaries around itself. Partly because Literature's "original" writers never established manageable relationships with the "minor" writers they both needed and feared, Literary writers were not able to establish enforceable boundaries around their work. Their work never really constituted a "discipline" during the nineteenth century, much less a "profession," partly because the definitions they were adopting to distinguish Literary merit made them either ambiguously positioned helpmates, as De Quincey was to Wordsworth, or rivals with each other, as reviewers were to writers, instead of consistent allies embarked on a common task, as (establishment) contemporary economic writers more often were. Partly, as I argue in a moment, Literary writers could not present their work as a discipline because, even though "English literature" was taught in some schools and universities, the way it was used there did not conform to the criteria they were developing in order to distinguish their work from inferior kinds of imaginative writing.

The division of labor among nineteenth-century economic writers that I described in chapters 3 and 4 worked so well, then, partly because economic writers did not consider originality the only criterion of status. It worked partly because all the economists whose work counted espoused variants of the same theoretical position. And it worked partly because the individuals who wrote popular versions of economic theory—imaginative writers like Harriet Martineau and financial journalists like Bagehot and Evans—neither disparaged their own work nor idealized the contributions of the theorists whose ideas they explained. The majority of imaginative writers, by contrast, did not conceptualize their work as divisible in this way because they did not consider all kinds of imaginative writing to be alike in any substantive way. As soon as writers like Wordsworth and Coleridge privileged originality over every other quality, as soon as they felt it imperative to discriminate absolutely between "genuine poetry" and inferior kinds of imaginative writing, and as long as they nevertheless continued to cultivate and depend on other, self-denominated minor writers to proclaim the value of their work, they allowed the possibility of disciplinary coherence and social status to slip away. With an inflexible yet unpoliced dichotomy between Literature and all other kinds of imaginative writing standing sentinel, like a Gorgon at the gate, Literary writers willingly—if inadvertently—helped consign the value of their work and that of their successors to the status of *merely* differential, despite their insistence that aesthetic value was the only kind that mattered.

Minor writers were not the only individuals to complicate the claims that "originals" like Wordsworth should take the lead in defining *Literary merit*. As publishing conditions began to change in the first decades of the nineteenth century, another set of writers also muddied the Literary waters—by offering another form of attention that Literary writers could not control. These authors wrote reviews for the new magazines, quarterlies, and miscellanies launched in ever-accelerating numbers after 1802. While the informal evaluation of imaginative writing had long been a role performed by British periodicals, the nature of reviewing began to change in that year, for, with the founding of the *Edinburgh Review*, contributors began to earn money (ten guineas per sheet of sixteen pages), editors began to be paid (£200 a year for Francis Jeffrey, the quarterly's first editor), and anonymous reviewing became the norm. The example set by the *Edinburgh Review* was soon followed by other quarterlies (the *Quarterly Review*, the *Westminster Review*, the *London Review*, and the *British Review*) and, a bit later, by additional monthly magazines (*Blackwood's*, the *New Monthly*, the *Edinburgh Magazine*, and the *London Magazine*) and weeklies devoted primarily to reviewing (such as the *Literary Gazette*).

The *Edinburgh Review* established yet one additional precedent. Under the direction of Jeffrey—and with the jurist himself writing many of the reviews—the *Review* began to publish reviews so vicious that Coleridge condemned their "damnatory style." As Coleridge characterized such writing, it featured "the substitution of assertion for judgment [and] . . . the frequency of arbitrary and sometimes petulant verdicts."[17] The result was what has been called "adjectival criticism," a mode of writing long on descriptive bombast, larded with personal innuendo, and short on tolerance for any stylistic or substantive innovation.[18] Jeffrey's lead was followed by the *Quarterly Review*, under the editorial direction of William Gifford, the *London Review*, under John Scott, and *Blackwood's*, under J. G. Lockhart. This mode of invective dominated the reviews that appeared in the British press for the first half of the nineteenth century. It was a sign of the demise of the eighteenth-century assumptions that human nature was universal and that "the true standard of taste" was available to everyone. It was also a product of the burgeoning market for all kinds of print that I have already described, for competition among periodicals led editors to seek increasingly extreme measures to attract and keep fickle readers. So fierce did the competition become, in fact, and so vicious were the reviews that at least one duel was fought over the charges and countercharges printed in periodical reviews.[19]

Wordsworth and the other "Lake Poets" were often the targets of such critical reviews. Jeffrey was particularly vicious in the invectives with which he dismissed Wordsworth's poems. In 1814, for example, he used the publication of *The Excursion* as an opportunity to publicly wash his hands of the poet: "The case of Mr. Wordsworth, we perceive, is now manifestly hopeless; and we give him up as altogether incurable, and beyond the power of criticism."[20] A year later, Jeffrey greeted *The White Doe of Ryleston* with an even harsher rebuke: "This, we think, has the merit of being the very worst poem we ever saw imprinted in a quarto volume." Calling the poem "a happy union of all the faults, without any of the beauties, which belong to his school of poetry," Jeffrey even hinted that the *Doe* might be a parody of Wordsworth's poetry, produced by some "wicked enemy of that school" to "instruct . . . Mr. Wordsworth, by example, in the nature of those errors, against which our precepts had been so often directed in vain." A reviewer for the influential *Quarterly Review* agreed with Jeffrey's negative evaluation, although the language he used was considerably milder; also in 1815, a reviewer for the lesser *Theatrical Inquisitor* chimed in, basically repeating the abuse already heaped on Wordsworth's latest offering.[21]

If reviewers could damn Literary writers in print, they could also help turn the tide of their reputations—at least with the readers of the periodicals. If Margaret Oliphant is correct, the first appreciation of Wordsworth's poetry not authored by one of the poet's followers was John Wilson's review, which appeared in *Blackwood's Edinburgh Magazine* in 1818.[22] Two years later, a reviewer for the rival *London Magazine* argued that Wordsworth's poetry had been allowed to "slumber in oblivion" because its novel "system" had yet to be fully realized in the poems—a neglect this reviewer seems to have wanted to correct: "The system which originates with themselves [the Lake Poets] is yet in embryo—the conception is great, but the machines are not yet sufficiently softened by practice." In 1822, another reviewer, writing for the politically conservative *New European Magazine*, voiced what was beginning to sound like a consensus: "Wherever the language of English shall be spoken . . . the Poems of William Wordsworth will be read, and admired." By 1835, the change in Wordsworth's reputation had come to seem worthy of comment in and of itself. "The common consent which once denied him a place amongst the bards of his age and country," declared the reviewer (probably W. J. Fox) for the *Monthly Repository*, "now seems to concede to him the highest rank."[23] By this time, the reversal of Wordsworth's reputation had been assured: he was awarded an honorary degree by Durham University in 1838; in 1839, Oxford followed suit, in a ceremony whose audience included John Keble, Matthew Arnold, John Henry Newman, and Arthur Hugh Clough. Wordsworth was asked to became the nation's poet laureate in 1843, a position he assumed in 1845, and, on his death in 1850, Matthew Arnold's two elegies ("Memorial Verses" and "The Youth of Nature") expressed the respect that had by then become nearly universal. By 1895, when Oliphant composed her history of Blackwood's publishing house, Wordsworth's reputation was so secure that she looked back on his first critics with open disbelief.[24]

It is worth noting that the elevation of Wordsworth's reputation—and, by extension, the more general acceptance of his aesthetic ideals—did not involve schools. Even Arnold, in his capacity as inspector of schools, did not recommend teaching Wordsworth's poetry *as the poet demanded it be read* in public schools, for, as we will see in a moment, this mode of reading was a coterie practice, cultivated outside the institutions of formal education.[25] Instead, the reputation of this poet, like those of his peers, was shaped in large part in the pages of the public press by the very periodicals created to capitalize on the burgeoning market for print. Given the competition for readers that raged *among* these periodicals, it does not seem surprising that reviewers' blame or praise sometimes strained toward hyperbole. Anything short of outright libel seemed fair game to reviewers, who were generally protected by anonymity and often urged on by their editors.[26] Somewhat more surprising is the competition that developed *between* reviewers and the authors of Literary works, especially since the same individuals so often published in both venues. Many Literary writers complained that reviewers were encouraged to be irresponsible by the institution of anonymity, which poets, at any rate, did not practice.[27] Until the 1860s, Literary writers repeatedly complained that reviewers' anonymity permitted a host of abuses, from double reviewing to damning an unread book, from reviewing one's own book to circulating scandalous personal rumors about authors.[28] The rivalry between book authors and reviewers was also fed by the different levels of compensation and respect afforded the two kinds of writing, especially in the first two decades of the nineteenth century.[29] While it is certainly true that abuses were committed by nineteenth-century reviewers, it is also the case that the two kinds of writing were ineluctably tied to each other. Not only did many of the same writers publish books and write reviews, but both sets of writers were attempting, in the broadest sense, to establish the terms by which the value of Literary writing could be conceptualized, measured, and rewarded. In his first review of the Lake Poets, Jeffrey made it clear that he viewed his primary function to be preserving and publicizing good writing in order to enhance Britain's cultural reputation. So important did he consider poetry, in particular, that he likened it to religion.[30] For a poet like Wordsworth, of course, the problem with this claim was that a culturally conservative reviewer like Jeffrey thought that the best way to preserve the nation's culture was to protect it from change—especially the kind of stylistic innovation that Wordsworth so vigorously promoted. In retrospect, then, we can say that reviewers tried to enhance the overall status of Literary writing and that their habitual comparisons of new writers' work to that of a few of their predecessors helped solidify the "old canon of English literature," which William St. Clair has described; but we must also acknowledge that, to contemporary writers of poetry and fiction, reviews did not always seem to contribute to a common enterprise, and reviewers did not always seem interested in assisting innovative young writers.

Understandably, Wordsworth was incensed by reviewers' treatment of his work, and the combination of disappointing sales and poor reviews probably does help explain the bitterness with which he elevated the judgment of posterity over that of his peers.[31] Nevertheless, Wordsworth's relationship to the approval of his contemporaries and his attitude toward the profits his works earned is more complicated than his professed indifference might imply. On the one hand, he clearly wanted to sell his works—in part at least because the estate he and Dorothy stood to inherit was tied up from 1802 and the Wordsworths needed money to support their modest establishment.[32] On the other hand, however, Wordsworth sometimes insisted that his poems be published initially in expensive quarto editions, thereby making them unaffordable for the vast majority of British readers. While the motive behind limiting *The Excursion* to a quarto edition, priced at 42s. (£2, 2s.) before binding and over 45s. (£2, 5s.) bound, may have been Wordsworth's desire for greater profits, the immediate result was to price the work beyond the market he claimed he wanted to reach. As St. Clair dryly remarks:

> *The Excursion* in quarto was, for its length, perhaps the most expensive work of literature ever published in England, and Wordsworth had to wait six years for most of the 500 copies to be sold before the book was reprinted in octavo. Wordsworth may have believed that the rural poor were more sensitive to literature than gentlemen, but he did not number many leech gatherers among his readers. For the price of one copy of *The Excursion* in quarto, a reader in Salisbury could have bought over a hundred fat pigs. Wordsworth's own income from his writing was below 100 shillings (£5) a week for most of his life, and he could not easily have afforded to buy his own books.[33]

Rather than expressing hypocrisy, as St. Clair implies, Wordsworth's insistence that *The Excursion* be priced for elite buyers may have articulated his preference for future readers over the attention of any of his contemporaries, for well-made, high-priced books would survive longer than cheap editions. Whatever Wordsworth's personal motives, the point to make is that, even though it had become possible to articulate the need for an aesthetic model of value, it was not possible simply to set aside market considerations. Whatever Wordsworth and other Literary writers thought about how Literary writing *should* be valued, it inevitably circulated in the market, where price and demand prevailed. Even Wordsworth must have realized this, for, when *The Excursion* was reissued in cheaper editions, beginning in 1820, his poems began to receive the recognition—albeit expressed in sales—that he always thought they deserved. Even after the upturn in Wordsworth's personal reputation, however, the general uncertainty about how Literary writing should be valued continued. Because the commercial interests of publishers did not always coincide with the aesthetic ideals (or even the commercial interests) of writers, the juxtaposition of the two models of value inevitably produced both what look to us like mixed agendas in individual writers and a contest among the various producers of imaginative work over how its value should be judged. As we will see in a moment, moreover, no consensus emerged among imaginative writers about how to deal with complicated issues like copyright, the pricing of new works, or the degree of control an author should have over his or her productions. With writers often viewing each other as rivals or enemies rather than allies, and with the financial interests of publishers and writers so frequently pitted against each other, it is difficult to imagine how they could have set aside their differences long enough to reach a consensus about how to challenge the market model of value that increasingly dominated British society.

The vexed struggle over how to define and adjudicate the value of imaginative writing was further complicated in the late 1820s by a shake-up in the hierarchy of kinds of imaginative work. Whereas poets continued to claim superior ethical status for their writing, soon after Byron's death in 1824 British publishers sharply curtailed their commitment to new volumes of poetry. As Lee Erickson points out:

> Despite an increase of 23 percent in the number of titles appearing annually between 1815 and 1828 (1,121 as compared with 1,377) and another 30 percent increase in titles between 1828 and 1832 (1,377 as compared to an estimated 1,789), by 1830 almost all publishers refused to publish poetry. John Murray refused any manuscripts of poetry after Byron's death in 1824; Longman said "nobody wants poetry now" and encouraged authors to write cookbooks instead of volumes of verse; John Taylor wrote to John Clare in 1830 saying that his firm "was no longer a publisher of poetry"; and Smith, Elder told Clare in the same year that they would publish poetry only at the author's risk. As Benjamin Disraeli said in *Vivian Grey* (1826–27), "the reign of Poesy is over, at least for half a century."[34]

The collapse of the market for new books of poetry was partly a result of the growing popularity of lavishly illustrated annuals, the magazines marketed primarily to young middle-class women beginning in the 1820s. These annuals, which also published poetry, included some titles that suggested their editors' aspiration to cultivate the "serious" reader—the *Literary Souvenir* sold six thousand copies in 1825—and others that placed the compilations in the tradition of Vicesimus Knox's anthologies of extracts; the *Forget Me Not* and *The Keepsake* belong to this category.[35] While the annuals undoubtedly undermined publishers' willingness to invest in new books of poetry, competition also came from another genre, whose numbers and status were on the rise in the 1820s. This genre was the novel, which, as we have already seen, had been appearing in increasing numbers ever since the early 1770s. The increase in the sheer number of new novels also put pressure on reviewers' efforts to establish their right to define *Literary value*. As early as the 1790s, some reviewers had begun to complain that the flood of new fiction made discrimination impossible, for critics and readers alike.[36] Others openly longed for a single group of readers to take over the labor of reviewing, which became more onerous as novel publication increased. Thus, in 1798, J. P. Malcolm wrote: "It would be well if some worthy persons were to engage in a review of all the Novels of the year in a monthly publication, pointing out such as were of an improper tendency with candour, and recommending those of merit. From such a work parents and guardians might select profit and entertainment for their pupils, and prevent their taste from being vitiated by scenes of depravity and wickedness too often to be found pourtrayed by the hand of real Genius."[37]

When in 1813 Walter Scott turned from writing poetry to writing novels, his reputation for producing high-quality work, as well as his unrivaled popularity, upended many of the commonplaces of the Literary world. On the one hand, no one was willing to dismiss anything Scott wrote (or was rumored to have written) as "wicked" or "depraved," and, largely as a consequence, reviewers and publishers began to reassess the status of the novel as a genre. On the other hand, no one could deny the profits his works generated, and this alone challenged the apparent incommensurability of popularity and merit.[38] Almost single-handedly, by his example and through the reviews he wrote of other novelists (including Jane Austen), Scott helped the nineteenth-century novel begin its slow ascent in the hierarchy of Literary genres; he laid the groundwork, that is, for the eventual consensus that, while some novels were merely entertaining (or worse) instances of imaginative writing, others were genuine Literature. While the novel did not displace poetry at the top of this hierarchy until late in the twentieth century, long after Literary studies had entered the university, the genre received increasingly serious attention from reviewers during the remainder of the nineteenth century—even though, as we will see, the popularity of this genre continued to vex efforts to discriminate absolutely between a model of value that privileged aesthetic ideals and a model that emphasized commercial success.

The respect increasingly accorded the novel as a genre thus posed a challenge to both reviewers' attempts to dictate the criteria by which Literary value could be identified and the model of aesthetic autonomy into which subsequent writers were refining Wordsworth's model of originality.[39] I return to the first of these issues in the next two sections, but, here, I want simply to note a further complication introduced by Scott's novels. When Scott decided to expand the already detailed descriptions of local Scots customs into the elaborate notes and appendices that characterize his Magnus Opus edition, which began to appear in 1829, he inadvertently made it more difficult for writers to identify connotation—as opposed to denotation—as the definitive characteristic of the Literary use of language.

As we will see, the wealth of historical and local details that distinguishes the Magnus Opus from earlier editions of the Waverley novels increased the appeal of this series; and, while it is possible, as St. Clair argues, that the combination of such accurate, quasi-accurate, and patently fictional details blunted Britons' desire for reliable information about "industrialization, urbanization, and population growth which were happening under their own eyes in their own country in their own times," it is also the case that the respect accorded Scott's novels made it difficult simply to dismiss such apparently referential material as non-Literary.[40] Until writers could find a way to include the novel in the hierarchy of Literary works—in a way that made sense of the novel's tendency to provide information, its denotative use of language, and its undeniable market appeal—the Romantic model would remain only one candidate among many in the campaign to define the terms of Literary value.

The contest over who would define the terms of Literary value remained vigorous for most of the nineteenth century. As we have already begun to see, the factors that animated this struggle were numerous, even in the first decades of the century; but the situation grew more complicated at midcentury, when the taxes that had been imposed to limit access to certain publications began to be repealed. These taxes, which had been slowly accumulating since the early eighteenth century, consisted of levies on advertising and paper; in addition, there was a window tax, which, according to Dickens, was even more effective than the stamp duties.[41] As long as these taxes existed, periodicals that contained news of current events remained prohibitively expensive, and, thus, they remained relatively unattractive venues for publishing imaginative writing of any kind. These taxes began to be repealed in the late 1830s, when it became apparent that they were not having the desired effect of restricting the number of working-class readers. In 1836, the newspaper tax was reduced to one penny, and it was abolished in 1855. The tax on paper was also reduced, then abolished in 1861.[42]

The result of these repeals was immediately felt by nearly everyone struggling to dictate the terms of Literary value. Reviewers still wanted to retain the role Jeffrey had claimed, but the rapid growth in the number and diversity of readers made it increasingly difficult for reviewers to claim to speak for a single public. Claiming to represent the public was also hard because the taste of many readers, as measured by what they read, was, frankly, beneath the level many self-respecting reviewers were willing to embrace. In 1858, writing anonymously in *Blackwood's Magazine*, Margaret Oliphant bemoaned the taste of contemporary readers as she surveyed with some bewilderment the "undiscriminated multitudes" of popular serial publications.[43] As beset journalists were eager to point out, moreover, the conventions the market had imposed on reviewing discouraged them from exercising careful judgment (even when they wanted to): editors could interfere with what a reviewer wrote, they were required to write with unseemly speed, and the number of titles they were expected to review in a single article had become unmanageable. Describing the variety and frequency of editorial interference, Oliphant noted that all magazine editors routinely rewrote articles; most were even willing to interpolate entire passages, "often to the confusion of the unfortunate writer." "[This practice] continued to be the habit of the *Edinburgh Review* down to very recent days," she wrote in the mid-1890s, "when an unhappy author might be made to say things quite foreign to his own opinion, even strictures upon his friends, without any power of protest."[44] At the end of the nineteenth century, even though reviewing had been improved in the ways I describe in a moment, Walter Besant could still complain about the pressure under which reviewers had to write. "I cannot conceive any kind of work more demoralising to a writer than that of reviewing a dozen novels every week in, say, two columns," he wrote. "The inevitable result is that . . . the reviewer, after a short course of this kind of work, loses the power of judgment; he scamps the reading so persistently that he becomes unable to read; he makes an effort to get at something like the story, which he proceeds to tell baldly and badly; appreciation is impossible where there had been no real reading: he cannot praise because praise is a definite thing which, unless it is general and meaningless, must be based on actual reading; but he can depreciate."[45]

Despite the uneven taste of the public, and in the context of the dismal state of reviewing, many imaginative writers continued to pay lip service to readers' right to define the terms of Literary value.[46] As we will see in the next interchapter, Harriet Martineau cited public need when she promoted her *Illustrations of Political Economy*, but this alternative was also appealing to novelists, whose respectable sales sometimes made readers seem like reliable judges. Thus, Charles Dickens praised "the great phalanx of the people" for having given Literature "at once its highest purpose, its natural range of action, and its best reward."[47] Other popular novelists agreed; Charles Reade, for example, called the public "the one incorruptible judge of authors."[48] Yet asking the public to evaluate Literary production was also problematic. Not only did the increased number and kind of readers make it difficult to interpret (or trust) their preferences, but imaginative writers had little control over the mechanisms by which their works were packaged for and distributed to readers in the first place. After 1842, this situation, which had always been complicated, was dramatically affected by the arrival

of a new participant in the world of British print. This participant was neither a publisher nor a reviewer but an institution uniquely able to accelerate, then capitalize on, the midcentury explosion of print. This participant,
moreover, soon began to vie with writers, reviewers, and readers to adjudicate the terms of Literary value and to dictate the particular form that new
imaginative works—especially novels—would take. This participant was the
great leviathan of the circulating library, epitomized by Mudie's Circulating
Library.

––––––––––

In 1897, after the reign of Mudie's had ended, Margaret Oliphant reflected
on the power that the "very energetic, very brisk and enterprising man,"
Charles Edward Mudie, had exercised over the market for new books. In
her account, Mudie was

> attached to the Dissenting interest, and with a curious understanding of that
> ocean of middle-class and unliterary readers which in its magnitude swamps
> all criticism and carries with flowing sail many an indifferent talent to success.
> Mr. Mudie himself carried a very flowing sail in those days, giving the best
> of advertisements to a book by announcing the number of copies of it he
> had in circulation in his libraries, and doing more, perhaps, than any other
> agency in existence to make a name, or at least to ensure a sale. He began with
> "100 copies of So-and-So at Mudie's Library" . . . until at the time of *Adam
> Bede* he had risen to 1000, thus giving an immediate proof of immense
> circulation and demand equally flattering to the writer and conducive to
> further triumphs.[49]

As we have already seen, circulating libraries had operated in England
since the 1740s, but Mudie's was the first to exercise so much control over
the distribution and format of new books.[50] It did so by two means: Mudie
kept the subscription price low, thus increasing the number of subscribers;
and his libraries placed large orders for each new book, thus guaranteeing
publishers that every suitable work would recoup its publishing costs.[51]
For an annual price of one guinea a year, a reader could borrow as many
books as she wanted, but she could take out only one volume of each work
at a time.[52] With a new work of fiction typically priced between 18s. and
31s., 6d. in the 1840s, and with many readers consuming dozens of books
a year, this fee made borrowing considerably more attractive than purchasing new books.[53] Under this system, the format that was most profitable
to the library and the publishers alike was the multivolume work, and the

genre that was best suited to this format was the novel. Thus, Mudie insisted that publishers accept and produce primarily three-volume novels, for the triple-decker format, which soon became the genre's norm, enabled each library to send a single work to three readers at the same time. Even though this format increased profits, however, Mudie's demand that publishers give discounts for bulk purchases undercut the publishers' share and made them less willing to grant lucrative contracts to authors. Oliphant reports that Blackwood's tried to hold out against "the famous 'deduction on taking a quantity'" but finally gave in when "it became known, to the great indignation of more important publishers, that such a firm as that of Messrs Newby, who published inferior novels by the thousand, were giving their three-volume novels boldly, at half the published price, to the great library which had grown up, like Jonah's gourd, in a moment, and threatened to change the very constitution of affairs for the English author and publisher."[54]

The main way a novelist could combat the tyranny Mudie's was thought to exercise was to appeal directly to the public, and one way to do this was to publish new fiction serially. Serial publication took one of several forms in the nineteenth century.[55] In the first, part-issue publication, Charles Dickens adapted the format of radical and working-class fiction that had begun to appear in the 1830s and 1840s, substituting for the weekly 1d. or 2d. parts nineteen monthly installments, each of which cost 1s. (except the last, double issue, which cost 2s.). This meant that a reader could purchase a novel that would otherwise have cost 31s., 6d. for one pound. While this price still put new fiction beyond the means of many readers, it did spread the cost of a novel over nineteen months. Dickens was particularly successful with part-issue publication; *The Old Curiosity Shop* (1840–41), his most successful venture in this format, was selling 100,000 copies a month by the end of its run.[56] Apart from Dickens, however, and a few others like Martineau, few people were able to turn a profit from part-issue publication, and the format all but disappeared with Dickens's death in 1870.[57]

A second, more common form of serialization was magazine or newspaper publication. This format offered the obvious advantages of propping a long work on the material that surrounded it (or vice versa), and, because the length of the work kept readers purchasing subsequent issues of the magazine, it also favored novels over (shorter) poems. Magazines and newspapers had been limited for the first half of the nineteenth century by the taxes on knowledge, but, when these were repealed, the number and kind of periodicals began to increase, as did the number of novelists who published in periodicals. We can see the results from the example of one prolific novelist: Anthony Trollope initially published twenty-five of the thirty-four full-length novels he composed between 1862 and 1882 in magazines.[58]

The various serial formats available at midcentury did impose constraints on imaginative writers, of course, especially novelists. At the very least, novelists who published serially had to compose for a deadline, and this sometimes created almost insuperable hardships. Even when deadlines did not loom, some novelists complained that serial publication replicated the abuses it was supposed to avoid, by making imaginative labor resemble factory work. With no agents to intercede between writer and publisher or editor and no professional organization to support their work,[59] some authors were engaged in almost constant negotiations over financial terms. And, because many publishing houses controlled both magazines and book publishing, writers were often prevented from shopping their books around or benefiting from market competition. Apart from the most successful authors—like Scott, Martineau, and Dickens—most imaginative writers in these decades faced a constant struggle for financial and imaginative independence.[60]

These infrastructural conditions also kept questions about Literary value suspended for much of the century. With circulating libraries and publishers colluding to keep the price of new fiction high, it remained difficult for imaginative writers to appeal directly to the public for affirmation of their merit. In any event, with an extended reading audience whose taste seemed to have declined, "the public" did not ensure the kind of evaluation that serious writers craved. Because reviewers continued to issue invective more often than praise, they also squandered much of the credibility they might have had. And, with Mudie's declaring, in practice if not explicitly, that a "good" book was published in three volumes and composed with women and young girls in mind, there seemed to be during the first three-quarters of the nineteenth century no reliable *system* for evaluating imaginative works and no consensus about the criteria that should be applied. In fact, until 1894, when the circulating libraries voluntarily agreed to abandon the triple-decker format, neither reviewers nor imaginative writers had much chance of establishing a definition of *value* that could simultaneously ensure respect for individual writers and protect the Literary reputation of Great Britain.

Hierarchies of Reading

Among the many reasons economic writers were more successful in establishing a single model of value than were their counterparts in the realm of Literature was that they never applied evaluative criteria to their own writing *as* writing, as Literary writers did. Economic writers never achieved complete agreement about the *content* of their theories, of course; on the contrary, their disputes with each other about theoretical matters and data were often as acrimonious as were reviewers' disputes with Literary writers. Nevertheless, because economic writing was conceptualized as transparent to its object—that is, as relying on the denotative capacity of language to describe and refer to the actual world without the mediation of style—it was assumed to convey useful *information*, which was also assumed to be more important than the way the information was presented. Arguably, even when mathematical formulae and graphs began to appear in economic works, it was the (presumed) stylistic minimalism of these forms of representation—their ability to present information without distracting mediation—that gave such figures authority, not the fact that they were intrinsically interesting stylistic features.

As we are about to see, imaginative writers' emphasis on the *meanings* their works conveyed, over the *information* economists emphasized, belonged to their insistence that the connotative capacity of language was more powerful than its ability to denote or refer. As the sign of originality, an imaginative writer's *style* was both the articulation of his or her innermost vision and the provocation for endless interpretations—precisely because language so used was not simply referential. Style—in the sense of the exact words in which an idea was formulated—was also the feature English courts identified as the site of a writer's *property*. Once printing made the production of multiple copies of a single work possible, it made no sense to say that a writer had property rights over his or her *books*. What copyright law after copyright law affirmed, instead, was the priority of style, as determined by the originality of particular words, set down in a particular order.

Of course, when considered as intellectual property, economic books and articles were also subject to this definition: a writer of an economic treatise earned money from his or her labor only if the resulting work was demonstrably original, in the sense the law identified. But most economic writers still did not privilege style in the same way or to the same extent that writers of imaginative works did, and many, like McCulloch, did not hesitate to include long passages of already-published material in new works packaged for a different audience. Such borrowing from oneself did not seem to diminish the value of economic writing, for, in general, the originality or style of economic writing—with the possible exception of the quasi-fictional financial journalism that I discussed at the end of chapter 4—was incidental to its ability to provide *economic explanations* or to deliver *information*; the original style of imaginative writing, by contrast, was precisely what writers wanted readers to value. For imaginative writers, style was the *object* of value as well as the vehicle by which definitions *of value* were typically implied; for economic writers, value was what their writing explained, *not* what stylistic originality conveyed *on* their writing.[61]

I begin this section with a discussion of style because privileging the style of writing, as Literary writers did, made *reading* a theoretical and practical problem for them in a way that it was not for their economic peers. Because economic and financial writers privileged information and theory, in other words, they did not concern themselves with *how* their readers read; for them, reading, like writing, seemed to be part of a simple delivery system, one that transmitted information intact and unproblematically. For imaginative writers, by contrast, the *way* a reader read mattered for several reasons. First, if a Literary writer wanted to be appreciated *in a certain way*, as Wordsworth did, he or she needed to dictate the terms in which the work would be read. Wordsworth tried to do this by appending instructive prefaces to his poems, by issuing new editions that altered the order of the poems, and, as with the *Prelude*, by simply withholding his work from publication. Other writers attempted to influence readers by depicting reading in their fiction or poems, as Jane Austen did in *Pride and Prejudice*; by showing Elizabeth Bennett reading and rereading Darcy's letter, Austen tried to promote the attentive consideration she sought for her novels. As this suggests, a second reason that imaginative writers needed to address reading was that, especially early in the century, when publishers produced many books (novels in particular) in formats that did not encourage repeated readings, a writer might want to promote rereading to increase the chances that her work might survive—literally as well as by reputation. One debt we undeniably owe to Mudie's was that the sturdy format the library encouraged dramatically increased the number of novels that survived from the years of its reign; by contrast, almost no copies of the novels that appeared between the 1790s and the mid-1830s now exist because the cheap formats in which they were published meant that they were literally read to pieces.[62]

Imaginative writers also addressed reading because, as writers tried to define the terms of Literary value, they increasingly implied that recognizing it depended on reading *in a certain way*. In fact, as we are about to see, many of the earliest attempts to theorize Literary reading belonged to efforts to improve the quasi-official evaluation of imaginative texts that appeared in the pages of periodicals—to specify the criteria by which respectable reviewers could identify some texts as Literature and others as "trash" so as to distinguish serious reviews from the vicious notices less conscientious reviewers continued to produce. Theorizing reading, in other words, went hand in hand with improving the practice of reviewing, and both constituted important facets of the attempt to distinguish Literary value from the market definition that equated value with popularity.

During the first half of the nineteenth century, relatively few writers explicitly addressed reading in theoretical terms, but even the scattered remarks about reading we do find help us understand how the kind of reviewing associated with Jeffrey became *criticism* in our modern sense; by extension, this helps us see how a particular kind of reading—what I call *Literary reading*—was delimited alongside the delimitation of Literature. The first extended discussions of reading appear in the second half of the nineteenth century in articles that took the form of reviews. As we have just seen, by the middle of the nineteenth century, reviewing had lost much of the prestige its eighteenth-century predecessor had enjoyed. The demise of reviewers' authority, as we have also seen, was partly the result of editors and reviewers having succumbed to the pressures of the competitive market, which privileged the kind of invective that Jeffrey practiced over any attempt to forge common criteria for evaluation. Partly, reviewing lost prestige because of the growth of the circulating library system and the adoption of various serial publishing formats, for both tended to encourage readers to consume imaginative works piecemeal rather than wait for a reviewer's judgment about a completed work. In the late 1850s, even though the social conditions that had accelerated this decline still obtained, reviewers began trying to regain some of the cultural authority they had lost. In 1859, when *Macmillan's Magazine* was founded, British journalists began seriously to debate the merits of anonymous reviewing, the practice that so many imaginative writers criticized. The debate about signature accelerated in the early 1860s, when France passed a *loi de signature*; then, in 1865, the prospectus of the *Fortnightly Review* openly called for signed articles.[63] Although the majority of periodicals continued to prefer anonymity or to mix signed with unsigned articles and reviews, the old rationales by which anonymous publication had been justified were increasingly difficult to defend.[64] While some Literary writers continued to complain about reviewing for the rest of the century, especially when reviews were unsigned, the kind of vicious or careless reviewing so common in the first half of the century began to be supplemented in the 1860s by more thoughtful and critically self-conscious reviews. In that decade, some journalists also began openly reflecting on the function of an expanded version of reviewing, a mode of commentary on matters more general than recently published books, which they frequently called *criticism*. In the wake of explicit attempts to improve the state of reviewing mounted by new periodicals like the *Oxford and Cambridge Magazine* and the *Saturday Review*, writers like Gerald Massey and W. C. Roscoe began to identify some of the features that distinguished good criticism, as well as good Literature, from bad. Matthew Arnold's essay "The Function of Criticism at the Present Time," published in 1864, can be taken as a barometer of this new and more self-consciously rigorous elaboration of criticism as a reputable participant in respectable writing.[65]

Efforts to discriminate among kinds of reading dovetailed with these late-century attempts to improve the quality of British reviewing and, more specifically, to distinguish a more capacious version of criticism from mere reviewing. Such discriminations were not new, of course, for attempts to rank kinds of imaginative writing always implied, although they rarely emphasized, that readers read different works in different ways. As early as the 1780s, Anna Seward had recommended that serious writing required the reader to *re*read,[66] and, in 1825, one "literary idler," who claimed to read "whatever [came] before [him]," distinguished between reading "deeply" and reading "lightly." Apart from saying that the former required him to consult older authors and the latter allowed him to enjoy the work of his contemporaries, however, he did not describe these practices in detail.[67] Nineteenth-century journalists only began to engage the issue of reading seriously after 1858, when, as we are about to see, several prominent novelists discovered in the expanded audience produced by the repeal of the taxes on knowledge a threat to British Literature. After this date, periodical writers addressed reading with increasingly frequency. While they offered some rough discriminations, however—distinguishing between "dipping and skimming" or "devouring without digesting," on the one hand, and "getting to the heart of great books" or simply serious reading, on the other[68]—such efforts remained relatively rudimentary until the late 1880s. Before then, most writers who reflected openly on reading were more interested in identifying subdivisions within the reading public or describing *what* readers should read than in describing *how* one should read a Literary work. Nevertheless, as they began to elevate the role of reviewer to the more culturally consequential role of critic, and as they subjected their own reading practices to scrutiny, journalists gradually made the kind of engaged interpretation that Literary writers like Wordsworth had demanded a subject for elaboration, in both theory and practice.

Journalists' intermittent interest in how readers consume imaginative writing acquired new urgency in 1858 when Wilkie Collins announced his discovery of a hitherto "unknown public" of 3 million, largely working-class readers. These readers, according to Collins, read almost exclusively the 1d. unbound weeklies fostered by the repeal of the stamp taxes, and they read these serials not for information, moral instruction, or aesthetic pleasure but simply for diversion and escape. This discovery provoked consternation even among relatively popular authors, like Collins, for, if the number of readers was really as great as he estimated and the quality of what they read as low, this audience had the potential to destroy the market for serious Literary work, which Collins equated with the nation's cultural heritage. To counteract this possibility, Collins offered an implicit, inchoate distinction between "literary reading" and another kind of consumption, to which he did not give a name. "The Unknown Public is, in a literary sense, hardly beginning, as yet to learn to read," Collins asserted; and, since "the future of English fiction may rest with this Unknown Public," it was imperative that its members "be taught the difference between a good book and a bad."[69]

In the same month that Collins exposed this "unknown public" to the readers of *Household Words*, Margaret Oliphant also reacted with horror to what she called "the byways of literature." Such writing, Oliphant complained, "requires no intellect; nay, we may go farther; . . . there are publications popular in this enlightened nineteenth century which reject the aid of mind more distinctly still—wastes of print, which nothing possessing intellect would venture on—wildernesses of words, where everything resembling sense is lost beyond description or recovery." What seems to have shocked Oliphant most about this backwash of print were the twin facts that such writing completely evaded the discrimination exercised by the periodicals' reviewers and that it so perfectly replicated this system of judgment in its own perverse mode of evaluation:

> In the underground, quite out of sight and ken of the heroes, spreads thick and darkly an undiscriminated multitude—undiscriminated by the critics, by the authorities, by the general vision, but widely visible to individual eyes, to admiring coteries, and multitudinous lower classes, who buy, and read, and praise, and encourage, and, under the veil of their own obscurity, bestow a certain singular low-lying Jack-o'-lantern celebrity, which nobody out of these regions is aware of, and which is the oddest travestie and paraphrase of fame.[70]

The language with which Collins and Oliphant recoiled from the penny journals is reminiscent of the terms in which early-nineteenth-century defenders of Literary originality condemned radical writing. This resemblance reminds us that the mid- and late-century attempts to discriminate among kinds of readers continued the project of social discrimination that was the other face of delimiting Literature.[71] This project of social discrimination was also practiced in the elementary schools where some (but not all) lower-class children were educated in the 1860s. In such schools, English Literary works *were* taught, but the primary purpose of doing so was to "improve" the morals and taste of the students, *not* to encourage in them the kind (or degree) of "self-expression" that elite readers were urged to cultivate outside the classroom.[72] In public schools, which served primarily middle- and upper-class boys, the composition of English-language essays and poems was encouraged, but Greek and Latin literature was held in highest esteem.[73]

Even though differential reading practices were beginning to be encouraged and practiced by midcentury—inside versus outside the classroom, for the majority versus the elite few, and in the vernacular or the ancient languages—Collins and Oliphant still did not see the issue in these terms. Instead, they cast the question as a matter of *what* readers read, not *the way* a text was consumed. Even though Collins noted that working-class readers had "in a *literary* sense" hardly begun to read, that is, he immediately turned from any consideration of what this phrase might mean to the texts these readers chose to read. And, even though Oliphant was reluctantly fascinated by the travesty of social discrimination in which the "multitudinous lower classes" engaged, she was finally more interested in the content these readers consumed than in the nature of their engagement with "the byways of literature."

What we see in the responses of these two writers is an idealistic, writer-centered (and noninstitutional) assumption that the way a reader reads is exclusively a function of the reading matter itself—not a function of the teaching that might occur in a classroom or the emulation a teacher-critic might inspire. This assumption repeated Wordsworth's claim that a writer could "*creat*[e] . . . the taste by which he is to be enjoyed" (*PW*, 3:80), and it implied that a novel—or, as Wordsworth would prefer, a poem—could teach the reader how to read, for, as the reader imaginatively approached the state of mind the writer had experienced while composing, the poem's meaning would simply be transferred intact to the reader. Paradoxically, moreover, and while none of these writers would have denied that style was one barometer of Literary value, this model of transmission repeated the ideal of linguistic transparency that economic writers also endorsed: implicitly, it downplayed connotation in favor of something like a denotative understanding of language, even though, in the case of imaginative writing, it was the vision or experience of the author, and not some quantum of information, to which language referred. As we are about to see, the similarities in these two models of reading—and, by extension, in these two ideas about language—did not survive the nineteenth century, for, even though many imaginative writers continued to insist that reading sought to duplicate the writer's experience, others began to associate what was distinctively Literary in a work with the use to which its language was put and the way this shaped the reader's engagement with the text.

The first writer to adumbrate this position was John Ruskin, the art critic, essayist, and poet (who, not incidentally, had received the Newdigate Prize for poetry from Wordsworth in 1839). In 1864, Ruskin delivered a lecture entitled "Of King's Treasuries" at Rusholme Town Hall in Manchester; later that year, he published the lecture, along with its companion, "Of Queen's Gardens," in a book entitled *Sesame and Lilies*. As a volume often awarded as a student prize, this work enjoyed a wide circulation in the second half of the nineteenth century; its sales are estimated to have reached several hundred thousand copies by the end of the century.[74] Most scholars today remember *Sesame and Lilies* for "Of Queen's Gardens," but, for its first audiences, "Of King's Treasuries" was arguably the more important of the two because of the role Ruskin assigned to reading in a boy's maturation.[75] Like previous treatments of reading, his account belonged to a ranking of books—he distinguished between "books of the hour" and "books of all time"—but, as he elaborated how a reader should approach the former, he began to formulate a more detailed description of what Collins called reading "in a literary sense." Significantly, Ruskin stressed the "meaning" of a "book of all time," and he cast this meaning not as self-evident because simply denoted by the author's words but as *difficult* and *evasive*. He did not exactly equate the difficulty of the Literary text with a connotative account of language, but he did equate this difficulty with the value of the Literary text:

> If the author is worth anything, . . . you will not get at his meaning all at once;—nay, . . . at his whole meaning you will not for a long time arrive in any wise. Not that he does not say what he means, and in strong words too; but he cannot say it all; and what is more strange, *will* not, but in a hidden way and in parables, in order that he may be sure you want it. I cannot quite see the reason of this, nor analyse that cruel reticence in the breasts of wise men which makes them always hide their deeper thought. They do not give it you by way of help, but of reward; and will make themselves sure that you deserve it before they allow you to reach it. . . . When you come to a good book, you must ask yourself, "Am I inclined to work as an Australian miner would? Are my

pickaxes and shovels in good order, and am I in good trim myself, my sleeves well up to the elbow, and my breath good, and my temper?" And, keeping the figure a little longer, even at cost of tiresomeness . . . the metal you are in search of being the author's mind or meaning, his words are as the rock which you have to crush and smelt in order to get at it.[76]

We can see here how Ruskin was transforming the problematic of representation so that the deferral inherent in it became an opportunity rather than a problem. In Ruskin's account of reading, it was precisely because words were not referential or transparent, because they did not immediately yield meaning, that the reader had to work. And it was this work—always a virtue for the Victorians[77]—that constituted the unique value the Literary work could provide. The process of interpretation conferred value on the Literary work, then, that exceeded the value accorded a mere commodity or a simply informative text.

In this account of reading, Ruskin almost immediately qualified the equation with which he flirted—the equation between deferral and value. By the end of the essay, in fact, he had returned to the more customary site of Literary value: value was located in the intention of the author, and the reading process was a search for this intention. As Ruskin described this search, it was ultimately a chastening experience, one that fully restored priority to the writer. The "kind of word-by-word examination of your author which is rightly called 'reading,'" he explained, required the reader to

> watch . . . every accent and expression, and put . . . ourselves always in the author's place, annihilating our own personality, and seeking to enter into his, so as to be able assuredly to say, "Thus Milton thought," not "Thus *I* thought, in mis-reading Milton." And by this process you will gradually come to attach less weight to your own "Thus I thought" at other times. You will begin to perceive that what *you* thought was a matter of no serious importance;—that your thoughts on any subject are not perhaps the clearest and wisest that could be arrived at thereupon:—in fact, that unless you are a very singular person, you cannot be said to have any "thoughts" at all; that you have no materials for them, in any serious matters;—no right to "think," but only to try to learn more of the facts.[78]

I return in the last section of this chapter to the crucial distinction with which Ruskin concluded this description—the distinction between "thought" and "facts." Before I do so, however, let me turn to two additional late-century attempts to theorize reading. Both of these were framed explicitly as responses to two events: the discoveries, which I have just described, by Collins and Oliphant of the "unknown public" and a lecture, delivered by Lord Iddesleigh in 1885 about what readers should read.[79] These essays, Edward Dowden's 1886 "The Interpretation of Literature" and Arnold Haultain's 1896 "How to Read," engaged the subject of reading with a depth that is rare in the period. Haultain's essay, which was published in *Blackwood's Edinburgh Magazine*, was one of the few attempts to break down the process he called "an attempt to understand another's mind" into individual steps. Haultain advocated performing "at least three readings" of any serious book; honing one's understanding of a book's argument by writing an essay to refute it; refraining from reading reviews until one had formed an opinion about the book; making marginal comments (in pencil) as one read; keeping a notebook that contained extracts of memorable passages; avoiding skimming; and mentally reviewing the contents of each chapter before going on to the next: "One excellent little plan . . . by which to master and impress upon the mind the matter of the printed page . . . is, when the chapter or the paragraph is finished, to close the book and try, in the simplest possible language, to convey its contents to a mind more ignorant than your own—if possible, to a child's."[80]

A modern reader will recognize in Haultain's method some of the strategies present-day professors teach our undergraduates: read carefully and more than once; avoid reading criticism until you have formulated your own ideas; take notes while you read. Significantly, of course, his method was not designed for classroom use; its publication in *Blackwood's* meant that it would be read by a relatively large number of late-Victorian readers, but its rules were not incorporated into the suggestions for classroom instruction issued by official school inspectors like Arnold. Instead, as extrainstitutional instruction aimed at a minority elite, Haultain's article was designed to help readers cultivate themselves through voluntary, private consumption. Even so, there were limits to the program. Haultain insisted that the "serious" books with which he was concerned ("books to be chewed and digested")[81] did not include what he held to be the highest form of imaginative (and, more narrowly, Literary) writing—poetry. Coming, as it does, in the course of such a detailed presentation of method, this refusal to apply his method to poems suggests that Haultain was reluctant to subject what had already emerged as the delimited category of Literary writing to any kind of reading that could be reduced to rules. We can begin to understand this reticence—and to see the restricted status of the audience he wanted to address—by turning to the slightly earlier treatment of Literary reading, Edward Dowden's 1886 essay "The Interpretation of Literature."

Dowden's essay, which appeared in the *Contemporary Review*, is the first article I have found to promote and theorize "interpretation" as a specifically Literary kind of reading. In it, Dowden, the respected Shakespearean critic and biographer of Shelley, acknowledged that *interpretation* was a controversial term: it was either redundant, because "literature itself [is] an interpretation," or irrelevant, because "a work of literature—a poem, suppose—which does not explain itself is not worth explaining."[82] Dowden answered both these objections with an account that would not have been out of place in one of Wordsworth's prefaces. "Literature is more than an interpretation of external nature and of human life," he explained; "it is a revelation of the widening possibilities of human life, of finer modes of feeling, dawning hopes, new horizons of thought, a broadening faith and unimagined ideals.... It cannot be comprehended all in a moment.... A great writer never fails ultimately to become his own interpreter; only this may need much time—perhaps the lifetime of a generation of men" ("Interpretation," 702, 703).[83]

Having established that interpretation was the proper mode of Literary reading, Dowden began to define this practice. Instead of offering a list of rules for reading, as Haultain did, he presented a sequence of increasingly elaborate and complex tropes that, by the end of the essay, make interpretation approach, without quite becoming, a homoerotic version of the sadomasochistic engagement that Ruskin described. In using tropes to explain how Literary writing works, of course, Dowden was implying—without directly stating—that the ability of (Literary) language to suggest or connote multiple meanings was one of Literature's distinctive features. The (homo)erotic overtones of the particular tropes he chose also suggest that the readers he most wanted to engage consisted primarily of elite, male graduates of public schools and universities:

> If some fine interpreter of literature would but explain to us how he lays hand on and overmasters the secret of his author, we should feel like boys receiving their lessons in woodcraft from an old hunter—and we are all hunters, skilful or skilless, in literature—hunters for our spiritual good or for our pleasure. How to stalk our stag of ten; how to get round to the windward of him; how to creep within range; how to bring him down while he glances forth with startled eye...; yes, and how to dismember him and cart him home. ("Interpretation," 702)

As Dowden's argument unfolds, the trope of hunting gives way to another image, one that both gives interpretation a different cast and makes it clear that it is *not* a search for information. This trope, the metaphor of swimming, carries over from the first simile the idea of sport and introduces the eroticism that pervades Dowden's concluding image:[84] "There are many great works of literature and art from which we learn little or nothing, at least consciously or in set term and phrase; but we go to them as a swimmer goes to the sea. We enter bodily, and breast the waves, and laugh and are glad, and come forth renewed and saturated with the breeze and the brine, a sharer in the free and boundless vitality of our lover, the sea" ("Interpretation," 710). This last phrase is elaborated in Dowden's climactic image, which describes the two phases or "movements of mind" that constitute interpretation:

> In the first stage of approach . . . the critic, while all the time full of athletic force, must cunningly assume a passive aspect, and to do so he must put restraint upon his own vivacity and play of mind. His aim is now to obtain a faithful impression of the object. His second movement of mind will be one of recoil and resilience, whereby having received a pure impression of the object, he tries to surprise and lay hold of the power which has produced that impression. (711)

Like so many nineteenth-century references to reading, this eroticized version repeated the Wordsworthian turn, for Dowden conceptualized Literary *reading* as an encounter with the writer's mind. Unlike some earlier formulations of this union, however, in its insistence that the writer's meaning is a *secret* his formulation stresses both the elusive quality of the meaning this mind contained and the allusive nature of the language in which it is conveyed. "Every great writer has a secret of his own," he explained at the beginning of the essay; and it was this "secret" that incited the "endless" pursuit of "fascinating" writing ("Interpretation," 701, 702). Thus, the pursuit of meaning yielded pleasure, in Dowden's account, but it did so not by allowing immediate access to the writer's meaning but by capitalizing on the impossibility of making (Literary) language mean only one thing. To use the terms I have been using in this book, Dowden was transforming the problematic of representation, by which a sign is always separated from its referent, into the site of Literary value. In so doing, he was providing a quasi-theoretical account of a process an earlier writer had called "self-culture":[85]

> Self-culture aims at the improvement of all the higher powers of our nature. Just so far, then, as reading contributes to self-culture, it contributes to

improve, and elevate, and refine our whole nature. By holding intercourse with the great minds of the world as they still live in their works, we can become like them. . . . Our moral feelings can become assimilated to theirs by inhaling their spirit.[86]

It was at least partly to preserve the distinction between this kind of "intercourse," which these writers considered unique to (nonclassroom) encounters with Literary writing, and the process by which one simply took information from lesser genres, like economic writing, that Victorians resisted providing step-by-step methods for reading Literary writing.

Dowden did offer the reader a substitute for the generalized account of reading he disdained: the image of the "organic whole," which was the prize engaged interpretation could yield: "When, after a period of patience and observation, the student of literature has obtained a faithful impression of the object, he casts his self-restraint aside, and leaps or darts forward to discover if possible the law governing the phenomena which he has observed. They are not isolated phenomena; they belong to an organic whole; they are determined by the law of its life" ("Interpretation," 715). This image, as we are about to see, was the figure that Henry James used in 1884 to raise the "art of fiction" to the level of "genuine poetry" and that Thomas Hardy elaborated in 1888 in his effort to make readers notice that novels were Literature too. As we will also see, the trope of organic unity is one of the elements of the late-nineteenth-century conceptualization of Literary writing and reading that survived the twentieth-century professionalization of Literary study. To see why it did so, we need to return once more to early- and midcentury efforts to delimit Literature and to rank kinds of imaginative writing.

Facts, Fictions, and Literary Value

As an adaptation of the Aristotelian criterion of unity, the concept of organic unity was applied to Literary writing early in the nineteenth century by Coleridge, who wanted to describe the relationship between the poet's imaginative act, the poem that embodies this passion, and the power the poem generates.[87] The "organism" to which Coleridge referred thus incorporated the poet, the poem, and the reader; what united these elements into a single whole was "the high spiritual instinct of the human being compelling us to seek unity by harmonious adjustment." This universal desire for "harmonious adjustment," in turn, produced a natural "compact"; Coleridge considered it "a previous and well understood, though tacit, compact between the poet and his reader, that the latter is entitled to expect and the former bound to supply this species and degree of pleasurable excitement."[88] The excitement, which Coleridge held to be the aim of poetry, was produced, by implication, not simply by the poet's exact rendition of what he or she had seen in or projected onto nature but by the reader's "endless" pursuit of that vision in his or her engagement with connotative poetic language. This, of course, is the process that Ruskin and Dowden elaborated.

Coleridge's use of this metaphor not only fused the trinity of poet/poem/reader into a single reified whole; it also severed the connection between the organism and the social context to which it might otherwise be said to refer. As compensation for the resulting isolation, the organic whole was said to form a new, autonomous whole composed of disembodied imaginations participating in a common passion, which was embodied in the poem. This objectification, along with its accompanying isolation from its social and material contexts, laid the groundwork for the critical formalism that was developed in the twentieth century by critics like René Wellek, I. A. Richards, Robert Penn Warren, and Cleanth Brooks. While I do not plan to rehearse this well-known chapter in the development of Literary criticism, it is important to note how Coleridge's description of this triad eventually helped generate an image of Literary writing—now, simply the Literary *text*—that seems wholly self-enclosed—that is, that does not even include the poet's original intention or the reader's reception of the poem. The stages by which Coleridge's triad was stripped of its first and last members were complex, and the resulting formulation was articulated only in the wake of twentieth-century British universities' adoption of Richards's Practical Criticism and the migration of New Critics like Warren and Brooks into American universities. Here, it will suffice to say that, once the poet/poem/reader triad was objectified and a vocabulary of critical expertise devised by which the reader (now critic) could "see the object as in itself it really is,"[89] it was relatively easy to develop rules for a critical practice suited to the classroom setting. In this institutional setting, and with the teacher-critic as a guide, all students could be encouraged to cultivate a version of the aesthetic and ethical encounter with Literature that had once been the practice of a minority elite. Even though it had moved into the social space of the school, however, this practice was inherently a- (or even anti-) social, for, in construing the Literary object as a purely linguistic organism, it identified the poem's "truths" solely in the language of the poem.[90] Thus, the hidden but "higher" truths that Wordsworth and many of his followers claimed to find in their interactions with nature, then to articulate and pass along to readers through poems, were gradually equated not just with originality and an elevated style but also with a certain use of language, one that derived its power from connotation and from allusions to other Literary writing, not from references to the external world or its delivery of informative facts.

This model of nonreferential Literary language continued to anchor the kind of value associated with poetry for most of the twentieth century, but, as early as the mid-nineteenth century, the increasing prominence of novels challenged efforts to generalize this model to Literature *tout court*. As long as novels were considered inferior to poetry, as they were at the beginning of the century, anyone who wanted to define the terms of Literary value could focus on connotative language, but, as novels were taken more seriously and accorded greater critical respect, reviewers (and novelists) increasingly tried to devise terms that would give this genre full membership in an increasingly delimited version of Literature.[91] Because Literature *was* still being delimited, they most often did so not by trying to specify the relevant features of this genre but by trying to make novels fit the norms that were being elaborated for poems. The contours of this challenge can be seen in James Fitzjames Stephen's 1856 review of *Robinson Crusoe*. This novel, Stephen explained, is valuable because the "story as it were tells itself . . . in a manner almost as natural and complete as if it were a real history of real facts."[92] A Wordsworthian poem may have been said to provide a valuable contribution to self-culture, in other words, because its allusive, connotative language engaged the reader in an endless pursuit of truth within a self-contained, linguistic universe, but a novel was considered valuable for reasons that harkened back to the fact/fiction continuum: its value was held to derive from its apparent artlessness and its fidelity to "facts," its ability, in other words, to use language in a referential manner to invoke the world outside its pages.

By the 1880s, as we will see in a moment, novelists themselves—writing as critics—found a way to square the circle of Literary value so that it would accommodate novels. To see why this was so important, however, we first need to understand why "facts" were simultaneously so critical and so problematic for writers who wanted to elevate the novel in the hierarchy of Literary kinds. We can get a sense of both from the revisions Wordsworth made to the "Preface" to *Lyrical Ballads* when he reissued the text in 1850. In the longest and most significant additions to the original "Preface," Wordsworth refined and elaborated the distinction he had once made between "Poetry" and "Science." He did so by adding four words to the second term of his original opposition. In the following quotation, I highlight Wordsworth's additions by placing them in square brackets and by italicizing the most important:

I here use the word "Poetry" (though against my own judgment) as opposed to the word Prose, and synonymous with metrical composition. But much confusion has been introduced into criticism by this contradistinction of Poetry and Prose, instead of the more philosophical one of Poetry and [Matter of Fact, or] Science. The only strict antithesis to Prose is Metre; nor is this, in truth, a *strict* antithesis, because lines and passages of metre so naturally occur in writing prose, that it would be scarcely possible to avoid them, even were it desirable. (*PW*, 1:135n)

In the body of the revised "Preface," Wordsworth elaborated this clarification. Both "Poetry" and "Matter of Fact, or Science," generate "knowledge," he explained, and both emanate from and produce "pleasure." Whereas science required effort, however, both to conduct scientific experiments and to master scientific laws, poetry was automatic and universal ("habitual," to use Wordsworth's term): "The knowledge both of the Poet and the Man of science is pleasure; but the knowledge of the one cleaves to us as a necessary part of our existence, our natural and unalienable inheritance; the other is a personal and individual acquisition, slow to come to us, and by no means a habitual and direct sympathy connecting us with our fellow-beings. . . . Poetry is the breath and finer spirit of all knowledge; it is the impassioned expression which is in the countenance of all Science" (140–41). Wordsworth clearly wanted to argue that poetry and "Matter of Fact, or Science," were related to each other, for he wanted to remind readers that the importance contemporaries attached to facts and information in non-Literary writing should be extended to poetry. He also wanted to distinguish between these two kinds of knowledge, however, for he wanted readers to understand that poetry was actually superior to "Matter of Fact" because poems promoted the sympathy that linked one human being to another. To make sure that the dichotomy between "Science" and "Poetry" did not privilege the former, he ultimately conflated the two, identifying the latter as the essence of knowledge, the category that contained both: "Poetry is the breath and finer spirit of all knowledge."

The dilemma that Wordsworth grappled with here repeated, at a more abstract level, the challenge that Thomas De Quincey, the poet's ever-eager disciple, had set out two years earlier. In an article entitled "The Poetry of Pope," De Quincey directly addressed the question central to the delimitation of Literary writing: "What is it that we mean by *literature*?"[93] De Quincey's answer involved drawing a central distinction *within* the general category that he denominates *literature* and that I have been referring to as *writing tout court*. This distinction, which was to prove extraordinarily influential for much of the rest of the century, distinguished between "literature of knowledge" and "literature of power":

> There is, first, the literature of *knowledge*; and, secondly, the literature of *power*. The function of the first is—to *teach*; the function of the second is—to *move*; the first is a rudder; the second, an oar or a sail. The first speaks to the *mere* discursive understanding; the second speaks, ultimately, it may happen, to the higher understanding or reason, but always *through* affections of pleasure or sympathy. ("PP," 14)

As Ruskin was to do, De Quincey argued that literature of power (*Literary writing*, to use my term) exploited the gap inherent in the problematic of representation, for it provoked the "exercise and expansion [of the reader's] latent capacity of sympathy with the infinite" (15).

Like Wordsworth, then, De Quincey sought to transform what others considered a continuum of kinds of print into a binary opposition. Even though he did not subsume one into the other, as Wordsworth did, he was forced to explain why this opposition was not self-evident. In a significant note, he explained:

> The reason why the broad distinctions between the two literatures of power and knowledge so little fix the attention lies in the fact that a vast proportion of books,—history, biography, travels, miscellaneous essays, &c.,—lying in a middle zone, confound these distinctions by interblending them. All that we call "amusement" or "entertainment" is a diluted form of the power belonging to passion, and also a mixed form; and, where threads of direct *instruction* intermingle in the texture with these threads of *power*, this absorption of the duality into one representative *nuance* neutralises the separate perception of either. Fused into a *tertium quid*, or neutral state, they disappear to the popular eye as the repelling forces which, in fact, they are. ("PP," 16n)

In all the passages I have quoted, Wordsworth and De Quincey sought both to align Literary writing with the other kinds of print that had so obviously gained authority by midcentury (such as economic writing) and to sever the continuum that might be said to link them; they severed this continuum by converting "literature" into a binary opposition, which, ideally, would elevate Literary writing over all forms of informational writing (as well as inferior kinds of imaginative writing). As De Quincey's note reveals, this theoretical effort was at odds with what others considered self-evident, for printed texts more frequently contained features associated with a variety of genres—and, thus, might be said to be hybrids ("history, biography, travels, miscellaneous essays, &c.")—than took the pure forms (Literary writing, informational writing) that Wordsworth and De Quincey invoked. Indeed, it was because mixed forms still predominated at midcentury that Wordsworth and De Quincey had to insist so adamantly that what looked like variants of each other, hybrids, or simply parts of a continuum were actually "repelling forces" trying to become the poles of a binary opposition. In the lingering power such mixed forms exercised, the campaign of the poet-turned-critic was to deny the existence of the continuum that everyone could see—or, rather, to assert that hybrids constituted departures from the norm, which was a *binary* that distinguished Literary from all other kinds of writing.

As we have seen, novels posed a challenge to such theoretical efforts—just as the binaries between fact and fiction and information and truth challenged writers' efforts to elevate the novel. This was true because the features critics used to distinguish between literature of power and literature of knowledge—the inclusion of "matter[s]of fact," information, and referential language—was what most readers prized in novels. Indeed, early-nineteenth-century novelists' willingness to embrace facts and capitalize on the referential capacity of language had frequently been singled out as the all-important sign that they were shrugging off the genre's old affiliation with romance and the Gothic, which had long compromised the novel's reputation. Thus, a writer for the *British Critic* used Scott's decision to include (supposedly) factual information in *Waverley* to distinguish this novel from rival romances, which he denigrated as "common": "We are unwilling to consider this publication in the light of a common novel, whose fate it is to be devoured with rapidity for the day, and afterwards forgotten for ever, but as a vehicle of curious accurate information."[94] Eager to increase his profits after the bankruptcy of Constable's publishing house (in which he had heavily invested), Scott had capitalized on the value readers accorded information by adding over one hundred pages of historical and explanatory notes to the Magnus Opus edition of *Waverley*. The best measure of the appeal Scott and his new publishers expected such material to have is their decision to expand the size of the edition—from the previous run of one thousand copies to twenty thousand copies.[95] In the 1840s, other novelists also capitalized on the genre's capacity to invoke real-life situations to enhance the appeal of their works. The entire subgenre we call *condition-of-England* novels (Elizabeth Gaskell's *Mary Barton* [1848], Benjamin Disraeli's *Sybil* [1845], Dickens's *Hard Times* [1854]) took information from government Blue Books and newspapers (sometimes verbatim); and some later novels, which did not explicitly advocate social reform, sought to enhance their authority by incorporating the results of painstaking research.[96]

By the middle decades of the century, reviewers began explicitly trying to address the challenge that information-rich novels posed to the Words-worthian definition of *Literary value*. They did so not through an explicit discussion of generic differences, however, but, initially, by attempting to distinguish between two tendencies they saw in contemporary novels. They called one tendency *idealism* and the other *realism*.[97] Idealism was held to use a variety of conventions, including (eventually) fantastic settings and supernatural events, to help readers perceive the higher "truths" that poets conveyed in verse. Realism relied heavily on information and the denota-tive capacity of language to produce another kind of truth, which, as we are about to see, needed to be carefully defined, lest it remind readers of the similarity between novels and writing that *merely* conveyed information. While writers who preferred idealism had no difficulty defending the merits of their approach—since it so closely approached the means and ends of the Wordsworthian ideal—authors who wanted their work to include more information and to refer more explicitly to actual events either tended to present idealism and realism as two related means of producing truth or tried to make realism seem as ethically responsible as idealism claimed self-evidently to be. Thus, David Masson, reviewing Dickens's and Thackeray's novels in 1851, commented that "idealism" and "realism" were "part of a continuous spectrum" and "a matter of artistic choice." Justin McCarthy, writing in 1863, agreed, although he attributed this "choice" to a "matured public opinion": "The novelist now obtains that leave and license by right of matured public opinion which he formerly obtained only by his outlawed social position. . . . He may be . . . a realist or an idealist. . . . He will be esti-mated for what he has done and for his manner of doing it."[98]

The persistence of the kind of hybrids De Quincey described in 1848—"history, biography, travels, miscellaneous essays, &c."—continued to trou-ble attempts to distinguish absolutely between a literature of power and a literature of knowledge, in part at least because this distinction, which De Quincey used to distinguish *between* one kind of writing and another, was increasingly used to *separate* an even more strictly delineated version of Literature from all other kinds of writing, including other variants of imag-inative writing. Critics writing in the wake of De Quincey's distinction, in fact, often tried to police the boundary *between* Literary and non-Literary writing by ordering the kinds *within* Literature; for this campaign, hybrid-ity of any sort seemed to be transgressive, for any mixture *within* a Literary work threatened to blur the all-important boundary necessary to define *Literature*. For these critics, it seemed essential to draw a line between the few works that counted as Literature and all the works that did not—even if some of the latter resembled some of the former in troubling ways. Thus, when Margaret Oliphant surveyed contemporary novels in 1867, she adamantly dismissed the vast majority for fear that calling everything that looked like a novel *Literature* would obliterate the category itself. "The novels which crowd our libraries are, for a great part, not literature at all," she emphatically declared.[99] By the late 1860s, the situation had grown more urgent, in part because of the extraordinary popularity of sensation novels, whose authors seemed indifferent to most of the qualities Wordsworth had associated with "good poetry." To try to draw a firmer line between one kind of novel and another, reviewers fixed their attention on the two categories they had identified in contemporary novels—idealism and realism.

Reviewers exposed the tension between these two tendencies in their attempts to evaluate one writer's self-conscious attempt to craft an aesthetic that elevated the referential capacity of language and its ability to convey information over the qualities Wordsworth and his followers admired. This writer was Charles Reade, a probationary fellow at Oxford who had tried his hand unsuccessfully at drama in the 1840s and 1850s, then turned to novel writing in 1853. Reade wanted to use narrative fiction to make contemporary issues come alive, and, to this end, he drew repeatedly, often word for word, on Blue Books and newspapers. What made his novels so controversial was not primarily that he copied directly from such sources but that he intentionally included information about disturbing situations that both poets and polite readers tended to ignore in order to make everyone experience the outrage he felt; among the topics that upset his audience (and made readers devour his books) were the brutal conditions that obtained in British prisons and the prevailing bias against marital infidelity. Because Reade took so many of his stories from the daily papers, moreover, his novels appealed both to elite readers, who constituted the target audience for serious poetry, and that "unknown public" whose members consumed the publications that explicitly and promiscuously mixed news, scandal, and fiction.

Reade insisted that the value of every Literary work, and of novels in particular, was directly proportional to its use of information and facts. He considered it essential to refer to actual situations and to cite factual information because he wanted to provoke readers to *act*. His endorsement of action was, in essence, an attack on the Wordsworthian idealization of contemplation, as the proper *tranquil*—and wholly mental—response to

Literary art. In his rebuke to one Canadian reviewer's charge that "the chiefs of Fiction did not found fictions on fact, and so told only truths," Reade exploded:

> Now, where does he discover that the chiefs of Fiction did not found their figments upon facts? Where?—why, in that little asylum of idiots, the depths of his inner consciousness! It could be proved in a court of law that Shakespeare founded his fictions on fact, wherever he could get hold of fact. Fact is that writer's idol. It was his misfortune to live in an age when the supplies of fact were miserably meager. Could he be resuscitated, and a copy of the *Toronto Globe* handed to him at the edge of the grave, he would fall on his knees, and thank God for that marvel, a newspaper. . . . As for Scott, he is one mass of facts.[100]

Reade's commitment to information-rich, fact-based fiction was so thorough that he developed an elaborate method for indexing the articles he clipped from newspapers, and he repeatedly challenged reviewers skeptical about his novels' accuracy to inspect these sources at his house in Mayfair.[101]

Even writers who admired Reade's talent were embarrassed by the way he chose and deployed his beloved facts. Margaret Oliphant, for example, who had assigned Reade "one of the highest places in his art" in 1867,[102] was forced to reconsider her judgment two years later when she realized that *Hard Cash* (1863) had violated what she considered a definitive criterion of Literature—respect for the distinction between fact and fiction. Oliphant focused on a character's sudden descent into insanity to highlight what she thought wrong in Reade's work:

> Such a thing might happen in fact; but fiction is bound as fact is not. To tell the truth, everything that is absurd and unlikely may, and does, happen in everyday life; and it is our own habit, when we meet with an incident in romance which is beyond measure improbable, to conclude at once that it is drawn from an actual model. But still we must add that this is not good practice; that fiction is bound by harder laws than fact is, and must consider *vraisemblance* as well as absolute truth.[103]

By the end of her review, Oliphant had found a way to exonerate Reade, whose work she still admired. She did so, however, not by agreeing that novels should incite action by animating facts, but by assimilating Reade's use of facts to "the necessities of art": "Mr. Reade, while taking from the theory of realism all that is best in it, has never been carried away by this common stream. With all his rapidity and sweep of movement, and all his vivid power of observation and detail, he has always preserved the ideal in his mind.... Even had the execution been less worthy, the higher aim is infinitely more accordant with all the canons and all the necessities of art."[104]

Oliphant's comment goes to the heart of the challenge that novels like Reade's posed to a model of Literary value that took Wordsworthian poetry as its norm. If it was the aim of all Literature to preserve an "ideal" according to the "necessities of art," then novels like Reade's, which explicitly referred to facts in order to incite action, fell short. Oliphant managed to salvage Reade's work only because she could momentarily reconcile his realism with the "higher aim" she associated with idealism. Other reviewers were less certain that such reconciliation was possible. Samuel Warren, another reviewer for *Blackwood's*, was skeptical that any novelist who used facts as Reade did could ever approach that coveted quality he called "truth." "Nature is not always to be painted as she really is," Warren declaimed. Is the appeal to fact "a reason why the minds of our sons and daughters should be polluted by what is notoriously the nearest thing to contact with absolute vice—namely, vivid and graphic descriptions of it by writers of undenied ability?"[105]

As this complaint suggests, it was precisely his abilities that made the example Reade set seem so pernicious. Since he was held to possess such talent—and because his novels were undeniably popular with readers—reviewers on both sides of the Atlantic repeatedly took issue with him because the delimited version of Literature they were trying to normalize no longer accommodated the generic mixture and the mixed use of language his novels flaunted. It was one thing for a novelist to gesture toward contemporary events, as Dickens and Trollope did, for, as we will see in the next chapter, the form these gestures took tended to subordinate information about factual matters to an aesthetic rationale—what Oliphant called "the necessities of art." It was something altogether different for a Literary writer to give information and facts center stage and to use language primarily to refer, for, by the 1860s, the hybrids that resulted from mixing fact and fiction and connotative with denotative uses of language seemed both to threaten the boundary between Literary and non-Literary writing and to undermine efforts to elevate the novel within the hierarchy of Literary kinds. In the early 1830s, as we will see in the second interchapter, Harriet Martineau had been able to please reviewers and readers alike with stories that animated information, but, when Charles Reade tried a version of the same thing two decades later, he transgressed boundaries that had begun to be fiercely defended, by reviewers and novelists alike. We can see how fierce this defense had become by 1870 in another of Oliphant's reviews of Reade's works. In the kind of omnibus review that betrays the pressures reviewers faced by that date, Oliphant accused Reade of failing to understand that the very definition of *Literary art* turned on the distinction between fiction and fact—or, as she refines this distinction to raise its stakes, between "truth" and fact:

> Truth is stranger than fiction, says the mustiest of proverbs; and Mr. Reade will probably plead that, as long as he does not go beyond that infallible guide, he cannot do wrong. But yet he does do wrong, and make the hugest blunder—a blunder unworthy of him, and of his unmistakable powers. Fact is no guide at all to art. This is a proposition which the realist will probably resist, but which we are ready to go to the stake for, did stakes exist in this tolerant age. Truth is one thing and fact is another. Truth is that grand general rule of humanity, the harmonious law which runs through everything, which tempers the wind, and varies the circumstances at once of good and evil, and makes it possible for a man to keep steadily along the path of his life, rarely driven to utter desperation by the combinations against him. Fact is the exceptional and contradictory, which breaks rudely into the sweet breadth of use and wont. . . . A man who follows fact in art at the expense of truth, is accordingly taking the lawless instead of the harmonious, the exceptional instead of the natural—a mistake which is fatal to a hundred novices, who attempt to copy where they should reproduce, and who are amazed to find that portraits of actual people, and stories "founded on fact," are not accepted by any audience as true to nature.[106]

If, as Oliphant insisted, the opposition between fiction and fact was based on an immutable, underlying opposition—between truth and (mere) fact—then no novel that conveyed information, as Reade's did, could pursue truth, as Literary writing ought to do. This criterion, of course, was explicitly Wordsworthian: it figured truth as a general "harmonious law" that "runs through everything" but manifests itself as such in no particular fact. Underwriting but transcending particulars, this law conferred comfort, rather than provoking the kind of agitation Reade desired (or the "utter desperation" Oliphant feared). By ensuring that a novel was an autonomous linguistic construct that invoked primarily other Literary texts, and not a tissue of references to actual situations, this law helped inspire the kind of contemplation poems produced, thereby keeping the reader inside the linguistic universe instead of expelling him outside, into the world of action.

By the first decades of the twentieth century, the repudiation of Reade's information-rich fiction was complete. Even authors who had once admired Reade, like William Dean Howells and George Orwell, could no longer see his appeal. When he was a boy, Howells remarked, everyone read Reade's novels, and Howells debated with his friends whether "we ought not to set him above Thackeray and Dickens and George Eliot." Thirty years later, by contrast, when Howells picked up one of Reade's novels, he reported being "amazed by its prevailing vulgarity, by its many aesthetic flaws, and by the sense that something fresh and new was about to be born, but not quite."[107] Writing in 1905, Orwell was equally puzzled by the discrepancy between Reade's aspirations and what by then looked like a dubious achievement. Reade "possessed vast stocks of disconnected information which a lively narrative gift allowed him to cram into books," Orwell declared. "He himself, of course, did not see his work in quite this light. He prided himself on his accuracy and compiled his books largely from newspaper cuttings, but the strange facts which he collected were subsidiary to what he would have regarded as his 'purpose.'" "What is the attraction of Reade?" Orwell mused; "it is the charm of useless knowledge."[108]

It is easy to interpret the critical demotion of Charles Reade's novels—not to mention their almost complete neglect today—as a minor chapter in the formation of the British Literary canon or as a parable about what happens to information when its occasion disappears (it becomes "useless knowledge").[109] But that demotion also helps us see how the metaphor of organic unity was being used to delimit the Literary field and to refine Literary value in the last decades of the nineteenth century. For my purposes, two features of this delimitation and refinement are particularly important. The first involves the way that apologists for the novel continued to recast the genre so that it fit into the evaluative system based on Wordsworthian poems. The second concerns the way that continuing efforts to specify the relationships *among* Literary kinds both depended on and ran afoul of efforts to distinguish *between* Literary writing and writing that was considered valuable *because* informational. This last topic will return us, at last, to the relationship between Literary and economic writing, and I save it for the remaining parts of my book. First, however, I turn to a debate about novels that took place in 1884. This debate enables us to see the complex negotiations by which this genre was finally shaped to fit into the delimited version of Literature that had triumphed by the end of the century.

The initial salvos in the debate about the "art of fiction" were launched in a public lecture, delivered by Walter Besant at the Royal Institution on 25 April 1884. This lecture provoked a written response from Henry James, which appeared in *Longman's Magazine* in September under the same title Besant had used: "The Art of Fiction." Finally, in December, Robert Louis Stevenson, whom James had praised in his essay, published a rejoinder to James's article, also in *Longman's*, entitled "A Humble Remonstrance." While these critics differed on some issues, they agreed about several crucial points. Among these, the most important for the refinement of the terms in which Literary value was understood (outside the classroom setting) was the argument that "fiction" is an "art." Besant (in James's paraphrase) insisted that fiction was one of the *"fine* arts," in fact, and that it deserved "all the honours and emoluments that have hitherto been reserved for the successful profession of music, poetry, painting, architecture." James agreed, stating emphatically: "It is impossible to insist too much on so important a truth."[110] By the time Stevenson chimed in, by more precisely defining the "art of fiction" as "the art of fictitious narrative in prose," he could simply assume that fiction was an art and go on to refine this claim by identifying fiction's art with its stylistic and formal features, not its referential use of language.[111]

For the purposes of my argument, the two most important contributions to this discussion are the essays by James and Stevenson. The first, which became a touchstone in twentieth-century discussions of the novel, made two substantive contributions to previous attempts to elevate the novel's status. On the one hand, James specified the terms in which novels should be evaluated in a manner that aligned them with Wordsworthian poems: "A novel is in its broadest definition a personal impression of life; that, to begin with, constitutes its value, which is greater or less according to the intensity of the impression" ("AF," 199). On the other hand, he imported Coleridge's metaphor of organic unity to explain how a novel could resemble the Wordsworthian poem: "A novel is a living thing, all one and continuous, like every other organism, and in proportion as it lives will it be found, I think, that in each of the parts there is something of each of the other parts" (203).[112] The Wordsworthian (and Coleridgean) strain implicit in both these definitions is clear in the paragraphs that separate the two quotations. Thus, for example, James explained that

> experience [the proper source of novels and poems] is never limited and it is never complete [cf. Wordsworth's "ever more about to be"]; it is an immense

sensibility, a kind of huge spider-web, of the finest silken threads, suspended in the chamber of consciousness and catching every air-borne particle in its tissue. It is the very atmosphere of the mind; and when the mind is imaginative—much more when it happens to be that of a man of genius [cf. Wordsworth's emphasis on genius]—it takes to itself the faintest hints of life, it converts the very pulses of the air into revelations.... The power to guess the unseen from the seen, to trace the implication of things, to judge the whole piece by the pattern, the condition of feeling life, in general, so completely that you are well on your way to knowing any particular corner of it—this cluster of gifts may almost be said to constitute experience. (201–2)

As my interpolations in this passage reveal, Wordsworthian themes appear repeatedly in this essay. What most interests me about these themes is the way that James shaped the novel to fit the paradigm of the Wordsworthian poem. Significantly, he did so by reworking the novel's characteristic relationship to information, reference, and facts. As we have seen, other critics, like Margaret Oliphant, tried to use the distinction between fiction and fact (or "truth" and fact) to secure novels an honorable place within the field of Literature. James, by contrast, simply displaced facts and information by highlighting the connotative capacity of novelistic language, its ability to create *the effect* of reality instead of simply referring to some actual situation. Acknowledging the "importance of exactness—of truth in detail," James gradually moved novelistic language from reference to art by emphasizing representation: "I may therefore venture to say that *the air of* reality (solidity of specification) seems to me to be the supreme virtue of a novel—the merit in which all its other merits . . . depend. If it be not there, they are all as nothing, and if these be there, they owe their effect to the success with which the author has produced the *illusion of life;* . . . it is here, in very truth, that he competes with life; it is here that he competes with his brother the painter, in *his* attempt to render *the look* of things, *the look that conveys their meaning"* ("AF," 202; all emphasis [except on *his*] added). From James's elevation of representation over reference, it is but a short step to identifying artistry and the connotative capacity of language as the criteria by which a novel, like a poem or a painting, should be judged: "It is of execution that we are talking—that being the only point of a novel that is open to contention. . . . We must grant the artist his subject, his idea, what the French call his *donnée;* our criticism is applied only to what he makes of it" (205). With such statements, James essentially obliterated the distinction between fiction and fact—or, more precisely, he rendered the facts that counted their *crafted* versions, the sum total of which enabled a novelist, in his words, to "compete with life" (196).

I return in a moment to the implications James's recasting of the novel had for criticism, but first let me briefly consider Stevenson's revision of James's terms. Stevenson's disagreement with James turned on the last point I quoted above:

> What, then, is the object, what the method, of an art, and what the source of its power? The whole secret is that no art does "compete with life." Man's one method, whether he reasons or creates, is to half-shut his eyes against the dazzle and confusion of reality. The arts, like arithmetic and geometry, turn away their eyes from the gross, coloured and mobile nature at our feet, and regard instead a certain fragmentary abstraction. . . . Literature, above all in its most typical mood, the mood of narrative, similarly flees the direct challenge and pursues instead an independent and creative aim. . . . Our art is occupied, and bound to be occupied, not so much in making stories true as in making them typical; not so much in capturing the lineaments of each fact, as in marshalling all of them towards a common end. . . . Life is monstrous, infinite, illogical, abrupt and poignant; a work of art, in comparison, is neat, finite, self-contained, rational, flowing and emasculate. . . . The novel, which is a work of art, exists, not by its resemblances to life, which are forced and material, as a shoe must still consist of leather, but by its immeasurable difference from life, which is designed and significant, and is both the method and the meaning of the work. ("HR," 216–17)

In Stevenson's account, the fact/fiction distinction has returned, but this time there was no question which was the superior term. According to Stevenson, value was not a function of Literature's factual basis, its informational content, or its ethical "truths." Instead, he considered Literature valuable precisely to the extent that it departed from life and constituted a self-contained, formally abstract world with purely aesthetic features.

Stevenson may have shifted James's emphasis—from a representation whose value depended on its ability to invoke reality to a representation whose value derived from its "difference from life"—but both Stevenson and James elevated the novel as a genre by presenting it as an organic whole, whose parts refer to each other, not to the world outside the text. James specifically used the term "organic whole" ("AF," 207); Stevenson invoked this image when he wrote that, "from all its chapters, from all its pages, from all its sentences, the well-written novel echoes and re-echoes its one creative and controlling thought; to this must every incident and character contribute" ("HR," 217). This metaphor appeared again in 1888, when Thomas Hardy sought to help readers "discriminate the best in fiction." "Briefly," he explained, "a story should be an organism."[113] As all three novelists used it, this image simultaneously captured the genre's ability to simulate *life* (by emphasizing the novel's "organic" nature) and stressed that the genre produced *only simulation* (because the novel is constructed). This image also assigned the reader two roles: recognizing the aesthetic *form* of the novel (what Hardy called its "beauty of shape" ["PR," 68]) and noticing the novel's ability to generate what James called "an air of reality" ("AF," 202).

Because all three of these novelists also wanted to distinguish between the "air of reality" a novel could create and the literal reality beyond its pages, they significantly amended Coleridge's version of the organic whole. Whereas Coleridge had depicted the poem as indissolubly joined to the poet's original passion and the reader's response, James in particular implied that the novel is autonomous ("a novel is a living thing, all one and continuous"). None of these novelists elaborated the idea that the novel might be considered separate from its *creator*, for they were as interested in the process by which a novelist produced art as they were in the "art of fiction" itself, but James did imply that the novel was separate both from the world to which its language might seem to refer and from its reader's moral response. In suggesting that the best Literary techniques were those that make artistry disappear, moreover, James also implied that criticism would be able to achieve its own autonomy—its difference from other kinds of writing—because only an expert critic could identify in apparently artless novels the traces of the "execution" that "generates" truth: "Catching the very note and trick, the strange irregular rhythm of life, that is the attempt whose strenuous force keeps Fiction upon her feet. In proportion as in what she offers us we see life *without* rearrangement do we feel that we are touching the truth; in proportion as we see it *with* rearrangement do we feel that we are being put off with a substitute, a compromise and convention" ("AF," 206).

The twin ideas of textual autonomy and critical expertise, which are the cornerstones of the formalism that came to characterize academic Literary criticism in the late twentieth century, rest on this paradox: invisible (but unmistakable) art produces truth; the reader-critic makes this truth visible, partly by illuminating invisible artistry. Implicit in this paradox is the idealism that Wordsworth and Coleridge described: only imaginative "seeing" can illuminate "deeper" truths. James supplemented this idealism in two ways: he implied that, when practiced by an expert reader, imaginative seeing is partly a function of critical method, *which is directed toward artistry and form*; and he adapted "organic unity" so that it began to isolate the individual text, at least from the (amateur) reader, whose engagement in the fiction now constituted a disqualification for (expert) judgment. "Few nonprofessional readers," Hardy explained, can "enjoy and appreciate" the novel's "artistic sense of form" "without some kind of preliminary direction" ("PR," 70).

Henry James did not elaborate the critical method that subsequent critics would claim made it possible to extract deeper truths from and about textual artistry, but he did lay the groundwork for this method. At the same time, and less happily, writers like James also created the conditions in which the rivalry that had simmered between Literary writers and reviewers for much of the nineteenth century would be reawakened—even though James, like Oliphant, Stevenson, and Hardy, wrote novels, reviews, and criticism as well. This rivalry stemmed from the emphasis Literary writers of all specializations continued to place on originality and their conviction that language could be the sole property of a uniquely creative individual. This proprietary view of language increasingly pitted Literary *critics* against Literary (*creative*) writers, as the former moved into the university system in the mid-twentieth century and the latter found themselves hostage to the belated largess that followed begrudging critical praise and the slow process of canonization. By the 1980s, in the name of restoring power to "interpretive communities" of Literary critics, some academic professionals tried to usurp the authority Wordsworth had wanted so desperately to claim for the poet.[114] One result, as many readers of this book will remember, was a version of "creative criticism" that all but obliterated the Literary writing critics had once claimed to serve.[115] Another was the development of the specialized, professionalized Literary practice to which this effort belonged—a practice limited almost exclusively to graduate programs of Literary studies and increasingly incomprehensible even to readers who have read and learned to love Literature on their own or in their secondary school and undergraduate classrooms. I return at the end of this book to the price professional Literary scholars have paid for this achievement, which seems to me only one possible outcome that could have followed these nineteenth-century efforts to rank kinds of writing and to delineate Literary value.

———

According to Walter Besant, by 1892 it was possible for an imaginative writer to supplement the production of poems or novels with enough periodical work to make a career as an imaginative writer. "The new fashion of journalism," he explained, "depends less upon its staff or regular leader-writers, with whom there is the danger that they may not keep abreast of the day, than upon the special papers invited by the editor, contributed and signed by men who happen to be authorities upon the subject. This opens up a great field. And the number of papers is simply enormous; there seems to be no end to them.... A literary man of the present day may carry on all his literary work—all that he can do—for as many hours of the day as is good for him, together with as much journalistic work as will suffice to render him independent of his publisher. This is an enormous gain."[116] While it was undeniably "an enormous gain" not to be beholden to dogmatic editors, this freedom still did not guarantee that a writer would know how to evaluate the work he or she produced. For the definition of *Literary value* remained ambiguous, even as—or precisely because—opportunities for publishing expanded. Even Besant, who was so optimistic about the future of Literature, realized that the task of defining *Literature* and ranking its numbers remained unfinished. "There are two values of literary works—distinct, separate, not commensurable—they cannot be measured, they cannot be considered together," he explained. "The one is the literary value of a work—its artistic, poetic, dramatic value, its value of accuracy, of construction, of presentation, of novelty, of style, of magnetism. On that value is based the real position of every writer in his own generation, and the estimate of him, should he survive, for generations to come.... The other value [is] the commercial value, which is a distinct thing."[117] In another essay, published the same year, Besant continued:

In any other profession there is a common standard for good work. In literature there is a kind—without doubt the highest kind—which pleases the refinement of five hundred or a thousand who possess the highest culture possible. That is a very rare kind. There are not a dozen living writers of our language who quite satisfy the standards of this small class. But there are lower standards—those which appeal to the better class, the class whose literary taste is not so keen, or so subtle, as that of the first class, yet is sound and wholesome. And there are lower standards and lower still, till we reach the depths of the penny novelette, the journal which is a scrap-book, the halfpenny sheet of ballads. Yet it is all literature, the literature of the nation, the literature of the people, from highest to lowest. At no point on this ladder of printed sheets can one stop and say, "Here literature ends."[118]

Besant's ecumenical dispensation—"it is all literature"—is a far cry from Oliphant's adamant assertion in 1867 that "the novels which crowd our libraries are, for a great part, not literature at all." The difference between the two judgments does not simply reflect a difference in temperament or the mellowing passage of time. Instead, it reminds us that, in a practice that increasingly valued originality, style, and the autonomy of the text and whose members could not agree about who could be trusted to evaluate properly Literary qualities, the exact definition of *Literature*—the features that distinguished it from other kinds of writing—would remain a matter of dispute. This dispute continued, as we are about to see, in part because novelists, practitioners of the most information-rich, referential kind of Literary writing, repeatedly engaged subjects that seemed properly the territory of other writers who did not claim the spoils of Literary writers and who more freely acknowledged the material conditions that enabled all writing to circulate in a credit economy.

Textual Interpretation and Historical Description

I have reached the point in my discussion at which I must pause. I can go no further forward—toward the historical and disciplinary position from which I write—or back—to the conditions that helped create this position—unless I go "into" some Literary texts. Partly, I have to engage these texts because some such immersion in textuality has become the signature methodology of the discipline in which I write, its characteristic—and, thus, its characterizing—disciplinary feature. Partly, I have to do so because, as I will argue in chapter 6, texts like the ones I examine there helped make the kind of formalism that governs the modern version of Literary study *and not some other mode of reading* the preferred method of engagement with Literary texts. Yet I do not want *simply* to offer conventional textual interpretations because, as the preceding chapters make clear, I am interested in the conditions—among them the generic conditions and the disciplinary divisions—that have *made* this method the characteristic feature of Literary studies. Thus, I need to discuss textual interpretation *as* a practice (however inadequately) before I begin to practice (a variant of) it. In this brief interchapter, I discuss textual interpretation alongside another methodology that might help shape a slightly different future for Literary studies. Following Ian Hunter, I call this methodology *historical description.*[1]

In order to get to the differential practices of textual interpretation and historical description, I need to assume a very large argument that I will not make here. This argument, which has been formulated in detail and with great care (and in significantly different terms) by Hunter and Guillory, concerns the way that the nineteenth-century elite practice of reading for aesthetic self-cultivation, which I discussed in chapter 5, was incorporated into the U.S. and British education systems during the first half of the twentieth century. As a result of this incorporation, the Literary text has become the privileged site where the (professional) teacher regularly meets the aspiring student, as part of a transaction that is simultaneously personal (a mode of development or educational "growth") and cultural (part of the moral management or "cultivation" of the nation's "population").[2] Because of the particular form taken by the late-twentieth-century professionalization of university teaching in the humanities, which emulates the research model developed in the natural sciences, the composition and publication of Literary commentary, in the form of "criticism" or some other kind of Literary scholarship, is now a required activity of nearly all professional university teachers. Indeed, despite the continued imperative to teach, one might say that publication has become *the* sign of one's status *as* a professional.[3]

The disciplinary position from which I write and the methodology that characterizes my discipline are outcomes of this twofold social process. Of most interest to me, in this transitional section, is the way that the institutionalization and professionalization of Literary studies have transformed the reading practice that James and Stevenson formulated at the end of the nineteenth century into an even more distinctive kind of "expert" reading that, when published as writing, is immediately recognizable as the product of a "theoretically sophisticated" Literary professional. It is recognizable as such partly because it is so different from the writing of (and for) what is sometimes referred to as the *educated general reader*. This is not the place to rehearse all the variants such professional reading and writing have taken in the last twenty years, for these express disputes within the discipline; nor is my main concern the discrepancy that has opened between professional writing and writing for a general reader. What I want to do here is simply to engage one variant of professional Literary reading/writing—which is sometimes called *New Historicism*, sometimes called *discourse analysis*—in order to explore some of the problems that arise when even expert readers try to use the textual interpretations such theoretically sophisticated practices yield to generate historical narratives. This brief, and admittedly inadequate, detour through the writings of a few contemporary Literary critics will enable me to return to the practice of historical description as a mode of (admittedly again) expert writing that seeks to curtail *interpretation* for the sake of a more elaborate mode of *description*.[4]

Reading Martineau's *Illustrations of Political Economy*: Exemplary Interpretations

I have selected two treatments of Harriet Martineau's *Illustrations of Political Economy* to discuss a historicist mode of textual interpretation for two reasons. Most practically, I do not want to stray too far from the subject of this book, and Martineau's *Illustrations* squarely occupies the generic overlap between economic and Literary writing that has by now been virtually eliminated by the division between economic and Literary studies as university disciplines. The second reason I have chosen treatments of this particular text is that the difference between the way our contemporaries interpret Martineau's work and the way her contemporaries responded to it is so striking. One of the things this difference dramatizes, of course, is the effect of changing assumptions about how certain kinds of readers *should* treat a text, particularly one that is either *both* economic *and* Literary or that fits comfortably into neither of these categories. That such assumptions *have* changed, along with the situation in which such texts are typically read, is one of the reasons why the products of *our* assumptions about (professional) reading have only limited value for the histories many Literary scholars now want to write.

Harriet Martineau's *Illustrations* was first issued in 1832–34, in twenty-five numbers printed and distributed by the London publisher Charles Fox. I will return in a moment to the history of the series' composition, publication, and nineteenth-century reception. For now, it is sufficient to note, as the work's most recent editor has done, that the *Illustrations* began to attract renewed attention, in the wake of the publication in 1960 of R. K. Webb's *Harriet Martineau: A Radical Victorian.*[5] Two of the most interesting modern analyses of the *Illustrations*, Catherine Gallagher's discussion in *The Industrial Reformation of English Fiction* and Claudia Klaver's chapter in *A/Moral Economics*, exemplify the practice developed by expert Literary readers in the last decades of the twentieth century in order to generate historical narratives from highly professionalized textual interpretations. This practice typically begins with the concept we also saw in Guillory's account of aesthetic value: discourse.[6] Thus, Gallagher explains that her subject is "the discourse over industrialism" sometimes known as the "Condition of England Debate" (*IREF*, xi), and Klaver says that hers is a "history of the uneven development of economic discourse in nineteenth-century England" (*A/M*, xi).

Emphasizing discourse enables these critics to make two important theoretical and methodological moves: modeling the relationship between a particular text (or group of texts) and other cultural artifacts and events, textual or otherwise, and escaping the evaluative constraints (i.e., the canon) imposed on Literary studies by the category of aesthetic value.[7] In so doing, the concept of discourse seems to distance these scholars' work from the formalism with which I associated Literary reading in chapter 5. As we will see, however, this is not quite the case, and the kind of formalism that persists carries with it some of the assumptions nineteenth-century theorists like Wordsworth and James associated with aesthetic value.

Traces of their formalist assumptions surface when Gallagher and Klaver focus on what each critic identifies as a "formal problem" in Martineau's text. Gallagher finds this "problem" in the lack of fit between two sets of narrative features, and she attributes it to contradictions that lie outside the text: "The formal discrepancy between content and tone, plot and narration, originates in the contradiction that runs through the author's model of causality, her combination of religious and 'scientific' elements" (*IREF*, 54). For Klaver, the "contradictions that open up within Martineau's novellas" also originate in a tension that is extratextual in nature; for her, this tension is located not in Martineau's *ideas*, as it is for Gallagher, but in the misalignment of form and content: textual contradictions "reveal the power of literary and other discursive forms to shape and deform the supposedly static content that they 'express'" (*A/M*, 59).

Gallagher and Klaver both consider the "formal discrepanc[ies]" and "contradictions" they find in Martineau's text important components of its relationship with the "discourse" in which it participates. Neither critic, that is, judges Martineau's text to be inferior *because* it is "plagued by internal contradictions" (*A/M*, 58). Even though Gallagher concludes that Martineau "left the writers of subsequent industrial fiction an ambiguous legacy" (*IREF*, 61), the source of this ambiguity—the tensions among the ideas Martineau embraced—produces *for the reader* an insight that was apparently only partially available to the author. Gallagher is discussing *A Manchester Strike*, one of the tales contained in *Illustrations*:

> The only hint of the author's awareness of any discrepancy between the story's implications and her providential beliefs is contained in the tale's very last paragraph. This is one of the rare places where the narrator expresses something other than bland acceptance. Seemingly exasperated by the short-sightedness of most workers and masters, she asks, "When will masters and men work cheerfully together for their common good, respect instead of proscribing [blacklisting] each other, and be equally proud to have such men as Wentworth and William Allen of their fellowship?" Both the tone and the content of the question are jarring, for until this very last moment Martineau's narrative methods have implied that the story could not have turned out differently.... The sudden introduction ... of an impatient protest against Allen's fate and of an exasperated appeal to a future state of "cheerful" harmony are both unexpected. They seem to express the author's bafflement at her inability to connect her sanguine assumptions about the marketplace with any-

thing that actually happens in the story, and they jar the reader into a full reali-zation of the discrepancy between the tale's content and its tone. (*IREF*, 60–61)

For Klaver, the reader is shown an even more revealing shortcoming of "economic discourse" by Martineau's "less than adequate" explanation of economic theory. Klaver is discussing *Berkeley the Banker*, another of the *Illustrations'* tales:

> *Berkeley the Banker* unintentionally makes visible an important theoretical slip-page or failure within scientific political economy. This failure, the inability of mathematical certainty to account for and quantify the irrational, "human" elements of trust and desire at the center of the capitalist system of money or "circulating credit," weakens the authority of the Ricardian economic model as an explanatory and prescriptive social and economic tool.... The early-nineteenth-century narrative forms that Martineau utilized in *Illustra-tions* were apparently able to embody certain kinds of "truth" that escaped the scientific calculations of Ricardian economics. In other words, through her fictional narratives, certain important cultural values were effectively rep-resented as naturally or self-evidently true in ways that had the capacity to strengthen the scientific authority of classical economic theory. The central irony of Martineau's popularizing project was that the very conventions that she so effectively mobilized to "humanize" political economy also contained the affective, moral, and even rational logics that could undermine the truth claims of the science. (*A/M*, 73, 77)

In other words, for both these critics, the text's lack of formal unity, in and of itself, registers *for the reader* some important insight about the "discourse" in which the text participates, even though that insight was not fully grasped by Martineau herself.

I want to make two points about these analyses. The first is that, despite what seems to be a departure from Literary formalism, both Gallagher and Klaver posit the formalists' ideal of organic unity as a norm in relation to which they interpret and evaluate Martineau's tales. Without such a norm, it would be impossible to identify *as departures* the "series of discrepancies between the tale's content, its form, and its emotional tone" (*IREF*, 54) that Gallagher finds or the "internal contradictions" that Klaver names (*A/M*, 58). While both critics begin with "discrepancies" and "contradictions" *with-in* the text, of course, both soon move to other sets of tensions, which they locate either in Martineau's ideas about economic principles (Gallagher) or between Martineau's narrative conventions and the ideas promoted by economic theorists (Klaver). In both cases, this apparent move away from a text, which a nineteenth-century critic like James would have evaluated in terms of its own autonomous organic unity, simply relocates the normative unity elsewhere—in the "discourse" with which these critics are primarily concerned. The failure of Martineau's text to fit perfectly into what should be the organic unity of "discourse" leads to these critics' judgments about the text's relative "success": Gallagher's reference to Martineau's "ambiguous legacy" suggests that she failed to leave subsequent authors a model on which they could build, and Klaver's judgment that Martineau's stories provide a "less than adequate" account of Ricardo's theories finds her achievement wanting. Significantly, however, the lack of fit between Martineau's text and its containing "discourse" also leads both critics to a quite different assessment, for both ultimately credit Martineau with enabling the reader to see tensions *in the discourse* that Martineau could not see.

This leads to my second point. For each critic presents the interpretation she generates, with the help of Foucault, Marx, and discourse analysis, as an emanation from or a product of Martineau's own text. By implication, that is, Gallagher and Klaver present their interpretations as *dictated by form* and, thus, by implication again, as identical to the interpretation any reader—even a nineteenth-century reader—would produce if she read Martineau's text. Gallagher does not elaborate this point; she simply conflates all readers by using the personal pronoun *we* and the article *the* (*IREF*, 58, 61 ["the reader"]).[8] Klaver is considerably more engaged by this theoretical issue. At the end of her discussion, she acknowledges that "it is impossible to gauge to what extent Martineau's readers registered the unintentional effects of her economic narratives" (*A/M*, 77), but, in the course of her analysis, she segues from descriptions that simply imply agreement among all readers ("the reader's sympathies are even further confused" [63]) to accounts that attribute so much agency to the text that every reader seems compelled to comply with its dictates: "the reader is forced," "the reader . . . cannot help" (67, 70).

We have seen this assumption about the relationship between a text's formal features and its reception before, of course. It is a variant of Wordsworth's claim that a writer can "create the taste" by which his works will be adequately appreciated and Haultain's description of the way an elite reader is drawn into engagement with the Literary text. In a moment, I argue that this assumption about the ability of form to dictate response belongs to the *ahistorical* bias of all variants of Literary formalism and, thus, to the incompatibility between this theoretical position and the desire to construct a historical narrative. First, however, let me quote a slightly more elaborate justification for a modern reader's extrapolation of a universal subject position from her own experience of a text. I take this passage from my own *Uneven Developments* not because mine is the best explanation of this tendency but because it exposes my own (past) investment in the assumption I am now calling into question.

> The reading I offer here of Dickens's *David Copperfield* is not an interpretation that a nineteenth-century audience would have been likely to devise—not least because the definitions and functions of "interpretation" have undergone such changes in the last one hundred years. Instead of attempting to reproduce whatever *meaning* the text might have held for its first readers, I am describing a set of structural patterns and transformations that are written into the novel as the very conditions of its intelligibility. I am arguing, in other words, that in so far as these substitutions and transformations constitute the terms of the novel's narrative development, they define the operations by which the text produces meanings; in so far as these operations organize the reading of *David Copperfield*, they construct the reader as a particular kind of subject—a psychologized, classed, developmental individual—even if the reader is not conscious of this pattern and even if the reader interprets the meaning of the novel differently from other readers or not at all.[9]

I have a particularly clear memory of writing these words and a very clear sense of why it seemed important to do so. Having spent weeks devising what I considered a theoretically sophisticated account of the narrative dynamics of Dickens's novel, I suddenly realized that I could not claim that my interpretation had any validity at all *as historical evidence* or as evidence for a historical argument. In trying to make an analysis informed by modern theoretical paradigms (all of which make one or more formalist assumptions) generate a narrative about a historical situation, I was unable to ignore the discrepancy between my formalist method and my historicist ambition. I ended up with an explanation that served my immediate purpose, but, because it simply substituted a theoretical model that privileged the conditions that made my own reading possible for a more detailed history of reading and (Literary critical) writing, my explanation could not really resolve the tension that persisted between formalism and historicism.

Historical Description

So, where does this leave those of us who want both to engage Literary writing and to write Literary (or other kinds of) history? Should modern

Literary critics simply abandon formalism altogether, stop producing textual interpretations, and adopt some other method? Some of my colleagues have taken this route (or advocated it): Franco Moretti, for example, has begun to substitute what he calls *distant reading* for the close reading associated with New Criticism and other modes of formalism; and Clifford Siskin has asked readers to "zoom out" to a vantage point sufficiently far from the individual text that large cultural patterns become visible.[10] While I see what motivates such projects, I cannot endorse them. Partly, my reluctance to do so is a matter of disciplinary definition. As I have already said, textual interpretation is the characteristic methodology of the discipline of academic Literary study; simply to abandon it for a more "scientific" or "quantitative" method is to deny the disciplinary specification that gives contemporary Literary study its institutional identity, its *raison d'être* in relation to—and as differentiated from—other academic disciplines. However textual interpretation may change or be combined with other analytic methods, it will remain a characteristic feature of this academic discipline *until the nature of the discipline*, and, hence, its *relation to* other disciplines, changes. Even if I cannot adopt the radical alternatives Moretti and Siskin propose, however, I can no longer simply assume that textual interpretation is *a mode of historical analysis* or can generate *historical evidence*. To make this assumption—to use textual analysis as a tool for writing history—Literary critics have to project from their own reading practice the universal subject position I have just described, and they have to ignore the historical specificity of the assumptions about organic unity and aesthetic value that persist in most textual interpretations. Even Literary critics as skillful as Gallagher and Klaver reproduce these problems, and, as a result, I am left feeling that their interpretations are so clever that they obscure the disjunction between discourse analysis and historical narratives.

To find an alternative to New Historicism and discourse analysis more generally—an alternative that might achieve historical specificity without sacrificing an intensive engagement with texts—I want to adapt Ian Hunter's notion of historical description. His account of this method is sketchy, and it remains unclear (at least to me) how a description of the "compositional technologies and historical deployments" of texts will "dissolve criticism's twin projects for 'man's' cultural completion . . . [and] so remove knowledge of literature from the domain of sensibility formation altogether."[11] While I do not fully understand what Hunter has in mind, what I take from his work is a sense of the role that *description* can play in helping us combine engagement with texts and the desire to write various histories. This description will need to focus not on the modern reader's experience of the text or on the meanings that contemporary theoretical paradigms enable us to attribute to it. Instead, it will need to focus on "compositional technologies," the material and generic conditions that made composition of particular texts possible, and on "historical deployments," the function to which texts were put by past readers. Such descriptions will not enable modern readers to recover the *meanings* a text once had, in other words, but they can help identify the *functions* a text once served. Admittedly, in substituting *function* for Hunter's "historical deployments," I am slightly altering his emphasis, for "deployments" seems closer to *use* than to *function*. I make this substitution because, like Guillory, I want to distinguish between *use* and *function*. The latter, in Guillory's account, is "the finite range of uses prescribed by the social classification of an object."[12] As a product of *classification*, function is, thus, a product of *genre, discipline,* and *institutional position.*[13] It is for this reason—to help recover the functions that particular texts served—that I have focused on these classificatory terms throughout this book. Descriptions of the ways in which various writers tried to differentiate among kinds of writing—so that they could rank them, acquire social authority for some but not others, produce disciplinary norms, and claim for themselves institutional positions (and professional status)—constitute an alternative to textual interpretation that does not simply replace reading with counting.

In chapter 6, I provide more elaborate examples of the kinds of engagement with Literary texts this emphasis on historical description encourages. First, however, I want to return to Martineau's *Illustrations of Political Economy.* If we examine this text in terms of classification and genre instead of discourse, it is possible to understand the function it served in terms that do not retain the assumptions associated with the implicit (and implicitly aesthetic) model of organic unity. Instead of imposing *our* theoretical categories on Martineau's text, this approach is actually consistent with the way Martineau and at least some of her contemporaries understood her accomplishment, for, to Martineau and many of her first reviewers, what was distinctive about the project was its generic mix. According to the history she recounted in her *Autobiography,* Martineau recognized that the "principles" of political economy could best be conveyed to readers by first embedding them in narrative "illustrations," then setting them apart from the fictional narrative in a concluding section that took the form of a list of declarative sentences.[14] Thus, for example, one of the principles that concludes *Berkeley the Banker* states simply: "The adoption of paper money saves times by making the largest sums as easily payable as the smallest." In the body of the text, Martineau conveyed a version of the same point, this time in a piece of dialogue that reveals something of its speaker's character in addition to the theoretical point: "'If there were no banks,' observed Mr. Craig, 'what a prodigious waste of time there would be in counting out large sums of money! A draft is written in the tenth part of the time that is required to hunt up the means of paying a hundred pounds in guineas, shillings, and pence, or in such an uncertain supply of notes as we have in a little town like this. And, then, good and bad coin—"[15]

Later in the *Autobiography*, Martineau called the parts of this generic mix "accessories" and "scientific erection" and their combination "exemplification." Her struggle, as she described it, was always to produce an effective relationship between features that belonged to different genres—to make sure that the "accessories," which belonged to imaginative writing, did not overwhelm the "erection," which she associated with the political economic theory that inspired her. It is worth quoting at some length Martineau's own description of her compositional process:

> Having noted my own leading ideas on the topic before me, I took down my books, and read the treatment of that particular subject in each of them, making notes of reference on a separate sheet for each book, and restraining myself from glancing even in thought towards the scene and nature of my story till it should be suggested by my collective didactic materials.... The next process, occupying an evening, when I had one to spare, or the next morning, was making the Summary of Principles which is found at the end of each number. This was the most laborious part of the work, and that which I certainly considered the most valuable. By this time, I perceived in what part of the world, and among what sort of people, the principles of my number appeared to operate the most manifestly. Such a scene I chose, be where it might.
>
> The next process was to embody each leading principle in a character: and the mutual operation of these embodied principles supplied the action of the story. It was necessary to have some accessories,—some out-works to the scientific erection; but I limited these as much as possible; and I believe that in every instance, they really were rendered subordinate.... The third day's toil was the severest. I reduced my materials to chapters, making a copious table of contents for each chapter on a separate sheet, on which I noted down, not only the action of the personages and the features of the scene, but all the political economy which it was their business to convey, whether by exemplification or conversation,—so as to absorb all the materials provided. This was not always completed at one sitting, and it made me sometimes sick with fatigue: but it was usually done in one day. After that, all the rest was easy. I paged my paper; and then the story went off like a letter. I never

could decide whether I most enjoyed writing the descriptions, the narrative, or the argumentative or expository conversations. I liked each best while I was about it. (1:194–95)

Martineau's sense that the generic mixture she called "exemplification" was "the grand principle of the whole scheme" (*Autobiography*, 1:169) was echoed by several of her first reviewers. In his *Eclectic Review* article published the same year Martineau's first numbers appeared, for example, Josiah Conder praised the unknown author for bringing to "abstruse subjects of inquiry, a masculine faculty of abstraction, with a feminine power of illustration." Because these qualities were "rarely united," he continued, Martineau's accomplishment was "extraordinary": "The combination of these qualifications for her difficult task *is* a phenomenon."[16] Writing for *Tait's Edinburgh Magazine* that same year, an anonymous reviewer agreed. This writer found in Martineau's tales "all the value of truth and all the grace of fiction" and applauded her for incorporating "the technical phraseology of the economists" in "narratives" filled with "characters" and "scenery."[17]

As we have already seen, by 1832 the aesthetic ideal had not only been formulated and published (in Wordsworth's *Preface* and Coleridge's *Biographia Literaria*, among other places); it had also attracted considerable attention from reviewers, attention that, by that date, had generally shifted from criticism to admiration. By that date as well, some of the century's most important treatises of political economic theory were in print: Ricardo's *Principles of Political Economy and Taxation*, McCulloch's *Discourse . . . on Political Economy*, his edition of Smith's *Wealth of Nations*, and numerous articles in the *Edinburgh Review*. By 1832, in other words, it would have been obvious to Martineau and her reviewers that her "exemplifications" *were* generic mixes—hybrids, to use the term I have suggested—that self-consciously brought together two different sets of features to overcome the limitations imposed by their separation. Her awareness of the need to close the gap opened by generic differentiation is clear in her defense of studying economic theory: "Enough has been said . . . to prove the *utility* of the study of political economy. Much . . . might also be said of its *beauty*. . . . Notwithstanding all that is said of its dryness and dullness, and its concentration in matter of fact, we see great attractiveness and much elegance in it."[18]

Not every early reviewer was so eager to embrace Martineau's generic hybridity. Indeed, the fact that some reviewers evaluated her text strictly in terms of its adequacy as economic writing, while others applied aesthetic criteria to it, demonstrates the extent to which these kinds had come to seem distinct by the early 1830s. Thus, for example, both George Poulett Scrope and John Stuart Mill reviewed the *Illustrations* as an example of political economic theory—the first harshly and the latter with qualified approval—and Edward Bulwar Lytton treated the tales purely as Literary writing, calling them "philosophical fiction" and "moral fiction."[19] As the decades passed and the two kinds of writing came to seem even more distinct, evaluations of Martineau's work tended to adopt one set of criteria to the exclusion of the other and to judge the *Illustrations* accordingly. In 1884, when Florence Fenwick Miller took up the tales, she found them "inevitably damaged, as works of art, by the fact that they were written to convey definite lessons."[20] In the 1930s, Mary Russell Mitford admitted having read Martineau, but she also remembered performing on them the generic discrimination that had by then come to seem natural: "The only things of hers I ever liked were her political economic stories, which I used to read, skipping the political economy."[21]

Martineau's most recent editor, Deborah Anna Logan, is one of the few contemporary Literary scholars to accord this generic hybridity the importance it deserves. Describing Martineau's accomplishment as "an entirely new genre," Logan argues that the "perfect timeliness" of Martineau's *Illustrations* "accounts both for its immediate success and for its lack of staying power or long-term relevance, the standard traditionally employed to measure literary worth. But the *Illustrations* requires a different sort of measure, as it is not a novel in the modern, generic sense of the term but a pivotal stage in the development of literary, economic, and social history."[22] Logan does not develop this last point at length, for her aim is not to chart the development of modern *disciplines*. Since I am concerned with the nineteenth-century chapter of that history, I want to linger for a moment over what Logan calls the "timeliness" of Martineau's generic mix and show how taking seriously the popularity the *Illustrations* enjoyed among Martineau's contemporaries enables us to understand part of this history.

When Martineau initially pitched the concept that became the *Illustrations* to various London publishers in 1832, she encountered silence, then rejection, then—when Fox reluctantly agreed to print the volumes—demands that she considered humiliating. The *Autobiography* stresses repeatedly and at considerable length the obstacles she faced: publisher after publisher either failed to respond at all or rejected her written overtures, citing as reasons the public's distress over the Reform Bill and the onset of cholera; they objected to her proposed title, even to putting the words *political economy* on the covers of the volumes (1:162–63). When she did not receive responses to her posted inquiries quickly enough, Martineau set off for London, where she took up solitary residence in her uncle's temporarily deserted house. In London, Martineau spent her days "trudging many miles through the clay of the streets, and the fog of the gloomiest December I ever saw" in pursuit of a receptive publisher (165). At night, she furiously scribbled away at the first of her tales. When Fox finally agreed to take the series, he demanded that she publish the *Illustrations* by the old method of subscription, and he required her to secure five hundred subscribers before the first issue appeared. He also insisted that he receive half the profits in addition to the usual bookseller's commissions and privileges; and, most dispiriting of all, he retained the right to cancel the entire series at the end of two numbers if each issue did not sell a thousand copies in a fortnight (167–70). In her own account, Martineau experienced these terms as a blow, but she refused to shrink before the obstacles Fox had put in her way:

> I set out to walk the four miles and a half to the Brewery [her uncle's house]. I could not afford to ride, more or less; but, weary already, I now felt almost too ill to walk at all. On the road, not far from Shoreditch, I became too giddy to stand without support; and I leaned over some dirty palings, pretending to look at a cabbage bed, but saying to myself, as I stood with closed eyes, "My book will do yet." I moved on as soon as I could, apprehending that the passers-by took me to be drunk: but the pavement swam before my eyes so that I was glad enough to get to the Brewery. I tried to eat some dinner; but the vast rooms, the plate and the liveried servant were too touching a contrast to my present condition; and I was glad to go to work, to drown my disappointment in a flow of ideas.... I wrote the Preface to my "Illustrations of Political Economy" that evening; and I hardly think that any one would discover from it that I had that day sunk to the lowest point of discouragement about my scheme.... I finished the Preface just after the Brewery clock had struck two.... I began now, at last, to doubt whether my work would ever see the light. I thought of the multitudes who needed it,—and especially of the poor,—to assist them in managing their own welfare. I thought too of my own conscious power of doing this very thing. Here was the thing wanting to be done, and I wanting to do it.... At last it was necessary to go to bed; and at four o'clock I went, after crying for two hours with my feet on the fender. I cried in bed till six, when I fell asleep; but I was at the breakfast table by half-past eight, and ready for the work of the day. (170–72)

Martineau persisted because she was convinced, in her words, that "the people wanted the book" (*Autobiography*, 1:161). Even though she had no proof that they "wanted" it—and it is not clear whether she always meant that "the people" *needed* these lessons, as the above quotation insists, or whether she sometimes imagined that they also *desired* "exemplifications" of political economic principles—Martineau began the quasi-disciplined, quasi-inspired compositional process whose description I have already quoted. However she may have imagined her readers' "want," they immediately expressed it in their actions. Priced at 18d., the first issue sparked such demand that, within ten days, Fox proposed increasing the edition from fifteen hundred to two thousand copies. So fevered were sales, however, that, before he could post his letter, he had to amend his proposal. In a series of frantic postscripts, he raised the figure—first to two thousand, then, to three thousand, then, to four thousand, and, finally, to five thousand copies (1:178). By 1834, according to one estimate, Fox was selling ten thousand copies of each monthly part, and the whole series is estimated to have reached over 140,000 readers.[23] Nor was Martineau's audience limited to members of "the people." Among the individuals we know to have read the *Illustrations*, we find government officials, poets, radicals, and scholars alike; these included Princess (soon to be Queen) Victoria, Coleridge, Florence Nightingale, Richard Cobden, and Robert Peel, who was already prime minister. Brougham, the lord chancellor, personally ferried Blue Books to Martineau to assist in her composition; Lord Althorp, the chancellor of the Exchequer, asked her to compose a number on tax reform; and Nassau Senior, the political economist and Oxford professor, also visited her.[24]

In light of this unmistakable popularity and the effect that Martineau undeniably had on legislators, what are we to make of the judgments that Gallagher and Klaver levy—that hers was merely an "ambiguous legacy" (Gallagher) or that her accomplishment was "less than adequate" (Klaver)? Certainly, one factor that separates the judgment of Martineau's peers (which was not universally positive) from the judgment of ours is that the former was shaped in and was partly responding to a period of social and economic uncertainty, when the agitation that had preceded passage of the Reform Bill was still fresh in readers' memories, as was the fallout of the bank failures of 1826. In such a context, simple tales that conveyed practical lessons in stories that were imaginatively engaging could seem like diverting solutions to actual problems—whether one read them in an overcrowded tenement, where necessities were scarce, or in the halls of Parliament, where concerns about how to manage the restive population predominated. Writing from the relative security of an academic position, by contrast, and in response to problems quite different from those Martineau's first readers faced, Gallagher and Klaver reflect on her works in relation to different issues—issues that are disciplinary, in the first instance, and only indirectly social (or political). It is not that our contemporaries' (or my past) evaluations are wrong, in other words; it is just that we made our evaluations for reasons that Martineau's first readers did not share, from professional contexts they did not occupy, and in terms that few of them would have recognized.

The function of Martineau's *Illustrations*, in other words, has changed, in part as a consequence of the transformation of the "classificatory discourse" through which this text is now read. This transformation, of course, is a result of the disciplinary division, the institutionalization of academic subjects, and the professionalization of Literary studies to which I have alluded, but what matters is that such transformations change the situation that motivates reading (and writing) along with the classificatory schema specifically positioned readers apply. While a few of Martineau's contemporaries read (and evaluated) the *Illustrations* as Literary writing (through aesthetic categories, generally pertaining to *style*) or as economic theory (in terms of the *ideas* political economists had advanced), for the most part the *Illustrations* were not read through either of the sets of terms that now belong to these categories. Gallagher and Klaver, by contrast, do read the *Illustrations* as Literary writing and through aesthetic categories *even though* their decision to dissolve Literature into "discourse"—or, rather, to treat all of culture *as* a (Literary) text—veils the persistence of these categories. Because the influence of these categories is veiled, and because their own positions as academic professionals can be taken for granted in writing generically marked "scholarly" writing, these writers do not stress the classificatory schema through which they read or the extent to which the aesthetic categories historically associated with the delimitation of Literature continue to inform their analyses.

What historical description cannot deliver should be clear. However this analytic mode is defined, it cannot recover the meanings a text once had, nor can it recover all of the uses to which a text was put by readers in different class, geographic, or gender positions. It cannot torque the interests past readers brought to texts or the significance they attributed to them to make them fit the interests of modern readers, political or otherwise. It cannot provide grounds for evaluating the style or the form or even the content of texts *apart from* making it clear that such grounds always exist, in any act of evaluation. What historical description might be able to deliver is a more useful method for understanding how the categories and classificatory schemes that do inform every evaluative act developed. At the very least, this might enable modern scholars to see that projecting ourselves into the past—or subsuming the past into our present—as we do every time we extrapolate a universal subject from our own reading experience, does not yield or amount to evidence for an argument about the past.

Viewed from the perspective of genre and discipline, the mixture of features that helped make Martineau's *Illustrations* so popular in her own day can now be seen to have helped accelerate the separation of imaginative and economic writing into the two distinct genres that anchor our modern academic disciplines of Literary studies and economics. After all, by making theoretical principles explicit and separable from the abstract, spare style preferred by theorists, Martineau helped make these principles available for appropriation by imaginative writers who wanted to embed them in plots, characters, and themes. As we have seen, by the end of the nineteenth century, even before the institutionalization and professionalization of Literary studies, readers who took up Martineau's work—or the novels of Charles Reade, for that matter—tended not to see a socially effective mixture of generic features but aesthetic failures. To show how other nineteenth-century Literary writers contributed to the aestheticization of the delimited form of imaginative writing we call *Literature*, I now turn to a series of texts that have become canonical in the academic discipline of Literary studies. The treatments I offer of some of these texts may disappoint academic readers who are expecting the kind of richly detailed textual engagements that Gallagher and Klaver have given us; others may be surprised that I insist that writers long associated with realism and historical accuracy were developing generic features that could foreclose, not elaborate, the referential capacity of language. However they are received by readers invested in the current discipline of Literary studies, the textual engagements I offer in chapter 6 all seek to recover the ways that generic and classificatory schema inevitably shape all acts of reading, writing, and evaluation.

CHAPTER SIX

Literary Appropriations

In preceding chapters, I have argued that nineteenth-century Literary writers cultivated an aesthetic model of value as part of a complex attempt to use generic differentiation to enhance their collective social prestige. As we saw in earlier parts of this book, emphasizing the distinction between kinds of writing associated with theory and information, on the one hand, and imaginative writing, on the other, was an important part of economic writers' bid for status, but we also saw that downplaying or denying the imaginative components of their work occurred in the context of other, supportive measures. These included what I have called the *division of labor* among economic writers, by which theoretical work was separated from popularizing efforts, and the compatibility between economic writing and a range of salaried positions (including university teaching, government work, and employment in private companies like the East India House). Because the conditions in which imaginative writers labored were different in significant ways—the publishing industry pitted subsets of authors against each other, and most imaginative writers did not hold salaried positions related to their writing—they were increasingly forced to invoke generic differentiation as the only basis for claiming prestige. As we have seen, differentiation could be used to cut through the ranks of imaginative writers, dividing the Literary genius from the merely opportunistic hack, or it could deny the overlaps between all kinds of imaginative writing—De Quincey's "literature of power"—and other forms that, as "literature of knowledge," did not explicitly aspire to enlarge readers' imaginative capacities. Elaborating an aesthetic model of value was critical to both modes of differentiation, for elevating the ideal of organic unity, along with the "poetic" (nonreferential) use of language, helped readers and writers alike identify genuine "art"; and, even though hybrids like Martineau's *Illustrations* and Reade's novels continued to appear, this ideal made it possible to distinguish between writing that merely delivered information and writing that improved its reader by calling attention to its own integrity and beauty.

It was relatively easy for nineteenth-century poets and visual artists to foreground the aesthetic features of their work, and it should come as no surprise that most of the theoretical formulations of the aesthetic model of value came from Wordsworth, Arnold, Ruskin, and the Pre-Raphaelites. Novelists faced a unique challenge in this campaign for at least three reasons. In the first place, the generic conventions of the novel form—its reliance on prose (and an apparently denotative use of language at that), its inclusion of characters often based on or similar to actual people, and its historical affiliation with nonfiction writing—so closely resembled the conventions of informational writing. Equally problematic was the undeniable fact that the boundary between some of the century's most popular novels—the sensation novels of the 1860s—and the sensational fiction printed in cheap weeklies was so difficult to draw. And, finally, as we saw in chapter 5, the very popularity of the novel form—as registered in sales—made the temptation to cater to the market almost irresistible, even for novelists like George Eliot and Henry James, who always aspired to elevate the genre. The theoretical claims that fiction is an "art," which proliferated in the 1880s, constituted late-century efforts to counter the genre's almost irresistible drift toward nonaesthetic forms, whether of the informational or the merely inferior kind.

In this chapter, I examine a series of nineteenth-century novels in which we can identify traces of writers' campaign to elevate the prestige of Literary writing by cultivating the generic features associated with the aesthetic model of value. Chronologically, this survey initially takes us back to the beginning of the century, for Jane Austen's novels, like Wordsworth's poems, constituted self-conscious attempts to foreground an aesthetic use of language and form that repudiated both the market definition of *value* and the generic conventions other novelists were using to capitalize on what seemed to be limitless market demand. In the second section, I turn from Austen to two other novelists also enshrined in the modern Literary canon—George Eliot and Charles Dickens—to show how midcentury novelists elaborated the gestural aesthetic Austen cultivated into the mode of formalism Literary critics now call *realism*. In my brief discussions of Dickens and Eliot, I focus on the formal conventions they developed to further police the boundaries of the text—that is, to direct the reader's attention to the pages of their novels by curtailing reference. In Dickens's case, these conventions include layering plots to manage the reader's attention, flattening out characters who have real-life referents, and various forms of abbreviation and emphasis; Eliot's preferred conventions emphasize the connotative (or figurative) capacity of language over its denotative (or referential) capacity. In the third section, I offer the most sustained textual engagement in this book, an examination of Anthony Trollope's *The Last Chronicle of Barset*. In this discussion, I focus on the way that Trollope managed both the relationships among the novel's parts and the novel's extratextual relationship to various nonfictional kinds of writing, including the bank check that plays a critical role in the novel. I present Trollope, who is often considered the most referential British novelist, as a formalist because I want to insist that the novel subordinates what looks like a referential use of language, reliance on contemporary events, and cultivation of a psychological mode of characterization to the production of a deliberately artful whole that transforms reference, allusion, and psychology into the kind of aesthetic surface that could help readers cultivate their own, apparently limitless "depths."

Let me make two additional prefatory remarks. The first concerns the terms *realism* and *realistic*, which a modern, nonexpert reader might use to invoke the resemblance between the world depicted in a fiction and its extratextual counterpart. Professional Literary critics, by contrast, typically use these terms as descriptions of the *formal conventions* that generate the *effect* of such a resemblance. As professional Literary critics shift attention from the world to which a novel seems to refer to the textual origins of that effect, as I do in this chapter, we carry to one logical conclusion the process of generic differentiation I have been describing in this book. In so doing, many Literary critics dehistoricize the problematic of representation: such critics treat representation as always and inherently problematic, instead of seeing its appearance *as a problem* as an effect of historically specific situations. Even though professional Literary critics often make this assumption, this does not prevent other readers from reading for the kind of pleasurable self-culture Hunter describes, of course: this mode of reading often entails assuming not that language refers to itself but that novels refer to an actual world and are "about" recognizable people (not characters). My argument in this chapter is that the nineteenth-century novelists whose works are now considered Literary used conventions that can be treated either as parts of aesthetic wholes or as windows onto the world. That they can be so treated suggests that these novelists did not intend that their works be read *only* as self-enclosed aesthetic objects or *only* as edifying entertainment; even Henry James, at the end of the nineteenth century, did not completely renounce his text's engagement with the nontextual world, nor was he completely indifferent to his readers' enjoyment. Nineteenth-century Britain constituted a transitional period—between the eighteenth century, in which the publishers' monopoly and the scarcity of schools limited what could be read, who could read, and the classificatory systems readers applied to print, and the twentieth-century's world of compulsory schooling, where print is systematically taught, albeit in various ways. Because they were transitional in these ways, these decades witnessed the emergence of various kinds of reading practices and various contexts for reading various kinds of work. All the novels I examine in this chapter have become part of the Literary canon because their features are amenable to the kind of analysis now taught in universities. But they were—and remain—popular because they also produce the effect of resemblance, which so many readers enjoy, even if the world they seem to resemble no longer exists outside their pages. This is the final twist of the paradox of generic differentiation: today's general reader, who likes these novels because they are "realistic" (true to life), keeps alive the informational function (they remind us of how things used to be), whose renunciation enabled nineteenth-century writers to elevate the genre; while today's Literary critics, who complete the differentiating agenda I have described in this book (the novels are aesthetic objects, whose ability to convey information is irrelevant), make reading them so difficult that doing so is indistinguishable from other kinds of highly technical work.

My second remark follows from my discussion of historical description. Given what I said in the last interchapter, it seems necessary to note that I do not engage at length with some of the most obvious "compositional technologies and historical deployments" associated with these novels. That is, I do not focus primarily on publishing format or finance, which I surveyed in chapter 5, nor do I deal with nineteenth-century reviews of these novels, as I did to identify the criteria by which contemporaries evaluated the works of Martineau and Reade. Instead, I offer descriptions of the narrative systems and conventions these novels contain—the conventions, that is, that enable them to generate the effect of reality to which I have just alluded. Inevitably, I view these novels through the classificatory terms and analytic procedures associated with my discipline, but I try not simply to repeat the formalism residual in many Literary critical methods. By emphasizing description, function, and classification—the elements of genre—instead of meaning and representation—the elements of interpretation—I try to reflect on the process by which novels *became* aesthetic objects and representation *became* problematic as part of that history of reading and schools that transformed (some) readers into Literary critics and left others simply loving to read.

Jane Austen's Gestural Aesthetic

From politics, it was an easy step to silence.
—*Northanger Abbey*

In order to grasp the importance of *Pride and Prejudice* in *classificatory* and *generic* terms, it is necessary to recover a number of the historical conditions that occasioned the novel. By using the verb *occasion*, I want to call attention to situations or events that were *occasions* for writing and that *encouraged* publication *of a certain kind*, first in the late 1790s, when Austen began *First Impressions*, and then in the early years of the nineteenth century, when she transformed this manuscript into *Pride and Prejudice*. The first of these occasions was set up by the conditions I described in the first interchapter: the dramatic upturn, at the end of the eighteenth century, in the number of new novels published each year. The second was created by the specific kinds of publications that proliferated in the 1790s: these included, on the one hand, the Gothic novels churned out by the Minerva Press and, on the other, the incendiary political writings inspired by revolutionary events in France. Identifying the third occasion admittedly involves more specula-tion on my part, for the unavailability of Austen's working papers makes it impossible to know exactly when or how *First Impressions* was revised. For reasons I will soon explain, I argue that the third occasion that provoked Austen not simply to write and publish but to develop the gestural aesthetic that became the signature of her craft was the passage, in 1797, of the Bank Restriction Act—or, more precisely, the changes this act caused in the epis-temological and social conditions in which the mature Austen lived and wrote.

In the first interchapter, I described the turn-of-the-century acceleration in print production that led Carlyle to christen these decades "the Paper Age." Here, I want simply to spell out some of the consequences this speedup would have had for a young clergyman's daughter, living at some distance from London, in the 1790s. First, the sheer number of new novels that made their way into print in the last two decades of the century must have been encouraging for a would-be author, for the increased possibility that even a first-time writer would find a publisher undeniably inspired more than one young lady to try her hand at print.[1] By any measure, this speedup is impressive. As we have seen, the volume of print began to increase in the late 1770s, to accelerate during the 1780s, and to continue to grow even during the revolutionary 1790s. The decade's most frightening years—1793–95—did see a decrease in the annual number of new novels (forty-five in 1793, fifty-six in 1794, and fifty-seven in 1795 instead of the seventy-four titles published in both 1790 and 1791), but the industry quickly rebounded, issuing ninety-one new novels in 1796, then seventy-nine and seventy-five in each of the next two years.

A second feature of this speedup must have been less encouraging for Jane Austen in particular. In 1798, when English publishers sent seventy-nine new novels into the market, twenty-eight of these were Minerva Press Gothics; and the great bulk of all printed materials consisted of political pamphlets or periodicals.[2] This last point should also remind us how important it was for anyone writing in the 1790s to compose work that would pass under the government's radar. For, even though the treason trials of 1794 did not result in convictions, ensuing events—specifically, the passage of the Treasonable Practices Act and the Seditious Meetings Act in 1795—made publication more dangerous than it had been in a century. As John Barrell has pointed out, these acts, by some interpretations at least, rendered "any speculative expression of republican sentiments . . . high treason."[3]

These two occasions—the increased likelihood that she could get a novel published and the *dissimilarity* between the kind of novel she was composing and the genres that dominated the market—seem to have encouraged Austen both to write and to shape what she wrote to fit a narrow market niche. For an author who wanted to distinguish her novel from the Minerva Press Gothics, that is, and from the potentially seditious publications issuing from the radical press, few models were available among her contemporaries' writing. Reviews of the novels published in 1798—the year Austen's first novel would have appeared if a publisher had accepted it—turn up a few works that were said to touch "the nicest feelings of the heart" or to show "an intimate acquaintance with life,"[4] comments that might be made about *Pride and Prejudice*, but Austen's principal models were the eighteenth-century novels that populated St. Clair's "old canon," along with works by a few of her illustrious female peers, like Frances Burney and Maria Edgeworth. In light of the various uses to which these publications were being put in the 1790s—escape, titillation, political agitation, or nostalgia—the young author tried to devise a writing *style* that would make readers engage her work in a very particular way.

In using style to shape consumption, of course, Austen was doing the same thing that Wordsworth was trying to do, and more than one modern Literary critic has yoked these two writers as similarly innovative.[5] In this section, I want to examine in some detail the aesthetic practice Austen developed both to engage her reader in her fiction and to limit the kind of reading practice that might lead the reader outside the novel—whether to events that the fictional episodes invoked or to some explicitly political response. Whether or not she was successful in dictating the way her novels were consumed, Austen did establish a model for subsequent novelists, who, as we will see, elaborated the gestural aesthetic she refined so that readers were increasingly encouraged to view novelistic language as more like the language of poetry than that of informational writing and fictional worlds as, at most, indirectly related to the world the reader inhabited.

Proving that Austen's aesthetic was a response to the three occasions I have named is impossible, for reasons I will soon explain, even if one engages the novel, as I do, at a level of textual detail that would ruin most readers' enjoyment.[6] Nevertheless, it seems important to speculate about the occasions for *Pride and Prejudice*, for these conjectures help explain features of the novel that are difficult to understand, not to mention why Austen's novels have both entered the Literary canon and continued to be eagerly read by millions of modern readers. The fact that Austen's novels can be engaged in different ways, the fact that they can be *classified* differently—as pure entertainment or as objects of a Literary professional's attention—is a function of their peculiar style, and, if this style was a response to particular occasions (as all style is), then identifying those occasions will help us see it as *having* a function as well as *being* one. For, even if the fact that I can engage this novel as the object of professional work and others can engage it as entertainment is partly a function of our different relations to university Literary studies, partly it is a function of one of the generic conventions Austen adapted to distinguish the way her novel *could* be consumed from the way most of her contemporaries' novels typically were. This convention—the use of a narrative system composed of multiple, carefully related parts—encourages at least two, very different kinds of reading. One focuses on plot and character, moves rapidly forward in a linear manner, sympathizes with the heroine, and enjoys the happy ending; the other focuses on Austen's language, as well as repeated patterns and themes, moves backward as well as forward, and enjoys nuance and complexity. The function of Austen's style, in other words, was—and is—to promote multiple kinds of engagements as well as many readings of the same work, and this has enabled her novels to attract readers of all types, even as the conditions in which readers read have multiplied too.

Before I explain why I identify the Bank Restriction Act as the third occasion for *Pride and Prejudice*, let me describe how Austen's narrative system works—both how it engages the reader in the fictional world the novel depicts and how it invites multiple engagements of different, but limited, kinds. The first will be familiar to anyone who has read the novel: Austen's characters, particularly Elizabeth Bennet, are sympathetic, interesting, and easily recognizable; they are revealed to the reader in a way that encourages both immediate identification and the sense that one is discovering in them complexities of which they are unaware; and they are engaged in a familiar plot (to find a suitable husband) that had—and still has—considerable appeal. These features are clearest, perhaps, in the episode in which Elizabeth reads, then rereads Darcy's letter, only to discover in herself past prejudices and present desires—including the desire to marry Darcy.

To show how the novel invites multiple but specific kinds of readings, I need to describe the way that Austen's narrative system manages the relationship among its parts. Together, this system and its management direct the reader's attention to various parts of the story and offer various perspectives on characters and events. In doing so, her narrative system performs some of the functions that previous novelists, like Fielding and Richardson, had achieved with chapter breaks and multiple letter writers: all these conventions shift attention from one scene or character to another, as speech prefixes and scene changes do in a play text. In addition to conventions favored by eighteenth-century novelists, Austen also adapted other conventions, like free indirect discourse, irony, and narrative focus, to layer multiple perspectives in the same chapter or scene and to offer the reader first one, then another of these perspectives as the scene unfolds. The density of these perspectives and the way the narrative rapidly shifts among them invite the reader to reread, for these devices create a first impression that one is seeing everything and a second impression that something has been missed. A good example of this occurs in volume 1, chapter 16, the scene that brings Elizabeth into contact with Wickham, the dashing young soldier who features so prominently in subsequent events. First, the narrative establishes that multiple characters are present—"they had all taken their seats." Then it aligns the reader's view with Mr. Collins's perspective—"Mr. Collins was at leisure to look around him and admire, and he was so much struck with the size and furniture of the apartment, that he declared he might almost have supposed himself in the small summer breakfast parlour at Rosings."[7] With the entry of Wickham, the narrative shifts the reader's attention from Mr. Collins's perspective to Elizabeth's—"when Mr. Wickham walked into the room, Elizabeth felt that she had neither been seeing him before, nor thinking of him since, with the smallest degree of unreasonable admiration." Five paragraphs later, the narrative leaves all the other characters with a detail that isolates Wickham and Elizabeth—"Allowing for the common demands of the game, Mr. Wickham was therefore at leisure to talk to Elizabeth" (*PP*, 75–76). With the entire party now excluded from the narrative's focus, the dialogue that cements Elizabeth's prejudice against Darcy (and her preference for Wickham) unfolds, in such a way as to confirm the impression left on Elizabeth by two previous social gatherings, her conviction that Darcy is proud.

On first reading, this scene seems simply to describe what it obviously narrates: a party where Elizabeth learns why Darcy behaves the way he does. But the particular details Austen includes—the word *small*, for example, in Mr. Collins's indirectly conveyed comment, the eagerness with which Elizabeth agrees with Wickham's judgment, even the narrative isolation of the whispering pair in what ought to be a "common" conversation—all suggest that something not directly narrated is occurring here, something one can discover only by reading the text again. On first reading, in other words, one cannot understand that Mr. Collins's allusion to the "small summer breakfast parlour at Rosings" uses a triple diminutive to reflect (badly) on his own grandiosity, or that Elizabeth's absorption in Wickham nurses her wounded pride, or that Wickham's eagerness to explain Darcy to Elizabeth expresses his need to get her on his side. Nor can a reader reap the particular rewards such rereading yields by going outside the novel, by thinking about what clergymen like Mr. Collins are usually like, what unmarried women like Elizabeth are likely to feel, or what might have led a handsome young man like Wickham to join the militia in the first place.

The conventions Austen deployed in this scene were not new, of course, nor did she attempt to derive from them an aesthetic that privileged originality, as Wordsworth and Coleridge were doing. She may have adopted and refined these conventions partly for the same reason that Wordsworth reviled the "frantic novels" his contemporaries were devouring, but, even if having her novels taken more seriously than Gothic fiction mattered to Austen, originality was never her goal. Instead, I suggest, she refined the conventions she borrowed primarily in order to draw distinct boundaries *around* her fictional worlds—that is, to invite multiple engagements with these worlds and to prevent readers mistaking the world depicted in each novel for the world they actually inhabited. Paradoxically, then, the conventions that eventually led readers to place Austen's novels in a different category from the works her contemporaries wrote—that prompted no less a judge than Walter Scott to single them out—were those that invisibly managed the reader's attention so that he or she was drawn "inside" fictional worlds that seemed self-sufficient and complete.[8]

Austen's management of the relationship between her narrative's parts— what I am calling the novel's *narrative system*—not only directs the reader's attention within each episode of the novel, inviting the reader always to visit again; it also seeks to curtail the capacity of language to invoke other, nontextual events—that is, to refer to things outside the novel. The narrative uses at least three sets of conventions to do so. The first is visible in Austen's references to the militia. If one were to read these passages referentially, they would invoke the war with France, which we know to have directly affected Austen through her brother Henry, who joined the Oxfordshire militia in 1793. While it is possible to use these passages to specify the novel's historical setting (1794 or 1795),[9] however, two features discourage the reader from treating these allusions simply as literal references. First, the name of the militia is blanked out, with the conventional eighteenth-century long dash formulation ("the—shire" [*PP*, 75 (vol. 1, chap. 16)]). Second, nearly every mention of the militia downplays the protective function that real militias played in the 1790s. Instead of representing the soldiers defending England, these passages either place individual soldiers in or adjacent to commercial establishments (as when Colonel Forster and Captain Carter are depicted "standing in Clarke's [circulating] library" [30 (vol. 1, chap. 7)]) or specifically associate the soldiers with the "double danger" of inappropriate romantic attachments and the allure of expensive finery (as when Brighton is said to pose the "double danger [of] a watering place and a camp" or when Lydia reports socializing with the soldiers and purchasing "a new gown, or a new parasol" [229, 230 (vol. 2, chap. 19)]).

The way the narrative presents the militia, then, tends to discourage readers from referring Austen's passages to real military men like Henry, much less to the war being waged while Austen was writing the novel. One function such curtailment would have played for Austen's first readers was to minimize the effect that references to the actual war might have had, especially for readers, like Austen, who had relatives in danger. A second set of conventions, which also alludes to a situation we know to have been familiar to Austen, is considerably more prominent in the novel and, correspondingly, more consequential. These conventions consist of a relationship among plots that manages the theme of money. Money, of course, was a constant concern for Jane Austen and her family, particularly during the years in which she worked on *Pride and Prejudice*. The family had never been wealthy, and, with Austen's father making less than £100 a year in 1797, the year she completed *First Impressions*, Jane's letters reveal constant worries about money. In that year, her personal savings totaled only £7; in 1801, when the family sold almost everything in preparation for the move to Bath, she watched her books and writing desk go with considerable sadness; and, in 1805, when her father's death further impoverished the family, Henry had to lend them £50 to help them stay afloat.[10]

In the first three-quarters of *Pride and Prejudice*, money is mentioned only twice, both in incidental ways: in the first mention of money, Lydia borrows a small sum from Jane and Elizabeth to "treat" her sisters to lunch at the Meryton inn (*PP*, 211 [vol. 2, chap. 16]); in the second, the Gardiners pay their bill at another inn when they are suddenly recalled to Longbourne (267 [vol. 3, chap. 4]). As soon as the narrative reveals that Wickham has eloped with Lydia, however, the subject of money virtually explodes into the narrative, and references to it quickly amass the coherence of a full-fledged plot. Even after it makes its presence known, however, this money plot initially unfolds away from the narrative's focus, for the events that concern money all occur in places that Elizabeth, the novel's principal focalizer, does not occupy. Thus, because Lydia has been allowed to follow the militia to Brighton and Elizabeth is traveling with the Gardiners, Elizabeth first hears about her sister's elopement through a letter from Jane, who has stayed behind in London. This same letter also reveals that Colonel Forster fears that Wickham might have no intention of marrying Lydia (262). Finally, when Elizabeth's father and Mr. Gardiner go to London, they discover (and then report) that Wickham is deep in debt and that he now demands money to marry Lydia. Thus, the subject of money erupts into the domestic plot through a mode of narration that calls attention to its status as representation (the letters), but it does so because of a role it has long played in an unnarrated, but profoundly consequential, money plot: all the while that he was flirting with Elizabeth and Lydia, Wickham was incurring bills he could not pay.

What we are seeing here is a narrative that embeds its allusions to real situations in a complex system that simultaneously invokes these situations and manages the effect of alluding to them—both in the narrative and, as a consequence, for the reader. This is what I call Austen's *gestural aesthetic*: it gestures toward extratextual events but so carefully manages these allusions that the reader is invited back into the text instead of encouraged to go outside its pages. Thus far, we have seen two of the forms this management takes: the foreclosure of reference, which is clearest in the military allusions, and the narrative's direction of the reader's attention, which is achieved by controlling access to various plots and the information they contain. This last dynamic foregrounds the mediation that representation performs, both as a theme in the novel and, through the embedded letters, as a distinctive mode of narration. In reading *Pride and Prejudice*, one can experience the real threat that war and family debt might have posed a young woman like Elizabeth only by—and through the buffer of—an imaginative engagement with the novel's domestic romance. As my description suggests, this narrative management operates within the narrative system at the same time that it polices its borders. Thus, for the novel's first three-quarters, the narrative's focus on the domestic plot blocks the reader's access to the money plot; as it does, it implicitly discourages a literal reading of the novel's events and actively modulates the reader's response to the danger an actual lack of money would have posed.

Over the course of the narrative, Austen uses a third device to manage the relationship between her fiction and reality. The best way I can describe this is as a kind of translation, for, by a series of substitutions, Austen gradually replaces the money plot's primary terms with a different set of terms that promise comfort instead of posing a threat. Thus, she transforms the fiscal jeopardy the Bennet girls face into a romantic threat, which, while potentially emotionally painful, can be solved within the domestic plot. Bringing the money plot out from under the romantic plot inaugurates this transformation, for only after events that are initially kept in the background of the narrative system become the primary strand of narration can Austen begin to rework their terms.

This reworking begins when it becomes obvious that Lydia poses a financial threat to her family. Initially, the amount Wickham demands seems like a sum the Bennets can manage: a settlement of the girl's share of the £5,000 she is to receive on her parents' death and £100 a year for her father's lifetime (*PP*, 286 [vol. 3, chap. 7]). But Mr. Bennet immediately realizes that this cannot be correct, and, in a conversation with his oldest daughters, he reveals the magnitude of the family's danger. "There are two things that I want very much to know," Mr. Bennet tells Jane and Elizabeth in his characteristically laconic way: "one is, how much money your uncle has laid down, to bring it about; and the other, how I am ever to repay him" (287). His daughters' shock forces their father to be more explicit: "'Money! my uncle!' cried Jane, 'what do you mean, Sir?'" When Mr. Bennet speculates that £10,000 is probably Wickham's real asking price, one of the girls bursts out again: "'Ten thousand pounds! Heaven forbid! How is half such a sum to be repaid?'" (288). At this point, the narrative details the monetary issues that, within the narrative system, have always underwritten the domestic plot and begins to lay out the monetary arrangements that will dictate the future: Austen reveals that Mr. Bennet never saved any money; Mr. Bennet says that he will not advance money for Lydia's wedding clothes; Mr. Gardiner uncovers exactly how much Wickham owes; and we find out that Wickham ran away with Lydia only because he was trying to evade his creditors.

The most important revelation about money, however, appears not in these scenes but in another letter, one that begins to neutralize the twin threats of poverty and disgrace. In this letter, Mrs. Gardiner informs Elizabeth that Darcy, not her uncle, paid off Wickham's debts (*PP*, 304ff. [vol. 3, chap. 10]). Instead of wondering how much money Darcy paid, Elizabeth's first response is to imagine that he has done this for her. Only after she has indulged this fantasy does she realize that the obligation the Bennets have thus incurred can never be repaid in kind. Soon, Mr. Bennet makes it clear that, *if Mr. Gardiner had paid Wickham*, the "obligation" would have been financial and the "return" would have had to be cash. Since Darcy has paid the money, however, this particular obligation has been dissolved: "And so, Darcy did every thing; made up the match, gave the money, paid the fellow's debts, and got him his commission! So much the better. It will save me a world of trouble and economy. Had it been your uncle's doing, I must and *would* have paid him; but these violent young lovers carry every thing their own way. I shall offer to pay him to-morrow; he will rant and storm about his love for you, and there will be an end of the matter" (356–57 [vol. 3, chap. 17]).

As this passage makes clear, Darcy's actions neutralize the threat that a monetary obligation would have posed to the Bennets by translating debt into a gift of love. Even before Mr. Bennet makes this explicit, in fact, Darcy has already alluded to this translation by rebuffing Elizabeth's attempt to thank him on behalf of her family. "Your *family* owe me nothing," he says to Elizabeth in the scene in which she expresses this gratitude. "Much as I respect them, I believe, I thought only of *you*" (*PP*, 346 [vol. 3, chap. 16]). Once Elizabeth says that she will marry Darcy, he completes this translation by saying that he "owes" her for the rebuke she has given his pride (349). Thus, by marrying Darcy, Elizabeth is able to "repay" him—not in money, but in love. And, by making the money plot first disrupt, then be absorbed by the domestic plot, Austen translates a monetary debt into mutual love.

In the narrative system that is *Pride and Prejudice*, these translations—the transformation of a financial payment into the bestowal of a gift, then the conversion of the gift into love—address and symbolically resolve the threat that the money plot posed to its romance counterpart. This resolution culminates when the money plot is banished from the novel, as the romantic relationships the narrative has long followed conclude successfully, in marriages. The event that initiates this resolution is actually not Darcy's decision to help Wickham but Elizabeth's change of heart about Darcy, for, as the passage I have just quoted reveals, he acts in order to respond to or communicate with her. Elizabeth begins to change her mind because of a series of portraits of Darcy: the letter Darcy writes to explain his relationship with Wickham, then two images of the gentleman that Elizabeth encounters at Pemberley. The letter inaugurates the change, but it is not until she arrives at his family estate, hears the admiring servant's praise of Darcy, and then sees the portrait that hangs in Pemberley's gallery that Elizabeth realizes she has been wrong. At this point, she knows that she would now accept Darcy if he offered again, and, for the first time, she imagines the fantastic scenario to which the narrative is leading: marriage with Darcy and herself as mistress of Pemberley.

In this scene, and in the events it precipitates, we see Austen foregrounding representation—moving it from a mode of narration (the letters) to a subject worthy of notice in and of itself. As a theme addressed in and as a component of *Pride and Prejudice,* representation first distorts, then reveals the true value that Darcy and his family estate embody. This has been obscured for much of the novel, for, until Elizabeth reads Darcy's letter, the reader has had access to him only through the perspectives other characters offer—first Wickham, who has a reason to misrepresent Darcy's character, and then Elizabeth, whose mediation, unbeknownst to the reader and to her, is prejudicial because prejudiced. This is why it is so important to reread *Pride and Prejudice.* Until Elizabeth—and, with her, the reader—learns to see the mediation that representation always involves, she—and we—do not have access to the value Darcy incarnates because we cannot see him as he really is. This is the lesson Elizabeth gradually learns from Darcy's letter, the housekeeper's words, and the portrait at Pemberley: seeing these objects as mediations gradually teaches Elizabeth to look at *how* information is conveyed, *who* conveys it, and *where* it surfaces instead of taking it at face value, instead of treating it *as* information. Once Elizabeth learns this—once Darcy's true value is revealed and the two lovers reach their mutual understanding—the subject of representation goes the way of the money plot: it disappears from the novel. As a theme, representation is banished from the novel when Darcy clears the way for Bingley and Jane to marry by explaining to his friend that he—Darcy—had previously not disclosed Jane's presence in London because he had misinterpreted her interest in Bingley. With misrepresentation and misunderstanding out of the way, the path is clear for the double marriages with which the novel culminates.

I need to describe one additional aspect of the novel's narrative system before I can explain why I call the Bank Restriction Act the *third occasion* for the novel. In *Pride and Prejudice,* Elizabeth's change of heart about Darcy is not quite sufficient to initiate the events that bring about the happy ending, for Elizabeth must find a way to convey this change to Darcy, who, as a man, must initiate any proposal. Austen narrates the sequence in which this happens in a manner that is extraordinarily complex, even for this extraordinarily complexly narrated novel. Elizabeth rehearses her revelation late in the novel, in the exchange in which she and Darcy playfully try to recover the "foundation" of their love (*PP*, 359 [vol. 3, chap. 18]). In this dialogue, Elizabeth associates her recognition that she had come to admire Darcy with what she describes as a "resolution" to thank him for finding Wickham and smoothing the way to Lydia's marriage. In retrospect, Elizabeth says this resolution is a "breach"—not just of etiquette, but of some "promise" she has presumably made. "My resolution of thanking you for your kindness to Lydia had certainly great effect," Elizabeth jokes. "*Too much*, I am afraid; for what becomes of the moral, if our comfort springs from a breach of promise, for I ought not to have mentioned the subject?" (360). This claim/disclaimer is interesting not simply because, syntactically, it takes the form of a declarative sentence that is also interrogatory but also because it concludes a sequence of references that has no origin in the text itself. In other words, this sequence violates the principle otherwise enforced by the system of narrative management I have been describing: it does not refer the reader to another part of this novel because it points to something that Austen does not narrate.

To see this, one must not only reread; one must work backward through the novel, following the clues Austen seems to leave. The trail begins with the passage I have just quoted (from vol. 3, chap. 18), in which the narrative describes Elizabeth remembering an earlier scene. If we turn to this scene (from vol. 3, chap. 16), which describes Elizabeth's "resolution," we find what seems to be a reference to a still earlier event; but, when we try to find a description of Elizabeth's initial decision to thank Darcy—or the promise she made not to do so—we find something else instead. In volume 3, chapter 16, the narrative reveals that Elizabeth has long contemplated thanking Darcy. "I can no longer help thanking you for your unexampled kindness to my poor sister," she blurts out. "Ever since I have known it, I have been most anxious to acknowledge to you how gratefully I feel it" (*PP*, 345). In the scene to which this refers, however—the scene that describes Elizabeth's discovery that Darcy found Wickham and paid his debts (vol. 3, chap. 10) there is no description of Elizabeth reaching such a "resolution." Instead, the narrative presents Mrs. Gardiner's letter, which conveys the information to Elizabeth, then devotes a paragraph to describing the "flutter of spirits" Elizabeth experiences, and then turns its attention to Wickham, who interrupts Elizabeth's reflections and the narrative's description of her response (308–11).

Matters get more complicated still, for, even if the narrative never describes the origin of Elizabeth's resolution to thank Darcy—or her promise not to do so—Austen does mention another "resolution" that her heroine makes between the time she learns of Darcy's generosity (vol. 3, chap. 10) and the moment she actually thanks him (vol. 3, chap. 16). Elizabeth reaches this resolution in apparently unpremeditated response to another character's "resolution," Lady Catherine De Bourgh's "resolution to prevent [Darcy's and Elizabeth's] marriage" (*PP*, 340 [vol. 3, chap. 15]). This resolution, moreover, is linked to a promise Elizabeth refuses, thereby taking the place of that other promise she presumably made. When Lady Catherine demands that Elizabeth promise not to enter into an engagement with Darcy, Elizabeth retorts: "I am only resolved to act in that manner, which will, in my own opinion, constitute my happiness, without reference to *you*, or to any person so wholly unconnected with me" (338 [vol. 3, chap. 14]). While it is difficult to see how this resolution could be the same resolution to which Elizabeth refers, in volume 3, chapter 18, as her "breach of promise," Austen does present it as the resolution that animates Darcy, for he says that it was Lady Catherine's reference to this outburst, and not Elizabeth's "eager desire of expressing [her] gratitude," that led him to renew his proposal. "My aunt's intelligence had given me hope, and I was determined at once to know every thing" (360).

It would obviously be difficult for a reader encountering the novel for the first time to notice that the narrative never describes Elizabeth deciding to thank Darcy or promising that she would not do so. It is virtually impossible to see this even when one rereads, for, as long as one is going forward, with the events Austen narrates, there are so many resolutions and promises that it is hard to keep track of what refers to what. There seems to be no reason to try and find this referent, in fact, for the absence of descriptions of Elizabeth's promise and her resolution to break it does not matter to the novel's action, its characters, or even the pleasure one gets from seeing more than the characters do: Elizabeth thanks Darcy, Darcy renews his offer to Elizabeth, the two laugh over their courtship of misunderstandings, and marriage brings the novel to a happy end. Nevertheless, a reader who is willing to go backward—not simply to reread, as Elizabeth does with Darcy's letter, but to follow the narrative clues, as I have just done—can discover this odd fact: in a narrative system that so carefully manages its reader's relation to it and its own relationship to the world toward which it gestures, this sequence leads to a dead end, either to two unnarrated events (Elizabeth's promise and her resolution to break it) or to a narrated event that resembles but is clearly *not* either of the events to which Elizabeth refers.

While the gestural aesthetic I have been describing makes it impossible to know for sure, I suggest that the peculiarity of this sequence gestures toward what I have been calling *Pride and Prejudice*'s *third occasion*, the changes introduced by passage of the Bank Restriction Act. For what this sequence enacts is the capacity of representation to block or waylay reference *not* in a manner *intended to reassure*, as the novel's narrative system is, but in a way that simply confuses and raises doubt. This subject, of course— the problematic nature of the relationship between representation and that to which it supposedly refers—was rendered inescapable by the Restriction Act, for, by making the *merely* representational nature of Bank paper visible, the act made Britons wonder whether paper money referred to anything at all, whether it had any value, whether it could support the "comfort" of England.

The Bank Restriction Act was passed in May 1797, as we have seen, and it was debated during the spring of that year, when Austen was, presumably, readying *First Impressions* for its (unsuccessful) submission to the publishers Cadell and Davies. This act also sanctioned a breach of promise, of course, like the breach of promise that Elizabeth associates with her resolution to thank Darcy; in the case of the act, the suspended promise was the notice printed on the face of every Bank note—the promise that the Bank would redeem the note with gold. Unlike Elizabeth's violated promise, however, which has no deleterious consequences in the novel, the Bank Restriction Act had consequences that were immediate and potentially disastrous. Not only did prices begin to rise as paper money proliferated, but, because the nation's security was tied to the creditworthiness of the Bank, calling that creditworthiness into question, as the Restriction Act did, could have undermined the government's ability to fund the nation's protection.

The formal homology between Austen's narrative treatment of Elizabeth's broken promise and the epistemological effect of the Restriction Act does not, by itself, *prove* that Austen had the Restriction Act in mind when she composed or revised *Pride and Prejudice*. I can—and will—adduce additional evidence to support this conjecture, but I want to insist that, given the merely gestural nature of her aesthetic, *no* evidence from inside or outside the text could conclusively prove such a claim. I have found no explicit reference to the Restriction Act in any of Austen's writing, and even her epistolary allusions to banks and high prices, which I cite in a moment, do not prove that she blamed the Restriction for the monetary volatility that persisted throughout the time she worked on *Pride and Prejudice*. Taken together, however, all this circumstantial evidence seems to me to make a strong case for this conjecture, and seeing the broken promises authorized by the Restriction behind the fictional promises whose violation brings *Pride and Prejudice* to a happy ending might explain why Austen used, not one, but *three* breaches of promise to end her novel. Austen developed a *gestural* aesthetic, in other words, and not one that completely occluded the world outside the novel (through the use of fantastical settings and supernatural characters, e.g.), because she wanted to acknowledge the situation caused by the Restriction so that she could use her fiction to manage the anxieties it caused.

Even if we do not know what Austen thought about the Bank Restriction Act, we do know that she was familiar with banks and with the relatively new banking industry more generally. We know this both because Jane joked with Henry about a "fantasy bank" in an early letter[11] and because Henry became a partner in an actual bank in 1805; this was the source of the £50 he gave his family that year. (The bank failed in 1816.) We also know that Jane was aware that the volatility of prices could have negative repercussions on the nation's ability to defend itself. In the spring of 1797, even before the act was passed, two platoons of sailors mutinied, partly to protest the fluctuating value of the military's wages. These mutinies, at Spithead and Nore, might well have reminded Austen of another mutiny that also occurred before the act (in 1795), one involving Henry's military unit, the Oxfordshire militia; this mutiny also protested inflated prices. While the Restriction Act was intended to stabilize prices, it did not have this effect, and, as we have already seen, in the wake of the act, money became a controversial and intensely political matter. As we have also seen, money remained a political issue for the almost quarter of a century in which the act remained in force—that is, for the remainder of Jane Austen's life.

We can only infer that Austen was putting the finishing touches on *First Impressions* during the months in which legislators discussed relieving the Bank of its obligation to pay, and we can only guess when she decided to include Elizabeth's enigmatic comment about her "breach of promise," but we know for certain that she revised the manuscript during the Restriction period. She had to have begun the revisions sometime after Cadell and Davies rejected the manuscript in November 1797; and, if B. C. Southam is correct in dating these revisions to 1809–12, then she reworked the manuscript during the height of the Restriction period, when it was clear that the act's original term had expired and no one could have known when—or even if—England would restore the Bank's money to its customary basis in gold.[12] Whether Elizabeth's allusion to her breach of promise and the entire sequence of references that lead to no textual point were incorporated into the novel during the composition of an early draft, a summer revision of *First Impressions*, or the final reworking that became *Pride and Prejudice*, Austen ultimately decided to leave this sequence in the novel that appeared in 1813, and she also decided not to include descriptions of the promise Elizabeth presumably made *not* to thank Darcy and her initial decision to violate her promise. The sequence of references that ought to, but does not, lead back to these unnarrated events remains a textual loose end, which violates the aesthetic autonomy of the text—whether intentionally or not we'll never know.

If the fiscal, political, and epistemological uncertainty provoked by the passage of the Restriction Act was one of the occasions for *Pride and Prejudice*, then both the nature and the limitations of Austen's narrative management make sense. The conventions she used to foreclose reference, after all, coexist in the novel with allusions to the very events she seems not to have wanted her readers to worry about. By alluding, however indirectly, to actual issues that might have concerned her readers—the war, unacknowledged debt, the role that representation had always played in Britain's credit economy—Austen was able to incorporate these matters into a safe, because textual, world of words, where they could be managed, translated into other terms, then simply dismissed. By foregrounding the theme and effects of representation, this narrative system could provide a symbolic resolution to real anxieties because the idea that representation was a *problem* was precisely what Austen's contemporaries had to learn to overlook.

Identifying the Restriction as an occasion for *Pride and Prejudice* also helps explain the tone in which the novel's famously fantastic conclusion is cast. Like the novel's narrative system, its tone is complex and multilayered, but each of its resonances, like the dynamics of the narrative, can be referred to the Restriction. Most obviously, the conclusion is gratifying and would have reassured readers, whether they read the novel once or a hundred times: if three broken promises could bring about Elizabeth's marriage to Darcy (Lydia's promise not to disclose that Darcy attended her wedding, Mrs. Gardiner's promise not to reveal Darcy's payment of Wickham's debts, and the promise Elizabeth made to someone not to thank Darcy), then surely the Bank's violation of its promise would bring no harm to the nation. Beneath this reassurance, however, the conclusion also sounds a second tone, the irony for which Austen is justifiably famous. As the signal of an author's awareness that a gap always separates words from the meanings they convey, irony is the signature of representation-made-visible—that is, of the very fact about representation that the Restriction exposed. And, third, the nostalgia the conclusion conveys, as the tonal mark of lost possibilities, expresses what passage of the Restriction Act made clear and what must have grown more obvious as the Restriction period dragged on: the power associated with land and with gentlemen like Darcy was beginning to be usurped by the moneyed men who backed the Restriction. Whatever its other effects, after all, the Restriction Act and its prolongation revealed that the Bank of England's directors were successfully equating the interests of the Bank—and not the landed gentry—with the welfare of the nation as a whole. Thus, the gentle rebuke Elizabeth deals to herself—"what becomes of the moral, if our comfort springs from a breach of promise"—preserves what Darcy represents in a kind of historical aspic, memorializing the comfort he can confer in the novel as an appealing, but increasingly distant, possibility for Austen and her readers. The way in which Austen memorializes the possibility associated with Darcy is also deeply ironic, of course, for sanctioning the violation of Lydia's and Mrs. Gardiner's and Elizabeth's promises can clear the way for Elizabeth to know, and for Darcy to act on, their mutual love, but sanctioning the Bank's violation of its promise to pay, as this resolution implicitly does, acceded to the transformation of political power that was already beginning to marginalize Britain's actual landed gentry.

Explicitly engaging the problematic of representation in a gestural aesthetic such as Austen's helped elaborate the formalism associated with the Romantic ideal of Literary value, even though it violated the text's organic unity. By simultaneously transforming reference into gesture and commenting thematically on the process of mediation, Austen's novels rendered their relationship to actual events less important than their ability to conjure up a self-contained, self-referential world. Thus, undecidability—in this case, the undecidability of referent—augmented the pleasure of reading, for it made the consumption of a novel gratifying no matter what happened in the reader's world. At the same time, undecidability also enhanced the value of the novel itself—in aesthetic *and* market terms—because undecidability—which, in this case, was a function of the complexity I have been describing—encouraged readers to reread the novel, not simply to devour it and cast it aside, as they did with the Minerva Press Gothics. Austen's model of reading anticipated the kind of Literary reading described at the end of the century by Ruskin and Dowden. That it directed the reader repeatedly back to the text and *not* to the world outside helped cut the ties between this kind of Literary text and the other prose genres that it otherwise so closely resembled while giving the Literary experience a value that seemed exempt from market price.

From Gesture to Formalism: *Little Dorrit* and *Silas Marner*

It is a truth universally acknowledged that mid-nineteenth-century novelists represented financial matters in ethical and moral terms. Many examples come to mind: Charlotte Brontë's Jane Eyre treats her inheritance as an instrument of justice; Thackeray's Becky Sharpe proves morally bankrupt when she whines that a "good woman" needs five thousand a year; Dickens's Bella Wilfer demonstrates her worth when she renounces her desire for gold; Elizabeth Gaskell allows Margaret and Thornton both love and worldly success only when the strong man acknowledges his dependence on the woman. As George Levine explains, in Victorian novels, if money is not used for some ethical end, it ruins heroes, debases higher goals, and threatens the aesthetic value of Literature; but denouncing money, as Amy Dorrit does at the end of Dickens's novel, can ennoble a character, just as preferring love to money, as Eliot's Dorothea Brooke does, can elevate a character over the degraded values of the market.[13]

As these and countless other examples demonstrate, money and financial matters are primarily semantic indices in mid-nineteenth-century British novels: as part of their generally critical relation to market society, midcentury novelists used a character's attitude toward money to indicate moral worth, and, more often than not, only a character's indifference to—or even repudiation of—money can signal virtue. To take the measure of the distance between such attitudes and treatments of the credit economy when it was new and relatively unfamiliar to writers and readers alike, we have only to remember Defoe's sense that the belief essential to all credit instruments was socially constructive because the ability to trust was essential to success in Britain's commercial society. By the middle of the nineteenth century, by contrast, the credit economy itself seemed to Literary writers to have grown distended and corrupt, and the attitudes it cultivated seemed dangerous, vicious, or both: too much trust could lead gullible investors to ruin, as Arthur Clennam discovers in *Little Dorrit*; and the lust for money, as Trollope's Melmotte reminded readers, could lead to unscrupulous schemes, outright lies, and intricate webs of deceit. The delimitation of Literature and the naturalization of the generic difference between Literary and other kinds of writing were complexly related to the emergence of this consensus, for distinguishing emphatically between Literary and informational writing made it easier for Literary writers to offer their work as a moralizing antidote to the attitudes and behaviors normalized by economic writing. The critical attitude toward money struck in so many midcentury novels, of course, belonged to this distancing campaign, even though there is plenty of evidence to show that the disgust with money expressed by so many mid-century novelists in their fictions was at odds with the active engagement they manifested in their own, real-life financial activities.

The narrative conventions refined by Jane Austen proved attractive to subsequent novelists looking both to critique and to profit from Britain's expanding credit economy. As the financial sector continued to grow in the ways I have described, and particularly after the scandals of the 1840s, numerous novelists elaborated Austen's gestural aesthetics so that it could simultaneously sharpen imaginative writers' critique of the market economy and draw an increasingly definite boundary between the imaginary world depicted in the novel, where ethical values could prevail, and the actual world outside, where corruption and greed seemed to make moral certainty impossible. Some novelists, like George Eliot and Margaret Oliphant, flirted with the boundary that sought to divide the fictional text from its social surround by elaborating Austen's mode of characterization so that fictional figures became readers' virtual friends. Others, like Charles Dickens and William Thackeray, experimented with various distancing devices—ranging from obtrusive narrators, to animated objects, to dehumanized characters—to reinforce the boundary that identified the textual world as *not* real, *non*referential, that is, as art. In this section, I examine this last practice, for the attenuated relationship such distancing conventions produced between the increasingly self-contained worlds conjured by realist fiction and the historical events toward which novels sometimes gestured constitutes a distinctive feature of the midcentury novelistic aesthetic.

———

Charles Dickens began publishing *Little Dorrit* in monthly parts in December 1855; the last of the twenty (as nineteen) parts appeared in June 1857. While not universally embraced by reviewers, the novel immediately attracted a large audience; so great was demand that sales of *Little Dorrit* soon surpassed those of Dickens's previous monthly serials, and Bradbury and Evans had to augment the first print run (thirty-two thousand copies) with six thousand additional copies.[14] The enthusiasm with which readers devoured *Little Dorrit* seems not to have been initially felt by the writer, however, for Dickens's manuscripts and letters show him struggling with the early numbers, changing the novel's title and emphasis, and vacillating between sweeping criticism of an entire society and a more optimistic focus on individual redemption. In October, just two months before the first number appeared, Dickens finally decisively shifted the narrative's attention to Little Dorrit, thereby signaling to readers his own interest in character and his decision to subordinate the novel's social commentary to his imaginative engagement with Amy Dorrit and her friends.[15]

In June 1855, while Dickens was mired in what he described as "a hideous state of mind" about his novel, journalists disclosed that the directors of the reputable banking firm of Strahan, Paul, and Bates had absconded with the bank's money.[16] Later that summer, another financial crime made news: the embezzlement (by forgery) of £150,000 from the Irish Tipperary Bank. The culprit was John Sadlier, a member of Parliament and a junior lord of the Treasury. Unable to face the shame of a trial, Sadlier committed suicide on 17 February 1856. Even after Dickens had figured out what the focus of his novel should be, the revelations of these crimes were obviously provocative: he began composing the sixth number of *Little Dorrit*, in which he introduced the financier Merdle, two days after Sadlier's suicide.

The financial crimes revealed in the summer of 1855 constitute one of the occasions for *Little Dorrit*, in an even more obvious sense than the events I associated with *Pride and Prejudice*. While Dickens openly acknowledged this—declaring, in the 1857 edition, that Merdle "originated after the Railway-share epoch, in the times of a certain Irish bank"[17]—the completed novel does not encourage readers to think about those crimes or to speculate about the conditions that made financial crime so common in the 1850s. Instead, the way that Dickens presented Merdle and his transgression, like his depictions of other contemporary events, made this character a part of the fictional world that existed within the pages of his novel.[18] Dickens might well have wanted to capitalize on readers' interest in Sadlier to support sales of *Little Dorrit*, but he did not want curiosity about the real-life financier to interfere with the moral lesson about the redemptive capacity of love that his reconfigured novel was shaped to deliver. Because the resemblance between Merdle and Sadlier had the potential to undermine this moralizing function—because it might make readers *classify* the novel as a journalistic revelation about contemporary events—he took pains to limit the reader's engagement with Merdle. Thus, the Merdle plot figures only briefly, the details of the financier's crimes remain vague, and the effects of the speculation he inspires are registered in a moral vocabulary that obscures his actual crimes. Even though Merdle's criminal activities lead to the collapse of the partnership formed by Clennam and Doyce, moreover, it is Arthur Clennam's insistence that he publicly take responsibility for the firm's debt that causes his creditors to bring suit against him; this, in turn, leads to Clennam's incarceration in debtor's prison; and it is this imprisonment that paves the way for his reunion with Amy Dorrit. This reunion

culminates in marriage, of course, but it also enables Clennam to be spiritually reborn; and, when a successful Doyce returns from the Continent, pays
Clennam's debts, and frees him from the Marshalsea, the novel dispenses
with the entire subject of financial speculation. Merdle's transgression thus
functions within the narrative as a blocking agent: it momentarily impedes
the romance plot that links Arthur Clennam to Amy Dorrit and decisively
colors the *bildung* chronicle of Clennam's reform. Because Clennam never
blames Merdle for the failure of the firm, and because Dickens presents Merdle's crimes only as abstractions ("Forgery and Robbery" [*LD*, 777]), the
narrative renders any attempt to refer Merdle to the men whose crimes inspired Dickens irrelevant to the function the character performs in the text.

Dickens does make the speculative mania that Merdle's actions spawn
serve an aesthetic role, for this theme enables him to link two plots that
otherwise barely overlap: the highly mannered treatment of high society,
which is populated by stereotypical characters like the Barnacles, and the
more detailed treatment of the Bleeding-Heart Yard plot, where individuated characters like Mrs. Plornish and her father appear. Rumors of riches
to be made from speculating in Merdle's ventures travel from the first plot,
where the Barnacles could afford to—but do not explicitly—risk money, to
the second, where the rent agent Pancks spreads the "contagion" to Clennam, even though both must borrow to speculate. In Dickens's characterization of Clennam, the desire to speculate becomes a psychological disorder, a monomania that must be cured before he can merit Little Dorrit.
While the character's ethical reform is crucial to the resolution of the novel,
the precise form of his moral affliction is less important than that it be
amenable to cure—not by an explanation that might enable readers to
discriminate between a sound investment and irrational speculation, but
simply through the moral transformation that Amy inspires.

As the narrative focus is increasingly trained on Clennam, the character
Merdle is relegated to ever more marginal positions. When Merdle meets
Mr. Dorrit in book 2, chapter 16, his presence is momentarily magnified by
an elaborate apostrophe that equates him with solar bodies ("Merdle! O
ye sun, moon, and stars, the great man!" [*LD*, 673]); but the figure rapidly
begins to deflate, reappearing only as an escort in Mr. Dorrit's "rapturous
dream" (677), then an inarticulate and shadowy presence in his stepson's
apartment (chap. 24), then an unidentified body (771), then a mere series
of words that dwindle to an adjective already demoted to a cliché ("the
Merdle lot" [869; see also 865, 873]). Even though Dickens mentions that
"the public mind" and "talk" inflate rumors about Merdle's wealth into the
"roar" that he is guilty of crimes (776), Merdle's influence in the narrative

is over. Almost immediately on his disappearance, Clennam takes responsibility for his company's debts, in a substitution that suggests that being in debt is equivalent to Merdle's forgeries and theft—even though the fictional version of the former, unlike the latter, can be redeemed by the rehabilitation Clennam has already begun to undergo.

Dickens's gestures toward actual financial crimes typify the way that many other midcentury novelists capitalized on the financial revelations of these decades. *Hard Times* also invokes a bank crime (embezzlement) to test a character's moral worth; Margaret Oliphant's *Hester* uses securities fraud to expose the fatal flaw in Edward Vernon's character; in Eliot's *Middlemarch*, the banker Bulstrode falls both because he lied about the legacy his wife left her daughter and because he has secretly invested in a manufacturer of toxic dyes; and, in *The Way We Live Now*, Trollope gestures toward another shadowy financier, one who draws young men too foolish for their own good into a speculative web as ruinous—and almost as imprecisely detailed—as Merdle's speculative ventures. While these thematic appropriations reveal how rich the vein of finance was for novelists looking both to entice readers with provocative reminders of actual events and to entertain them with morally edifying tales of perfect justice, they also show how thoroughly the aesthetic agenda had triumphed by midcentury.

———

Like *Little Dorrit*, George Eliot's *Silas Marner* was a popular (i.e., a commercial) success (although, by the standard that Dickens set, the success of nearly any midcentury novelist is only relative): during its first six months, the one-volume edition of *Silas Marner*, which was priced at 12s., sold eight thousand copies. As with *Little Dorrit* again, *Silas Marner* received mixed responses from the periodical reviewers. Most reviewers praised the novel for its lifelike depictions of the poor: unlike the "ordinary tales of country life that are written in such abundance by ladies," observed the *Saturday Review*, Eliot's fictional poor "are like real poor people." Some reviewers, however, were puzzled by Eliot's decision to feature such depressing poor people. "We see the people amid all their groveling cares, with all their coarseness, ignorance, and prejudice—poor, paltry, stupid, wretched, well-nigh despicable," wrote E. S. Dallas in the *Times*.[19] *Silas Marner* also resembles *Little Dorrit* in another sense: in their final versions, both novels were products of their authors' change of mind. Just as Dickens initially thought that the novel tentatively entitled *Nobody's Fault* would be a social critique, so the story of the linen weaver initially came to Eliot as "a sort of legendary tale." Dickens, as we have seen, eventually focused his attention on a smaller scale, and Eliot shifted hers from legend to something that might also be construed as smaller. "As my mind dwelt on the subject," Eliot explained to John Blackwood, "I became inclined to a more realistic treatment."[20]

The similarities between these two novels reveal some significant facts about midcentury novelistic practice. First, the gulf between the commercial success of both novels and the mixed reception they received from reviewers reminds us that the debate about how to measure Literary value, which I described in chapter 5, dominated the middle decades of the century. The particular reservations expressed by Eliot's reviewers reflect obliquely on this debate, moreover, for the feature that reviewers praised in her work—her ability to create "real poor people"—was the same quality that led so many ordinary readers to appreciate (and buy) her works: her ability to create characters so real that they seemed like virtual friends. The shared appreciation for this quality in the nineteenth century means that the disciplinary sense of "realism," which modern Literary critics emphasize, had not yet been articulated as a term *expert* readers could use to differentiate their responses from those of ordinary readers. In other words, even though reviewers were trying to acquire the social authority to make their judgments more decisive than the crude measure of popularity or sales, they had yet to cultivate a *technical* vocabulary that would immediately distinguish between the way they evaluated novels and the way less expert readers did. We can also see the lack of a modern, *disciplinary* system of classification in the fact that cultural biases—in this case, class biases—informed the judgments of reviewers and ordinary, middle-class readers alike. Finally, the change of mind Eliot described, which led her to give "a more realistic treatment" to a topic that had once seemed "legendary," like Dickens's decision to subordinate social commentary to a tale of individual redemption, reminds us that, at midcentury, a narrower focus promised larger returns. Both readers and writers assumed, that is, that cultivating an imaginatively engaging relationship between readers and individuated characters was an essential component of even the most ambitious Literary art.

These complexities remind us once more how difficult it is to provide a historical description of these works. For, on the one hand, such a description aspires to recover the novels' "compositional technologies"—the historically specific material and generic conditions that occasioned them—and, to do so, we need to invoke the terms and categories that prevailed when the novels were written, published, and consumed. On the other hand, however, in order to count *as a disciplined* description—in order to be *disciplinary knowledge now*—this account has to be formulated in the technical terminology used by today's professional Literary critics. Throughout this book, I have tried to manage the tension between these two demands by stressing both the terms in which a work was initially understood and the way that a retrospective view alters what we see by altering the categories through which our now-disciplined analysis proceeds. In this brief engagement with *Silas Marner*, I do not make these two perspectives speak to each other, as I did in my discussion of *Roxana*, so much as I highlight the way the novel now appears, when viewed in relation to a fully aestheticized model of Literary writing. The "historical deployments" of this novel, to invoke Hunter's term, obviously varied in the 1860s, as responses to it show, but its historical *function*, when viewed retrospectively and in relation to the discipline of Literary studies, was to help demarcate certain uses of language as specifically *Literary* and, as a consequence, as the appropriate object for disciplined (professional) Literary work.

To emphasize only Eliot's treatment of language, as I do here, is admittedly to overlook features that other readers have justifiably celebrated, but it does enable me to isolate a development that was essential to the aestheticization of novels; it was difficult for readers to classify a novel as an aesthetic object, as Henry James urged them to do, until novelistic language came to seem different in some important way from the other uses of prose that seemed superficially so similar to it. We have already seen how Austen and Dickens curtailed the referential capacity of fictional worlds—by elaborating the formal complexities of overlapping plots as crafted interventions rather than simple depictions of everyday life and by flattening out characters that had real-life referents so that the situations that had inspired them would not distract readers from the function a character played within the novel itself. What this brief engagement with Eliot adds to my argument is some sense of how one novelist tried to alter her readers' understanding of language itself so that they would value the way a Literary novelist could augment the referential capacity of words with the mode of connotation Wordsworth had attributed to poetry.

In *Silas Marner*, Eliot uses the figure of gold to shift her reader's attention from the denotative capacity of language to its ability to conjure more than words can say. As the embodiment of a particular kind of value, of course, and the referent of all paper money, gold, even when invoked in a tale set in the not-too-distant past (i.e., a fiction), would have made most nineteenth-century readers think first of money. Lest her readers think that *Silas Marner* is simply a story about money, however, Eliot pushes such a denotative understanding aside. By presenting the weaver's relationship to gold as affective rather than instrumental, she begins to redefine how the word *gold* means as well as what it can be seen to signify. Having been driven out of the narrow religious community in which he was raised, Marner has settled at the outskirts of the obscure village of Raveloe, where he begins to hoard the gold he is paid for weaving. Marner hoards not in order to amass more money but because, in his eyes, the gold has become a quasi-sentient companion. Thus, the narrative informs us that the weaver loves the "bright faces" of the coins, that he imagines they are "conscious of him," and that he considers them "his familiars."[21] It is not immediately clear what, if anything, the gold represents, either to Marner or in the narrative. Instead of treating it as a symbol, the narrative depicts the weaver's obsession with it as a parody of a human relationship, one in which an arid simulacrum of love barely sustains, but emphatically is not, the genuine article: "His life had reduced itself to the functions of weaving and hoarding, without any contemplation of an end towards which the functions tended. . . . He loved the guineas best. . . . He spread them out in heaps and bathed his hands in them; then he counted them and set them up in regular piles, and felt their rounded outline between his thumb and fingers, and thought fondly of the guineas that were only half earned by the work in his loom, as if they had been unborn children" (*SM*, 20–21). Given how much life Marner has invested in the coins, it comes as no surprise that, when the gold is stolen, he falls into a state of near catatonia. In the thematic system Eliot has thus far established, he has attributed life to his gold so that it can sustain his life. Having given the gold a meaning it has for no one else in order to confer on himself what little meaning he can bear, Marner can barely survive its loss.

In the episode that awakens Marner from this state of suspended animation, the narrative extends the logic enacted in this transaction. Whereas Marner had substituted for an instrumental understanding of gold a meager set of meanings that just kept his heart alive, the narrative now begins to infuse the word *gold* with a new set of meanings that expand its animating capacity. This episode also signals Eliot's shift from a merely mimetic form of "realism"—the kind of writing that could convey information about "real poor people" to an audience curious to learn—to a mode of aesthetic representation that infuses even pictures of poor people with a "poetic" dimension. This dimension—the aura or excess that Literary writers consistently associated with poetry—was what novelists like Eliot wanted to produce in novelistic prose. The episode in which this double shift occurs, which appears in part 1, chapter 12, describes Marner's first encounter with a child who, having sought refuge in the weaver's cottage, has fallen asleep on his floor. The narrative relates this encounter through a version of the indirect discourse Austen refined, with the result that the reader's perspective is simultaneously aligned with that of the weaver and trained on him. When we read that Marner has "contracted the habit of opening his door and looking out from time to time, as if he thought that his money might be coming back to him" (*SM*, 109), for example, the phrase that begins with *as if* allows the reader to look at the weaver instead of looking with him, with the result that we interpret the weaver's action in a way that might or might not coincide with his understanding. When Marner reenters his cottage, this double perspective persists:

> He thought he had been too long standing at the door and looking out. Turning towards the hearth, where the two logs had fallen apart, and sent forth only a red uncertain glimmer, he seated himself on his fireside chair, and was stooping to push his logs together, when, to his blurred vision, it seemed as if there were gold on the floor in front of the hearth. Gold!—his own gold— brought back to him as mysteriously as it had been taken away! He felt his heart begin to beat violently, and for a few moments he was unable to stretch out his hand and grasp the restored treasure. The heap of gold seemed to glow and get larger beneath his agitated gaze. He leaned forward at last, and stretched forth his hand; but instead of the hard coin with the familiar resisting outline, his fingers encountered soft warm curls. In utter amazement, Silas fell on his knees and bent his head low to examine the marvel: it was a sleeping child.... How and when had the child come in without his knowledge?... But along with that question, and almost thrusting it away, there was a vision of the old home and the old streets leading to Lantern Yard— and within that vision another, of the thoughts which had been present with him in those far-off scenes. The thoughts were strange to him now, like old friendships impossible to revive; and yet he had a dreamy feeling that this child was somehow a message come to him from that far-off life. (110–11)

Parts of this passage clearly reproduce Marner's thoughts: "Gold!—his own gold—brought back to him as mysteriously as it had been taken away!... How and when had the child come in?" Insofar as these sentences align the reader's perspective with the weaver's "agitated gaze," we, too, see gold in the body of the child, then wonder at the girl's arrival. Insofar as Eliot allows the reader a point of view that does not coincide with Marner's, however, we know that the weaver is mistaken both in believing that his gold has returned and in imagining that the child is a message from his previous life. But the double perspective created by free indirect discourse does not simply correct Marner's literalism; nor does it provide only a clinically accurate depiction of a recluse's delusion. Instead, this passage paves the way for the child to *become* gold in a manner that differs from the literal sense Marner initially imagines. For, as the story unfolds, the value that most people would attribute to literal gold, and that the word *gold* would ordinarily denote, migrates to the child, where it is transformed into an altogether different kind of value. Thus, Marner is right in imagining that the child is gold, but only because he gradually learns that *gold* is not necessarily literal or limited to the coins the word usually denotes.

The plot of *Silas Marner* enacts another version of this displacement of literal meaning by connotation, for, as love for Eppie replaces the love he had once lavished on the gold, Marner ceases to miss his hoard and to view the money he now earns in quite a different way. At first, the weaver dismisses the monetary function of gold as incidental—not because the gold seems too alive to spend, as it once had seemed, but because gold no longer seems to matter at all. Soon, however, he restores the monetary function to gold because his interest is fixed on something other than himself: "The disposition to hoard had been utterly crushed at the very first by the loss of his long-stored gold: the coins he earned afterwards seemed as irrelevant as stones brought to complete a house suddenly buried by an earthquake.... And now something had come to replace his hoard which gave a growing purpose to the earnings, drawing his hope and joy continually onward beyond the money" (*SM*, 131). That which "replace[s]" the weaver's hoard, of course, is something literal gold could never buy; and, as his hopes are directed forward, "beyond the money," the monetary function can return, for the values the novel promotes are no longer jeopardized by the values associated with money.

Substituting the child for gold in the episode I have quoted enables Eliot to transform the weaver's initial nonmonetary relation to gold into a human relationship that puts money in its proper place: it becomes the mere "function" that sustains the "end" of a genuinely meaningful life. Such a life, of course, is what De Quincey's "literature of power" was also said to sustain by enlarging the reader's sympathies; by analogy, then, the "literature of knowledge" De Quincey described could do no more than provide the conditions in which such a life could be lived, as literal gold purchased the necessities of life. This expansion of sympathy is what Eliot depicts in the remainder of the narrative, for she shows Eppie so engaging Marner's sympathies that, when her real father appears and offers to make her rich, the weaver can allow her to make the choice for herself. When Eppie elects to remain in her humble surroundings, the narrator makes explicit what everything in the story has implied: the metaphoric "treasure"

Eppie incarnates has brought Marner more than money can buy; in the process, it has "exalted" these humble characters beyond the ordinariness of prose to the heights associated with "poetry": "Perfect love has a breath of poetry which can exalt the relations of the least-instructed human beings" (*SM*, 146). Even her disappointed father, the landowner Godfrey Cass, ultimately has to accept that the rules associated with literal money have been rendered obsolete by the love whose value Marner and Eppie have demonstrated. "'There's debts we can't pay like money debts, by paying extra for the years that have slipped by,'" Cass admits as he relinquishes his claims to Eppie (174).

Silas Marner provides a particularly clear example of the way that mid-century novelists subjected economic matters—in this case, the monetary value of gold—to the alchemy of a moral lesson by emphasizing the connotative capacity of language—that is, the elevation of figuration and suggestion over denotation and reference. Marner initially mistakes Eppie for actual gold because he thinks that her blonde hair is literal "gold on the floor" (*SM*, 110), but, when the young girl is called a "treasure" (137, 172), metaphor trumps such literalness. When Eppie chooses her adopted "father," Marner, over her actual father, she repeats this logic: what a linguistic figure can be made to mean, through imaginative elaboration and the power of connotation, is more valuable than what reference, denotation, or quantification can convey. Eliot's emphasis on language's ability to transfigure and ennoble also helps explain why the historical inaccuracies of this tale and the textual contradictions it contains do not matter to the ethical lesson it confers: in the first decades of the nineteenth century, when the events of *Silas Marner* are explicitly set, a weaver would have been far more likely to be paid in some kind of paper money than in gold; and, in the novel itself, Eppie's "auburn" hair (138) inexplicably metaphorizes into "gold" again at the end of the novel (181).

Eliot's attempt to make readers appreciate the connotative capacities of Literary language by troping terms associated with the market model of value is echoed in numerous Victorian novels. When, at the end of Dickens's *Our Mutual Friend*, Bella Wilfer becomes "the true golden gold" of feminine virtue, for example, Dickens also implies that metaphor can trump reference because the moral value a writer can cultivate in a novel is more powerful than the mere monetary value of literal gold in the merely actual world. Even if novels did circulate in the marketplace as commodities, such tropes suggest, they were able to create for readers experiences money could not buy and modes of imaginative engagement merely informational writing could never inspire.

The Rewards of Form: *The Last Chronicle of Barset*

In identifying the occasions for the three nineteenth-century novels I have examined, I have thus far emphasized extratextual situations and events: the transformation of the publishing industry and the epistemological fallout of the Restriction Act in Austen's Regency novel; financial scoundrels and readers' expectations behind Dickens's and Eliot's midcentury fictions. The last novel I consider also seems to have been occasioned by an identifiable historical event, and, in part, it undeniably was. What Trollope did with this event, however, was to so completely alter the function its representation plays that its fictional version differs radically from his contemporaries' descriptions of the same event. In some important ways, in fact, all the extratextual situations and events that his novel seems so faithfully to reproduce constituted less compelling occasions for *The Last Chronicle of Barset* than did one that was generic in nature. As the last of the six novels that compose the "Barsetshire novels"—as the novel that transformed the previous five *into* a series by bringing the series to a close—this novel prepared Trollope's readers to view the novel he had just completed, *Can You Forgive Her?* as the beginning of a *new* series, the "Palliser novels." Thus, the generic occasion for this novel coincided with its generic novelty, for Trollope's Barsetshire series was the first such series (in English), the series that taught readers not to assume that a story's conclusion would always coincide with the end of a particular book.[22]

To cast *The Last Chronicle* as a formalist work of art—as a novel that approaches James's ideal of organic unity—might seem perverse, for it threatens to ignore both the novel's position in the series of Barsetshire novels and the way generations of readers, including Henry James, have understood Trollope's works.[23] Many nineteenth-century readers, whether they loved Trollope's novels or despised them, considered them accurate representations of English life, and many modern Literary critics view them as the most referential of all Victorian fiction.[24] In this section, I risk the charge of perversity because treating *The Last Chronicle of Barset* as an example of midcentury formalism enables me to show both how deep the strain of formalism runs in the modern discipline of Literary studies and what even a novel that seems to refer to nontextual events contributed to this emphasis. The description I offer of this novel, in other words, seeks to capture the way Trollope made the worlds his novels depict so compelling, so detailed, and apparently so artlessly crafted that even the events to which they seem most obviously to refer, even the craft that creates this impression, and even the series to which this novel undeniably belongs become irrelevant to the experience of *this* novel, to the experience of this *as* a novel that is virtually, if not completely, self-contained.

The most obvious extratextual occasion for *The Last Chronicle of Barset* was the failure, on 10 May 1866, of Overend, Gurney, and Company, the prestigious London bill-broking house.[25] We saw in chapter 4 how political economists and financial journalists dealt with the panic this collapse briefly caused, and we also saw that, to one journalist at least, the collapse of Overend and Gurney provided an opportunity to remind Britons that the nation's overall financial system was stable and safe. I begin my discussion of *The Last Chronicle of Barset* by returning to Walter Bagehot's response to the 1866 panic because both the novel and Bagehot's articles focus on the same credit instrument—the bank check. What interests me about the novel's use of the check—especially in light of Bagehot's articles—is that, even though a check constitutes the axis of the novel's complex plots, Trollope did not take advantage of or even mention some of this monetary form's most important features, which were the very points Bagehot stressed about it. Reading Trollope's novel in relation to Bagehot's articles enables us to see how little it mattered *for the coherence of the fiction* that a Literary appropriation of an actual instrument got the details of its use wrong. Let me emphasize at the outset that I am not treating Trollope's novel and Bagehot's articles as parts of a single discourse. Even though both can be said, in some sense, to be about the same subject, and even though both undeniably helped mediate readers' relation to that aspect of the credit system represented by the bank check, the two men use in their writing such different generic conventions to perform functions so different from each other that they are best viewed as being engaged in different *kinds* of writing. At the end of this discussion, I show that the pictures of the credit economy these kinds of writing produced were radically different too. That the two could coexist in the late 1860s reminds us that economic theorists had not yet succeeded in making their account of "the economy" the only plausible way of understanding the complex dynamics of credit and debt. Of course, because *The Last Chronicle of Barset* is *only* a novel, because it is only incidentally concerned with economic matters, it posed no challenge to the authority economic writers sought to claim in this regard.

Bagehot's articles appeared in the *Economist* on 12 and 19 May, immediately after the collapse of Overend and Gurney. As we saw in chapter 4, in these articles Bagehot singled out the check for special attention for two reasons: first, as a form of "refined credit," the bank check required and epitomized the public confidence that, in ordinary times, allowed the British financial system to work so well; and, second, as the most vulnerable part of the credit system, checks provided a fail-safe, for creditors' unwillingness to accept them both signaled that the credit system was in trouble and shifted public confidence back to that "coarser" form of credit, the Bank of England note.[26] Paradoxically, then, in periods of panic, the public's distrust of checks increased its trust in Bank of England notes, and, as long as legislators allowed the Bank to issue enough notes (by suspending the Bank Act), the system could be restored to its former equilibrium.

To explain this paradox and calm his panicked readers, Bagehot described the role the London Clearing House played in the British financial system.[27] The way that Bagehot described this institution—he both assumed that his readers understood the Clearing House system and implied that they needed to remember what they had temporarily forgotten—reveals that the central instrument of this system, the bank check, was poised on the threshold of cultural taken-for-grantedness in 1866, as the Bank of England note had been in 1850: people inside the financial industry, who dealt with checks every day, simply took this instrument for granted and examined individual checks only to see whether they conformed to type, while people outside the financial industry—ordinary people—might still be skeptical, not just about a particular check, but about checks in general. We can see that the check occupied this threshold position precisely because it could become—or be made—visible in a period of panic like May 1866; and it could be made visible, in turn, because it was a representative of a representative of the ground of value (a deposit in a bank) instead of a representative of this ground (gold), as a Bank of England note was assumed to be.

In Bagehot's account, the threshold status of the English bank check was easiest to see when the reader considered what happened when a foreign country tried to introduce the "Anglo" system of banking:

> Persons who have been connected with, or who have watched what we may call *Anglo* banking—the introduction of an English system of banking into continental countries—well comprehend how useful, how refined, how incomprehensible to most foreigners is this cheque currency. The bank note is a most coarse form of credit as compared with it. Taking a bank note (even when not a legal tender) only involves trusting the bank; but taking a cheque presumes also a trust in the cheque-giver. He says he has a balance, and the bank says it will pay that balance. It is so familiar to us that we forget the anomaly; but it is strange that thousands' worth, millions' worth we might say, of solid securities are daily parted with in London on the credit attached to

assertions like these. It is right; the confidence is well repaid; but if you try to explain the *rationale* to a sceptical and inexperienced foreigner, you will not find it very easy to put the argument convincingly. ("What," 89)

With the "sceptical and inexperienced foreigner" rhetorically standing in for the frightened English reader, Bagehot patiently explained what every Briton ought to know: "In a panic, this currency of cheques—this currency of refined credit—is much disturbed, and is in part destroyed; and, therefore, we fall back on credit of the first order—on credit of the coarser sort—upon bank notes. We require *more* bank notes, just because the *feeling*, the confidence which made *few* bank notes effectual has disappeared" (89).

The sudden visibility to which the check was susceptible, then, ensured that distrust would not carry over to the next monetary instrument in the chain of Britain's credit, the Bank of England note. All that was necessary to halt the panic was to restore the *"feeling"* that generally allowed few Bank notes to suffice, and all that was necessary to restore this feeling was to allow the Bank of England to issue more notes by making it easier to suspend the 1844 Bank Act in periods of distress ("What," 91). As we saw in chapter 4, Bagehot did not think that amending the act would end the need for suspension, but he did insist that an amendment would allow the government "to deal with an internal panic, not as an exceptional monstrosity to be destroyed by an illegal act; but as a calculable, though unpleasant, piece of business" (92).

For the purposes of this argument, Bagehot's articles are important because he insisted that checks constituted a special kind of money, one that differed from both Bank notes (in being more "refined") and bills of exchange (in requiring no discount at point of origin).[28] Checks could be represented as a special kind of credit paper because of their unique features: unlike a bill of exchange, a check did not require an endorsement; unlike a Bank note, a check conferred value only if it was returned to a bank within a "reasonable time." As we saw in the preamble, this reasonable time was determined not by law but by convention. By the middle of the nineteenth century, bankers and the public alike generally interpreted the reasonable time a check could be held as two days—the period between the receipt of the check and the end of the next business day.[29] After this period, the person who had accepted the check could not assume that the bank would honor it. For this reason, and because a check accrued no interest, there was no reason for anyone to hold a check longer than the time required to take it to a bank.[30]

We do not know whether Anthony Trollope read Bagehot's two articles, but we do know that the composition of *The Last Chronicle of Barset* overlapped with the fall of Overend and Gurney and the appearance of Bagehot's essays. Trollope composed the novel between 21 January and 15 September 1866.[31] He published the work, in the unusual format of thirty-two stand-alone parts priced at 6d. each, between December 1866 and July 1867, in a frankly commercial experiment designed both to rival magazine publication and to challenge the tyranny of Mudie's. We also know that Trollope was familiar with at least some of Bagehot's work, for the first part of the latter's *English Constitution* ran in the *Fortnightly Review*, the periodical Trollope helped found, in May 1865. From Trollope's repeated trips to London during this period as well as his intense interest in the state of his own finances, we can also assume that he knew about Overend and Gurney's failure and that he would have registered, at least indirectly, the shock waves that subsequently roiled the British financial system.[32] Thus, even if Trollope decided long before the crash of Overend and Gurney to focus the novel on a check, the firm's failure, the ensuing panic, and Bagehot's articles all appeared while he was composing the novel, and it makes sense to try to determine how, if at all, these events register in the completed text.

The central question of *The Last Chronicle* is how the Reverend Josiah Crawley, the poor clergyman of Hogglestock, came into possession of a check for £20 that was initially drawn by Lord Lufton on his London bank and given to his agent, Mr. Soames, in exchange for ready money (Bank notes). At the beginning of the novel, Crawley has been accused of stealing the check, which Mr. Soames claims to have lost at Crawley's house. Crawley has undeniably cashed the check in order to pay his creditors, by sending it to a Barchester bank by way of a brickmaker from Hoggle End. Even though Crawley is repeatedly asked how he obtained the check, however, the confused and befuddled clergyman cannot say, and Trollope spins a novel of almost nine hundred pages out of the speculation, rumor, charges, and conjectures that fill the vacancy left by Crawley's silence.

The centrality of the check is established in the first pages of the novel, for the story of its loss is the first thing the reader encounters. Before Mr. Crawley has even made an appearance, the narrator tells us: "The crime laid to his charge was the theft of a check for twenty pounds, which he was said to have stolen out of a pocket-book left or dropped in his house, and to have passed as money into the hands of one Fletcher, a butcher of Silverbridge, to whom he was indebted."[33] A few pages later, the narrative elaborates further:

Some six weeks after this [Fletcher's receiving his money], inquiry began to be made as to a certain cheque for twenty pounds drawn by Lord Lufton on his bankers in London, which cheque had been lost early in the spring by Mr. Soames, Lord Lufton's man of business in Barsetshire, together with a pocket-book in which it had been folded. This pocket-book Soames had believed himself to have left at Mr. Crawley's house, and had gone so far, even at the time of the loss, as to express his absolute conviction that he had so left it. He was in the habit of paying a rentcharge to Mr. Crawley on behalf of Lord Lufton, amounting to twenty pounds four shillings, every half-year.... This amount was, as a rule, remitted punctually by Mr. Soames through the post. On the occasion now spoken of, he had had some reason for visiting Hogglestock, and had paid the money personally to Mr. Crawley. Of so much there was no doubt. But he had paid it by a cheque drawn by himself on his own bankers at Barchester, and that cheque had been cashed in the ordinary way on the next morning. On returning to his own house in Barchester he had missed his pocket-book, and had written to Mr. Crawley to make inquiry.... Mr. Crawley had answered this letter by another, saying that no pocket-book had been found in his house. All this had happened in March.

In October, Mrs. Crawley paid the twenty pounds to Fletcher, the butcher, and in November Lord Lufton's cheque was traced back through the Barchester bank to Mr. Crawley's hands. A brickmaker, of Hoggle End, much favoured by Mr. Crawley, had asked for change over the counter of this Barchester bank—not, as will be understood, the bank on which the cheque was drawn—and had received it. The accommodation had been refused to the man at first, but when he presented the cheque the second day, bearing Mr. Crawley's name on the back of it, together with a note from Mr. Crawley himself, the money had been given for it; and the identical notes so paid had been given to Fletcher, the butcher, on the next day by Mrs. Crawley. When inquiry was made, Mr. Crawley stated that the cheque had been paid to him by Mr. Soames, on behalf of the rentcharge due to him by Lord Lufton. But the error of this statement was at once made manifest. There was the cheque, signed by Mr. Soames himself, for the exact amount—twenty pounds four shillings. As he himself declared, he had never in his life paid money on behalf of Lord Lufton by a cheque drawn by his lordship. The cheque given by Lord Lufton, and which had been lost, had been a private matter between them. His lordship had simply wanted change in his pocket, and his agent had given it to him. (*LC*, 38–39)

Here is the case in a nutshell, complete with details about people, figures, and dates. There were originally two checks: one, for an odd amount, was drawn by Mr. Soames on his Barchester bank (to pay Lord Lufton's rent), delivered to Crawley and cashed in the "ordinary way the next morning"; the other, for an even amount, was drawn by Lord Lufton on his London bank, given in exchange for cash to Mr. Soames, lost, then, some seven months later, cashed at another Barchester bank, by a brickmaker of Hoggle End, on behalf of Crawley, who had signed its back.

This straightforward narration leaves two questions unanswered: How did Mr. Crawley get Lord Lufton's check? Where was the check during the seven-month period between its loss and its presentation at the bank? At the end of the novel, some seven hundred pages after this passage, the reader learns part of the answer to both questions. Mrs. Arabin, the wealthy wife of the dean of Barset and a friend of the Crawleys, states simply: "I gave him [Mr. Crawley] the cheque" (*LC*, 737). In response to further questioning, Mrs. Arabin explains that she obtained the check "as part of the rent due to her from the landlord of 'The Dragon of Wantley'" (739), the inn she inherited from her first husband. She admits knowing that she could have deposited the check in her own bank, but, since she "kept [her] account at the other bank" (i.e., not the Barchester bank where Lord Lufton had an account [740]), she simply put the check into her desk, and, when her current husband, Dean Arabin, wanted to give Mr. Crawley a gift of fifty pounds, she impulsively put the check into an envelope along with the five ten-pound Bank of England notes her husband intended to give (739). "I thought that cheques were like any other money," Mrs. Arabin says in some embarrassment; "but I shall know better for the future" (809).

As even this truncated summary suggests, Trollope places a check at the center of his narrative because of two of its unique features. Because the check did not have to be endorsed, it could pass through various hands without signature; this means that, unlike a bill of exchange, the check would not have carried a record of its history on its back; and *this* means that, when Mrs. Arabin received the check, she would not have known that Mr. Soames and Jem Scuttle had once had it. Second, because the check was a representative of a representative of value, it was the only credit instrument whose value was simultaneously so mediated and so deferred—yet without any loss or increase in worth; this means that Trollope could use the check as an objective correlative for Mr. Crawley himself. Like an actual check, that is, which yielded its monetary value (in Bank notes) only belatedly, when it was returned to the bank, so Mr. Crawley yields his own value—the truth of his innocence—only belatedly, when Mrs. Arabin admits that she gave him the check. Before that moment, the narrator tells us, he remembers where he got the check ("with an exactness" that seems to him "almost marvellous" [*LC*, 772]), but he still does not know, and cannot say, whether he stole it.

This peculiarity in Mr. Crawley's character—he remembers but does not know—is apparently explained by two details: when he is initially confronted with his signature on Lord Lufton's check, Crawley mistakenly says that Mr. Soames gave it to him (*LC*, 40); and, when Dean Arabin is asked whether he gave Crawley the check, as Crawley subsequently claims, Arabin answers definitively that he did not (41). Yet the peculiarity that is Crawley's character is more than a response to his initial blunder and Arabin's denial; it also expresses the effort, on Trollope's part, to alter the mode of characterization that prevailed in midcentury novels and that he had used to such effect in his own previous works. Trollope emphasized the two features of checks I have just named—they did not require endorsement, and they deferred but did not necessarily lose the value they represented—because these features could be used to launch a mode of characterization that encouraged the reader to do more than simply identify with a fictional character. In order to make sense of Mr. Crawley, the reader has to recognize patterns; she must see that details that are distributed throughout a long and complex narrative belong to a single pattern and that this pattern, once assembled, constitutes the secret that even Crawley does not know. Thus, Trollope did not emphasize either the property of checks that Bagehot stressed, that they constituted "refined" credit whose fragility could signal an impending crash, or the property that most Victorians would probably have thought of first, that a check was guaranteed only if it was returned to the bank in reasonable time. He did not emphasize these characteristics (or allude to the financial panic that erupted midway through his writing) because, for him, the fictional check served an *aesthetic* function, not the financial function an actual check served for economists, bankers, and ordinary Britons.

To show how Trollope used the check to help develop this mode of characterization, I need to describe the way that Trollope managed the novel's complex narrative system. What I am about to describe constitutes an elaboration of the system of narrative management we saw in *Pride and Prejudice*, although I argue that Trollope managed the relationship between various plots *and* between the events that compose the *story* and his *narration* of these events to produce an even more attenuated relationship between the novel and everything outside it than Austen's gestural aesthetic did.[34] Instead of simply revealing in a single narration where the check has been and why (as he did with the controversy about the check's whereabouts, which I have just quoted), Trollope broke up this story and distributed its parts throughout the novel. Thus, for example, the narrative reveals in chapter 5 that Lord Lufton issued Mr. Soames a second check as soon as he learned that the first one was lost (*LC*, 65); this, we are told in chapter 8, led Mr. Soames to stop payment on the first check at the London bank where it had been issued (105). It was because the check was stopped at its point of origin that the bankers attempted to trace its recipients, for, when the Barchester bank where the brickmaker cashed the check sent it to London to clear, the London bank dishonored it; this caused the Barchester bank to pursue Mr. Soames, who had stopped payment in London, and who was then forced to tell the story of losing the check at the clergyman's house. The reader can see this sequence only by patiently reconstructing it, just as one can understand Elizabeth's allusion to her broken promise only by working back through *Pride and Prejudice*. Unlike the sequence I described in Austen's novel, however, which is inconsequential *in* and *for one's experience of* the novel, this sequence is integral to one's understanding of *The Last Chronicle*, for, unless one reconstructs these events, it is impossible to understand why Soames brings charges against Crawley in the first place.

A second example reveals more about this complex mode of narration. This example involves, on the one hand, the sequence at the level of the story that reveals how Mrs. Arabin obtained the check and, on the other, the sequence at the level of the narration by which the reader learns about these events. To enable the reader to reconstruct the story, Trollope used two characters: Mrs. Arabin, who discloses, in chapter 70, that she got the check from Dan Stringer, the innkeeper's cousin; and the attorney Mr. Toogood, who is a cousin of Mrs. Crawley's acting on the clergyman's behalf. Toogood first visits the inn in Barchester in chapter 42; and he returns to the inn in chapter 72. On the first visit, the narrator mentions that Toogood sees Dan Stringer, who is hanging about the inn, and that he learns about another servant, Jem Scuttle, who left for New Zealand soon after the check disappeared. Because Toogood does not yet realize the significance of these figures, however, and because the narrative is focalized through Toogood, the reader is not encouraged to notice these characters any more than Toogood does. On the second visit, which is narrated after Mrs. Arabin has revealed to Johnny Eames—and, thus, to the reader—that she got the check from Dan Stringer, Toogood, who has received Mrs. Arabin's news by telegraph, confronts Stringer. At this point, Toogood is able to infer that Stringer probably got the check from Scuttle, who probably stole it from Mr. Soames as he was driving him to Crawley's house. Thus, long after the theft of the check occurred, the reader and Mr. Toogood can put the pieces of the puzzle together, and, belatedly, we can also see why Dan Stringer was hanging around in chapter 42.

One final example of this dynamic is even more revealing. In chapter 42, Mr. Toogood learns that Mrs. Arabin's father, old Mr. Harding, has "mentioned" the mystery of the check to his daughter in a letter he sent to Paris; Toogood also learns that, having already left Paris, Mrs. Arabin did not receive the letter. But Mr. Harding does *not* tell Mr. Toogood one more detail, which is immediately conveyed to the reader in a second letter that Mr. Harding writes to his daughter and that Trollope includes verbatim in the novel. In this letter, Mr. Harding tells Mrs. Arabin that the solution to Mr. Crawley's situation "has something to do with the money which was given to Mr. Crawley last year, and which, if I remember right, was your present" (*LC*, 433).

Coming, as it does, precisely halfway through the novel, this detail has the potential to solve the mystery. Yet, because Mr. Harding does not realize the significance of what he remembers, because he does not tell Mr. Toogood what he recalls, and because the pronoun *your* could either be singular, referring only to Mrs. Arabin, or plural, referring to her and her husband, no one—not even the reader—is encouraged to see why it matters. Like the first two examples, this one detaches the events in the story from the narration of them; but it also detaches the understanding a *character* is able to achieve from that of the *reader* because Trollope gives the reader access to information a character does not have. This last example thus demonstrates that Trollope was making *detection* a prominent component of reading, just as it is, in a different sense, in the novel's story. Detection, of course, would have been easier for someone who was *rereading* the novel, for this reader would be able to identify as *clues* details that might seem inessential on first reading. Thus, *deferral* at the level of story both cultivated and yielded to *detection* in the process of reading, and it made rereading yield understanding that was superior to what even a careful first reading could produce. If deferral installed belatedness at the heart of significance, then detection and the kind of pattern recognition facilitated by rereading were the reading practices by which that significance could, belatedly, be conferred.

The complexities of the check's journey and the disjunction between the story and the narration can be graphically conveyed by two simple synopses:

1. *The journey of the check (the story)*:

Lord Lufton → Mr. Soames (the cheque is lost in early spring) → Jem Scuttle → Dan Stringer → Mrs. Arabin → Dean Arabin → Mr. Crawley → brickmaker → Barchester bank → London bank/// → the Barchester Bank → Mr. Soames (who has stopped the check) → Mr. Crawley.

(The "///" indicates the moment when the check loses its value, which occurs when Soames stops it at the bank. Having lost its value, the check becomes a clue, not a monetary instrument.)

2. *The narration of this journey:*

The narrative reveals in chapter 1 that the check passed from Lord Lufton to Mr. Soames, who lost it in the "early spring."

In chapter 42, Mr. Toogood sees Stringer but does not know that he belongs to this mystery. In this chapter, Mr. Harding's letter also informs the reader that Mrs. Arabin gave money to Crawley.

In chapter 70, Mrs. Arabin tells Johnny Eames that she gave the check to Crawley. She also says that she received it from Dan Stringer. All this took place in mid-April.

In chapter 72, Mr. Toogood discovers that Stringer got the check from Jem Scuttle, who probably stole it from Mr. Soames.

The dynamic captured by these two summaries is one in which the narration's revelation of plot details and a character's or a reader's understanding are both detached from the events to which they refer, then allowed, belatedly, to infuse those events with the only meaning they ever have. This, of course, is also the dynamic of credit—the dynamic by which monetary instruments like checks acquired their value in relation to gold in nineteenth-century Britain. Checks, that is, circulated as value because they were both detached from gold and, implicitly and belatedly, linked to it. As instruments whose value rested solely on trust, checks also obliquely shored up the trust that underwrote the value of the Bank's gold—the belief that enough of it was actually in the Bank's reserve. This dynamic had enormous social and material significance in nineteenth-century Britain, of course, for it was the mechanism by which collective belief supported the entire credit system and, thus, the foundation for the economic and political stability of the nation—and, beyond that, Britain's worldwide empire. But, in *The Last Chronicle of Barset,* Trollope also used this dynamic as a narrative strategy that supports an aesthetic system: it generates *interest* for the reader and attaches this interest to the reader's ability to find and recognize clues, not just the ability to identify with a character. Indeed, because Crawley knows but cannot believe that he did not steal the check, the reader who simply identifies with him can only share his uncertainty for most of the novel. Recognizing clues and using them to construct a larger pattern, instead of identifying with Crawley, enables the reader to produce for herself the certainty that Crawley only belatedly achieves *and* to recognize that characterization—the belated formation (not recognition) of what character is—is a matter of effort and a response to *art*.

The mode of narration I have been describing would have been familiar to any reader of nineteenth-century novels, just as it is to a modern reader: it is the mode of narration cultivated by Victorian sensation novels and split off into the subgenre of the detective novel. While both these novel forms proliferated in the last half of the century, however, the function this narrative strategy served in Trollope's novel differs slightly from its function in novels like Wilkie Collins's *The Woman in White* or Arthur Conan Doyle's Sherlock Holmes stories. In sensation and detective fiction, the dislocation of narration from story functioned primarily to generate suspense about the outcome of the plot, to convert apparently insignificant details into clues, or to highlight the ingenuity of the detective; the function of these narrative effects, in turn, was to entice the reader to read on—to consume the novel as rapidly as possible. In Trollope's novel, by contrast, the dislocation of narration from story constituted a mode of *characterization*; the narrative deferral, the scattering of clues, and the belated ascription of meaning that both fostered constituted the process by which the reader could know who Mr. Crawley *is*—through the careful kind of reading I have been describing, not through rapid consumption. For Trollope, moreover, narrative dislocation emanated *from* character; it did not stem from circumstances in which a character is enmeshed. In *The Last Chronicle of Barset*, this belated ascription of identity is necessary because Mr. Crawley's peculiar inability to trust his own memory means that he looks to other characters to tell him who he is. Instead of looking inward, in other words, Crawley looks outward, to other characters in the novel, and this means that, while the answer to the mystery lies within himself, making what he knows credible (to himself and to the reader) requires consulting other characters. Thus, Trollope uses Crawley's inability to believe what he knows and the other characters' failure to agree to generate plot, instead of using plot to generate character, as Collins was often accused of doing. Only when the mystery of the check is solved and Dean Arabin belatedly admits that it passed through his hands to Crawley can Crawley see the mystery for what it has always been: the mystery of a self whose identity is not fixed because of its dependence on someone else. "So far have I been from misdoubting the dean," Crawley exclaims when confronted with the truth, "that I postponed the elaborated result of my own memory to his word. . . . Gentlemen, I did not believe my own memory" (*LC*, 772).

Just as Trollope's use of narrative dislocation distinguishes *The Last Chronicle of Barset* from contemporary sensation novels, so the mode of characterization he developed produced a different kind of character from the ones we find in the novels of many of his contemporaries. For, unlike the kind of developmental characters Austen and Eliot depicted, for example, Mr. Crawley does not achieve self-knowledge through maturation. Nor is the truth about his character depicted as a secret to himself, as is the case with characters like Elizabeth Bennet and Maggie Tulliver. Such characters reveal what seems to be a true self by fictitiously growing into self-knowledge, and the reader shares this process of maturation by identifying with them; this is one of the principal means by which a novel was said to promote "self-culture." Mr. Crawley, by contrast, is an old man when the novel opens, and his true character—at least insofar as this is implied by what he did—seems always to be elsewhere and otherwise, awaiting the kind of consensus that only a social tribunal like a trial can confer. For such a character—dislocated, dissociated, not present to itself—the narrative devices that Austen and Eliot used to reveal the latent or immature self are simply inadequate. Instead of using strategies like free indirect discourse to take the reader "deeper" into a character that is complex because divided or hidden, Trollope relocated the complexities that presumably ought to belong inside a psychologized character *outside* the fictional individual, in the complexities of plot. As an effect of plot and narration, Crawley's "character" is available, but only if the reader is willing to pay as much attention to the pattern revealed by narrative dynamics as to what looks like the explicit characterization of Crawley. The reader, in other words, is encouraged not simply to identify with a complex character but to assemble parts of the complex narrative system into a pattern that represents—or stands in for—the character with whom the reader might want to identify.

The ability to cultivate readers' identification with characters had been considered a distinctive feature of the novel since the early eighteenth century, whether this led to dismay from critics worried that impressionable young girls would crave novelistic excitement in their actual lives or to praise from those who argued that identification constituted a vital part of a moral education. As we have seen, Austen also used identification with a maturing or divided character to cultivate a form of undecidability that cultivated the ethical and aesthetic potential of the problematic of representation. Trollope was also cultivating this undecidability, of course, for the reader's inability to know where the check is at any given point in the novel presumably enhanced the pleasure reading this novel could yield. Even though this kind of undecidability constituted an equally aesthetic variant of pleasure, however, Trollope's refusal to encourage readers to identify with a maturing character or one who was simply internally divided made the formalism implicit in Austen's gestural aesthetic produce a new level of textual autonomy. We will see in a moment that my insistence that Trollope's mode of characterization led to a more refined version of formalism *instead of* identification with lifelike characters runs counter to Trollope's explicit claim that novels could—and should—promote identification: repeatedly, ardently, Trollope spoke of himself as having lived with his own characters as if they were cherished friends. Nevertheless, in several of his late novels—in *The Last Chronicle of Barset* and especially in *The Way We Live Now*—he also began to experiment with the kind of characterization I have been describing, which, taken to its logical extreme (as it was by modernists like Virginia Woolf), frustrated readers' attempts to identify with characters or to use this identification to judge or mature. Before I specifically address the apparent contradiction between the mode of engagement I have been describing and Trollope's own explicit commitment to identification with characters, let me turn to another part of *The Last Chronicle of Barset*'s complex narrative system. For Trollope used a secondary plot not simply to hide details essential to the primary plot, as Austen so effectively did, but also to elaborate the complex relationship between imaginative fictions like this one and the actual operations of the credit economy that it seems to, but does not, help readers understand.

———

The Last Chronicle of Barset contains an extensively developed secondary plot that revolves around London and the City. In so doing, this City plot constitutes a counterpoint to the plot that centers on Crawley, which takes place almost exclusively in the country. The City plot involves a number of interrelated stories, all of which are introduced in chapter 24. These include a flirtation between Johnny Eames, who loves Lily Dale, and Madelina Demolines, who wants to prevent her ex-suitor, Conway Dalrymple, from marrying Clara Van Siever, whose portrait he is currently painting; another flirtation between Mrs. Dobbs-Broughton, the wife of an apparently successful financier, and Dalrymple, an artist who specializes in expensive portraits of society women; the shady financial dealings of Mr. Dobbs-Broughton and his partner, Mr. Musselboro; and the even shadier activities of Mrs. Van Siever, the sleeping partner in the business these two men run and the mother of Clara, whose portrait Conway Dalrymple secretly paints in Mrs.

Dobbs-Broughton's London house. These plots culminate in an equally complicated series of denouements: Madelina tries and fails to lure Johnny Eames into marriage; Dobbs-Broughton, having been ruined by Mrs. Van Siever, gambling, and drink, kills himself, leaving Mrs. Dobbs-Broughton financially and emotionally dependent on Conway Dalrymple; Conway extracts himself from the distraught widow and marries Clara Van Siever, whose mother promptly disowns her; and Mr. Musselboro, having failed in his attempt to marry Clara, marries Mrs. Dobbs-Broughton. Finally, Johnny Eames, who has proved himself a "hero" by pursuing Mrs. Arabin to Europe, fails to persuade Lily Dale to marry him, in part at least because Madelina has sent Lily anonymous letters, enclosing with them notes that Johnny Eames had sent Madelina that prove—or at least insinuate—that Johnny has been untrue to Lily.[35]

The link between the City plot and the country plot is Johnny Eames, who sets off to find Mrs. Arabin, who holds the key to the mystery of the check. Johnny Eames is the nephew of Mr. Toogood, who, in turn, is the cousin of Mrs. Crawley, the clergyman's wife. In the overall narrative, there are also obvious parallels between the City and the country plots. The courtship in the country plot between Mr. Crawley's daughter Grace and Major Grantley has its City counterparts in the flirtations between Mrs. Dobbs-Broughton and Conway Dalrymple, on the one hand, and Johnny Eames and Madelina Demolines, on the other; and, more significantly still, the chronic, escalating debt that reduces Mr. Crawley to his miserable, querulous state in the country plot has its counterpart in two minor scenes of indebtedness in the City plot: in the first, Mr. Cradell, a clerk who works in the office alongside Johnny Eames, borrows £3 from his wealthy coworker; in the second, Augustus Crosbie, Lily Dale's ex-lover, borrows £500 from Mr. Butterwell, once his superior, but now his office subordinate, to pay off the debt incurred by Crosbie's late wife's attorney.

Two features of the City plot deserve special attention. The first has to do with the precise financial activities that take place in the City. In a series of disclosures that, like the financial details in *Pride and Prejudice*, are conveyed only incidentally and in passages of description, the narrator reveals that Dobbs-Broughton and Musselboro engage in various financial activities. They speculate in shares, but, more important, "they len[d] money on interest" (*LC*, 379). Because they lend money on short notice, renew loans when they fall due, and risk credit for scant security, Dobbs-Broughton and Musselboro charge unusually high interest rates. They are, in other words, what we would call *loan sharks*, and Mrs. Van Siever, as the sleeping partner who provides the capital, always gets her share. Thus, we learn from various conversations that the partners charge at least 12 percent (440) and that Mrs. Van Siever gets 10 of this 12 for supplying the cash. We also learn, again from a conversation, that Dobbs-Broughton, who also gambles, currently owes Mrs. Van Siever over £950. Because he does not have the money, Dobbs-Broughton proposes giving Mrs. Van Siever a check for £500 and a note of hand, payable at two weeks time, for the rest (385).

Like the gestures toward financial events we have seen in other nineteenth-century novels, these revelations only indirectly instance actual financial transactions, they receive little elaboration in the narrative, and, as a consequence of the latter, they could easily escape the notice of an in-attentive reader. In this sense, they seem to belong to the same kind of gestural aesthetic that I have associated with Austen, Eliot, and Dickens. In *The Last Chronicle of Barset*, however, these narrative gestures serve an even more elaborately aesthetic function than do their counterparts in the novels I have thus far examined: by establishing a relationship within the fiction among details that seem referential (but are not), Trollope simultaneously set up a self-referential system that is confined to the novel and used this system to comment obliquely on the financial system that actually existed in 1866. He did so, moreover, in a way that presented a substantially different picture of the credit system from the one that Bagehot offered that same year.

In *The Last Chronicle of Barset*, as we have just seen, Trollope juxtaposed the check to a note of hand (a promissory note) by making Dobbs-Broughton offer both to Mrs. Van Siever to satisfy (actually, to extend) the debt he owes her. But these are not the only credit instruments mentioned in the novel. Coins, Bank notes, checks, bills of exchange, promissory notes, and informal (unwritten) promises to pay all make an appearance, just as they would have done in the daily transactions of a nineteenth-century Briton. It was this variety of credit instruments to which Walter Bagehot also referred in 1866; but, whereas Bagehot wanted to draw a sharp distinction between one credit instrument and another, Trollope simply placed them on a continuum—at least until the moment in the novel when Mrs. Arabin exclaims that a check is not "like any other money." Until that moment, Trollope not only treats all forms of credit as virtually interchangeable; he also positions the least formal of these, the unwritten promise to pay, on the boundary *between* the credit economy and an older economy of obligations and presents that scholars call the *gift economy*.[36] He extends the credit continuum into the world of gifts by suggesting that, even though the clerk Cradell may not make good on the vow he gives Johnny Eames in exchange for a £3 loan ("upon my solemn word and honour" [*LC*, 167]), Cradell's default will not disrupt their friendship. Johnny Eames has loaned money to Cradell before; other loans have morphed into gifts; and so many other gifts circulate in the novel that they create the impression that Trollope's credit economy is paralleled, and sometimes permeated, by a gift economy that is its virtual twin. Indeed, the proximity between the two—the £800 allowance that Archdeacon Grantly allows his son, which the latter considers an obligation to "marry a lady" (82), and the indiscriminate generosity of Mrs. Thorne, who treats her wealth as if it "belonged to a common stock" (544)—makes it seem that, in this novel, any extension of credit might suddenly become a gift and, vice versa, that a gift might suddenly confer obligation of some kind.

The continuum that Trollope suggests between the credit and the gift economies therefore differs from the relationship Austen implied when she translated Mr. Bennet's monetary obligation to Darcy into Darcy's gift of love. Austen substituted a fictional invocation of the gift for her gestures toward actual financial debt in order to neutralize the anxiety that references to the latter might have caused her readers; Trollope, by contrast, implied that all such transactions were the same in some important ways: all promises to pay, like all bestowals of gifts, deferred the transfer of value, and, as they did, they reinforced the social links among individuals, whether for good or ill. In some ways, this equation must have been reassuring to Trollope's readers, for it suggested that the social ties that linked individuals within families, friendships, parties, and neighborhoods were as important as the economic bonds that reduced every individual to his or her cash worth. In other ways, however, Trollope's credit continuum could have been deeply unsettling, for it reminded readers that every credit instrument, like every debt of any kind, conferred the obligation of relationship, which—as we see in the case of Major Grantley's worry that he will not be able to marry Grace Crawley—restricted one's independence; by making the individual dependent on others, credit and gifts made everyone's character like the character of Mr. Crawley: distended, displaced, a function of relationship, not an expression of a developmental self.

Unlike Bagehot, then, who wanted to draw an absolute distinction between one credit instrument and another (not to mention between the obligation credit represented and the freely given gift), Trollope linked all these forms of indebtedness together. For Bagehot, as we have seen, drawing an absolute distinction between the Bank of England note and the check was intended to reassure his readers by reminding them that Britain's credit system was secure; but, as Trollope's novel suggests, this distinction was, in some ways, a fiction, for it denied both the social component inherent in all forms of credit and the fact that a social relation—mutual belief—was, finally, the only basis for any credit instrument, even Bank of England notes, which, by 1866, were fully taken for granted. Like the absolute distinction so many nineteenth-century writers wanted to draw between fact and fiction as a way to enhance the value of one kind of writing over another, Bagehot's distinction between the Bank of England note and the check required his readers to not acknowledge what was so clearly before them, to not credit what they could otherwise know, and to not worry about what they did not fully understand. Even the economic expert, in other words, by drawing so narrow a compass around how the credit system should be understood, helped make his readers' ignorance about the details of this tolerable, for the belief such ignorance supported was necessary to make credit work in the first place.

As I have repeatedly asserted in this book, imaginative writers also helped neutralize the problematic of representation inherent in the credit economy. This is true in the case of Trollope as well, for his blurring of the boundary between the credit and the gift economies in *The Last Chronicle of Barset* did not systematically or explicitly expose the extent to which credit always depended on people's collective belief—their willingness to not know (or care) that credit instruments worked by deferring the value they supposedly represented. Instead of showing that gifts were different from credit instruments, in other words, in the sense that gifts do not defer value but are simply valuable *in a different sense*, Trollope distinguished between the two in other terms: even though he linked various forms of credit to gifts, in other words, Trollope also implied that gifts *ought* to be different from credit, *not* because the gift is valuable in terms that money cannot represent, but because one is properly the domain of women and the other the business of men. By mapping the difference between a monetary obligation and a gift, both of which he presents as social, onto another distinction, which he clearly considered natural, Trollope tried to provide a natural ground for the gift and money economies. For him, nature is the ground of value that is deferred in modern society: when a woman gives a man a gift, she emasculates him; when a man gives money to a woman, he treats her as a prostitute or another man.

The gendering of the gift and credit economies is visible everywhere in *The Last Chronicle*: when Mrs. Thorne hires a horse for Lily Dale or Mrs. Lufton gives presents of game to Mrs. Crawley (*LC*, 210–11), these are acceptable transactions because they occur between women; when Johnny Eames loans his clerk £3, this is acceptable too, even though the loan might eventually become a gift, because it passes between two men. It is when the alignment of exchange and gender is disturbed that things go horribly wrong in the novel; this explains why Mrs. Arabin's presentation of the check to Mr. Crawley precipitates the novel's crisis. As Trollope tells the story of the check, it does not matter that, in the nineteenth century, a check was different in kind from a Bank note, as it did for Bagehot; nor does it matter that Mrs. Arabin does not cash the check in reasonable time, as it would have for an actual person accepting a check at midcentury. Instead, in the novel, this transaction matters because, in treating the check as a gift, and in giving it to Mr. Crawley, Mrs. Arabin obliterates the natural boundary that ought to separate men from women and masculine business from feminized gifts. In doing so, Mrs. Arabin upsets what Trollope presents as the natural order of things: in conferring a gift of money on a man—even though he has expressly refused such gifts before—Mrs. Arabin reduces Mr. Crawley to the position of a mere woman, and she impugns her husband's masculinity in the process.

Mrs. Arabin's gift expresses the gender disorder that already obtains in the Arabin household. Having inherited money from her first husband, Mrs. Arabin is financially independent: she keeps a separate bank account (*LC*, 500), she is the sole owner of the Wantley inn, and she makes decisions about money without consulting her husband—even, as the case of the check proves, without his knowledge. When she makes Mr. Arabin deliver the envelope to Mr. Crawley, Mrs. Arabin spreads this disorder beyond her home. In the process, she symbolically emasculates both men, by making one her agent and the other the unwilling recipient of the unwanted, because feminizing, gift. Trollope's description of this transaction shifts focalization from one man to another, as the debilitating shame radiates outward from the sealed envelope through the hands of the men who take it:

> [The dean] would willingly have picked the Crawleys out from the pecuniary mud into which they were ever falling, time after time, had it been possible. For, although the dean was hardly to be called a rich man, his lines had fallen to him not only in pleasant places, but in easy circumstances—and Mr. Crawley's embarrassments, though overwhelming to him, were not so great as to have been heavy to the dean. But in striving to do this he had always failed, had always suffered, and had generally been rebuked. Crawley would attempt to argue with him as to the improper allotment of Church endowments—declaring that he did not do so with any reference to his own circumstances, but simply because the subject was one naturally interesting to clergymen. And this he would do, as he was waving off with his hand offers of immediate assistance which were indispensable. Then there had been scenes between

the dean and Mrs. Crawley—terribly painful—and which had taken place in direct disobedience to the husband's positive injunctions. "Sir," he had once said to the dean, "I request that nothing may pass from your hands to the hands of my wife." "Tush, tush," the dean had answered. "I will have no tushing or pshawing on such a matter. A man's wife is his own, the breath of his nostril, the blood of his heart, the rib from his body. It is for me to rule my wife, and I tell you that I will not have it." After that the gifts had come from the hands of Mrs. Arabin—and then again, after that, in the direst hour of his need, Crawley had himself come and taken money from the dean's hands! (809–10)

The shame of the gift is so great, for both men, that it vests the check with the debilitating ignorance that will follow it for the remainder of its journey. So powerful is the association between the feminizing gift and not knowing that Trollope tells us that, even if Arabin had opened the envelope, he would not have understood what he saw: "The interview had been so painful that Arabin would hardly have been able to count the money or to know of what it consisted, had he taken the notes and cheque out of the envelope in which his wife had put them" (810).

In the dynamic of Trollope's novel, it is as if Mrs. Arabin's removing the check from the credit economy, keeping it out of circulation, then giving it as a gift, has neutralized its monetary function—or, more precisely, Mrs. Arabin has stripped the check of its monetary meaning and transformed it into a weapon that neuters every man who touches it. This transfer of the check from the masculine domain of money to the feminized domain of the gift, then, is the origin of the gargantuan plot that is *The Last Chronicle of Barset*. This is the transgression that must be uncovered and corrected before Mr. Crawley can undo the effects of ignorance—before he can know his own mind. The correction occurs, of course, when Mrs. Arabin is tracked down and humbled, by being forced to acknowledge her own ignorance, which motivated her emasculating gift ("I thought that cheques were like any other money, but I shall know better for the future"). While the lesson Mrs. Arabin must learn, however, is the same principle Bagehot wanted to teach his readers in 1866—checks are not the same as Bank notes—the implications of these two lessons could not be more different. It was in order to restore the natural order of gender in his novel that Trollope chastised Mrs. Arabin, by an aesthetic administration of justice that consumes the entire plot. To restore trust in Britain's financial system, by contrast, Bagehot wanted to remind all readers—male and female alike—that the socially most significant binary opposition was between one form of money and another, not between men and women or credit money and gifts; to deliver this lesson, a simple reminder could suffice, for, in 1866, Britain's financial system was already meting out its own justice, in the form of instability and price volatility. For Trollope, then, restoring the ground of moral value—the natural hierarchy of gender—required nine hundred pages of aesthetic reworking and transvaluation; for Bagehot, the ground of value was simply gold, which Bank of England notes transparently represented, and restoring this ground required nothing more than reminding readers that they could believe again, as they had become accustomed to doing.

––––––––

I will return to the subject of gender in a moment, but first let me explore the way that Trollope elaborated the problematic of representation so that it could generate both the pleasures that came from engaging a self-contained aesthetic work and the ethical reform that this engagement could yield. I have been arguing that, in *The Last Chronicle of Barset*, Trollope began to experiment with a mode of characterization that depends partly on plot. Such characterization encouraged a mode of reading in which the reader gathered up disparate clues, then assembled them into a coherent story that is not available through a sequential engagement with the novel. To read in this way is not entirely to leave identification behind, of course, and, at most, we can say that a reading practice focused on recognizing patterns supplements or enhances a reader's engagement with lifelike characters. While its generic novelty was somewhat obscured by Trollope's use of more conventional features that permitted identification, the kind of reading this novel encouraged was relatively new in 1867. I want now to place Trollope's experiment within the context of the discussions about reading that I examined in chapter 5. This will also enable me to locate this generic experiment in the context of Trollope's own discussions of contemporary novels, which, in so many ways, depart from the analysis I have been developing.

As we have seen, an explicit debate about what and how to read did not saturate the Victorian press until the mid-1880s, but a few individuals broached these subjects in the middle decades of the century. In 1859, for example, Samuel Smiles included a chapter entitled "Self-Culture" in his popular *Self-Help* in which he asserted that good reading is characterized not by the quantity of books one reads but by the quality of attention one devotes to the book at hand: rather vaguely, he described this attention as "the concentration of the mind for the time being on the subject under consideration."[37] In general, however, *Self-Help* qualifies any endorsement it gives to attentive reading by the pervasive suspicion Smiles cast on all reading, which he considered "much less influential than practical experience and good example in the formation of character."[38] The first unqualified endorsement of a more serious mode of reading was issued three years later, by Matthew Arnold in a lecture entitled "On Translating Homer." Arnold made this lecture more generally available when he published it, along with his other Oxford lectures, later that year. The relatively specialized nature of his addressee limited the impact of his remarks, however, and his concentration on classical poetry simply ratified the hierarchy of Literary genres that had traditionally relegated the novel to an inferior position.

We saw in chapter 5 that Ruskin's 1864 "Of King's Treasuries" supplied more general terms for the debate—terms that were, potentially, at least, applicable to the novel as well as poetry. Like other midcentury writers, Ruskin was concerned about how the acceleration of print and the growth of the reading audience might affect the nation's reading skills, and he tried to counteract any deleterious effects by setting up a hierarchy of books, which, like many midcentury hierarchies, shaded into a hierarchy of reading practices. Ruskin began with the question many of his contemporaries asked: "What to read?" To answer this question, he offered a distinction that drew on, but significantly altered, De Quincey's distinction between "literature of power" and "literature of knowledge." For Ruskin, the salient distinction separated "books of the hour"—"bright accounts of travels; good-humoured and witty discussions of question; lively or pathetic story-telling in the form of novel; firm fact-telling, by the real agents concerned in the events of passing history"—from "books of all time." The first he dismissed because they were not crafted and because their primary function was to convey information. They were "not books at all," he insisted, "but merely letters or newspapers in good print.... [Such works] may not be, in the real sense of the word, a 'book' at all, nor, in the real sense, to be 'read.'" Real reading Ruskin reserved for "books of all time." Such works, he insisted, were not "communication," which he associated with both information and oral delivery; instead, they were *writing*: "A book is essentially not a talking thing, but a written thing; and written, not with a view of mere communication, but of permanence. The book of talk is printed only because its author cannot speak to thousands of people at once; if he could, he would—the volume is mere *multiplication* of his voice.... But a book is written, not to multiply the voice merely, but to perpetuate it" ("KT," 32).

Placing serious books in the realm of "writing" has important implications for the Literary practice of reading. Certainly, the kind of reading that I have associated with *The Last Chronicle* cannot proceed in the absence of writing, if for no other reason than that it is nearly impossible to reconstruct the events of the story without taking notes.[39] The patterns that a reader can recognize as she reads, moreover—between events and characters in the City and country plots, for example—require either a prodigious memory or some written help. Beyond notes like this, which might supplement or collect the marginalia a reader jots alongside a book's type, *writing* also includes all the other printed books the reader (or writer) might have read in a lifetime. Invoking this implicit library as the backdrop to a single book encourages the reader to make sense of a writer's allusions to Shakespeare, Homer, or the other novels in the Barsetshire series, for that matter, by going to another Literary text, not by referring the words to experiences or objects outside the text. When Ruskin placed serious books in the realm of writing, then, he not only removed them from the realm of speech, but he also curtailed the referential function that language so obviously performed in informational writing in favor of a mode of allusion that operates best within Literature construed as an autonomous domain.

When Ruskin explicitly addressed the topic of reading in "Of King's Treasuries," his emphasis fell on the "value" that Literary reading could extract from the worthwhile book. I quoted part of this discussion in chapter 5, but a section I omitted there is relevant here:

If the author is worth anything, . . . you will not get at his meaning all at once. . . . Not that he does not say what he means, and in strong words too; but he cannot say it all; and what is more strange, *will* not, but in a hidden way and in parables, in order that he may be sure you want it. I cannot quite see the reason of this, nor analyse that cruel reticence in the breasts of wise men which makes them always hide their deeper thought. They do not give it you by way of help, but of reward; and will make themselves sure that you deserve it before they allow you to reach it. But it is the same with the physical type of wisdom, gold. There seems, to you and me, no reason why the electric forces of the earth should not carry whatever there is of gold within it at once to the mountain tops, so that kings and people might know that all the gold they could get was there; and without any trouble of digging, or anxiety, or chance, or waste of time, cut it away, and coin as much as they needed. But Nature does not manage it so. She puts it in little fissures in the earth, nobody knows where: you may dig long and find none; you must dig painfully to find any.

And it is just the same with men's best wisdom. When you come to a good book, you must ask yourself, "Am I inclined to work as an Australian miner would? Are my pickaxes and shovels in good order, and am I in good trim myself, my sleeves well up to the elbow, and my breath good, and my temper?" And, keeping the figure a little longer, even at the cost of tiresomeness, for it is a thoroughly useful one, the metal you are in search of being the author's mind or meaning, his words are as the rock which you have to crush and smelt in order to get at it. ("KT," 34–35)

This image conveys the familiar Victorian respect for work, as Stephen Arata has argued,[40] but it also simultaneously reverses the priority the literal ordinarily enjoys over the connotative capacity of language: in Ruskin's account, gold is merely a "type," not a physical thing. At the same time, Ruskin's passage genders reading; or, more precisely, it makes it clear that one kind of reading—call it *Literary reading*—is a fully masculine activity, not the effeminate, indiscriminate consumption so long associated with women, girls, and—not incidentally—novels.

This kind of reading—the "word-for-word examination" of the text that Ruskin recommends ("KT," 43)—is, of course, the ancestor of the professionalized, disciplinary reading taught in modern graduate programs of Literary study. As such, it is also one prototype of the kind of reading with which I have engaged Trollope's novel. While the protocols for this kind of reading were only systematically laid out a century later, I am arguing that novels like *The Last Chronicle of Barset*, whose disjunctive plots and embedded patterns encourage attentive engagement, note taking, and rereading, and that challenge the reader's desire to identify with characters by encouraging the kind of painstaking reconstruction in which I have been engaged, promoted this kind of reading even before it was described, theorized, or presented as a recognizable practice. By placing an individual Literary text within the larger field of Literary writing, moreover, this kind of novel also helped draw the boundaries around Literature, making allusions to other Literary texts more important than references to external reality. This, in turn, helped obscure whatever similarities continued to exist between Literary and informational writing: even when two texts address issues that seem to be identical, as Trollope's novels and Bagehot's articles did, we do not read them in the same way because we classify them differently and, thus, assign different functions to them.[41]

Even if my own reading practice can be said to have descended from the mode of engagement encouraged by *The Last Chronicle of Barset*, two important questions remain. The first concerns the discrepancies between the account of reading I have just given—or the one outlined by Ruskin, for that matter—and the descriptions of reading that Trollope offered in the autobiographical account he wrote in 1875–76. The second has to do with another discrepancy—this one between my description of the novel, which highlights the check, a mode of characterization that impedes identification, and the discrepancy between story and narration, and what seems to have been one of Trollope's most cherished concerns, one that emphasizes gender. As a means of moving toward a conclusion, let me address each of these issues in turn.

The contrast between Trollope's autobiographical account of reading and the description Ruskin offered in *Sesame and Lilies* seems even more significant when we factor in Trollope's opinion about Ruskin's book, which he published in an 1865 review. In the review, Trollope criticized Ruskin for a multitude of sins: the art critic had strayed too far from his area of expertise; his preaching was heavy-handed; and the lessons he wanted to convey, especially in "Of Queen's Gardens," were irrelevant when it came to actual women ("nothing is to be learned from them by any woman living or about to live").[42] Most pertinent to my argument is Trollope's explicit criticism of Ruskin's description of reading. Far from recognizing in Ruskin's account a mode of reading that might be encouraged by or illuminate his own novels, Trollope ridiculed Ruskin's version of reading:

> He first advises men to read, and tells them that they should read attentively. This in itself is very well, and an excellent treatise on reading might probably be given by a man so well instructed as Mr. Ruskin. But when he attempts to define the way in which the general reader should read, he mounts so high into the clouds, that what he says,—if it were not altogether so cloudy as to be meaningless and inoperative,—would quench all reading rather than encourage it. Young or old, boys or girls, we should have our Greek alphabets, and get good dictionaries in Saxon, German, French, Latin, and Greek, in order that we may trace out the real meaning of the words which we read! After this, he is carried away by his wrath against the nation, and tells us that, after all, we are not good enough to read. "My friend, I do not know why any of us should talk about reading. We want some sharper discipline!" "We have despised literature," Mr. Ruskin says, and this he proves by asserting that men will give more for a large turbot than for a book;—but cheap literature he does not like; and he tells us that we are "filthy," because we all thumb the same books from circulating libraries! . . . That such a man should write on Art may be well, but that he should preach to us either on morals or political economy is hardly to be borne.[43]

In part, Trollope's objections to Ruskin articulate the class and educational differences that separated these two men and the assumptions about genre that their respective experiences would have imparted. As the product of a public school, Ruskin assumed that his readers knew Greek and Latin and could recognize Saxon roots, and he also assumed that poetry was self-evidently superior to fiction. Trollope, with his irregular education and his long employment with the postal service, always smarted under the accusation that he did not read Greek and repeatedly took offense at the claim that poetry was generically superior to novels.[44] Protecting the right of the "general reader" to read however and whatever he or she wants, Trollope clearly resented Ruskin's hectoring tone and his unmistakable assumption of educational and generic superiority.

But even recognizing the personal investment Trollope had in defending the "general reader" (and the novel as a Literary form) does not fully explain the gap between the reading practice I have applied to his novel and the way he seems to have imagined readers approaching his work. For, far from claiming that his mode of characterization was innovative or that it discouraged identification, Trollope explicitly described both reading and writing as character centered and as cultivating precisely the kind of identification I have said his novel impedes. Repeatedly in his autobiography, he insisted that characters constitute the center of his fictions, that "plot . . . is the most insignificant part of a tale," that people read in order to learn how to behave, and that a reader's identification with characters—his or her ability to live with characters imaginatively and to believe that they are real—is what makes novels effective as didactic instruments. For Trollope, in short, the ethical role of a novel was fulfilled by an aesthetic that privileged character, not an aesthetic that rendered character elusive by privileging artistry or plot. "No novel is anything," Trollope insisted, "for purposes either of comedy or tragedy, unless the reader can sympathise with the characters whose names he finds upon the page."[45] While other comments do suggest that, in some ways at least, his practice was consistent with the formalism I have been describing—he thought that the parts of a novel should all fit together and that readers should view his Barsetshire novels as parts of a single whole[46]—his insistence that readers must identify with lifelike characters is so emphatic that it threatens to make my analysis seem completely at odds with his stated aesthetic.

As I have already explained, the difference between the analysis I have offered and the way Trollope imagined readers engaging his works *is* both considerable and significant, for it articulates the gap that has opened in the last century and a half between institutionalized modes of "expert" reading and the way a "general reader" typically reads a book. I do not want to understate this difference. Indeed, one of the arguments of this book is that the process of generic differentiation I have been describing produced different modes of reading, including both the disciplined, expert approach to a Literary work and the way a general reader engages a novel. Nevertheless, I think that it is also the case that, even in the mid-nineteenth century, when Trollope composed both *The Last Chronicle of Barset* and his autobiography, elements of the reading practice subsequently refined in the university system were already beginning to appear. The terms in which contemporaries introduced these elements do not coincide with a modern Literary critic's terms, of course, for the specialized vocabulary of the modern discipline had yet to be formulated. But, in debates about what makes a novel "art," and even in the pages of *The Last Chronicle*, we can find adumbrations of the classificatory schema on which subsequent Literary critics would build.

In *An Autobiography*, Trollope alluded to the distinction many midcentury reviewers used to sort and rank contemporary novels, that between novels of character and novels of plot.[47] When he initially addressed the topic, he impatiently dismissed this distinction as critics' useless meddling in the novelist's "art": if a novel is good "Art," he insisted, it had to contain both an effective plot and realistic characters; "if a novel fail in either, there is a failure in Art."[48] When he turned to specific novelists, however, Trollope let the critics' distinction back in, for he, like they, needed categories that would enable him to differentiate among novelists. Thus, he often observed that a given novelist's work tends to favor *either* plot *or* character, not both. Of Edward Bulwer Lytton, for example, Trollope wrote that "the reader with him never feels, as he does with Wilkie Collins, that it is all plot, or, as with George Elliot [*sic*], that there is no plot"; and, of Charlotte Brontë, he approvingly noted that "she lived with those characters" (of *Jane Eyre*).[49] Trollope's discussion of Wilkie Collins, while respectful, dismissed the novel of plot as *too* contrived, too obviously artful: "The construction is most minute and most wonderful. But I can never lose the taste of the construction.... Such work gives me no pleasure."[50]

Trollope's tendency to see a distinction *between* a novel that privileges plot and one that features character reminds us of how important even such imprecise categories were to someone trying to discriminate among novels. As long as this distinction dominated critical discussions of the novel, moreover, as it did in the 1860s and 1870s, novelists who aspired to elevate the status of the genre in the hierarchy of Literary kinds, as Trollope did, almost invariably expressed a preference for the novel of character. They did so largely because of the history of the genre: as we have seen, because of the skepticism that reviewers had long directed toward the novel, writers who wanted to promote this genre tried to stress the beneficial effects readers could achieve by identifying with characters who matured, implicitly, this was the defense advanced by both Austen and Eliot, in their different ways. In light of the relative success of this claim, it is not surprising that Trollope, who was intent on "vindicat[ing his] own profession as a novelist, and also . . . that public taste in literature which has created and nourished the profession [he] follow[ed]," insisted that lifelike characters were the centerpieces of his novels and sometimes implied that character was opposed to plot.[51]

Modern Literary critics no longer use these categories, of course, and the description I have offered of *The Last Chronicle of Barset* presents plot as *a mode of characterization*, not something that is separable from or opposed to characterization. In my account, however, this mode of characterization emphasizes the divisions and inability to know *within* a character rather than the maturation of a conflicted or immature individual, as the more typical nineteenth-century mode of characterization did. I have also argued that Trollope used the disjunction between story and narration to create a different *kind* of plot than what one finds in a Collins novel. Trollope wanted to make plot *function* differently, to make it not simply prolong suspense but engage the reader in discovering the patterns I have identified. Even though I have abandoned the terms Trollope and his contemporaries used, then, insofar as I have respected the difference he created, I think that I have produced a description of Trollope's writing that he would have recognized. Insofar as I have invoked another distinction, however—one that opposes identification with characters to an engagement that focuses on a novel's form (artistry)—I have clearly moved further from Trollope's accounts of the novelist's craft.[52] While it is inevitable that my analytic categories differ from the ones Trollope used, I suggest that his own novel contains passages that support this emphasis on art. These passages typically depict reading or writing.

One episode in *The Last Chronicle of Barset* is particularly significant in this regard, for it reveals that Trollope, like so many of his contemporaries, wanted to distinguish kinds of reading practices from each other, just as he wanted to describe and rank novels. In chapter 62, Mr. Crawley, still suffering under the suspicion that he has stolen the check, tries to decide whether to resign his ministry. Filling his mind are two alternatives: the advice that the Barsetshire clergyman Mr. Tempest has offered in a letter (stay the course, do not resign, and await the clerical court's decision) and the suggestion that he resign implied by the brickmaker Hoggett's mantra, "It's dogged as does it." Before completing his own letter to Dean Arabin, which will convey his decision, Crawley undertakes two mental exercises: he reminds himself of his accomplishments; and he rereads part of the Greek poem that inspired Milton's *Sampson Agonistes*. Among his considerable achievements, Crawley cites the fact that "he knew 'Lycidas' by heart; and as for Thumble [his rival for the curacy], he felt quite sure that Thumble was incompetent of understanding a single allusion in that divine poem" (*LC*, 661). When he takes up the Greek poem, by contrast, Crawley does not recall the ways he outshines the competition but immediately identifies with the fictional character:

> Before he commenced his task [of writing to the dean], he sat down with his youngest daughter, and read—or made her read to him—a passage out of a Greek poem, in which are described the troubles and agonies of a blind giant. No giant would have been more powerful—only that he was blind, and could not see to avenge himself on those who had injured him. "The same story is always coming up," he said, stopping the girl in her reading. "We have it in various versions, because it is so true to life.
>
> > Ask for this great deliverer now, and find him
> > Eyeless in Gaza, at the mill with slaves.
>
> It is the same story. Great power reduced to impotence, great glory to misery, by the hand of Fate—Necessity, as the Greeks called her; the goddess that will not be shunned! . . . 'At the mill with slaves!' Can any picture be more dreadful than that?" . . . His wife was sitting stitching at the other side of the room; but she heard his words—heard and understood them; and before Jane could again get herself into the swing of the Greek verse, she was over at her husband's side, with her arms round his neck. "My love!" she said. "My love!"
>
> He turned to her, and smiled as he spoke to her. "These are old thoughts with me. Polyphemus and Belisarius, and Samson and Milton, have always been pets of mine. The mind of the strong blind creature must be sensible of the injury that has been done to him! The impotency, combined with his strength, or rather the impotency with the memory of the former strength and former aspirations, is so essentially tragic!"
>
> She looked into his eyes as he spoke, and there was something of the flash of old days, when the world was young to them, and when he would tell her of his hopes, and repeat to her long passages of poetry, and would criticise for her advantage the works of old writers. "Thank God," she said, "that you are not blind. It may yet be all right with you."
>
> "Yes—it may be," he said.

"And you shall not be at the mill with slaves."

"Or, at any rate, not eyeless in Gaza, if the Lord is good to me." ... Then he took up the passage himself, and read it on with clear, sonorous voice, every now and then explaining some passage or expressing his own ideas upon it, as though he were really happy with his poetry. (661–62)

In this complex passage, Crawley segues from a mode of reading that paralyzes him because it makes him identify with the blind giant to another mode of reading, one in which memories of other, similar Literary passages and his own engagements with them inspire a new critical attention to the text, thus renewing his sense of possibility. By imaginatively liberating him from his crippling identification with the eyeless giant, memories of the (here unnamed) *Odyssey* (Polyphemous) and Procopius's *Anecdota* or *Secret History* (Belisarius) reanimate Crawley, moving him from imaginative paralysis to critical engagement; just as this novel's dense web of allusions encourages the reader to range freely through other Literary texts, "every now and then explaining some passage or expressing [her] own ideas upon it."[53]

At the end of chapter 62, Mr. Crawley completes his resignation letter. Even though this action may seem to renege on Crawley's newly recovered sense of power, Trollope infuses it with the glow of an inner life reinvigorated by the curate's engagement with Literary writing. Even penniless, this juxtaposition suggests, Crawley will neither dwell among the "slaves" who cannot recognize Milton's allusions nor suffer from the kind of blindness that compounds the pain of impotence. Rejecting a mode of reading that turns on imaginative engagement because it threatens to engulf him with self-pity, Crawley allows the book to lead him into an apparently limitless world where other books await the avid reader. In so doing, this character models a reading practice that Trollope does not theorize in *An Autobiography* but that this novel repeatedly encourages. That one of the many allusions in this chapter invokes "Lycidas," moreover, strengthens the connection I have drawn between the kind of reading Ruskin advocated in "Of King's Treasuries" and the reading practice Trollope models here, for "Lycidas" is the poem Ruskin chose to demonstrate how to read, and he, too, engaged it by elucidating Milton's allusions.

No analysis of a single chapter can prove conclusively that Trollope was developing the experimental formalism I have described, for Literary analysis cannot yield the kind of evidence that is said to prove disputes about information conclusively. Nevertheless, that this chapter juxtaposes Crawley's paralyzing identification with character to a more enabling engagement with Literary allusion suggests that, at some level at least, Trollope *practiced* writing in a way that did not fully correspond to the theoretical formulations he offered. If I am correct—if Trollope's practice encouraged a mode of reading he never theorized as such—then it matters less that he did not use the terms I have used to describe it, for his terms, like mine, inevitably derived from the classificatory schema that was available. This leads, at last, to the final issue I want to address: the gap between what I have stressed in my description of the novel and the emphasis Trollope seems to have preferred. To understand how engagements that resemble each other in their method can generate understandings that are so different in content, we need briefly to return to the process I have been describing in the second half of this book: the process by which kinds of writing came to seem so different during the course of the nineteenth century.

As I have argued, during the nineteenth century the continuum of generic kinds—along with the continuum that linked fact and fiction—was decisively broken up into the separate genres I have described. Even though writers continued to publish what I have called *hybrids*—indeed, even though *every* publication might be said to have been, in important ways, only and always a hybrid—writers and publishers increasingly insisted that all publications were not alike, that informational writing was different from Literary writing, and that Literary writing differed, in crucial (if not universally agreed-on) ways, from what Oliphant disdainfully called "reading for the million." While Literary writers were not typically associated with formal institutions or routinely supported by related, salaried jobs, as economic writers more often were, by the last decades of the century it was possible for writers like Walter Besant to argue that Literature was becoming, if it had not already become, a profession.[54] Both Trollope's career and—more specifically—the chapters on novel writing, novel reading, and criticism included in *An Autobiography* were enabled by and contributed to this development, for, as Trollope and his contemporaries tried to identify the terms by which they could discriminate among kinds of writing—as they tried to discover how novels could be seen as "art"—they helped lay the groundwork for the disciplinary refinement that occurred in twentieth-century universities and graduate programs.

As we have also seen, the delimitation and internal ordering by which Literary practitioners ranked kinds of imaginative writing had counterparts in the way that other kinds of writers conceptualized and presented their work. Among the economic or financial writers I have examined here, one criteria that distinguished economic *theory* from the local accounts of financial events a journalist might publish was the relative abstraction of the former, its ability to produce not just an accurate description of immediate economic factors but an ahistorical model of "the economy" itself. As we saw in chapters 3 and 4, during the early and middle decades of the century, political economists like David Ricardo and John Stuart Mill identified the properties and laws of this abstraction; they devised an analytic language capable of describing its dynamics; and their followers established protocols for credentializing experts, who were then considered reliable guides to economic matters. The writings of these experts (some retrospectively identified as such)—Smith, Ricardo, Mill, Jevons, Marshall, and others—now constitute the nineteenth-century canon of economic theory, and, even though most modern economists disavow any relation between the work of these writers and their own "science," the process of disciplinary and generic specification in which they engaged undeniably helped create the conditions in which modern economic experts work, not to mention the prestige they now enjoy.

Precisely because of the division of labor among kinds of economic and financial writers that I have already described, most "general readers" in the nineteenth century would have been more likely to read financial journalism than economic theory. For such readers, who might have been experts in Literary writing but not in economic matters, the "economy" was not necessarily visible as the law-governed entity the theorists described. Because of the inevitable gap between the production of knowledge and its acceptance by a population of general readers, the dynamics professional economists now describe became visible piecemeal—as discrete events, contested sets of principles, and apparently inexplicable, if alarmingly periodic, disruptions. Even though economic theorists had begun to formulate an abstract model of the "economy" as a whole by 1866, in other words, this model had yet to become the culture's commonsense understanding of events that could still seem unrelated to each other. In 1866, the "economy" had yet to achieve the cultural transparency, the taken-for-grantedness, that Bank of England notes had finally achieved and that other financial instruments would soon acquire. The inescapable fact of financial crimes and the unmistakable importance of economic transactions made such topics available for imaginative writers, but the still-emergent state of the theoretical model also made it possible for a writer to treat such issues *either* as parts of a single conceptual whole (as economic writers did) *or* as features appropriated for a totality that seemed whole in a different sense—in the way an organism was unified, as art was said to be. Given the transitional state of economic science in the 1860s and 1870s—despite the relative professional coherence I have described—it should not surprise us that a Literary writer like Trollope would simply appropriate a detail from financial transactions with which he was familiar (a check is different from a Bank note) and subordinate its treatment to an ethical agenda, conducted through the dynamics and according to the rationale of aesthetic form. To Trollope and his readers, it did not matter that the most characteristic features of a Victorian check do not feature in the novel; what mattered was that he could use the check in an aesthetic pattern—as a formal counterpart to the characterization of Mr. Crawley, as the provocation for an enormously distended plot, and as the last link in the narrative chain that connects Mr. Crawley to Mrs. Arabin and to the City plot.

This brings me once more to the place that gender occupies in *The Last Chronicle of Barset*. I have said that, for Trollope, gender constituted the ground of value, which is displaced and disordered when Mrs. Arabin takes monetary matters into her own hands and gives Mr. Crawley the check. The check thus plays a symbolic role as well as the role of provocation for the plot: it both signals that the gendered ground of value is in jeopardy and provokes the intricate series of negotiations and admissions that finally restore that order, when Mrs. Arabin is humbled and Mr. Crawley finally discovers who he is. To modern readers, by contrast—certainly to *this* modern reader—gender is at most *one* of the norms that might be said to ground value, and the idea of a woman presenting a gift to a man does not seem to me particularly troubling. For Trollope, by contrast, the threat that naturalizing all kinds of monetary transactions seemed to pose was precisely a threat to the natural hierarchy of gender. To Trollope, but not to me, the role a Literary text could best play was to restore this natural order, to reassure its readers—no matter what their actual experience—that, in the world of art, money belonged to men, as power did as well, and the gifts women circulated among themselves did not trouble these undeniable truths.

It is because the passage of time changes the contexts in which readers read that the protocols for reading change too. And, because time passes, truths that once seemed self-evident can also lose their pertinence. It is not that gender no longer matters to a reader like me. It is just that it matters in a different way—and for different reasons—than it did to Trollope, who needed to prop the entire edifice of his novel on what he saw as its eternal truths. For Trollope, a novel that rose to the status of "art" needed to rest not simply on the order and harmony of its internal parts but also on the natural order of gender, which, he presumed, any reader would recognize as self-evidently true.

CODA

In modern universities—at least in the United States and the United Kingdom—economics typically enjoys greater prestige than Literary studies. The latter may teach students how to analyze texts and write clear prose, after all, but the former conveys useful information and skills that can be put to work. A degree in economics leads to gainful employment, the argument goes; a degree in Literature drives parents to despair.

In the current array of disciplinary and employment options, all this may be true. But simply seeing these disciplines as options, which students must weigh against each other, fails to register what we have lost in allowing them to become so separate. Because the questions economists ask, the ways they ask and answer these questions, and the form in which they give their answers differ so radically from the practices of their counterparts in Literary studies, students who must choose to study one discipline or the other are also choosing between two models of value, models that seem to have almost nothing in common. The incompatibility of these models does not usually bother those of us who teach, for professors of economics and professors of Literature rarely read each other's work, generally talk to each other only on university committees, and do not often ask their undergraduates what shift of mental gears is necessary to go from a lecture course on macroeconomics to a seminar on Shakespeare. Professors don't ask, students don't tell, and the scholarship in the two disciplines grows ever more different in kind.[1] As a result, most students graduate having chosen much more than a major: they have chosen a set of disciplinary blinders to wear (or chafe at) for much of the rest of their lives.

In the account I have given in this book, responsibility for this state of things falls on both sides of the disciplinary divide. As I explain in chapters 3 and 4, if economic writers had not pursued natural philosophical, then mathematical models *to the exclusion of other ways of modeling value,* if these writers had not been successful in popularizing a theoretical consensus about which economic questions mattered, and if they had not embraced marginal utility theory in a way that narrowed the discipline and ignored what their models could not explain, economics as a discipline might not have assumed the form it now takes. By the same token, as I demonstrate in chapters 5 and 6 and in the second interchapter, if Literary writers had not cloaked their participation in the market economy with an ideology that emphasized originality and textual autonomy, if they had not embraced a version of formalism at the end of the nineteenth century that denies virtually every relation except critique between imaginative writing and the market, and if twentieth-century Literary critics had not incorporated aesthetic formalism into the rarified practice promoted in today's graduate programs, then imaginative writing of all kinds might now seem to have something to contribute to the discussions about value we need so desperately to restart. Capitalism and globalization have taken their current forms in part at least because these discussions did not take place, alongside and as part of the social and economic developments that have accompanied specialization. These discussions did not take place—at least in a language comprehensible to all sides—partly because writers developed genres that seemed to be different in kind and that were arranged in an increasingly rigid hierarchy that divided their audiences into ever-more-differentiated segments too.

Some readers may say that focusing on generic and disciplinary differentiation misses the point, for the source of Literary studies' devaluation is simply the increased importance advanced societies now assign to *information,* whether or not it comes from departments of economics. As a discipline devoted to self-culture and the elaboration of ambiguities, Literary studies seems irrelevant not because it promotes a model of value that ignores the market but because it fails to produce information that one might use.

There are plenty of reasons to think we live in an information age, one that is enamored of the modern fact. As John Guillory has reminded us, the memorandum was the dominant genre of the twentieth century; and, as Geoff Bowker notes, the modern memory practices—electronic databases and digital retrieval systems—were designed to manage only the most minute nuggets of data.[2] Yet even if information abounds—and it undeniably does—it is also clear that information genres like the memorandum now compete with a vast array of other genres that are neither information rich nor designed for easy access and use. These genres—the blogs, video diaries, virtual worlds, wikis, and audio-mash-ups that proliferate in cyberspace—are sometimes completely indifferent to information; they flirt with the distinction between fact and fiction or openly mock it; and they often seemed designed not to facilitate efficient use but precisely to immerse users in an apparently endless experience of some alternative universe. These genres not only frustrate the efficiency so valued by the corporate world; they also threaten to make conventional categories useless and academic disciplines obsolete.

For now, at least, the genres of cyberspace do not seem poised to *rival* the genres of the credit economy, nor do they visibly threaten them. Unlike nineteenth-century Literary genres, in other words, most cyberspace genres are comfortable with their place in the market economy: making money while having fun may seem like the best revenge against the otherwise remorseless demand that one spend one's life working just to buy more things. But what the proliferation of such genres indicates to me is not that the market model of value can co-opt everything—even a technology as potentially ungovernable as cyberspace. Instead, these new genres say to me that the longing for an alternative to the market model is alive and well at the beginning of the twenty-first century, just as it was for Wordsworth and Coleridge at the end of the eighteenth. This longing no doubt coexists with students' understandable desire to earn a marketable degree and their genuine respect for the kind of skills they acquire in advanced economics courses. Even so, the longing is clearly there—for some other source of value, some other way of making sense of what we do.

I do not believe that the genres of cyberspace will replace academic disciplines or the genres they have bred anytime soon. Disciplines are too inertial, and too many people have too much invested in systems of credentialization and evaluation simply to let established practices go. Nor do I believe that this society's appetite for easily managed information is likely to diminish in the near future. But I do not believe that the desire for alternatives—to the market model of value, to the genres of the credit economy, to the academic division of knowledge—is likely to go away either. The inertia of these forms and the persistence of such desires may simply remain in tension. Or those of us who work in academic disciplines may find ways to reach beyond the constraints of our highly disciplined vocabularies to create new genres that invite more readers of different kinds, instead of limiting who can read what we write by the language and the forms we use.

I do not have much faith in speculations about the future. But I do know that, whatever happens next in university disciplines and the cyberworld, what we and our students will be able to know will always be shaped by the genres we create. Because these genres will be forged from the ones we have inherited, understanding their history is a step toward writing that future.

NOTES

INTRODUCTION

1. In *A History of the Modern Fact*, I argue that the modern fact is an epistemological unit that presents apparently value-free, descriptive data as if doing so involved no interpretation. Such facts are interpretive, of course, but the conceit is that they are somehow outside or prior to interpretation. See the introduction to Poovey, *History of the Modern Fact*. Given the emphasis that modern Literary studies places on interpretation, it seems difficult to understand how it could be compatible with this assumption about (or preference for this kind of) facts.

    Here, and throughout this book, I capitalize the word *Literary* when I use it in the modern (post-eighteenth-century) sense of canonical imaginative writing, or imaginative writing that meets the prevailing criteria for canonization. Canon formation is a complex social process in its own right, of course, one that has been analyzed in compelling detail by Guillory (see *Cultural Capital*, esp. chap. 1). Siskin makes the argument for distinguishing typographically between *literature* and *Literature* (see *Historicity*, 11 and chaps. 4 and 5; "More Is Different," 810, 810 nn. 20–22, 811).

2. My understanding of genre is loosely derived from the work of Cohen ("History and Genre"), but Cohen's theories about genre are spelled out more clearly in Siskin, *Historicity*, 10–11, 20, 22, 28, 41, and 131. Following Cohen and Siskin, I view a genre as an ensemble of formal features that are ranked hierarchically within the genre in order to perform a specific social function; these features are also interrelated with the features of other forms of writing produced at the same time. Thus, e.g., the genre of economic theory contains features like abstractions, the use of select examples, references to other theoretical works, and (sometimes) mathematical or numerical language. The most important feature of the nineteenth-century version of this genre is the use of abstractions, for the function of the genre was to produce a model of the economy in the abstract. Other kinds of nineteenth-century writing also contained abstractions, like Dickens's references to "imagination" in *Hard Times*, but such abstractions are not the most important feature of a Literary work, nor was the primary function of a nineteenth-century novel to produce abstract models. One advantage of this understanding of genre is that it enables us to view each text both as a member of a larger set (its genre) and in relation to other texts produced at the same time that belong to other genres. Another advantage is that it enables us to see that genres change: as the social function of a particular genre changes, the hierarchy of its

features and its relations to other genres change too. Then, too, this model of genre allows us to understand the various genres produced at any given time as themselves hierarchically arranged in relation to each other. As a concept that emphasizes grouping, classification, and social function, genre enables us to understand the past uses of individual texts; in so doing, it deemphasizes interpretation, which is inevitably informed by the theoretical and cultural assumptions that we take to the text.

3.   I take the term *delimited*, as an alternative to *created* or *originated*, from Guillory's *Literary Study*.

4.   I am concerned here with the distinctively *modern* modes of fact and fiction, for Aristotle discussed both categories long before the seventeenth century. For my specification of the distinction between the ancient sense of facts and the modern one, see Poovey, *History of the Modern Fact*, 8–11. McKeon also describes the modernity of what he calls "*our* kind of fiction" and "the realist and aesthetic formulation of fiction" (*Secret History of Domesticity*, 109, 746 n. 159).

5.   Not all forms of money involve writing. The tallies initially used by goldsmiths and revenue officials to keep track of credits and tax payments under Charles II, e.g., were simply notched sticks that, on completion, were split down the middle so that each party could keep one part of the tally. These sticks were soon outmoded, however, precisely because they could not be endorsed and, thus, could not circulate as money. See Feavearyear, *Pound Sterling*, 100–101.

6.   Barchus discusses the physical features that called attention to the commodity status of eighteenth-century books. See *Graphic Design*, esp. 6–7.

7.   The other form of representation on which early modern Britons tried to impose a rigid distinction between some version of fact and fiction was the Bible. Debates over various vernacular translations of the Bible can be seen as attempts to distinguish between "authorized" and inauthentic versions of a text that had many versions and possible translations.

   As we will see, debates about how to define *money*—and what instruments and forms of value should be included in calculations of a nation's circulating medium—occurred repeatedly in the period I examine in this book. These debates became increasingly intense and frequent during the second half of the nineteenth century, as the kinds of credit instruments increased in number, the English banking system was organized into a more coherent trunk-and-branch system, and the country banks' issue of paper notes was restricted. All these factors made it seem more imperative and more feasible to determine the volume of the circulating "money." See interchapter 1 below.

8.   *Print commerce* is a phrase coined by McDowell (see "Fugitive Voices") to distinguish between the "print culture" that writers like Jonathan Swift could embrace and the debased trade in paper that Swift scorned.

9.   "Such scholarship may consider, first, an individual author's views about money, his/her financial practices, profits from artistic labor, positioning within the marketplace, etc. Second, it may analyze the wider economy in which the author and his or her work may reside, which includes the reception and evaluation of art or literary texts within the larger marketplace; it may examine the other cultural discourses (e.g., advertisements, popular cultural artifacts and practices) that impinge upon, influence, or parallel the text(s) under consideration; it may address the economic and social effects of gender, ethnicity, and sexual orientation on textual production. Finally, it should take account of the national, regional, or transnational economies

during the time of a work's composition" (Woodmansee and Osteen, "Taking Account," 35).

10. Ibid., 38 (see generally 36–38).

11. McCloskey, *Rhetoric of Economics*, *If You're So Smart*, and *Knowledge and Persuasion*; Mirowski, "Doing What Comes Naturally"; Klamer, McCloskey, and Solow, eds., *Consequences of Economic Rhetoric*; Klamer, *Value of Culture*, 13–28; and Klamer and Leonard, "So What's an Economic Metaphor?"

12. Feavearyear, *Pound Sterling*; Pressnell, *Country Banking*; Kynaston, *City of London*; Michie, *London Stock Exchange*; Robb, *White-Collar Crime*.

13. Kauffman, *Business of Common Life*; Gagnier, *Insatiability of Human Wants*; Gallagher, *Nobody's Story*; Cruise, *Governing Consumption*; Lynch, *Economy of Character*; Shell, *Economy of Literature, Money, Language, and Thought*, and *Money and Art*; Goux, *Symbolic Economies*; Copeland, *Women Writing about Money*; Thompson, *Models of Value*; Bellamy, *Commerce*; Brantlinger, *Fictions of State*; Nicholson, *Writing and the Rise of Finance*.

14. McDowell, *Women of Grub Street*; Raven, *Judging New Wealth*; Garside, Raven, and Schöwerling, eds., *English Novel*; St. Clair, *Reading Nation*.

15. Altick, *English Common Reader*; Sutherland, *Victorian Authors*; Griest, *Mudie's Circulating Library*; Erickson, *Economy of Literary Form*; Finkelstein, *House of Blackwood*.

16. Cohen, "History and Genre"; Siskin, *Work of Writing*; Warner, *Licensing Entertainment*; and Guillory, *Cultural Capital*.

17. For an important discussion of the role played by the East India Company in generating this debt, see Bowen, *Business of Empire*, chaps. 1 and 6.

18. See Joshi, *In Another Country*, pt. 1.

PREAMBLE

1. Goux, *Symbolic Economies*, 2; and Shell, *Economy of Literature*, 4.

2. See Hunter, *Before Novels*; Davis, *Factual Fictions*; and McKeon, *Origins of the English Novel*, and *Secret History of Domesticity*. My thanks to Holly Bryan for reminding me of this bias, which persists in my own discussion of eighteenth-century imaginative writing. A more comprehensive discussion of this material would trace the ways that various kinds of imaginative writing, including play texts and poems, participated in preserving or breaking up the fact/fiction continuum.

3. See Hunter, *Before Novels*, pt. 3; McKeon, *Origins of the English Novel*, esp. chaps. 2 and 6 and pt. 3, and *Secret History of Domesticity*, chaps. 8, 11, and 13; and Davis, *Factual Fictions*, chaps. 2–5.

4. McClusker and Gravesteijn, *Beginnings of Commercial and Financial Journalism*, 291.

5. See Barker, "Patchwork Screen," 31.

6. Parsons, *Power of the Financial Press*, 18.

7. Koss, *Rise and Fall of the Political Press*, 32.

8. See Gilmartin, *Print Politics*, chap. 2.

9. Parsons, *Power of the Financial Press*, 20; Edwards, *Pursuit of Reason*, 15. Erickson says that the *Edinburgh Review* reached a peak number of 13,500 sales in 1818 (*Economy of Literary Form*, 32). The larger numbers that Parsons and Edwards provide refer to the expanded number of readers who encountered the *Review* in libraries, clubs, and reading rooms.

10. Parsons, *Power of the Financial Press*, 22–23.

11. Edwards, *Pursuit of Reason*, 35.
12. Bagehot quoted in Parsons, *Power of the Financial Press*, 27, 25.
13. Ibid., 28.
14. See Porter, "Trusted Guide," 7.
15. In a similar gesture, Jevons distinguished between "credit documents" and coins. His category "representative money" is also relevant here, but, since it includes nonpaper money, it does not quite correspond to my concept of paper credit. See *Money*, 191, 194–206, 238.
16. For a telling discussion of insurance documents as a form of value in this period, see Baucom, *Specters of the Atlantic*, 80–112.
17. I am admittedly finessing the intense debates about exactly which paper instruments constituted money, debates that intensified during the nineteenth century as more credit instruments were invented. See, e.g., Walker, "Money," 790–91; and Jevons, *Money*, 248–50. Among the instruments I do discuss, I do not take up promissory notes because, by law (3 & 4 Anne, c. 9), these notes were governed by the same conventions that covered bills of exchange. The promissory note differed from the bill of exchange in that the former was a direct commitment by the drawer to pay the acceptor without an intermediary and on demand. Promissory notes, like bills of exchange, were negotiable on endorsement.
18. Currie quoted in Kynaston, *City of London*, 392.
19. Gilbart, *History, Principles, and Practice* (hereafter *HPP*), 1:264. Volume and page numbers for subsequent citations are given in the text.
20. McCulloch notes that "no precise form of words is required to constitute a bill of exchange" (McCulloch, *Dictionary*, 596), but the bills presented as models by Gilbart and others follow the same conventions of wording and format.
21. Women could endorse and use bills of exchange, but, because these bills were mostly used by merchants, the number of women who did so was relatively small. The Married Women's Property Act of 1870 had to stipulate the changes in the legal treatment of a bill signed by an unmarried woman on marriage. See Gilbart, *HPP*, 1:271–72.
22. Jevons, *Money*, 244. Page numbers for subsequent citations are given in the text. Here is McCulloch's definition of *discount*: "an allowance paid on account of the immediate advance of a sum of money not due till some future period" (McCulloch, *Dictionary*, 496). McCulloch also explains that the method typically used by banks and bill brokers to calculate the discount of any bill routinely extracted larger fees than the law allowed.
23. The standard account of the bill-broking industry is King, *London Discount Market*.
24. See, e.g., letters 11 and 12 in Rae, *Country Banker*, esp. 81.
25. McCulloch, *Dictionary*, 593, 595.
26. Some of the features of this system of banking could also be found in the Roman Empire, in the Italian city-states, and in medieval London, but English banks first began to assume something resembling their modern form under Queen Elizabeth, when the usury laws were repealed. In 1546, Sir Thomas Gresham advanced money "upon interest according to the King's Majesty's statute at ten per cent" (Fitzmaurice, *British Banks*, 5). Underscoring the problem that financial institutions' preference for secrecy poses for historians (particularly historians of visual images), Fitzmaurice comments: "Banking is a trade which keeps its records in print rather than pictures and with a traditional secrecy destroys them when no longer of use" (ibid.). Another modern historian, by contrast, marvels that the method by which banks make

money does not constitute a *greater* mystery: "The process by which banks create money is so simple that the mind is repelled. Where something so important is involved, a deeper mystery seems only decent" (Galbraith, *Money*, 18).

27. The first scriveners' guild was medieval in origin. Its work diminished when the advance of printing contracted the demand for handwritten documents and when, in 1621, James I assigned the work previously done by scriveners to the Crown's clerks. See Melton, *Sir Robert Clayton*, 22–25.

28. Price, "Some Notes," 271.

29. Richards, *Early History of Banking*.

30. Melton, *Sir Robert Clayton*, 19.

31. This was a major source of the fortune amassed by Sir Robert Clayton (who figures so prominently in Defoe's *Roxana*). As Melton explains: "Legal interest and broker-age restraints did not circumscribe his wealth to that of an ordinary moneylender, if the banker's wealth did not, by and large, derive primarily from the constant reinvestment of his fees, charges and interest, but rather from the clandestine in-vestment of his pool of clients' deposits. In this way the role of the cashier and the role of the moneylender were integrated, though in a way partly concealed from his clients" (*Sir Robert Clayton*, 39).

32. Paper banknotes became acceptable on the Continent in an uneven fashion. They were common in Rome, as well as in Denmark and Sweden, by the mid-eighteenth century, e.g., but they were discredited in France during the Revolution (Booker, *Travelers' Money*, 11–12).

33. Running cash notes were derived from the goldsmiths' deposit receipts. The running cash note was also a receipt for a deposit, made out to the bearer, and negotiable either in business or at the Bank, where it could be exchanged for gold or silver. These notes were made out in odd amounts (Duggleby, *English Paper Money*, 30).

34. The charter of 1694 authorized the Bank to issue paper notes only to order. Paper notes also seem to have been interest-bearing instruments, and, for both reasons, they could not have circulated widely. Permission to issue notes payable to the bearer on demand was given by the 1697 revision to the charter (8 & 9 Will. 3, c. 20). See Dunbar, *Chapters*, 193 n. 2.

35. Duggleby, *English Paper Money*, 26, 30–31.

36. In 1708, Parliament vetoed the issue of notes payable on demand or at less than six months by any joint-stock banks with more than six partners. "This was," according to Duggleby, "arguably the most important development in the early history of banking and was confirmed in the renewal of the Bank's charter in 1709 for 21 years and again when a 30 year renewal was enacted in 1713 following the Treaty of Utrecht" (*English Paper Money*, 27). While this legislation did not grant an official monopoly over note issue, it did dissuade other London banks from issuing notes.

37. Swift quoted in Nicholson, *Writing and the Rise of Finance*, 72.

38. Pressnell, *Country Banking*, 106–7.

39. Fitzmaurice, *British Banks*, 57, 64, 63.

40. Pressnell, *Country Banking*, 140–41; Duggleby, *English Paper Money*, 31. While Bank of England notes were all printed in round numbers, the word *pounds* was not printed on them until 1759. This allowed a cashier to write an odd amount on the note by hand. Duggleby reports: "The Bank has one such note for £28. 10s. on which the words 'eight pounds ten shillings' have been written after the printed 'Twenty'" (31).

41. Walker points out that cattle and sheep constituted "living money" in Britain after the Romans deserted the islands ("Money," 788).

42. The Restriction was repealed in 1819, but the Bank was not required to redeem its notes for gold until 1821.
43. Feavearyear, *Pound Sterling*, chap. 9.
44. Keyworth, *Forgery*, 14.
45. [Wills], "Review of a Popular Publication," 426. As we will see in chapter 4, while the Bank Act of 1844 secured the circulating medium to a specified amount of reserve gold, this measure did not prove adequate. The Bank Act was suspended in 1847, 1857, and 1866, and it continued to spark controversy until the 1880s.
46. Walker and Jevons both note this aspiration as one of the achievements of any credit system. See Walker, "Money," 791; and Jevons, *Money*, 285–86.
47. LiPuma and Lee, *Financial Derivatives*, chap. 2.
48. Nevin and Davis, *London Clearing Banks*, 19–21.
49. McCulloch notes that, for a brief period in the nineteenth century, between 1853 and 1859, two kinds of checks were issued. The first, unstamped checks on plain paper, had to contain a date of issue and to be drawn on a bank at no greater distance than fifteen miles. Checks on stamped paper did not have to contain their date or place of issue, they could be drawn on anyone, they could be issued at any distance from where they were to be paid, and they could be made out to bearer or to order. 21 Vict., c. 20, extended the stamp duty to all checks. McCulloch also describes the innovation of the printed checkbook, which he says originated "within the last twenty years"— i.e., in the 1840s (McCulloch, *Dictionary*, 290). Jevons notes that checks came in several forms, including bankers' checks (drawn from one banker on another) and certified checks (equivalent to promissory notes of the banker) (*Money*, 242–43). Like nineteenth-century commentators, I focus on personal checks drawn on a bank.
50. Rae, *Country Banker*, chap. 11.
51. McCulloch, *Dictionary*, 301.
52. See Poovey, *History of the Modern Fact*, xvi–xvii, 54–55.
53. Walker, "Money," 791.

CHAPTER ONE

1. Muldrew has estimated that the increase in demand between 1540 and 1600 was 500 percent and that the increase in supply was only 63 percent (*Economy of Obligation*, 100). The gulf between supply and demand continued into the eighteenth century; see Mathias, "People's Money."
2. Yoking the value of money to a ground of precious, relatively consistently priced metal was not the only condition necessary to counteract the gap between monetary instruments and value, however. As modern analysts remind us, five additional conditions have to obtain for the slippage associated with this gap to be controlled: it has to be possible to exchange metal for money, and vice versa, at a fixed rate; there has to be a free trade in the monetized metal across national boundaries; all coins that circulate have to be issued by an official mint that can certify weight and fineness; the coins have to be protected from clipping, sweating, and other abuses intended to extract their precious metal; and there has to be some provision for regularly replacing worn coins at a fair price. While the British government tried to implement some of these measures before the end of the eighteenth century, for the entirety of the seventeenth and eighteenth centuries at least two were not enforced. First, clipping and sweating continuously debased the actual coins that circulated; and, second, before Peel's Act of 1819, which opened a free market in the trade of precious metals, it was illegal to export unstamped bullion from Britain. These two factors—the debased condition of

British coinage and the ban on bullion export—meant that it was always possible for the value of British money to fall below the value of bullion. And this meant that the relationship between money's function as a common medium of exchange (a universal equivalent) and its status as a commodity (a product that derives its value from market conditions) remained puzzling and worrisome to the men and women who had to negotiate the market system every day. See Feavearyear, *Pound Sterling*, 2–3.

3. Craig, *The Mint*, 128–29, 82.

4. Valenze, *Social Life of Money*, 37. See also Whiting, *Trade Tokens*, 17–20.

5. Valenze, *Social Life of Money*, 92.

6. See ibid., chap. 3.

7. Ibid., 38, 39.

8. See ibid., 39; and Appleby, "Natural Law of Money," 48.

9. McCulloch, preface to *Select Collection... Paper Currency and Banking* (hereafter SCPCB). Page numbers for subsequent citations are given in the text.

10. Lamb, *Preserving the Self*, 4.

11. The *OED* attributes several sets of meanings of the term *value* to the fourteenth century. The oldest refers to the monetary sense of the word and dates to the early part of the century ("that amount of some commodity, medium of exchange, etc., which is considered to be an equivalent for something else; a fair or adequate equivalent or return"). The ethical meaning was in use by the 1380s ("the relative status of a thing, or the estimate in which it is held, according to its real or supposed worth, usefulness, or importance"). The best studies of this elusive transformation are Agnew, *Worlds Apart*; and Muldrew, *Economy of Obligation*.

12. Supple, *Commercial Crisis*; Appleby, *Economic Thought*; Poovey, *History of the Modern Fact*, chap. 2; Finkelstein, *Harmony and Balance*; Ogden, *Indian Ink*, chap. 4.

13. The political stakes of the opposition between property and paper money became clear for these writers during the French Revolution, which was funded, in part, by the form of paper money called *assignats*. Burke, e.g., wrote that, in France, "everything human and divine [was] sacrificed to the idol of paper credit, and national bankruptcy [was] the consequence; and to crown all, the paper securities of new, precarious, tottering power, the discredited paper securities of impoverished fraud and beggared rapine, [were] held out as a currency for the support of an empire, in lieu of the... great recognized species that represent the lasting conventional credit of mankind, which disappeared and hid themselves in the earth from whence they came, when the principle of property, whose creatures and representatives they are, was systematically subverted" (*Reflections on a Revolution in France* [1790], quoted in Pocock, "Mobility of Property," 197). Thanks to Nathan Hensley for reminding me of this argument.

14. When Benjamin Disraeli reanimated this position in the 1840s in his Young England movement, it seemed not only old-fashioned but also suspiciously self-interested and biased against the middle class. I acknowledge that a more comprehensive treatment of the eighteenth-century discussions of money *as a debate* would need to take this position seriously, and I realize that I risk simply repeating McCulloch's Whig assumptions in not doing so. Other scholars, including Pocock, have done more justice to this position than I have been able to do here.

15. McCulloch, preface to *Select Collection... Money* (hereafter SCM). Page numbers for subsequent citations are given in the text.

16. McCulloch is discussing a tract by Rice Vaughan entitled "A Discourse of Coins and Coinage," composed probably in the 1630s and printed in 1675.

17. The latter meaning, which the *OED* assigns to the period between 1250 and 1867, departs in significant ways from another meaning of the word *tale*, which precedes this definition: "a story or narrative, *true or fictitious*, drawn up so as to interest or amuse, or to preserve the history of a fact or incident; a literary composition cast in narrative form" (emphasis added). This definition captures the equivocation ("true or fictitious") that I call the *fact/fiction continuum*.

18. William Petty, "Quantulumcunque concerning Money" (1682), in *SCM*, 162. The other anthologized opponent of this practice is Sir Robert Cotton, who states that debasing the value of a nation's coin "will trench both into the Honor, the Justice, and the Profit of my Royal Master very far" ("A Speech . . . Touching the Alteration of Coin" [written 1682; published 1695], in ibid., 125).

19. "An Essay upon Money and Coins, Part II: Wherein Is Shewed, That the Established Standard of MONEY Should Not Be *Violated* or *Altered*, under Any Pretense Whatsoever" (1758), in *SCM*, 445, 448.

20. In the article entitled "Money" published in the first edition of the *Encyclopaedia Britannica* (1771), the author argues that another reason that money challenges the idea of a standard is that there are two precious metals that can serve as the standard (gold and silver). But the issue of the standard is really not complicated by this fact, for, as this author acknowledges, most nations choose between gold and silver, thereby effectively making one function as the standard.

21. For a discussion of the relationship between eighteenth-century economic writing and natural philosophy, see Schabas, *Natural Origins of Economics*, chaps. 1 and 2.

22. Jones, "Harris, Joseph."

23. McCulloch defines *paper money* as "notes which are legal tender without being convertible at the pleasure of the holder into certain amounts of coin. The value of this variety of paper currency depends upon the extent to which it may be issued compared with the demand, or rather with the business it has to perform. Whether those by whom it is issued are in good or bad credit is immaterial. It obtains currency by its issuers having power to make it legal tender; and nothing more is required to sustain its value than that it should be issued in moderate quantities" (*SCPCB*, v). The examples he gives are French assignats and the currencies of Russia and Austria—not, significantly, Bank of England notes during the Restriction period (1797–1819).

24. See, e.g., McCulloch's criticisms of the country banks in "Banks—Banking," esp. 87–88.

25. In Macaulay's account, the national debt was the cornerstone of the nation's honor: "If it be true that whatever gives to intelligence an advantage over brute force, and to honesty an advantage over dishonesty, has a tendency to promote the happiness and virtue of our race, it can scarcely be denied that, in the largest view, the effect of this system [financing the government through a permanently funded debt] has been salutary. For it is manifest that all credit depends on two things, on the power of a debtor to pay debts, and on his inclination to pay them. The power of a society to pay debts is proportioned to the progress which that society has made in industry, in commerce, and in all the arts and sciences which flourish under the benignant influence of freedom and of equal law. The inclination of a society to pay its debts is proportioned to the degree in which that society respects the obligations of plighted faith" (*History*, 4:401).

26. Ibid., 396, 400.

27. I am not referring to the use of the words *fiction* or *fact*, which have a long and complex history. For the former, see Williams, *Keywords*, 111–13. For the latter, see the introduction to Poovey, *History of the Modern Fact*.

28. I place *news* in quotation marks because much of what appeared in these ballads reported events we would consider questionable or fictitious, such as monstrous births. Reporting anything about the government and actual current events was prohibited in this period; the earliest news sheets were translations from the Dutch. On news and the overlap between fact and fiction, see Davis, *Factual Fictions*, chap. 3; and Hunter, *Before Novels*, chap 7. Robert Mayer discusses early modern histories in *History and the Early English Novel*. St. Clair explains the fact/fiction continuum in almanacs in *Reading Nation*, 81–82. Travel writings are the subject of work by Hulme and Youngs (see the introduction to Hulme and Youngs, eds., *Cambridge Companion to Travel Writing*). McKeon examines the role of reference in secret histories in *Secret History of Domesticity*, pt. 3. Kerby-Miller discusses satire in the preface to his edition of *The Memoirs of . . . Martinus Scriblerus*, 29–36.

29. Robert Boyle, "Origins of Forms and Qualities," in Stewart, ed., *Selected Philosophical Papers*, 74–75.

30. Davis, *Factual Fictions*, 51.

31. St. Clair, *Reading Nation*, 81, 82.

32. Ibid., 82.

33. On the *Athenian Mercury*, England's first literary periodical, see Clery, *Feminization Debate*, chap. 2. On periodicals and the rise of writing, see Siskin, *Work of Writing*, chap. 6; and Mackie, "Introduction: Cultural and Historical Background," esp. 22–30.

34. Thus, when the *Tatler* announced the death of the astrologer John Partridge in 1709, it provoked the still-living man to write back and angrily deny his demise. In response, Steele simply reiterated the news of Partridge's death, thus proving that, in this case, print had more power than flesh and blood. See Mackie, "Introduction: Cultural and Historical Background," 27–28.

35. Gallagher, *Nobody's Story*; Davis, *Factual Fictions*; McKeon, *Secret History of Domesticity*. See also Terdiman, *Body and Story*, chap. 1.

36. See Poovey, *History of the Modern Fact*, chap. 1.

37. Ogden, *Indian Ink*, chap. 5.

38. George White, *An Account of the Trade to the East-Indies* (London, 1691), 5, quoted in Ogden, *Indian Ink*, 165–66.

39. See, e.g., Mackay, *Extraordinary Popular Delusions*, chap. 2.

40. In an issue of the *Craftsman* published in 1727, e.g., Nicholas Amhurst, writing in the persona of "Usbeck," charged that stockjobbers "out-lie one another": "They call the chief commodity which they deal in *South Sea stock*; this is worth more or less in idea only, as the lie of the day takes or does not take. . . . They told me that in the year 1720, they carried this ideal value of their stock so high, that what, in the beginning of the year, was not valued above 1000 piasters, mounted to more than 10,000 in less than the space of seven moons; that is, every man had agreed to call himself exceedingly rich" ([Amhurst], "Nicholas Amhurst: From *The Craftsman* No. 47").

41. All these examples come from Mackay, *Extraordinary Popular Delusions*, 70, 55, 80.

42. Clery, *Feminization Debate*, chap. 3.

CHAPTER TWO

1. Pocock mentions John Locke's belief that money is a "partly fictitious and partly perdurable entity," but, as long as money consisted of gold or silver, Locke thought that the perdurable quality of the metals could offset money's fictitious nature.

Locke also realized, of course, that the belief that gold and silver were inherently valuable was also based on a fiction. *Machiavellian Moment*, 435.

2. Valenze usefully points out that, in Britain, especially in the seventeenth century and the early eighteenth, some individuals resisted the commercial use of money by preserving alternative attitudes toward coins that treated them as magical or spiritually devalued instruments. See *Social Life of Money*, esp. 1–29.

3. Pocock, "Mobility of Property," and *Machiavellian Moment*, 451–59.

4. "Facts for Enquirers," 4.

5. Walker argued that the development of credit was essential to the division of labor that launched modernity. See "Money," 790.

6. I stress that a reader able to recognize these features had to be "educated" not to invoke a specific level of formal schooling but to acknowledge that, even after writers devised conventions to signal that a given work was factual or fiction, some readers would have missed or misread these pointers. If lower-class readers were still reading primarily seventeenth-century chapbooks and ballads well into the nineteenth century, as St. Clair argues, then they would not have been trained *by their reading* to discriminate between fact and fiction. The official ban on abridgments and anthologies, which obtained for almost the entire eighteenth century, along with the high price of most books, would have meant that the very texts in which writers were developing the modern distinction between fact and fiction had only a limited audience. See *Reading Nation*, esp. chap. 4.

7. Appleby mentions Defoe eight times, but she quotes from only two texts and gives his writing no sustained attention (*Economic Thought*, 134, 144, 165, 172, 182, 197, 210, 262 n. 44). In Letwin's *Origins of Scientific Economics*, Defoe makes no appearance at all. Schumpeter has a more complicated attitude. He mentions Defoe only three times, always in notes, but, in his final reference, he calls him "a most brilliant and prolific writer." "But even his most ambitious efforts in our field remained in the sphere of economic journalism," Schumpeter continues. Defoe's writings "did not contribute anything new to economic analysis" (*History of Economic Analysis*, 372 n. 15).

8. Literary historians often credit Defoe with originating the English novel, but they also tend to draw a sharp line between Defoe's novels and his nonnovelistic writing. See, e.g., Watt, *Rise of the Novel*, chaps. 3 and 4. One exception to this generalization is Davis, who devotes the majority of his chapter on Defoe to the nonnovelistic writing—in this case, the political writing. See *Factual Fictions*, chap. 9. I discuss Davis below.

9. Defoe, *Essays upon Several Projects*, 9.

10. See Poovey, *History of the Modern Fact*, 159–66.

11. McKeon also discusses what he calls the "radically discontinuous allegory of Lady Credit" in Defoe's writings (*Secret History of Domesticity*, 441 [see also 441–47]). I discuss McKeon's argument below.

12. Defoe, "Villainy of Stock-Jobbers," 71. Page numbers for subsequent citations are given in the text.

13. The practice of stockbroking seems to have become an independent business at about the time Defoe published "The Villainy of Stock-Jobbers," and, since a formal stock exchange did not exist in London, the practice was unregulated. Later commentators distinguished between stockbroking, the practice in which the agent bought or sold shares for another person, and stockjobbing, in which the agent bought and sold for himself with the intention of profiting from subsequent sales

and purchases. Defoe does not distinguish between the two here, nor does he consistently distinguish between the actions of independent jobbers and those of the directors of the old East India Company, whom he also held responsible for driving up the price of company shares.

14. Morris and Morris, *Wall Street Journal Guide*, 46, 34.
15. The classical source is Erasmus, *On Copia*, 14.
16. For a discussion of the antecedents of Defoe's figure and the way its emphasis shifted, see Backscheider, "Defoe's Lady Credit." See also Pocock, *Machiavellian Moment*, 452–55.
17. Defoe, *The Review*, 3, no. 5:17–18 (facsimile bk. 6).
18. In 1711, Joseph Addison published his famous allegorical depiction of "Publick Credit" in the *Spectator*, the periodical he had recently founded with Richard Steele. Addison's account is explicitly allegorical; he places the female figure on a throne of gold in the Bank of England's Great Hall, surrounds her with the documents that ratified the Glorious Revolution (the Act of Uniformity, the Act of Settlement), and makes her complexion wane and wax according to the news she hears. When threatened with the Stuart Pretender, "she would fall away from the most florid Complexion, and the most healthful State of Body, and wither into a Skeleton," but, when greeted by George Augustus (soon to become George I), she is restored "into a Habit of the Highest Health and Vigour" (*Spectator* 3 [3 March 1711], in Ross, ed., *Selections*, 431).
19. See Shapin, *Scientific Revolution*, chap. 2, and *Social History of Truth*, chap. 5; and Poovey, *History of the Modern Fact*, chap. 3.
20. For a discussion of these events, see Novak, *Daniel Defoe*, 350–59. The gender issues of Defoe's *Essay on Public Credit* are discussed in Mulcaire, "Public Credit." For an important discussion of Lady Credit, see O'Brien, "Character of Credit."
21. Defoe, *Essay*, 7. Page numbers for subsequent citations are given in the text.
22. It might seem that the primary difference between the treatments of credit I have examined is that one is private credit and the other public—i.e., the national debt. In his late treatise *The Complete English Tradesman*, however, Defoe makes it clear that he considered public credit to be *like* private credit—only on a greater scale: "Credit, next to real stock, is the foundation, the life and soul, of business in a private tradesman; it is his prosperity; it is his support in the substance of his whole trade; even in public matters, it is the strength and fund of a nation" (*Complete English Tradesman*, 233).
23. Gildon's demand appears in his *Epistle to Daniel Defoe* (1719), which Davis describes as one of the first texts to specifically attack a work "on the grounds that it is fictional—that is, not a lie, a libel, or a distortion, but simply a fiction" (*Factual Fictions*, 156).
24. Although she does not use the term, Gallagher associates fictionalization with novels published in the 1740s. See *Nobody's Story*, esp. chaps. 9 and 14.
25. For two eighteenth-century letters that either document the truth of Mrs. Bargrave's story or demonstrate that this tale circulated in the eighteenth century independently of Defoe's text, see Sherman, ed., *Restoration and the Eighteenth Century*, 2374–80.
26. Defoe, "The Apparition," 254. Page numbers for subsequent citations are given in the text.
27. McKeon, *Secret History of Domesticity*, 108–9.
28. Shapin and Shaffer, *Leviathan and the Air Pump*, chap. 1; Shapin, *Social History of Truth*, esp. chaps. 1, 3, and 5; Poovey, *History of the Modern Fact*, chap. 1.
29. Gallagher, *Nobody's Story*, 174.

30. See Dickson, *Financial Revolution*, chaps. 5 and 6; Nicholson, *Writing and the Rise of Finance*, esp. chap. 2; Clery, *Feminization Debate*, chap. 3; and Liss, *Conspiracy of Paper*.

31. Nicholson, *Writing and the Rise of Finance*, esp. 60–69.

32. Clery, *Feminization Debate*, esp. chaps. 4 and 5.

33. Defoe, *Roxana*, ed. Blewett, 35. All references are to this edition; page numbers for subsequent citations are given in the text.

34. See Patey, *Probability and Literary Form*, esp. pt. 2.

35. Ibid., 144.

36. James Harris, *Discourse on Music* (1744), quoted in ibid., 85.

37. Patey, *Probability and Literary Form*, 138.

38. Defoe, *Conjugal Lewdness; or, Matrimonial Whoredom* (1727), quoted in McKeon, *Secret History of Domesticity*, 450.

39. See Alkon, *Defoe and Fictional Time*, 53–58; and Blewett, *Defoe's Art of Fiction*, 126–27.

40. It is easy for a modern reader to reconcile the inconsistencies manifested by the character Roxana, for we have available a number of theoretical paradigms that postulate a "deeper" level at which contradictions express psychological conflicts. Numerous modern Literary critics have applied this model of depth psychology or psychoanalysis to *Roxana*, but, to do so, they have had to ignore the fact that this model was not available to Defoe. See Warner, *Licensing Entertainment*, 168–75; and Castle, "'Amy, Who Knew My Disease.'"

41. Patey argues that character began to climb in the hierarchy of a fiction's features by the 1760s. See *Probability and Literary Form*, 89, 122.

42. Mullan, "Textual History of *Roxana*," 332. Mullan notes that the original title might also have been given by a publisher or a bookseller, but, since this was the only title used during Defoe's lifetime, the author must have at least tacitly approved of the longer title.

43. Ibid., 332.

44. Mullan, introduction to *Roxana*, ix. Richardson printed this letter as a preface to the second edition of his novel, thereby underscoring his ambition to create a new template for a new "kind of Writing."

45. Cloud points out that Shakespeare's characters began to undergo a similar editorial unification beginning with Alexander Pope's 1723 edition of the plays. Cloud cites various textual anomalies that Pope "resolved" by assigning them to particular speakers; he also notes that Pope began to preface each play with a list of dramatic characters that also encouraged readers to unify each character. See "'Very Names.'"

46. Mullan, introduction to *Roxana*, vii. The 1750 edition states that Roxana "repeated all the Passages of her ill spent Life to me," and the 1775 edition inserts an intermediary: "Here the conclusion is left for me to relate, as I had it from Mr. Worthy himself [Roxana's last husband]" (both quoted in ibid., vii).

47. Quoted in ibid., vii.

48. Ibid., xiii.

49. See Clery, *Feminization Debate*, 68–72.

50. This model of interior, secret complexities that are revealed to a sympathetic reader through print is, of course, another legacy of the kind of fiction produced by Richardson and Fielding in the 1740s. The norms of this kind of fiction—of what we now call *the English novel*—are familiar to every modern reader: the central character (often, but not invariably, a woman) is constructed around an ever-receding horizon

of interior complexity, glimpses of which entice the reader both to identify with her and to continue reading; these interior "depths" are subject to moral interpretation, either because the character "learns" or "develops" in the course of the fiction or because we can treat them as "psychological" complexities that are, for this reason, beyond judgment; and the character, like everything else in the fiction, belongs to a semantic field that is credible in forming a whole that is coherent, in sum, if not in every single detail.

51. For my discussion of Hutcheson and experimental philosophy more generally, see *History of the Modern Fact*, 144–213. Hutcheson's *Inquiry into the Originals of Our Ideas of Beauty and Virtue* was published in 1728, and *An Essay on the Nature and the Conduct of the Passions* appeared in 1729.

52. Defoe, *Complete English Tradesman*, chaps. 15, 24.

53. This is the most common way that Literary critics have described the relationship between imaginative and economic (or financial) writings in this period. See Cruise, *Governing Consumption*, esp. chap. 2; Thompson, *Models of Value*, 146; and Lynch, *Economy of Character*, chap. 1.

54. For a biographical account, see Skinner, introduction to *Principles*.

55. Schumpeter says that Steuart's work was "intentionally and laboriously systematic" and that his *Principles of Political Economy* was "of first-rate importance" (*History of Economic Analysis*, 176). See also Kobayashi, "Section 2," lxx. Kobayashi explains that Steuart had more admirers in Germany, and he argues that "what cast [Steuart's] work into oblivion [in Britain] was the post-Ricardian academic environment of the classical school, which owes most, for better or worse, to none other than Adam Smith" (lxix–lxx). In *The Wealth of Nations*, Smith mentions Steuart only once and then in a note in which he simply uses Steuart to corroborate a source. See *Wealth*, 208 n. 146. Page numbers for subsequent citations are given in the text.

56. Kobayashi, "Section 2," lxxiv–lxxv. See also Thompson, *Models of Value*, 75–78.

57. Steuart, *Principles*, 1:3. Volume and page numbers for subsequent citations are given in the text.

58. See Skinner, introduction to *Principles*, lxvii–lxviii.

59. Kobayashi, "Section 2," lxxxiv, lxxxvi.

60. Fielding, *Tom Jones*, 413. Page numbers for subsequent citations are given in the text.

61. Kobayashi, "Section 2," lxx, lxxi.

62. Thompson, *Models of Value*, 144.

63. Thompson determines that these "notes," which Fielding also refers to as "bills," must have been "bank notes or bills drawn on a London bank," but "they are unlikely to have been Bank of England notes" (ibid., 136, 137). He also notes, parenthetically, that, in figuring this out, he might have generated "an assumption of detail and verisimilitude inappropriate to Fielding's form of fiction" (136–37). This last point is the one I want to stress: Fielding was simply not interested in identifying the exact nature of the notes Allworthy gave to Tom because they do not function as monetary counters in the novel; their loss and recovery belong to the ethical and aesthetic rationales of the novel.

64. Siskin describes the system as the characteristic genre of the eighteenth century. See "Problem of Periodization." While I do not call the system a *genre* in this book, I see why Siskin wants to do so, and I have learned much from his work on eighteenth-century systems.

65. See Poovey, *History of the Modern Fact,* 223 and chap. 4.
66. In saying that the market system was a product of *The Wealth of Nations,* I am not making an extreme Foucauldian claim that representation creates reality. Certainly, market transactions occurred before Smith put pen to paper; had this not been the case, he would not have been able to observe or to write. But saying that economic transactions belong to a *system* requires more than observation; it requires either a belief in the superiority of regularity to the heterogeneity of individualized instances or an aesthetic preference for order over discord. Smith had both the belief and the preference, as his *Lectures on Rhetoric* makes clear. See Poovey, *History of the Modern Fact,* 243–47.
67. Kobayashi, "Section 2."
68. Marx, *Critique of Political Economy,* 65. It might be worth noting that, in *Capital,* Marx followed Smith's organizational plan rather than Steuart's: he opened discussions with theoretical analysis before offering a historical narrative.
69. "Money-centered narratives" is the phrase used by Lynch, *Economy of Character,* 94–102; "it narratives" is used by Douglas, "Britannia's Rule," 70–89, and by Lamb, "Modern Metamorphoses"; "object narratives" appears in Flint, "Speaking Objects," 212–26; "spy narrative" is used by Raven, *Judging New Wealth,* 45–46; "novels of circulation" is Bellamy's phrase in *Commerce,* 119–28; "novels about non-human characters" appears in Olshin, "Form and Theme," 41–53; and "traveling coins" is Valenze's phrase in *Social Life of Money,* 81–88.
70. One exception to this generalization is the discussion of "traveling coins" in *Social Life of Money,* 81–88, but Valenze does not discuss Bridges's text. Such narratives also appeared in the format of short fiction during the eighteenth century. In 1710, e.g., Joseph Addison published an essay in the *Tatler* (Saturday, 11 November 1710) chronicling a "delirium" in which the author imagines that a shilling "reared it self upon its Edge, and turning the Face towards me, opened its Mouth, and in a soft Silver Sound gave me the following Account of his Life and Adventures" (Mackie, ed., *Commerce of Everyday Life,* 184). Another essay of this type appeared in the *Adventurer* in 1752; this one chronicles the story of a transmigrated soul that takes up residence in a flea. The first British example of this subgenre seems to have been Charles Gildon's *The Golden Spy* (1709–10). Bellamy argues that "the novel of circulation became established as an autonomous narrative form within Britain" in 1751, with the publication of Francis Coventry's story of a Bologna lapdog, *Pompey the Little* (*Commerce,* 119).
71. Bellamy, *Commerce,* 119.
72. On the takeoff of print, see Raven, *Judging New Wealth,* chap. 2.
73. See Flint, "Speaking Objects," 225 n. 9. The texts published in magazines are cataloged in Mayo, *English Novel,* 442–43.
74. By the 1860s, when *Middlemarch* began to appear, the object-narrated tales that appeared in print were typically essays again, not extended fictions like *Chrysal* or *Adventures of a Bank-Note.* Nineteenth-century examples of this kind of tale include [Blanchard], "Biography of a Bad Shilling"; [Oliphant], "Autobiography of a Joint-Stock Company"; "The Catalogue's Account"; and [Head], "The Mechanism of the Post Office."
75. Bridges, *Adventures,* 1:6. My citations refer to the original volume numbers, which the Garland edition retains: vol. 1 of the Garland edition contains Bridges's first two volumes, vol. 2 the last two. Volume and page numbers for subsequent citations are given in the text.

76. For a description of the process by which the Bank of England selected these numbers, see [Wills], "Review of a Popular Publication," 428.

77. See Pressnell, *Country Banking*, 16, 22–23, 26, and chap. 6.

78. Early examples of merchants' handbooks include *The Merchants Avizo* (1607) and Lewes Roberts's *Merchants Mappe of Commerce* (1638) (see Poovey, *History of the Modern Fact*, 59–62; and Valenze, *Social Life of Money*, 39). American guidebooks to the competing currencies of the 1860s include *A Bank Note Reporter* and *Counterfeit Detector* (see Galbraith, *Money*, 90).

79. The *Encyclopaedia Britannica* was issued serially. The first bound volume, containing entries for the letters A and B, was published in 1769, and the last bound volume, containing entries for the letters M–Z, appeared in 1771. The entry "Money," which appeared in 1771 in vol. 3, is largely a theoretical discussion, and the only remotely practical information it contains is the "Table of Coins" that shows the quantity of fine metal contained in the coins of four nations. The entry "Bank" contains marginally more useful information about the amount of interest banks of various kinds charged for securing or changing money.

80. Repeatedly, Steuart voiced his irritation that notes issued "on one side of a river, running through the same country, should not pass on the opposite bank" (*Principles*, 3:152), but he could offer no effective solution to this problem, given the geographic limits to the circulation of credit.

81. In 1750, when the Irishman Edmund Burke arrived in England, he said that there were no more than a dozen "bankers' shops" outside London (*Regicide Peace*, in *Works*, 2:203, quoted in Pressnell, *Country Banking*, 4). It should be noted that historians disagree about the number of private banks in operation throughout this period.

82. Bridges's first work was *A Travestie of Homer* (1762, with additional editions in 1764, 1767, 1770, and 1797); his second was *The Battle of the Genii* (1764), which was a burlesque of a scene from Milton's *Paradise Lost* (Knight and Baylis, "Bridges, Thomas," 592).

83. "Novels" (*Critical Review*).

84. Lynch is the only scholar who notices that the narrator of Bridges's tale is a paper note, not a coin, but she mistakenly conflates the note and a bill of exchange (*Economy of Character*, 97). Her argument is that Bridges's depiction of the Note's circulation, like other "narratives that put money's mobility center-stage[,] may well have afforded their readers a kind of comfort.... The banknote's travels can make circulation seem more tidily circular.... [Such narrators] assuage fears that the social is of unlimited and hence inapprehensible extension. Like the conversible gentleman, the protagonist in this style acts as broker of differences. His social work demonstrates how people are connected" (98).

INTERCHAPTER ONE

1. Feavearyear, *Pound Sterling*, 177, 194, 218–19.

2. One exception to its willingness to increase issue in response to demand was 1826, when the Bank refused to help the "men of paper," the country bankers whose overissue seemed to have fuelled the speculative mania and crash of 1825–26. See ibid., 218–21.

3. Thomas Carlyle, *The French Revolution*, in Carlyle, *Works*, 2:29, 51. Among the nineteenth-century novelists who dramatized the Paper Age, the most notable is Honoré Balzac, whose *Lost Illusions* (1837–43) examines the connection between

papermaking, revolutionary sentiment, and the rise of commercial society. See also Thomas Love Peacock's *Paper Money Lyrics* (1825).

4. Carlyle, *Works*, 2:61, 29.

5. McLaughlin, *Paperwork*, esp. chap. 1. On the history of papermaking, see Coleman, *British Paper Industry*; and Hunter, *Papermaking*.

6. The first mass-produced paper was introduced in France in the 1790s, and its first use was to print paper money, the assignats. The machine that made this continuous-roll paper was invented by Nicholas Louis Robert. It was the model for the Foudrinier brothers' paper machine, which was imported into England in 1810 but not adopted by most English printers until the 1820s. When adopted, these machines immediately increased the production of all kinds of paper, from legal documents to advertisements, and they eventually made possible the invention of today's high-speed rotary printing machines. See Hunter, *Papermaking*, 257–64; St. Clair, *Reading Nation*, 88; and Erickson, *Economy of Literary Form*, 20–48. The Bank of England continued to use the special watermarked paper produced by Henry Portal's firm that it had initially adopted in 1725. See Duggleby, *English Paper Money*, 30–52. Country banks probably used locally available paper, but I have found no reliable information about this.

7. Raven notes, in fact, that, in the 1790s, booksellers began to charge fixed prices for their books instead of automatically extending the credit that customers had come to expect. This caused anger and recrimination, but, because it does not seem to have undercut sales, it would have required the exchange of a greater volume of banknotes. He also comments that, toward the end of the century, imaginative writing began to stress the risks associated with too much credit, but he does not make the further observation that such subject matter helped swell the volume of available printed reading materials. In other words, it became fashionable to comment on the dangers of the very credit represented by the paper notes required to purchase books. See *Judging New Wealth*, 197–99.

8. Raven argues that the commodification of Literary writing was well under way by 1790 (ibid., 42–43).

9. In addition to Raven's *Judging New Wealth*, see St. Clair's *Reading Nation*.

10. St. Clair, *Reading Nation*, 35 and chaps. 3 and 5.

11. Queen Anne's Act theoretically established limits on prices and the duration of copyright, but St. Clair argues that the English courts did not enforce these provisions: "At the beginning of the eighteenth century, the London book industry thus found itself with all of the privileges and institutions of the guild system, but without any of the controls which normally accompanied such a regime. They were able to act as an unregulated and unrestrained private commercial monopoly over the whole text-based culture of England, and this is what they proceeded to do" (ibid., 93).

12. Ibid., 109.

13. Raven, *Judging New Wealth*, 38, 35. Note that Garside, Raven, and Schöwerling limit their studies to what Raven calls "imaginative literature," not all publications. See Garside et al., eds., *English Novel*.

14. Raven, *Judging New Wealth*, 35, 54. The circulating libraries charged substantial fees, so, even though the "imaginative literature" that Raven has cataloged was "popular," it was not "cheap," as was much of the output of the radical presses in the 1790s. Raven points out that, by 1760, London circulating libraries charged subscribers from between fifteen shillings and one guinea annually; in 1760, two shillings could buy a stone of beef or a pair of shoes (57).

15. St. Clair, *Reading Nation*, 79.
16. Ibid., 133–34. The old canon of English poets, according to St. Clair, consisted, in alphabetical order, of Samuel Butler, Chaucer, Collins, Cooper, Dryden, Falconer, Gay, Goldsmith, Gray, Milton, Pope, Shakespeare, Spenser, Thomson, and Young. The old canon of prose fiction included *Robinson Crusoe, Gulliver's Travels*, the novels of Richardson, Fielding, and Smollett, *The Vicar of Wakefield, Rasselas*, and *Tristram Shandy* as well as translations of *Don Quixote* and *Gil Blas*. The "English classics" included much material that had originally been published in periodicals, including the *Spectator*, the *Tatler*, the *Rambler*, the *Adventurer*, the *Idler*, the *Mirror*, the *Observer*, the *Lounger*, the *Guardian*, the *World*, and the *Connoisseur*. While the materials from these periodicals were considered "classic," in part, because they appealed to and were considered suitable for women, women writers are notably absent from all these lists (128, 130, 131).
17. Ibid., chap. 16.
18. The first figure comes from Feavearyear, *Pound Sterling*, 177. Feavearyear says that there were 900 country banks by 1815 (194). Newmarch's figure appears in his "Bills of Exchange," 168. He also found 360 bank offices in Scotland and 51 in London (in addition to the Bank) (169, 170).
19. The Bank of England had been granted the right to issue £5 notes in 1793, so, even before the Restriction Act, it did circulate relatively small notes—although not £1 notes.
20. Newmarch, "Bills of Exchange," 173–74, 180.
21. Boyd, whose pamphlet I discuss in chapter 3, actually maintained that bills of exchange and other kinds of negotiable paper did not form part of the circulating medium: "The latter... is the circulator; the former are merely objects of circulation" (Boyd quoted in Francis Horner, "Thornton on the Paper Credit," 31). Horner emphatically disagrees with Boyd and points out that Thornton and all other reputable commentators considered bills of exchange part of the circulating medium. In 1819, the Bullion Commission decided that bills of exchange were *not* money.
22. Newmarch, "Bills of Exchange," 154–58.
23. Ibid., 167, 180.
24. Newmarch tried to capture the interrelations of the parts with this succinct formula: "Cheques are bank notes drawn against deposits, and bills of exchange are cheques drawn against commodities" (ibid., 161). Accepting this formula, however, required one to accept his even more fundamental distinction between the "ready capital" that notes and checks represented and the "floating capital" that bills of exchange and account ledgers represented (161–62).
25. The notion of a misrecognition of imaginative works' relation to the market comes from Pierre Bourdieu. See, e.g., Bourdieu, *Distinction*, 491–93, and *Rules of Art*, 286–95; and Guillory, *Cultural Capital*, chap. 5.
26. Raven does not elaborate this point, beyond commenting that "attention to the dangers of fashion and the isolation of specific exemplars of the ton was the direct result of the vulnerability of... lighter literature to charges of frivolity and immorality" (*Judging New Wealth*, 155).

CHAPTER THREE

1. Warner discusses Charlotte Lennox's *Female Quixote* as the eighteenth-century novel whose treatment of fiction and its relationship to reality provided the kind of meta-commentary necessary to enable contemporaries definitively to recognize fiction. See *Licensing Entertainment*, 286–87.

2. Alborn, *Conceiving Companies,* 57. On Ricardo as a currency radical, see ibid., 62–63.

3. Hilton, *Age of Atonement,* 126–27.

4. For histories of the South Sea Bubble and contemporary responses to it, see Dickson, *Financial Revolution,* 90–156, 286–87; and Nicholson, *Writing and the Rise of Finance,* 65–69. For discussions of eighteenth-century credit, see Hoppit, "Use and Abuse of Credit," 64–78, and *Risk and Failure,* chaps. 4 and 5. On the spectacular growth of the national debt, see Dickson, *Financial Revolution,* 199–215.

5. See Pressnell, *Country Banking,* chap. 6, esp. 139.

6. Elibank, "Essay on Paper Money and Banking," 215, 217, 216. Lord Elibank (1703–78) was a Tory landowner in Scotland who was a friend of Hume, a member of the Select Society, and a partner in a bank in Dumfries. He was suspected of Jacobitism but never charged with any crimes.

7. Hume, "Of Money," 284. See also Hume, "Of the Balance of Trade."

8. Steuart, *Principles,* 3:198.

9. Smith, *Wealth,* 284 (bk. 2, chap. 2).

10. My account of these events draws heavily on Feavearyear, *Pound Sterling,* 160–77.

11. Pressnell, *Country Banking,* 443.

12. White, *Free Banking,* 55 (see also 55–58); Hilton, *Age of Atonement,* 125–31.

13. Feavearyear, *Pound Sterling,* 175–81.

14. Copleston quoted in Hilton, *Age of Atonement,* 126. Alborn refers to the "discipline" of the gold standard in *Conceiving Companies,* 59.

15. Alborn, *Conceiving Companies,* 59.

16. Boyd, "Letter," 41, 65, 84–85.

17. The Bank issued credit (and increased note issue) by two methods: it discounted bills by issuing its own notes, and it simply issued notes in response to perceived demand (Feavearyear, *Pound Sterling,* 178, 190).

18. Boyd, "Letter," 61–64.

19. Ibid., 72.

20. Baring's response was also published in 1801. See his "Observations." Lord King also mentions the impact of Boyd's pamphlet. See his "Thoughts."

21. Thornton, "Enquiry," 204–5, 208.

22. Hilton, *Age of Atonement,* 127; Alborn, *Conceiving Companies,* 62–63.

23. Howison, "Investigation," 169.

24. Ibid., 142, 145, 156.

25. King, "Thoughts," 349, 376.

26. Ibid., 467, 468.

27. Scotland had no single bank with the power or government mandate that protected the Bank of England, nor was Scottish provincial banking hampered by legislation forbidding investment by more than six partners. As a consequence, Scotland's entire banking system was less subject to the kind of turmoil that repeatedly led to bank failures in England. Despite the autonomy of Scotland's banking system, its banks also agreed to stop payment in gold after the Restriction Act. Had they not done so, all England's paper would have rushed to Scotland for redemption, and all Scotland's gold would have migrated into the hands of Englishmen.

28. On the campaign to make note issue fully competitive, as other industries increasingly were, see White, *Free Banking,* 76. White usefully supplements the categories that most economic historians use to describe these debates—the Currency school vs. the Banking school—with a third category—the Free Banking school. Proponents of free banking argued against the near monopoly in note issue exercised by the Bank of

England and, in general, supported the principles that underwrote the Scottish banking system. This position was rendered obsolete when the Buillionist controversy was laid to rest by the passage of the 1844 Bank Charter Act. The act implemented a moderated version of the Currency school position, as we will see below.

29. Spater, *William Cobbett*, 2:315. For sales figures, see ibid., 314–15, 556 n. 16. Thompson maintains that Cobbett "*created* th[e] Radical intellectual culture, not because he offered its most original ideas, but in the sense that he found the tone, the style, and the arguments which could bring the weaver, the schoolmaster, and the shipwright, into a common discourse. Out of the diversity of grievances and interests he brought a Radical consensus. His *Political Registers* were like a circulating medium which provided a common means of exchange between the experiences of men of widely different attainments" (*Making of the English Working Class*, 746). Thompson says that, at the *Register*'s point of greatest popularity (between October 1816 and February 1817), its issues, at 2d. per copy, ran at something like forty to sixty thousand copies per week, thereby outselling all competitors "of any sort" (718).

30. Cobbett, *Paper*, 69n (letter 7). Page numbers for subsequent citations are given in the text.

31. *Monthly and Commercial Report* quoted in Spater, *William Cobbett*, 2:313.

32. Bordo and White, "Tale of Two Currencies," 305–7. *Unfunded debt* refers to short-term obligations. These included army, navy, ordnance, and Exchequer bills.

33. The argument of Linda Colley's influential study of this period is that participation in local militia organizations did just this: it encouraged the feeling of national unity that enabled individuals in various parts of Great Britain to imagine that they belonged to a nation, instead of first and foremost to a parish or a village. See *Britons*, esp. chap. 7. This is precisely the campaign that Cobbett resisted, although he did so not by consistently attacking military voluntarism or patriotism per se but by focusing on the system of public credit, which was another appeal to collective, as opposed to local, affiliation. When Cobbett insinuated that rumors that the French were about to invade England were being circulated (or at least endorsed) by the British government, he was implicitly charging that the Pitt administration was using fear to promote patriotism. When he argued that certain developments in France (such as that country's default on its national debt) set a positive example for England or that French hypocrisy was no worse that its English counterpart, he was approaching what could have been (and was) interpreted—and prosecuted—as treasonous support for the enemy.

34. Nattrass makes the point that Cobbett's style led to the charge of seditious libel. See *William Cobbett*, 142–43.

35. For additional discussions of Cobbett's style, see Thompson, *Making of the English Working Class*, 748–55; Klancher, *Making of English Reading Audiences*, 121–29; and Nattrass, *William Cobbett*, esp. chaps. 3 and 5. Nattrass also emphasizes Cobbett's reliance on the dialogue form. See ibid., 137, 141–43.

36. Hazlitt, "Character of Cobbett," 53, cited in Klancher, *Making of English Reading Audiences*, 122.

37. See Nattrass, *William Cobbett*, 111; and Klancher, *Making of English Reading Audiences*, 122–23.

38. Klancher, *Making of English Reading Audiences*, 122.

39. This phrase comes from "Mr. Cobbett," *Athenaeum* 1 (1828): 97, quoted in ibid., 122.

40. Nattrass, *William Cobbett*, 89. Nattrass also comments on Cobbett's use of style to appeal to two audiences (109–11). On Coleridge as a monetary relativist, see Hilton, *Age of Atonement*, 128–29.

41. Shelley, *Letters*, 27, quoted in Klancher, *Making of English Reading Audiences*, 129.

42. Leigh Hunt, *White Hat* (13 November 1819), quoted in Nattrass, *William Cobbett*, 9.

43. This is the argument brilliantly developed by Russett in *De Quincey's Romanticism*, introduction and chap. 1. Russett points out that imaginative writers could also be marginalized, either by contemporaries (John Clare, James Hogg) or by subsequent students of Literature (Felicia Hemans, Mary Robinson, and Ann Racliffe) (5).

44. Nattrass, *William Cobbett*, 221n.

45. This was the Bullion Commission, which was appointed in 1810 to examine the state of the nation's currency. Chaired by Francis Horner, one of the founders of the *Edinburgh Review*, this committee concluded that the high price of bullion and the depreciated state of the currency resulted from the Bank of England's overissue of paper money. The House of Commons was skeptical about what was perceived as an attack on the Bank, and Horner's resolutions failed (Feavearyear, *Pound Sterling*, 186–88). When he reissued *Paper against Gold* in 1828, Cobbett claimed that a second reason he wrote the letters was so that he could be seen to have gone on record as an opponent of the government's decision.

46. Spater points out that this component of Cobbett's argument derives from and elaborates ideas that Thomas Paine developed in a pamphlet entitled "The Decline and Fall of the English System of Finance," published in 1796. "Cobbett accepted as certainties two of Paine's principles: first, that the paper or funding system was sure to collapse in the near future, and second, when it did, there would be a permanent revolution in government. To this Cobbett added a third principle, peculiarly his own, but an extension of Paine's ideas, that there would be no change in government, and no reform, *until* the funding system collapsed" (*William Cobbett*, 2:316).

47. Thompson, *Making of the English Working Class*, 757. It should be noted that Thompson's overall assessment of Cobbett emphasizes his contributions to early-nineteenth-century radicalism. Alborn calls Cobbett's writings "radical bluster" (*Conceiving Companies*, 61).

48. Unlike later radicals (and the position he later endorsed), Cobbett at this point did not believe that political representation alone could reform Britain's endemic inequality. See Spater, *William Cobbett*, 2:316.

49. For a discussion of this idea of value, see Thompson, "Moral Economy."

50. For a table listing thirty-three of the pernicious systems Cobbett identified in various writings, see Gilmartin, *Print Politics*, 161.

51. Klancher makes a slightly different point when he argues: "Cobbett attempts to locate his audience both within and without a world of signs. . . . He seeks a stance outside the social text, a ground where all representations become inadequate to their pragmatic effects" (*Making of English Reading Audiences*, 128).

52. Raymond Williams notes Cobbett's use of "punching italics" (*Cobbett*, 55).

53. Nattrass, *William Cobbett*, 90. Paine's pamphlet, which was written before the Restriction Act, was both prescient and extremely influential. One modern editor, in fact, states that it "probably hastened the gold suspension of the Bank of England" (Paine, *Writings*, 7:286 n. 1). Thomas Paine also provided Cobbett with a stylistic model, for his plain style was a calculated departure from the style practiced by eighteenth-century "refined" writers. For a discussion of the influence of Paine's

style, see Haywood, *Revolution in Popular Literature*, 17–25; Gilmartin, *Print Politics*, chap. 1; and Klancher, *Making of English Reading Audiences*, 103–7.

54. Paine, "Decline," in *Writings*, 7:307.
55. Paine's *Rights of Man* (1790, 1792) was explicitly a counter to Burke's *Reflections on the Revolution in France* (1790).
56. This restates the slogan Paine repeatedly used: "Public credit is suspicion asleep" ("Decline," in *Writings*, 7:298).
57. Spater, *William Cobbett*, 2:368. Cobbett outlined this plan in his *Weekly Political Register* 35 (1819–20): 48–50. Gilmartin argues that this plan articulates "a first principle of radical opposition," one of the "canny and subversive emulations of the state's own potent specters." "They can make nothing that cannot be imitated," in Cobbett's words (*Print Politics*, 5).
58. Cobbett, *Rural Rides*, 1:123–24 (30 October 1822).
59. Feavearyear provides an example of the first, more typical account (*Pound Sterling*, 240–50); White supplements this traditional account by emphasizing the Free Banking school (*Free Banking*, chaps. 3 and 4).
60. The Joplin and Gilbart figures and the McCulloch quote are taken from White, *Free Banking*, 47.
61. Gilbart's estimate and the Macleod quote are taken from ibid.
62. Lord King's pamphlet appears in King, *Selection*, 231–59.
63. The notes ceased to be legal tender, in even this restricted sense, in 1823. The Bank Act of 1833 made all Bank notes above £5 legal tender again, as long as the Bank could maintain their convertibility (Feavearyear, *Pound Sterling*, 218, 235). For a discussion of Lord King's actions, see ibid., 190–91.
64. Cobbett quoted in ibid., 209. Here, we might note that, in *Paper against Gold*, Cobbett did not systematically distinguish between Bank of England notes and country banks' notes; all paper notes, to him, were equally fictitious. In the wake of the resumption of payments, he began to blame country bankers for issuing too many notes and to take a softer position on the Bank: "The Bank is blamed for putting out paper and causing high prices; and blamed at the same time for not putting out paper to accommodate merchants and keep them from breaking. It cannot be to blame for both, and indeed it is blamable for neither. It is the fellows that put out the paper and then break that do the mischief" (*Rural Rides* quoted in Feavearyear, *Pound Sterling*, 223).
65. A second act required note-issuing banks to publish quarterly statements of their average weekly note circulation (Feavearyear, *Pound Sterling*, 235). The 1833 Bank Act also ended the 5 percent cap on interest for the Bank of England.
66. White explains these concepts. See *Free Banking*, chap. 4.
67. Pitt quoted in Feavearyear, *Pound Sterling*, 242.
68. Scrope quoted in White, *Free Banking*, 83. White points out that this equation overlooks the elements of time, risk, and profit that were inherent in bills of exchange, as opposed to banknotes, which constituted demands to pay immediately (84). Here is White's succinct summary of the three schools' positions regarding the volume of note issue: "Whereas the Currency School held that any bank could overissue, and the Banking School that no bank could overissue, the Free Banking School held that only a central bank like the Bank of England could overissue" (53). Checkland, who does not include the Free Banking school in his summary of these debates, describes the positions of the other two groups: "The [Banking school] said, in effect, 'Trust the Bankers.' Demand convertibility of the note issue, but beyond that leave discretion

to those in charge of banking policy. . . . Do not impair the scope and flexibility of the Bank's actions by an insistence upon rigid rules. The Currency school, on the other hand, denied that the bankers should be left so free of control. They said, in effect, that the issue of notes by the Bank of England should be backed pound for pound, by gold reserves. Paper currency would thus be convertible at all times, with the result, so it was argued, that liquidity crises could not occur. . . . The essential need was for a 'regulation based upon principle'" (*Rise of Industrial Society*, 198).

69. See Reid, *Life and Adventures.*

70. Bailey, *A Defense of Joint-Stock Banks and Country Issues* (1840), quoted in White, *Free Banking*, 131.

71. Hodgskin, *Popular Political Economy* (1827), quoted in ibid., 133.

72. Boyd, "Letter," 33–34, 68.

73. Cobbett quoted in Gilmartin, *Print Politics*, 163.

74. The act extended the definition of a newspaper to any publication that printed news within twenty-six days and that sold for less than 6d. This made the cheap radical weeklies subject to the 4d. stamp tax and effectively placed them outside the purchasing power of their mass readership (Haywood, *Revolution in Popular Literature*, 100).

75. Ibid., 102.

76. Ibid., 114. Haywood discusses the unstamped wars in chap. 5.

77. Altick, *English Common Reader*, 287–89. See also Haywood, *Revolution in Popular Literature*, 104–7.

78. Ibid., 112–13.

79. Ibid., 139 (see also chap. 6).

80. Jay and Jay, eds., *Critics of Capitalism*, 36. The second part was also published separately as an Owenite pamphlet in 1842. Taylor refers to Owen, along with William Thompson and Thomas Hodgskin, as "neo-Ricardian" economists (*Eve and the New Jerusalem*, 84).

81. Marx, *Critique of Political Economy*, 106.

82. Thompson, *Making of the English Working Class*, 826–28.

83. "The productive classes are bewildered amidst the multiplicity of remedies offered for their consideration. They have as many remedies as wrongs—one contradicting another, and most of them equally valueless; for they are alike based merely on passing events, instead of resting on the broad foundation of some great principle. . . . There is wanted, not a mere governmental or particular remedy, but a general remedy—one which will apply to all social wrongs and evils, great and small" (Bray, *Labour's Wrongs* [hereafter *LW*], 8). Page numbers for subsequent citations are given in the text.

84. See Taylor, *Eve and the New Jerusalem*, chap. 4; and Thompson, *Making of the English Working Class*, 711–830.

85. The other radical who assigned money a prominent place in the coming revolution was the retired naval lieutenant Thomas Hodgskin, who published *Labour Defended against the Claims of Capital* anonymously in 1825. On Hodgskin, see Thompson, *Making of the English Working Class*, 778–79.

86. Owen, *Reports of Meetings in Dublin* (1823), quoted in Bonar, "Labour Exchange," 520. Even though Bonar denigrates Owen's writings as "propaganda," he gives a thorough account of the way the labor exchange notes functioned (520–23). Valenze points out that the nineteenth-century schemes to print labor notes built on a project described by the Quaker John Bellers (1654–1725) at the turn into the eighteenth century. See *Social Life of Money*, 121–33.

87. *Crisis* (16 June 1833), cited in Bonar, "Labour Exchange," 521.

88. *Crisis*, ii, cited in ibid.

89. Bonar explains that "men bought goods that were unsaleable in the ordinary market, turned them into labour-notes, and with these notes drew useful and saleable articles from the stores" (ibid., 522).

90. This comment continues: "Still, the principles on which the system was founded remain unimpeachable, and ought to be cherished in the public mind" (Allen Davenport in the 15 March 1851 *National Co-Operative Leader* quoted in Thompson, *Making of the English Working Class*, 798). Writing in 1901, Bonar was less enthusiastic about the underlying principles, especially the decision to value all labor at 6d. per hour: "If careful valuation had been made for [the notes] by a common pawnbroker, the exchange societies might, at a small expense of dignity, have purchased a longer lease of life" ("Labour Exchange," 522). Labor notes are still used in some U.S. communities, including Ithaca, NY, and Lawrence, KS. For a discussion of the former, see Maurer, "Uncanny Exchanges."

91. Bonar, "Labour Exchange," 522–23.

92. Owen quoted in ibid., 522.

93. Bray also exposes "the knavery and mystery of banking" (*LW*, 147). Joint-stock bankers, he explains, "make and issue bank-notes of the nominal value of one millions pounds of sterling, although there may not be amongst the whole of them even the one-thousandth of this part of gold. The bank-notes, however, imply that they may at any time be exchanged for gold at the bank from whence they have been issued; and they are taken by the public on this security, although it is almost universally known that there is never in the coffers of a bank one-half the quantity of gold that would be required to cash the notes issued" (148–49). This is "a vile and cunning robbery," Bray complains, for banks issue worthless paper in exchange for the commodities workers have actually produced (148).

94. [De Quincey], "Dialogues"; and Bailey, *Critical Dissertation*. The latter volume also includes John Stuart Mill's 1826 review of Bailey's pamphlet as well as three additional pamphlets by Bailey. For Bailey's tabulation of Ricardo's various uses of *value*, see *Critical Dissertation*, 239 n. a.

95. "On the broad principle of equal rights will Labour now take its stand,—not Labour in the United Kingdom only, but in France, and the United States, and the world at large. This principle will apply equally to all men of all countries, all colours, and all creeds. . . . Let Labour, then, come to the battle fearlessly" (Bray, *LW*, 13). Unlike some other radicals, Bray did not include women among the "men" whose rights were equal. On the question of gender equality in the radical movement, see Taylor, *Eve and the New Jerusalem*, chaps. 2–8.

CHAPTER FOUR

1. Acts of 1833, 1845, and 1928 made Bank of England notes of five pounds and higher legal tender, but one-pound and ten-shilling notes were not declared legal tender until 1928.

2. Country banks that were issuing notes on the day that Peel introduced his resolutions, 6 May 1844, were allowed to continue doing so unless they became bankrupt, ceased to exist, or interrupted issue. In addition, banks with fewer than six partners in England or Wales were forbidden to issue notes in the future if, through incorporation or amalgamation, they increased their partners beyond six. Any bank that continued to issue was allowed to circulate only in the amount of its average circulation

in the twelve weeks preceding 27 April 1844. If a bank ceased to issue, the Bank of England could petition to take over two-thirds of the lapsed issue. These provisions immediately led to a decrease in country bank issue, and the last bank to issue its own notes, Fox, Fowler, & Co. of Wellington, Somerset, lost its right when it amalgamated with Lloyds Bank Ltd. See Feavearyear, *Pound Sterling*, 254–55.

3. The 1844 Bank Charter Act established two departments in the Bank of England. The Issue Department was charged with note issue and the Banking Department with all other business. The act restricted the Bank's note issue to £14 million. Any issue above that amount had to occur in exchange for, and be covered by, gold or silver in the amount of the face value of the issue. In addition, the act required the Bank to publicize its position in a weekly account printed in the *London Gazette*, and it strictly limited (although it did not end) note issue by country banks. See Feavearyear, *Pound Sterling*, 253–55.

4. Francis Horner articulated this principle as early as 1802, in his review of Thornton's pamphlet on credit. Horner explicitly described the distinction between accumulating facts and generating theories as a division of labor, and he clearly intended this division to characterize political economy as a distinctively modern *science*. See "Thornton on the Paper Credit," 28.

5. "Almost all the absurd theories and opinions which have successively appeared have been supported by an appeal to facts. But a knowledge of facts, without a knowledge of their mutual relation—without being able to show why the one is a cause and the other an effect—is, to use the illustration of M. Say, really no better than the indigested erudition of an almanack-maker, and can afford no means of judging the truth or falsehood of a general principle" (McCulloch, *Discourse*, 14–15).

6. See Poovey, *History of the Modern Fact*, chaps. 4 and 5; Fontana, *Rethinking*, chaps. 2 and 3; Klaver, *A/Moral Economics*, chaps. 1–3; Yeo, *Defining Science*; Checkland, "Advent of Academic Economics"; Winch, *Riches and Poverty*; Letwin, *Origins of Scientific Economics*; Olson, *Science Deified*; Schabas, *World Ruled by Number*; and Porter, *Rise of Statistical Thinking*, chaps. 1 and 2.

7. Klaver, *A/Moral Economics*, chap. 1. Other scholars who have assigned Ricardo this position in the history of political economy include Winch, *Riches and Poverty*; Blaug, *Ricardian Economics*; Checkland, "Propagation of Ricardian Economics"; Fetter, "Rise and Decline," 67–84; Polanyi, *Great Transformation*; and Himmelfarb, *Idea of Poverty*. Klaver devotes extensive attention to Ricardo's style.

8. Klaver, *A/Moral Economics*, 19–20.

9. McCulloch, *Discourse*, 74. McCulloch continues: "Those, however, who give to his works the attention of which they are so worthy, will find them to be no less logical and instructive than they are profound and important" (ibid.).

10. Ricardo quoted in Klaver, *A/Moral Economics*, 20.

11. Deane, "McCulloch, John Ramsay," 185.

12. Klaver, *A/Moral Economics*, 35–52.

13. Deane, "McCulloch, John Ramsay," 185. Like Deane, I use the terms *profession* and *professionalize* in a less rigorous way than do modern sociologists, who have developed strict criteria for what counts as professionalization. See, e.g., Larson, *Rise of Professionalism*, chap. 1. Perkin points out that, in this sense, there were few professions in Britain until 1880 (*Rise of Professional Society*, chaps. 1 and 2). As I use these terms, they refer to the achievement of a recognizable degree of social authority that is organized by supporting institutions, even though official criteria for attaining this authority may not have been codified.

14. This was still a large run in comparison with the print runs of most novels. St. Clair points out that most publishers in this period issued new novels in runs of between 500 and 750. See *Reading Nation*, 564, 578 n. 2.

15. Reid, "Biographical Notice," xxiv.

16. Rauch points out that readers often wanted to acquire knowledge about current events to enhance their own social prestige. See *Useful Knowledge*, 28–29.

17. An edition of *The Wealth of Nations* had been published in 1814, but it was abridged to conform to its editor's ideas. See Fontana, *Rethinking*, 70.

18. In addition to the two collections I have already discussed, this series included *Paper Currency and Banking* (1857), *The National Debt and the Sinking Fund* (1857), *Commerce* (1859), and *Economical Tracts* (1859).

19. Deane, "McCulloch, John Ramsay," 185.

20. Ibid.

21. McCulloch, "Banks–Banking." Page numbers for subsequent citations are given in the text.

22. The principle to which McCulloch alluded turned on the international acceptance of a gold standard, which Britain had ratified in 1821. In theory, the gold standard allowed the international money market to set the price of gold in spite of attempts by individual governments to regulate prices. Because the free trade of gold would "automatically" cause gold to flow away from countries where prices were "unnaturally high," these countries would be forced to lower prices. As they did so, gold would flow back, and the countries would expand their money supplies by printing more paper and extending more credit, thus raising prices again.

23. In the wake of the 1826 Bank Act, which permitted joint-stock banks to form (outside a sixty-five-mile radius of London), considerable controversy developed over whether joint-stock banks were more trustworthy than private banks (those with fewer than six investors, many of which were family-owned companies). In "Banks–Banking," McCulloch explicitly targets joint-stock banks as the threat to the Bank, but many of his contemporaries were equally skeptical about private bankers. In addition to Harriet Martineau's *Berkeley the Banker* (1832), which I examine in the second interchapter, see also [White], "Murdering Banker" (1838); and [Gore], "London Banker" (1843). The attitude of these two writers is captured by the former's determination "to deposit the whole of [his] worldly goods in [his] breeches-pocket, convinced, from long and melancholy experience, that every man is his own best banker" ([White], "Murdering Banker," 823).

24. This presentation of different events as versions of the same kind is consistent with the theory of history that McCulloch invokes in his *Discourse*. There, he approvingly cites Sir James Mackintosh's *Discourse on the Law of Nature and Nations*: "History, if I may be allowed the expression, is now a vast museum, in which specimens of every variety of human nature may be studied. From these great accessions of knowledge, law-givers and statesmen, but, above all, moralists and *political philosophers*, may derive the most important instructions. They may plainly discover in all the useful and beautiful variety of governments and institutions, and under all the fantastic multitude of usages and rites which have prevailed among men, the same fundamental comprehensive truths, the sacred master principles which are the guardians of human society, recognized and revered (with few and slight exceptions) by every nation upon earth, and uniformly taught (with exceptions still fewer) by a succession of wise men, from the first dawn of speculation to the present moment" (18n).

25. Lalor, *Money and Morals*. See Ingram, *History of Political Economy*, 216.

26. On Chalmers's popularity, see Hilton, *Age of Atonement*, 36–70; Watt, *Thomas Chalmers*, 103–7; and Poovey, *Making a Social Body*, 99–106.

27. Chalmers's three works on political economy were the third volume of *Christian and Civic Economy* (1826), *On Political Economy* (1832), and *On the Adaptation of External Nature to the Moral and Intellectual Constitution of Man* (1833). As Hilton points out, contemporary reviewers were indifferent (or worse) to these volumes (*Age of Atonement*, 64–65).

28. Schumpeter, *History of Economic Analysis*, 487.

29. Chalmers, *Works*, 6:266.

30. Ibid., 16:56.

31. *Christian Observer* quoted in Hilton, *Age of Atonement*, 132.

32. This appears in a letter written by S. J. Loyd, Lord Overstone, in 1856, quoted in ibid., 135.

33. *Ecclesiastic and Theologian* quoted in ibid.

34. On limited liability, see Poovey, *Making a Social Body*, 157–64; and Hilton, "Chalmers as Political Economist."

35. Mill quoted in Hilton, *Age of Atonement*, 70.

36. In bk. 3, chap. 14, Mill's subject is the "under-supply of money" (*Principles*, 561); in bk. 3, chap. 23, his subject is "fluctuations in the rate of interest" (641); and, in bk. 4, chap. 4, his subject is "the downward tendency of prices" (733). Page numbers for subsequent citations are given in the text.

37. See Mackay, *Extraordinary Popular Delusions*.

38. In 1896, W. E. Johnson, himself a well-known practitioner and historian of political economy, demonstrated that the claim to be a science, by which McCulloch distinguished political economy from Adam Smith's moral practice of jurisprudence, had by century's end been appropriated by "economics." In Johnson's definitions, as in McCulloch's, the decisive distinction between science and art is the distinction between theory and practice. While the definitions Johnson offers are not strict, he associates political economy with the "ethical survey of the value of human ends" and economics with "a general theory of the action of industrial forces." The first, he states, is an art; the second is a science: "A *science* of economic causes and effects must precede the *art* of political economy; and . . . this art is related to the science in the same way as any branch of applied knowledge is related to the corresponding theoretical knowledge" ("Method of Political Economy," 740). For a discussion of economists' aspiration to attain for economics the status of a science, see Schumpeter, *History of Economic Analysis*, 534–36. The word *scientist* was coined by William Whewell in 1843.

39. I quote from Mill's self-quotation (in 1843); the original essay was published in the *Westminster Review*. See Mill, *Logic of the Moral Sciences*, 90–91. This is a reprint of the sixth book of Mill's *A System of Logic Ratiocinative and Inductive, Being a Connected View of the Principles of Evidence and the Methods of Scientific Investigation* (1843).

40. Jeffrey, "Madame de Staël," 20–21.

41. Walter Bagehot, "The First Edinburgh Reviewers" (1855), quoted in Klaver, *A/Moral Economics*, 1.

42. Lee, *Origins of the Popular Press*, 108. On journalism in this period, see also Brake, *Subjugated Knowledges*; Cross, *Common Writer*, chap. 3; and Hampton, "Journalism."

43. Besant, "Literature as a Career," 325, 326–27.

44. See Poovey, "Writing about Finance," 22–26.

45. Cross, *Common Writer*, 93–114.

46. Bagehot famously complained that "sums are matters of opinion," and he disliked both the need for precision and the routine of banking. See Barrington, ed., *Works and Life*, 10:213.
47. Ibid., 246.
48. Bagehot, "What a Panic Is" (hereafter "What"), 92. Page numbers for subsequent citations are given in the text.
49. Edwards, *Pursuit of Reason*, 6.
50. *London Times*, 11 May 1866, 11, and 14 May 1866, 8.
51. *London Times*, 12 May 1866, 8.
52. Bagehot quoted in Kynaston, *City of London*, 240.
53. Bagehot, "The Panic" (hereafter "Panic"), 93. Page numbers for subsequent citations are given in the text.
54. Kynaston, *City of London*, 238–39. The quotation comes from the prosecuting counsel's opening speech.
55. *London Times*, 14 May 1866, 8.
56. See, e.g., Mackay, *Extraordinary Popular Delusions*. For other attempts to theorize the collective emotions that fueled manias and panics, see my discussion of Jevons below.
57. Parsons, *Power of the Financial Press*, 26.
58. Evans, *History of the Commercial Crisis* (hereafter *History*), v, and *Commercial Crisis, 1847–48* (hereafter *Commercial*), vii. Page numbers for subsequent citations of both are given in the text. Kindleberger commented in 1978 that Evans's records of bankruptcies give "some sense of the spread of the crisis" of 1847. "Unhappily," Kindleberger continued, in a comment that reveals his interest in the national or aggregate economy, "these are by number rather than by volume of assets of failed banks and firms, which would give a better idea of their importance" (*Manias*, 140).
59. See, e.g., Evans, *Commercial*, 31n., 48n.
60. Evans, *City Men*, 116. Page numbers for subsequent citations are given in the text.
61. Evans repeatedly insisted that legislation would never curtail financial transgressions. See, e.g., *History*: "Practical experience teaches that no legislation will properly restrain speculation or adventure; it will check, but not effectively prevent business being carried out on an unsound basis" (27).
62. See Faller, *Turned to Account*.
63. Evans, *Speculative Notes*, xi. Page numbers for subsequent citations are given in the text.
64. The first passage is from "A Singular Development," the second from "Shadows of the Past.—A Walk Round 'Change.'"
65. Evans does both in "Dark, Sombre Morning—Bright, Glowing Eventide." The essay opens with this striking image: "Gaunt panic, with uncertain gait and distorted visage, stalks hurriedly through the land. Like the leper of old, downcast in mien and paralyzed in limb, his presence is the signal for immediate apprehension, lest his contagious touch should strike with disease sound constitutions, and bleach white the bones of living men. The slightest blast from his lividly scorching breath remorselessly crumbles up credit, and destroys, as by the fell wand of the necromancer, the good fame and fortune acquired by long years of toil and steady accumulation" (*Speculative Notes*, 36). Later in the sketch, the narrator has a vision that an unnamed "great financier" halts the panic and saves all the banks (40).
66. This send-up, *Piccadilly*, was serialized in 1865 but not published in volume form until 1870. The best source for information about Oliphant is Margaret Oliphant's *Memoir*.

67. Oliphant, *Memoir*, 2:152. This satire is thought to be based on the activities of Albert Grant, who founded the Credit Foncier and Moblier of England in 1864. By 1877, Grant and the company were bankrupt.

68. Here is Margaret Oliphant's assessment: "The excitement of the struggles of business life roused all his faculties, and I have always heard that his capacity was great in financial matters. No doubt, too, a man so formed for activity of mental life enjoyed more or less the keen conflict of wits, more tremendous than any conflict of literature, in which each man has to keep his eye upon the other, lest he should be overreached and checkmated. But I do not know that Laurence entered upon any further commercial or speculative enterprise on so large a scale as the Cable Company. His experience in that did not tempt him to further exertions" (*Memoir*, 2:153–54). Laurence might have been one model for the character Roland, the London stockbroker who appears in Margaret Oliphant's 1883 novel *Hester*.

69. [Oliphant], "Autobiography of a Joint-Stock Company" (hereafter "Autobiography"), 121. Page numbers for subsequent citations are given in the text. The sketch was later reprinted in Oliphant's *Traits and Travesties: Social and Political* (1882).

70. The companies acts were passed between 1844 and 1867. Intended to ease restrictions on business by making it easier to incorporate and by limiting the liability of company owners and investors, this legislation included the 1844 Registration Act; an 1856 act, which further eased the process of registration; the 1857 repeal of the Joint-Stock Bank Act, which repeal allowed banks to incorporate; and the 1862 and 1867 Consolidating acts, which extended the privileges granted by the 1856 Company Act to banks and insurance companies, and which granted limited liability to shareholders in all corporations.

71. The use of a naive character, often referred to as a "green 'un," as a stand-in for the reader can be found in other nineteenth-century texts, both fictional and investigative. See, e.g., Dickens's *Oliver Twist*; and [Blanchard], "Biography of a Bad Shilling."

72. Robb, *White-Collar Crime*, 15.

73. Ibid., 28. This figure represented about one-fifth of the nation's wealth and more than doubled the investments in French and German companies combined.

74. Michie, *London Stock Exchange*, 72, 95.

75. Robb, *White-Collar Crime*, chap. 2.

76. On the historical relationship between print and the growth of the credit economy, see Poovey, "Writing about Finance," 17–26; and Parsons, *Power of the Financial Press*.

77. Winch, "Emergence," 564–65. See also Robbins, "Nature and Significance of Economic Science"; and Gagnier, *Insatiability of Human Wants*, 4–5, 40–53.

78. "It is clear that Economics, if it is to be a science at all, must be a mathematical science. Many persons seem to think that the physical sciences form the proper sphere of mathematical method, and that the moral sciences demand some other method,—I know not what. My theory of Economics, however, is purely mathematical in character. Nay, believing that the quantities with which we deal must be subject to continuous variation, I do not hesitate to use the appropriate branch of mathematical science, involving though it does the fearless consideration of infinitely small quantities. The theory consists in applying the differential calculus to the familiar notions of wealth, utility, value, demand, supply, capital, interest, labour, and all the other quantitative notions belonging to the daily operations of industry. As the complete theory of almost every other science involves the use

of that calculus, so we cannot have a true theory of Economics without its aid" (Jevons, *Theory of Political Economy*, 3). As Schabas points out, however, Jevons was also aware of the limitations of science, and he used mathematics as a convenient tool rather than a privileged epistemological key to the mysteries of the universe. See *World Ruled by Number*, 81–84.

79. Jevons, "Commercial Crises and Sun-Spots," in *Investigations*, 4. Jevons's papers on this subject were composed in the last sixteen years of his life. They include "On the Study of Periodical Commercial Fluctuations" (1862), "On the Frequent Autumnal Pressure in the Money Market, and the Action of the Bank of England" (1866), "The Solar Period and the Price of Corn" (1875), "The Periodicity of Commercial Crises and Its Physical Explanation" (1878), and "Commercial Crises and Sun-Spots" (1878). The papers were collected in Jevons, *Investigations*. Page numbers (keyed to *Investigations*) for subsequent citations of all these papers are given in the text.

80. The Marxist Hyndman, e.g., charged: "The spots on the sun had as much influence on industrial crises as the spots on the leopard in the Zoological Gardens" (*Commercial Crises*, 9–10).

81. John Mills, "On Credit Cycles," 17; Purdy, *City Life*, 21–41, 81–93, 195–207. In 1860, Clement Juglar also tried to account for commercial crises, this time by arguing that economic downturns were simply parts of a "trade cycle" (*Of Commercial Crises and Their Periodical Return in France, England, and the United States*). On Juglar, see Niehans, "Juglar's Credit Cycles."

82. Wilson also thought that variations in harvests caused fluctuations in gold. See Checkland, *Rise of Industrial Society*, 425–26.

CHAPTER FIVE

1. I stress the *Literary* as opposed to the more general *aesthetic* definition of *value* because I want to emphasize print forms of art. A more sustained discussion of this topic would need to trace the way that the pre-Raphaelites adapted what I call the *Romantic definition* of *value* for visual and mixed media.

2. I use the term *Romantic* here even though I am examining some of the conditions that helped naturalize such technical Literary critical terminology. As I argue in my introduction, I am aware of the limitations of accepting the periodization implicit in the term *Romantic*, but, given how widely this term is now used, it seems perverse to discard it.

3. Hunter, *Culture and Government*, 5, 115.

4. Guillory, *Cultural Capital*, 315–16 (see also 269–340). "Double discourse of value" is a phrase used by Barbara Herrnstein Smith, whose work Guillory engages, to invoke the separate models of value associated with the market and the work of art.

5. Ibid., 303, 307, 315, 316–17.

6. I say that the latter is more complex both because, as Guillory notes, aesthetics remains a subset of the discipline of *philosophy*, which has, at best, an oblique institutional relation to modern Literary studies, and because Literary study only belatedly became a properly *disciplinary* subject (in the twentieth century) and then one that was also divided into two large kinds of practice.

7. I do realize that Wordsworth (and Coleridge) might also be viewed as having taken a more radical attitude toward the future of imaginative writing, in keeping with the radical political position he took in the 1790s, instead of the defensive posture I describe here. The radical Wordsworth and his conservative counterpart seem to me to be the same person. That is, like Jarrells, I view Wordsworth's efforts to delimit

imaginative writing as an attempt to substitute one kind of "revolution" (a poetic revolution) for another (a revolution by and for the people). See *Britain's Bloodless Revolutions*, 77–96.

8. Wordsworth, "Preface to *Lyrical Ballads*," in *Prose Works* (hereafter *PW*), 1:126. Page numbers for all subsequent Wordsworth citations (keyed to *PW*) are given in the text.

9. In their commentary on the "Preface" to *Lyrical Ballads*," Owen and Smyser note that, in 1808, Wordsworth implied that he had some notion of a "moral sense," akin to the faculty Francis Hutcheson described in the 1720s, and that he connected this to aesthetic appreciation, or "taste." They also note that Wordsworth never explained the precise connection between aesthetic judgment and moral feelings. They quote Henry Crabb Robinson saying that Wordsworth "wished popularity for his *Two voices are there, one is of the Sea* as a test of elevation and moral purity" (*PW*, 1:175).

10. Andrew Bennett helpfully paraphrases these claims in order to explain the connections among them: "In order to discriminate the poet from the scribbler or hack, the poem from common, everyday verse, Romantic theories of poetry produce an absolute and non-negotiable opposition between writing which is original, new, revolutionary, writing which breaks with the past and appeals to the future, and writing which is conventional, derivative, a copy or simulation of earlier work, writing which has an immediate appeal and an in-built redundancy. The sign of the great poem, then, is originality. Originality, in turn, generates deferred reception since the original poem is defined as one which cannot (immediately) be read. The original poem is both new and before its time. . . . And since the original and autonomous poem is *only* one which has been produced by the genius, the guarantee of true poetry inheres, finally, in the identity of the poet himself, his signature leaving its indelible trace throughout the work. We can only know that we are reading a 'great' poem because of the signature of the genius, that ineffable but theoretically unmistakable identification of the work by and with the poet himself, an identity which will live on in the future, will, indeed, come to life in posterity" (*Romantic Poets*, 3–4).

11. "Even a theoretical preface cannot suffice," Klancher comments of this passage. "It, in turn, demands a larger theory of language, social order, and historical development that Wordsworth, in the opening of the Preface, apologizes for *not* writing. . . . It has now become impossible to write the smallest, humblest poem of worth without framing it with an ambitious theory of social transformation, individual and collective psychology, literature and the interpretation of signs" (*Making of English Reading Audiences*, 139).

12. Coleridge, *Biographia Literaria*, quoted in Russett, *De Quincey's Romanticism*, 29.

13. De Quincey quoted in Russett, *De Quincey's Romanticism*, 174.

14. See ibid., chap. 4.

15. See ibid., chap. 5.

16. Harriet Martineau is another example of a woman who occupied the position of minor writer, this time in relation to David Ricardo and the other economic theorists whose ideas she popularized in her *Illustrations of Political Economy*. I return to Martineau in the second interchapter.

17. Coleridge quoted in Woolford, "Periodicals," 112.

18. "Adjectival criticism" is Woolford's phrase (ibid., 111–12). These reviews also featured long quotations from the book under review. When the review was not damning, these excerpts functioned to "puff," or advertise, the book.

19. John Lockhart challenged John Scott, the editor of the *London Magazine*, to a duel over the latter's charge that Lockhart was "a professional scandal-monger." Scott was killed by Lockhart's friend and intended second, James Christie (Oliphant, *Annals*, 1:231–33; Russett, *De Quincey's Romanticism*, 109; Jones, "Scott-Christie Duel," 605–29). On *Blackwood's* vicious reviews, see Wheatley, "*Blackwood's* Attacks." For a discussion of the proliferation of periodicals in these decades, see Erickson, *Economy of Literary Form*, chap. 3.

20. Jeffrey, in the *Edinburgh Review* 24 (November 1814), quoted in Reiman, ed., *Romantics Reviewed*, 2: pt. A, 439.

21. Jeffrey quoted in ibid., 454. For the *Quarterly Review* and the *Theatrical Inquisitor*, see ibid., 817, 833, 835, 843, 875.

22. Oliphant, *Annals*, 1:171. In 1825, Wilson published another assessment of Wordsworth, this one negative. Oliphant was not able to explain his change of opinion (see ibid., 278–86).

23. Reiman, ed., *Romantics Reviewed*, 2: pt. A, 626 (*London Magazine*), 497 (*New European Magazine*), 699 (*Monthly Repository*).

24. See Oliphant's frank incomprehension of Wilson's negative review (*Annals*, 1:278–86).

25. "Nowhere in his School Reports does Matthew Arnold advocate that *this* practice of culture—focused for him in the astringent dialectic of his literary criticism—should be democratically disseminated as the basis of popular education" (Hunter, *Culture and Government*, 68).

26. Oliphant's description of the early years of *Blackwood's* is filled with accounts of the ruses with which periodical writers tried to attract readers as well as their editors' complicity in these schemes. See *Annals*, vol. 1, chaps. 3 and 4.

27. In the first decades of the nineteenth century, only novels were routinely published anonymously. As St. Clair explains: "Writers of novels . . . were still more like piece workers than independent 'authors,' and most novels of the period were still published, as had been a custom in the eighteenth century, without the author even being named" (*Reading Nation*, 173).

28. In the last decades of the nineteenth century, even after reviewers had adopted higher standards for their work, Charles Reade was still complaining about the abuses anonymity sanctioned: "I find that Literature, directly or indirectly, owes its sad degradation in England to an excess of anonymous writing; one branch is directly degraded by it, and from a great height. I mean the branch which is blasphemously miscalled 'criticism.' I find that anonymous criticasters are often contemptible and scarcely ever scientific in their judgments. There is scarcely a writer in the island, whose name signed at the bottom of his critique would not rather weaken than strengthen its authority; and this is a terrible phenomenon in any art or science. . . . The anonymous criticaster is deprived of these two great guides, without which no *class* of men ever yet went straight, reward, and punishment: he is neither punished for dishonesty and blunders, nor rewarded for purity and infallibility" (quoted in Reade and Reade, *Memoir*, 2:226–27). Double reviewing was the practice of a journalist reviewing the same publication for several different periodicals. William Hepworth Dixon, the editor of the *Athenaeum*, reviewed his own work in the 1860s. For a discussion of double reviewing, see Dahl, "Fitzjames Stephen." See also Brake, *Subjugated Knowledges*, 20.

29. On the discrepancy in status of the two occupations, see Russett, *De Quincey's Romanticism*, chap. 3.

30. See Jeffrey's review of Southey's *Thalaba* in the *Edinburgh Review* 1 (October 1802), in Reiman, ed., *Romantics Reviewed*, 2: pt. A, 415.
31. This is suggested by Owen and Smelser, Wordsworth's editors (see Wordsworth, *PW*, 3:55–60).
32. For a helpful discussion of the profits Wordsworth made from his works, see Erickson, *Economy of Literary Form*, chap. 2.
33. St. Clair, *Reading Nation*, 201–2.
34. Erickson, *Economy of Literary Form*, 26.
35. On the annuals, see ibid., 28–33. For declining sales in poetry after 1824, see chap. 1.
36. Writing anonymously in 1791, e.g., John Noorthouck compared the production of imaginative writing with manufacturing, to the disparagement of both: "When a manufacture has been carried on long enough for the workmen to gain a general proficiency, the uniformity of the stuffs will render it difficult to decide on the preference of one piece beyond another" (*Monthly Review*, ser. 2, 5 [July 1791], quoted in Williams, ed., *Novel and Romance*, 373).
37. Review of *Santa Maria*, *Gentleman's Magazine* 48 (September 1798), quoted in ibid., 448.
38. By any account, Scott was the most popular and best-selling poet of Wordsworth's generation. Scott's son-in-law J. G. Lockhart, who published *The Life of Scott* in 1837, gleefully chronicled the extraordinary sales of his major poems. *The Lay of the Last Minstrel* (1805) sold 12,500 copies in two years; *Marmion* (1808) sold 16,000 in its first two years and 25,000 by the end of the fourth; *The Lady of the Lake* (1810) sold out its expensive, quarto edition of 2,050 in days and its octavo of 18,250 by the end of the first year; and even *Rokeby* (1813), which Scott considered a failure, sold 10,000 in its first three months. Wordsworth's *Lyrical Ballads*, by contrast, which was relatively successful among Wordsworth's poems, went through four editions in eight years but sold only about 1,500 copies in its first three; his *Poetry in Two Volumes* (1807) sold very few copies; and his collected edition, published in 1820, sold only about 500 copies in four years. These sales figures are from Murphy, *Poetry as an Occupation*, 138–39, 195. When Scott began to publish novels in 1814, his sales remained unusually high, averaging about 10,000 in the first year of each novel (ibid., 139). St. Clair gives more complete figures for Scott's sales in *Reading Nation*, app. 9, pp. 632–43. For a nineteenth-century assessment of Scott's popularity, see Oliphant, *Annals*, 1:49, 59.
39. For a discussion of the aesthetic model of value, see Psomiades, *Beauty's Body*, chap. 1. In Psomiades's perceptive account of aesthetics, femininity constitutes both the site of contradiction and the figure through which this contradiction is managed. This account seems compatible with my argument, for the gap I associate with the problematic of representation could also be described in Psomiades's terms. I tend to emphasize the way Literary writers took advantage of this gap, however, whereas she tends to stress the way images of women were manipulated in the process, especially, although not exclusively, in visual images.
40. St. Clair, *Reading Nation*, 425.
41. See ibid., 310. The Stamp Act of 1819 had imposed a duty of 4d. on any periodical containing news or commentary; paper was taxed at a rate of 3d. a pound; and newspaper advertisements were taxed at a rate of 3s., 6d. each week.
42. Eliot, "Business of Victorian Publishing," 44.
43. [Oliphant], "Byways of Literature," 204, 211.
44. Oliphant, *Annals*, 2:235.

45. Besant, "The Start in Fiction," 192–93.
46. On this point, see Woolford, "Periodicals," 114–15.
47. Dickens quoted in Patten, *Charles Dickens*, 12.
48. Reade, *Readiana*, in *Works*, 9:354.
49. Oliphant, *Annals*, 2:457–58.
50. For a discussion of circulating libraries, see Erickson, *Economy of Literary Form*, chap. 6.
51. Eliot, "Business of Victorian Publishing," 50–51.
52. Griest, *Mudie's Circulating Library*, 39–40.
53. For a brief overview of the financial dimension of Victorian publishing, see Eliot, "Business of Victorian Publishing," 37–60. See also St. Clair, *Reading Nation*, chap. 11. St. Clair points out that the price of the triple-decker novel represented a 300 percent increase over the previous price of novels (202).
54. Oliphant, *Annals*, 2:459. John Blackwood referred to the library as "the Leviathan Mudie," although the dislike this phrase implies softened considerably over the years. See ibid., 459–62. In an anonymous essay entitled "The Monster-Misery of Literature," the author (probably the novelist Catherine Gore) railed against what she called "the miserable decline and fall of the great empire of letters" (556).
55. On serial publication, see Hughes and Lund, *Victorian Serial*, chap. 1.
56. Eliot, "Business of Victorian Publishing," 44.
57. Another kind of part-issue serialization was pioneered by George Eliot when she published *Middlemarch* in 1871–72. This format spread the novel over eight volumes that appeared every other month at a price of 5s. each. This format enabled Eliot to publish a novel that was longer than the triple-decker, to command a higher price for the whole (40s.), and to keep more of the book's profits, which were substantial. So successful was this format that she also used it for her last novel, *Daniel Deronda* (1876).
58. These included the *Cornhill Magazine*, the *Fortnightly Review*, *Blackwood's Edinburgh Magazine*, *Macmillan's Magazine*, *Good Words*, the *Graphic*, the *Temple Bar*, *All the Year Round*, the *Manchester Weekly Times*, and *Life* (Eliot, "Business of Victorian Publishing," 49).
59. Literary writers did try several times to create a professional organization that would solve problems like the lack of an international copyright law and the deplorable state of reviewing. In 1843, e.g., Harriet Martineau welcomed the idea of a Society of British Authors because such a society would help turn reviewing into "criticism": "From this may we not hope that an improved criticism will induce an improved temper among its subjects? If the conduct of criticism should ever become a department of the operations of the Association, I believe our influence upon Society would be deepened and strengthened, as it could be by no other employment of our united resources" (letter of 25 April 1843, quoted in Besant, "First Society," 293). With reviewers being paid to savage aspiring writers, few university positions available for teachers of Literature, no government support for the Literary establishment, and writers believing that they had to compete against each other to survive, however, the chances that such an organization would succeed were slim. Of the eight writers' associations formed between 1736 and 1843, none proved successful, and a "science" of criticism did not wholly supplant anonymous reviewing. See Bonham-Carter, *Authors by Profession*, 1:80–86, 226–27 n. 35. On efforts to establish a Society of British Authors after 1842, see Besant, "First Society," 272–305, and *Autobiography*, chap. 12.

60. Hughes and Lund, *Victorian Publishing,* chap. 1. See also Martineau, *Autobiography,* 1:252–53.
61. The different valuations of style I am describing here are complexly related to the different sources of income typically open to the two groups of writers. As I explained in chapter 3, from early in the nineteenth century economic writers had a range of institutional or quasi-institutional positions open to them, from the clerkship held by John Stuart Mill at the East India House, to the lectureships that McCulloch held, to the newspaper positions of Bagehot and Evans, to the university posts staffed by Malthus and Marshall. These positions did not all directly support writing, of course, but, apart from Martineau, few of the individuals whose economic writing I have discussed depended solely on writing for a livelihood. Imaginative writers sometimes held other posts as well—Thomas Love Peacock worked at the East India House, and Anthony Trollope worked for the postal service. By and large, however, partly because they linked their identities to self-expression, and partly because more of them looked to their writing for the bulk of their income, imaginative writers typically viewed writing as *the* definitive activity of their lives.
62. The discovery of the Corvey Collection in a castle in Germany has enabled scholars to have access to many of these novels, which have otherwise completely vanished. For a description of the collection, see http://www.unl.edu/sbehrend/html/sbsite/projects/Corvey/Corvey%20Index.htm.
63. On the debate about signature, see Maurer, "Anonymity vs. Signature"; Everett, *Party of Humanity;* and Brake, *Subjugated Knowledges,* 19–32.
64. Surprisingly, some editors were relieved to have their power lessened, as the turn to signature surely did, for with a decrease of power came a reduction of responsibility and blame. For an expression of what this burden felt like to Macvey Napier, the editor of the *Edinburgh Review* between 1829 and 1847, see Small, "Liberal Editing," 82.
65. This is the argument elaborated by Woolford, "Periodicals," 124–35. See also Kent, "Higher Journalism."
66. Seward's recommendation (which appeared in *Variety: A Collection of Essays, Written in the Year 1787, 1788,* xxx, xxvi) is quoted in Williams, ed., *Novel and Romance,* 361.
67. "Note-Book of a Literary Idler," 736, 737.
68. Collins, "Our Audience," 161; Butterworth, "Overfeeding Reading"; Dowden, "Interpretation of Literature," 701.
69. [Collins], "Unknown Public," 222.
70. [Oliphant], "Byways of Literature," 202, 204.
71. Russett notes that the process of canonization is also a process of narrowing—not just the number of works "worth" reading, but also the number of readers who can read (properly). Canonization makes (certain) texts more "expensive" in the sense that they require "greater investments of educational capital" (*De Quincey's Romanticism,* 245). See also Guillory, *Cultural Capital,* esp. chaps. 1 and 3.
72. Before the Education Act of 1870, primary education was not compulsory. Those working-class children who did attend school went to one of the religious schools established by various denominations, the ragged schools that had operated since 1844, or schools for girls like the dame schools. In these schools, when Literary writing was taught, it was used either for memory work or to encourage respect for middle-class culture. Many (but not all) middle- and upper-class boys attended public schools, like Eton and Rugby. The 1870 Education Act made primary education compulsory and encouraged (but did not require) the state to sponsor schools. There were additional education acts in 1880 and 1902.

73. Hunter points out that the "literary pedagogies" that were practiced before the nineteenth century focused on the teaching of classical grammar and rhetoric. Such pedagogies were not "Literary" in the modern sense because they were limited to teaching Greek and Latin and the skills of rhetoric and oratory. While what Hunter calls "Romantic aesthetic education" was introduced into some schools in the nineteenth century, to replace the monitorial system, it was not until the first decades of the twentieth century that its features—"self-expression, the 'mass' teaching of English literature, and the exemplary role of the teacher-critic"—assumed a dominant role (*Culture and Government*, 3, 4, 3). We might note that Arnold, who encouraged more people to read Literature (but not the teaching of criticism in schools), won a prize at Rugby for composition of a critical essay (in English) and at Oxford for the composition of a poem. Nevertheless, he always considered Greek literature the highest example of Literary writing.

74. Koven, "How the Victorians Read *Sesame and Lilies*," 165.

75. Samuel Smiles followed this example in *Self-Help*, but his discussion of reading did not offer instructions about how to read.

76. Ruskin, "Of King's Treasuries," 31, 34–35.

77. Arata, "On Not Paying Attention."

78. Ibid., 43.

79. In the wake of Lord Iddesleigh's Edinburgh lecture, the *Pall Mall Gazette* solicited numerous writers and cultural authorities to submit their suggestions for the "Best Hundred Books." The magazine published these lists in 1886, both in regular issues of the periodical and in a special supplement. This debate about what to read, in turn, sparked additional inquiries into what readers were *actually* reading. Secondary articles on the debate about what to read include Mays, "Disease of Reading"; and Arata, "On Not Paying Attention." A useful nineteenth-century review of the primary contributions to this debate is Murray, "Books and Reading." Primary sources that tried to survey what actual readers read include Salmon, "What Boys Read," "What Girls Read," and "What the Working Classes Read"; Gattie, "What English People Read"; Humphery, "Reading of the Working Classes"; and Maxwell, "Craving for Fiction." On this topic, see Rose, *Intellectual Life*, chap. 4.

80. Haultain, "How to Read," 263, 265.

81. Ibid., 263.

82. Dowden, "Interpretation of Literature" (hereafter "Interpretation"), 701.

83. Carolyn Williams has pointed out to me that this observation is a paraphrase of Walter Pater's comments in the 1873 *Introduction to the Renaissance* (private conversation). Pater is most probably the link between Ruskin and Dowden.

84. The sexual overtones also appear when Dowden says that "the lover of literature" must "lie open" to a wide range of impressions, "submit" to all great writers, and avoid "being seduced" by only one writer ("Interpretation," 711, 712, 713). We should note that it was precisely such sexualized accounts of reading that had long undermined imaginative writers' efforts to justify their work. As we have seen, in the eighteenth-century version of the charge that reading led to immorality, female readers were moralists' primary concern, the genre most often faulted was the novel, and reading was called not "interpretation" but a "dangerous recreation." See Pearson, *Women's Reading*, chap. 4. Dowden's apparent indifference to this history suggests two things: first, assumptions about gender remained asymmetrical in relation to reading, for, by calling the community of readers and writers a "fraternity," he could neutralize the hostility that still chastised women readers for their "indiscretion"; and,

second, by 1886, the nature of the value that serious Literary writing was assumed to convey was conceptualized as sufficient to offset any threat of a sexualized taint.

85. Hunter discusses this model of reading in "Reading Character," 226–43, and *Culture and Government*, 64–67, 235–45, and passim.

86. "Reading as a Means of Culture," 316.

87. For a discussion of the "exceptionally complicated" history of *organic*, see Williams, *Keywords*, 189–92. The most influential critical discussion of the place that organic theories played in Romantic literature and theory is Abrams, *The Mirror and the Lamp*, chaps. 7 and 8.

88. Coleridge, *Biographia Literaria*, 211, 206.

89. Arnold, "Function of Criticism," 261.

90. In addition to Abrams, *Mirror and the Lamp*, see Poovey, "Model System."

91. We should note that, even though the category of Literature was undeniably narrower in the 1840s and 1850s than it had been a century earlier, its boundaries were still a matter of dispute. When R. H. Horne published a collection of the best forty living representatives of what he called "general literature" in 1844, e.g., only seventeen of the figures he included could conceivably pass muster with the editors of a modern Literary anthology like the *Norton*. Some of the writers Horne included— Southwood Smith and T. N. Talfourd, e.g.—would no longer be considered Literary writers, and others—Thomas Ingoldsby and A. Fonblanque—have fallen below the level of the Literary canon. See *New Spirit*, iv, v.

92. Stephen, "Relation of Novels to Life," 112, 118.

93. De Quincey, "Poetry of Pope" (hereafter "PP"), 13. Page numbers for subsequent citations are given in the text.

94. *British Critic* quoted in Hayden, *Scott: The Critical Heritage*, 69.

95. Millgate, *Scott's Last Edition*, 1.

96. Mary Ann Evans (George Eliot) is famous for the extent of her historical research, but huge groups of novels, many now forgotten, also counted on the appeal that their presentation of genuinely, quasi-, or pseudoaccurate information would hold for readers. The nautical novels that were popular in the 1830s, e.g., are often said to have flourished because readers wanted information about life at sea in the wake of Napoleon's defeat. See Gettmann, *Victorian Publisher*, 167–68. But see also the discussion of mid-nineteenth-century novels in chapter 6 below.

97. One example of the idealist position can be found in Bulwer Lytton, "On Certain Principles of Art." George Eliot is generally taken as an advocate of the realist position. See her review of Rhiel's *Natural History of German Life*. For discussions of this debate, see Stang, *Theory of the Novel*, esp. chap. 1; Pyckett, "The Real *versus* the Ideal"; and Lively, "Truth in Writing."

98. Masson's "British Novelists since Scott" and McCarthy's "Novels with a Purpose" quoted in Pyckett, "The Real *versus* the Ideal," 65, 66.

99. [Oliphant], "Novels" (1867), 261.

100. Reade, *Readiana*, in *Works*, 9:356–57.

101. For accounts of the notebook and index system that Reade developed in order to construct these matter-of-fact romances and his relation to realism in general, see Haines, "Reade, Mill, and Zola"; Sutcliffe, "Fact, Realism, and Morality"; and Burns, "Pre-Raphaelitism." Reade published numerous accounts of this method. See Reade and Reade, *Memoir*, 1:324–30; and Reade, *A Terrible Temptation*, in *Works*, vol. 8, chap. 22. Here is one of Reade's challenges to his critics: "I offered, in print, to show these [sources], at my own house, to any anonymous writer who might care to profit

by my labor—the labor of Hercules" ("A Terrible Temptation," *Readiana*, in *Works*, 9:360). In 1857, James Fitzjames Stephen, publishing anonymously in the *Saturday Review*, accused Reade of exaggerating the facts he took from a Royal Commission report on the Birmingham Jail (*"Edinburgh Review* and Modern Novelists"). To document the veracity of his fictional episodes, Reade also routinely reprinted letters from his critics and the corroborating evidence supplied by his readers in subsequent editions of his novels. See, e.g., the exchange printed as the preface to the new edition of *Hard Cash*, in *Works*, 2:4–12.

102. [Oliphant], "Novels" (1867), 280.

103. [Oliphant], "Charles Reade's Novels," 510.

104. Ibid., 513. Oliphant associates "realism" with Thackeray, whose impatience with "the vague ideal of virtue which had long held a conventional sway" led him to create novels without a "respectable" hero (ibid.).

105. [Warren], "Advice," 595.

106. [Oliphant], "New Books," 185. In this review, Oliphant also finally works out the link between lower-class readers' desire for information and their appetite for salacious stories. "It is the natural first impulse of the mind towards fact and history" that attracts readers to cheap newspapers (166). The press then responds to this appetite, but, instead of supplying readers with ennobling materials, it gives them "a literature which exaggerates all their worst tendencies and accustoms their minds to nothing but evil" (167).

107. Howells quoted in Smith, *Charles Reade*, 157, 152.

108. Orwell quoted in ibid., 105.

109. This is my emphasis in "Forgotten Writers."

110. James, "Art of Fiction" (hereafter "AF"), 197. Page numbers for subsequent citations are given in the text.

111. Stevenson, "Humble Remonstrance" (hereafter "HR"), 214. Page numbers for subsequent citations are given in the text.

112. Graham points out that James was not the first nineteenth-century writer to apply this metaphor to the novel. See *English Criticism*, 115.

113. Hardy, "Profitable Reading of Fiction" (hereafter "PR"), 63, 69. Page numbers for subsequent citations are given in the text.

114. See, e.g., Fish, *Is There a Text in This Class?* and Hartman, *Criticism in the Wilderness*.

115. See Poovey, "Creative Criticism."

116. Besant, "Literature as a Career," 325, 326–27.

117. Besant, "Society of Authors and Other Societies," 227–28.

118. Besant, "Literature as a Career," 309–10.

INTERCHAPTER TWO

1. Here is Hunter's brief description of the genesis and potential of historical description: "Historical philology is, in principle at least, capable of dissolving the Romantic aesthetic and the (cultural) human sciences. It can do so by deploying a description of texts—of their compositional technologies and historical deployments—which is not contingent on the ethical or theoretical transformation of the bearer of the description. In other words, it deploys a description which does not generate a 'pedagogical imperative,' and is not therefore part of the system of sensibility training or self-problematisation" (*Culture and Government*, 289). While I am not sure my practice is precisely what Hunter has in mind, his provocative comments have inspired the commentary I provide in this interchapter.

•

2. In Hunter's account, today's Literary education is characterized by "the use of texts as morally charged environments in which students must 'discover for themselves' the growth of their own personalities" under the supervision of a teacher-critic (ibid., 64). In pt. 1 of *Culture and Government*, Hunter describes the process by which the "morally managed space of the school" was gradually contracted "into the landscape of the literary text," which is presented as having "depths always withdrawing into an experience never quite grasped" (65, 67). In pt. 2, he provides an account of the way criticism has become "a special kind of pedagogy or moral training" (153) by taking over and extending the function of classroom teaching. Missing from this compelling account is full recognition of one side effect of the professionalization of teaching/criticism: the gulf that has opened between the content and methods of most forms of undergraduate Literary instruction, which generally follows the model Hunter describes, and those of graduate instruction, which is typically conducted according to the research model pioneered in the natural sciences.

3. See Guillory, *Literary Study*.

4. I realize, of course, that separating interpretation and description in this way risks creating a false dichotomy because any interpretation entails description and all description is inevitably interpretive. Nevertheless, I want to maintain these terms as facets of an antinomy so that I can pursue the limits of a particular mode of textual interpretation.

5. On twentieth-century responses to Martineau, see Logan, introduction to *Illustrations*, 40–46.

6. *Discourse* is also, and most often, associated with the work of Michel Foucault, but contemporary Literary critics profess a more or less faithful adherence to Foucault's definition. For Klaver's account of her relation to Foucault's work, see *A/Moral Economics* (hereafter *A/M*), xvii–xx. Gallagher does not discuss Foucault explicitly in *Industrial Reformation of English Fiction* (hereafter *IREF*), but her description of the "Condition of England Debate" becoming "a discourse unto itself" (xi) calls Foucault's work to mind. (Page numbers for subsequent citations of both Klaver and Gallagher are given in the text.) For Gallagher's extended discussion of Foucault's influence on New Historicist practice, see Gallagher and Greenblatt, *Practicing New Historicism*, 66–74. Guillory's relationship to Foucault is considerably more distant; his explicit affinity is with the work of Pierre Bourdieu.

7. Gallagher describes her practice not as escaping the evaluation associated with the aesthetic but as enlarging this category so that it will accommodate more texts. Treating "whole cultures as texts," she explains, enables her to value texts that are often excluded from the canon: "Works that have been hitherto denigrated or ignored can be treated as major achievements, claiming space in an already crowded curriculum or diminishing the value of established work in a kind of literary stock market" (Gallagher and Greenblatt, *Practicing New Historicism*, 10). What this description fails to acknowledge is the *discriminatory function* that the category of aesthetic value has historically performed.

8. In the introduction she coauthored with Greenblatt, Gallagher comes closer to making this assumption about the universality of the reading experience explicit. After describing the complex experience "we" feel when reading, the authors suggest that past readers must have had a similar response: "In a meaningful encounter with a text that reaches us powerfully, we feel at once pulled out of our own world and plunged back with redoubled force into it. It seems arrogant to claim such an expe-

rience for ourselves as readers and not to grant something similar to the readers and the authors of the past" (Gallagher and Greenblatt, *Practicing New Historicism*, 17).

9. Poovey, *Uneven Developments*, 89–90.

10. Moretti, introduction to *Graphs, Maps, Trees*. In "Textual Culture" and *Blaming the System*, Siskin expresses the preference for "zooming out" to larger patterns that can be found across a number of texts, instead of "zooming in" to particular textual features.

11. Hunter, *Culture and Government*, 289, 291.

12. Guillory, *Cultural Capital*, 294.

13. Guillory's account of the "aesthetic function" is helpful, even though he anchors his analysis in the Foucauldian term *discourse*: "The relevant consideration is the specific social functions of objects produced or received in a given historical context *as* works of art, since it is only as works so classified that they can have certain *other* social functions.... The 'aesthetic function' does not name one possible use of an object among many, contingent on the 'personal economy' of an individual subject, but the pre-determination of social function by a classificatory discourse" (ibid., 295).

14. Martineau, *Autobiography*, 1:169. Page numbers for subsequent citations are given in the text. Martineau explained that she chose the method of fictional illustration "not only because it is new, not only because it is entertaining, but because we think it the most faithful and the most complete.... The reason why we chose the form of narrative is, that we really think it the best in which Political Economy can be taught" (preface to *Illustrations* [new ed., 1836], 1:xiii).

15. Martineau, *Berkeley the Banker*, pt. 2, p. 144, and pt. 1, pp. 15–16. The 1833 reprint that I cite reproduces the first edition.

16. Conder, "Review," 413.

17. "Miss Martineau's *Illustrations*," 416.

18. Martineau quoted in Logan, introduction to *Illustrations*, 32–33 n. 2.

19. Bulwer Lytton, "On Moral Fiction," 427, 429.

20. Miller, *Harriet Martineau*, cited in Logan, introduction to *Illustrations*, 37.

21. Mitford quoted in Courtney, *Adventurous Thirties*, as cited in ibid.

22. Logan, introduction to *Illustrations*, 29, 39–40.

23. Martineau gives her account in the *Autobiography*, 1:177–78. Additional sales figures appear in Klaver, *A/Moral Economics*, 58; and Logan, introduction to *Illustrations*, 34. Klaver usefully compares these figures to the 3,000 copies that John Stuart Mill's *Principles of Political Economy* sold during a four-year period, and we can also compare them to the pressrun of 500–750 copies for the first edition of Jane Austen's *Pride and Prejudice*. For a discussion of the role played by Martineau's text in the popularization of political economy, see Freedgood, *Victorian Writing about Risk*, chap. 1. Other useful discussions of Martineau include David, *Intellectual Women*; Sanders, *Reason over Passion*; and Webb, *Harriet Martineau*.

24. Logan, introduction to *Illustrations*, 35. Logan also notes that the *Illustrations* was popular in America and that it was translated into Dutch, German, Spanish, French, and Russian: "It was purchased by the courts of Russia and Austria, and France adopted the series for use in public schools" (ibid.).

CHAPTER SIX

1. An anonymous article published in the *Monthly Magazine* in 1797 presented novel writing as so easy and so common a pastime that the result was a kind of

"terrorism"—a deluge of formulaic novels that threatened to overwhelm the English reader. See "Terrorist System."

2. I reached these figures by counting the titles listed for these years in Garside et al., eds., *English Novel*, vol. 2. Anthony Jarrells and Marilyn Butler have both pointed out that, during the 1790s, Gothic novels were often thought to be political as well, either because of their excessive violence or because they were thought to articulate moral relativism. See Jarrells, *Britain's Bloodless Revolutions*, 60; and Butler, *Jane Austen*, 31.

3. Barrell, *Imagining the King's Death*, 588.

4. [Thomas Wallace], review of Charles Lamb, *A Tale of Rosamund Gray and Old Blind Margaret*, from the *Monthly Review*, quoted in Garside et al., eds., *English Novel*, 2:749; [Samuel Rose], review of Charlotte Smith, *The Young Philosopher*, from the *Monthly Review*, quoted in ibid., 761.

5. See Siskin, *Historicity*, chap. 7, and *Work of Writing*, chaps. 8 and 9; and Jarrells, *Britain's Bloodless Revolutions*, 190–95.

6. Many Literary critics have offered suggestive and interesting accounts of the historical events that inspired Austen's novels, of course. Among these, I particularly recommend Miles, "'A Fall in Bread'"; Butler, *Jane Austen*; and Roberts, *Jane Austen*. Galperin has offered his account of why identifying such sources is so difficult. See *Historical Austen*, esp. the introduction.

7. Austen, *Pride and Prejudice* (hereafter *PP*), ed. Jones, 74 (vol. 1, chap. 16). All references are to this edition; page numbers (as well as volume and chapter numbers) for subsequent citations are given in the text.

8. Scott's review of *Emma*, published in the *Quarterly Review* in 1815, is generally taken as a sign (along with the dedication to the prince regent) of Austen's reputation as a serious (Literary) writer. Scott praised Austen for using "common incidents" and "such characters as occupy the ordinary walks of life" to arouse the same interest that other novelists achieved only with "uncommon events" and elevated characters. See Scott, *Scott on Novelists*, 231.

9. This is what Irvine does in his edition (see Irvine, "Appendix F," 449).

10. Austen, *Letters*, 84, 85.

11. Nokes, *Jane Austen*, 134.

12. Southam says that the revisions were undertaken in 1809–10, 1811, and 1812 (*Austen's Literary Manuscripts*, 60–61). Fergus argues, on the basis of one of Jane's letters to Cassandra, that the revisions were all done in 1811–12 (*Jane Austen*, 82).

13. Levine, "Form of the Novel." Literary scholars who have discussed the moralizing tendency of Victorian novelists in relation to money include Russell, *Novelist and Mammon*; and Klaver, *A/Moral Economics*.

14. By early February, forty thousand copies had been sold, and, even though the last number sold only thirty-one thousand, *Little Dorrit* brought Dickens more readers than he had ever had (Schlicke, "*Little Dorrit*," 349).

15. Schlicke summarizes the history of the novel's composition (ibid., 335–36), but the most sustained discussion of this topic is Butt and Tillotson, *Dickens at Work*, 222–33.

16. Schlicke, "*Little Dorrit*," 335.

17. Dickens, *Little Dorrit* (hereafter *LD*), 35 ("Preface to the 1857 Edition"). Page numbers for subsequent citations are given in the text.

18. Russell offers the following observation about Dickens's treatment of mercantile firms, an observation that also applies to his treatment of financial topics more generally: "Dickens creates four mercantile firms in his major works. They are all

initially depicted with some fidelity to reality, and then shaped into an imaginative mould to conform with Dickens's preoccupation with theme or character" ("Money and Finance," 381). The best scholarly treatment of Dickens's moralizing is Klaver, *A/Moral Economics*, chap. 4.

19. Both reviews are reprinted in Carroll, ed., *George Eliot*, 171–72, 179.

20. Eliot quoted in Carroll, introduction to *Silas Marner*, viii.

21. Eliot, *Silas Marner* (hereafter *SM*), 17, 19. Page numbers for subsequent citations are given in the text.

22. ApRoberts notes that *The Last Chronicle of Barset* established "something new" in English literature, "the *roman fleuve*, made famous in France by Balzac's *La Comedie humaine*": "Thackeray had made some connections between novels, but it is Trollope who really establishes the genre, to be later practiced by such as Galsworthy and Anthony Powell. Trollope does not seem to have been influenced by Balzac and so we might be the more inclined to give him credit for his profound originality" (*"The Last Chronicle of Barset,"* 310).

23. James's early reviews of Trollope's novels all disparaged the works for their lack of artistry. In his 1866 review of *The Belton Estate*, e.g., James complained: "Trollope is a good observer; but he is literally nothing else." By 1883, James had come to appreciate Trollope's art more, although it seems unlikely that, even then, he would have considered *The Last Chronicle of Barset* an example of the organic unity he celebrated. See Terry, "James, Henry."

24. Miller, e.g., considers Trollope's novels so artless that they seem simply business "as usual," and Butte considers Trollope's Palliser novels a reliable window onto Victorian politics. See Miller, *The Novel and the Police*, 107–45; and Butte, "Trollope's Duke of Omnium." A few critics have examined Trollope's novels as self-conscious works of art. See, in particular, Kendrick, *Novel Machine*. Particularly interesting is chap. 6, "The Rhetoric of Reality."

25. In his 1882 revised edition of Gilbart's *History, Principles, and Practice of Banking* (1859), A. S. Michie detailed the impact of this crash. In London alone, six prominent banks failed: the English Joint-Stock Bank, the Imperial Mercantile Credit Company, the European Bank, the Bank of London, the Consolidated Bank, and the Agra and Masterman's Bank (the last two eventually resumed business). Michie also quotes the *Bankers' Magazine* on the impact of the crash: "A greater crash has never taken place in any one week in any country in the world" (Gilbart, *HPP*, 2:344 [see also 343–56]).

26. Bagehot, "What," 88–89. Modern economists call the money that is preferred in periods of panic *quality money*.

27. The London Clearing House had been formed as a secret organization in 1775. It became a public institution that sought to increase its influence in the nineteenth century, admitting the London joint-stock bankers to the association in 1854, country bankers in 1858, and the Bank of England in 1864. For other nineteenth-century accounts of the Clearing House, see Gilbart, *Practical Treatise*, 251–59, and *HPP*, 2:310–33; and Jevons, *Money*, chap. 20. Bank checks, which were also called *drafts* (and sometimes spelled *cheques*), were orders drawn on a banker against deposited sums and payable on demand. They originated in the late seventeenth century as a credit instrument resembling the receipt goldsmiths offered for deposited securities. The form of bank checks varied from bank to bank but remained relatively constant until the middle decades of the nineteenth century. As individuals began to take advantage of banks' willingness to accept and hold deposits, and as traffic on the stock

exchanges increased in volume, the use of checks became more common, and banks began to print uniform books of blank checks for their depositors. To prevent fraud, the checks in each book were sometimes numbered and registered with the issuing bank. See Nevin and Davis, *London Clearing Banks*, 19–21. In 1848, John Stuart Mill commented that the use of checks was "spreading to a continually larger portion of the public" (*Principles of Political Economy*, 520). Writing in 1849, Gilbart commented that the use of checks began to become more widespread when operations on the London Stock Exchange increased in volume (*Practical Treatise*, 255).

28. In insisting on this distinction, Bagehot was departing from the argument of at least one other nineteenth-century political economist. To John Stuart Mill, who focused on how the quantity of paper monetary instruments affected the *price* of money, checks seemed exactly like banknotes. See *Principles of Political Economy*, 357, 359.

29. The convention of reasonable time was originally adopted in order to protect both the drawer and the recipient of a check from the possibility that the issuing bank would fail in the time between a check's draft and its being returned for cash or deposit. On the legal complexities of "reasonable time," see Gilbart, *HPP*, 1:247.

30. This last point led Jevons to distinguish between checks and banknotes, as Bagehot also did: "The salutary effect of this law [the law of reasonable time] and of other conditions is, that cheques do not circulate in this kingdom in place of money, but are usually presented within one or two days of receipt. Hence they come to serve as mere instruments of transfer of money, and involve no considerable length of credit. Nothing can be gained by holding an ordinary cheque, for there is no interest, and something may be lost" (Jevons, *Money*, 242). Bagehot's reference to *bank notes* reminds us that, in 1866, several country banks still issued their own paper money. For the most part, however, his use of the term *bank note* in this essay refers to Bank of England notes, which had become the country's normal currency (if not its legal tender) by that time. That Bagehot did not capitalize the *bank* in *bank notes* indicates the invisibility that Bank notes had attained by 1866: by that time, it was no longer necessary to distinguish typographically between Bank of England notes and a country bank's notes.

31. Hamer, "Working Diary," 1606.

32. At the time of Overend and Gurney's collapse, Trollope was living just twelve miles from London; he belonged to numerous London clubs and made frequent visits to the metropolis. He also owned and took personal interest in company shares of various kinds (Trollope, *Autobiography*, 156). For all these reasons, it is unimaginable that he would not have registered the company's collapse.

33. Trollope, *The Last Chronicle of Barset* (hereafter *LC*), 34. Page numbers for subsequent citations are given in the text.

34. The distinction I am making between *story* and *narrative* is the same distinction that narratologists make between *fabula* and *story*. Despite the risk of confusion, and because narratologists do not all agree on this terminology, I prefer the more commonsense terms.

35. Readers familiar with the novel will recognize how inadequate my summary is to the intricacies of this plot. In particular, the narrator tells us that Lily Dale ultimately refuses Johnny not simply because of Johnny's inconstancy but also because Lily, having once loved Augustus Crosbie (who abandoned her), cannot imagine herself belonging to another man.

36. See Mauss, *The Gift*.

37. Smiles, *Self-Help*, 199.

38. Ibid., 201. Elsewhere in *Self-Help*, Smiles expressed even more doubts about reading. "How much of our reading is but the indulgence of a sort of intellectual dram-drinking," he exclaimed (ibid.). "The habitual novel-reader indulges in fictitious feelings so much, that there is a great risk of sound and healthy feeling becoming perverted or benumbed" (205). Smiles considerably softened his criticism of reading in later books. See, e.g., *Character*, chap. 10.
39. Thanks to Richard Miller for this observation.
40. Arata, "On Not Paying Attention," 200.
41. Freedgood also notices how modern reading practices curtail the referential ability of language. See *Secret Life of Things*, chap. 4.
42. Trollope, "*Sesame and Lilies*," 635.
43. Ibid., 634–35.
44. In his *Autobiography*, Trollope referred to the *Contemporary* review in which a critic said that he did not understand Greek as "the most ill-natured review that was ever written upon any work of mine": "That charge has been made not unfrequently by those who have felt themselves strong in that pride-producing language. It is much to read Greek with ease, but it is not disgraceful to be unable to do so" (201).
45. Ibid., 229. Such assertions appear too frequently to cite them all, but see in particular chaps. 8 and 12 of the *Autobiography*.
46. Ibid., 139, 184.
47. Trollope discusses this topic in ibid., 226–29. This distinction had been drawn by Bulwer Lytton in "Art and Fiction" (1838). Debates about the relative merits of the two "kinds" of fiction appeared again in the 1850s but erupted in earnest in the 1860s in relation to sensation novels. Among the critics who drew this distinction in the 1860s, one of the most prominent was E. S. Dallas, in *The Gay Science* (1866). For a discussion of this distinction, see Eigner and Worth, introduction to *Victorian Criticism*, 14–17.
48. Trollope, *Autobiography*, 227.
49. Ibid., 251, 252.
50. Ibid., 257.
51. Ibid., 216.
52. Trollope explicitly stated that young people, in particular, read novels in order to learn what to expect in life and how to behave: "A vast proportion of the teaching of the day,—greater probably than many of us have as yet acknowledged to ourselves,—comes from these books, which are in the hands of all readers. It is from them that girls learn what is expected from them, and what they are to expect when lovers come; and also from them that young men unconsciously learn what are, or should be, or may be, the charms of love" (ibid., 220).
53. It would be impossible to catalog all the Literary allusions contained in *The Last Chronicle of Barset*, but, with the help of my graduate students, I can say with some confidence that allusions to Shakespeare's tragedies, the Old Testament, and Greek tragedies predominate. The novel also contains allusions to poems by Byron, eighteenth-century novels (including *Sir Charles Grandison*), and the other novels in the Barsetshire series.
54. See chapter 5 above; and Poovey, "Forgotten Writers."

CODA

1. Recently, some economists have published books and articles designed to engage readers not trained in graduate economics. Often these books apply relatively technical

economic principles to everyday life situations. See, e.g., Shiller, *Irrational Exuberance*; and Levitt, *Freakonomics*. While these are important efforts to supplement the technical language and specialized genres that most academic economists use, such books rarely question the methodological and disciplinary biases of their discipline. On the other side of the disciplinary divide, few Literary scholars have attempted to reach out to general readers, and those who have—Harold Bloom comes to mind—are often ridiculed by their academic peers precisely because they do not use the rarefied vocabularies and theoretical paradigms that govern most academic Literary scholarship.

2.   Guillory, "Memo and Modernity," 111; Bowker, *Memory Practices*.

BIBLIOGRAPHY

Abrams, M. H. *The Mirror and the Lamp: Romantic Theory and the Critical Tradition*. New York: Oxford University Press, 1953.

Agnew, Jean-Christophe. *Worlds Apart: The Market and the Theater in Anglo-American Thought, 1550–1750*. Cambridge: Cambridge University Press, 1986.

Alborn, Timothy L. *Conceiving Companies: Joint-Stock Politics in Victorian England*. London: Routledge, 1998.

Alkon, Paul. *Defoe and Fictional Time*. Athens: University of Georgia Press, 1979.

Altick, Richard D. *The English Common Reader: A Social History of the Mass Reading Public, 1800–1900*. Chicago: University of Chicago Press, 1957.

[Amhurst, Nicholas (as "Usbeck")]. "Nicholas Amhurst: From *The Craftesman* No. 47 [27 May 1727]." In Sherman, ed., *The Restoration and the Eighteenth Century*, 2422.

Appleby, Joyce C. *Economic Thought and Ideology in Seventeenth-Century England*. Princeton, NJ: Princeton University Press, 1978.

———. "Locke, Liberalism, and the Natural Law of Money." *Past and Present* 71 (1976): 43–69.

ApRoberts, Ruth. "*The Last Chronicle of Barset*." In Terry, ed., *Oxford Reader's Companion to Trollope*, 306–11.

Arata, Stephen. "On Not Paying Attention." *Victorian Studies* 46 (Winter 2004): 193–205.

Armstrong, Nancy. *Desire and Domestic Fiction: A Political History of the Novel*. Oxford: Oxford University Press, 1987.

Arnold, Matthew. "The Function of Criticism at the Present Time." In *Lectures and Essays in Criticism*, vol. 3 of *The Complete Prose Works of Matthew Arnold*, ed. R. H. Super, 234–67. Ann Arbor: University of Michigan Press, 1962.

Austen, Jane. *Jane Austen's Letters: New Edition*. Edited by Deirdre Le Fay. New York: Oxford University Press, 1997.

———. *Pride and Prejudice*. Edited by Robert P. Irvine. Peterborough, ON: Broadview, 2002.

———. *Pride and Prejudice*. Edited by Vivien Jones. London: Penguin, 2003.

Backscheider, Paula R. "Defoe's Lady Credit." *Huntington Library Quarterly* 44, no. 2 (Spring 1981): 89–100.

Bagehot, Walter. *The Collected Works of Walter Bagehot*. Edited by Norman St. John-Stevas. 15 vols. London: The Economist, 1978.

———. "The Panic." *Economist* 24 (19 May 1866). Reprinted in Bagehot, *Collected Works*, ed. Stevas, 10:93–100.

———. "What a Panic Is and How It Might be Mitigated." *Economist* 24 (12 May 1866). Reprinted in Bagehot, *Collected Works*, ed. Stevas, 10:88–92.

Bailey, Samuel. *A Critical Dissertation on the Nature, Measure, and Causes of Value*. 1825. Reprint, New York: Augustus M. Kelley, 1967.

"Bank." In *Encyclopaedia Britannica* (facsimile ed.), 1:518–19.

Barchus, Janine. *Graphic Design, Print Culture, and the Eighteenth-Century Novel*. Cambridge: Cambridge University Press, 2003.

Baring, Francis. "Observations on the Publication of Walter Boyd, M.P." In Capie, ed., *History of Banking*, 8:101–29.

Barker, Jane. "A Patchwork Screen for the Ladies." In *Women Critics, 1660–1820: An Anthology*, ed. Folger Collective on Early Women Critics, 30–33. Bloomington: Indiana University Press, 1995.

Barrell, John. *Imagining the King's Death: Figurative Fantasies of Regicide*. Oxford: Oxford University Press, 2000.

Barrington, E. I., ed. *The Works and Life of Walter Bagehot*. 20 vols. London: Longmans, Green, 1915.

Baucom, Ian. *Specters of the Atlantic: Finance Capital, Slavery, and the Philosophy of History*. Durham, NC: Duke University Press, 2005.

Bellamy, Liz. *Commerce, Morality, and the Eighteenth-Century Novel*. Cambridge: Cambridge University Press, 1998.

Bennett, Andrew. *Romantic Poets and the Culture of Posterity*. Cambridge: Cambridge University Press, 1999.

Besant, Walter. *The Art of Fiction*. London: Chatto, 1902.

———. *Autobiography of Sir Walter Besant*. New York: Dodd, Mead, 1942. Reprint, St. Clair, MI: Scholarly Press, 1971.

———. *Essays and Historiettes*. 1903. Reprint, Port Washington, NY: Kinnikat, 1970.

———. "The First Society of British Authors." In *Essays and Historiettes*, 271–307.

———. "Literature as a Career." In *Essays and Historiettes*, 308–31.

———. "The Society of Authors and Other Societies." In *Autobiography*, 215–42.

———. "The Start in Fiction: Critics and Criticasters." In *Autobiography*, 180–97.

[Blanchard, Sidney Laman]. "A Biography of a Bad Shilling." *Household Words* 2, no. 44 (25 January 1851): 420–26.

Blaug, Marc. *Ricardian Economics*. New Haven, CT: Yale University Press, 1958.

Blewett, David. *Defoe's Art of Fiction*. Toronto: University of Toronto Press, 1979.

Bonar, J. "Labour Exchange." In Palgrave, ed., *Dictionary of Political Economy*, 2:520–23.

Bonham-Carter, Victor. *Authors by Profession*. 2 vols. Los Angeles: William Kauffman, 1978.

Booker, John. *Travelers' Money*. Dover, NH: Alan Sutton, 1994.

Bordo, Michael D., and Eugene N. White. "A Tale of Two Currencies: British and French Finance during the Napoleonic Wars." *Journal of Economic History* 51, no. 2 (June 1991): 303–16.

Bourdieu, Pierre. *Distinction: A Social Critique of the Judgment of Taste*. Translated by Richard Nice. Cambridge, MA: Harvard University Press, 1984.

———. *The Rules of Art: Genesis and Structure of the Literary Field*. Translated by Susan Emanuel. Stanford, CA: Stanford University Press, 1995.

Bowen, H. V. *The Business of Empire: The East India Company and Imperial Britain, 1756–1833*. Cambridge: Cambridge University Press, 2006.

Bowker, Geoff. *Memory Practices in the Sciences.* Cambridge, MA: MIT Press, 2006.

Boyd, Walter. "A Letter to the Right Honourable William Pitt." In Capie, ed., *History of Banking*, 8:9–100.

Brake, Laurel. *Subjugated Knowledges: Journalism, Gender, and Literature in the Nineteenth Century.* New York: New York University Press, 1994.

Brantlinger, Patrick. *Fictions of State: Culture and Credit in Britain, 1684–1994.* Ithaca, NY: Cornell University Press, 1996.

Bray, John. *Labour's Wrongs and Labour's Remedy; or, The Age of Might and the Age of Right.* Leeds: David Green, 1839. Facsimile ed., London: London School of Economics, 1931.

Bridges, Thomas. *Adventures of a Bank-Note.* 4 vols. 1770–71. Reprint, 4 vols. in 2, New York: Garland, 1975.

Bulwer Lytton, Edward. "On Art in Fiction." In Eigner and Worth, eds., *Victorian Criticism of the Novel*, 22–38.

———. "On Certain Principles of Art in Works of Imagination." *Blackwood's Edinburgh Magazine* 93 (May 1863): 545–60.

———. "On Moral Fictions: Miss Martineau's *Illustrations of Political Economy.*" *New Monthly Magazine and Literary Journal* 37 (1833): 146–51. Reprinted in Martineau, *Illustrations*, ed. Logan, 427–29.

Burns, Wayne. "Pre-Raphaelitism in Charles Reade's Early Fiction." *PMLA* 40 (1945): 1149–64.

Butler, Marilyn. *Jane Austen and the War of Ideas.* Oxford: Oxford University Press, 1975.

Butt, John, and Kathleen Tillotson. *Dickens at Work.* London: Methuen, 1957.

Butte, George. "Trollope's Duke of Omnium and 'the Pain of History': A Study of the Novelist's Politics." *Victorian Studies* 24, no. 2 (1981): 209–27.

Butterworth, C. H. "Overfeeding Reading." *Victoria Magazine* 1, no. 2 (1869): 500.

Capie, Forrest H., ed. *History of Banking.* 10 vols. London: William Pickering, 1993.

Carlyle, Thomas. *The Works of Thomas Carlyle.* Edited by H. D. Traill. 30 vols. New York: Scribner's, 1903.

Carroll, David, ed. *George Eliot: The Critical Heritage.* New York: Barnes & Noble, 1971.

———. Introduction to *Silas Marner*, ed. David Carroll, vii–xxv. London: Penguin, 1996.

Castle, Terry. "'Amy, Who Knew My Disease': A Psychosexual Pattern in Defoe's *Roxana.*" *ELH* 46, no. 1 (Spring 1979): 81–96.

"The Catalogue's Account of Itself." *Household Words* 3, no. 74 (23 August 1851): 519–23.

Chalmers, Thomas. *The Works of Thomas Chalmers.* 14 vols. Glasgow: William Collins, 1836–42.

Chandler, James, ed. *The Cambridge History of English Literature, 1780–1830.* Cambridge: Cambridge University Press, forthcoming.

Checkland, S. G. "The Advent of Academic Economics in England." *Manchester School of Economic and Social Theory before 1870* 19 (1951): 43–70.

———. "The Propagation of Ricardian Economics in England." *Economica*, n.s., 16 (February 1949): 40–52.

———. *The Rise of Industrial Society in England, 1815–1885.* London: Longman, 1964.

Clery, E. J. *The Feminization Debate in Eighteenth-Century England: Literature, Commerce, and Luxury.* Houndsmills: Palgrave Macmillan, 2004.

Cloud, Random. "'The Very Names of the Persons': Editing and the Invention of Dramatick Character." In *Staging the Renaissance: Essays on Elizabethan and Jacobean Drama*, ed. David Scott Kastan and Peter Stallybrass, 88–96. New York: Routledge, 1991.

Cobbett, William. *Paper against Gold; or, The History and Mystery of the Bank of England, of the Debt, of the Stocks, of the Sinking Fund, and of the Other Tricks and Contrivances, Carried on by the Means of Paper Money.* London: W. M. Cobbett, 1828.

———. *Rural Rides.* London: Everyman's Library, 1912. Reprint, London: Dent, 1973.

Cohen, Ralph. "History and Genre." *New Literary History* 17, no. 2 (1986): 201–18.

Coleman, D. C. *The British Paper Industry, 1495–1860: A Study in Industrial Growth.* Oxford: Clarendon, 1958.

Coleridge, Samuel Taylor. *Biographia Literaria.* Edited by George Watson. London: J. M. Dent, 1975.

Colley, Linda. *Britons: Forging the Nation, 1707–1837.* New Haven, CT: Yale University Press, 1992.

Collins, Charles Allston. "Our Audience." *Macmillan's Magazine* 8 (June 1863): 161.

[Collins, Wilkie]. "The Unknown Public." *Household Words* 18, no. 439 (21 August 1858): 217–22.

Conder, Josiah. "Review of *Illustrations of Political Economy* by Harriet Martineau." *Eclectic Review* 8 (1832): 44–72. Reprinted in Martineau, *Illustrations*, ed. Logan, 413–14.

Copeland, Edward. *Women Writing about Money.* Cambridge: Cambridge University Press, 2004.

Corvey Collection. http://www.unl.edu/sbehrend/html/sbsite/projects/Corvey/Corvey%20Index.htm.

Courtney, Janet. *The Adventurous Thirties: A Chapter in the Women's Movement.* London: Oxford University Press, 1933.

Craig, Sir John. *The Mint: A History of the London Mint from A.D. 287 to 1948.* Cambridge: Cambridge University Press, 1953.

Cross, Nigel. *The Common Writer: Life in Nineteenth-Century Grub Street.* Cambridge: Cambridge University Press, 1985.

Cruise, James. *Governing Consumption: Needs, Wants, Suspended Characters, and the "Origins" of Eighteenth-Century Novels.* Lewisburg, PA: Bucknell University Press, 1999.

Dahl, Christopher C. "Fitzjames Stephen, Charles Dickens, and Double Reviewing." *Victorian Periodicals Review* 14, no. 2 (Summer 1981): 51–58.

Dallas, E. S. *The Gay Science.* 2 vols. 1866. Reprint, New York: Garland, 1986.

David, Deirdre. *Intellectual Women and Victorian Patriarchy: Harriet Martineau, Elizabeth Barrett Browning, George Eliot.* Ithaca, NY: Cornell University Press, 1987.

Davis, Lennard J. *Factual Fictions: The Origins of the English Novel.* New York: Columbia University Press, 1983.

Deane, Phyllis. "McCulloch, John Ramsay." In *Oxford Dictionary of National Biography*, ed. H. C. G. Matthew and Brian Harrison, 35:184–86. Oxford: Oxford University Press, 2004.

Defoe, Daniel. *The Complete English Tradesman.* 1726. Edinburgh: William & Robert Chambers, 1839. Reprint, Gloucester: Alan Sutton, 1987.

———. *Essay on Public Credit.* 1710. Reprint, London: Charles Reynell, 1742.

———. *Essays upon Several Projects; or, Effectual Ways for Advancing the Interests of the Nation.* London: Booksellers of London and Westminster, 1702.

———. *The Review.* Facsimile Text Society. 23 vols. New York: Columbia University Press, 1928.

———. *Roxana.* Edited by David Blewett. London: Penguin, 1982.

———. *Roxana.* Edited by John Mullan. New York: Oxford University Press, 1998.

———. "A True Relation of the Apparition of One Mrs. Veal . . . to One Mrs. Bargrave." In Defoe, *Works*, 15:251–65.

———. "The Villainy of Stock-Jobbers Detected and the Causes of the Late Run upon the Bank and Bankers Discovered and Considered." In Capie, ed., *History of Banking*, 1:69–121.

———. *The Works of Daniel Defoe.* 16 vols. New York: Jenson Society, 1905.

[De Quincey, Thomas]. "Dialogues of Three Templars on Political Economy, Chiefly in Relation to the Principles of Mr. Ricardo." *London Magazine* 9 (April 1824): 341–55.

———. "The Poetry of Pope." *North British Review* (1848). Reprinted in Keen, ed., *Revolutions in Romantic Literature*, 13–16.

Dickens, Charles. *Little Dorrit.* Edited by John Holloway. London: Penguin, 1967.

Dickson, P. G. M. *The Financial Revolution in England: A Study in the Development of Public Credit, 1688–1756.* London: Macmillan, 1967.

Douglas, Aileen. "Britannia's Rule and the It-Narrator." *Eighteenth-Century Fiction* 6 (1993): 70–89.

Dowden, Edward. "The Interpretation of Literature." *Contemporary Review* 49 (May 1886): 701–19.

Duggleby, Vincent. *English Paper Money: Treasury and Bank of England Notes, 1694–2002.* 6th ed., Sutton, Surry: Pam West, 2002.

Dunbar, Charles F. *Chapters on the Theory and History of Banking.* 1891. 2nd ed., New York: Putnam's, 1901.

Edwards, Peter. "*An Autobiography.*" In Terry, ed., *Oxford Reader's Companion to Trollope*, 23–27.

Edwards, Ruth Dudley. *The Pursuit of Reason: The Economist, 1843–93.* Boston: Harvard Business School Press, 1993.

Eigner, Edwin M., and George J. Worth. Introduction to Eigner and Worth, eds., *Victorian Criticism of the Novel*, 1–21.

Elibank, Lord. "Essay on Paper Money and Banking." 1755. In Capie, ed., *History of Banking*, 1:212–20.

Eliot, George. "Review of W. H. Rhiel, *Natural History of German Life.*" *Westminster Review* 66 (July 1856): 51–79.

———. *Silas Marner.* Edited by David Carroll. London: Penguin, 1996.

Eliot, Simon. "The Business of Victorian Publishing." In *The Cambridge Companion to the Victorian Novel*, ed. Deirdre David, 37–60. Cambridge: Cambridge University Press, 2001.

Encyclopaedia Britannica; or, A Dictionary of Arts and Sciences. 3 vols. 1771. Facsimile ed., Chicago: Encyclopaedia Britannica, 1979.

Erasmus, Desiderius. *On Copia of Words and Ideas.* Translated by Donald B. King and H. David Rix. Milwaukee: University of Wisconsin Press, 1963.

Erickson, Lee. *The Economy of Literary Form: English Literature and the Industrialization of Publishing, 1800–1850.* Baltimore: Johns Hopkins University Press, 1996.

Evans, D. Morier. *City Men and City Manners: The City; or, The Physiology of London Business; with Sketches on 'Change, and at the Coffee Houses.* London: Groombridge & Sons, 1852.

———. *The Commercial Crisis, 1847–48: Being Facts and Figures Illustrative of the Events of That Important Period Considered in Relation to the Three Epochs of the Railway Mania, the Food and Money Panic, and the French Revolution.* 1849. Reprint, New York: Burt Franklin, 1970.

———. *Facts, Failures, and Frauds: Revelations Financial, Mercantile, Criminal.* 1859. Reprint, New York: Augustus M. Kelley, 1968.

———. *The History of the Commercial Crisis, 1857–58, and the Stock Exchange Panic of 1859.* 1859. Reprint, New York: Augustus M. Kelley, 1969.

———. *Speculative Notes and Notes on Speculation, Ideal and Real.* 1864. Reprint, New York: Burt Franklin, 1968.

Everett, E. M. *The Party of Humanity: The "Fortnightly Review" and Its Contributors, 1865–1874.* Chapel Hill: University of North Carolina Press, 1939.

"Facts for Enquirers: The National Debt." In *English Chartist Circular, and Temperance Record for England and Wales* 2, no. 53 (1843): 4. Originally appeared in *Hobson's Poor Man's Companion.*

Faller, Lincoln. *Turned to Account: The Forms and Functions of Criminal Biography in Late Seventeenth- and Early Eighteenth-Century England.* Cambridge: Cambridge University Press, 1987.

Feavearyear, A. E. *The Pound Sterling: A History of English Money.* Oxford: Clarendon, 1931.

Fergus, Jan. *Jane Austen: A Literary Life.* New York: St. Martin's, 1991.

Fetter, Frank. "The Rise and Decline of Ricardian Economics." *History of Political Economy* 1 (1969): 67–172.

Fielding, Henry. *The History of Tom Jones, a Foundling.* Edited by George Sherburn. New York: Random House, 1950.

Finkelstein, Andrea. *Harmony and Balance: An Intellectual History of Seventeenth-Century English Economic Thought.* Ann Arbor: University of Michigan Press, 2000.

Finkelstein, David. *The House of Blackwood: Author-Publisher Relations in the Victorian Era.* University Park: Pennsylvania State University Press, 2002.

Finn, Margot C. *The Character of Credit: Personal Debt in English Culture, 1740–1914.* Cambridge: Cambridge University Press, 2003.

Fish, Stanley. *Is There a Text in This Class? The Authority of Interpretive Communities.* Cambridge, MA: Harvard University Press, 1980.

Fitzmaurice, R. M. *British Banks and Banking: A Pictorial History.* Truro: B. Bradford Barton, 1975.

Flint, Christopher. "Speaking Objects: The Circulation of Stories in Eighteenth-Century Prose Fiction." *PMLA* 113, no. 2 (March 1998): 212–26.

Fontana, Biancamaria. *Rethinking the Politics of Commercial Society: The Edinburgh Review, 1802–1832.* Cambridge: Cambridge University Press, 1985.

Foucault, Michel. *The Order of Things: An Archaeology of Knowledge.* New York: Random House, 1970.

Freedgood, Elaine. *The Secret Life of Things: Fugitive Meanings in Victorian Novels.* Chicago: University of Chicago Press, 2006.

———. *Victorian Writing about Risk: Imagining a Safe England in a Dangerous World.* Cambridge: Cambridge University Press, 2000.

Gagnier, Regenia. *The Insatiability of Human Wants: Economics and Aesthetics in Market Society.* Chicago: University of Chicago Press, 2000.

Galbraith, John Kenneth. *Money: Whence It Came, Where It Went.* Boston: Houghton Mifflin, 1975. Rev. ed., Boston: Houghton Mifflin, 1995.

Gallagher, Catherine. *The Body Economic: Life, Death, and Sensation in Political Economy and the Victorian Novel.* Princeton, NJ: Princeton University Press, 2006.

———. *The Industrial Reformation of English Fiction, 1832–1867.* Chicago: University of Chicago Press, 1985.

———. *Nobody's Story: The Vanishing Acts of Women Writers in the Marketplace, 1670–1820.* Berkeley and Los Angeles: University of California Press, 1994.

Gallagher, Catherine, and Stephen Greenblatt. *Practicing New Historicism.* Chicago: University of Chicago Press, 2000.

Galperin, William. *The Historical Austen*. Philadelphia: University of Pennsylvania Press, 2003.

Garside, Peter, James Raven, and Rainer Schowerling, eds. *The English Novel, 1770–1829: A Bibliographical Survey of Prose Fiction Published in the British Isles*. 2 vols. Oxford: Oxford University Press, 2000.

Gattie, Walter Montagu. "What English People Read." *Fortnightly Review*, n.s., 46 (August 1889): 307–21.

Gettmann, Royal A. *A Victorian Publisher: A Study of the Bentley Papers*. Cambridge: Cambridge University Press, 1960.

Gilbart, J. W. *History, Principles, and Practice of Banking*. 1859. Rev. ed., edited by A. S. Michie. 2 vols. Philadelphia: G. D. Miller, 1882. Reprint, New York: Greenwood, 1968.

———. *A Practical Treatise on Banking*. 1827. Reprint, Philadelphia: G. D. Miller, 1855.

Gilmartin, Kevin. *Print Politics: The Press and Radical Opposition in Early Nineteenth-Century England*. Cambridge: Cambridge University Press, 1996.

Godwin, William. *An Enquiry Concerning Political Justice, and Its Influence on General Virtue and Happiness*. 1793. Reprint, London: Penguin Books, 1976.

[Gore, Catherine]. "The London Banker." *Bentley's Miscellany* 14 (1843): 598–604.

[———]. "The Monster-Misery of Literature: By a Mouse Born of the Mountain." *Blackwood's Edinburgh Magazine* 55 (May 1844): 556–60.

Goux, Jean-Joseph. *Symbolic Economies: After Marx and Freud*. Translated by Jennifer Curtiss Gage. Ithaca, NY: Cornell University Press, 1990.

Graham, Kenneth. *English Criticism of the Novel, 1865–1900*. Oxford: Oxford University Press, 1965.

Griest, Guinevere. *Mudie's Circulating Library and the Victorian Novel*. Bloomington: Indiana University Press, 1970.

Guillory, John. *Cultural Capital: The Problem of Literary Canon Formation*. Chicago: University of Chicago Press, 1993.

———. *Literary Study in the Age of Professionalism*. Chicago: University of Chicago Press, forthcoming.

———. "The Memo and Modernity." *Critical Inquiry* 31, no. 1 (Autumn 2004): 108–32.

Haines, Lewis F. "Reade, Mill, and Zola: A Study of the Character and Intention of Charles Reade's Realistic Method." *Studies in Philology* 40, no. 4 (October 1943): 463–80.

Halperin, John. *The Life of Jane Austen*. Baltimore: Johns Hopkins University Press, 1984.

Hamer, Mary. "Working Diary for *The Last Chronicle of Barset*." *Times Literary Supplement*, 24 December 1971, 1606.

Hampton, Mark. "Journalism." In *Encyclopedia of the Victorian Era*, ed. James Eli Adams, Tom Pendergast, and Sara Pendergast, 2:320–23. Danbury, CT: Scholastic, 2004.

Hardy, Thomas. "The Profitable Reading of Fiction." In *Life and Art: Essays, Notes, and Letters Collected for the First Time*, ed. Ernest Brennecke Jr., 56–74. New York: Greenberg, 1925.

Hartman, Geoffrey. *Criticism in the Wilderness: The Study of Literature Today*. New Haven, CT: Yale University Press, 1980.

Haultain, Arnold. "How to Read." *Blackwood's Edinburgh Magazine* 159 (February 1896): 249–65.

Hayden, John O. *Scott: The Critical Heritage*. New York: Barnes & Noble, 1970.

Haywood, Ian. *The Revolution in Popular Literature: Print, Politics, and the People, 1790–1860*. Cambridge: Cambridge University Press, 2004.

Hazlitt, William. "Character of Cobbett." In *Collected Works of William Hazlitt*, ed. P. P. Howe, 8:50–59. New York: AMS, 1967.

[Head, F. B.]. "The Mechanism of the Post Office." *Quarterly Review* 87 (June 1850): 69–115.

Hilton, Boyd. *The Age of Atonement: The Influence of Evangelicalism on Social and Economic Thought, 1785–1865*. Oxford: Clarendon, 1988.

———. "Thomas Chalmers as Political Economist." In *The Practical and the Pious: Essays on Thomas Chalmers (1780–1847)*, ed. A. C. Cheyne., 141–56. Edinburgh: St. Andrew, 1988.

Himmelfarb, Gertrude. *The Idea of Poverty*. New York: Knopf, 1984.

Hoppit, Julian. *Risk and Failure in English Business, 1700–1800*. Cambridge: Cambridge University Press, 1987.

———. "The Use and Abuse of Credit in Eighteenth-Century England." In *Business Life and Public Policy: Essays in Honour of D. C. Coleman*, ed. Neil McKendrick and R. B. Outhwaite, 64–78. Cambridge: Cambridge University Press, 1986.

Horne, R. H., ed. *A New Spirit of the Age*. New York: Harper & Bros., 1844.

Horner, Francis. "Thornton on the Paper Credit of Great Britain." In *The Economic Writings of Francis Horner in the Edinburgh Review, 1802–6*, ed. Frank Whitson Fetter, 28–56. London: London School of Economics, 1957.

Howison, William. "An Investigation into the Principles and Credit of the Circulation of Paper Money, or Bank Notes, in Great Britain." In Capie, ed., *History of Banking*, 4:131–203.

Hughes, Linda K., and Michael Lund. *Victorian Publishing and Mrs. Gaskell's Work*. Charlottesville: University Press of Virginia, 1999.

———. *The Victorian Serial*. Charlottesville: University Press of Virginia, 1991.

Hulme, Peter, and Tim Youngs, eds. *The Cambridge Companion to Travel Writing*. Cambridge: Cambridge University Press, 2002.

Hume, David. "Of Money." In *Essays Moral, Political, and Literary*, ed. Eugene F. Miller, 281–94. Indianapolis: Liberty Fund, 1985.

———. "Of the Balance of Trade." In *Essays Moral, Political, and Literary*, ed. Eugene F. Miller, 316–21. Indianapolis: Liberty Fund, 1985.

Humphery, George R. "The Reading of the Working Classes." *Nineteenth Century* 33 (April 1893): 690–701.

Hunter, Dard. *Papermaking: The History of an Ancient Craft*. New York: Knopf, 1943.

Hunter, Ian. *Culture and Government: The Emergence of Literary Education*. London: Macmillan, 1998.

———. "Reading Character." *Southern Review* 16 (July 1983): 226–43.

Hunter, J. Paul. *Before Novels: The Cultural Contexts of Eighteenth-Century Fiction*. New York: Norton, 1990.

Hyndman, H. M. *Commercial Crises of the Nineteenth Century*. London: Swan Sonnenschein, 1892.

Ingram, John K. *A History of Political Economy*. London: A. C. Black, 1915.

Irvine, Robert. "Appendix F: The Militia Regiments on the South Coast of England in 1793–95." In Austen, *Pride and Prejudice*, ed. Irvine, 449–77.

———. Introduction to Austen, *Pride and Prejudice*, ed. Irvine, 9–35.

James, Henry. "The Art of Fiction." In Eigner and Worth, eds., *Victorian Criticism of the Novel*, 193–212.

Jarrells, Anthony S. *Britain's Bloodless Revolutions: 1688 and the Romantic Reform of Literature*. Houndmills: Palgrave Macmillan, 2005.

Jay, Elisabeth, and Richard Jay, eds. *Critics of Capitalism: Victorian Reactions to "Political Economy."* Cambridge: Cambridge University Press, 1986.

Jeffrey, Francis. "Madame de Staël, *Sur la literature.*" *Edinburgh Review* 21 (February 1813): 1–50.

Jevons, W. Stanley. *Investigations in Currency and Finance.* 1884. 2nd ed., ed. H. Stanley Jevons, London: Macmillan, 1909.

———. *Money and the Mechanism of Exchange.* 1875. London: Kegan Paul, Trench, Trubner, 1908.

———. *The Theory of Political Economy.* 1871. 4th ed., ed. H. Stanley Jevons. London: Macmillan, 1911. Reprint, London: Macmillan, 1931.

Johnson, Claudia. *Jane Austen: Women, Politics, and the Novel.* Chicago: University of Chicago Press, 1988.

Johnson, W. E. "Method of Political Economy." In Palgrave, ed., *Dictionary of Political Economy,* 2:739–48.

Jones, Leonidas M. "The Scott-Christie Duel." *Texas Studies in Language and Literature* 12 (1971): 605–29.

Jones, R. M. D. "Harris, Joseph." Revised by D. J. Bryden. In *Oxford Dictionary of National Biography,* ed. H. C. G. Matthew and Brian Harrison, 25:453–54. Oxford: Oxford University Press, 2004.

Jordan, John, and Robert L. Patten, eds. *Literature in the Marketplace: Nineteenth-Century Publishing and Reading Practices.* Cambridge: Cambridge University Press, 1995.

Joshi, Priya. *In Another Country: Colonialism, Culture, and the English Novel in India.* New York: Columbia University Press, 2002.

Kaplan, Deborah. *Jane Austen among Women.* Baltimore: Johns Hopkins University Press, 1992.

Kauffman, David. *The Business of Common Life: Novels and Classical Economics between Revolution and Reform.* Baltimore: Johns Hopkins University Press, 1995.

Keen, Paul, ed. *Revolutions in Romantic Literature: An Anthology of Print Culture, 1780–1832.* Peterborough, ON: Broadview, 2004.

Kendrick, Walter M. *The Novel Machine: The Theory and Fiction of Anthony Trollope.* Baltimore: Johns Hopkins University Press, 1980.

Kent, Christopher. "The Higher Journalism and the Mid-Victorian Clerisy." *Victorian Studies* 8 (1969): 181–98.

Kerby-Miller, Charles, ed. *The Memoirs of the Extraordinary Life, Works, and Discoveries of Martinus Scriblerus.* New York: Oxford University Press, 1988.

Keyworth, John. *Forgery, the Artful Crime: A Brief History of the Forgery of Bank of England Notes.* London: Bank of England Museum, 2001.

Kindleberger, Charles P. *Manias, Panics, and Crashes: A History of Financial Crises.* 1978. Rev. ed., New York: Basic, 1989.

King, Lord Peter. *A Selection from the Speeches and Writings of the Late Lord King.* Edited by the Earl of Fortesque. London, 1844.

———. "Thoughts on the Effects of the Bank Restriction." In Capie, ed., *History of Banking,* 8:347–526.

King, W. T. C. *History of the London Discount Market.* London: Routledge, 1936.

Klamer, Arjo. *The Value of Culture: On the Relationship between Economics and Arts.* Amsterdam: Amsterdam University Press, 1996.

Klamer, Arjo, and Thomas C. Leonard. "So What's an Economic Metaphor?" In Mirowski, ed., *Natural Images in Economic Thought,* 20–51. Cambridge: Cambridge University Press, 1994.

Klamer, Arjo, Donald M. McCloskey, and Robert M. Solow, eds. *The Consequences of Economic Rhetoric.* Cambridge: Cambridge University Press, 1988.

Klancher, Jon P. *The Making of English Reading Audiences, 1790–1832*. Madison: University of Wisconsin Press, 1987.

Klaver, Claudia. *A/Moral Economics: Classical Political Economy and Cultural Authority in Nineteenth-Century England*. Columbus: Ohio State University Press, 2003.

Knight, Joseph, and Gail Baylis. "Bridges, Thomas." In *Dictionary of National Biography*, ed. H. C. G. Matthew and Brian Harrison, 7:592. Oxford: Oxford University Press, 2002.

Kobayashi, Naboru. "Section 2: The First System of Political Economy." In Steuart, *Principles of Political Economy*, ed. Skinner, 1:lxix–cxvii.

Koss, Stephen. *The Rise and Fall of the Political Press in Britain: The Nineteenth Century*. Chapel Hill: University of North Carolina Press, 1981.

Koven, Seth. "How the Victorians Read *Sesame and Lilies*." In Nord, ed., *Sesame and Lilies*, 165–204.

Kynaston, David. *The City of London: A World of Its Own, 1815–1890*. Vol. 1 of 2. London: Random House, 1994.

Lalor, John. *Money and Morals: A Book for the Times*. London: John Chapman, 1852.

Lamb, Jonathan. "Modern Metamorphoses and Disgraceful Tales." In *Things*, ed. Bill Brown, 193–226. Chicago: University of Chicago Press, 2004.

———. *Preserving the Self in the South Seas, 1680–1840*. Chicago: University of Chicago Press, 2001.

Larson, Magali S. *The Rise of Professionalism*. Berkeley and Los Angeles: University of California Press, 1977.

Leask, Nigel. *The Politics of Imagination in Coleridge's Critical Thought*. London: Macmillan, 1988.

Lee, Alan J. *The Origins of the Popular Press in England, 1815–1914*. London: Croom Helm, 1976.

Letwin, William. *The Origins of Scientific Economics: English Economic Thought, 1660–1776*. London: Methuen, 1963. Reprint, Westport, CT: Greenwood, 1975.

Levine, George. "The Form of the Novel and the Spirit of Secularity." Plenary address, North American Victorian Studies Association, 1 October 2005.

Levitt, Steven, and Stephen J. Dubner. *Freakonomics: A Rogue Economist Explores the Hidden Side of Everything*. New York: HarperCollins, 2005.

LiPuma, Edward, and Benjamin Lee. *Financial Derivatives and the Globalization of Risk*. Durham, NC: Duke University Press, 2004.

Liss, David. *A Conspiracy of Paper*. New York: Ballantine, 2000.

Lively, Cheryl. "Truth in Writing: The Standard of Realism for the Novel in *Fraser's Magazine*, 1830–1850." *Victorian Periodicals Review* 4, nos. 3/4 (December 1973): 3–10.

Logan, Deborah Anna. Introduction to Martineau, *Illustrations*, ed. Logan, 9–50.

Lynch, Deirdre. *The Economy of Character: Novels, Market Culture, and the Business of Inner Meaning*. Chicago: University of Chicago Press, 1998.

Macaulay, Thomas Babington. *The History of England from the Accession of James II*. 5 vols. Philadelphia: Porter & Coates, n.d.

Mackay, Charles. *Extraordinary Popular Delusions and the Madness of Crowds*. 1852. Reprint, New York: Farrar Straus Giroux, 1932.

Mackie, Erin, ed. *The Commerce of Everyday Life: Selections from the Tatler and the Spectator*. New York: St. Martin's, 1998.

———. "Introduction: Cultural and Historical Background." In Mackie, ed., *Commerce of Everyday Life*, 1–32.

Martineau, Harriet. *Berkeley the Banker*. 2 vols. London: William Clowes, 1833.

———. *Harriet Martineau's Autobiography*. Edited by Gaby Weiner. 2 vols. 1877. Reprint, London: Virago, 1983.

———. *Illustrations of Political Economy*. New ed. 9 vols. London: Charles Fox, 1836.

———. *Illustrations of Political Economy: Selected Tales*. Edited by Deborah Anna Logan. Peterborough, ON: Broadview, 2004.

Marx, Karl. *A Contribution to the Critique of Political Economy*. Translated N. I. Stone. 1859. Reprint, Chicago: Charles H. Kerr, 1904.

Masson, David. "British Novelists since Scott." *North British Review* 15 (May 1851): 157–89. Reprinted in Eigner and Worth, eds., *Victorian Criticism of the Novel*, 148–58.

Mathias, Peter. "The People's Money in the Eighteenth Century: The Royal Mint, Trade Tokens, and the Economy." In *The Transformation of England: Essays in the Economic and Social History of England in the Eighteenth Century*, 190–208. New York: Columbia University Press, 1979.

Maurer, Bill. "Uncanny Exchanges: The Possibilities and Failures of 'Making Change' with Alternative Monetary Forms." *Environment and Planning D: Society and Space* 21 (2002): 317–40.

Maurer, Oscar. "Anonymity vs. Signature in Victorian Reviewing." *Studies in English* 27 (June 1948): 1–27.

Mauss, Marcel. *The Gift: The Form and Reason for Exchange in Archaic Societies*. Translated by W. D. Halls. London: Routledge, 1990.

Maxwell, Herbert. "The Craving for Fiction." *Nineteenth Century* 33 (June 1893): 1046–61.

Mayer, Robert. *History and the Early English Novel: Matters of Fact from Bacon to Defoe*. Cambridge: Cambridge University Press, 1997.

Mayo, Robert D. *The English Novel in the Magazines, 1740–1815*. Evanston, IL: Northwestern University Press, 1962.

Mays, Kelly J. "The Disease of Reading and Victorian Periodicals." In Jordan and Patten, eds., *Literature in the Marketplace*, 165–94.

McCarthy, Justin. "Novels with a Purpose." *Westminster Review* 82 (July 1864): 24–49.

McCloskey, Deirdre. *If You're So Smart: The Narrative of Economic Expertise*. Chicago: University of Chicago Press, 1990.

———. *Knowledge and Persuasion in Economics*. Cambridge: Cambridge University Press, 1994.

———. *The Rhetoric of Economics*. Madison: University of Wisconsin Press, 1985.

McClusker, John J., and Cora Gravesteijn. *The Beginnings of Commercial and Financial Journalism: The Commodity Price Currents, Exchange Rates Currents, and Money Currents of Early Modern Europe*. Amsterdam: NEHA, 1991.

McCulloch, J. R. "Banks—Banking." In McCulloch, *Dictionary of Commerce and Commercial Navigation*, 86–134.

———. *A Dictionary, Practical, Theoretical, and Historical of Commerce and Commercial Navigation*. London: Longmans, Green, 1871. This is a reprint of the 1869 edition, the last edition to appear in McCulloch's lifetime. It also includes all McCulloch's prefaces to the various editions.

———. *A Discourse on the Rise, Progress, Peculiar Objects, and Importance of Political Economy: Containing an Outline of a Course of Lectures on the Principles and Doctrines of that Science*. Edinburgh: Archibald Constable, 1825.

———, ed. *A Select Collection of Scarce and Valuable Tracts on Money*. 1856. Reprint, New York: Augustus M. Kelley, 1966.

———, ed. *A Select Collection of Scarce and Valuable Tracts on Paper Currency and Banking: From the Originals of Hume, Wallace, Thornton, Ricardo, Blake, Huskisson, and Others.* 1857. Reprint, New York: Augustus M. Kelley, 1966.

McDowell, Paula. "Fugitive Voices." Lecture, New York University, September 2005.

———. *The Women of Grub Street: Press, Politics, and Gender in the London Literary Market-place, 1678–1730.* Oxford: Oxford University Press, 1998.

McKeon, Michael. *The Origins of the English Novel, 1600–1740.* Baltimore: Johns Hopkins University Press, 1987.

———. *The Secret History of Domesticity: Public, Private, and the Division of Labor.* Baltimore: Johns Hopkins University Press, 2005.

McLaughlin, Kevin. *Paperwork: Fiction and Mass Mediacy in the Paper Age.* Philadelphia: University of Pennsylvania Press, 2005.

Mellor, Anne. *Romanticism and Gender.* New York: Routledge, 1993.

Melton, Frank T. *Sir Robert Clayton and the Origins of English Deposit Banking, 1658–1685.* Cambridge: Cambridge University Press, 1986.

Michie, Ranald C. *The London Stock Exchange: A History.* Oxford: Oxford University Press, 1999.

Miles, Robert. "'A Fall in Bread': Speculation and the Real in *Emma.*" *Novel* 37 (Fall 2003–Spring 2004): 66–85.

Mill, John Stuart. *The Logic of the Moral Sciences.* Edited by A. J. Ayer. La Salle, IL: Open Court, 1988.

———. "On Miss Martineau's Summary of Political Economy." *Monthly Repository* 8 (1834): 318–22. Reprinted in Martineau, *Illustrations,* ed. Logan, 430.

———. *Principles of Political Economy with Some of Their Applications to Social Philosophy.* 1848. Rev. ed. Edited by W. J. Ashley. London: Longmans, Green, 1909.

Miller, D. A. *The Novel and the Police.* Berkeley and Los Angeles: University of California Press, 1988.

Miller, Florence Fenwick. *Harriet Martineau.* London: W. H. Allen, 1884.

Millgate, Jane. *Scott's Last Edition: A Study in Publishing History.* Edinburgh: Edinburgh University Press, 1987.

Mills, John. "On Credit Cycles and the Origin of Commercial Panics." *Transactions of the Manchester Statistical Society* 8 (1868): 9–40.

Mirowski, Philip. "Doing What Comes Naturally: Four Metanarratives on What Metaphors Are For." In Mirowski, ed., *Natural Images in Economic Thought,* 3–19.

Mirowski, Philip, ed. *Natural Images in Economic Thought: "Markets Read in Tooth and Claw."* Cambridge: Cambridge University Press, 1994.

"Miss Martineau's *Illustrations of Political Economy.*" *Tait's Edinburgh Magazine* (August 1832). Reprinted in Martineau, *Illustrations,* ed. Logan, 416–18.

"Money." In *Encyclopaedia Britannica* (facsimile. ed.), 3:253–68, 1768–71.

Moretti, Franco. *Graphs, Maps, Trees: Abstract Models for a Literary History.* London: Verso, 2006.

Morris, Kenneth M., and Virginia B. Morris. *The Wall Street Journal Guide to Understanding Money and Investing.* New York: Lightbulb, 1999.

Mulcaire, Terry. "Public Credit; or, The Feminization of Virtue in the Marketplace." *PMLA* 114 (October 1999): 1029–42.

Muldrew, Craig. *The Economy of Obligation: The Culture of Credit and Social Relations in Early Modern England.* New York: St. Martin's, 1998.

Mullan, John. "Appendix: The Textual History of *Roxana.*" In Defoe, *Roxana,* ed. Mullan, 331–39.

———. Introduction to Defoe, *Roxana*, ed. Mullen, vii–xxvii.

Murphy, Peter. *Poetry as an Occupation and an Art in Britain, 1760–1830*. Cambridge: Cambridge University Press, 1993.

Murray, John. "Books and Reading." *Quarterly Review* 162 (April 1886): 501–18.

Nattrass, Leonora. *William Cobbett: The Politics of Style*. Cambridge: Cambridge University Press, 1995.

Nevin, Edward, and E. W. Davis. *The London Clearing Banks*. London: Elek, 1970.

Newmarch, William. "Bills of Exchange in Circulation, 1826–47." *Journal of the Statistical Society of London* 14 (May 1851): 143–83.

Nicholson, Colin. *Writing and the Rise of Finance: Capital Satires of the Early Eighteenth Century*. Cambridge: Cambridge University Press, 1994.

Niehans, Jurg. "Juglar's Credit Cycles." *History of Political Economy* 24, no. 3 (1992): 545–69.

Nokes, David. *Jane Austen: A Life*. Berkeley and Los Angeles: University of California Press, 1997.

Nord, Deborah Epstein, ed. *Sesame and Lilies*. New Haven, CT: Yale University Press, 2002.

"Note-Book of a Literary Idler." *Blackwood's Edinburgh Magazine* 17 (June 1825): 736–44.

Novak, Maximillian E. *Daniel Defoe, Master of Fictions*. Oxford: Oxford University Press, 2001.

"Novels." *Critical Review*, December 1781, 477–78.

O'Brien, John. "The Character of Credit: Defoe's 'Lady Credit,' *The Fortunate Mistress*, and the Resources of Inconsistency in Early Eighteenth-Century Britain." *ELH* 63, no. 3 (1996): 603–31.

Ogden, Miles. *Indian Ink: Script and Print in the Making of the East India Company*. Chicago: University of Chicago Press, 2007.

[Oliphant, Laurence]. "The Autobiography of a Joint-Stock Company (Limited)." *Blackwood's Edinburgh Magazine* 120 (July 1876): 96–122.

Oliphant, Margaret. *Annals of a Publishing House: William Blackwood and His Sons, Their Magazine and Friends*. 2 vols. London: William Blackwood, 1897. Reprint, New York: Scribner's, 1897.

[———]. "The Byways of Literature: Reading for the Million." *Blackwood's Edinburgh Magazine* 84 (August 1858): 200–16.

[———]. "Charles Reade's Novels." *Blackwood's Edinburgh Magazine* 106 (October 1869): 488–514.

———. *Memoir of the Life of Laurence Oliphant and of Alice Oliphant, His Wife*. 2 vols. New York: Harper & Bros., 1891.

[———]. "New Books." *Blackwood's Edinburgh Magazine* 108 (August 1870): 166–88.

[———]. "Novels." *Blackwood's Edinburgh Magazine* 102 (September 1867): 257–80.

Olshin, Toby A. "Form and Theme in Novels about Non-Human Characters, a Neglected Sub-Genre." *Genre* 2, no. 1 (1969): 41–53.

Olson, Richard. *Science Deified and Science Defied: The Historical Significance of Science in Western Culture*. Berkeley and Los Angeles: University of California Press, 1983.

Paine, Thomas. *The Writings of Thomas Paine*. Edited by M. D. Conway. 4 vols. New York: AMS, 1967.

Palgrave, R. H. Inglis, ed. *Dictionary of Political Economy*. 4 vols. London: Macmillan, 1896. 2nd ed., New York: Macmillan, 1900.

Parsons, Wayne. *The Power of the Financial Press: Journalism and Economic Opinion in Britain and America*. New Brunswick, NJ: Rutgers University Press, 1989.

Patey, Douglas Lane. *Probability and Literary Form: Philosophic Theory and Literary Practice in the Augustan Age.* Cambridge: Cambridge University Press, 1984.

Patten, Robert L. *Charles Dickens and His Publishers.* Oxford: Oxford University Press, 1978.

Pearson, Jacqueline. *Women's Reading in Britain, 1750–1835: A Dangerous Recreation.* Cambridge: Cambridge University Press, 1999.

Perkin, Harold. *The Rise of Professional Society: England since 1880.* London: Routledge, 1989.

Pocock, J. G. A. *The Machiavellian Moment: Florentine Political Thought and the Atlantic Republican Tradition.* Princeton, NJ: Princeton University Press, 1975.

———. "The Mobility of Property and the Rise of Eighteenth-Century Sociology." In *Virtue, Commerce, and History*, 103–23.

———. *Virtue, Commerce and History: Essays on Political Thought and History, Chiefly in the Eighteenth Century.* Cambridge: Cambridge University Press, 1985.

Polanyi, Karl. *The Great Transformation.* Boston: Beacon, 1944.

Poovey, Mary. "Creative Criticism: Adaptation, Performative Writing, and the Problem of Objectivity." *Narrative* 8, no. 2 (May 2000): 109–33.

———. "Forgotten Writers, Neglected Histories: Charles Reade and the Nineteenth-Century Transformation of the British Literary Field." *ELH* 71 (2004): 433–53.

———. *A History of the Modern Fact: Problems of Knowledge in the Sciences of Wealth and Society.* Chicago: University of Chicago Press, 1998.

———. Introduction to *The Financial System in Nineteenth-Century Britain*, ed. Mary Poovey, 1–33. Oxford: Oxford University Press, 2003.

———. *Making a Social Body: British Cultural Formation, 1830–1864.* Chicago: University of Chicago Press, 1995.

———. "The Model System of Contemporary Literary Criticism." *Critical Inquiry* 27 (Spring 2001): 408–38.

———. *Uneven Developments: The Ideological Work of Gender in Mid-Victorian England.* Chicago: University of Chicago Press, 1988.

———. "Writing about Finance in Victorian England: Secrecy and Disclosure in the Culture of Investment." *Victorian Studies* 45, no. 1 (Autumn 2002): 17–41.

Porter, Dilwin. "A Trusted Guide of the Investing Public: Harry Marks and the *Financial News*, 1884–1916." In *Speculators and Patriots: Essays in Business Biography*, ed. R. P. T. Davenport-Hines, 1–17. London: Frank Cass, 1986.

Porter, Theodore. *The Rise of Statistical Thinking, 1820–1900.* Princeton, NJ: Princeton University Press, 1988.

Pressnell, L. S. *Country Banking in the Industrial Revolution.* Oxford: Clarendon, 1956.

Price, F. G. Hilton. "Some Notes on the Early Goldsmiths and Bankers to the Close of the 17th Century." *Transactions of the London and Middlesex Archaeological Society* 5, no. 2 (August 1877): 255–81.

Psomiades, Kathy Alexis. *Beauty's Body: Femininity and Representation in British Aestheticism.* Stanford, CA: Stanford University Press, 1997.

Purdy, William. *The City Life: Its Trade and Finance.* London, 1876.

Pyckett, Lyn. "The Real *versus* the Ideal: Theories of Fiction in Periodicals, 1850–1870." *Victorian Periodicals Review* 15, no. 2 (Summer 1982): 63–74.

Rae, George. *The Country Banker: His Clients, Cares, and Work from an Experience of Forty Years.* 1885. Rev. ed., London: John Murray, 1930. A very short version of *Country Banker* appeared in 1852. The 1885 text is not a revision but a new text.

Rauch, Alan. *Useful Knowledge: The Victorians, Morality, and the March of Intellect.* Durham, NC: Duke University Press, 2001.

Raven, James. *Judging New Wealth: Popular Publishing and Responses to Commerce in England, 1750–1800.* Oxford: Clarendon, 1992.

Reade, Charles. *The Works of Charles Reade.* 9 vols. New York: Peter Fenelon Collier, n.d.

Reade, Charles L., and the Rev. Compton Reade. *Charles Reade, Dramatist, Novelist, Journalist: A Memoir, Compiled Chiefly from His Literary Remains.* 2 vols. London: Chapman & Hall, 1887.

"Reading as a Means of Culture." *Sharpe's London Magazine,* n.s., 31 (December 1867): 316–23.

Redman, Deborah A. *The Rise of Political Economy as a Science: Methodology and the Classical Economists.* Cambridge, MA: MIT Press, 1997.

Reid, Hugh G. "Biographical Notice." In McCulloch, *Dictionary of Commerce and Commercial Navigation,* xxi–xxx.

Reid, William. *The Life and Adventures of the Old Lady of Threadneedle Street; Containing an Account of Her Numerous Intrigues with Various Eminent Statesmen, of Past and Present Times, Written by Herself.* London, 1832.

Reiman, Donald H., ed. *The Romantics Reviewed: Contemporary Reviews of British Romantic Writers.* 2 2-pt. vols. New York: Garland, 1971.

Richards, R. D. *The Early History of Banking in England.* Cambridge: Cambridge University Press, 1992.

Robb, George. *White-Collar Crime in Modern England: Financial Fraud and Business Morality, 1845–1929.* Cambridge: Cambridge University Press, 1992.

Robbins, Lionel. "The Nature and Significance of Economic Science." In *The Philosophy of Economics,* ed. Daniel M. Hausman, 113–40. Cambridge: Cambridge University Press, 1984.

Roberts, Warren. *Jane Austen and the French Revolution.* New York: St. Martin's, 1979.

Rose, Jonathan. *The Intellectual Life of the British Working Classes.* New Haven, CT: Yale University Press, 2001.

———. "Was Capitalism Good for Victorian Literature?" *Victorian Studies* 46 (2004): 489–501.

Rosenberg, Charles E. "Florence Nightingale on Contagion: The Hospital as Moral Universe." In *Healing and History,* ed. Charles E. Rosenberg, 116–36. New York: Dawson, 1979.

Ross, Angus, ed. *Selections from "The Tatler" and "The Spectator" of Steele and Addison.* New York: Penguin, 1982.

Ruskin, John. "Of King's Treasuries." In Nord, ed., *Sesame and Lilies,* 27–67.

Russell, Norman. "Money and Finance." In Schlicke, ed., *Oxford Reader's Companion to Dickens,* 378–81.

———. *The Novelist and Mammon: Literary Responses to the World of Commerce in the Nineteenth Century.* Oxford: Clarendon, 1986.

Russett, Margaret. *De Quincey's Romanticism: Canonical Minority and the Forms of Transmission.* Cambridge: Cambridge University Press, 1997.

Salmon, Edward G. "What Boys Read." *Fortnightly Review,* n.s., 39 (1886): 248–59.

———. "What Girls Read." *Nineteenth Century* 20 (October 1886): 515–29.

———. "What the Working Classes Read." *Nineteenth Century* 20 (July 1886): 108–17.

Sanders, Valerie. *Reason over Passion: Harriet Martineau and the Victorian Novel.* New York: St. Martin's, 1986.

Schabas, Margaret. *The Natural Origins of Economics.* Chicago: University of Chicago Press, 2005.

———. *A World Ruled by Number: William Stanley Jevons and the Rise of Mathematical Economics.* Princeton, NJ: Princeton University Press, 1990.

Schlicke, Paul. "*Little Dorrit.*" In Schlicke, ed., *Oxford Reader's Companion to Dickens*, 335–41.

———, ed. *The Oxford Reader's Companion to Dickens*. Oxford: Oxford University Press, 1999.

Schumpeter, Joseph A. *A History of Economic Analysis*. Edited by Elizabeth Boody Schumpeter. New York: Oxford University Press, 1954.

Scott, Sir Walter. *Sir Walter Scott on Novelists and Fiction*. Edited by Ioan Williams. New York: Barnes & Noble, 1968.

Scrope, George Poulett. "Review of *Illustrations of Political Economy*." *Quarterly Review* 49 (1833): 137–52. Reprinted in Martineau, *Illustrations*, ed. Logan, 422–25.

Shapin, Steven. *The Scientific Revolution*. Chicago: University of Chicago Press, 1996.

———. *A Social History of Truth: Civility and Science in Seventeenth-Century England*. Chicago: University of Chicago Press, 1994.

Shapin, Steven, and Simon Shaffer. *Leviathan and the Air Pump: Hobbes, Boyle, and the Experimental Life*. Princeton, NJ: Princeton University Press, 1985.

Shell, Marc. *The Economy of Literature*. Baltimore: Johns Hopkins University Press, 1978.

———. *Money and Art*. Chicago: University of Chicago Press, 1995.

———. *Money, Language, and Thought: Literary and Philosophical Economies from the Medieval to the Modern Eras*. Berkeley and Los Angeles: University of California Press, 1982.

Shelley, Percy Bysshe. *The Letters of Percy Bysshe Shelley*. Vol. 10 of *The Complete Works*, ed. Roger Ingpen and Walter E. Peck. New York: Gordian, 1965.

Sherman, Stuart, ed. *The Restoration and the Eighteenth Century*. Vol. 1C of *The Longman Anthology of British Literature*. 2nd ed., New York: Addison-Wesley, 2003.

Shiller, Robert J. *Irrational Exuberance*. Princeton, NJ: Princeton University Press, 2000.

Siskin, Clifford. *Blaming the System: Enlightenment and the Forms of Modernity*. Chicago: University of Chicago Press, forthcoming.

———. *The Historicity of Romantic Discourse*. New York: Oxford University Press, 1988.

———. "More Is Different: Literary Change in the Mid and Late Eighteenth Century." In *The Cambridge History of English Literature: 1660–1780*, ed. John Richetti, 797–823. Cambridge: Cambridge University Press, 2005.

———. "The Problem of Periodization: Enlightenment, Romanticism, and the Fate of System." In Chandler, ed., *Cambridge History of English Literature*.

———. "Textual Culture and the History of the Real." *Textual Culture* (forthcoming).

———. *The Work of Writing: Literature and Social Change in Britain, 1700–1830*. Baltimore: Johns Hopkins University Press, 1998.

Skinner, Andrew S. Introduction to Steuart, *Principles of Political Economy*, ed. Skinner, 1:xi–lxviii.

Small, Helen. "Liberal Editing in the *Fortnightly Review* and the *Nineteenth Century*." *Publishing History* 53 (2003): 75–96.

Smiles, Samuel. *Character*. 1871. Reprint, New York: A. L. Burt, n.d.

———. *Self-Help and Illustrations of Conduct and Perseverance*. 1859. Abridged ed., ed. George Bull, New York: Viking Penguin, 1986.

———. *Thrift*. 1875. Reprint, New York: A. L. Burt, n.d.

Smith, Adam. *An Inquiry into the Nature and Causes of the Wealth of Nations*. Edited by Edwin Cannan. 1776. Reprint, New York: Modern Library, 1937.

———. *Lectures on Rhetoric and Belles Lettres*. Edited by J. C. Bryce. Indianapolis: Liberty Fund, 1985.

Smith, Elton E. *Charles Reade*. Boston: Twayne, 1976.

Southam, B. C. *Jane Austen's Literary Manuscripts*. London: Oxford University Press, 1964.

Spater, George. *William Cobbett: The Poor Man's Friend*. 2 vols. Cambridge: Cambridge University Press, 1982.

Stang, Richard. *The Theory of the Novel in England, 1850–1870*. New York: Columbia University Press, 1959.

St. Clair, William. *The Reading Nation in the Romantic Period*. Cambridge: Cambridge University Press, 2004.

[Stephen, James Fitzjames]. "The *Edinburgh Review* and Modern Novelists." *Saturday Review* 4 (18 July 1857): 57–58.

———. "The Relation of Novels to Life." In *Cambridge Essays Contributed by Members of the University*. London, 1855. Reprinted in Eigner and Worth, eds., *Victorian Criticism of the Novel*, 93–118.

Steuart, Sir James. *An Inquiry into the Principles of Political Economy*. 1767. Edited by Andrew S. Skinner. 4 vols. London: Pickering & Chatto, 1998.

Stevenson, Robert Louis. "A Humble Remonstrance." In Eigner and Worth, eds., *Victorian Criticism of the Novel*, 213–22.

Stewart, M. A., ed. *Selected Philosophical Papers of Robert Boyle*. Indianapolis: Hackett, 1991.

Supple, Barry. *Commercial Crisis and Change in England, 1600–1642: A Study in the Instability of a Mercantile Economy*. Cambridge: Cambridge University Press, 1964.

Sutcliffe, Emerson Grant. "Fact, Realism, and Morality in Reade's Fiction." *Studies in Philology* 41 (1944): 582–98.

Sutherland, J. A. *Victorian Authors and Publishers*. Chicago: University of Chicago Press, 1976.

Tawney, R. H. Introduction to Thomas Wilson, *A Discourse upon Usury by Way of Dialogue and Orations*, ed. R. H. Tawney, 1–172. London, 1925.

Taylor, Barbara. *Eve and the New Jerusalem: Socialism and Feminism in the Nineteenth Century*. New York: Pantheon, 1983.

Terdiman, Richard. *Body and Story: The Ethics and Practice of Theoretical Conflict*. Baltimore: Johns Hopkins University Press, 2005.

Terry, R. C. "James, Henry." In Terry, ed., *Oxford Reader's Companion to Trollope*, 275–76.

———, ed. *The Oxford Reader's Companion to Trollope*. Oxford: Oxford University Press, 1999.

"The Terrorist System of Novel-Writing." *Monthly Magazine* 4, no. 21 (1797): 102–5.

Thompson, E. P. *The Making of the English Working Class*. New York: Random House, 1966.

———. "The Moral Economy of the English Crowd in the Eighteenth Century." *Past and Present* 50 (February 1971): 76–136.

Thompson, James. *Models of Value: Eighteenth-Century Political Economy and the Novel*. Durham, NC: Duke University Press, 1996.

Thompson, William. *Inquiry into the Principles of the Distribution of Wealth*. 1824. Reprint, New York: Augustus M. Kelley, 1963.

———. *Labour Rewarded: The Claims of Labour and Capital Conciliated; or, How to Secure to Labour the Whole Product of Its Exertion by One of the Idle Classes*. 1827. Reprint, New York: Augustus M. Kelley, 1969.

Thornton, Henry. "An Enquiry into the Nature and Effects of the Paper Credit of Great Britain." In Capie, ed., *History of Banking*, 8:131–228.

Trollope, Anthony. *An Autobiography*. Edited by Michael Sadlier and Frederick Page. 1883. Reprint, New York: Oxford University Press, 1950.

———. *The Last Chronicle of Barset*. Edited by Peter Fairclough. New York: Penguin, 1984.

———. "*Sesame and Lilies.*" *Fortnightly Review* 1 (15 July 1865): 633–35.

Valenze, Deborah. *The Social Life of Money in the English Past*. Cambridge: Cambridge University Press, 2006.

Walker, F. A. "Money." In Palgrave, ed., *Dictionary of Political Economy*, 2:787–96.

Wallerstein, Immanuel. "Should We Unthink the Nineteenth Century?" In *Rethinking the Nineteenth Century*, ed. Francisco O. Ramirez, 185–91. New York: Greenwood, 1988.

Warner, William B. *Licensing Entertainment: The Elevation of Novel Reading in Britain, 1684–1750*. Berkeley and Los Angeles: University of California Press, 1998.

[Warren, Samuel]. "Advice to an Intending Serialist." *Blackwood's Edinburgh Magazine* 60 (November 1846): 590–605.

Watt, Hugh. *Thomas Chalmers and the Disruption, Incorporating the Chalmers Lectures for 1840–44*. Edinburgh: Thomas Nelson, 1943.

Watt, Ian. *The Rise of the Novel: Studies in Defoe, Richardson, and Fielding*. Berkeley: University of California Press, 1957.

Webb, R. K. *Harriet Martineau: A Radical Victorian*. New York: Columbia University Press, 1960.

Wheatley, Kim. "The *Blackwood's* Attacks on Leigh Hunt." *Nineteenth-Century Literature* 47 (1992): 1–31.

[White, J.]. "The Murdering Banker." *Blackwood's Edinburgh Magazine* 44 (December 1838): 823–32.

White, Lawrence H. *Free Banking in Britain: Theory, Experience, and Debate, 1800–1845*. Cambridge: Cambridge University Press, 1984.

Whiting, J. R. S. *Trade Tokens: A Social and Economic History*. Newton Abbot: David & Charles, 1971.

Williams, Ioan, ed. *Novel and Romance, 1700–1800*. New York: Barnes & Noble, 1970.

Williams, Raymond. *Cobbett*. Oxford: Oxford University Press, 1983.

———. *Keywords: A Vocabulary of Culture and Society*. New York: Oxford University Press, 1976.

———. *The Long Revolution: An Analysis of the Democratic, Industrial, and Cultural Changes Transforming Our Society*. New York: Columbia University Press, 1961.

[Wills, W. H.]. "Review of a Popular Publication, in the Searching Style." *Household Words* 1, no. 18 (27 July 1850): 426–31.

Winch, Donald. "The Emergence of Economics as a Science, 1750–1870." In *The Industrial Revolution: 1700–1914* (Fontana Economic History of Europe, vol. 3), ed. Carlo Cipolla, 507–73. Glasgow: William Collins Sons, 1975.

———. "Marginalism and the Boundaries of Economic Science." In *The Marginal Revolution in Economics*, ed. R. D. Collison Black, A. W. Coats, and Craufurd D. W. Goodwin, 59–77. Durham, NC: Duke University Press, 1973.

———. *Riches and Poverty: An Intellectual History of Political Economy in Britain, 1750–1834*. Cambridge: Cambridge University Press, 1996.

Wollstonecraft, Mary. *A Vindication of the Rights of Woman*. Edited by Carol H. Poston. New York: Norton, 1975.

Woodmansee, Martha, and Mark Osteen, eds. *The New Economic Criticism: Studies in the Intersection of Literature and Economics*. London: Routledge, 1999.

———. "Taking Account of the New Economic Criticism: An Historical Introduction." In Woodmansee and Osteen, eds., *The New Economic Criticism*, 3–50.

Woolford, John. "Periodicals and the Practice of Literary Criticism, 1855–64." In *The Victorian Periodical Press: Samplings and Soundings*, ed. Joanne Shattock and Michael Wolff, 109–42. Leicester: Leicester University Press, 1982.

Wordsworth, William. *The Prose Works of William Wordsworth*. Edited by W. J. B. Owen and Jane Worthington Smyster. 3 vols. Oxford: Clarendon, 1974.

Yeo, Richard. *Defining Science: William Whewell, Natural Knowledge, and the Public Debate in Early Victorian Britain*. Cambridge: Cambridge University Press, 1993.

INDEX